P9-CRQ-566

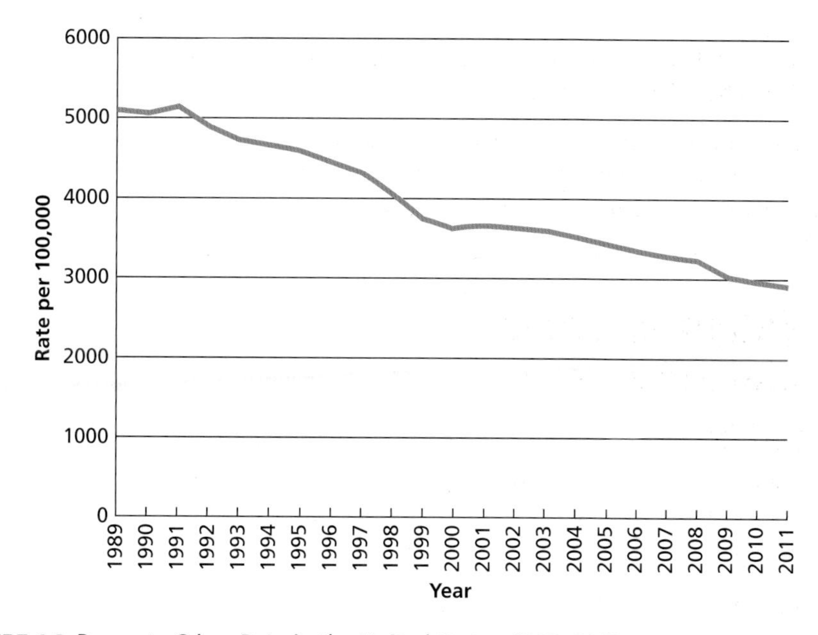

FIGURE 1.2 Property Crime Rate in the United States, 1989–2011.
Source: Federal Bureau of Investigation, n.d.

offenses ÷ population of area) × 100,000. The result allows us to determine how many offenses occur per 100,000 residents of an area. This, in turn, allows us to compare data over time and between different places with different populations, by presenting them in a standardized format.

The offenses included in the violent crime rate are murder, forcible rape, robbery (i.e., taking another person's property through the use or threat of force, such as a holdup), and aggravated assault (Federal Bureau of Investigation, 2012d). The offenses included in the property crime rate are burglary (i.e., breaking and entering), larceny (i.e., stealing another person's property, such as shoplifting), motor vehicle theft, and arson (Federal Bureau of Investigation, 2012b). The graphs in Figures 1.1 and 1.2 tell an important story. In the 1990s, the violent crime rate decreased dramatically, and that decrease has continued (though less dramatically) through the 2000s. Over the same time period, property crime rates have also declined noticeably.

Criminologists and criminal justice scholars and practitioners are very interested in why crime has declined. As with many issues in criminal justice, no absolute answer fully explains it. However, research (Blumstein & Wallman, 2000; Conklin, 2003) has identified a variety of factors that may have contributed to the reduction in crime; for further discussion, see Box 1.3. Criminologists will continue to study the various forces that affect the crime rate and the effect of criminal justice policy decisions on the level of crime in society.

The UCR also provides data about **clearance rates**, referring to the percentage of cases that are solved, or cleared, usually by arresting a suspect. Figure 1.3 shows the clearance rate for the major crimes included in the UCR. Murder has the highest clearance rate because homicide cases are often given the highest priority in terms of investigative resources.

clearance rate
A statistic indicating the percentage of cases that are solved, or cleared, usually through the arrest of a suspect.

The above data are for the United States as a whole. However, it is important to recognize that there are regional variations in the amount of crime. Figure 1.4 shows the amount of crime by region. The southern United States consistently experiences the highest crime rates for both violent and property crimes. There has long been a debate among criminologists as to why this is the case, much of it focused on whether

BOX 1.3

Research in Action

EXPLAINING THE CRIME DECLINE

Much of what is written in this text is based on research, as you will note in the numerous citations throughout. We encourage you to pursue further reading about topics that you find interesting. The purpose of each chapter's "Research in Action" box is to look in more depth at research related to a particular issue that is important to criminal justice. This is important because doing so moves toward evidence-based practice, a model that is gaining increased popularity in criminal justice. Evidence-based practice "seeks to increase the influence of research on policy, or, in a manner of speaking, put systematic research evidence at center stage in the policy-making process" (Welsh & Farrington, 2011, p. 62). The idea is to bridge theory and practice, ideally leading to more effective criminal justice policies.

Here, we will focus on the crime drop that was described in the text and depicted in Figures 1.1 and 1.2. The decrease in crime over the past 20 years has been nothing short of dramatic. It is important to understand what factors may have contributed to the crime drop. Doing so would allow the criminal justice system, or others in society, to structure policies that might sustain low crime rates or even cause them to decrease further. Of course, there has been significant debate over what caused the crime drop—and some perspectives have been grounded in evidence, while others have not. So what does the evidence say?

Perhaps the main conclusion is that there is no single factor that has led to the crime drop. Research has identified a number of possible explanations that may, in fact, have worked together to lead to reductions in crime. One of the first attempts to disentangle these explanations was the publication of a volume by Blumstein and Wallman (2006), which included contributions by prominent criminologists who are experts in their respective fields of study. Consider these findings. Wintemute (2000) suggested that interventions identifying the places, persons, and weapons that were used in gun violence could reduce crime. Rather than focusing too broadly, a selective approach to supply and demand reduction for guns appeared to be successful. Spelman (2000) studied the impact of prisons, considering whether the increase in prison populations that began in the late 1970s and early 1980s could have had contribued to the crime drop. Based on statistical modeling, he concluded that approximately 25% of the crime drop could be attributed to the increased rate of imprisonment. Rosenfeld (2000) focused on homicides (i.e., murders) committed by adults, speculating that (once again) increased use of imprisonment, a decline in intimate partner homicide due to a decrease in marriages and a decreased tolerance for domestic violence, and processes leading to a more civil society have led to crime reductions.

Research by Johnson, Golub, and Dunlap (2000) turned to the relationship between drugs and crime. Central to their analysis was noting that the popularity of heroin and crack has diminished, with marijuana becoming more prevalent. The authors note that the subculture surrounding marijuana distribution and use is a less violent one than was associated with heroin and crack. Eck and Maguire (2000) reflected on the role of policing, arguing that specific, highly focused policing strategies (such as problem-oriented policing or hot spots policing, which you will learn about in Chapter 11) may have contributed to the decline. Grogger (2000) offered an economic analysis, suggesting that increased job opportunities and a movement away from illegal drug dealing led to a drop in violence. Finally, Fox (2000) offered a demographic analysis, considering the relationship between the age structure of the population and crime, acknowledging that much violence—particularly homicide—is committed by the 18–24-year-old age group; from the late 1970s to the late 1990s, the proportion of the U.S. population in that age group declined.

The analyses described above offer insight into the crime drop, but research did not stop in 2000. Subsequent research has considered a variety of other possible explanations, such as the following: a decline in high-risk behavior, such as fighting, risky driving, risky sexual activity, and dropping out of school, which are associated with crime (Mishra & Lalumière, 2009); reductions in airborne concentrations of lead, as lead exposure causes negative behavioral effects (Mielke & Zahran, 2012); increased immigration, as increases in immigration in cities was associated with decreases in crime in those cities, over time (Stowell, Messner, McGeever, & Raffalovich, 2009); and the "security hypothesis," which is the notion that improved security measures adopted by individuals and businesses can reduce crime (Farrell, Tilley, Tseloni, & Mailley, 2010, p. 25). No doubt the research will continue into the future, as criminologists and others seek to deterime what factors produced the crime decline.

Q What do you think are the benefits in pursuing evidence-based practice? What do you think are the challenges in using research as a basis for criminal justice policy making?

Q Do you find any of the above explanations for the crime drop more persuasive than others? Why or why not? What other explanations do you think there might be, beyond those listed above?

Q Drawing upon a model of evidence-based practice, what policies do you think would be helpful to keep crime levels low, based on the above findings?

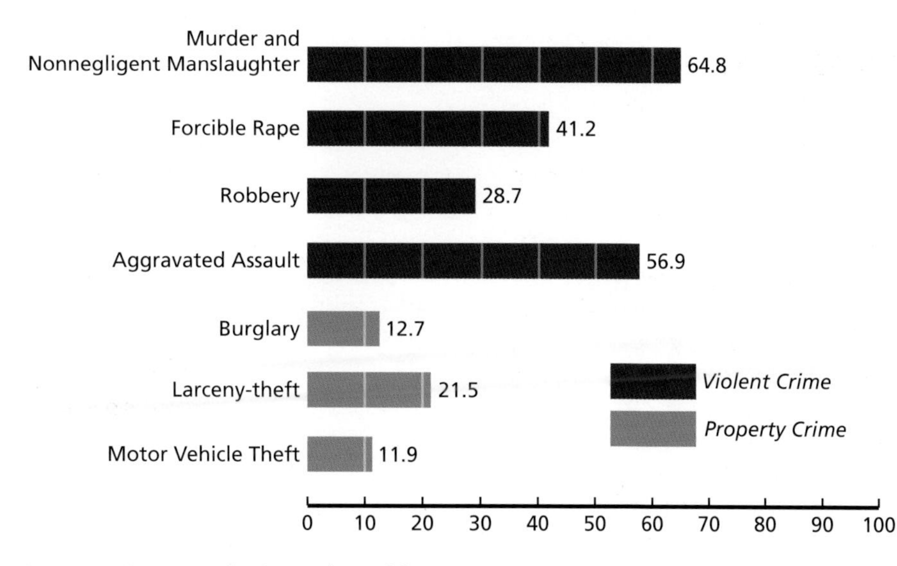

FIGURE 1.3 Percent of Crimes Cleared for Arrest or Exceptional Means, 2011.
Source: Federal Bureau of Investigation, 2012a

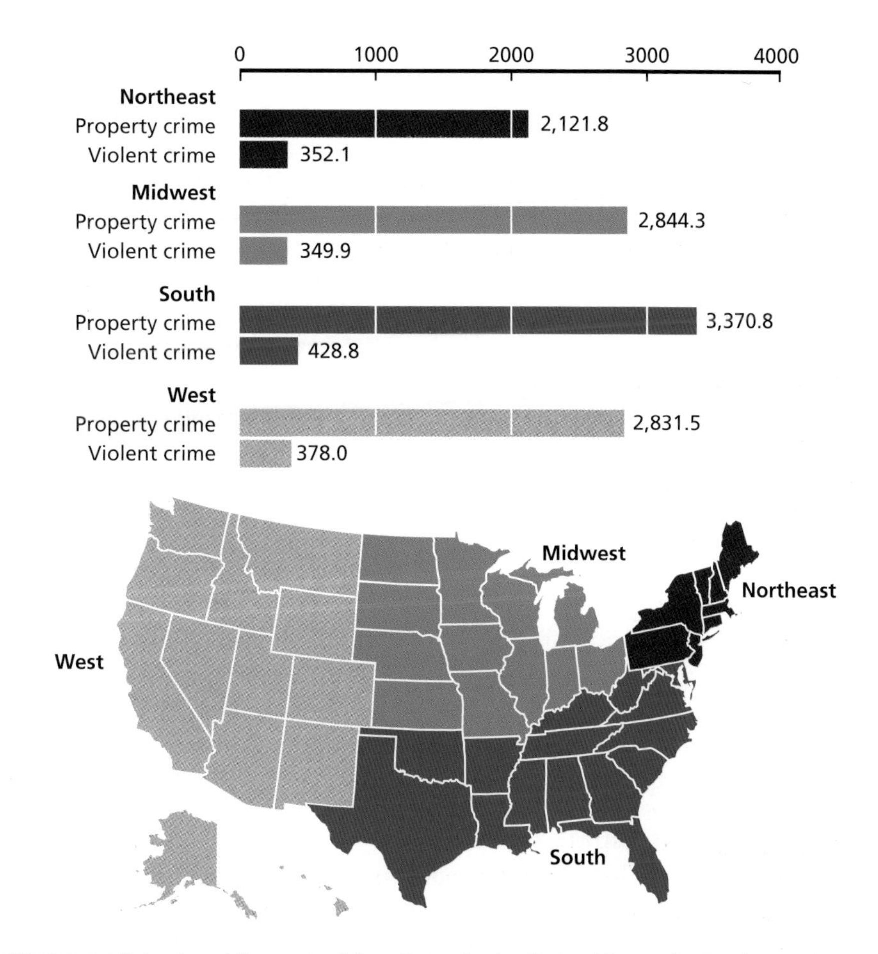

FIGURE 1.4 Violent and Property Crime Rates in the United States by Region, 2011.
Source: Federal Bureau of Investigation, 2012c

Many police agencies now employ crime analysts, who look for patterns in crime data and who prepare maps to show the distribution of crime within a jurisdiction. Information prepared by crime analysts is used to guide decision making about police strategy. Why do you think it would be useful to understand the spatial distribution of crime?

there are attributes that lead the southern states to experience higher crime rates. Although there is not a firm resolution on this question, the following explanations have been proposed: a southern subculture that favors violence (Cohen, 1996); higher temperatures in the South (Cohn, Rotton, Peterson, & Tarr, 2004), as more potential offenders and victims may venture out when the weather is nice or because hot weather makes tempers flare; differences in patterns of social relationships among people, known as social capital, in which lower levels of social capital in the South lead to increased crime (Rosenfeld, Messner, & Baumer, 2001); and higher poverty levels in the South being associated with crime (Huff-Corzine, Corzine, & Moore, 1986).

Finally, in a global society, it is useful to consider how crime rates in the United States compare to those in other countries. Criminologists Franklin Zimring and Gordon Hawkins (1997) observe,

> Other industrial democracies have rates of crime comparable to those found in the United States . . . But the death rates from all forms of violence are many times greater in the United States than in other comparable nations. *Lethal violence is the distinctive American problem* [emphasis added]. (p. 51)

The rate of lethal violence in the United States is a concern that policy makers must work to address. Its causes are complex and its solutions elusive, although the reduction in violent crime since the mid-1990s is encouraging.

OTHER SOURCES OF CRIME DATA

The UCR provides useful data to help us understand the nature and prevalence of crime in the United States. However, one substantial limitation is that it relies on data from crimes that were actually reported to the police. If a crime occurred that was not reported to the police, it is not included in the UCR data (for a useful overview of measurement

issues related to crime data, see Lynch & Addington, 2007). Evidence suggests that not all persons report their victimizations to the police. Reporting rates vary by crime. Here are a few examples of the percentages of victims who report the crime to the police: motor vehicle theft, 79.6%; robbery, 60.5%; burglary of a home, 56.2%; rape and sexual assault, 41.4%; and theft of an item costing under $50, 19.5% (U.S. Department of Justice, 2010).

To gain a more complete perspective on the amount of crime in the United States, there are two sources of data other than the UCR that can be used. The first of these is a victimization survey in which researchers ask members of the public whether they have been victimized by crime (see generally Cantor & Lynch, 2000). The Bureau of Justice Statistics, an agency within the U.S. Department of Justice, conducts the annual **National Crime Victimization Survey (NCVS)**. The NCVS is not directly comparable to the UCR because it uses a slightly different system for classifying offenses. In addition, the NCVS does not measure homicide because the victim is deceased. However, it does provide informative data about the amount of crime that occurs in the United States.

National Crime Victimization Survey
A survey conducted by the Bureau of Justice Statistics to determine how many persons have been the victims of criminal acts. Also known as the NCVS, this is an example of a victimization survey.

For instance, according to the most recently available NCVS at the time of this writing (U.S. Department of Justice, 2010), of every 100,000 persons, 1,980 would be victimized by a violent crime and 13,470 would experience a property crime. Note that these figures are considerably higher than those detected by the UCR, as presented in Figures 1.2 and 1.3. The gap between the official UCR crime rate and the NCVS victimization rate is one measure of the **dark figure of crime**, meaning the volume of crime that goes unreported to authorities. Although NCVS rates are higher than those in the UCR, they do illustrate the same trend over time, showing a substantial decrease in crime since the mid-1990s.

dark figure of crime
Refers to the amount of crime that is not reported to the police or other authorities. An example is the gap between the official Uniform Crime Report crime rates and those suggested by the National Crime Victimization Survey.

The NCVS (U.S. Department of Justice, 2010) provides other interesting facts about victimization as well. Persons with a family income below $7,500 have the greatest risk of being victimized by a violent crime, as do persons below 25 years of age. Violent crimes are almost equally likely to involve offenders known to the victim (50.1%) as they are to involve strangers (49.9%). The greatest percentage of violent crimes occurs during the daytime (defined as 6AM–6PM; 53.6%), and the most frequent location is at or near the victim's home (29.3%). When a weapon is used in a violent crime (26.3% of all cases), it is most likely to be a firearm (used in 33% of all violent crimes in which a weapon was used). The sorts of data that the NCVS provides can be informative in developing crime prevention programs and in making decisions about criminal justice agency strategies and priorities.

A second form of crime data is the **self-report study**. This, too, is a survey administered to the public, but instead of asking about whether persons have been victims of crime, it asks whether persons have committed certain criminal acts. Research suggests that, with some exceptions, persons completing the surveys are generally truthful about their participation in illegal activities (for additional background, see Thornberry & Krohn, 2000). Unlike official crime data and victimization studies, there is no single survey recognized as the designated national self-report study for the United States.

self-report study
One way of measuring the amount of crime in society by administering surveys that ask persons to report whether or not they have committed certain criminal acts.

One example of a self-report study is the Youth Risk Behavior Survey (YRBS), conducted every other year by the Centers for Disease Control. The YRBS is administered to high school students and has found that, of the students who completed the study, 8.2% reported driving under the influence of alcohol within the past 30 days, 32.8% reported being in a fight within the past 12 months, 5.4% reported carrying a weapon on school property within the last 30 days, 39.9% reported having ever used marijuana, 6.8% reported having ever used cocaine, and 20.2% reported having ever taken a prescription drug without having a prescription for it (Eaton et al., 2012). Follow-up questions on self-report studies can also gain useful information about what factors are associated with engaging in illegal behavior and why individuals are motivated to do so.

CRIME DATA: TRADE-OFFS AND POLITICS

Each of the above measurements—official data, victimization surveys, and self-report studies—has strengths and weaknesses that we must keep in mind when interpreting crime data (for a general discussion, see Rand & Rennison, 2002; U.S. Department of Justice, 2004). The UCR and NCVS share the advantage of being national programs, each of which provides information about crime in the United States, as a whole. Another advantage both share is that they are collected on an annual basis, allowing for comparisons over time.

The UCR is often viewed by those in the criminal justice system as the definitive account, as it is based on actual police records. This is an advantage, because it provides data about the type and volume of offenses that come to the attention of criminal justice agencies and to which they must respond. However, disadvantages include that reporting to the UCR program is not mandatory, so some police agencies may not submit their data; also, the UCR does not record what we have seen above, which is the large number of crimes that are never reported to the police. In addition, UCR data may be impacted by the way police agencies collect and process their data, since there may be inconsistencies between departments, or even within a department, in terms of how crime information is recorded and verified (McCleary, Nienstedt, & Erven, 1982). The UCR also applies what is known as the hierarchy rule, which only counts the most serious offense that occurs in an incident. For instance, if during a bank robbery the offender committed an aggravated assault on a bank patron, only the most serious offense—the robbery—would be counted (for additional examples, see Federal Bureau of Investigation, 2004, pp. 10–12).

The NCVS does not have a hierarchy rule and does count unreported crimes, thereby differing from the UCR. In addition, the NCVS provides data about many aspects of a victimization, including information about the victim, the offender, the location and time of the offense, and more. But it, too, has drawbacks. One is that the NCVS is not a full count of all crime, but rather is based on a survey administered to a sample of individuals (approximately 67,000–85,000 persons per year; Survey Methodology, n.d.). This means that, statistically, it is possible to have sampling error, if the individuals who complete the survey are not representative of (i.e., similar to) the general population. The NCVS also relies on the accuracy of individual memories about the crimes that are addressed in the survey, which may have occurred months prior to the administration of the survey.

Self-report studies differ from the UCR and NCVS in that they are generally not designed for the purpose of reporting on crime trends in the United States as a whole. The purpose of YRBS, for instance, is "[t]o monitor priority health-risk behaviors . . . among youth and young adults" (Eaton et al., 2012, p. 2); other self-report studies may be conducted as components of individual criminal justice research studies, but are not intended to capture general trends in crime. These studies can provide useful understandings of offender behavior or measures of crime among the general public, but like the NCVS, they presume that samples are representative and memories and reporting are accurate.

As this discussion indicates, there is no perfect way to measure the amount of crime in society. There will always be some amount of offending and victimization that is unknown, so any measure is best viewed as an approximation, which must be interpreted carefully and with knowledge of the above strengths and limitations. This is of importance because, as discussed briefly below, crime data can influence criminal justice policy. As a result, it is important that the data be used and interpreted properly.

Policy advocates often, and understandably, use crime data to support their positions (e.g., Best, 1990; Best, 1999). But make no mistake, the use of data can be political, as individuals and groups marshal the numbers that are most supportive to their causes (see Stone, 2012, chapter 8). Consider recidivism, which is a measure of how often

former offenders commit new crimes. A report released in 2002 found that 67.5% of inmates released from prison in 1994 were rearrested within three years of their release. The same report noted that 25.4% of inmates released from prison in 1994 were sentenced to another prison term within three years of their release (Langan & Levin, 2002). Both are measures of the same concept—recidivism—and both could be offered as evidence of either high (67.5%) or low (25.4%) recidivism. And, the data are incomplete. What about an offender who committed a crime three years and one day after release? What about an inmate who is sentenced to a local jail, rather than a state prison? You can see the difficulties associated with measuring a seemingly simple concept.

Data can also be used for political purposes. If crime rates go up, there is often a rush to point fingers, as individuals and agencies accuse one another of not doing enough to reduce crime. If crime rates go down, there is often a rush to claim credit for the decrease, as individuals and agencies claim that it was their doing. For intance, following news that firearms deaths had declined by 56% in California, both sides of the gun control debate claimed credit for the reduction. Gun control advocates claimed that it was due to gun control measures adopted by the state. Gun rights advocates claimed that gun ownership by the public deterred would-be criminals (Fagan, 2013). Of course, both sides are responding to the same fact, with different arguments.

Numbers are often accepted with scientific certainty. However, we encourage you to critically assess crime data and to reflect upon how the data were collected and what conclusions may reasonably be drawn from them.

Q Do you find the crime data presented in this section surprising? Why or why not?

Q Look back to the scenario at the beginning of the chapter. If you wanted to gather a fairly comprehensive set of data to measure the amount of crime before and after the implementation of your preferred policy, what sort of crime data would you utilize? Be as specific as possible in your answer.

Q Locate an actual crime statistic used in a policy debate. Is there any additional information you would want to know in order to better understand the data and how they are being used?

Looking Ahead

You will see from the Contents that the book is divided into five units. This chapter introduced the concepts of crime and criminal justice in preparation for the later units. Unit I explores how philosophies of criminal justice and law influence decisions about which acts to criminalize and about the strategies to use in responding to crime. Unit II focuses on the concept of social control, considering how individual behavior is regulated and why persons sometimes turn to deviant activities. Knowledge of social control may lead to more effective justice policy by helping justice agencies develop strategies that focus effectively on the root causes of crime and its control. Unit III asks the question, what is justice? There is no single definition, but this unit explores various models of what justice means as well as how justice policy is actually made. Unit IV considers the role of criminal law and punishment in accomplishing social control and achieving justice. Finally, Unit V turns to the agencies of criminal justice themselves, exploring the work of the police, the courts, and corrections.

Conclusion

As illustrated in this chapter, criminal justice can be understood from a variety of perspectives, each of which has the potential to shape the field in different ways.

Ultimately, criminal justice centers on the study of society's responses to crime. The good news is that, as of this writing, crime in the United States has declined substantially since the mid-1990s. The challenge for criminal justice students and professionals alike is to consider what policies are most promising to continue reducing crime, while also protecting the rights and liberties valued by Americans. Understanding criminal justice as a system, profession, bureaucracy, moral agent, and academic discipline is a starting point for meeting this challenge. Also important is a survey of the key foundational ideas in criminal justice, as presented in subsequent chapters. Throughout the text, examples will draw connections between theory and practice and illustrate how philosophical concepts are applied in policing, law, corrections, and more.

We encourage you to think critically about the ideas in each chapter and to work through the case studies and questions that are presented in the text. In addition to providing interesting and important points for reflection and discussion, this will help you become a sophisticated observer of the criminal justice system and its workings.

DNA Evidence

Criminal Justice Problem Solving

Deoxyribonucleic acid (DNA) contains individualized genetic material that can, after scientific testing, be used to identify persons. You may have seen news reports, television shows, or movies that illustrate its use in criminal justice settings as a valuable tool of forensic science. If an offender leaves at the scene of the crime any material containing DNA, that DNA can potentially be matched to a sample taken from the offender at a later time. A DNA match between an offender and material left at the scene of a crime does not result in an automatic guilty verdict, but it can be used to establish that an offender was present or that an offender left biological material behind (e.g., blood, semen, saliva), which could be instrumental in linking the offender to the crime.

There are many unsolved crimes for which DNA evidence is available. However, without a suspect to whom the DNA sample from the crime scene can be compared, the DNA is of little use by itself. All states, as well as the federal government, have established DNA databases that archive samples from known offenders. When DNA is retrieved in an unsolved case, it can then be compared to the profiles in the database. If there is a match, or "hit," a formerly cold case (i.e., one that was not solved and for which investigators had insufficient leads to continue the investigation) can potentially be solved.

This is the foremost advantage of DNA databases—the potential to solve cold cases, increasing the clearance rate. In addition, the use of DNA databases is cost efficient as an investigative tool, particularly when balanced against the costs, both social and financial, of crime to society. Finally, DNA databases can in some instances help to ensure that the correct offender is identified and charged with the crime. For instance, a match acquired through a DNA database analysis could, depending on the circumstances of the case, result in the exoneration of other (actually innocent) suspects against whom there was circumstantial or questionable evidence (Grinnell & Burke, 2005).

DNA databases can also have the potential to identify offenders through the novel use of familial DNA (see Lerch, Burke, & Owen, 2008). Familial DNA rests on the premise that close relatives have similar, though not identical, DNA profiles. If a DNA sample from a crime scene is compared to samples in a DNA database, and the result is that a partial match is found between the crime scene and database sample, analysts can infer that the person who left the DNA at the crime scene is a close relative of the person whose sample is in the database. This is because the partial match would indicate shared genetic material consistent with that of a family member. Investigators could then focus on family members of the person whose DNA was in the database, in hopes of discovering a lead in the case.

While DNA evidence and DNA databases have the potential to contribute to criminal investigations, they have also been controversial. Consider the following questions:

- **Q** If a DNA database is used, who should be required to submit samples to the database? The U.S. Supreme Court recently upheld the collection of DNA samples for inclusion in the database from persons who had been arrested (but not convicted) for serious crimes (*Maryland v. King*, 2013). Do you agree with this decision? Should it be extended to persons arrested for any crime, serious or not? Persons accused of traffic violations? The general public as a whole? Why or why not?
- **Q** Would any moral concerns arise from the use of DNA databases? If so, what would they be? If not, why not?
- **Q** Currently, familial DNA is controversial, and its use is not permitted in most jurisdictions. Should it be? Why or why not?
- **Q** Is there any further information about DNA and its role in criminal justice that you would want to know before making a decision? Why?

Chapter One: Appendix

The Criminal Justice System

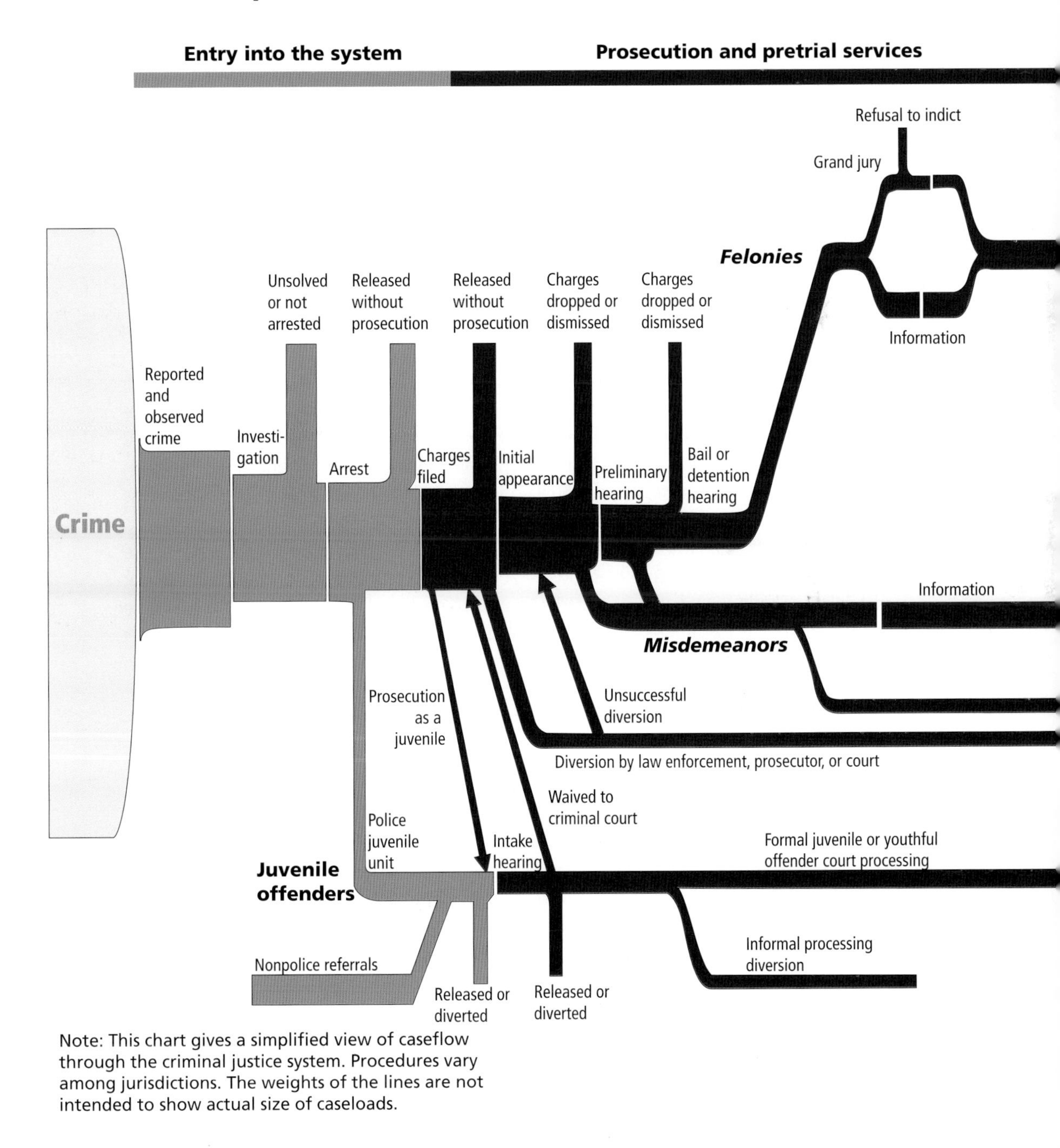

FIGURE 1.5 The Sequence of Events in the Criminal Justice System.
Source: Bureau of Justice Statistics, 2010

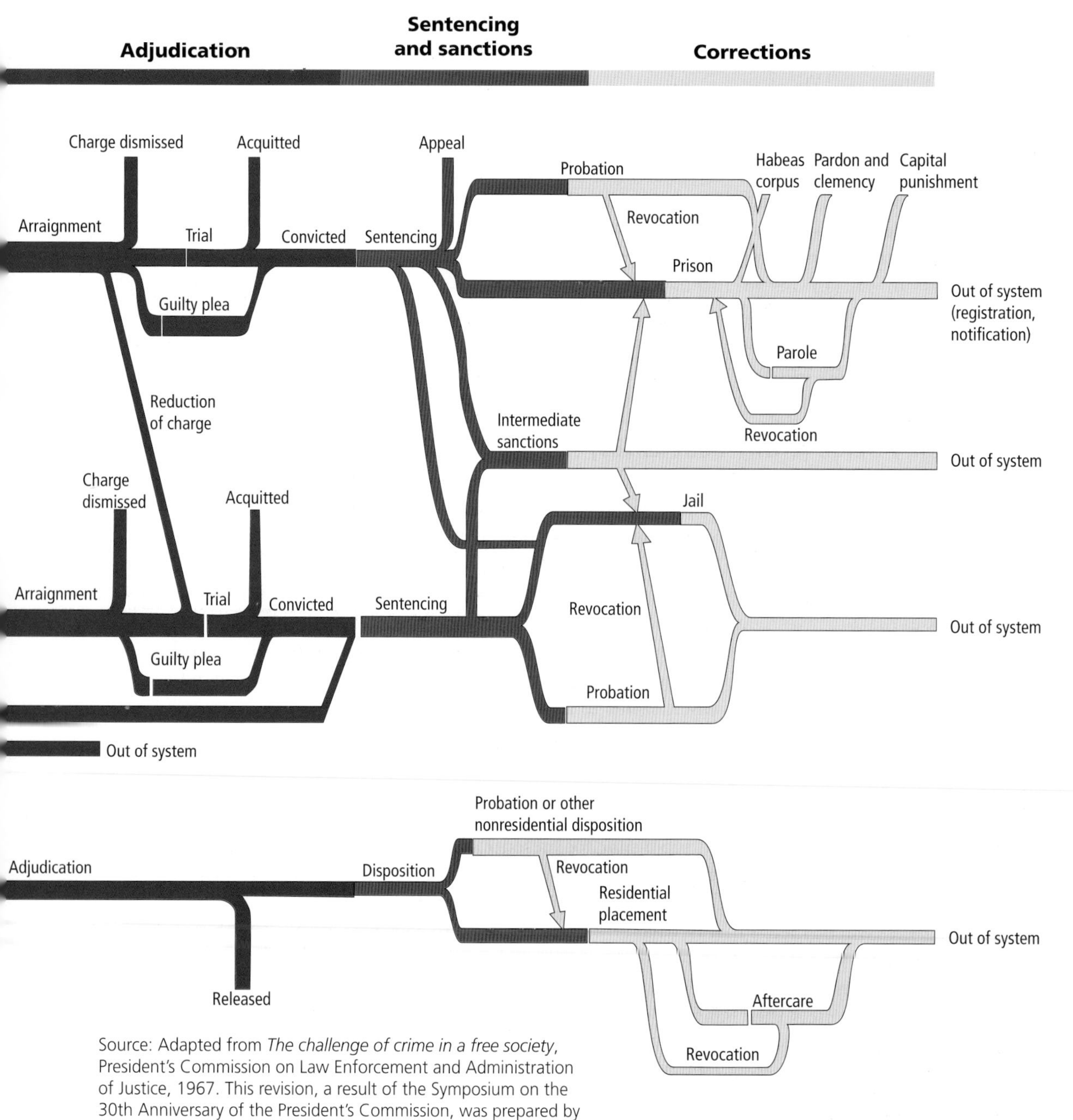

Source: Adapted from *The challenge of crime in a free society*, President's Commission on Law Enforcement and Administration of Justice, 1967. This revision, a result of the Symposium on the 30th Anniversary of the President's Commission, was prepared by the Bureau of Justice Statistics in 1997.

Further Explanation of Figure 1.5

The flowchart in Figure 1.5 depicts the criminal justice system. This narrative will introduce you to the processes diagrammed in the flowchart, but recognize that it will likely take additional study and coursework to fully understand all aspects of the criminal justice system that are illustrated here.

First, note that the flowchart branches off into four separate lines. The top line is labeled "Felonies," the second "Misdemeanors," the third "Diversion by law enforcement, prosecutor, or court," and the fourth "Juvenile offenders." In this discussion, we will focus solely on the processing of felony cases, as they are the most serious cases addressed by the criminal justice system. However, it is important to note that the misdemeanor (less serious crimes) processes have some differences from how felonies are handled, and juvenile cases have not only a different process, but also a different vocabulary for the names of the various steps in the system.

You should view the flowcart as the processes that offenders go through between the time they commit their crimes and the time they complete their sentences. Note that the thickness of the lines narrows as the flowchart proceeds from left to right. This illustrates a funnelling effect, as at each stage of the process, some offenders leave the system. This means, for instance, that of the offenders who commit a crime, not all will be caught, prosecuted, found guilty, and sentenced.

Let's begin at the left and move to the right, following a felony case. The various colors indicate which component of the criminal justice system is involved at each stage. As you read through the descriptions, follow along on the lines in the flowchart.

THE POLICE (LIGHT BLUE LINES)

Note that crime is depicted at the far left of the chart and then the line instantly narrows to only include reported or observed crimes. This is consistent with the discussion in this chapter about the large volume of unreported crime that never makes it into the criminal justice system. Some reported crimes will receive further investigation, but others will not, particularly if they are minor offenses and there are no visible leads. Of cases that are investigated, some go unsolved. In the flowchart, the vertical lines leading to the top of the chart represent instances in which offenders leave the system—in this case because the crime remains unsolved. For crimes that are solved an arrest will be made, but in some cases, whether due to lack of evidence, violation of police protocols, or perceived triviality of the offense, persons who are arrested may be released without further processing.

THE PROSECUTOR (DARK BLUE LINES)

The prosecuting attorney is reponsible for presenting in court the case against a person who has been charged with a crime (you will learn more about prosecutors, and criminal court processes, in Chapter 12). The prosecutor makes the decision as to what charges will be filed—that is, what crimes were alleged to have been committed. Sometimes, the prosecutor declines to file charges, for the same types of reasons that the suspect may have been released after arrest as described above. And sometimes the prosecutor offers the chance to participate in a diversion program, in which an individual participates in a rehabilitative, educational, counseling, or community service program, which if successfully completed results in the charges being dropped.

If charges are filed, there are next a series of hearings. These include: an initial appearance in which the accused appears before a judge to be informed of the charges being filed against him or her; a preliminary hearing in open court in which the prosecutor and defense attorneys present evidence and the judge makes a decision as to whether there is probable cause that the accused committed the crime (in which case a document called an information is issued); a bail hearing, to determine whether the accused must

remain in jail prior to trial or can be released into the community; and a grand jury, in which the prosecutor (the defense attorney and accused may not attend) presents evidence to a group of citizens who determine if there is probable cause that the accused committed the crime (in which case a document called an indictment is issued).

There are three points to note about these processes. First, they are designed to ensure fairness to persons accused of a crime, by ensuring that they understand the charges against them and that the case cannot proceed unless there is proable cause to believe the accused committed the crime. Second, at each stage (other than the bail hearing), the charges may be dismissed if probable cause is not found. And third, to complicate matters, the order of these steps may vary by jurisdictions, and some jurisdictions may have a preliminary hearing or grand jury, but not both.

THE COURTS (PURPLE AND RED LINES)

An arraignment is a hearing in which a person accused of crime, known as a defendant, is asked how he or she pleads to the charges. If the defendant pleads "not guilty," a trial is held before a judge or a jury. The defendant may be found guilty (resulting in a conviction) or not guilty (resulting in an acquittal). If the defendant pleads "guilty," there is no trial and the accused is convicted on the basis of admitting guilt. At any point prior to this stage, the defendant may enter into a plea bargain with the approval of the prosecutor and judge. A plea bargain occurs when the defendant agrees to plead guilty to a crime in exchange for a lesser sentence, reduced charges, or some other benefit. The overwhelming majority of criminal cases are resolved through a guilty plea, often the result of a plea bargain. Trials are rare occurrences.

After a conviction, the defendant is sentenced to some form of punishment. If the defendant plead "not guilty" and believed that trial processes were unfair, or that the sentence was inappropriate, or that the law or Constitution had not been followed in the processing of the case, he or she may file an appeal to a higher court.

CORRECTIONS (YELLOW LINES)

Once a sentence has been issued, correctional agencies are responsible for implementing it. Sentences can include: time spent in a local jail, which would generally be a sentence of less than a year; time spent in a state or federal prison, which would generally be for a sentence of a year or more; time spent on probation, in which the offender remains in the community under the supervision of a probation officer (if the offender commits another crime or breaks a rule of probation, he or she may have probation revoked and be sent to jail or prison); and intermediate sanctions, such as electronic monitoring, boot camp, or day reporting centers, which you will learn more about in Chapter 13 (noncompliance in these sanctions can sometimes lead to revocation and a jail or prison sentence).

Most offenders sentenced to prison will be released, either by serving the full term of their sentence, by earning early release on parole, by receiving a pardon or similar measure, or by successfully challenging their imprisonment through what are known as *habeas corpus* appeal proceedings. Other offenders will remain in prison for their entire life, and a small number will be executed if under the sentence of death.

The above is a very brief overview of the criminal justice system; much more could be written about the dynamics and mechanics of each stage. While the system may appear complex (and in reality, it is), the more courses you take in criminal justice, the more familiar it will become.

Unit One

Perspectives on Law

Photo Essay: Morality and the Law

Chapter 1 described the variety of perspectives through which criminal justice may be viewed. Consistent across these perspectives is the reality that the criminal justice process contains many points where discretionary decisions can be made. It is important that these decisions are ethical and informed by research. In reality, discretionary decisions are far from simple and can pose challenging dilemmas, many of which lie at the heart of debates about philosophies of morality and law. It is a consideration of these ideas, and their effects on criminal justice theory and practice, to which Unit I will turn.

To what extent should notions of morality influence the law and criminal justice? In his book *Hellfire Nation*, political scientist James Morone suggests that American politics (and by extension, American law and its enforcement) has been profoundly shaped by moral forces "entangled in two vital urges—redeeming 'us' and reforming 'them'" (2003, p. 3). In this way, he argues, law and policy are shaped by sequential "moral storm[s]" (2003, p. 10), as public debate rages over moral ills and their remedies. However, what is defined as a moral ill—and who and what society views as in need of reform—changes over time.

The response to crime has always contained a moral element. To borrow from Morone's argument, punishment was applied to the "them" who had violated social expectations that had been encoded into law. Whether it was a debtor being placed in the pillory (as shown here) or a murderer being hanged, it was perceived as a justified response to the problem of crime in colonial days. Not all punishment was meted out equally, however. For instance, "In Massachusetts . . . anyone guilty of drunkenness was fined five shillings; offenders unable to pay spent three hours in the stocks [a device similar to the pillory, but securing the feet rather than the head and arms]. If . . . the criminal was an outsider to town, he would most often be whipped and then banished" (Rothman, 1995, p. 112). How do you think morality was defined at that time and place? What do you think Massachusetts was trying to accomplish with the law described above? Do you think the punishments were fair?

Criminal laws in the colonial era were often grounded in religious morality. This included laws punishing blasphemy, heresy, and inappropriate conduct on the Sabbath day (e.g., traveling, drinking, shopping, and in some cases, failure to attend religious services). In addition, some colonies used the law to enforce adherence to their desired religion, prohibiting members of other religious groups from even entering the colony. For instance, the Massachusetts colony at one time required the banishment of Jesuits and Quakers; those who returned to the colony after being banished were executed (Friedman, 1993), such as Quaker Mary Dyer, pictured here, who was hanged in 1660. To what extent do you think laws should be driven by religious morality? Why?

As time progressed, the means of punishment turned more toward the use of prison but with an emphasis on reforming the prisoner. In this era, a moral punishment became one that provided an opportunity for the offender to repent for his or her sins that had led to the commission of a crime. As one observer noted at the time, "Can there be a combination more powerful for reformation than that of a prison which hands over the prisoner to all the trials of solitude, leads him through reflection to remorse, through religion to hope" (de Beaumont & de Tocqueville, [1833] 1964, p. 84). At Eastern State Penitentiary in Philadelphia, pictured here, inmates were confined in solitary cells with little to no human contact for the duration of their sentences, but the goal was for each inmate to experience a religious reformation as a result of a monastic life in the penitentiary. How would you assess this idea of punishment?

As society turned to the scientific study of social problems, views of morality became less dependent on religion and more focused on social conditions. Crime came to be understood not just as a matter of failing to be pious, but rather as being driven (at least in part) by social conditions that could influence individual behavior. In particular, criminologists began to seriously consider the impact on crime of issues such as poverty, socioeconomic status, education, medical conditions, mental health, and more (see Chapter 5 for a survey of various perspectives on explanations for crime). If these issues are related to crime, does society have an obligation to provide shelters or housing for the homeless, health care for those who are unable to obtain insurance, education for all persons, and a law requiring persons to be paid at least minimum wage? Why or why not?

As views of crime changed, so did views of punishment and its morality. Punishment became less about religious reformation and more focused on other goals. Among the goals for modern correctional agencies are the rehabilitation of offenders through programming, including education, vocational training, recreational activities, health care services, and more (see Carlson & Garrett, 2008). What would you identify as the characteristics or qualities that make punishment moral? Is there a moral obligation to provide these types of correctional programming?

Ideas about morality still underlie debates about law and justice in America and are often the subject of substantial controversy. However, there is not always agreement about how to decide what is or is not moral. Often in today's society, some people will attempt to discover a version of morality drawing upon historical roots. Others will advocate new conceptions of morality. What will morality mean in our future? Although that is difficult to predict, we find ourselves confronted by choices from the past as well as designing new options for the next generation. As we strive for consistency, fairness, and justice under the law, continued debates about morality will no doubt shape our

response to crime, the laws we make, and how we decide to enforce them. What do you think are the most important issues facing criminal justice today? How can you contribute to these conversations? What difference can your work make in the criminal justice system?

The chapters in Unit I explore the intersections between morality and law, including how philosophies of idealism and pragmatism shape the criminal justice system. Given the tremendous power that is accorded to justice professionals through their use of discretion, it is most important to consider the theoretical ideas that have shaped and will continue to shape the reality of criminal justice practice.

2

Concepts of Law and Morality

Learning Objectives

1 Explain the need for criminal justice systems. 2 Describe criminal justice strategies and tactics. 3 Explain how philosophical arguments about morality relate to criminal justice. 4 Compare and contrast idealism and pragmatism as related to criminal justice issues. 5 Apply the five concepts of morality to idealism, pragmatism, and criminal justice issues.

Key Terms

social contract theory
legitimacy
strategy
tactics
data
empiricism
idealist
pragmatist
harmony
ultimate truth
a priori
a posteriori
self
deity
teleology
paradigms

Key People

Thomas Hobbes
John Locke
Jean-Jacques Rousseau
Charles Sanders Peirce
Lawrence Kohlberg
Plato

Justice on Lover's Lane

Case Study

You are a police officer assigned to patrol Lover's Lane. Numerous assaults and robberies have recently occurred in this area. While on evening patrol, you notice a van that is parked and appears to be rocking. As a tactically trained officer on patrol, you know how to approach suspicious persons and suspicious vehicles. Should you stop to investigate the van that's rocking? Why or why not? If so, how far would you take the investigation?

If you decide *not* to stop, you fear the possible headlines in the news: VICTIM SEXUALLY ASSAULTED IN VAN AS OFFICER DRIVES BY. It is not just the potential for personal embarrassment or harm to your professional integrity that requires you to stop. Rather, you have an obligation to obey your department's orders, which include instructions from your sergeant to "keep a close eye on Lover's Lane." Therefore, you decide to investigate the van.

You discover that the van was rocking because the two teenagers inside the vehicle, a male and a female, were engaged in sexual activity. Both teenagers were of legal age to engage in sexual activity, and the behavior was completely consensual. How would you handle the situation? Why?

There is no single correct answer to this scenario (nor will there be for many other scenarios you encounter in this book). Although police officers are required to implement an agency's strategies by using acceptable tactics, they have much discretionary judgment in deciding *how* to best do so. This makes policing, and all criminal justice professions, very complex. In rendering their decisions, police officers and other criminal justice professionals must work only within the bounds of law and agency policy. However, their actions also illustrate perspectives on morality.

Q Generate a list of possible responses to this scenario. Think broadly to identify many possible approaches that an officer might take in addressing the situation. Then, determine what your preferred response would be. What criteria did you consider in choosing your preferred response?

Q Consider your preferred response to the scenario. Did your beliefs about the morality of sexual activity or the morality of other issues affect your decision? If so, how and why? If not, why not? Do you believe your answer could be viewed as a decision involving morality? Explain.

Facing page: Assisted-suicide advocate Dr. Jack Kevorkian and his "suicide machine." Do you think physician-assisted suicide violates social morality?

Q Would your preferred response be different if the teenagers were disrespectful or angry? If they were consuming alcohol? If they were consuming illegal drugs? If you knew the teenagers? If you knew their parents and also knew they would disapprove of this activity? If it was a same-sex rather than heterosexual couple? Why or why not?

Q Do your responses to the above questions differ from those of your friends or classmates? Why or why not? If they do, what factors might have influenced the differing decisions?

Criminal Justice and Society

FOCUSING QUESTION 2.1

Why do societies need criminal justice systems?

Consider for a moment why society needs police departments, or for that matter, other criminal justice agencies, such as courts and prisons. Another way of thinking about this is to ask the question: what would society be like if we *did not* have police departments, courts, and prisons? As you think about this question, you would probably reach one of two answers.

One possible answer is a society so perfect that there is no crime, no disorder, and therefore, no need for the agencies of criminal justice. While such a society may be theoretically possible, it is unlikely in reality. French sociologist Émile Durkheim (1938) observed that a truly crime-free society would require unanimous agreement on all aspects of life, as that is the only way that all persons would come to unanimous agreement on the laws and also agree to abide by them without exception. As Durkheim noted, this is something that is difficult to imagine given the wide variety of differing human opinions, tastes, and preferences.

Another possible answer is that a society without police, courts, and prisons would operate in a state of nature, a free-for-all environment where there is little order. After all, if there were no police to enforce rules, no courts to resolve disputes, and no prisons to punish wrongdoers, what would life be like? In describing a state of nature, British philosopher Thomas Hobbes suggested that life would be "solitary, poor, nasty, brutish, and short" ([1651] 1963, p. 143). Individuals would be responsible for enforcing their own self-interest, potentially by taking revenge against wrongdoers, while also fearing that they would accidentally offend others and then be the victim of someone else's revenge. Without a justice system, there would be little to protect the weak from being victimized by the strong, who could take or do what they wished without fear of punishment. Certainly, the chaotic state of nature is not an ideal lifestyle.

Let's return to the question posed earlier: why do we need criminal justice agencies? The simplest and most direct answer is that we need the police, courts, and corrections so we can *maintain order* in society. We do not live in a crime-free utopia. And we do not want to live in a Hobbesian state of nature. The criminal justice system helps us live in an orderly society that is a middle ground between the two extremes.

social contract theory A philosophical explanation for the origins of government, in which individuals willingly give up complete freedom to do as they please in exchange for a more secure society governed by laws enforced by a government.

This notion is actually a fairly sophisticated concept called **social contract theory**. Several philosophers have written about different perspectives on social contract theory (including Hobbes, [1651] 1963; Locke, [1689] 1963; Rousseau, [1762] 1963), but the basics go something like this. In a state of nature, individuals have the complete freedom to do whatever they want to do, good or bad—that is, until a stronger person or group stops them—because there are no agencies to enforce laws or maintain order. Because this is an undesirable way to live, individuals agree to give up some of their

freedom in exchange for security. That is, individuals no longer have complete freedom but instead are bound by a series of laws governing their behavior, which are enforced by a government. This is the social contract between the government and the governed, promising security in exchange for compliance with the law and its processes. As an example, in a state of nature, individuals could freely take the property of others and, there being no government or laws, there would be no penalty for doing so unless the property owner sought revenge. Under the social contract, individuals would give up their freedom to steal, as the government would pass laws against stealing in the interest of promoting safety and well-being in society.

But this raises an important question: how much freedom should be exchanged for security under the concept of the social contract? In the United States, the courts and public opinion are often the arbiters who determine whether the exchange is appropriate.

Consider the issue of police roadblocks. In what circumstances should the police be permitted to stop vehicles at a roadblock in order to investigate potential criminal activity? There is a liberty-security balance at play here. The liberty interest is the freedom to travel without interference, and the security interest is the prevention of criminal activity that could pose risks to the public. The U.S. Supreme Court has allowed police roadblocks for the purpose of detecting drunk drivers (*Michigan Department of State Police v. Sitz*, 1990), has permitted roadblocks to check for driver's license and registration (*Delaware v. Prouse*, 1979) and has allowed vehicles to be briefly stopped at permanent checkpoints near borders for the purpose of preventing smuggling and illegal immigration (*U.S. v. Martinez-Fuerte*, 1976). In each of these cases, the security interest was deemed to outweigh the freedom interest, especially given that such stops are brief. However, the U.S. Supreme Court rejected the City of Indianapolis's practice of using roadblocks to investigate for drug crimes, in which officers made "an open-view examination of the vehicle from the outside [and a] narcotics-detection dog walks around the outside of each stopped vehicle" (*City of Indianapolis v. Edmond*, 2000, p. 35). As this type of roadblock went beyond the narrow traffic safety and border safety rationales permitted in prior cases, the Court held that it went too far, especially given that the vehicles at the roadblock were detained without suspicion of wrongdoing. As illustrated by the roadblock issue, there are limits to the amount of freedom that may be curtailed in the name of security.

Furthermore, the social contract is dynamic, as the amount of freedom exchanged for the amount of security received may vary over time, and is often influenced by public opinion. For instance, after the terrorist attacks of September 11, 2001, the public and politicians seemed willing to accept more regulation in exchange for greater security. Within the month following September 11, 2001, 61% of persons polled "thought it necessary for [the] average person to give up some civil liberties to curb terrorism" (see Newman, 2003, p. 227); by 2011, the number had declined to 25% (Gallup, n.d.), as the public became more critical of homeland security policies. In 2013, a majority of the public (53%) disapproved of a government program that "obtained records from larger U.S. telephone and Internet companies in order to compile telephone call logs and Internet communications" (Gallup, 2013, para. 2). The balance was tipped toward privacy of communications as opposed to security interests—although in the same poll, almost 40% of those who disapproved of the program indicated that there could be some circumstances in which they would support it. Again, the social contract's balance between freedom and security is a fluid one.

Therefore, the social contract is a *metaphor* that helps us explain the role of government, of which criminal justice is one part, in society. An important feature of a social contract is the notion that the government must be responsive to the people. English philosopher John Locke ([1689] 1963) quoted the Latin dictum *salus populi supreme lex* (p. 193), meaning "the good of the people is the supreme law." This is important

legitimacy
Exists when citizens accept that their government has the right to govern them. Governments without legitimacy may face protest, disobedience, or revolution.

because it leads to the concept of **legitimacy**. A government has legitimacy when the people accept that it has the right to govern them. When a government does not have legitimacy, there may be protest, widespread disobedience of laws, or revolution.

The above has provided a perspective on why societies have criminal justice systems and the balances that they must strike in order to retain legitimacy. We will now turn to a discussion of how criminal justice agencies and personnel utilize strategies and tactics to enforce the law. Then, we will focus on how the selection of strategies and tactics, as well as the adoption of the laws themselves, reflects and reveals deeper moral and philosophical foundations. Debates about these very ideas shape understandings of the criminal justice system and perceptions of its legitimacy.

Q Do you agree with Durkheim that a crime-free society would be impossible? Explain why or why not.

Q What factors would you consider in determining how to reach an acceptable balance between freedom and security in the development and enforcement of the law? From the perspective of the social contract, what do you think should be the primary goals of the criminal justice system?

Q What are some factors that you think would contribute to government legitimacy? How could the criminal justice system promote them?

Choosing Strategies and Tactics

FOCUSING QUESTION 2.2

What judgments are involved in making decisions about criminal justice strategies and tactics?

When enforcing the law, justice professionals must determine how to promote security while maintaining basic freedoms under the social contract theory described above. In doing so, they make many discretionary decisions on a daily basis. These decisions help clarify the meanings of law, morality, and justice. With each accumulated decision, we gain a better understanding of how decision making proceeds and how the law is implemented in practice. An examination of strategies and tactics will provide further insight to this discussion.

Reflect on your decision in the Lover's Lane case at the beginning of this chapter. There are numerous ways you could have responded. It would be within your authority as a peace officer to make an arrest for fornication or public indecency or to simply advise the couple to "move along." This is the power of discretionary decision making: the couple in the van will perceive your decision, whatever it is, to be *the law* on the matter. Unless they visit Lover's Lane frequently, they may have no other experiences or ideas about what the law is or how it is enforced. In this way, through your actions, you have defined what the law means in practice (by choosing from a set of possible responses), at least as far as the couple in this case is concerned. Because you are an officer of the law, your decision will likely hold legitimacy. And in making your decision, you have consciously or unconsciously invoked notions of morality, as we will discuss later in this chapter. Of course, other officers in similar situations might make different choices, resulting in a different definition of law.

It quickly becomes clear that in studying the law, it is as important to consider how the law is enforced and defined by criminal justice professionals as it is to consider what is written in legal codes. Yet it is important to dispel the notion that criminal justice professionals act impulsively or without guidance in making discretionary decisions. Agency leaders (e.g., chiefs, wardens, and other supervisors) often set broad strategies for accomplishing agency goals, which they expect their employees to understand and

follow. And individuals within an agency, especially sworn personnel, receive training, guidance from peers, and sometimes briefings on current research to help guide them in identifying the specific tactics for accomplishing agency strategies. It is within this framework of strategies and tactics that many discretionary decisions are made.

STRATEGIES

strategy
The broad approach that an agency or organization uses to address a problem or issue. A strategy is a broad plan that is put into effect through the use of various specific tactics.

Strategy refers to the broad approach that a criminal justice agency uses to address crime. Often generated by agency leaders, strategies provide the plan or framework within which employees are expected to work when approaching an issue or problem. For instance, what strategies could a police department use to address driving under the influence of alcohol or drugs (DUI)? One strategy might be to drive DUI offenders home rather than taking them to jail. Another strategy might be to publicize the dangers of DUI through a media campaign. Still another strategy might be to promote aggressive enforcement through DUI checkpoints. Or an agency could use all of these strategies, in combination. Strategies have moral consequences stemming from value debates. Is it fair to take DUI offenders home instead of holding them accountable for their actions? Is it a good use of police resources to spend money on an advertising campaign rather than to spend it on other things? Would aggressive enforcement strategies violate anyone's constitutional rights? These are important questions to consider when weighing the various strategies. An individual's values and beliefs would likely influence how he or she would answer these questions and would shape strategic decisions accordingly.

Strategies develop the big-picture plan for an agency to address a particular problem or conduct its business. However, even when strategies are established, they rely on individuals' judgments and decisions to carry them out. And again, this includes questions about morality and value debates related to criminal justice practice.

Many police agencies operate SWAT (special weapons and tactics) teams or SORTs (special operations response teams). Here, a team makes entry into a structure thought to be associated with drug offenses; upon entry, officers discovered that it was the wrong house (Narain, 2008). One strategic decision for SWAT teams or SORTs is determining in what types of incidents, and for what purposes, the teams should be used; what do you think? What do you think would be the most important considerations when a team plans the tactics for completing its assignments?

tactics
Specific actions that are taken to implement the broad idea outlined in a strategy.

data
Careful and systematic observations that are analyzed to draw a conclusion about a research question. Examples of data include statistics, interviews, survey responses, and more.

TACTICS

Tactics consist of deciding *how* to implement a strategy. As noted above, the decision to use DUI checkpoints would be a strategic choice. Perhaps the captain of patrol operations determined that use of checkpoints would lead to a reduction in automobile accidents (and the evidence suggests that they do; see Erke, Goldenbeld, & Vaa, 2009; and Elder et al., 2002). Determining where, when, and how to administer the checkpoints are tactical decisions. For instance, the crime analysis division could produce **data** indicating where and when most alcohol-related accidents occur, and that could guide the tactical decision of when and where checkpoints should be operated. Another tactical decision might include whether to use technologies such as the passive alcohol sensor, a device which can alert officers to the presence of alcohol in the vicinity of an individual (Burke, 2001).

Therefore, strategies broadly identify problems and how to address them, while tactics identify specific ways to put the strategy into effect. A reasonable strategy coupled with sufficient tactics should result in effective criminal justice policies. Tactics may be developed through a number of sources. Agency personnel could share what they have learned and make recommendations for tactics, academy and on-the-job training can demonstrate tactical choices, personnel can learn through their own or others' experiences, and research can provide insights about effective practices. Unfortunately, pre-planned tactics may not be able to consider all possible aspects of a situation. This is why the use of discretion is required to determine how to best resolve situations for which there is not firm tactical guidance.

Tactics involve moral decisions because they must be evaluated in terms of fairness, justice, equality, and other overarching values and philosophies. Let's take another example. Assume that an agency adopts a *strategy* of aggressively enforcing a state's law requiring seat belts to be worn by the occupants of a vehicle (and that failure to do so results in a $50 fine). Now assume that one *tactic* used to implement this strategy is to arrest any persons whose vehicles are pulled over and who are not wearing seat belts. What beliefs, values, and standards need to be balanced to assess this tactic on moral grounds? Certainly, you would want to consider issues such as officer safety, whether an arrest for a such a minor offense would infringe on a person's rights, the value to society of ensuring that seat belts are worn, and how far an officer's right to make an arrest should extend in a democratic society (to see how the Supreme Court ruled in a similar case, see *Atwater v. City of Lago Vista,* 2001). Therefore, as you make decisions about tactics, you simultaneously shape the moral foundations of criminal justice. Box 2.1 will help you think more about tactics, using the Lover's Lane case from the chapter's opening as an example.

CRIMINAL JUSTICE: POPULAR CONCEPTIONS VERSUS ACADEMIC SCHOLARSHIP

Again flowing from the notion of social contract theory, it is in everyone's best interest to have a criminal justice system to maintain order. In a democracy, where government agencies must be legitimate and responsible to the public, that criminal justice system must meet a number of ideals, including fairness, equality, and effectiveness. But how do we judge whether the criminal justice system is meeting its obligation? How do we determine the appropriate strategies and tactics for criminal justice agencies to use? Often, there is disagreement between members of the general public, to whom the criminal justice system must answer, and criminal justice scholars, who have dedicated careful study to the system and its functioning. Each may reach different conclusions about criminal justice strategies and tactics.

To the public, it is tempting to focus only on the goals of the criminal justice system without considering precisely how those goals are accomplished and with what implications. For instance, if prisons are meant to promote public safety by

BOX 2.1

TACTICS ON LOVER'S LANE

Refer back to the case study at the beginning of the chapter. The department's strategy has been to "keep a close eye on Lover's Lane." When you see the van, you must decide what tactics to use in approaching it so you can figure out what's going on. Remember, it is nighttime, you do not know how many people are in the van, you do not know who is in the van, and you do not know for sure what they are doing in the van. Assume that the van has tinted windows and that the interior is not lit. Here are some of the resources you have in your police vehicle: flashing police lights; siren; spotlight; headlights; loudspeaker; in-car video camera; two-way radio; handcuffs; mace; Taser; nightstick; sidearm; and shotgun.

Prepare a description of your tactics that includes these issues:

- Q Where will you park your car in relation to the van?
- Q How will you approach the van?
- Q How will you get the attention of the occupants?
- Q Will you ask them to leave the van? If so, how? If not, why?
- Q What precautions will you take for your own safety?
- Q What precautions will you take for the safety of the persons in the van?
- Q What questions will you ask?
- Q If you believe that sexual relations were occurring in the van, how would you determine whether it was consensual?

Discuss your tactics with those of your classmates. (You may also wish to discuss your solutions with a trained law enforcement officer. What do you think you would learn if you did so?) How do your tactics reflect ideas about morality, as described in the chapter?

What you have done in this exercise is engage in tactical decision making. But in the development of tactics, as you receive new information, your tactics may change. How would the following information change your tactical approach? Why?

- It is daytime instead of nighttime.
- The area is a suburb instead of a Lover's Lane.
- When you shine your lights through the van's windows, five heads pop up.
- As you approach the van, you receive a radio call alerting you to a prowler in the area.

locking up offenders, persons might believe that what happens inside the prison is inconsequential as long as they also believe that prisons can meet their goals of keeping society safe. This leads some to give common-sense but overly simplistic responses to the complex questions of criminal justice. When asked about strategies related to inmate rights or privileges (e.g., visits, education, recreation, etc.), a typical response would revert back to the perceived purpose of prisons—to promote public safety—leading to responses such as, "But how does *that* keep society safe?" An outcry could result, perceiving rights and privileges as unnecessary and extraneous. Little evidence is typically offered beyond what is reported in the media. As a result, much of the argument relies on notions of what the system should accomplish ("lock 'em up to keep us safe") without considering what must occur for that to happen. Much popular discourse on criminal justice, then, relies on arguments about the purpose of criminal justice agencies without careful analysis of how agencies go about their work. That is, the ends (i.e., the actual or desired outcomes) are the focus rather than the means (or methods) by which those ends are achieved.

Public perceptions of criminal justice are also guided by intuitive perceptions of what works (or ought to work), rather than being driven by data. Charles Sanders Peirce, a nineteenth-century philosopher, developed an idea that still influences education and decision making in the twenty-first century. In his article "The Fixation of Belief" (1877), he claimed there are four ways of knowing something. The first three are those most commonly relied upon by the public; they include tenacity, authority, and common sense.

Tenacity is believing that something is true based on the sheer desire to believe it, often because it is something that a person wants to be true. Individuals often use tenacity to support positions that are intractable, or not subject to measurement with data (e.g., "justice is good"). To return to the above example, tenacity could be used to structure arguments by those supporting or opposing inmate rights and privileges. For instance, persons could argue that prisons should be unpleasant environments, or that inmates are entitled to recreation and education, solely because that is how they believe prisons ought to be, based on their worldview.

The use of authority to support a position occurs when persons base their opinions on what they are told by others whom they perceive to be credible, or believable. There are many reasons that a person might be perceived as credible. Perhaps the person holds a position that provides expertise in a topic, such as a warden who explains the benefits of educational and recreational programming (a position that correctional administrators and staff do tend to hold—Tewksbury & Mustaine, 2005). Or credibility might be based on personal relationships, such as a friend whose advice has been useful in the past. If that same friend then expresses an opinion that prisons are like country clubs, that opinion may be accepted as true (this is a popular, though inaccurate, perception about prisons—see Beckett & Sasson, 2000). Regardless, the focus is on accepting what others say, rather than on an independent review of data.

Common-sense arguments are those that sound logical but are made without the use of actual data or observations. On the surface, these arguments sound logical and well thought out. However, this can cause some questionable arguments to masquerade as reasonable when in fact they are not supported by the weight of the evidence. For instance, it may be logical to reason that prison amenities do little to promote rehabilitation or to reduce reoffending, because they make the prison environment too pleasant. However, as indicated below, this common-sense notion is not supported by research.

Compare each of these approaches to that used by criminal justice scholars. First and foremost, scholars are concerned with data. The answers to all questions are grounded in the collection of data, such as statistics, careful observations, and in-depth interviews. This is also known as **empiricism** (see Box 2.2). To continue with the prisons example, a scholar may take as a starting point that the goal of prisons is to protect society. But the scholar would then consider what would need to happen within prisons for them to truly serve as protection for society. The scholar might find, for instance, that most individuals who are sentenced to prison commit a new offense when they are released (Langan & Levin, 2002). The scholar would then conclude that prisons currently do not fully provide protection from future crime. However, the scholar would also find that data indicate that inmates are less likely to commit new offenses if they utilize the right to receive visitors while in prison (Mears, Cochran, Siennick, & Bales, 2012), if they complete even one college-level class while in prison (Burke & Vivian, 2001), and that artistic programming may contribute to offender rehabilitation (Johnson, 2008). On the basis of empiricism, then, the scholar might reach a different moral conclusion

empiricism
The notion that the answers to questions should be grounded in the collection and analysis of data. This approach guides scholars in criminal justice and other fields.

BOX 2.2

PROBLEM-SOLVING METHOD

There is a five-step method for solving problems through empiricism (this is also the process that pragmatists favor, as described in the chapter). The method is the basis for social science research as well as evidence-based criminal justice tactics and strategies (e.g., problem-oriented policing; Goldstein, 1990). Anyone can use the method for any problem; however, problems that are more difficult require more research and analysis.

- Step 1. Become aware of a problem. (*Example: Citizens complain to you about neighborhood disorder.*)
- Step 2. Locate, define, and analyze the problem. (*Example: You find that the disorder comes from a group of juveniles loitering in a nearby parking lot on weekend nights.*)
- Step 3. Entertain possible hypotheses for addressing the problem. (*Examples: Implement a curfew; play loud classical music on speakers in the parking lot; increase police patrols; provide alternative weekend entertainment.*)
- Step 4. Choose one hypothesis to test. (*Example: Play loud classical music on speakers in the parking lot.*)
- Step 5. Collect data to verify the results. (*Example: Observe how many juveniles congregate at the parking lot the weekend before the speakers are installed; compare that to how many juveniles congregate at the parking lot after the speakers are installed.*)

If playing loud classical music on speakers in the parking lot causes the juveniles to stop loitering there, you have implemented a successful solution (as long as they haven't just relocated to another parking lot!). If it turns out that the juveniles groove on classical music and now more of them loiter at the parking lot, you have not implemented a successful solution, and you would return to Step 3 (for a discussion of the actual impact of this type of solution, see Lucas, 2009).

Q How much of this process did you use to resolve the Lover's Lane scenario? Can this process be applied to that scenario?

Q Select a criminal justice issue or problem that you find interesting. Explain how this method could be applied to resolve it. Compare this pragmatic approach to idealistic decision making, described later in this chapter.

from the public. For the scholar, it is the means that are of the most interest. The means of accomplishing a goal may determine how well it is accomplished and whether the goal itself is valid.

Determining what criminal justice agencies should do is indeed a difficult task. It is sometimes complicated when the public and scholars use different processes to arrive at answers about the goals, strategies, and tactics that the criminal justice system should follow. As the next section will address, reaching these answers often includes a consideration of morality as applied to criminal justice issues.

Q Select a criminal justice issue of your choice. What are the possible strategies that could address it? What tactics might accompany each strategy? What do you think is the best solution? Why? In considering possible strategies and tactics, are there any data that you would find helpful to guide your decisions?

Q What role should researchers play in making criminal justice policy? What role should public opinion play? How can they be reconciled when there are disagreements?

Morality and Justice Studies

FOCUSING QUESTION 2.3

How are philosophical arguments about morality related to criminal justice?

The concept of morality underlies the above discussions. As described in Chapter 1, because it cannot avoid addressing issues of right and wrong—whether through determining what behaviors ought to be prohibited, how offenders should be punished, what the limits of the social contract are, and more—criminal justice functions as a moral agent. It is important to reflect on what this means, both for the study and practice of criminal justice.

It is also important to understand what the term "morality" means in this context. As McCollough (1991) explains, "*morality* refers to commonly accepted rules of conduct, patterns of behavior approved by a social group, values and standards shared by the group. It consists of beliefs about what is good and right held by a community with a shared history" (pp. 6–7). As such, this definition of morality does *not* assume that there is a master list of moral or immoral actions against which all others are judged. Nor does the definition assume that morality is grounded in any particular ideology, be it religious, political, economic, or any other. Rather, morality may be viewed as an ongoing *process* in which society continuously reflects on the items in McCollough's definition with the goal of determining the best solution to a dilemma.

As such, morality does not imply wagging a finger and saying, "that's immoral." In fact, issues of morality in criminal justice are often *implicit*, meaning that factors such as those listed by McCullough *shape* debates, but the debates are not about morality itself. Instead, the debates are about what should happen in policy and law, with proponents of various sides basing their answers on considerations that have a moral context.

Let's consider an example. Under social contract theory, prisons may be used to deprive offenders of their freedom in order to maintain security in society. But what happens when inmates are released from prison? In the past 10 to 15 years, there has been an effort to focus on offender re-entry programming, which is designed to help inmates re-enter society and maintain a crime-free lifestyle after their release from prison. As such, offender re-entry is a strategy pursued by a variety of criminal justice agencies. Tactics to implement the strategy often include educational programming, job skills and job search training, addressing health care needs, and assisting with housing after release (e.g., Lattimore, Steffey, & Visher, 2010). Tactics may also include the development of partnerships between correctional agencies, policing agencies, researchers (to determine program effectiveness), and the community, to collaborate on how to best provide services and supervision to released offenders (e.g., Bureau of Justice Assistance, 2007). But why pursue offender re-entry as a goal? One argument is that it has the potential to reduce recidivism (Lattimore, Steffey, & Visher, 2010), but there is also a moral context in which re-entry policies were developed.

In his 2004 State of the Union Address, President George W. Bush spoke in favor of re-entry programming, in fact pledging $300 million toward re-entry efforts. In doing so, he said, "America is the land of second chance, and when the gates of the prison open, the path ahead should lead to a better life" (Bush, 2004, para. 63). This is fundamentally a value statement about right and wrong, with the message that the right approach to addressing the needs of ex-offenders is contextualized in providing them opportunities for success. Defining re-entry programming as the best solution therefore conveys a moral message drawing upon the value of second chances.

Of course, finding the "best solution" is easier said than done, and it is typical to see spirited debate over criminal justice issues that raise questions of morality.

For instance, recall the discussion of physician-assisted suicide from Chapter 1. In some U.S. states, there is a process by which terminally ill patients may obtain drugs for the purpose of ending their own lives. What beliefs, values, and standards may help us understand the moral implications of this issue? Some would argue that physician-assisted suicide for terminally ill patients protects an individual's dignity and freedom to choose how to end one's life. Others would argue that life is sacred and no life should be voluntarily terminated, even if in the course of a serious illness. Still others might argue that physician-assisted suicide gives too much power to the medical industry in determining who does or does not have a terminal illness and that society should instead value the role of family or nontraditional therapy in end-of-life decisions. Yet others might argue that, in states in which physician-assisted suicide was approved by a public vote, it is an example of democracy in action and that the will of the people should prevail. Certainly, many other perspectives exist as well.

How, then, do we assess the morality of physician-assisted suicide? The answer lies in considering issues such as those raised earlier, by carefully studying what scholars, practitioners, and the public have to say about the issue, and by seeing how the arguments develop over time. As such, determining morality is much more complex than a gut reaction of "that's right!" or "that's wrong!" But understanding the morality of criminal justice issues is essential, for it provides the foundation, albeit a foundation that shifts over time, for our criminal justice system and its operation.

Criminal justice practitioners make seemingly routine decisions on a daily basis that require them to grapple with difficult and complex issues, and the collection of those decisions (and the debates surrounding them) helps shape the moral conceptions that serve as the foundation of criminal justice. But what factors, other than those described above, can shape understandings of morality as related to criminal justice? One answer is that moral decision making varies according to a series of stages, each with its own prescription for identifying the "right" answer to a moral dilemma.

KOHLBERG'S MORAL STAGES

Psychologist Lawrence Kohlberg argued that there are six moral stages, each of which prescribes its own method for determining what is or is not moral (for an overview of Kohlberg's theory, see Kohlberg & Hersh, 1977). According to Kohlberg, individuals proceed through these stages over the course of their lives, although they may do so at different paces; Table 2.1 lists the stages. Here, our interest is noting that different persons may have different ideas about how morality is

TABLE 2.1 Kohlberg's Moral Stages

Level	Stage	Focus
Preconventional	1	Avoiding punishment
	2	Individual needs and exchange relationships
Conventional	3	Do what's nice
	4	Law, order, and respect for authority
Postconventional	5	Advocate for rights and values through democratic processes
	6	Adherence to ethical principles

defined, resulting in differences in their positions on moral issues (for continued development of the theory, which is beyond the scope of this book, see Rest & Navárez, 1994; Gibbs, 2014). Understanding the different stages can therefore help in understanding differences of opinion about the moral premises underlying criminal justice decision making.

The six stages are grouped into three levels: preconventional, conventional, and postconventional. The preconventional level focuses on punishments and power. In Stage 1, avoiding punishment forms the basis for moral decision making. As long as a behavior avoids punishment, it is deemed acceptable. In Stage 2, decisions are made in a way such that the individual's needs come first, and the needs of others are only met through exchange relationships, such as deal making that benefits both parties. The conventional level focuses on the loyalty to the social structure, including friends, family, and country. Stage 3 can be summarized by stating that being perceived as "nice" is what matters. Doing that which is viewed by others as being good matters (or trying to do so, even if the actual outcome is negative), as one key goal of this stage is to conform to societal expectations. Stage 4 was described by Kohlberg and Hersh (1977) as focusing on "law and order," meaning "doing one's duty, showing respect for authority, and maintaining the given social order for its own sake" (p. 55). As in Stage 1, abiding by the rules matters—but here, it is not out of a desire to avoid punishment (as in Stage 1), but rather for a desire to uphold the social order and to respect authorities. The postconventional level focuses on the identification of moral principles that might supersede the law or existing social order. Stage 5 begins with the idea that there are certain rights and societal values that are worth promoting, even if these rights and values are not recognized under current law. If the latter is the case, then it becomes morally right—perhaps obligatory—to use the democratic process to advocate for change through existing political structures. Stage 6 is the only stage to entirely transcend existing legal and social structures. In this stage, individuals identify consistent ethical principles, such as a belief in justice, or in equality, or in the categorical imperative (as described in Box 1.2). It is important to note that this is not a listing of specific rules that must be followed, but rather an identification of abstract principles that represent what is "right." Moral decisions are then made on this basis, even if the decision requires breaking an existing law or violating an existing social norm.

Consider how these perspectives could shape moral debates about criminal justice policy, returning to the example of physician-assisted suicide. In states prohibiting physician-assisted suicide (which is the majority of states), persons in Stages 1, 3, and 4 would likely oppose the practice—Stage 1 because it could result in an undesired punishment, Stage 3 because it violates the social expectations that lead to the approval desired from others, and Stage 4 because it violates the existing law and authority. Persons in Stage 2 would do whatever is in their best interest—that could be supporting physician-assisted suicide to alleviate their own pain and suffering, opposing it to prevent the immediate death of a friend or family member, or any other outcome consistent with their interests. Persons in Stage 5 would recognize that a decision about the legality of physician-assisted suicide had been made through the democratic process, and would respect that—but also would advocate to change the law if they believed that it should be legalized. Persons in Stage 6 would assess physician-assisted suicide based upon their own view of moral principles and, if they thought that it is morally justified, they would support its use regardless of what the laws were.

In making moral decisions, individuals vary. The concept of moral development, with the notion that individuals may function at different stages of moral reasoning, has been researched in criminal justice. Results suggest that the level of moral

BOX 2.3

Research in Action

POLICE MORALITY

The police must negotiate multifaceted moral dilemmas in their everyday work. As Muir (1977) observed in his classic study of police officers: "The policeman was beset by the same profound questions of moral philosophy as any other member of mankind . . . The substance of the policeman's moral philosophy was critical in how he performed his job" (p. 190).

How do police officers approach questions of morality? Steve Herbert's 1997 book, *Policing Space*, addresses that, and other issues. Herbert spent hundreds of hours in the field, observing Los Angeles Police Department officers as they worked the streets. During the observations, he took notes, which formed the basis for the arguments made in his book.

Herbert found that the police identified themselves in relation to others in the community, while also observing that the police divide the community into two distinct categories—police and non-police. The police saw their job "as a deeply moral enterprise" (p. 142). Herbert described police perceptions of morality as a tendency to view things in dualistic terms, meaning that actions and persons were often viewed as either good or evil. The police saw themselves as good and criminals as evil. The police also saw one of their responsibilities as defending the moral order, which gave them a sense of duty for "doing the right thing" (p. 151).

In some cases, the right thing could mean community-oriented interventions. Herbert tells the story of officers who, upon encountering potential gang members, talked with them to try to persuade them to follow a law-abiding path. "In these situations, the officers believed that by interfering in people's lives they could be not just agents of the law but also agents of positive change" (p. 156). In other cases, the right thing could mean an arrest, which officers viewed as morally correct not only because it provided justice to individual offenders, but also because it preserved the safety of the neighborhood.

The benefit of a dualistic view of morality is that it provides "a refuge from . . . ambiguity" (p. 158), which can serve as an aid for decision making. Having a clear sense of right and wrong can reduce the need to grapple with uncertainty in moral judgment. For the police, "actions become more meaningful if they are understood in terms of moral rightness and goodness, in terms of the overarching goals of peace and freedom." (p. 160).

And with that, we come full circle back to Muir—moral philosophy is of critical importance to police officers in their daily work. Similarly, the concepts of morality outlined in this chapter are of critical importance to criminal justice professionals.

Q How do you think police officers in your community develop their sense of the "right thing?"

Q How do you think Kohlberg's stages of moral reasoning would impact police officer determinations of the "right thing?" How would officers at different stages reach different conclusions?

reasoning can influence police officer attitudes (Musgrave & Stephenson, 1983; Morgan, Morgan, Foster, & Kolbert, 2000), offender recidivism (Van Vugt et al., 2011), and perceived legitimacy of judicial opinions (Daneker, 1993). As such, understanding different approaches to moral reasoning can aid in understanding the positions that individuals take on criminal justice issues, as well as differences in how discretion is used in criminal justice decisions. For further discussion of how moral reasoning impacts decision making, see Box 2.3.

Q What questions of morality are raised by the case study at the beginning of the chapter? How do they reflect debates about beliefs, values, and standards?

Q Can you think of other examples, besides physician-assisted suicide, in which there are debates about differing moral perspectives on issues of law and justice? How could each be analyzed under the frameworks presented in this chapter?

Three Tendencies of Idealists and Pragmatists

FOCUSING QUESTION 2.4

How do idealistic and pragmatic philosophies influence criminal justice?

In the next two sections of this chapter, we will ask you to think about some philosophical ideas. As you do so, think about how they can be applied to criminal justice policy debates and to the exercise of discretion by criminal justice professionals. You will see that each is related to the questions of morality that underlie these debates and uses of discretion.

To begin to better understand the foundations of criminal justice, we will compare and contrast the philosophical perspectives of idealism and pragmatism. Not everyone agrees on what morality means or how it is established. Understanding the differences between idealism and pragmatism can help us understand why there are disagreements on questions involving morality, crime, and justice.

The preceding discussion of the difference between public and academic conceptions of criminal justice lays the groundwork for the distinction between idealism and pragmatism. Like many members of the public, **idealists** are concerned with the overall goals of the criminal justice system. An idealist would first identify what he or she believed to be the broad goals of the system (perhaps that the police should keep the public safe and prisons should punish offenders). These goals would become the basis for the idealist's analysis of morality. The idealist would structure strategies and tactics toward meeting these goals, however they may be defined. Anything perceived (rightfully or wrongfully, based on evidence or not) as contrary to these goals would be criticized and disavowed.

idealist
An advocate of the philosophical perspective of idealism, which evaluates actions and decisions based on how well they meet broad goals or theoretical ideas.

pragmatist
An advocate of the philosophical perspective of pragmatism, in which actions and decisions are evaluated based on empiricism and the analysis of data.

Pragmatists, on the other hand, more closely represent most scholars. They are primarily interested in using empiricism to assess the performance of the criminal justice system, using the results of their analyses to inform moral discussions and decisions (the philosopher Charles Sanders Peirce, discussed earlier in this chapter, was a noted American pragmatist). To the pragmatist, the goals of the system are important, but equally important are information and evidence about how the system actually works and how that, in turn, informs discussions about strategy, tactics, and discretion.

As a simple example, consider the concept of a *dog*. The idealist might think of the grand *concept* of an ideal dog—perhaps a heroic dog, or a dog well-known from movies or television, or a beloved childhood pet. This would then be the standard against which all dogs would be judged. The pragmatist might think of a more scientific notion of dog—perhaps distinguishing canine from feline or considering what biological characteristics define a dog. This would then be the standard against which the pragmatist would judge a dog.

To take a criminal justice example, consider the use of private prisons, in which private corporations (rather than state or federal governments) operate prison facilities. While there are some variations, the way private prisons generally work is for the state to pay the company a certain amount per day for each inmate who is held in the facility. The private company then staffs and operates the facility. In 2011, 8.2% of the nation's prison inmates were held in private facilities, an increase from 6.8% in 2000 (Carson & Sabol, 2012). There has been significant debate as to whether the use of private prisons is a good idea or a bad idea. Some idealists might argue that the goal of the criminal justice system should be, pursuant to social contract theory, for the government to sanction offenders under the law; such an idealist would oppose private prisons, because the government has ceded at least part of its authority to a private corporation. Other idealists would argue that the goal of the criminal justice system is to provide services in the most cost-effective manner possible; these

idealists would likely support private prisons, perceiving that private business is more efficient and less costly than the government. As this example illustrates, persons on any side of an issue can function as idealists, and disagreement among idealists may occur. But regardless of their views, idealists use the same basic method: identifying a grand goal as moral doctrine and then judging all details based on whether or not they meet that goal.

The pragmatist, on the other hand, would acknowledge that there are goals that drive the criminal justice system. But the pragmatist would want to study the prison privatization in practice. The pragmatist would use data and statistics to reach conclusions about private prisons, which would likely include the following: Private prisons do not generate lower recidivism rates than public prisons, and may be at greater risk of recidivism (Duwe & Clark, 2013); private prisons do tend to be more cost-effective, costing less than public facilities (Perrone & Pratt, 2003); and "publicly managed prisons tend to provide better skills training programs and seemed to generate fewer complaints or grievances" (Lundahl et al., 2009, p. 392); of course, these are but few of the many research studies that have explored prison privatization. For the pragmatist, findings such as those above would be made solely on the basis of data. If scholars were to disagree, it would be about how the data were analyzed and not about their individual opinions about the use of private prisons as a policy option. However, these data would inform moral decisions about prison privatization, including how it does or does not support the traditional American values of equality, fairness, and efficiency. Whether or not a pragmatist chooses to support the use of private prisons remains a moral decision, as it cannot be separated from these values, but it is a moral decision based on data and analysis rather than adherence to broad goals.

As noted earlier, the purpose of these discussions is not to dictate what is or is not moral but rather to examine the processes by which individuals decide for themselves. This helps us understand how working criminal justice professionals reach their decisions about strategy, tactics, and discretion and why different professionals may reach different decisions.

In Table 2.2, three additional philosophical tendencies of idealism and pragmatism are compared. As we proceed, we will see how this relates to criminal justice.

HARMONY

Harmony is the idea that when things are in their proper order, this represents beauty. The ancient Greek philosophers believed that true justice would result when groups of people were in harmony with one another (Grube, 1992).

While we all may *hope* for harmony in our own lives and in society, the idealists truly consider it a natural guiding principle for making moral criminal justice decisions. Idealists seeking harmony sometimes draw upon philosopher Immanuel Kant's

harmony
The idea that when things are in their proper order, it represents beauty.

TABLE 2.2 Tendencies of Idealists and Pragmatists

Philosophical Concept	Idealism's Tendencies	Pragmatism's Tendencies
Harmony	Serves as the verification of truth and the ultimate goal	Not relevant because it is not based on experience
Truth	Truth is found beyond normal experience	Truth beyond experience cannot be verified
Mind/Body Relationship	Split	Connected

([1785] 2002) categorical imperative, which states that people should only engage in an action if they would also be willing for others to do so as a universal rule. Kant's classic example is that, under the categorical imperative, it would not be acceptable for one person to lie because it would not be desirable to have a society in which all persons felt that it was appropriate to lie. It would be difficult to achieve harmony when it was unclear whether any particular statement is a truth or a falsehood, so Kant's solution was to define all lying as morally wrong.

The officer responding to the Lover's Lane example might see the rocking van as out of place and therefore threatening to social harmony, be unwilling for it to be a universally accepted norm of behavior, and as a result, feel the need to take whatever actions are necessary to restore harmony. (However, the persons in the van might feel that their actions were harmonious and should be imitated by all, so you can see how disagreements about harmony can arise!) Therefore, it is harmony with universal principles—whether religious, ideological, or otherwise motivated—that guides an idealist's moral reasoning. This has resulted in profound expressions in American government of beautiful ideas that are indeed central to moral reasoning about justice issues, including the Declaration of Independence (harmony exists when all persons have rights to life, liberty, and pursuit of happiness) and the Bill of Rights (harmony exists when all persons may live according to their rights).

Conversely, pragmatism does not seek harmony. To the pragmatist, harmony is an *idea,* but its truth cannot be *verified.* Just because two or more things seem to fit together or appear to be pleasant does not mean that they are correct or appropriate. For instance, a correctional theorist might believe that all offenders benefit from hard work and discipline, leading to harmony by instilling universal values in offenders. If, on this basis, the theorist implemented a correctional boot camp in which offenders participate in military-style drills and discipline, she would be functioning as an idealist. The pragmatist, on the other hand, would not find this belief a satisfactory reason to implement a program. Instead, the pragmatist would seek to gather data about the boot camp programs to verify their usefulness or appropriateness (and in so doing would find many to be ineffective; see MacKenzie, 2006). If harmony happens to result from a pragmatist's analysis, that is fine, but harmony need not be a required outcome.

TRUTH

For years now, you have probably been taught to tell the truth. This is an important concept to criminal justice. After all, criminal justice seeks to determine the truth in various venues, including investigations (with their interviews and analyses of evidence), trials, and interpretations of law. But what is truth? This is actually a profound question. For our purposes, we will consider two perspectives, one from idealists and one from pragmatists.

ultimate truth
A belief held by idealists that there are certain absolute notions or ideas (i.e., truths) that guide or should guide human action.

Idealists believe there is an **ultimate truth** that guides, or should guide, human action. As an example, recall that the Declaration of Independence stated, "We hold these truths to be self-evident, that all men are created equal . . ." This is a statement grounded in idealism. By being held as self-evident, the truth is something that is accepted as a statement of how things ought to be, but it cannot be "proven" with data. You either accept or do not accept that all persons are equal; there is no mathematical equation that proves or disproves the proposition. As such, an idealist's truths are often used as the barometers by which harmony is judged. If something is in line with the accepted truth, whatever it may be, then the world is harmonious.

This is a very important argument to understand. For instance, idealists who accept as self-evident truth the idea that people commit crime because of the environment in which they are raised would advocate a range of social policies aimed at child rearing

(improved schools, adequate childhood health care, parent training, positive after-school activities, etc.) in the hopes that these policies would make a person less likely to commit crime later in life. Criminal justice solutions that run contrary to this idea would be viewed as neither harmonious nor acceptable. On the other hand, if a person accepted as self-evident truth the idea that crime was caused by an offender's free will, in which he or she makes the conscious choice to commit a crime, then the aforementioned solutions would be irrelevant, and that person would likely advocate for harsh punishments to deter offenders from committing crimes. Therefore, disagreement about policies, especially among idealists, often occurs due to disagreements about what constitutes the truth.

Pragmatists tend not to focus on the ultimate truths. Rather, pragmatists define as truth only observations that could be verified in some way, whether through observation or through the analysis of data. Agreeing that something is a reasonable argument, a good idea, or an important value is not enough to constitute a truth for a pragmatist. Therefore, the concept of truth is much narrower to the pragmatist, referring only to that which is verifiable. In considering why people commit crime, a pragmatist would likely avoid broad statements such as "environment causes crime" or "biology causes crime," instead preferring more nuanced, specific, and empirically verified findings, such as that low blood glucose (Virkkunen, 1987) or childhood abuse (Widom & Maxfield, 2001) has been found to be related to crime among some individuals. Because crime is so complex, any broader claims seeking to explain all crime with a simple statement would go beyond what could be verified empirically. Pragmatists and idealists sometimes disagree about issues because of differences in perceiving truth. The idealist might become frustrated with the pragmatist's focus on empirical verification, arguing that it loses sight of the "big picture"; conversely, the pragmatist might become frustrated with the idealist's desire to work from philosophical ideas that may not be precisely verified with data.

THE MIND/BODY RELATIONSHIP

Idealists and pragmatists also differ in terms of how they see the connection between the mind, referring to the world of ideas, and the body, referring to the physical world around us. This runs into deeper questions about how we perceive ourselves and the world in which we live. This raises a question: is the reality as perceived in our mind different from the reality in the physical world, as idealists might believe (a mind/body split)? Or is there only one true reality based on observable truth, as pragmatists might believe (a mind/body connection)?

Idealists believe that mind and body can be split because each deals with different realities in different realms. As a result, idealists believe that the strength of mind may serve to displace weaknesses in the physical world. For instance, idealists point to the human ability to use the mind to focus on happiness derived from positive mental images even in the face of negative physical conditions. Consequently, idealists view this as an advantage and believe that the mind's world of ideas is superior to the physical world, and they give it priority in their lives. This is known as a mind/body split.

Let's consider how this applies to criminal justice decision making. Recall the example from earlier in the chapter about how we know what a dog is. This goes back to ancient Greek philosophy in Plato's book *The Republic*. Plato argued that for any object or concept (be it a dog, a chair, a triangle—or justice), there exists in the mind a perfect example (or model) of that concept. When identifying an object or concept in the physical world, we do so by comparing it to our notion of what the perfect example looks like. Reality, then, is whatever conforms to these perfect examples or models (Plato called them "forms"). This helps account for the passion with which idealists argue for their positions. When advocating for a concept, including those related to

BOX 2.4

STERLING V. MINERSVILLE

On April 17, 1997, a police officer observed a vehicle in a parking lot with its lights off adjacent to a beer distribution center. The officer indicated that he was concerned about recent burglaries in the area and found the vehicle to be suspicious for that reason. Upon investigation, the officer found two males in the vehicle, an 18-year-old adult and a 17-year-old juvenile. The officer found no signs of a burglary to the establishment but did determine that the young men had been drinking. When questioned, the occupants of the vehicle were evasive with their answers. A legal search of the vehicle revealed two condoms, at which point the officer questioned the boys as to their sexual activity. Although the testimony remains debated, the officer testified that both boys acknowledged that they were gay and were in the parking lot to engage in consensual sexual activity. There was no law in the jurisdiction that prohibited either homosexuality or same-sex sexual behavior, and the two were both of legal age in their jurisdiction to engage in consensual sexual activity. However, because they were under the required drinking age of 21, the two boys were arrested for alcohol violations and were taken to the police station.

While at the stationhouse, the officer lectured them on the Bible and counseled them against homosexual activity. The officer then told the 18-year-old that if he did not inform his grandfather he was gay, the officer would do it for him. Shortly after that statement, the 18-year-old confided to his friend that he was going to kill himself, and upon release from custody, he committed suicide in his home. The Third Circuit Court of Appeals ruled that the officer had violated the young man's right to privacy (see Owen & Burke, 2003).

criminal justice issues (e.g., justice, rehabilitation, morality, or anything else), idealists are advocating for the *perfect* version of that concept as they envision it in their mind, regardless of how it may appear in reality, and anything short of that is both unacceptable and ultimately unreal.

Pragmatists view things differently. Rejecting the concept of mind as a separate realm of ideas, they instead hold that thought processes are part of the brain, which is part of the body, which is part of the physical world. Pragmatists then believe that the thought processes in the brain are sufficient to solve the very real problems that are presented in the physical world. Indeed, one of the most important aspects of life for pragmatists is the ability to solve problems in the physical world. This is called the mind/body connection, because it does not recognize the two realities that idealists perceive (that of the mind's ideas and of the body's physical world).

Again, let's consider how this is related to criminal justice. Pragmatists do not accept Plato's idea that there are perfect examples of concepts beyond the physical world. To the pragmatist, the world is what it is, and reality is limited to that which can be directly observed. When advocating for a concept, pragmatists are less concerned about the perfect version of the concept but instead base their ideas on observations and data. A pragmatist arguing for rehabilitation, for instance, would be less concerned about the "perfect" version of rehabilitation but would be much more interested in whether or not particular rehabilitation programs work, as observed, and what could be done to strengthen them.

Q Do you think criminal justice professionals should follow idealism, pragmatism, neither, or both? Or would it depend on the circumstances? Why?

Q How can differences in idealistic and pragmatic understandings of harmony, truth, and the mind/body relationship help to explain differing opinions on controversial issues? Provide an example.

Q How would ideas about idealism, pragmatism, harmony, truth, and the mind/body relationship influence the resolution of the scenario at the beginning of the chapter? The scenario in Box 2.4?

Five Concepts of Morality

FOCUSING QUESTION 2.5

How do the five concepts of morality illustrate the distinction between idealism and pragmatism, as applied to criminal justice?

Idealism and pragmatism are competing philosophies with very different ideas about morality. Whether drawing upon idealism, pragmatism, or a combination of each, decisions about morality can be of great consequence to the justice system and the persons it affects.

Idealists and pragmatists have different ideas about knowledge, self, the nature of the universe, the nature of a deity, and death, as illustrated in Table 2.3. These five concepts form the basis for their decisions about morality. We will consider each concept to show how they relate to idealism, pragmatism, and criminal justice.

KNOWLEDGE

Addressing questions about morality requires us to consider the logic that we apply when seeking answers to moral questions, whether they are questions of fact, questions of legal interpretation (i.e., what a law means), or questions about values. Idealists generally pursue these questions in an a priori manner. **A priori** reasoning occurs without empiricism and may stem from a number of sources, such as tenacity, authority, or "common-sense" arguments offered without empirical evidence, as described earlier. As long as the decision is in accord with harmony and truth as perceived by the idealist, it is acceptable. On the other hand, pragmatists rely on **a posteriori** reasoning, drawing upon empirical verification grounded in observations, data, and experiences. Even conclusions about abstract ideas about morality draw upon actual experience and actual conditions in the world.

For instance, consider analyses about whether burglary is right or wrong. The idealist would likely reason that burglary is wrong because it violates principles of security in one's property, thus leading to disharmony in the world. A pragmatist would likely reason that burglary is wrong based on the observable harm to others that it directly causes.

a priori
Reasoning that occurs without empiricism and which may stem from sources including tenacity, authority, or common-sense arguments offered without evidence. Most associated with idealism.

a posteriori
Reasoning that is based on empiricism, grounded in observations, data, and experiences. Most associated with pragmatism.

SELF

The concept of **self** represents how one views humanity. Does humanity have a timeless higher purpose or goal? Or is humanity primarily concerned with the day-to-day matters of the present time? Idealists see humanity as subject to rules that are not necessarily of their own making. The author of the rules could be a supreme being or it could

self
A philosophical concept that represents how one views humanity.

TABLE 2.3 Five Concepts of Morality

Moral Concept	Idealism	Pragmatism
Knowledge	a priori	a posteriori
Self	Higher purpose	Independent organism
Deity	Important role	Less important role
Universe	With overall purpose	Without purpose
Death	New beginning	The end

be other forces in the universe, including a deep belief in certain values or ideas. By extension, idealists also believe that there is some sort of meaning or purpose to life. However, pragmatists believe that humanity is composed of organisms capable of thought, and as a result, they create their own individual meanings about what life is or should be. These meanings may change from time to time and are generally based on the pragmatist's experiences and do not necessarily include an emphasis on deeper meanings or purposes of life.

Some police or correctional officers, attorneys, or judges may take an idealistic perspective and see the pursuit of justice as the guiding force for humanity, suggesting the need for swift action to be taken anytime a law is broken, without exception. Others may take a pragmatic perspective and not perceive any particular guiding force, treating each situation differently and reaching resolutions that do not necessarily demonstrate any goals other than the resolution of the immediate situation. The ways criminal justice professionals view the nature of humanity, its purposes, and its goals can influence perceptions of justice and the exercise of discretion. This can also help explain disagreements about decisions involving morality.

deity
What one believes about the nature of a supreme being.

THE NATURE OF A DEITY

The concept of a **deity** refers to what one believes about the nature of a supreme being. Beliefs about the concept of a deity vary. To some, this may be the embodiment of a supreme being, such as a "God" in monotheistic faiths, or more than one supreme being, such as multiple "gods" in polytheistic faiths. Some who view the concept of a deity in this manner believe that a supreme being is omnipotent, omniscient, and omnipresent; others believe that while such a being exists, he or she does not interfere in the lives of human beings. Others reject the existence of a supreme being and view as a deity the primal matrix of energy that provides the natural order of the cosmos. And still others reject the notion of a deity entirely. There is no single perspective that all idealists or all pragmatists take regarding their beliefs, so in many ways, it is the nature of the belief, rather than idealistic or pragmatic worldviews, that determines the influence on moral positions.

In 2012, the Kentucky Supreme Court (*Gingerich v. Commonwealth*) and the Kentucky legislature (Slow moving vehicle . . . , 2012) debated whether the horse-drawn vehicles of the Old Order Swartzentruber Amish would be permitted to substitute white or silver reflective tape instead of the bright orange and red placard required of slow-moving vehicles; the color and shape of the placards were offensive to Amish religious beliefs. While the Court denied permission, the legislature enacted a new law to permit the substitution. What arguments and moral concerns do you think could be raised on either side of the debate?

Although idealists hold widely disparate views on the divine, most (but not all) idealists accept the concept of the divine as an important influence in human life and, therefore, use their spiritual beliefs as a foundation for their ideas of morality, fairness, and justice. Pragmatic concepts of deity tend to vary from belief in a supreme being or beings who make limited interventions in human lives, to atheistic beliefs holding that humanity fends for itself in the universe without the aid of a greater force. Of course, there are exceptions to these generalized statements. For the purposes of this chapter, what becomes most important is how an individual's concept of a deity affects his or her decisions about issues related to criminal justice.

Some idealists and pragmatists set aside their private ideas about their beliefs in a deity as they consider law and public policy; others do not. In fact, some believe that they *should not* put aside these personal beliefs. Rather, they view it as their moral obligation to ensure that the moral commands that stem from their belief in a deity become law or public policy (recall from Box 1.2 that this reflects the divine commandment theory of ethical decision making).

Indeed, there are some societies in the world where entire legal codes are based on religious law (see generally Bracey, 2006, chapter 5). In the United States, there are frequent debates about the separation of church and state and the extent to which belief systems grounded in theology should influence public policy. For instance, in the Lover's Lane case, should officers consider moral perspectives that are derived from their belief in a deity? How would this influence decisions? Courts in the United States have generally ruled against instances that can be viewed as the government imposing a specific theological or religious belief system, but there is often controversy about where the lines should be drawn.

UNIVERSE

Some may see the universe as a natural entity with orderly processes and purposes. Others may see the universe as a chaotic environment with a disorienting series of problems. Idealists tend to see the universe as vast and purposeful, with an underlying order that, even if not directly observable, creates meaning (in philosophy, this is known as a **teleology**). Idealists also believe that humanity struggles to understand the principles that govern the order of the universe and to abide by those principles in making moral decisions. Pragmatists are more likely to believe in a universe without a recognizable purpose. This is consistent with the pragmatist's emphasis on that which is observable. To the pragmatist, it is irrelevant whether or not the universe has a purpose because it does not change either the universe itself or the problems that arise and must be resolved on a daily basis.

teleology
A philosophical concept suggesting that a vast and purposeful universe with an underlying order creates meaning.

Referring back to the Lover's Lane example, an officer working from an idealistic perspective might consider (subconsciously, at least) the situation in terms of universal ideals. Of course, there are different possible interpretations of the universe's purpose. One idealist might see the universe as promoting the message "if it feels good, do it" and therefore feel that the proper moral decision is not to interfere with the couple's happiness and instead allow them to continue their activities. Another idealist might see the universe as requiring a celibate lifestyle outside of marriage and therefore feel that the proper moral decision is to arrest the couple to stop the sexual activity and to deter them from engaging in similar behavior later. Both approaches could be justified as uses of discretion, and both involve making moral decisions. The pragmatist, on the other hand, would not see larger universal purposes as relevant, instead focusing on the harm that could come from the situation at hand, what rights could be affected, and how to respond accordingly.

DEATH

Appropriately, understandings of death are the final concept of morality. One unique quality among human beings is that we know, to borrow from Benjamin Franklin, that "nothing can be said to be certain, except death and taxes" (Isaacson, 2003, p. 463). Idealists often believe in an afterlife in some form (heaven, nirvana, reincarnation, or something else), which often includes being judged by a greater or higher force (which may or may not be a deity, depending on their belief system). This leads some idealists to believe that in making moral decisions, they should judge others by the same criteria against which they believe they will be judged (this also relates to the pursuit of harmony). Pragmatists do not see death as having any special significance to moral decisions or actions. The pragmatist takes death seriously, especially when it results from a crime, negligence, or as a form of punishment. However, in these cases, it is the death itself that is important in the pragmatist's construction of a situation, and what happens after death is not significant. Events after death are not subject to direct observation and therefore do not play a strong role in the pragmatist's decision-making processes.

BOX 2.5

Ethics in Practice

POLITICAL PATRONAGE (PART I)

In the context of a legal argument, a serious moral issue was presented to the U.S. Supreme Court in the 1990 case, *Rutan v. Republican Party of Illinois*. The case was based on a 1980 executive order issued by the Governor of Illinois, a Republican, which stated that no employees of state government would be hired, promoted, or transferred without the governor's consent. This created a formal patronage system in Illinois for 60,000 state employees, including officers in the Illinois State Police and the Illinois Department of Corrections. Patronage refers to hiring practices that are based on political favor rather than on an individual's qualifications. The Supreme Court described how the process worked when an agency recommended an employee to be hired, promoted, or transferred:

> Permission has been granted or withheld through an agency expressly created for this purpose, the Governor's Office of Personnel (Governor's Office) . . . In reviewing an agency's request that a particular applicant be approved for a particular position, the Governor's Office has looked at whether the applicant voted in Republican primaries in past election years, whether the applicant has provided financial or other support to the Republican Party and its candidates, whether the applicant has promised to join and work for the Republic Party in the future, and whether the applicant has the support of Republican Party officials at state or local levels. (p. 66)

It should be noted that prior to this order, both Republicans and Democrats in Illinois used political patronage for hiring state employees (for a political history of Illinois, see Gove & Nowlan, 1996). This order by the Governor simply formalized the patronage system. For example, before hiring a prison guard, his voting record in primary elections would be examined, and if the individual had voted Republican, then he could be hired; this decision was often left to Republican county chairmen.

APPLYING PHILOSOPHY AND MORALITY TO CRIMINAL JUSTICE

Criminal justice is complex because it relates to complex human behavior. The criminal justice practitioner must be prepared to make difficult decisions about strategy, tactics, and discretion, and those decisions are fundamentally about morality. In making these complex decisions, individuals often follow the philosophical tendencies of idealism or pragmatism. These tendencies serve as **paradigms**, or worldviews that help individuals make decisions. By relying on idealism and pragmatism as paradigms, an individual does not start from scratch when addressing a problem. Rather, the paradigm—through its conception of harmony, truth, the mind/body connection, and the five concepts of morality—aids the individual in choosing the preferred methods and philosophies to apply in a situation.

paradigms
Philosophical tendencies or worldviews held by individuals that they use to help them make decisions.

Idealism and pragmatism may be viewed as endpoints on a continuum. There is much variation in human behavior and human thought. Some idealists may not believe in *all* of the elements of idealism that have been described, and some pragmatists may not believe in *all* of the elements of pragmatism that have been described. Nonetheless, the descriptions do approximate two common perspectives on how to engage in the sorts of moral decision making necessary to address criminal justice questions. It is important to understand both models because doing so can help you understand why disagreements about criminal justice policy and practice occur and how they might be reconciled based on an individual's philosophical position.

The ultimate question for the criminal justice professional is, what is the right thing to do? Clearly, it is not as simple as making a choice that can be defended based merely on the situation at hand; instead, one must develop a consistent philosophy that

The majority opinion of the Supreme Court, written by Justice Brennan, decided that this practice violated the First Amendment rights by chilling free speech—that is, persons seeking an employment, promotion, or transfer may feel as though they could not engage in expression that would convey a lack of support for the majority party. Justice Scalia's dissenting opinion argued that the Supreme Court should not intervene in such cases because patronage has historically been practiced, and doing so was justifiable in order to support the party discipline necessary to sustain the two-party system; Justice Scalia also argued that it was up to the Illinois legislature and voters to determine whether or not they wanted to use patronage, rather than a matter for the Supreme Court.

The alternative to patronage is to use a civil service system, in which applications for hiring, promotion, and transfer would be evaluated based on the merit and qualifications of the applicants. Party affiliation, voting records, and the like, would not be considered in personnel decisions.

Consider the following questions about patronage systems.

- Q Do you agree with the majority opinion or with the dissenting opinion in this case? Or do you have a different opinion on the issue entirely? Explain your answer.
- Q How may criminal justice institutions be affected by patronage? If the affected parties are non-policy-making employees, is there any harm that can come to the criminal justice system? Is it possible for criminal justice institutions to be used to promote political agendas (with or without patronage)?
- Q Is this a moral issue? Why or why not? If it is, how would the concepts of idealism and pragmatism and the concepts of morality apply to it?

produces the type of criminal justice best suited for a democratic society. See Box 2.5 for an ethical scenario regarding a moral dilemma in criminal justice, related to employee hiring and promotion.

- Q Consider the issue of capital punishment (the death penalty). How can it be analyzed through the five concepts of morality?
- Q Drawing upon the five concepts of morality, explain how an idealist and a pragmatist would differ in their handling of the case presented in Box 2.4. Explain your answer.
- Q Do you think the criminal justice system more closely represents idealism or pragmatism? Provide examples.

Conclusion

Criminal justice professionals are called upon to make discretionary decisions on a daily basis. Whether addressing broad strategies or the tactics to implement them, these decisions have the potential to impact individuals and society in profound ways. This chapter has considered the role that academic scholarship, morality, and idealistic and pragmatic philosophies may play in shaping decisions about the practice of criminal justice. In the next chapter, we will draw upon the ideas presented here—particularly about idealism and pragmatism—to consider the different ways law can be understood and how these understandings can further shape the goals and activities of the criminal justice system.

Criminal Justice Problem Solving

Alcohol Policy

American alcohol policy has had a long and varied history. "In early America, drinking was no vice" and was in fact common and accepted (Morone, 2003 p. 283). The importance of alcohol may be illustrated by the 1794 Whiskey Rebellion. In response to a national tax on whiskey levied in 1791 (to pay down the national debt), one congressman stated that citizens in his district "have long been in the habit of getting drunk and that they will get drunk in defiance of . . . all the excise duties [taxes] which Congress might be weak or wicked enough to pass" (Boyer et al., 1993, p. 220). In 1794, citizens in Pennsylvania took up arms to resist the whiskey tax, and George Washington himself commanded federal troops to put down the uprising. This became a notable event in American history because it helped to establish the power of the federal government in the new republic.

However, there have also been numerous anti-alcohol movements in American history (Morone, 2003), the most notable leading to the prohibition of alcohol between 1920 and 1933. While there have been few calls to return to the Prohibition era, with its inconsistent enforcement, corruption, and attendant increase in crime (MacCoun & Reuter, 2001), debates about the legality of alcohol have continued, with a particular focus on the age at which individuals should be permitted to drink.

Worldwide, there is not a clear consensus on the appropriate drinking age. Some countries have no minimum drinking age. For those that do, the age tends to vary from 16 to 21 years old (Stimson, Grant, Choquet, & Garrison, 2007). And some countries prohibit the consumption of alcohol entirely.

In the United States, state governments are responsible for establishing the drinking age. Prior to 1988, there was variation in state laws: some set the drinking age at 18, others at 21. In 1984, Congress passed a law stipulating that states whose drinking age was lower than 21 would lose federal highway funding. Not wanting to lose highway funding, by 1988, all 50 states had set their drinking age at 21 (Richardson & Houston, 2009). Recently, there has been considerable debate about lowering the drinking age to 18. In 2008, seven state legislatures considered measures that would lower the drinking age; none passed (Jolley, 2008). And, as of this writing, 136 college and university presidents have publicly expressed support for revisiting the drinking age (Amethyst Initiative, n.d.).

Q Lowering the drinking age from 21 to another age (most likely 18) would represent a substantial change in criminal justice policy. Would you be in favor of or opposed to this change? Why?

Q Discuss how an idealist would approach the answer to this question based on any of the concepts in this chapter.

Q Discuss how a pragmatist would approach the answer to this question based on any of the concepts in this chapter.

Q How would this change in law change criminal justice strategies, tactics, and discretion?

3

Concepts of Legal Philosophy

Learning Objectives

1 Explain the role of legal philosophies, principles, and rules in understanding law. 2 Describe the six concepts of law. 3 Compare and contrast legal moralism and legal positivism. 4 Describe the various schools of legal philosophy as they relate to idealism and pragmatism.

Key Terms

six concepts of law
Hart-Devlin Debate
Wolfenden Report
legal moralism
collective judgment
harm principle
legal positivism
jurisprudence
idealistic theories of law
legal naturalism
natural law
critical theories of law
legal paternalism
legal pragmatism
legal realism

Key People

Patrick Devlin
Ronald Dworkin
H. L. A. Hart
John Stuart Mill
Mortimer Adler
Joel Feinberg
Richard Posner
Jeffrey Segal
Harold Spaeth
Michael Lipsky

Case Study

Working the Corner

You are a police officer beginning your evening shift patrol with your partner, who is driving the squad car. At roll call, your sergeant reminded you that complaints about prostitution were increasing in your patrol area. In particular, citizens have expressed concern about prostitutes who openly solicit clients on the street and who perform sexual acts in alleyways and parked cars.

That evening, you find a young woman, whom you and your partner have previously arrested for prostitution, occupying her usual street corner. Your partner stops the squad car and confronts the woman, asking her, "What are you up to tonight?" The young woman responds, "You know what I do." Your partner interprets this as an admission of guilt for prostitution and arrests her for that offense, although he did not witness any specific illegal behavior other than perhaps loitering. Later, your partner explains to you that he was just doing his job by giving the people what they want, which is streets free of immoral behavior. He knew the charges would likely be dismissed, but said, "At least she'll be off the streets for a while."

Q Do you agree with your partner's attitude and actions? Why or why not? If not, how would you have handled the situation differently?

Q Do you agree with your partner's description of a police officer's job: "giving the people what they want"? Why or why not?

Q Should police officers consider their own personal morality when they make discretionary decisions? Should officers consider the public's sense of morality concerning issues? Should legislators consider morality when determining what acts to define as crimes? Why or why not?

Previous page: A "No cursing" sign in Virginia Beach, Virginia. Why do you think a locality would want to prohibit cursing?

Studying Approaches to the Law

FOCUSING QUESTION 3.1

Why is it important to study the various philosophies of law?

It is important for criminal justice scholars, professionals, and policy makers to understand the distinctions between idealism and pragmatism and how they relate to questions of law and morality. We live in a diverse society where there is disagreement about what the law ought to accomplish and how it should do so, and debates grounded in idealistic and pragmatic thought certainly influence perceptions about the law.

The legal philosophies presented in this chapter also influence perceptions about the law. The goal of this chapter is to survey some of the classic and significant theories about the role of law in society. Recall from Chapter 1 that crimes are those activities or behaviors that governments have chosen to prohibit under the law. Each of the theories in this chapter provides its own explanation about how governments should decide which activities or behaviors to make illegal and define as criminal.

As you read, do not presume that there is a single legal philosophy that all persons agree upon. Likewise, do not presume that individuals simply select one philosophy and follow it when making all of their own personal decisions about what the law should accomplish. In reality, there is not uniform agreement about the role of law in society, and individuals may reflect on multiple legal philosophies when making a decision pertaining to law. The world is a complex place, but understanding a variety of (competing) legal philosophies will help to make some sense of it—at least in terms of the role of law in society.

This study is important because the perspective that an individual holds about the role of law in society can have several implications. It can affect how an individual enforces the law or thinks it should be enforced. It can affect how an individual behaves or thinks others should behave. It can affect how an individual votes or advocates for policies and it helps explain why there are sometimes differences that are difficult to reconcile on controversial policy issues. And it can affect an individual's satisfaction with the legal system based on whether or not he or she believes the legal system, in practice, matches his or her concept of what the law should be. This, in turn, affects perceptions about whether the system is legitimate or whether it is in need of reform.

Consider the consequences of the latter point. If individuals perceive that the law has failed by not accomplishing the goals they desire, they may lose confidence in the legal system. They may protest or engage in civil disobedience (deliberately disobeying a law they believe is unjust). They may simply ignore the law. Or they may engage in vigilantism and enforce the law themselves in the way they think it should be done rather than relying on the criminal justice system.

For all of these reasons, it is essential for criminal justice professionals, as well as policy makers and legislators, to give careful consideration to the role of law in society. For instance, it would not be enough for the police officer in the scenario at the beginning of the chapter to argue that he is "just enforcing the law." To appreciate the development of law and the pursuit of justice, we must understand the ideas that underlie the law, which can also help us better understand our own positions.

PRINCIPLES AND RULES IN CRIMINAL JUSTICE

This is a good point at which to introduce the distinction between principles and rules. As you can imagine, it is time-consuming and challenging to evaluate all behaviors and actions and to independently evaluate each to determine whether or not it should be legal. A heuristic is a tool—usually a philosophical idea or perspective—used to reduce decision-making complexity by providing guidance in answering questions. One form

of heuristic is the application of broad principles in the evaluation of specific legal questions. Let's consider how that might work.

Rules are externally imposed guidelines that shape our behavior in some way. Rules can include laws that must be followed, policies that must be implemented, strategies that are directed as means to address criminal justice issues, guidance on appropriate tactics, and more. In short, then, many decisions made by the criminal justice system fall under this definition of rules. We may follow rules for a variety of reasons. Thinking back to Kohlberg's moral stages from Chapter 1, rules may be followed out of fear of punishment (Stage 1); because it benefits us or results from a mutually beneficial negotiation (Stage 2); because they cause us to be liked or valued by those whose opinions we value (Stage 3); because they uphold the social order that we support (Stage 4); because they are the product of democratic processes (Stage 5); or because they support the principles we hold dear (Stage 6).

Note a key distinction between following the rules in Stages 1–4 versus Stages 5–6. In Stages 1–4, rule following provides a benefit (avoiding punishment, providing individual benefits, producing positive feedback, or maintaining current social order), but there is not significant consideration given to the reason behind the rule. In Stages 5–6, consideration is given to the principles that the rule ought to accomplish, which may be pursued through the democratic process (Stage 5) or through actions that apply the principle in practice (Stage 6).

Rules are designed to provide order and consistency. Rather than guessing at what is required, the rules provide us with a (hopefully) clear understanding that all persons to whom the rule applies must follow. At the same time, we may sometimes resent rules. The resentment for rules may exist in situations where the reason or purpose for the rule is unclear. However, even when persons resent rules, they often still follow them. And, at one level, we may ask whether it matters—if a rule is followed, the outcome is the same, whether or not the reason for the rule is understood or accepted. But at another level, rules that are established without a clear purpose, or for which the purpose is rejected, may threaten the legitimacy of the criminal justice system. This is particularly true for individuals functioning in Stages 5 and 6, where the need for rules to reflect sound principles is paramount.

This brings us to principles, which are the reasons for the rules. As such, they are generally expressions of broad ideas about how the world (or some part of it) ought to work. Principles can include the legal philosophies that will be presented in this chapter; the concepts of morality presented in the previous chapter; ideas about justice that will be described in Chapter 6; and broad values that individuals may hold. If the principle is understood and individuals accept it as a valid idea, then the rules become acceptable. Let's consider an example. Most states have laws against littering, or the illegal disposal of trash, which is generally punished with a fine (National Conference of State Legislatures, 2008). What principles could underlie this rule? One principle could be *to prevent harm to others,* which could include the effort to clean up litter on one's property, unsightly environments that lower property values, or polluted water supplies, depending on the type of items discarded (see Tunnell, 2008). Another principle could be *to promote morality,* by arguing that nature has moral value that must be protected (see Taylor, [1981] 2005). We will revisit these principles later in the chapter. Note that each principle is indeed broad—preventing harm and promoting morality—as principles are statements that can be applied to a wide range of issues. Of course, there are numerous other principles that could be applied, both for and against littering laws.

Principles can work as a heuristic, or decision-making aid, in three ways. First, individuals can identify the principles that matter most to them and then *develop rules* that reflect those principles. For instance, proponents of each of the two principles described above would advocate for specific laws against littering, because such laws are consistent with the principles. They would also likely advocate for related laws, such as those regulating pollution and other environmental concerns.

Second, individuals can *evaluate existing or proposed rules* based on their principles. That is, they can review a rule, determine whether or not it matches their preexisting principles, and then make a determination as to whether they think the rule is good or bad on that basis. Suppose a law was proposed that would significantly reduce the penalties for small amounts of littering. Individuals supporting the principles identified above would consider whether the proposed law corresponded to their principles and might find that it does not, because it reduces penalties for undesired behavior. As a result, they might find that they could not support the proposed law.

Third, *rules and principles can clarify one another.* Observing the specific rules related to a broad principle can help us better understand that principle. The opposite is also true; knowing the principle that underlies a rule can help us understand why that rule was created. For instance, consider the principle of preventing harm to others. What are the actions that are harmful? Perhaps the principle would lead to laws against littering but would allow the use of landfills. Knowing this set of rules would indicate that one key component of the principle is identifying the times and places in which actions, such as dumping of trash, can occur. Likewise, if a person were skeptical of anti-littering laws, wondering why they were enacted, one answer that could be given is the explanation that littering has the potential to cause harm, and that the law was designed to prevent harm.

Different individuals may identify different principles that they support. Perhaps you had a principle other than those listed above that supported or opposed littering laws. Furthermore, individuals may differ in terms of how they define their principles. Perhaps you believed that littering does cause harm or is a moral wrong; on the other hand, you could have thought that the two principles were sound, but that littering was not that harmful or that littering was not such a moral wrong. Many times, debates about criminal justice issues are more about the principle to be used, or how that principle should be interpreted, than they are about the actual issue under question. This sometimes becomes important in decisions about who to hire and fire for high-level criminal justice positions (see Box 3.1).

In these types of debates, idealists and pragmatists (discussed in chapter 2) often reach different conclusions. Idealists identify principles that reflect abstract ideas, based on the pursuit of truth, harmony, and idealized concepts. As such, these are not verified through empirical techniques, but are conceptual worldviews. The principle that rules should support morality is a philosophy known as legal moralism, which we will discuss later in the chapter. It is an idealistic principle, as its basis is non-empirical, relying on value judgments as opposed to data. Pragmatists ground their principles in the empirical analysis of data. The principle that the law should prevent harm is a philosophy grounded in legal positivism, which we will also discuss later in the chapter. It is a pragmatic principle, as the amount and magnitude of harm can be measured empirically, which then informs the application of the principle.

The concern we have for justice in society requires us to examine the relationship between rules and principles. Doing so can clarify our understandings of controversial issues. In the remainder of this chapter, we will explore legal philosophies that can serve as the principles underlying the development of laws.

Q How can conflicts be resolved when two (or more) persons have differing philosophies of law that lead to differing opinions on a legal issue?

Q Before reading about the various legal philosophies in this chapter, how would you explain what role you think the law should play in society? How would you apply your ideas to the scenario at the beginning of the chapter?

Q Take a few minutes and examine a rule (i.e., law, strategy, tactic, policy) related to criminal justice. What is the principle behind this rule? How does the principle clarify the rule? How does the rule clarify the principle?

BOX 3.1

Ethics in Practice

PATRONAGE AND SHARED PRINCIPLES IN PRACTICE

Box 2.5 (Chapter 2) summarized the U.S. Supreme Court case, *Rutan v. Republican Party of Illinois* (1990). Take a moment to review the facts of the case. What could motivate the decision to require party allegiance in order to receive a job, a promotion, or a transfer? Some might argue that it was purely politically motivated and designed to reward loyal party members. However, a less cynical interpretation, or at least a more sympathetic interpretation, is that the goal of patronage was, from a governor's perspective, to create a better state. For instance, if the governor believed he was pursuing morally justified policies and a political agenda in the best interest of the state, would he not want state employees to share that moral and political vision?

As you recall from Chapter 2, the U.S. Supreme Court thought not, holding that party support was not an appropriate criterion for state jobs. But this is an issue pertaining to principles, and one that is still relevant today. If we accept the latter explanation for patronage, above, then it is fundamentally the same as arguing that it is best to employ a workforce of persons who agree on what the principle underlying state laws and policies ought to be. This is still the case in some positions today. The *Rutan* case and other decisions (*Elrod v. Burns,* 1976; *Branti v. Finkel,* 1980) clarified that there are some positions where political affiliation can be considered as a criterion not only for hiring, promoting, and transferring, but also for firing employees. These are generally understood to be executive level jobs with responsibilities for setting agency strategies and policies.

For instance, police chiefs often serve at the pleasure of the mayor, meaning they may be hired or fired by the mayor, and may be replaced when a new mayor is elected. Directors of departments of corrections, and sometimes prison wardens, often serve at the pleasure of the governor, meaning that they may be hired or fired by the governor, and may be replaced when a new governor is elected. The argument that is implied by this arrangement again relates to principles, namely, that elected officials wish for their policy-making employees to share their view of the principles that ought to underlie the policies or strategies they are pursuing.

Q Do you think criminal justice agency leaders should be able to be hired and fired based on political party affiliation? Why or why not? Do you think they should be able to be fired for disagreeing with an elected official's principles, even if not based on political party affiliation? Why or why not?

Q What criteria do you think should be considered in hiring a police chief, prison warden, or other criminal justice agency administrator? What criteria do you think should be impermissible to consider?

Analyzing the Law

FOCUSING QUESTION 3.2

What are the six concepts of law?

The chapter's opening scenario suggests an important question: should the law regulate morality? In the previous chapter, we saw that criminal justice decisions are often moral decisions because practitioners must, in the course of their jobs, resolve difficult questions about what is right and wrong. Here, we are interested in a slightly different question. When *making* the laws and determining what behaviors should or should not be punished under the law, should *legislators* (or the public or others) consider morality? If a group of legislators believe that prostitution is an immoral activity, is that a sufficient reason to make it illegal? Or should prostitution only be made illegal if it is found to harm persons? In fact, prostitution is not an issue on which there is unanimous agreement under the law. For instance, in some counties in Nevada, prostitution is not only legal but also regulated by the state (Brents & Hausbeck, 2001). In part, disagreements stem from different legal

philosophies, each of which provides its own viewpoint about the role of law in society. As noted above, these legal philosophies form the principles that are applied to debates about what activities and behaviors the law should, or should not, regulate.

There are **six concepts of law** that provide a full understanding of the role law plays in society, from its creation through its actual use in guiding behavior. Too often, we may think of the law as doing only one thing or having one use without realizing that it is a much more complex concept. The six concepts of law help us organize that complexity, and we will apply them to the legal philosophies in this chapter. The six concepts are:

six concepts of law A framework for understanding the role of law in society by considering the foundation, rationale, formation, application, focal point, and use of discretion in law.

1. What is the *foundation of law?* On what ideas or notions is the law based? The answer is either a public morality or a private morality. While the mechanisms for doing so vary, public moralities find the basis for the law in a moral code that is universally applicable to all persons, while private moralities do not.

2. What is the *rationale for law?* What purpose does the law serve in society? The answer may be the enforcement of morality or the protection of individual rights. To enforce morality suggests that a prescribed vision for society is promoted through the law; to protect individual rights suggests that freedoms are protected even if they permit behaviors that some may find immoral.

3. How do we conceptualize the *formation of law?* How is the law created? The formation of law may be rational or irrational. Here, rational refers to processes that are both logical and empirical. Irrational refers to processes that lack an empirical base. Irrational is not intended as a negative term, but merely to indicate that the basis for decision making is something other than that which can be accounted for through data.

4. What is the *application of law* to actual problems? How is the law applied? The terms "rational" and "irrational" are again used, but with different meanings. Here, rational suggests that the law sets a clear standard that is applied uniformly by all. Irrational suggests that there is room for interpretation, and therefore differing opinions, in terms of how the law is applied in practice. Again, irrational is not intended as a negative term, but instead indicates a lack of precision in applying the law.

There is an important observation about the relationship between the formation and application of law. Legal philosophies are not rational in both areas, nor are they irrational in both areas. They are not rational in both areas because human beings are simply not rational all of the time. Sometimes emotions, moods, and personal preferences come into play and unavoidably cloud rational decision making. Consider this question: could you structure data analysis that was entirely objective, and then accept the conclusions it offers without question, and then apply it universally without exception? This is a difficult scenario to imagine, as it suggests a process so automated and mechanical that human judgment is not necessary; we might borrow from sociologist Max Weber to call this an "iron cage" that limits the contributions of individual persons (e.g., Swedberg, 2005, pp. 132–133). At the same time, legal philosophies are not irrational in both areas because that would result in chaotic unpredictability. Consider this question: should laws be developed based on ideas that are not verified through data, and then be applied so imprecisely or inconsistently that their meanings are unclear? If that were the case, there would be little tangible basis for the law, leaving individuals to grasp for proverbial straws in order to understand its meaning. In the development of law, some rationality is necessary; but total rationality and total irrationality are not realistic.

5. What is the *focal point of law?* What does one focus on to determine whether the law is successful? Some argue that the law is successful based on its product, or outcome. Others argue that the law is successful based on process, meaning the way in which it is applied by criminal justice professionals.

BOX 3.2

RELATIONSHIPS OF LAW AND MORALITY

The relationships between law and morality in Figure 3.1 illustrate the differences between the theories of Patrick Devlin and H. L. A. Hart. Devlin believed that law and morality are inextricably joined. Hart believed that there is no necessary connection between law and morality.

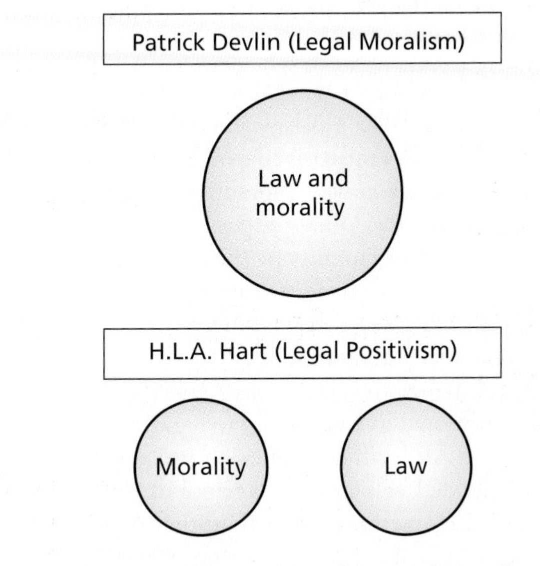

FIGURE 3.1 Relationships of Law and Morality

Q Which of these illustrations best represents your idea of how law and morality are connected? Can your ideas be illustrated in a better way?

Q Discuss which model would offer the best approach to the issue of animal abuse. Explain your answer.

6. What is the role of *discretion in law?* Is it to be encouraged or discouraged? Discretion can be viewed as a beneficial practice that allows for individuals to determine how best to handle specific situations. It can also be viewed as a negative practice that undermines the value of the law as it is written.

There is no single correct answer to the above questions. Each legal philosophy approaches them differently, as legal philosophers disagree about the proper approach to the law. One example of this is the Hart-Devlin debate. The **Hart-Devlin debate** refers to an intellectual exchange between Patrick Devlin and H. L. A. Hart, both British legal scholars who wrote in the mid-twentieth century. Devlin fit the philosophical model of an idealist, and Hart fit the philosophical model of a pragmatist. The debate focused on the question of whether the law should attempt to regulate morality. We begin with this debate because it helps lay the groundwork for other idealistic and pragmatic legal theories.

Hart-Devlin debate
An intellectual exchange between British legal philosophers H. L. A. Hart and Patrick Devlin focused on the role of morality in the law.

Wolfenden Report
A report issued by a British government commission in 1963 regarding the legal status of homosexuality and prostitution. The report formed the basis for the Hart-Devlin debate.

The Hart-Devlin debate was sparked by the ***Wolfenden Report*** (1963), which was issued by a British government commission studying laws about prostitution and homosexuality. The report recommended legalizing private acts of homosexuality between consenting adults, in part because of "the importance which society and the law ought to give to individual freedom of choice and action in matters of private morality" (*Wolfenden Report,* 1963, p. 48). The recommendations regarding prostitution were more complex but essentially drew a distinction between public acts of prostitution,

which were to be prohibited, and private acts of prostitution, which were to be tolerated. The report noted that the prostitution law "should confine itself to those activities which offend against public order and decency or expose the ordinary citizen to what is offensive or injurious" (*Wolfenden Report,* 1963, p. 143). Note that for both issues, the report recommended drawing a distinction between public and private behavior, and in the case of prostitution, the report was more concerned about disorder and harm than about the morality of the act. As you read, you may wish to refer to Box 3.2, which illustrates the difference between Hart's ideas and Devlin's ideas.

Q What do you think should be the relationship between the law and morality?

Q Review the six concepts of law. If you were to create your own legal philosophy, how do you think each of the questions should be answered? Why?

Q Do you agree or disagree with the *Wolfenden Report*'s recommendations? What criteria did you consider in making your decision?

Patrick Devlin's Legal Moralism

FOCUSING QUESTION 3.3

What did Devlin believe was the law's role in society?

British legal philosopher Patrick Devlin ([1965] 1977) disagreed with the recommendations of the *Wolfenden Report* because he believed that the law should enforce public morality, a philosophy known as **legal moralism**. To Devlin, religion and morality were linked because he believed that morality must be the basis for law and that religion must be the basis for morality. While religious foundations shaped Devlin's thinking, his philosophy was articulated through his consideration of three questions.

Devlin's first question was, "Has society the right to pass judgment at all on matters of morals?" (Devlin, [1965] 1977, p. 54). He answered this in the affirmative. To Devlin, a society's "**collective judgment**" (p. 55) would create a sense of public morality in which the members of a society would reach consensus about which behaviors are morally acceptable and which behaviors are morally unacceptable. Even *private* behavior could violate the *public* morality if it was perceived to affect society negatively in some way. And if it did, Devlin would argue that society could indeed pass judgment on it.

We will briefly compare Devlin's perspective to the work of John Stuart Mill, a nineteenth-century British philosopher. Mill ([1859] 1981) argued that society should only concern itself with actions that pose a direct harm to others. This notion has come to be known as the **harm principle**. Mill was not concerned about actions that might cause persons to harm themselves, nor was he concerned with actions that might *indirectly* lead to the potential for harm to occur. Also, Mill did not believe that society should concern itself with morality because he believed that doing so promoted conformity while discouraging the individuality that was necessary to allow a society to progress. Mill's position was reflected in the *Wolfenden Report.*

In contrast to Mill, Devlin believed that regulating public morality was necessary to allow a society to progress, as we see in the discussion of his second question, which was: "Has [society] also the right to use the weapon of the law to enforce [morality]?" (Devlin, [1965] 1977, p. 54). Devlin answered with a resounding "yes." To Devlin, a shared public morality was the bedrock of any society, and without this moral bedrock, the society would collapse. As a result, he believed that morality was essential to the very survival of society. Devlin noted that "societies disintegrate from within more frequently than they are broken up by external pressures" (Devlin, [1965] 1977, p. 59), and this could occur through two means—treason against the government and immorality. Because both means could promote the downfall of society, Devlin argued that both

legal moralism
The idea that popular notions of morality should influence decisions about what behaviors the law ought to regulate. This was the perspective held by Patrick Devlin in the Hart-Devlin debate.

collective judgment
The consensus that members of a society would reach about which behaviors are morally acceptable and which behaviors are morally unacceptable. This was instrumental to Patrick Devlin's theory of legal moralism.

harm principle
The idea advanced by John Stuart Mill that a society (through the law) should only concern itself with actions that pose a direct harm to others.

should be addressed with equal vigor through the law. Therefore, Devlin's philosophy does not distinguish between public and private acts; if the public believes the act is immoral, then Devlin would argue it threatens society and must be addressed in law.

Devlin's third question asked about how the government should go about creating a legal code reflecting moral interests. He recognized that there was the risk of creating a society in which *all* individual behavior is controlled by the public's opinion of morality, which would be undesirable. Devlin defines public morality as that "about which any twelve men or women drawn at random might after discussion be expected to be unanimous" (Devlin, [1965] 1977, p. 61). The unanimity should be guided by feelings of "intolerance, indignation, and disgust" (Devlin, [1965] 1977, p. 62) toward the issue in question. Without such strong feelings, Devlin believes it would be inappropriate to restrict an individual's behavior. Thus, he thought that the criminal law could be used to control behaviors that "lie beyond the limits of tolerance" (Devlin, [1965] 1977, p. 62).

Devlin also issued cautions in developing a morally driven legal code, as follows. First, it is important for the law (and for society) not to be overly restrictive but instead to focus only on aspects of morality that meet the rather strict criteria provided earlier. Otherwise, individuals should have freedom in their personal lives. Second, laws based on morality must be carefully considered and not made in haste. Over time, laws prohibiting a practice may remain on the books even if society no longer deems the practice immoral. It is then difficult to remove these laws "without giving the impression that moral judgment [overall] is being weakened" (Devlin, [1965] 1977, p. 63). Therefore, lawmakers should work to ensure that only the most significant moral issues are addressed by the law. Third, when enforcing laws based on morality, law enforcement should respect the legal requirements for privacy, such as procuring a warrant based on probable cause before entering a person's home to search for evidence of a crime. Finally, while the law can tell individuals not to engage in certain immoral acts, that does not mean that all people will then act morally in all other circumstances.

As an example of Devlin's legal moralism, consider a brief history of gambling law in the United States. From the early years of the United States into the twentieth century, the collective judgment expressed a public morality opposed to gambling. In part, the moral objection to gambling was that it flouted the individual work ethic that was part of the national fabric: "Gambling was odious, then, because it was the wrong way to make money: it mocked the ideal of slow, steady progress through hard work" (Friedman, 1993, p. 134). As a result, laws against gambling of all sorts were enacted in the American states. Even private gambling was prohibited as a violation of society's morals. Gambling laws could not ensure that all financial transactions were moral, but they did help alleviate concerns that gambling would undo the stability of society. As the twentieth century unfolded, however, attitudes about gambling began to change. For instance, lotteries were increasingly viewed as engines for enhancing state budget revenues (Pierce & Miller, 2004), and riverboat casinos became a popular way for localities to increase tourism and to stimulate the economy (Deitrick, Beauregard, & Kerchis, 1999). As Devlin predicted, changing the laws to permit lotteries and casinos proved difficult because some persons believed that doing so indicated an abandonment of social morality. However, the collective judgment on the issue clearly had shifted, as many laws were changed not by elected officials but by votes of the public as a whole (known as initiative or referendum elections) (Pierce & Miller, 2004).

DEVLIN AND THE SIX CONCEPTS OF LAW

Devlin's legal moralism can be assessed using the six concepts of law presented earlier. Table 3.1 summarizes how Devlin's theory fits the concepts. The left column lists the concepts of law. The middle column identifies the basic positions of the theory which, in Devlin's case, is idealistic, drawing upon the elements of idealism as described in the

TABLE 3.1 Devlin's Six Concepts of Law

Concepts	Idealist Perspective	Devlin's Position
Foundation of Law	*Public Morality*	Law is based on morality derived from religion
Rationale of Law	*Enforce Morality*	To preserve society by maintaining its morality
Formation of Law	*Irrational*	Underlying morality is the key principle to consider
Application of Law	*Rational*	Logical principles to ensure careful application
Focal Point of Law	*Product*	If society is preserved, then the law is successful
Discretion within the Law	*Discouraged*	One person's private moral judgments should not replace society's views of public morality

prior chapter. In particular, it seeks the truth in terms of a higher moral code, and it works to ensure that society is in harmony with that moral code as enforced through the law. The third column provides further description of Devlin's position. Exploration of the six concepts of law will help you to compare and contrast the various theories presented in this chapter, to assess others as you discover them, and to arrive at your own philosophy about what the law should be.

Foundation of Law. Public morality is the foundation of law for Devlin. For legal moralists, the morality on which law is based often (though not always) has its foundation in religious beliefs of some sort. Devlin asserts that the public is duty bound to follow morality. This firm grounding in morality causes idealists to perceive great legitimacy in their efforts and to pursue them vigorously because they believe the stakes include not only the moral welfare of society but also its very survival.

Rationale of Law. For Devlin and legal moralists, the purpose of law is to enforce morality. Legal moralists argue that doing so preserves society by maintaining its underlying morality, arguing that a failure to do so would allow a society to crumble as its moral foundation shatters beneath it. Because proponents of legal moralism believe strongly in their underlying values, they often advocate firmly for laws supporting their values with only a limited willingness to compromise (see Sabatier & Jenkins-Smith, 1993). This is coupled with arguments that a failure to adopt a particular morality-driven law or policy will be a step toward society's decline.

Formation of Law. In legal moralism, the formation of law is categorized as irrational. As conceptualized by Devlin, the legal moralist forms law by considering what the average person believes is morally offensive and then criminalizing it. This is a non-empirical method because it does not involve careful and systematic study of the issue that is being criminalized (which a pragmatist would favor); rather, it relies on beliefs about ultimate values and truths, which in their own right cannot be proven or disproven.

Application of Law. The application of law is categorized as rational. For Devlin and the legal moralists, the law must be applied carefully. Recall Devlin's principles to be considered as the law is implemented: that it permit freedom, that it is made carefully with a recognition that things may change over time, that it account for privacy in enforcement, and that it is realistic in recognizing that law will not cause all people to be virtuous all the time. This balances law and liberty and rationally considers the realities of what law can and cannot accomplish.

Focal Point of Law. Idealists tend to judge the success of the law by assessing its products, or end results. For instance, if the law punishes those who tamper with society's moral code and as a result the moral code remains intact, thereby preserving society, then the law has been successful. It is of less consequence whether or not the means (or techniques) used to accomplish the ends (or products) were proper, or appropriate, as long as the ends themselves are accomplished. Of course, this is an ethical question which has challenged criminal justice for centuries: what happens if a good result is obtained using improper or questionable methods? As Devlin perceived the law's regulation of morality as essential to society's survival, it is the outcomes that matter the most to legal moralism.

Discretion within the Law. As discussed in Chapter 1, the use of discretion is an unavoidable component of criminal justice practice. The legal moralist does not take the position that there should never be discretionary decision making because that would be unrealistic. However, the legal moralist would discourage discretion, instead arguing that criminal justice practitioners should follow the public morality underlying the law rather that replacing it with their own individual views of morality. If the rationale of the law is indeed to preserve society by maintaining its underlying morality, then legal moralists would want that underlying morality to be uniformly enforced.

Q What is your opinion of the theory of legal moralism? Why?

Q How would legal moralism resolve the scenario at the beginning of the chapter?

Q Can you identify any examples of legal moralism? How do they meet the six concepts of law described in this section?

Q Do you believe there are any issues today that "lie beyond the limits of tolerance" using the criteria of "intolerance, indignation, and disgust"? Should they be controlled under the law? Explain your answer.

H. L. A. Hart's Legal Positivism

FOCUSING QUESTION 3.4

What did Hart believe was the law's role in society?

legal positivism
A philosophy that views the law solely as a human creation rather than as an attempt to discover, confirm, or enforce higher moral standards. This was the perspective held by H. L. A. Hart in the Hart-Devlin debate.

Legal positivism has been profoundly influenced by the work of British legal philosopher H. L. A. Hart ([1961] 1994). **Legal positivism** views the law solely as a human creation and not as an attempt to discover, confirm, or enforce higher moral standards. The legal positivist would not accept Devlin's notion that the law should even attempt to regulate morality. Hart (1958, pp. 601–602) identified five criteria for law that further illustrate the theory of legal positivism:

1. "Laws are commands of human beings";
2. "There is no necessary connection between law and morals";
3. "The analysis (or study of the meaning) of legal concepts is . . . worth pursuing and . . . to be distinguished from" . . . an assessment of morals;
4. "A legal system is a 'closed logical system' in which correct decisions can be deduced by logical means from predetermined legal rules" alone; and
5. "Moral judgments cannot be established or defended, as statements of fact can, by rational arguments, evidence, or proof."

Let's work to understand the meaning of these five criteria. It will become apparent that Hart is not an idealist because truth, harmony, and Devlin's concept of public morality play little role in his theory. Hart's beliefs draw upon the pragmatic tradition

because of his emphasis on viewing law as a rational creation of humans designed to address the observable reality of society, rather than non-empirical moral codes.

We will continue the example of gambling to explore the five criteria. If a state were to pass a law against gambling based on legal positivism, it would be only because a group of individuals decided that such a law was necessary. There would be no presumption that the law was derived from any higher source (criterion 1). Simply believing that gambling is immoral would not be a sufficient reason to pass a law prohibiting it. Further, the mere fact that gambling is illegal would not necessarily be an indicator that the behavior is immoral (criterion 2). The rationale for laws about gambling would be empirically based, whether for it (such as promoting economic development, e.g., Koo, Rosentraub, & Horn, 2007) or against it (such as concerns about gambling addiction, e.g., Room, Turner, & Ialomiteanu, 1999). However, evidence would not be used to prove or disprove the morality of gambling, which is a judgment not subject to empirical proof (criterion 5). When passed, the law should be clear enough so that a criminal justice professional would understand what it meant, to whom it applied, and how it should be enforced (criterion 4). And the law, its creation, and its impact could be subjects of legal scholarship and writing, **jurisprudence** (the study of law) being recognized as a legitimate area of academic study (criterion 3).

jurisprudence
The academic and philosophical study of law.

Hart's approach differs greatly from Devlin's. Hart himself wrote about his differences with Devlin, making several observations. Hart ([1959] 1971) observed that Devlin's approach is based largely on feelings, or emotions, in determining what is immoral. This means that, for Devlin, the law is also based on these feelings. Hart believed that feelings are not enough on which to base morality and not enough on which to base the law. In addition, Hart noted that emotionally based decisions about morality may infringe on individual liberties. This is problematic when "the popular limits of tolerance . . . shift" (p. 51)—that is, when collective judgment has changed and a behavior is no longer viewed as immoral but remains illegal because people are reluctant to change the law (as Devlin predicted). At that point, based on an initial decision grounded in legal moralism, the law would continue to infringe on individual liberties but without a moral basis for doing so.

As a result, Hart believed that making decisions about the law must be more complex than reducing it to questions about perceptions of morality. Instead, he suggested that the first question should instead be whether the issue causes some sort of harm aside from concerns about morality. Hart did not believe society is threatened by acts that pose no harms aside from being viewed as immoral. To return to the recommendations of the *Wolfenden Report,* Hart wrote that there is no reason to believe society would be threatened because consensual sexual acts that are unpopular with the public are permitted to occur. In fact, Hart suggested that permitting legislation solely on the basis of Devlin's "intolerance, indignation, and disgust" ([1965] 1977, p. 62) can have dangerous results, as he illustrated with a striking example: "We once burnt old women because, without giving our reasons, we felt in our hearts that witchcraft was intolerable" (Hart, [1959] 1971, p. 53).

Hart ([1959] 1971) ended his critique of Devlin by issuing a caution to democratic societies: "it is fatally easy to confuse the democratic principle that the *power should be in the hands of the majority* with the utterly different claim that the majority, with the power in their hands, *need respect no limits*" [emphasis added] (p. 54). Hart's concern was that Devlin's approach places no limits on lawmakers; if something is viewed as immoral through society's collective judgment, it can (and to Devlin, must) be made illegal. Hart was not opposed to morality. However, he believed that morality is not a *sufficient* reason, by itself, to enact law, even if the majority is morally opposed to a practice. Instead, Hart believed it is important for government to protect the rights and freedoms of the public.

Let's consider one more example, this time about swearing (e.g., cursing or foul language). In some jurisdictions, cursing in public is against the law, and individuals have been arrested and cited for violating such laws (Associated Press, 2002). Some of these laws date back to early American history and are clearly grounded in collective judgments about public morality (Parkes, 1932). How would Hart assess this kind of law? He would likely raise several objections. First, Hart might wonder what harm cursing actually causes and whether it would damage the fabric of society. Second, he might wonder what would happen if cursing later became an accepted behavior, as evidence suggests that it has, in particular judging from the mass media content (Jay, 1992). Could the law then be used against individuals whose behavior is no longer viewed with "intolerance, indignation, and disgust"? Third, Hart might be concerned about the impact of this law. What, exactly, is considered a curse word or inappropriate language? Could the law infringe upon free speech? These sorts of questions are those that Hart would want lawmakers to consider *before* making a law to ensure that it addresses legitimate concerns, grounded in empirical findings beyond general notions about the morality of swearing.

HART AND THE SIX CONCEPTS OF LAW

Hart's legal positivism can be assessed using the six concepts of law presented earlier. Table 3.2 summarizes how Hart's theory fits the concepts, reflecting the pragmatic approach described in the previous chapter.

Foundation of Law. Whereas Devlin believed that a public morality accepted by society is the foundation of law, Hart asserted that its foundation is private morality. Hart believed that individuals should be entitled to follow their own morality as long as it is not "harmful to the legitimate interests of others. People have . . . a legal right to do (what others consider to be a) moral wrong" (Raes, 2001, p. 31). This notion sets clear limits as to what the law can and cannot do. Again, Hart was not opposed to morality, but he found morality, *by itself*, to be an insufficient reason for enacting a law.

Rationale of Law. Following from his foundation of law, Hart was concerned about protecting individual rights. Devlin would be willing to sacrifice individuals' rights by prohibiting them from doing things they would like to do, if doing so was necessary to protect society's moral views. On the other hand, Hart believed that individuals should have the freedom to do as they please as long as they do not harm others. For Hart, the law is not designed to create a model society (as Devlin believed) but rather to protect people's rights so they can live freely, but safely, within society.

TABLE 3.2 Hart's Six Concepts of Law

Concepts	Pragmatic Perspective	Hart's Position
Foundation of Law	*Private Morality*	Allow individuals the right to create their own morality
Rationale of Law	*Protect Individual Rights*	Individual needs are valued, even if scorned by society
Formation of Law	*Rational*	Laws are formed based on careful study and analysis
Application of Law	*Irrational*	Professionals may reach different conclusions based on imperfect data
Focal Point of Law	*Process*	If the law follows its own rules, then it is successful
Discretion within the Law	*Encouraged*	Discretion is inevitable and can strengthen the system

Formation of Law. In creating law, Hart and legal positivists follow a rational process that is both logical and empirical. Rather than relying on feelings about what is moral and immoral, crafting the law about a particular issue requires careful study of that issue, its nature, its impact, its causes, and so forth. This demonstrates a desire for the empiricism that is characteristic of pragmatists. In doing so, lawmakers must work to identify the line between individual rights and harm to society, to strike the balance described in Hart's foundation of law, and to respect the rights described in Hart's rationale of law.

Application of the Law. Legal moralists discourage the use of discretion in law. This is sometimes accomplished through the development of guidelines for criminal justice professionals to follow (see Box 3.3 for one example). Rather than relying on guidelines, legal positivists would want to collect multiple data points (e.g., information about the offender's background, needs, employment, schooling, nature of the crime, etc.) and analyze them to reach the best decision in each individual case. This is also consistent with how legal positivists approach the formation of the law based on a careful study of data.

Table 3.2 labels this as irrational. In the application of law, the legal positivist is driven by two noble ideas. First, life's most important decisions are often made with insufficient information, and this should be remedied whenever possible. Second, human judgment should not be taken out of the law. As to the first observation, data will always be imperfect, especially when trying to make sense of complex human behavior. As to the second observation, infusing human judgment raises the possibility that different people will reach different conclusions based on the same data. For these reasons, the discretionary application of law becomes irrational in that outcomes are not driven by a strict set of rules and guidelines that guarantee the same result across different cases.

Focal Point of Law. For legal positivists, the law is successful only if it follows a clearly articulated, fair, and accepted process. Therefore, the means by which the law operates become more important than the end results. This is not to say that the effectiveness of the law in responding to harmful behavior is unimportant—quite the contrary. Like good pragmatists, legal positivists want to collect data to see if the law is helping to reduce harms in society. However, remember that for legal positivists, promoting a private morality and protecting individual rights are most important and that careful study is required when forming and applying the law. For this all to occur, the process *must* be carefully followed, and if the process is not carefully followed, the law will likely not fully reflect the wishes of the legal positivist.

Volunteer Carlos Arredondo, in the cowboy hat, assists Jeff Bauman, in wheelchair, after the 2013 Boston Marathon bombing. In crisis and disaster situations, members of the public often help one another. Should the law, through "good Samaritan" statutes, require persons to provide assistance to others in emergency situations? How would Devlin and Hart approach this question?

Discretion within the Law. Hart acknowledges that the substantive criminal law, as written, cannot cover all possible scenarios of human behavior. This makes the use of discretion inevitable for criminal justice professionals. Furthermore, Hart would argue that

BOX 3.3

SENTENCING GUIDELINES

In some jurisdictions, including the federal court system and a number of state court systems, judges utilize sentencing guidelines when deciding the appropriate punishment for an offender. Sentencing guidelines were created to reduce the amount of discretion that judges had in determining sentences and to produce more consistency in sentences (for a general overview, see Spohn, 2009, chapter 6). Most sentencing guidelines incorporate two factors: an offender's prior record and the seriousness (or other characteristics) of the crime committed. Based on these pieces of information, a judge consults a table to arrive at the appropriate sentence. A sample appears in this box. Across the top are column headings based on an offender's prior record. Down the left side, there are six rows (labeled A through F) representing the seriousness of the offense. The most serious offenses fall in the A category, and the least serious offenses are in the F category.

Let's say that theft is an F-level offense, and that it is the third offense for a particular offender. Looking at the table, this would indicate that the punishment should be 18 months in prison. All judges using this table would reach the same conclusion based on the facts.

Sentencing Matrix

Offense Seriousness	1st Offense	2nd Offense	3rd Offense	4th Offense
A	360	Life	N/A	N/A
B	120	240	Life	N/A
C	72	144	240	Life
D	36	72	144	240
E	18	36	72	144
F	Fine	Probation	18	36

This is intended as a conceptual example, as actual sentencing guideline systems are much more sophisticated, accompanied by volumes of explanation as to how the system works. To the idealist, sentencing guidelines help to reduce discretion, ensuring that sentences are consistent, reflecting the uniformity of law viewed as necessary to protect the morality of society.

To the pragmatist, sentencing guidelines omit an individualized consideration of possibly relevant information—other than that included in the guidelines—that would be useful in sentencing the offender, therefore reducing not only discretion but also empiricism in sentencing. The alternative used by states without sentencing guidelines is to allow judges to use their discretion in determining the appropriate sentence, which usually may be selected from a very broad range of alternatives (e.g., 1–10 years in prison).

Q Do you think judges should be required to utilize sentencing guidelines? Subsequent court cases (e.g., *U.S. v. Booker,* 2005; *Blakely v. Washington,* 2004) have questioned the extent to which guidelines may be *required*, as opposed to *recommended*; which do you think is the better approach? Explain your answer.

Q Which of the sentencing systems—guidelines or use of judge's discretion—would you prefer if you were a judge? If you were an offender? Explain.

Q What principle do you think sentencing guidelines rules illustrate?

the use of discretion could actually produce a better criminal justice system. For instance, better judgments, more informed by data and analysis, can be made by the criminal justice professional who is closest to the behavior or issue in question. This is closely related to the legal positivist's application of the law, discussed earlier, which relies on this sort of discretion. Discretion then becomes part of the process to ensure that the law is properly implemented and that individual rights are acknowledged.

Q What is your opinion of the theory of legal positivism? Explain.

Q How would legal positivism resolve the scenario at the beginning of the chapter?

Q Compare and contrast how Hart and Devlin would approach a law regulating foul language. Which approach do you most agree with? Why? You may wish to review the Michigan Court of Appeals case *Michigan v. Boomer* (2002).

Q How do legal moralism and legal positivism compare to the characteristics of idealism and pragmatism described in the previous chapter?

Other Schools of Legal Philosophy

FOCUSING QUESTION 3.5

What are some other idealistic and pragmatic ideas about law?

Societies have long struggled to develop orderly legal systems. Two foundational approaches are the legal moralism advocated by Devlin and the legal positivism advocated by Hart. Other theorists have also written about the law. Table 3.3 lists additional theories of law that we will briefly consider.

The theories are grouped according to whether they most closely reflect idealism or pragmatism. Although we do not attempt to cover all possible theories of law, this discussion will give you the flavor of some theoretical variations. The theories described serve as excellent examples that further distinguish between legal idealism and legal pragmatism. Expanding your understanding with these additional theories will help you to further appreciate others' ideas about law and justice, to see how those ideas lead to the creation and interpretation of laws, and to give you the opportunity to reflect on your own ideas about what the law should do. As you reflect on the previous section and begin reading this section, read Box 3.4 about hate crime and consider how the philosophies of law may apply to it.

THEORIES OF LEGAL IDEALISM

Our discussion begins with **idealistic theories of law**. While all subscribe to the basic tenets of idealism, there is variety in how they do so. However, the theories tend to share the following ideas:

1. A systematic method is used to develop a legal system based on beliefs held as truths without empirical evidence.

idealistic theories of law
Theories of law grounded in the idealistic perspective. The theories include legal naturalism, rights and interpretive jurisprudence, critical theories of law, and legal paternalism.

TABLE 3.3 Legal Theories

Legal Idealism	Legal Pragmatism
Legal Moralism	Legal Positivism
Legal Naturalism	Legal Realism
Rights and Interpretive Jurisprudence	Everyday Pragmatism
Critical Theories of Law	
Legal Paternalism	

BOX 3.4

Research in Action

HATE CRIME

According to the Federal Bureau of Investigation (2012e), hate crime broadly refers to offenses that are committed on the basis of "an offender's bias against a race, religion, sexual orientation, ethnicity/national origin, or disability" (para. 1). Some jurisdictions also include gender, gender identity, age, and political affiliation (Anti-Defamation League, 2012). Hate crimes affect many persons each year. In 2012, Uniform Crime Report data indicated 5,796 hate crime incidents (Federal Bureau of Investigation, 2013), but National Crime Victimization Survey data indicated 148,400 victimizations, many of which were not reported to the police (Langton & Planty, 2011).

Research has identified two primary motives that lead offenders to commit hate crimes. The first, and most common (66% of cases in one study, based on an examination of incident records), was "for the thrill or excitement of the attack" (McDevitt, Levin, & Bennett, 2002, p. 307) in which the victim was deliberately sought out based on one or more characteristics. The second (25% of cases in the same study) was to cause persons who had moved into a neighborhood, and against whom the offender was prejudiced, to leave the neighborhood (McDevitt, Levin, & Bennett, 2002).

Advocates for legislation against hate crimes (e.g., Wellman, 2006) cite tragic and high-profile cases to illustrate the need for such laws. Such cases include the 1998 murder of Matthew Shepard in Wyoming (Loffreda, 2001), an anti-gay hate crime, and the 1998 murder of James Byrd, Jr., in Texas (King, 2003), based on the race of the victim, who was African American. Hate crime laws generally take one of two forms: either creating a new hate crime offense with which offenders can be charged; or making provisions to increase sentences when an existing offense is committed due to a bias or prejudice against one of the groups protected under the law.

Wellman (2006) argues that hate crime laws demonstrate the prevailing public attitude which decries hate crimes, appropriately punish hate crime offenders, and educate those who may not otherwise understand that there is a need to reinforce our moral standards with such laws. Further justifications for hate crime laws include research findings suggesting that hate crimes are more violent and more psychologically harmful than other crimes, including emotional distress felt by other members of the targeted group even if they were not directly victimized (Gerstenfeld, 2004).

At the same time, others are critical of hate crime laws. For instance, Jacobs and Potter (1997) noted that the actual criminal act should be the primary focus, rather than the motive, particularly as it may be difficult to determine when a crime is actually hate based. They ask, "Must the criminal conduct have been wholly, primarily, or slightly motivated by the disfavored prejudice?" (p. 4). In addition, they express concern that hate crime laws may have the effect of "further dividing an already fractured society" (p. 42) by highlighting divisions between groups.

Consider how the material in this chapter can apply to discussions of hate crime laws.

Q How would the philosophies of law described in this chapter apply to hate crime laws? That is, what would they recommend the law do about hate crime, and why?

Q Other than the philosophies of law, what other principles do you think might underlie hate crime laws?

Q After reviewing your answers to the above two questions, how do you think the law should address hate crimes? What can be done to prevent them?

2. Legal decisions draw upon history and tradition, attempting to reflect long-held understandings of the truth.
3. The purpose of the legal system is to create and serve a moral society (however "moral" may be defined), and if it does not do so, the law has failed.
4. Laws that do not correspond to the standards of public morality, and which do not work to create and serve a moral society, are viewed as invalid.
5. The legal system should consistently follow precedents (i.e., prior decisions) when dealing with similar cases rather than treating similar cases differently.

6. Legal idealism competes with other legal theories, and proponents of the theory work to demonstrate its superiority to other theories.

Individual philosophers vary in the degree of emphasis they give to each idea, and some may even alter these ideas or add new ones. However, your ability to recognize these concepts will help you to explain and interpret idealistic legal thought and behavior.

Legal Naturalism

Proponents of **legal naturalism** believe in the concept of natural law. So far, you have read about theories in which humans create law either by attempts to define the public morality on which individuals agree (for legal moralists) or by empirical processes focusing on the prevention of harm (for legal positivists). A belief in **natural law**, on the other hand, presupposes that there are *universally accepted principles* of human behavior that are meant to apply to all persons everywhere. For instance, a natural law theorist would argue that just as gravity is a natural law of physics applicable everywhere on Earth, there also exist standards of human behavior that should apply to all persons without exception.

legal naturalism
A legal theory espousing a belief in the concept of natural law.

natural law
A belief that there are universally accepted principles of human behavior meant to apply to all persons in all places and that law should discover, reflect, and enforce these principles.

But how does a natural law theorist know what these universal standards of behavior are? Because natural law assumes that these principles are inherent within the universe and not created by humans, there is no easy answer to this question. Some base their answers on what they believe to be universal religious principles, but others draw upon various conceptions of the state of nature to distill basic principles necessary for the peaceful coexistence of multiple persons. As an example, some natural law theorists might argue that universal principles suggest that all persons have a right to live without fear of violence. This principle would suggest that murder, assault, and war must be prohibited under law (interestingly, in 1928, the Kellogg-Briand Pact unsuccessfully attempted to criminalize war under international law; Paterson, Clifford, & Hagan, 1991). Therefore, laws against murder, assault, and war would not be made by humans but rather would be implemented because it was natural to do so and would be presumed to apply in all societies across the globe. It is worth reiterating the distinction from legal moralism. Law is not made because a group of people gathered to decide what was moral or not. Here, law is made because it is simply following the natural principles, design, order, or intent of the universe.

Table 3.4 describes how legal naturalism corresponds to the six concepts of law. The foundation, rationale, and formation of law emphasize the use of the law to promote universal standards of morality. In doing so, the focal point of the law emphasizes the importance of generating moral outcomes as the product of the law, based on the universal standards that are identified. Legal naturalism presumes a

TABLE 3.4 Legal Naturalism and the Six Concepts of Law

Concepts	Idealistic Perspective	Legal Naturalism
Foundation of Law	*Public Morality*	Universal principles of human conduct
Rationale of Law	*Enforce Morality*	Law should promote universal standards
Formation of Law	*Irrational*	Laws should be made after identifying natural principles
Application of Law	*Rational*	The law should be clear and enforced uniformly
Focal Point of Law	*Product*	Follow a natural process to achieve a moral outcome
Discretion within the Law	*Discouraged*	Law should not be individualized, but should be enforced uniformly

rational application of the law, ensuring that it is applied uniformly with minimal use of discretion; to do otherwise would result in an inconsistent application of the moral standards being enforced.

In a provocative paper, Robinson (2013) studied situations in which persons had to fend for themselves, whether due to disasters, exploration of frontier territories, or situations in which law enforcement was (even temporarily) absent. In these situations, Robinson argues, there is "a tendency of humans toward social cooperation, even when it is not obvious to a person at the time that such is in his or her individual interest" (p. 505), which is stable enough to suggest that its origins may include "genetic predisposition or some form of universal social learning" (p. 442). This is consistent with computer-based simulations conducted among adult populations (Axelrod, 1984) and with research conducted among 15-month-old infants (Schmidt & Sommerville, 2011), each of which revealed an ethic of altruism and cooperation. Does this suggest that cooperative behavior is a principle grounded in natural law? Such a notion could influence the development of law related to criminal justice issues, such as appropriate punishments and the structure of court proceedings (Robinson, 2013).

Philosopher Mortimer Adler (1947) argued that to make law "without a foundation in natural law is purely arbitrary" (p. 83) because doing so would mean that any legislator or politician could propose any law for any reason without having to reference grander truths. This could make the law appear very subjective, responding to the whims of the time. There would be nothing to prevent arbitrary changes to the law. At the same time, Adler noted that natural law, by itself, "is ineffective for the purposes of enforcing justice and keeping peace" (p. 83). Even if natural law issues moral absolutes, someone must still identify those principles and incorporate them into a written legal code—a process which can be sidetracked by politics, debates about legal philosophies, or other distractions, resulting in outcomes other than the reflection of natural law in the legal code. For instance, if legal naturalism specifies that there is a right to live without fear of violence, does this mean that violence is never authorized? Would self-defense, police use of force, capital punishment, or war be permitted? How is the natural law rule to be interpreted? This is a dilemma that is difficult to resolve, perhaps because once again it illustrates the differences between idealists in search of overarching principles and pragmatists seeking to make law based only on what is measurable and directly observable in the world.

RIGHTS AND INTERPRETIVE JURISPRUDENCE

American legal philosopher Ronald Dworkin may be classified as an idealist due in part to his position on the role of morality in law. Although Dworkin was not quite as adamant as Devlin about the risks that immoral behavior posed to society, he did believe that legislators and judges could not ignore moral considerations when framing and interpreting law. Another point of difference between Devlin and Dworkin is in how morality is defined. Dworkin strongly criticized Devlin's methods of determining public morality, instead advocating for a more comprehensive approach:

> The claim that a moral consensus exists is not itself based on a poll. It is based on an appeal to the legislator's sense of how his community reacts to some disfavored practice. But this same sense includes an awareness of the grounds on which that reaction is generally supported. If there has been a public debate involving the editorial columns, speeches of his colleagues, the testimony of interested groups, and his own correspondence, these will sharpen his awareness of what arguments and positions are in the field. *He must sift these arguments and positions,* trying to determine which are prejudices or rationalizations, which presuppose general prejudices or theories vast parts of the population could not be supposed to accept, and so on. It may be that *when he has finished this process of reflection* he will find that the claim of a moral consensus has not been made out. [emphasis added] (Dworkin, 1966, p. 1001)

Therefore, we see that Dworkin shares the idealist's emphasis on morality in the foundation and rationale of law. He also shares idealistic tendencies in the application, focal point, and discretion of law. In his "right answer thesis," Dworkin (1978) argues that there is a correct answer even to the most difficult legal problems. It is the obligation of a judge to strive for identifying that right answer through a careful interpretation of legal materials (and that interpretation includes the consideration of moral contexts in which the law was made). Dworkin disavows the idea of having judges create their own versions of the law to fill in gaps in the written legal code, meaning that Dworkin is focused on a single proper (or correct) outcome as the focal point of law and does not advocate for frequent use of discretionary decisions. Although Dworkin has a well-respected moral theory, his critics note that he appears to rely on a single interpretation of morality to determine what the law should be (Tamanaha, 2004).

The protection of rights is important to Dworkin, and he believes that society should take rights seriously (1978). Should a legal conflict come down to the question of whether or not rights should be protected, Dworkin would generally favor protecting the rights. While his focus on morality remains a key emphasis in terms of the law's foundation and purpose, it is therefore tempered by an appreciation for individual rights, which was less prominent in Devlin's theory. The formation of law may still be considered irrational because its primary focus is the identification of a common morality, which plays an important role in idealistic philosophy—even though the identification of that morality is achieved through the in-depth process quoted earlier. Table 3.5 describes how Dworkin's theory corresponds to the six concepts of law.

Legal debates about flag burning may illustrate elements of interpretive jurisprudence. In 1989, the U.S. Supreme Court ruled on the case *Texas v. Johnson,* which challenged a law criminalizing the desecration of the American flag. The law was overturned on the grounds that flag burning was freedom of expression as protected under the First Amendment. However, Chief Justice Rehnquist dissented with the majority ruling, expressing moral disapproval of flag burning. In his opinion, rather than relying primarily on prior court cases, Rehnquist cited song lyrics, historical documents, poetry, quotations, excerpts from a legislative hearing, and more, in support of his argument. While his argument ultimately did not prevail, it represents an application of interpretive jurisprudence.

CRITICAL THEORIES OF LAW

Critical theories of law represent a relatively new field with roots in the 1970s. It is also a somewhat diverse field comprising a variety of different—but overlapping—perspectives. According to most critical theorists, the law was created by powerful individuals to help them remain in power. Here are a few ideas shared by critical theorists.

critical theories of law A legal philosophy holding that the law was created and is used by powerful individuals to help them remain in power.

1. Throughout American history, laws have been created by those with wealth and power to maintain their interests.

TABLE 3.5 Interpretive Jurisprudence and the Six Concepts of Law

Concepts	Idealistic Perspective	Interpretive Jurisprudence
Foundation of Law	*Public Morality*	Morality discovered after careful interpretation
Rationale of Law	*Enforce Morality*	Law is grounded in morality but with protection of rights
Formation of Law	*Irrational*	Morality is the key principle in the creation of law
Application of Law	*Rational*	Interpret laws to identify the single correct answer
Focal Point of Law	*Product*	Discovering the proper answer leads to better law
Discretion within the Law	*Discouraged*	Deviation from reasoned morality is avoided

2. The interests of those with power differ from the interests of those without power.
3. The motives and hidden meanings of the law should be questioned to determine whether (and how) they marginalize and dehumanize those without power.
4. Developing a critical theory of law can raise awareness of these concerns, articulate the value of all persons, and prevent the law from being used to restrain or harm those without power in society.

Critical legal theorists have undertaken two distinct but related tasks. One task is to be critical of the status quo as described in the first two items on the list. Another task is to offer a better approach and to remedy problems they have identified in the law by accomplishing the third and fourth items on the list. Critical theory is often associated with calls for larger social reforms beyond the law, including the consideration of an array of social problems and the promotion of justice in law and society. This means that the focal point of law for critical theorists is in the outcomes, by accomplishing the reforms and achieving the move toward justice and equality that they desire.

While some critical theorists would disagree, it seems that critical theory fits more neatly in an idealistic framework than in a pragmatic framework, although there is some degree of overlap. Critical theorists are attempting to accomplish and enforce morality under the law, which places them in the framework of idealism. However, the morality that they draw upon is precisely focused, exploring issues related to the values of justice, fairness, and equality for all persons, and how they are related to societal power structures. These values are held as ultimate truths that are used in the pursuit of harmony in the world.

The formation of the law is listed as irrational. Critical theorists generally structure their beliefs around deeply held values that are not subject to empirical verification. At the same time, critical theorists often draw upon sophisticated bodies of empirical data to offer evidence in support of their arguments, such as providing information about poverty, inequalities in arrests and sentencing, and so forth. However, the primary focus is on the underlying values relating to power structures and concern about inequities, which the empirical data are offered to support.

The application of law and use of discretion also follow idealistic principles. Critical theorists are generally fighting inequalities, and permitting widespread use of discretion or flexible application of law would have the potential to exacerbate those inequalities. In fact, discretion could be perceived as one tool that is utilized to favor those in power and punish those who lack power. Table 3.6 summarizes the six concepts of law for critical legal theory.

TABLE 3.6 Critical Legal Theory and the Six Concepts of Law

Concepts	Idealistic Perspective	Critical Theory
Foundation of Law	*Public Morality*	Morality emphasizing the needs of all citizens rather than the elite
Rationale of Law	*Enforce Morality*	Protect individuals with an emphasis on justice, fairness, and equality
Formation of Law	*Irrational*	Law is based on deeply held values about power structures and equality
Application of Law	*Rational*	Strict adherence to law to ensure fairness for all
Focal Point of Law	*Product*	Harmonic society for all citizens, not just the elite
Discretion within the Law	*Discouraged*	Enforce law fairly without bias or special treatment

You may sense that critical legal theory is controversial; it is. Some critical theorists broadly criticize criminal justice institutions. For instance, Irwin ([1985] 1998) argued that jails are used to manage "the rabble" (p. 228), by which he means persons who are isolated from mainstream society and who are perceived by society as offensive. Irwin went on to suggest that "the police are at least as interested in managing the rabble as in enforcing the law" (p. 229). This perspective illustrates the first three characteristics of critical theory, and comes with recommendations for reforming the system to meet the fourth.

Critical theorists also examine how specific offenses are treated under the law. One example that illustrates critical theory is the disparity in sentencing between white-collar crimes and street crimes. White-collar crimes can result in injury and death, largely due to negligence or toxic environments (see Kappeler & Potter, 2005). However, sentences for white-collar crimes are often lenient, especially when compared to sentences for street crimes that cause less harm financially or otherwise (Reiman, 2001). Is this because the law was deliberately structured to protect the wealthy and financial wrongdoings? Some critical theorists would argue that to be the case. Or does society perceive street crime as more serious? In either case, critical theorists would work toward promoting fairness in the system, and in doing so they challenge the status quo, its assumptions, and its values, which can raise controversial questions.

LEGAL PATERNALISM

Under the philosophy of **legal paternalism**, the government can pass laws "to protect individuals from self-inflicted harm or, in its extreme version, to guide them, whether they like it or not, toward their own good" (Feinberg, 1971, p. 3). That is, if persons engage in behaviors that are likely to harm them, but do not harm anyone else, should the law intervene? Legal paternalists would answer that the law should. Some laws do attempt to protect people from making dangerous decisions; one example is requiring a prescription for medications about which individuals might not know the proper uses and side effects.

legal paternalism
A legal theory holding that the government creates and enforces law to protect individuals from engaging in risky behaviors or making decisions that might harm them.

All behavior, even something as routine as crossing the street, carries some risk of harm. Therefore, the challenge for the paternalist is to determine which behavior is sufficiently risky to need regulation. Joel Feinberg (1971) notes several factors that can be considered in this decision, including whether the behavior is voluntary, whether the risks are known or unknown, and the probability and severity of the potential harm. When a behavior is deemed risky enough to be regulated, legal paternalism can proceed in two ways. The first is a weak paternalism in which the law may intervene to ensure that individuals understand the potential risks of their behavior and are indeed willing to accept them; if they are, they may engage in the behavior. The second is a strong paternalism in which the law discourages (through higher taxes on items deemed to be risky, limiting where risky behavior can take place, etc.) or actually prohibits a risky behavior.

As an example, consider whether or not motorcycle riders should be required to wear helmets. A weak paternalistic response might be a state-funded media campaign alerting drivers of the risks of not wearing a helmet. The goal would be to increase awareness to hopefully ensure that a choice *not* to wear a helmet was made voluntarily and with full information about possible risks. A strong paternalistic response might be to require that helmets be worn while a motorcycle is in operation and to fine drivers who fail to do so.

Legal paternalism meets the general criteria of an idealistic legal philosophy. The morality that paternalists perceive as the foundation and rationale of law is a belief that society has a moral obligation to protect its citizens, with the metaphor of the law acting as a parent to its subjects (a concept known as *parens patriae*). The formation of paternalistic law is labeled as irrational, because it is based on the notion that regulation of behavior by the state produces better results than if people are left to make their own

TABLE 3.7 Legal Paternalism and the Six Concepts of Law

Concepts	Idealistic Perspective	Legal Paternalism
Foundation of Law	*Public Morality*	Value of protecting all citizens from harm
Rationale of Law	*Enforce Morality*	Views law and government in the role of a "parent"
Formation of Law	*Irrational*	Based on idea that the law leads to better results than people would reach on their own
Application of Law	*Rational*	Law must be applied to all persons, as written, to minimize risks of harm
Focal Point of Law	*Product*	Minimizing risk
Discretion within the Law	*Discouraged*	It is morally wrong to pick and choose whom to protect through enforcement of law

choices. Like critical theorists, legal paternalists may use empirical data to support their arguments, such as citing the number of motorcycle accidents and injuries that occur yearly. However, the emphasis remains on the moral value of protecting people from their own potential decisions. Paternalistic law does not support discretion. The focal point of law lies in its outcomes because the assumption is that all persons engaging in a prohibited risky behavior must be stopped for their own safety no matter what their intentions might be. This makes for a clear but rigid application of the law. Table 3.7 summarizes the six concepts of law for legal paternalism.

THEORIES OF LEGAL PRAGMATISM

legal pragmatism
A legal theory arguing that the law should be based on empirical evidence rather than on grand concepts such as morality.

Richard Posner (2003) is a leading spokesperson for **legal pragmatism**. Posner and other legal pragmatists would prefer to see the law based on empirical evidence rather than grand concepts such as morality. Again, this is consistent with Hart's approach as well. We will consider two additional legal philosophies that have their roots in the ideas of legal pragmatism.

LEGAL REALISM

Legal realists give their primary focus to the decision-making processes of the courts because they believe that the courts *create* law through their accumulated decisions. The law, then, becomes whatever the courts say it is.

legal realism
A legal theory with a primary focus on the decision-making processes of the courts. The theory holds that the courts create law through their accumulated decisions, meaning that the law becomes whatever the courts say it is.

A modern perspective related to the roots of **legal realism** is the attitudinal model, which was developed by political scientists Jeffrey Segal and Harold Spaeth (1993) to explain U.S. Supreme Court behavior. The attitudinal model argues "that the Supreme Court decides disputes in light of the facts of the case vis-à-vis the ideological attitudes and values of the justices" (p. 65). Almost any Supreme Court case provides an example. When the Supreme Court decides a case, it issues a majority opinion that becomes the law of the land. Justices who disagree with the majority can write a dissenting opinion, which does not become law but serves as a statement of a justice's beliefs (the opinion written by Chief Justice Rehnquist about flag burning, described earlier, is an example).

For instance, in the 2001 case *Kyllo v. United States*, the Supreme Court addressed the question of whether a search warrant should be required before taking thermal images outside a home (i.e., the use of infrared images to detect heat emanating from a structure, which could indicate whether marijuana was grown inside). Five justices agreed that a warrant should be required; four justices argued that it should not. Each side issued a written opinion supported by facts, law, and rational argument; the side supported by the most justices becomes the law of the land. But how could the justices reach opposite conclusions based on the same facts and one body of law? Because, as

TABLE 3.8 Legal Realism and the Six Concepts of Law

Concepts	Pragmatic Perspective	Legal Realism
Foundation of Law	*Private Morality*	Morality need not be the basis for law; realists do not focus on foundations of law
Rationale of Law	*Protect Individual Rights*	Balance rights, societal needs, and other factors to provide meaningful results
Formation of Law	*Rational*	Analyzes the immediate situation under review
Application of Law	*Irrational*	The law as written is not always clear or applicable and must be interpreted
Focal Point of Law	*Process*	Outcomes depend on the process that is followed by professionals
Discretion within the Law	*Encouraged*	Professionals make judgments to give law meaning

the legal realists suggest, the law is what the judges *interpret* it to be, and different judges may reach different (though legitimate) interpretations.

Unlike idealists, legal realists do not claim that the law has a specific foundation. They believe it may be presumptuous to assume what the foundation of law might be. Legal realists do not rely on public morality as a foundation for law because they are more likely to rely on interpretive and problem-solving skills to discover the meaning of the law through the consideration of individual cases. Legal realism does ask whether the law makes society a better place to live by solving problems. A successful law does not need to determine the morality or immorality of an offense. A successful law is one that (through the interpretive actions of criminal justice professionals) provides a meaningful answer to the victim of the crime, to the offender, and to society. Table 3.8 summarizes the six concepts of law for legal realism.

Legal realists focus primarily on the courts. However, similar questions could be asked of other criminal justice professionals. Do a police officer's discretionary decisions on the street serve to create law? Are a correctional officer's discretionary decisions in a prison based on interpretations of what policies mean or ought to mean? This is the basis of Michael Lipsky's (1980) theory of street-level bureaucracy, which argues that the individual decisions made by practitioners do in fact create policy. This is because the public accepts what practitioners do or say as being the real policy on an issue, regardless of what may be written in the law or policy documents. Note that legal realists cannot simply make up whatever they want, but are generally deciding how to interpret the written laws and policies. Clearly, discretion and independence in the application of law are key values to the legal realist.

For instance, in some jurisdictions persons on probation must follow a rule such as, "I will obtain advance permission from my probation and parole officer before I associate with any person convicted of a felony or misdemeanor" (Missouri Department of Corrections, 2013, p. 4). This could apply to coworkers, friends, and family (also, take a moment to consider what principle might underlie the rule). Different officers might interpret the rule differently. For instance, is going to lunch with a group of coworkers, one of whom has a prior misdemeanor for a motor vehicle violation, a violation of the rule? Is talking to a next-door neighbor with a felony record while picking up the mail a violation of the rule? Officers make these decisions, and their interpretations are viewed as policy by persons under their supervision. Officers may also differ in their responses to violations of the rule (evidence does suggest variation in how probation officers respond to probation rule violations—see Clear, Harris, & Baird, 1992). Depending on the officer or the situation, a probationer violating the rule could be given a warning, subjected to increased supervision, or even sent to prison.

Many jurisdictions have debated and passed laws that prohibit smoking in various locations. Depending on jurisdiction, some places where smoking has been banned include restaurants, bars, schools, workplaces, parks, beaches, shopping centers, bus stops, sidewalks, and apartments. Do you agree or disagree with smoking bans in these locations? What philosophy or philosophies of law do you think they illustrate?

EVERYDAY PRAGMATISM

We conclude with everyday pragmatism. We do not present the six concepts of law for this perspective because it is more centered on a realistic view of the process by which law is developed than on a full exposition of the six concepts.

Richard Posner, a judge on the U.S. Seventh Circuit Court of Appeals, argues that the pragmatism of everyday people has become the basis of the law (2003). The law is capable of functioning in our society because the citizenry allows it to do so. If the law was unsatisfactory, everyday people could protest or rebel against it, at which point the law would no longer be legitimate (i.e., no longer have the public support it needs to be effective). Posner is not suggesting that the people have assembled and agreed upon any legal concepts. Rather, the law is dynamic and has evolved into its present form, which is acceptable to the public's interests.

One of Posner's ideas is that the law is an *activity* (1993). The importance of this idea is that, again, law is dynamic, changing over time as a result of the interactions between people. It would be a dramatic oversimplification to suggest that law is adopted and then enforced. Law is created through negotiations, often in a political context, and then shaped by the discretionary decisions of criminal justice professionals. And as the public, the media, interest groups, scholars, and others see areas that are in need of reform or revision, they are raised and reconsidered, all of which involves human interaction. The law, then, in addition to being an activity, is shaped by a multitude of individuals, and the responsibility for the law ultimately lies with all people in a democratic society. Reviewing the history of any legal issue, or following debates about current legal controversies, can illustrate the many forces that ultimately shape the law in a dynamic and active process.

Q Of the theories presented, which do you think are useful perspectives on shaping or implementing the law? Which are not useful? Why?

Q How would each of the theories address the case study at the beginning of the chapter? What are the differences and similarities?

Conclusion

Whether police officers, attorneys, judges, correctional officers, or serving in other areas of the justice system, criminal justice professionals are charged with upholding the laws of society. On the surface, this sounds simple enough, but the complexities reveal themselves when we discover that there are multiple—sometimes conflicting—opinions about what the law should accomplish. Before attempting to enforce the law, it is important to reflect on its purpose(s) by considering perspectives such as those described in this chapter. Although it is not likely that there will ever be complete agreement about the role of law in society, understanding the debates can help place into context the variety of laws that are on the books or that are proposed in legislatures each year. As we move to Unit II, we will consider why some persons violate the laws that have been established and the forms of social control that attempt to regulate behavior.

Nudist Camps

Criminal Justice Problem Solving

The previous chapter was about moral reasoning pertaining to criminal justice under the idealistic and pragmatic models. This chapter was about legal theory under the idealistic and pragmatic models. This material need not be considered in isolation but should be integrated. Consider *White Tail Park v. Stroube* (2005), a case from the Fourth Circuit of the U.S. Court of Appeals.

> AANR-East [American Association for Nude Recreation—Eastern Region, Inc.] is one of several recreational organizations affiliated with the American Association for Nude Recreation, a national social nudism organization. In June 2003, AANR-East opened a week-long juvenile nudist camp at a licensed nudist campground operated by White Tail near Ivor, Virginia. AANR-East leased the 45-acre campground that ordinarily attracts about 1,000 weekend visitors who come to engage in nude recreation and interact with other individuals and families who practice social nudism . . .
>
> Modeled after juvenile nudist summer camps operated annually in Arizona and Florida by other regional divisions of AANR, the 2003 AANR-East summer camp offered two programs: a "Youth Camp" for children 11 to 15 years old, and a "Leadership Academy" for children 15 to 18 years old. The camp agenda included traditional activities such as arts and crafts, campfire sing-alongs, swimming, and sports. The camp also included an educational component designed to teach the values associated with social nudism through topics such as "Nudity and the Law," "Overcoming the Clothing Experience," "Puberty Rights Versus Puberty Wrongs," and "Nudism and Faith." A total of 32 campers attended the 2003 summer camp [and AANR-East planned to operate the camp the subsequent year].
>
> Prior to the scheduled start of AANR-East's 2004 youth camp, the Virginia General Assembly amended the statute governing the licensing of summer camps specifically to address youth nudist camps. The amended statute requires a parent, grandparent or guardian to accompany any juvenile who attends a nudist summer camp (p. 455).

Prior to this new law, there was no requirement that guardians accompany their children at nudist camps. AANR-East, White Tail, and three sets of parents sued Robert B. Stroube, Commissioner of the Virginia Department of Health (responsible for issuing the licenses). The complaint stated that the new law violates parents' rights to raise their children as they see fit. In other words, the complaint alleges that parents should have the right to send their children to a properly licensed nudist summer camp, without having to accompany them for the duration of the camp.

- Q Using the concepts presented in Chapter 2, describe the perspectives you could use to engage in moral reasoning about this issue. Explain your response.
- Q Using the concepts presented in this chapter, describe how this issue would be addressed under the various philosophies of law. Which do you think provides the best response to the issue?
- Q In what ways are your responses to the preceding questions connected? Do you see any common themes that might be important in guiding your own interpretation of the law?
- Q Considering all of the above, how do you think this situation should be resolved, and why?

Unit Two

Perspectives on Deviance and Crime

Photo Essay: What Behaviors Are Deviant?

The study and practice of criminal justice involve pragmatic and idealistic questions about the relationship between law and morality and the role of law in society. These ideas help shape decisions about how the law ought to be developed and enforced. This unit continues the discussion by exploring how societies decide what behaviors should be permitted and what behaviors should be prohibited. We also consider competing explanations for reasons that individuals engage in behaviors that society has labeled as deviant or illegal.

What makes us describe some behaviors as acceptable and others as unacceptable? There is no simple answer to this question, nor is there full agreement about what is deviant and what is not. Although there is consensus that serious crimes such as murder, rape, robbery, and assault should be labeled as deviant and criminalized, other behaviors have been the subject of legal debate, as the following examples illustrate.

Would you wrestle a bear? In 1998, the citizens of Missouri went to the polls and voted to make bear wrestling a crime (Bear Wrestling, 2010). But is it deviant? Statistically, it is safe to assume that not many individuals have wrestled a bear—but some have. In Ohio, at least one venue in the state allowed members of the public to wrestle bears, as it was not in violation of state law (Associated Press, 2006). However, following pressure from animal rights advocates, the U.S. Department of Agriculture intervened to halt the bear wrestling exhibitions that occurred there (Sims, 2008). What do you think are the arguments on either side of bear wrestling? What principles would you consider in determining whether the practice is deviant? How would this shape your opinions about what, if any, laws should govern the practice? How does this compare to issues such as dog fighting or cockfighting?

What would you be willing to endure in order to gain membership in a group? Among a wide variety of high school (Hoover & Pollard, 2000) and college (Owen, Burke, & Vichesky, 2008) student organizations, hazing is used in the membership process. While there is no common definition of hazing, it essentially includes any dangerous, demeaning, or humiliating act that is required for membership in the group. This can include a wide range of activities, including but not limited to forced consumption of

food, alcohol, or other drinks; deliberate deprivation of sleep; being hit or slapped; being addressed with insulting language or names; requirements to engage in dangerous or illegal activity; required removal of clothing or wearing of undesired attire; being prohibited from speaking with persons outside the group; and much more. Virtually all schools, colleges, and universities have rules against hazing, which can result in disciplinary proceedings. Should hazing also be defined as a crime under the law? Most states do have laws against hazing. While there is variation among the states, the laws generally prohibit those forms of hazing that can result in physical injury or which involve the commission of other crimes (StopHazing.org, n.d.). Consider the forms of hazing that result in humiliation or embarrassment, but not physical injury. Should these actions be defined as deviant? Should they be criminalized? Why or why not? Again, reflect on what principles you would consider in making your decision.

Bear wrestling and hazing may have little in common, except that both have the potential to inflict pain and injury, depending on the circumstances. But is the causation of injury a consistent principle that is used to define deviance? The answer is "no." The law is generally willing to accept, or even encourage, some activities that have the potential to cause harm. For instance, athletes may participate in activities that can result in or cause physical harm, even for juveniles (high school football games can be rough!). But is there a limit? What is the dividing line between physical harm a player consents to as part of the game and physical harm that crosses the line into an unacceptable assault? Even for those acts that go too far, where is the line between wagging a finger and saying, "That's bad sportsmanship," versus deciding to file criminal charges (see Yates & Gillespie, 2002)?

Part of the dilemma about injuries related to sporting activities stems from the fact that athletes know that there is a risk of harm and accept it as part of the game. Does consent, then, become a significant aspect of defining deviance? If an adult voluntarily chooses to wrestle a bear but a student does not choose to experience hazing, does that influence perceptions of the social or legal acceptability of those acts? Consent is a complex issue, but it, too, is inconsistent as a predictor of what is deviant. Like sports, the law is generally willing to allow individuals to modify their bodies through tattooing,

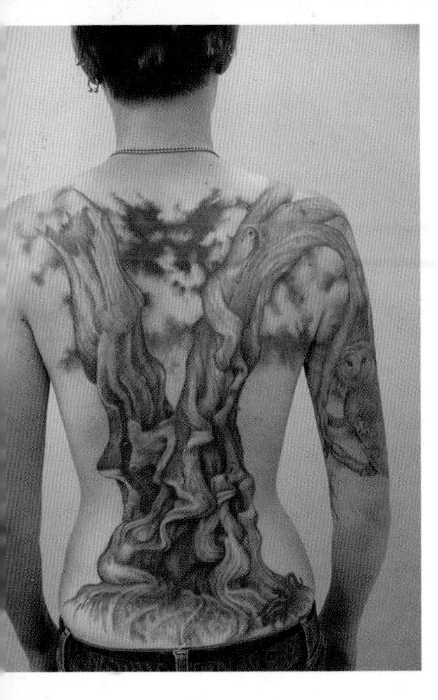

piercing, and other practices, although doing so may cause pain, physical alteration, scarring, or other outcomes that, if committed without consent would certainly be viewed as criminal (Egan, 2007).

Compare body modification, such as piercing and tattooing, to sadomasochistic sexual practices, also known as S&M. One definition of S&M practices is: "The knowing use of psychological dominance and submission, and/or physical bondage, and/or pain, and/or related practices . . . in order for the participants to experience erotic arousal or personal growth" (Egan, 2007, p. 1616). Generally, the law has been reluctant to permit consent to injuries that result from S&M, unlike those which result from body modification or sports (Egan, 2007). Does this reflect inconsistencies in law and in definitions of deviance? Or does it reflect a divergence in attitudes about the sexual versus the nonsexual, the mainstream versus a subculture, or other distinctions? It becomes clear that there is not a so-called bright line, to borrow a legal term, that distinguishes what is deviant from what is not, and much less a line that determines when the law should get involved and when it should not.

Much of this photo essay has focused on activities that have some potential for harm. But what about behaviors that are not inherently harmful; may they be defined as deviant and subject to social control? "Sagging" is the colloquial term to describe the practice in which individuals, usually male, wear their pants low enough that their undergarments are readily visible. Is this deviant? What arguments do you think could be made on either side? Those who believe that it is deviant have used a variety of strategies to curtail the behavior. For instance, one New York legislator sponsored billboards, such as the one pictured here, to use informal social control to encourage individuals not to sag (Peltz, 2010). Others have promoted more formal social control, as local ordinances have been passed in some communities that would punish sagging through fines and jail time (Koppel, 2007). Would you define sagging as deviant?

The focus of this unit is deviance. As you will see, there is no single explanation as to why certain acts are labeled as deviant whereas others are not. Nor is there a single explanation for why some behaviors that are labeled as deviant are controlled through the law (prisons and fines), while others are controlled more informally (through peer pressure or scolding). And there is no single explanation for why some individuals choose to engage in behaviors that have been labeled as deviant. However, all of these topics are essential to the study of criminal justice because a natural starting point is understanding the behaviors to which the criminal justice system ultimately responds (or equally important, does not respond) through its law enforcement powers. As you read the chapters in this unit, pause to consider issues like these, reflecting on the human behavior (as well as the debates around it) that is the central focus of criminal justice.

4

Deviance and Social Control

Learning Objectives

1 Explain how the concepts of deviance, social norms, and socialization are related. 2 Compare and contrast how informal and formal social controls affect human behavior. 3 Differentiate the four main styles of formal social control. 4 Analyze the process of "medicalizing" deviance and its consequences for criminal justice. 5 Evaluate how medicalization and other forms of social change affect the ways in which society exerts social controls.

Key Terms

deviance
social norms
subcultures
socialization
social control
informal social control
formal social control
penal social control
compensatory social control
conciliatory social control
therapeutic social control
medical model of deviance
stratification
medicalization of deviance
insanity
deinstitutionalization
mental health courts

Key People

Donald Black
Talcott Parsons
Peter Conrad
Joseph Schneider

Case Study

A Crime of Fantasy?

The *New York Times* declared, "'Ugly Thoughts' Defense Fails as Officer Is Convicted in Cannibal Plot."

> A New York police officer was convicted . . . in a bizarre plot to kidnap, torture, kill and eat women, ending a trial whose outcome hinged on a delicate distinction between fantasy and reality. The trial had drawn widespread attention, in part because it involved an officer's disturbing behavior, but also because it raised a fundamental question: When does a virtual crime, contemplated in Internet chat rooms, become an actual crime? There was no evidence that any of the women whom the officer, Gilberto Valle, was accused of plotting to kill were harmed. But prosecutors argued that the officer took actual steps to further his plot, like conducting surveillance of potential victims. (Weiser, 2013a, paras. 1–3)

Using the alias "Girlmeat Hunter," Valle exchanged messages on the Internet that the jury concluded were detailed and specific plans to kidnap, sexually torture, and cannibalize roughly 100 women. Valle's defense was that he was merely engaging in online "'fantasy role play' with like-minded 'death fetishists'" (Gregorian, Gearty, Molloy, & Miller, 2013, para. 16). The jury rejected the defense's claims after reviewing the contents of the family computer that Valle's wife had turned over to investigators. It was loaded "with crime-scene pictures of dead and mutilated women, twisted images of women being tortured and sexually assaulted, pictures of female friends he'd downloaded from Facebook, Google searches for terms like, 'How to kidnap a woman' and 'human meat recipes . . .'" (para. 15). According to one of the jurors, the key evidence on the computer was the chat logs of the people with whom he communicated on websites devoted to sadistic fetishes. At first, the jury considered these conversations to be fantasies. Over time, however, "the picture that emerged was that of a man who was stepping out of the world of fantasy and into reality. . . . He was speaking to what [the jury felt were] serious people and he didn't back away from them. He willingly continued the conversations and sometimes was the provocateur of the conversations" (paras. 21–22). Moreover, Valle then took steps to carry out his plan by going to Maryland to meet a women he described in a document entitled, "Abduction and Cooking of Kimberly: A Blueprint."

Previous page: A drug user injecting heroin. What are some ways that deviant behavior can be controlled?

A forensic psychiatrist who conducted an evaluation of Mr. Valle concluded that Valle "suffered from a deviancy that involved fantasies of sexual sadism, in which he derived excitement from the imagined psychological or physical suffering of female victims" (Weiser, 2013b, para. 5). There was no evidence, though, that Valle suffered from any mental illness or personality disorder associated with violence.

The criminal charge on which Valle was convicted was kidnapping conspiracy. The possible sentence is up to life in prison (Weiser, 2013a).

Q Do you think engaging in online chats about kidnapping, sexual torture, and cannibalism is within the realm of normal fantasy, or is such activity deviant? Explain your reasoning.

Q Is there a distinction between having thoughts, communicating those thoughts, and acting on those thoughts? Does the distinction matter in terms of determining whether or not something is deviant? At what point do you think the law may intervene?

Q Do you think Valle was inappropriately prosecuted in this case for having entertained deviant thoughts? Why or why not? Would your answer vary for a different case with online conversations about child pornography? What about acts of terrorism?

An Overview of Deviance

FOCUSING QUESTION 4.1

How are the concepts of deviance, social norms, and socialization related?

Deviance refers to any departure from behaviors that are typical, acceptable, or expected. Deviance is often confused with crime. However, these concepts are distinct, as crime is only one form of deviant behavior. For example, shoplifting is both a crime, because it is prohibited under criminal law, and an example of deviance, because it is viewed as an unacceptable behavior. On the other hand, consider door-holding behavior. Holding the door open for the person immediately behind you is often viewed as an acceptable, even expected, behavior. Failure to do so could then be viewed as deviant—though certainly not criminal. Therefore, deviance refers to a range of behaviors including, but not limited to, crime.

deviance
Behaviors that violate society's expectations, beliefs, standards, or values. As such, deviance refers to any departure from behaviors that are typical, acceptable, or accepted. Crime is one form of deviance.

The broad definition provided above does not capture the negative connotation that the term "deviance" has come to have in everyday use. We tend to restrict our everyday usage of the term "deviance" to refer only to those behaviors that are negatively viewed or condemned in society (Conrad & Schneider, 1980). However, deviance can also refer to atypical or unexpected behaviors that are, in fact, positive. For example, men who become Buddhist monks are "deviant" under the broadest definition of the term, because separating oneself from mainstream society in order to live in a religious community is a departure from "typical" social behavior. Yet, we do not condemn these monks for their lifestyle; indeed, they are held in high regard. Therefore, while their behaviors may meet the *definition* of deviance, the monks would not be *labeled* by society with the negative term "deviants." Spreitzer and Sonenshein (2004) use the term "positive deviance" to describe "behaviors that are honorable [and] voluntary" (p. 839), but yet which differ from those which are typical or expected in society.

NORMS

Many of the social sciences define deviant behaviors as those that depart from accepted social norms (McCaghy, Capron, Jamieson, & Harley, 2007). **Social norms** are societal rules. The norms that tell us what we *ought* to do—become educated; respect our elders; obey the law—are called *prescriptive norms*. The norms that tell us what we *ought not* to do—commit crimes, lie, drop out of high school—are called *proscriptive norms*.

social norms
Societal judgments about what individuals should or should not do. Norms are based on widely shared values about what are good or bad, correct or incorrect, behaviors.

Norms are based upon widely shared values regarding that which is "good" or "correct," and, conversely, that which is "bad" or "incorrect." Norms may be formal or informal. Formal norms, also known as *mores,* tend to have moral underpinnings. The values expressed in the Ten Commandments (e.g., not killing, stealing, committing adultery, etc.) or other religious doctrines are examples of mores. In contrast, informal norms, also known as *folkways,* do not have as strong a moral foundation, but are social expectations nonetheless. Folkways include rules governing etiquette and acceptable standards of behavior, like how to dress for a particular occasion.

Norms vary across both situation and time (Curra, 1999). For example, language that may routinely be used while hanging out with your friends after school may be inappropriate to use at home with your family. Similarly, behaviors that may be considered perfectly acceptable by today's standards, such as teenage males wearing earrings, would have been taboo, or unacceptable, to many of our grandparents or great-grandparents.

Norms also vary across cultures. For example, belching at the dinner table is considered rude in many Western cultures, but is considered to be a compliment to the host or cook in some African and Asian countries (see Sinha, 1996).

subculture
A group that shares a set of norms that are different from those of the larger society.

Even within a given culture, there may be subcultures that have their own set of norms. **Subcultures** are groups that share a set of norms that are different from those of the larger society. Subcultures may exist based on race, ethnicity, religion, sexual orientation, and occupation. For example, in certain ethnic subcultures, wine is routinely served with dinner, even to family members under the legal drinking age. Similarly, certain professions have their own subculture. Police, for example, tend to socialize among themselves, often socially isolating themselves from people who do not work in law enforcement. As you will learn in Chapter 11, this behavior in the policing subculture fosters a type of solidarity in which the officers come to value bravery, secrecy, and loyalty (see, e.g., Cochran & Bromley, 2003; Van Maanen, 1974).

It is important to note that the norms and behaviors of members of subcultures may or may not be criminal. For example, the members of a biker gang may be deviant (that is, have different norms from those of the larger society) insofar as the way they act and dress. However, these same members may be law-abiding citizens. In contrast, "swingers" are members of a deviant subculture, with norms (different from the larger society) that permit having multiple sexual partners other than one's spouse (Walshok, 1971). In some jurisdictions, adultery (i.e., engaging in sexual activity with persons other than one's spouse) is illegal. However, in other jurisdictions, it may be legal behavior (remember that norms vary between places). As you can see, identifying social norms, identifying subcultures and their norms, and defining deviance, both criminal and noncriminal, can be a complex process, indeed.

SOCIALIZATION

In legal and justice-related studies, we tend to think of the law as the primary means of controlling human behavior. It is, after all, easy to imagine that passing a law against an undesired behavior will make people stop doing it. However, there are many other and arguably more important factors that account for human behavior, besides the law. These range from genetics and the biochemistry of the brain to the influences of friends, families, teachers, religion, the media, and so on (see Mohr, 1996). Different social sciences focus on different causes of behavior. For example, psychology tends to focus on the individual, while sociology tends to focus on the role of social institutions (e.g., family, religion, peers, etc.). Two related processes, socialization and social control, are key concepts in understanding the role that "society" plays in shaping our behavior. As you read about these concepts, bear in mind that they are as important, *if not more so,* as law in controlling human behavior (see Black, 1976).

socialization
The process by which individuals learn a society's or culture's norms and also learn to conform to them.

Socialization is the process by which "people learn to conform to social norms; a process that makes possible an enduring society and the transmission of its culture

between generations" (Abercrombie, Hill, & Turner, 2006, p. 363). Socialization works in two ways: internally and externally. Internal socialization occurs when a person learns social norms from others so the norms become a part of the individual's own personality (p. 363). When we internalize norms, our own behavior is guided by the rules we have learned. For example, when we learn that it is wrong to steal, we refrain from stealing even though there may be opportunities to do so with no one around to catch us. Our own moral compass or conscience guides our behavior because societal norms have been "internalized" to become a part of us. Thus, our behavior is controlled by self-imposed regulation, rather than by external forces. In other words, through internal socialization norms are followed because it is perceived as the right thing to do, rather than out of a fear of punishment or disapproval.

In contrast, external socialization occurs when interactions with other important people cause us to behave in accordance with social norms so that we gain "acceptance and status in the eyes of others" (Abercrombie, Hill, & Turner, 2006, p. 363). External socialization may occur in three stages. *Primary socialization* takes place at home in early childhood when social norms are taught to children by family members, especially by parents. Gender roles, including how to act and dress according to gender-specific norms, are examples of primary socialization. Later, *secondary socialization* occurs throughout childhood and adolescence. Secondary socialization occurs through our interactions with the educational system, religion, peer groups (first in neighborhoods, then at school), and the media—especially through television, cinema, music, and the Internet (e.g., Saracho & Spodek, 2007). Keep in mind, though, that secondary socialization is not a separate process. Rather, it is a continuation of the process initiated by primary socialization. The key distinction is that primary socialization is provided by family members, while secondary socialization is provided by people and institutions with which we do not have as close a relationship. For example, learning how to interact socially with other people starts with primary socialization, as family members model and teach these behaviors. As children get older, their social skills are refined by secondary socialization, through interactions with classmates, in clubs and organizations, and so on. This process continues into adulthood, through *adult socialization,* when new work environments socialize people into "roles for which primary and secondary socialization may not have prepared them fully" (Abercrombie, Hill, & Turner, 2006, pp. 363–364). This could include understanding the culture, politics, tasks, and processes that are involved in a workplace (Morgan, 1986).

A failure of normal socialization processes is one of the most widely accepted ways in which sociology explains deviance (Deflem, 2006). Under this view, the institutions of socialization, whether primary or secondary, fail to properly "impart the knowledge and opportunities that result in rule-abiding behavior" (Heitzeg, 1996, p. 38). Another sociological explanation for deviance is that people may be socialized into a subculture with deviant norms, rather than being socialized with widely accepted social norms. This may cause people to behave deviantly for two reasons. First, through the process of internalization, the deviant norms may become a part of a person's personality. Second, if socialized into a deviant subculture, a person may conform to that deviant subculture's norms in order to win social approval from the other members of the group (Delfelm, 2006; Akers & Jensen, 2007).

Q Provide an example of a deviant behavior that is not a crime, but is viewed negatively by society. Provide an example of a deviant behavior that is viewed positively by society.

Q What are some examples of norms that likely shaped your grandparents' behavior as teenagers that would not be viewed as norms today? What are some examples of norms that shaped your behavior, but which might not have been viewed as norms for your grandparents?

Who or what were the most important agents of primary socialization in your life? How did the influence of secondary socialization change your own behavior from the ways in which you were first brought up?

Return to your answer to the first question following the case study at the beginning of the chapter, regarding whether or not you found Valle's actions to be deviant. How were ideas about norms and socialization reflected in your answer?

The Social Control of Deviance

FOCUSING QUESTION 4.2

How do informal and formal social controls affect human behavior?

social control
The processes by which society controls individual and group behaviors. The term is now often used to refer to the ways deviant behaviors are controlled, both informally and formally.

Social control refers to the processes by which society controls individual and group behaviors. Social control was originally defined by Edward A. Ross in 1901 as "virtually all of the human practices and arrangements that contribute to social order and . . . that influence people to conform" (Ross, as cited in Black, 1998, p. 4). However, largely due to the work of Talcott Parsons (1951) and Donald Black (1989; 1984), the term is now used to refer to the ways in which deviant behaviors are specifically controlled, both informally and formally.

INFORMAL VERSUS FORMAL SOCIAL CONTROL

informal social control
Tools used to control behavior in everyday social life, including social control exercised by peers, communities, families, and groups. This forms the basis of the socialization process.

Informal social controls are the tools used to control behavior in everyday social life—"within families, friendships, neighborhoods, organizations, and groups of all kinds" (Dawson, 2006, p. 1435). As such, informal social controls form the basis of the socialization process. They are both internal (often referred to as "self-control") and external (often referred to as "relational controls").

Internal or *self-control* is akin to one's conscience—one's "internalized norms, beliefs, morals, and self-concept" (Conrad & Schneider, 1992, p. 7). Sociologists explain the development of conscience via the socialization process, which is similar to the way that psychologists explain its development. *External* or *relational social control* is dependent upon a person's interactions with others. Virtually any type of positive or negative reaction from others constitutes informal social control. Positive reactions from others—such as praise, a smile, tangible rewards, and emotional support—encourage and positively reinforce desired behaviors.

Such positive responses are designed to cause the recipient to continue to engage in those behaviors that are encouraged or accepted by society. In contrast, negative reactions from others—such as ridicule, gossip, corporal punishment, shaming, ostracism, and even something as simple as a stern, disapproving look—discourage and punish undesired behaviors. Such negative responses are designed to cause the recipient to change his or her behaviors by conforming to desired social norms. See Box 4.1 for a discussion of informal social control of drinking and driving.

formal social control
Mechanisms exercised by the government to control human behavior and to cause persons to conform to norms and obey laws. Criminal justice and criminal law are the most important tools of formal social control.

Formal social controls are those mechanisms exercised by the government to control human behavior. While criminal justice tends to focus on criminal law, which is the most important tool of formal social control, other forms of law (e.g., constitutional law and civil law, which are discussed later in this text) are also tools of formal social control. It is important to note one distinction between informal and formal social control. Informal social control may be used to reinforce virtually any norms and to avoid negative deviant behaviors. However, formal social control is primarily—though not exclusively—concerned with regulating those deviant activities that have been defined as crimes. For instance, both formal and informal social control are utilized to teach the norm that stealing is wrong. However, informal social control would be the most likely to address norms related to sharing or etiquette, as violations of norms on these matters are not usually defined as crimes.

BOX 4.1

THE SOCIAL CONTROL OF DRUNK DRIVING

Laws against drinking and driving have been around since shortly after the advent of the automobile. However, drinking and driving was not considered to be a particularly important social problem for much of the twentieth century. In fact, it was not until the early 1980s that widespread public attention was given to the problem of drinking and driving. It was at that time that Candy Lightner, whose daughter was killed in an alcohol-related traffic accident, formed Mothers Against Drunk Driving ("MADD"). Through MADD's activism, drinking and driving "gained recognition as a prominent social concern" (see Applegate et al., 1996, p. 57) and the issue was addressed by politicians and policy makers (see Reinarmann, 1988).

In response to the increased recognition of the DUI (driving under the influence) problem in the United States, policy shifted "toward an increased emphasis on deterrence, retribution, and incapacitation . . . the common thread of this social climate [being] harsher punishment of offenders" (Appelgate et al., 1996, p. 58). For example, in the years following the establishment of MADD, specifically between 1980 and 1989, the number of DUI arrests nationwide increased nearly 22% while the number of licensed drivers increased only 14% (Bureau of Justice Statistics, 1992). Yet, the increasing severity of criminal punishments for DUI had little effect on drinking and driving. Rather, research has found that the activities of grassroots organizations like MADD and SADD (Students Against Destructive Decisions), and anti-DUI educational and public service campaigns are far more effective at curtailing drunk driving than the criminal law (e.g., Ross, McCleary, & LaFree, 1990; Fradella, 2000).

Q Why do you think informal social controls are more effective than formal social controls in controlling drunk driving?

Q What do you think should be done to reduce drinking and driving? What kinds of solutions could utilize informal social control? Formal social control? Both?

Clearly, the criminal justice system represents the ultimate in formal social control, with its government-authorized power to arrest, hold trials, and punish as a means of regulating behavior. Nevertheless, the criminal justice system increasingly bridges formal and informal social control with policies such as community policing, community courts, victim-offender reconciliation programs, and the like, all of which involve the criminal justice system working in collaboration with community partners. In such arrangements, the criminal justice system can leverage its formal social controls and the community partners can leverage their informal social controls, working jointly to promote the same desired behaviors. As you read this book, look for examples of how modern criminal justice utilizes elements of both formal and informal social control.

AGENTS OF SOCIAL CONTROL

The institutions of social control are similar to those of socialization. Eitzen and Baca-Zinn (1998) classified the institutions of social control into two types of agents: agents of ideological social control and agents of direct social control.

Agents of ideological social control attempt to shape the consciousness of people in society. Such agents include the family, educational institutions, religion, organized sports, media, and the government. These agents influence ideas, attitudes, morals, and values. In doing so, they help to maintain the status quo by reinforcing governing ideologies and persuading citizens to comply willingly with laws.

According to Eitzen and Baca-Zinn, the family teaches the child to "fit" into society. Educational institutions uphold the behavioral standards of the community and indoctrinate in their students social norms about work, respect for authority, and patriotism. Most major religions support the status quo in American society by honoring the American way of life and by teaching acceptance of an imperfect world, with the promise of rewards in the next life if believers strive to achieve that which is defined by society as "good." Sports promote local, regional, and national pride; allow for a cathartic and productive channeling of aggressive energies; provide an avenue for upward social mobility; and build character. The media similarly promote adherence to basic social values by shaping how we evaluate ourselves and others; by influencing, via advertising, what we view as desirable; and by molding how the public perceives and interprets events. Finally, the government sets educational standards; acts in the name of national security; and promotes solidarity and patriotism through public services and the public appearances of elected leaders. In acting as they do, these institutional agents of social control successfully promote social norms in a manner that leads most Americans to accept the legitimacy of the social, political, and economic order. Moreover, even when the status quo is questioned, it tends to be done in an "acceptable" manner, such as through critical commentary and peaceful demonstration.

In contrast, *agents of direct social control* attempt to punish or neutralize both organizations and individuals who deviate from society's norms. These need not be "bad" people. Rather, they may be "deviant" only insofar as their behavior departs from what is expected by others in society. Examples include the poor, the mentally ill, and political dissidents. In each case, the behaviors and norms of individuals in these groups may, sometimes through no fault of their own, run counter to social norms or expectations.

The agents of direct social control include welfare agencies, science and medicine, and government. Welfare agencies provide and administer public assistance programs that function to prevent social unrest. However, they also may exert social control through the stigmatization that is often associated with being on such public assistance programs. This may reinforce and legitimize the value of work and self-sufficiency. Science and medicine have developed a number of devices that are aimed at controlling the behavior of some members of society. These devices will be explored in more detail later in this chapter. Finally, the government also acts as an agent of direct social control. When the government does so, it acts in one of the four styles that we will explore in the next section.

Q Which type of informal social control do you think is the most powerful—internal, self-controls or external, relational controls? Explain. Do you think the answer might vary depending on the behavior in question? Why or why not?

Q How would informal and formal social control apply to the Valle case study presented at the beginning of the chapter? Which (or neither, or both), do you think would be most appropriate to address the situation?

Q Legal sociologist Donald Black (1984, 1989) argued that societies with strong informal social controls have less need for formal social control, and conversely, societies with weak informal social controls have greater need for formal social control. Why do you think this is? Give examples to support your reasoning.

Q Educational institutions are generally classified as an ideological agent of social control. Yet, they have the ability to punish students who are norm violators. Do you think that schools serve as ideological agents of social control, direct agents of social control, or both? Explain.

Styles of Social Control

FOCUSING QUESTION 4.3

What are the four main styles of formal social control?

Donald Black (1984), a leading scholar of law and society, argued that law is used as a tool of formal social control in four related, yet distinct, ways. As summarized in Table 4.1, he termed the four styles of formal social control penal, compensatory, therapeutic, and conciliatory.

Black argued that there is an inverse relationship between law (as formal social control, including any combination of those in Table 4.1) and informal social control. In other words, in societies where informal social control is strong and effective in controlling behavior, there is less need to rely on law to do so. Conversely, in societies lacking strong and consistent systems of informal social control, it becomes necessary to have a greater reliance on law to control behavior (Black, 1976). Let's consider why that may be the case.

In tightly knit, highly structured communities, the need for formal social control should be very low because both socialization and informal social control should be highly effective, given how closely members of the community are connected to one another. In contrast, as societies become larger and more complex, close relationships with family and community become less important and more difficult to maintain. In addition, stratification increases. **Stratification** refers to differences among members of a society, which are divided in a hierarchical manner. This results in levels of inequality, for which those persons at the top of the hierarchy benefit while those at the bottom suffer (from discrimination, reduced opportunity, and so on). Examples may include differences based on "social class, race, gender, birth [order], age," ethnicity, or any other characteristic which might be associated with prestige or social status (Abercrombie, Hill, & Turner, 2006, p. 381). Simply having differences does not automatically result in stratification; rather, stratification occurs when individuals are judged on the basis of these differences.

stratification
Differences between members of a society that occur when persons and groups are divided in a hierarchical manner. This results in levels of inequality from which persons at the top of the hierarchy benefit, whereas those at the bottom suffer.

TABLE 4.1 Donald Black's Styles of Formal Social Control

Style of Social Control	Summary of Style
Penal	Views the violator of a social norm which has been codified into criminal law as an offender who is deserving of official condemnation and punishment through the criminal justice system. Four main justifications are proffered for using criminal law as a tool of formal social control: retribution, deterrence, rehabilitation, and incapacitation. These concepts are explored in depth in Chapter 10.
Compensatory	Focuses on providing restitution to the victim of an act. In other words, it attempts to compensate a wronged or aggrieved person in a way that restores them as closely as possible to the *status quo ante*—the way they were before the deviant person wronged them. This is typically accomplished via the civil justice system. The victim sues the rule-breaker and is compensated for his or her injuries or losses, usually financially.
Therapeutic	Views the deviant person as someone who needs help to become non-deviant or "normal." This is often accomplished via science and medicine, especially psychology and psychiatry. Because of this fact, it is clear that science and medicine are major institutions of social control.
Conciliatory	Attempts to create and preserve social harmony via dispute resolution. Mediation is an example of conciliatory social control. The focus is on allowing both sides to express their displeasures or concerns and then work toward a compromise that allows not only the removal of the irritants in a relationship, but also perhaps even some semblance of social harmony.

penal social control
Views the violator of a social norm that has been codified into criminal law as an offender who is deserving of official condemnation and punishment. This is accomplished through the criminal justice system.

compensatory social control
Focuses on providing restitution to the victim of a harmful act. This is typically accomplished through the civil justice system.

conciliatory social control
Attempts to create and preserve social harmony via dispute resolution. This is accomplished through practices such as mediation.

therapeutic social control
Views the deviant person as someone who needs help to become nondeviant or "normal." This is often accomplished through science and medicine.

medical model of deviance
A way of explaining deviance that underlies therapeutic social control. Under the model, deviance is defined objectively as a disease, and treatment of the disease is sought in accordance with the therapeutic style of social control.

In societies where people share similar belief systems or have similar backgrounds, there tends to be little stratification (because there are few differences, or persons are not judged based on differences that do exist). As a result, there is greater consensus on behavioral norms, and socialization and informal social control may be effective in teaching and enforcing those norms. When informal social controls fail, then the formal mechanisms of social control used tend to be compensatory and conciliatory, relying on the tight bonds between community members. Consider, for example, the Amish. This group of Swiss-German ancestry is known for very simple living, primarily in rural, self-contained communities. They dress plainly and resist most modern conveniences like electricity, telephones, and automobiles. They value humility, family, community, and devout adherence to their religious beliefs. As you might imagine, informal social controls are quite effective in bringing about conformity with desired behavior.

In contrast, complex and stratified societies may produce less consensus about social norms, in part stemming from perceived or actual inequalities produced by stratification. Socialization then becomes less consistent and complete, and informal social controls less effective, as communities are less tightly bound together. Formal social controls in such complex societies tend to be more punitive and more therapeutic than in less complex societies. Life in contemporary urban areas is a good example of this. Few people care what others think of them. In fact, in a large city, you may not even know the other people who live on the same block or on the same floor of your apartment building. In such an environment, informal social controls would have little effect in changing people's behavior. Hence, there is a greater need for more formal social controls.

All four styles of formal social control listed in Table 4.1 are important for the justice system. **Penal social control** is exclusively the province of the criminal justice system, and is explored throughout this text. **Compensatory social control** is usually achieved through lawsuits brought in the civil justice system, which will be discussed in Chapter 7. **Conciliatory social control** is increasingly being integrated into the criminal justice system, through programs emphasizing restorative justice or restitution, as described in Chapters 6 and 10. In the balance of this chapter, we will consider **therapeutic social control**, as it is not covered elsewhere in the book. To best understand therapeutic social controls, it is necessary to explore the roles that medicine, especially psychiatry and psychology, play in defining and treating deviant behavior.

Q Provide a specific example of each of the four styles of social control. What do you think are the advantages and disadvantages of each?

Q As described in the case study at the beginning of the chapter, Gilberto Valle was subjected to penal social control for his online discussions with others concerning plans to kidnap, rape, kill, and eat women. How might the other styles of formal social control have been applied in this case? Which (alone or in combination) do you think is most appropriate? Why?

The Medicalization of Deviance

FOCUSING QUESTION 4.4

What is "the medicalization of deviance"?

The **medical model of deviance** is, historically speaking, a relatively new way of explaining deviance, and one that underlies therapeutic social control. The emergence of the medical model was made possible by the development of medicine as an established science. The medical model purports to define deviance objectively, as a disease. As such, the medical model advocates "treatment" of the underlying disease in accordance with the therapeutic style of formal social control.

Talcott Parsons (1951) was the first to conceptualize medicine as an institution of social control. Parsons viewed illness itself as a form of deviance, primarily because the sick could not perform their normal roles in society (and thereby threatened the stability of the social order). Sick persons are viewed as ill through no fault of their own. They are viewed as being in need of treatment so they can get well. Such treatment is sought from a health care professional, with whom the sick persons are expected to cooperate. The health care professional, especially the physician, seeks to return sick persons to wellness, thereby removing the deviance and allowing the sick person to resume his or her normal role in society. In this way, health professionals promote social control.

One of the most comprehensive treatments of medicine as an institution of social control was Peter Conrad and Joseph Schneider's (1980) book entitled *Deviance and Medicalization: From Badness to Sickness.* Conrad and Schneider traced the history of how "moral-criminal definitions of deviance [changed] to medical ones" (p. 32). By labeling something as a disease, the moral blame is shifted away from the individual, who comes to be viewed as "sick" and in need of treatment, instead of being viewed as "bad" and in need of punishment. For example, the excessive consumption of alcohol was once considered sinful and immoral, requiring punishment. Through the process of medicalization, such behavior is now understood as the disease of alcoholism, which requires treatment. Similarly, in the past, an unruly, unfocused child was thought to need discipline. Today, however, such behaviors may be symptoms of a condition called attention-deficit/hyperactivity disorder (ADHD), which may be treated instead of punished. Defining a deviant behavior as an illness or a symptom of an illness, then providing medical intervention to treat the illness, is what Conrad and Schneider mean by the **medicalization of deviance.**

medicalization of deviance
Defining a deviant behavior as an illness or a symptom of an illness and then providing medical intervention to treat the illness. Incorporates elements of the medical model of deviance and therapeutic formal social control.

Medicalization of deviance can occur through the processes described above, by redefining behavior previously labeled as criminal, as a medical issue. In the criminal

Hyperactive children were once labeled as "bad" kids and were punished for their inability to pay attention in school. Today, through the process of medicalization, many such children are diagnosed with attention-deficit/hyperactivity disorder (ADHD) and are prescribed medications. Critics complain that medicine is being used to control children who need more structure, discipline, and educational interventions that promote more active learning. What role do you think medicalization should play in contemporary social control?

justice system, offenders may also seek the insanity defense, a tool illustrating another perspective on the medicalization of deviance.

MEDICALIZATION AND CRIMINAL RESPONSIBILITY

The criminal justice system is premised upon the assumption that people have free will to choose their actions and, therefore, that it is fair to hold people accountable for any actions they take that violate the criminal law. In contrast, medicalization suggests that an individual's behavior may be controlled or determined, at least in part, by a medical condition. This, then, raises questions about the extent to which individuals can or should be held accountable for their actions, if those actions were caused by a medical or mental condition, rather than being the product of voluntary free choice. This principle is embedded in the criminal justice system in the centuries-old insanity defense.

Insanity

A legal defense that refers to the defendant's state of mind at the time a criminal offense is committed. Definitions of insanity vary by jurisdiction.

Insanity is a legal term, not a medical one, even though its application is very much dependent on the process of medicalization. What insanity refers to is the defendant's state of mind at the time a criminal offense is committed. Most generally speaking, insanity means that an offender was unable to know right from wrong at the time of the offense. Thus, the very nature of the insanity defense is retrospective. The law requires the judge or jury to go back in time to evaluate the defendant's state of mind in the past. Note that the determination of whether or not an offender is insane rests with a judge or jury. Medical professionals provide examinations and testify regarding their findings to assist the judge or jury in reconstructing the defendant's past mental state—a complicated task. Their work is often guided by the diagnostic framework provided in the *Diagnostic and Statistical Manual of Mental Disorders* published by the American Psychiatric Association (2013).

On July 20, 2012, James Holmes entered a movie theater in Aurora, Colorado. Dressed in bullet-resistant gear, a ballistic helmet, and gas mask, he opened fire, killing 12 people and injuring more than 70 others. Prosecutors announced that they would seek the death penalty in their trial of Holmes for multiple counts of murder, attempted murder, and various weapons charges. Holmes subsequently entered a plea of not guilty by reason of insanity. What issues do you think the defense and prosecution would be likely to address in a trial for this case?

It is important to note that there is no specific medical diagnosis of insanity, since it is strictly a legal matter. Likewise, having a mental illness does not mean that a judgment of insanity will occur. While mental illnesses can influence offenders' thought patterns, it is only when a judge or jury determines (with the aid of information from medical experts) that the criteria for legal insanity are met that an offender is declared insane (more on this below).

When we excuse what would otherwise constitute criminal conduct on this basis of insanity, a court does not impose criminal punishment on the defendant. Instead, the defendant is typically sent to a secure psychiatric hospital for treatment of the underlying mental illness—often for a longer period of time than he or she would have served in prison had a verdict of guilt been reached (Fradella, 2007). In other words, defendants who are found to be legally insane are not subjected to penal social control, but rather therapeutic social control. While some disagree with this concept, the criminal justice system maintains the insanity defense for a number of important philosophical reasons, discussed below.

Justifying the Insanity Defense. Why do we have an insanity defense? First, it is unfair to punish people for acts that result from mental illness. Noted jurist David Bazelon summarized the moral basis of the insanity defense when he explained, "Our collective conscience does not allow punishment where it cannot impose blame" (*Durham v. United States*, 1954, p. 876). Why is this? It is because our assumption of rational decision making by a person of free will is inapplicable when dealing with someone who is severely mentally ill, when that mental illness has led to a crime; the criminal behavior in question was the product of the illness, rather than an action freely undertaken by the offender. With the assumption of rational decision making either undercut or eliminated, the reasons for criminal justice system intervention and the role it can play are likewise eroded.

Second, none of the major justifications for imposing penal social control through criminal punishment (you will learn more about these in Chapter 10) is applicable to the mentally ill criminal offender. From the standpoint of retribution theory, which focuses on the imposition of unpleasant consequences as a punishment for bad acts, what evil is there to punish if someone acted not out of criminal intent, but rather out of thought processes caused by a mental illness? Punishment of the mentally ill also cannot be justified under deterrence theory, in which the threat of punishment is used as a tool to discourage persons from committing crimes, because it is nearly impossible to deter acts resulting from mental illness. Deterrence is based on the idea that individuals weigh the benefits and costs of possible actions, and choose only those in which the benefits outweigh the costs. If decisions are based on thought patterns influenced by a mental illness, then this rationale is not applicable. Rehabilitation (i.e., therapeutic social control) is cited as a justification for penal social control, but realistically, treatment of the mentally ill in the correctional setting leaves much to be desired and is better accomplished through the mental health system. Incapacitation, the confinement of offenders in a correctional institution (i.e., a prison or jail) so they cannot continue to commit crimes against the public, is equally likely to be accomplished if legally insane offenders are held in a secure psychiatric hospital instead of a correctional institution.

Third, those who commit criminal acts as a result of their mental illness do not fit neatly into the criminal law's definitions of *mens rea.* As you will learn in Chapter 9, *mens rea* is Latin for "a guilty mind"; today, we use it to refer to criminal intent. For most crimes, it must be shown that the offender had the *mens rea,* or intent, to commit the crime. But those who are mentally ill may not have criminal intent at the time of the commission of an offense. Even if they do, their mental illness may have caused *mens rea* to have been formed defectively—meaning that their intent to commit the crime could be a product of the illness, rather than an actual desire to engage in

criminality. As early as the thirteenth century, English courts recognized this principle by excusing crimes committed by a "madman . . . who lacks mind and reason, and is not much removed from a brute" (Bracton, ca. 1265, as cited in Elkins, 1994). Since then, our understandings of mental illness have advanced considerably, but American law has retained the premise that someone should not be held criminally responsible for any offense committed while the person was legally insane (Fradella, 2007).

The above reasons are those that underlie the insanity defense. While there are numerous references to mental illness throughout this discussion, it is important to note once more that not all mentally ill persons will qualify for or use the insanity defense—in fact, most will not. But when mental illness does lead to a legal judgment of insanity, it is the above principles that are used to justify the insanity defense.

Public Misperceptions about Insanity. In a two-year research study on the insanity defense, Michael Perlin (1997) found two trends in public opinion about it. First, he found that people believed the defense was much more widely used than it really is, and second, he found that public sentiment toward the defense was overwhelmingly negative. Here is how the insanity defense was portrayed in the news media:

> According to the news media, the allegedly "popular" insanity defense—nothing more than a "legalistic slight of hand" and a "common feature of murder defenses"—is a reward to mentally disabled defendants for "staying sick," a "travesty," a "loophole," a "refuge," a "technicality," one of the "absurdities of state law," perhaps a "monstrous fraud." It is used—again, allegedly—in cases involving "mild disorders or a sudden disappointment or mounting frustrations . . . or a less-than-perfect childhood." It is reflected in "pseudoscience [that] can only obfuscate the issues," and is seen as responsible for "burying the traditional Judeo-Christian notion of moral responsibility under a tower of psychobabble." (Perlin, 1997, p. 1403)

In reality, defendants raise an insanity defense in less than 1% of all felony cases; when invoked, the defense is successful less than 25% of the time (Callahan, Steadman, McGreevy, & Robbins, 1991; Janofsky, Vandewalle, & Rappeport, 1989; Kirschner & Galperin, 2001; Silver, Cirincione, & Steadman, 1994). That means that a judgment of insanity is made in less than one-quarter of one percent of all cases. Defendants plead insanity nearly twice as often for non-homicide offenses than for those offenses involving a human death (Perlin, 1997; Rodriquez, 1983). When used in homicide cases, juries are reluctant to excuse a killing based on the mental state of the defendant. Consider the sensational criminal prosecutions of Jack Ruby, Sirhan Sirhan, John Wayne Gacy, Jeffery Dahmer, Charles Manson, Colin Ferguson, and John Salvi. All pled insanity; and in each case insanity was rejected and the offender was convicted. In contrast, Andrea Yates killed her children by drowning them in a bathtub and was found insane after a second trial based on a diagnosis of postpartum depression. The outcome in her case, however, is the exception and not the rule.

Perlin also found much public concern about defendants who fake their mental illnesses in order to escape a conviction, and who simply hire clinicians who will testify on their behalf and engage in an expert battle with the prosecution's clinicians at trial. Although this scenario might make for good media play, it is unrealistic. In cases where both the prosecution and the defense hire medical experts to testify about the defendant's mental state, there is overwhelming agreement on a diagnosis between the clinicians on both sides of the case. One study placed the agreement rate at 88% (Rogers, Bloom & Manson, 1984) and another at 92% (Fukunaga, Pasewark, Hawkins, & Gudeman, 1981). Moreover, the media—particularly Hollywood movies—exacerbate the fears of a defendant feigning mental illness to avoid criminal punishment. Such fears are ill-founded. "Recent carefully-crafted empirical studies have clearly demonstrated that malingering [i.e., faking illness] among insanity defendants is, and

traditionally has been, statistically low" (Perlin, 1997, p. 1405). In practice, modern diagnostic instruments and procedures allow clinicians to correctly distinguish those who are truly mentally ill from those who are faking with 92–95% accuracy (Schretlen & Arkowitz, 1990). Thus, when defendants attempt to fake mental illness, it is extraordinarily difficult for them to get away with it.

The Insanity Defense and the Problem of Medicalization. Although there are several formulations of the insanity defense, most versions of it require proof that, at the time of the offense, the defendant suffered from a "mental disease or defect"—often one that is "severe"—that caused the defendant to be unable to appreciate either the nature and quality of his or her acts, or their wrongfulness or criminality (Fradella, 2007). The part concerning the inability to understand the nature and quality of one's acts is sometimes referred to as the *cognitive incapacity* prong of the insanity test; it excuses a defendant from criminal liability when he or she is so severely disturbed that he or she is incapable of forming *mens rea,* or criminal intent. For example, if a man strangled another person believing that he was squeezing the juice out of a lemon, then he did not understand the nature and quality of his act (Rosen, 1999), and there was no *mens rea.* Much more frequently, insanity involves the inability to appreciate the wrongfulness or criminality of an act. In this situation, a defendant knows what he or she is doing; in other words, the defendant forms *mens rea,* such as an intent to assault or kill. But such intent is formed not out of a sense of malice, but rather as a function of some mental illness causing *moral incapacity*—the inability for a defendant to appreciate that their intended conduct is wrong. For instance, a defendant forms the intent to assault if he brutally attacks another person because he hears what he believes to be the voice of God ordering him to attack a demon (which psychiatry calls command hallucinations). But due to his psychotic symptoms induced by mental illness, he may believe he is doing something good, not understanding the wrongfulness or criminality of the action.

The insanity defense raises important ethical questions. For example, which conditions should constitute a bona fide "mental disease or defect" for insanity defense purposes? Should a diagnosis of alcoholism qualify as an excuse for driving under the influence? "And why not accept a plea of pyromania by an arsonist, of kleptomania by a thief, of nymphomania by a prostitute, or a similar plea of impulse and non-volitional [e.g., not consciously controlled] action by the child molester" (*Burger v. State*, 1968, p. 332)? As Schouten and Silver (2012) note:

> While any mental or medical condition could theoretically serve as a basis for an insanity defense, the law limits the conditions that can be considered for that purpose. These restrictions are aimed at insuring that only those who truly deserve to be relieved of responsibility are eligible for it. To that end, voluntary intoxication is excluded, as are conditions that have antisocial behaviors as their primary characteristic . . . and appear to have no physiological basis. Some legal standards require that the mental illness serving as the basis for the defense be "severe." (para. 10)

Accordingly, most insanity cases involve defendants who suffer from major psychotic disorders, like schizophrenia or bipolar disorder, or from abnormal brain functioning caused by traumatic injuries, tumors, lesions, or other medical conditions. But medicalization has caused a dramatic increase in the number of psychiatric diagnoses. And advances in neuroscience suggest that certain controversial conditions, like psychopathy—"an extreme form of personality disturbance, with no established effective treatment, marked by indifference to right and wrong, lack of empathy, conning and manipulation, and aggressive pursuit of self-interest"—may be the function of "anatomic and physiological abnormalities" (Schouten & Silver, 2012, para. 13).

BOX 4.2

Ethics in Practice

THE INSANITY DEFENSE

Consider each of the following cases in which the insanity defense was raised.

- *Commonwealth v. Tate* (1995): Gregory Tate was a drug addict who resorted to robbery to obtain funds to buy drugs, the ingestion of which would allow him to avoid suffering withdrawal symptoms and pain. The court rejected his claim of insanity, ruling that drug addiction was not a qualifying "mental disease or defect."
- *Robey v. State* (1983): Joy Robey suffered from intermittent explosive disorder. She claimed this disorder caused her to go into fits of rage during which she would beat her infant. The court accepted that Joy was insane when she beat her child, but, once lucid, the disorder did not excuse Joy's subsequent failure to get treatment for her daughter after a particularly brutal battering incident, which led to the death of the child. Joy's conviction for involuntary manslaughter was upheld on appeal.
- *Bieber v. People* (1993): Donald Bieber shot a stranger in the head. For several hours prior and subsequent to the murder, he had come in contact with various individuals at different locations. In addition to singing "God Bless America" and the "Marine Hymn," he told these people that he was a prisoner of war and that he was being followed by communists. He also fired shots at some of the people, without injuring anyone, and aimed his gun toward others. After the murder, he told people that he had killed a communist on "War Memorial Highway." Bieber suffered from amphetamine delusional disorder. The court rejected his insanity plea reasoning that, although Bieber's mental illness prevented him from understanding the criminal nature and quality of his acts at the time of the murder, his insanity was "settled," meaning that he contracted a psychotic disorder by having voluntarily engaged in long-term amphetamine use that caused permanent damage to his brain. Finding Bieber to be at fault for causing his insanity, the court refused to excuse his criminal conduct.
- *State v. Grimsley* (1982): Robin Grimsley suffered from dissociative identity disorder (i.e., she had multiple personalities). After learning of a lump on her breast, she dissociated from her primary personality; Jennifer, one of Robin's alternate personalities, took over. Jennifer drank and drove while intoxicated. Expert testimony established that when Jennifer was in control, Robin did not exist; there was a complete break in consciousness between the two personalities. Even though Robin was not in control when Jennifer was driving (indeed, Robin was not even conscious), the court concluded that her mental disorder did not impair her reason such that she—whether as Robin or as Jennifer or as both—would not know that drunk driving was wrong, or would not have the ability to refrain from driving while drunk.

As more deviance becomes medicalized, the more the criminal justice system will need to struggle with ethical issues regarding who deserves punishment and who deserves treatment, determining the appropriate balance between penal and therapeutic social control. Some of these ethical questions are explored in Box 4.2.

CONSEQUENCES OF MEDICALIZATION

The medicalization of deviance through the therapeutic model of social control offers both advantages and drawbacks. On the positive side, the medical model's rehabilitative focus responds to the specific needs of each individual, rather than assuming that there is a single solution, like imprisonment, that fits all deviant persons. On the other hand, focusing on the individual may come at the expense of solving larger social problems, such as poverty and inadequate educational systems. For instance, individual drug users may receive treatment for drug addiction, but the socioeconomic pressures that may have caused them to start using drugs in the first place remain unresolved.

Similarly, medicalization offers the benefit of reducing moral blame, by attributing wrongdoing to a medical condition rather than blaming the individual; this, in turn, eases the reintegration of the person into society after treatment (Braithwaite, 1989). But medicalization is not always beneficent or morally neutral. In fact, labeling something as

- *State v. Crenshaw* (1983): Because Rodney Crenshaw suspected his wife had been unfaithful, he beat her unconscious, stabbed her 24 times, and then decapitated and hid her body. He claimed he did not know his actions were wrong because he followed the Moscovite religious faith. He asserted that he delusionally believed it would be improper for a Moscovite not to kill his wife if she committed adultery. The court stressed that it is society's morals, and not the individual's morals, that are the standard for judging knowing right from wrong in the insanity context.
- *Clark v. Arizona* (2006): In the early hours of June 21, 2000, Officer Jeffrey Moritz of the Flagstaff Police responded in uniform to complaints that a pickup truck with loud music blaring was circling a residential block. When he located the truck, the officer turned on the emergency lights and siren of his marked patrol car, which prompted petitioner Eric Clark, the truck's driver (then 17), to pull over. Officer Moritz got out of the patrol car and told Clark to stay where he was. Less than a minute later, Clark shot the officer, who died soon after but not before calling the police dispatcher for help. Clark ran away on foot but was arrested later that day with gunpowder residue on his hands; the gun that killed the officer was found nearby, stuffed into a knit cap (p. 2717).

Eric Clark suffered from paranoid schizophrenia. He believed that his hometown was under invasion by aliens. Furthermore, he believed that some of the aliens impersonated government officials and were out to kill him. In fact, Clark rigged a fishing line with beads and wind chimes as part of an alarm system at his house to alert him to when alien invaders came near. Similar unusual behavior included his insistence on keeping a bird in his truck to ward off airborne poisons. On the day he killed Officer Moritz, Clark believed that the officer was an alien who was trying to kill him. Clark was convicted because the court concluded that his mental illness "did not . . . distort his perception of reality so severely that he did not know his actions were wrong" (p. 2718). Clark was sentenced to 25 years to life in prison. The U.S. Supreme Court upheld his conviction.

Q In which cases do you agree with the courts' rulings regarding whether a particular diagnosis should be accepted as a "mental disease or defect" that excuses criminal culpability on the basis of insanity? In which do you disagree? Explain your reasoning for each scenario.

Q What ethical obligation(s) does the criminal justice system have in cases in which the insanity defense is raised? Explain your answer.

a sickness can mask underlying motives and value judgments in ways that inhibit social change. For example, Victorian society viewed masturbation as both an illness and as a cause of other illnesses, like epilepsy (see Baker-Brown, 1866). For women, the so-called "cure" was a gruesome medical technology called a clitoridectomy—the removal of the clitoris. By treating masturbation as an illness, the moral condemnation was removed from the person masturbating. However, the "treatment" repressed sexuality, especially in women. Thus, medical social control reinforced sexually repressive views and male dominance in society.

Q Identify a behavior or action that has been medicalized. In what way has medicalization, or therapeutic social control, been used to address the behavior? What might be the consequences of the medicalization?

Q What do you think should be the role of the insanity defense in the criminal justice system? If you were a judge, what factors would you consider when determining whether a person's actions met the threshold for insanity, as defined under the law?

Q What do you think ought to be the role of therapeutic social control, or the medicalization of deviance, in criminal justice? Why?

Therapeutic Social Control and Public Policy

FOCUSING QUESTION 4.5

How do medicalization and other social changes affect the ways in which society exerts social controls?

Conrad and Schneider (1980) noted the impact that the medicalization of deviance has had on social policy. As decisions are made about which behaviors to address through penal social control and which behaviors to address through therapeutic social control, public policies change accordingly.

deinstitutionalization A movement in the 1960s and 1970s in which persons were released from mental hospitals in favor of community-based, often therapeutic, social control.

Conrad and Schneider pointed to the **deinstitutionalization** movement of the 1960s and 1970s as a dramatic shift in social control. During deinstitutionalization, people were released from mental hospitals and prisons in favor of community-based, often therapeutic, social control. In sentencing new offenders and determining which services were appropriate for new referrals to mental health agencies, community-based solutions were increasingly sought. Social service agencies, diversion programs, halfway houses, and group homes are examples of social controls that were to be created or strengthened as a part of the deinstitutionalization movement. For example, as public drunkenness was widely decriminalized (i.e., controlled by tools other than the law), outpatient medical treatment of alcoholism increased dramatically. Deinstitutionalization resulted in a substantial change in how social control was supposed to be accomplished in the United States, and it reflected an increased use of medical technologies and medical collaborations.

However, the principles of deinstitutionalization were not completely realized in practice. Advocates of deinstitutionalization hoped that community-based treatment would be more effective and more economical, particularly as new medications were available to manage even fairly serious mental illnesses. The community-based treatment facilities, however, never fully materialized, due to inadequate planning, a lack of funding, a lack of assistance in helping deinstitutionalized persons find the variety of programs that they needed, and disagreements about what deinstitutionalization was supposed to accomplish in the first place (Talbott, [1979] 2004).

As a result, the deinstitutionalization movement failed to achieve its goals. Many persons who were released from mental institutions became homeless because they did not have access to treatment services, and as a result the symptoms of their illnesses worsened (Talbott, [1979] 2004). The criminal justice system then sometimes became involved, as homelessness created "more opportunities for [persons with mental illness] to come to the attention of the police for what is perceived to be criminal behavior. Such behavior is often a manifestation of their illness" (Lamb & Bachrach, 2001, p. 1042).

Consider what has happened in the deinstitutionalization movement. The approach taken by the medical model shifted as new medical technologies developed (in the form of prescription medications) and as the mental health community recommended the promotion of community-based medical collaborations as an alternative to mental hospitals. This was grounded firmly in notions of therapeutic social control. However, due to imperfect implementation of necessary programs, mental illness has become, at least in part, regulated through penal social control, as there is a "pressure to institutionalize persons who need 24-hour care wherever there is room, including jail" (Lamb & Bachrach, 2001, p. 1042). Contrary to public perceptions, persons with mental illnesses who are confined in jail or prison often do not have access to a full range of treatment services. In fact, research indicates that mentally ill offenders often do not receive adequate treatment while incarcerated. "The lack of adequate mental health resources exacerbates existing serious mental conditions for inmates, resulting in decompensation in inmate mental and physical health, inmate suicides, and related complications in inmate management for correctional officials"

and the courts (Stone, 1997, p. 285; see also Fradella, 2003). What the future holds, and whether there will be a return to a therapeutic emphasis, remains to be seen.

The deinstitutionalization movement is but one example of how styles of social control may shift over time. Clearly, social control is not static, but rather changes in response to social, political, and economic contexts. Such shifts have the capacity to change societal views on particular forms of behavior viewed (or once viewed) as deviant, leading to acceptance of the behavior or, alternatively, a backlash against it.

VINDICATION AND PUTATIVE BACKLASH

Some behaviors may be decriminalized and demedicalized—that is, removed from the control of either law or medicine. When this happens, Conrad and Schneider (1980) predict two possible outcomes. The first possibility is that the underlying behavior will become vindicated. *Vindication* occurs when the behavior is no longer viewed as deviant. Alternatively, some *putative backlash* may occur that either recriminalizes the behavior or redefines the deviant nature of the behavior. To illustrate this proposition, Conrad and Schneider used the example of homosexuality. The American Psychiatric Association (APA) removed homosexuality from its official list of mental disorders in 1973. Between 1971 and 2000, 34 states removed their sodomy laws (which were essentially criminal laws against same-sex sexual activity). Moreover, in the 2003 Supreme Court case of *Lawrence v. Texas,* the remaining sodomy laws in the United States were ruled unconstitutional, as violations of the right to privacy and personal liberty embodied in the Fourteenth Amendment's Due Process Clause. Therefore, homosexuality has been both demedicalized (as it is no longer viewed as a mental illness) and decriminalized (as it is no longer a criminal offense).

A fair argument can be made that homosexuality has been largely vindicated. The arrival of the twenty-first century brought a new social perspective on homosexuality. No longer does it hold the social stigma that it once did. By 2013, laws banning discrimination based on sexual orientation have been enacted in hundreds of counties and cities nationwide, as well as in 21 states and the District of Columbia (AFL-CIO, 2013). Nearly 90 percent of all Fortune 500 companies have policies that prohibit discrimination based on sexual orientation, while close to 60 percent offer domestic partnership benefits (Human Rights Campaign, 2013). As of this writing, 16 states (California, Connecticut, Delaware, Hawaii, Iowa, Illinois, Maine, Maryland, Massachusetts, Minnesota, New Hampshire, New Jersey, New York, Rhode Island, Vermont, and Washington) and the District of Columbia have legalized same-sex marriage; Colorado offers civil unions; and Nevada and Oregon offer legal recognition of domestic partnerships that confer many of the same state rights associated with marriage, while Wisconsin offers limited rights to same-sex couples in registered domestic partnerships (National Conference of State Legislatures, 2013). In the wake of the U.S. Supreme Court's decision in *United States v. Windsor* (2013), the federal government now recognizes same-sex unions in all of the aforementioned states. And gay and lesbian characters have become commonplace in a variety of media, including television, cinema, and even comics (Anderson, 2005; Dennis, 2012). This is indeed evidence of vindication.

On the other hand, there can be no doubt that putative backlash has also occurred. For instance, antigay violence remains. Consider that 2011 marked the highest number of antigay murders ever reported since the National Coalition of Anti-Violence Programs (2012) began collecting such data in 1998. Antigay violence in the form of assaults and batteries often goes unreported in the mainstream press, even though it occurs in significant numbers. In fact, the Southern Poverty Law Center (2010), an organization that tracks hate crimes, reports that gay, lesbian, bisexual, and transgender people are significantly more likely to be the victims of hate crimes than members of any other minority group in the United States. Antigay initiatives, seeking to repeal hate crime laws, domestic partnership laws, and nondiscrimination laws, are one of the

hottest topics in politics. And the legal status of same-sex relationships has proven to be one of the most divisive issues of our time. Thus, as Conrad and Schneider predicted in 1980, putative backlash has occurred as debate continues about rights that are not completely vindicated.

OTHER CONSEQUENCES OF SHIFTS IN THE STYLE OF SOCIAL CONTROL

There can be no argument that medicine acts as a powerful institution of social control. The medicalization of deviance has produced what the *New York Times* described as "a veritable epidemic of mental illness," as the U.S. Surgeon General asserted in 1999 that "22 percent of the population has a diagnosable mental disorder" (Sharkey, 1999, para.1). And that figure may increase to nearly half the population in light of significant increases in the number of relatively common behaviors that are now labeled as mental disorders, including excessive drinking, over- and under-eating, and compulsive gambling (Rosenberg, 2013). Indeed, the most recent edition of the APA's *Diagnostic and Statistical Manual of Mental Disorders* ([DSM-5], 2013) has been severely criticized for a number of its diagnoses:

> Disruptive Mood Dysregulation Disorder [turns] temper tantrums into a mental disorder. Normal grief will become Major Depressive Disorder, thus medicalizing and trivializing our expectable and necessary emotional reactions to the loss of a loved one and substituting pills and superficial medical rituals for the deep consolations of family, friends, religion, and the resiliency that comes with time and the acceptance of the limitations of life. The everyday forgetting characteristic of old age will now be misdiagnosed as Minor Neurocognitive Disorder, creating a huge false positive population of people who are not at special risk for dementia. . . . And the DSM-5 obscures the already fuzzy boundary been Generalized Anxiety Disorder and the worries of everyday life. (Frances, 2012, paras. 11–19)

The medical model of deviance is driven, in part, by a profit motive. Several commentators have derided the fact that approximately 70% of the APA's task force members for the DSM-5 are associated with the pharmaceutical industry (Cosgrove & Krimsky, 2012). Might market forces be driving the creation of diagnoses for the benefit of the profession and the pharmaceutical industry such that these "disorders" can be treated with the products sold by the companies with which the APA's DSM task force members are affiliated (Frances, 2012; Sachdev, 2013)? And as more behaviors qualify as sickness, aren't more specialists needed to diagnose and treat those sicknesses? Certainly, more clients mean more money. That is not to say that the members of the APA are not acting with the best of intentions, but there can be no doubt that the medicalization of deviance has been a major contributor to the ever-rising costs of health care.

In addition to the economic consequences of medicalization, putative backlash against medicalization, itself, has created many other problems with real cost—both economic and human. Consider the fact that in the last 20 years, we have heard repeated calls for people to "take responsibility" for their own actions, with science being perceived as offering excuses for their deviant behavior (e.g., Dershowitz, 1994). In spite of the fact that insanity defenses rarely work, people often get angry when they see high-profile criminal defendants arguing that they should not be held responsible for their actions. This backlash against medicalization has led to significant changes in the legal definitions of insanity for a host of criminal and civil justice proceedings (Fradella, 2007). For example, for the insanity defense to be used successfully today, it is no longer sufficient in some jurisdictions to demonstrate that the defendant suffers from a mental illness that causes him or her to be unable to

appreciate the difference between right and wrong. Rather, in some states, to qualify for the insanity defense, the mental illness must be so "severe" that the defendant did not even know what he or she was doing. In others, even severe psychiatric conditions causing the formation of *mens rea* cannot excuse conduct that is a direct product of delusional beliefs (*Clark v. Arizona*, 2006).

BOX 4.3

Research in Action

MENTAL HEALTH COURTS

Mental health courts are a specialized type of problem-solving court designed to apply formal social control to mentally ill offenders using the therapeutic style, rather than the penal style of social control traditionally applied to criminal offenders. Since the first mental health court was established in 1997, these specialty courts have grown in use and popularity. By 2013, some 300 mental health courts were operating in the United States. These courts are staffed by specially trained personnel experienced in working with mentally ill offenders and are based on a therapeutic jurisprudence model, rather than an adversarial justice style (Council of State Governments Justice Center, 2013; Mann, 2011). Mental health courts typically include judges, social workers, probation officers, and attorneys who have received special training regarding mental illness, psychotropic medication, and substance abuse. This stands in sharp contrast to the "mixed bag" of training and education that would be found in traditional criminal courts.

Mental health courts are remarkably diverse. The clinical diagnoses that qualify arrestees for participation in mental health court varies significantly across the country, as do court procedures and completion requirements (Mann, 2011; Redlich, Hoover, Summers, & Steadman, 2010). The types of cases that mental health courts adjudicate also vary; 85% accept misdemeanor cases and 75% handle felony cases, although only 20% accept violent felony cases and only 1% handle seriously violent felony cases (Mann, 2011).

Technically, participation in mental health court programs is supposed to be voluntary. Upon agreeing to participate, new participants are required to sign contracts that typically include commitments to take prescribed medications, attend and engage in treatment appointments, return to the court for status review hearings, come to court on time, meet with case managers or probation officers, and follow any other individual requirements deemed necessary (Mann, 2011; Redlich et al., 2010). The use of sanctions to enforce these provisions varies significantly across mental health courts. Redlich and colleagues (2010), however, found that although 65–76% of mental health court participants reported that they chose to enroll in the programs, most indicated that they did not know the court was voluntary, had not been informed of the program requirements prior to enrolling, and were unaware that they could stop participation if they so desired.

Empirical evaluations of mental health courts have generally found them to be effective at reducing recidivism (Herinckx, Swart, Ama, Dolezal, & King, 2005; Moore & Hiday, 2006; McNeil & Binder, 2007; Trupin & Richards, 2003). For example, Dirks-Linhorst and Linhorst (2012) found that the rearrest rate of 351 defendants who successfully completed a mental health court program was 14.5%, as compared to 38% among defendants negatively terminated from the program and 25.8% among defendants who chose not to participate. But at least two studies have concluded that there is little difference in reoffending levels between mental health court graduates and those who do not complete such programs (Christy, Poythress, Boothroyd, Petrila, & Mehra, 2005; Cosden, Ellens, Schnell, & Yamini-Diouf, 2005). The intense variations in how each mental health court structures its own policies and programs may explain these divergent findings.

Q What do you think are the advantages and disadvantages of mental health courts? Do you think their use should be expanded in the criminal justice system? Why or why not?

Q As described above, there are many different ways that mental health courts can be structured. How do you think they should be structured in order to be the most effective? Why?

Q How do mental health courts illustrate therapeutic social control? Do you think they illustrate any aspects of other forms of social control?

Source: Schug & Fradella, 2014

These definitional changes affect criminal justice processes. People found guilty and sentenced to prison sometimes find themselves labeled as mentally ill upon being released. This can result in an involuntary commitment to a mental health setting, in the name of therapeutic social control (Miller, 1997). To provide mental health services at the time an offender is initially brought into the criminal justice system, some jurisdictions have created **mental health courts**, which focus on therapeutic social control. Box 4.3 presents an overview of these specialty courts and the research evaluating their effectiveness.

mental health courts
A specialized type of problem-solving court for offenders with mental illnesses. Mental health courts focus on therapeutic social control.

Q Do you think there are any types of deviance that should be medicalized? Are there any types of deviance that you think should be decriminalized or demedicalized? If they are, do you think vindication or putative backlash would occur?

Q How has the debate regarding same-sex marriage been shaped by the process of the medicalization of deviance? Would national legalization of same-sex marriage vindicate homosexuality as a nondeviant behavior in the twenty-first century, or would there be further putative backlash? Why?

Q How would you determine when persons should be subjected to penal versus therapeutic social control? In part, this requires considering how you would weigh the role of individual responsibility versus the medicalization of deviance.

Conclusion

Human behavior is the complex product of many forces, both internal and external. Bringing behavior into compliance with a society's norms is the function of the socialization process and of social control mechanisms. The social control function is not limited to criminal justice but can also include family, peer groups, the medical profession, and more. One balance that must be struck is determining how the combination of penal, compensatory, therapeutic, and conciliatory social control can be used to promote adherence to norms and compliance with the law. One increasingly important form of social control is the therapeutic, or medical model, which has grown in significance and impact over time. However, the various forms of socialization and formal and informal social control described in this chapter sometimes do not result in full compliance with social norms, in which case deviance results. The next chapter will further explore the nature and causes of deviant behavior.

Gun Control and Mental Illness

Criminal Justice Problem Solving

The Second Amendment to the U.S. Constitution states, "A well regulated Militia, being necessary to the security of a free State, the right of the people to keep and bear Arms, shall not be infringed." In *District of Columbia v. Heller* (2008), the U.S. Supreme Court invalidated a ban on handgun possession in Washington, D.C., reasoning that Second Amendment rights are exercised individually. The Court went on to say, though, that "nothing in our opinion should be taken to cast doubt on longstanding prohibitions on the possession of firearms by felons and the mentally ill" (p. 626). Two years later in *McDonald v. City of Chicago* (2010), the Court extended *Heller's* holding to the states.

Federal law has prohibited people with serious mental illnesses from possessing firearms since at least 1968, when the Federal Gun Control Act was adopted. As amended over the years, it provides, in relevant part, that "it shall be unlawful for any person who has been adjudicated as a mental defective or who has been committed to a mental institution" to purchase or possess a firearm. Such adjudication occurs when someone has been declared legally incompetent, has been involuntarily civilly committed to mental health treatment, or has been adjudicated legally insane; in contrast, this law does not reach people in mental institutions either for observation or as a function of voluntary admission (Vars & Young, 2013). Individual states vary in their gun regulations. However, while some states have no laws on point, most either mirror federal legislation or in fact have more stringent prohibitions on gun ownership or possession by people with mental illnesses, including those without any history of commitment. "For example, Hawaii prohibits gun possession by anyone who 'is or has been diagnosed as having a significant behavioral, emotional, or mental disorder. . . .'" (p. 12). Such laws, however, did not prevent the tragedies committed by Jared Loughner in Tucson, Arizona; Seung Hui Cho at Virginia Tech; James Holmes in Aurora, Colorado; and Adam Lanza in Newtown, Connecticut. Lanza used guns his mother had purchased legally. Loughner, Holmes, and Cho each purchased "the firearms they used for the murders they committed from federally licensed firearms dealers," even though all three of them had shown signs of serious mental illnesses (McCreary, 2013, p. 813). Similarly, Russell Weston, who shot and killed two police officers at the U.S. Capitol Building in 1998 to "prevent the United States from being annihilated by disease and legions of cannibals" (p. 829), had purchased the gun he used from a firearms store in Illinois even though he had been involuntarily hospitalized in Montana—a commitment Montana seemingly had never reported.

In the wake of the Virginia Tech shooting, Congress enacted the National Instant Check System (NICS) Improvement Amendments Act (McCreary, 2013, p. 836). The law required state and federal agencies to report information about people who were prohibited from possessing firearms to the U.S. Attorney General who, in turn, would enter the data in a searchable electronic database that firearms dealers need to check before selling a gun. The law authorized the withholding of certain federal funds to states who failed to comply. Yet, after the deadline for compliance had come and gone, at least nine states had failed to provide any information and the threatened loss of funds has never been imposed (McCreary, 2013).

Even if NICS were fully implemented and working properly, there are reasons to doubt whether it would be effective in preventing mass shootings by those with serious mental illnesses. First and foremost, only federally licensed firearm stores are required to use NICS. In contrast, no background checks occur for the roughly 40 percent of all U.S. firearm sales that occur either between private sellers or at gun shows. Second, even if universal background checks were required, neither Jared Loughner nor James Holmes had been committed. Hence, a NICS search would have failed to prevent either of them from having obtained the weapons they used in their respective massacres.

Criminal Justice Problem Solving

Gun Control and Mental Illness

continued

As this chapter should make clear, psychiatric terms like "mental illness" and "mental disorder" do not map well onto legal language like "mental defect" that is used in federal gun control laws. Which mental illnesses render people significantly "mentally defective" such that they forfeit their Second Amendment rights? And who would make this determination? Should a formal adjudication be necessary, or should the types of behaviors exhibited by Seung Hui Cho while a student at Virginia Tech or by Jared Loughner while a student at Pima Community College trigger restrictions on the ability to obtain firearms legally?

Q Would you support or oppose the following changes in law and public policy designed to reduce gun violence while preserving Second Amendment rights? Explain your answers.

- Closing the "gun show loophole" by requiring universal background checks?
- Requiring mental health professionals to report a patient to county governments if they believe the patient is "likely to engage in conduct that would result in serious harm to self or others," as the State of New York does?
- Barring a person from purchasing firearms for five years, as California does, after being placed on a 72-hour psychiatric hold in a facility?
- Restricting gun sales not only for those involuntarily committed, but also for those who voluntarily admit themselves to in-patient psychiatric care, as Georgia and Mississippi both do?
- Insisting that anyone who wants to purchase a gun be required to prove his or her medical and mental health fitness to do so by obtaining a permit based on a physician's approval, as suggested by law professor Jana McCreary (2013)?

Q What other ideas do you have to prevent persons with serious mental illnesses from accessing firearms? How would you define "serious mental illness" for purposes of these laws?

Source: Fradella, 2013.

5

Deviance and Criminal Behavior

Learning Objectives

1 Identify the characteristics of deviance in society. **2** Explain why some people engage in criminal deviance. **3** Apply psychological theories to the explanation of crime and criminal behavior. **4** Apply sociocultural theories to the explanation of crime and criminal behavior. **5** Explain why the study of deviance is important for criminal justice.

Key Terms

serial murder
criminologist
deviance
social constructionism
criminology
classical criminology
positivist school of criminology
rational choice theory
routine activities theory
psychodynamic theory
differential association theory
neutralization theory
antisocial personality
social disorganization theory
concentric zone theory
strain theory
social bond theory
labeling theory
conflict criminology
Marxist criminology
feminist criminology
peacemaking criminology
life course theory

Key People

Kai Erickson
Émile Durkheim
Franz Gall
Cesare Lombroso
Charles Goring
William Sheldon
Richard Dugdale
Henry Goddard
Francis Galton
Karl Christiansen
Lawrence Cohen
Marcus Felson
Sigmund Freud
August Aichhorn
Edwin Sutherland
Gresham Sykes
David Matza
Hans Eysenck
Michael Gottfredson
Travis Hirschi
Robert Park
Ernest Burgess
Roderick McKenzie
Clifford Shaw
Henry McKay
Robert Merton
Albert Cohen
Walter Miller
Richard Cloward
Lloyd Ohlin
Robert Agnew
Edwin Lemert
Frank Tannenbaum
Richard Quinney

Case Study

The Case of Carl Panzram

serial murderer
Offenders who have killed two or more victims over time.

Serial murder (also known as serial killing) is defined as "[t]he unlawful killing of two or more victims by the same offender(s), in separate events [i.e., not in the same incident]" (Behavioral Analysis Unit, 2008, p. 9). Serial killing is rare when compared to other crimes. In fact, between 1800 and 2004, there have been more fictional serial killers (well over 500 in novels and movies) than actual offenders (approximately 430). Nonetheless, the investigation of serial murders is a high priority for law enforcement agencies (Hickey, 2010).

Carl Panzram may not be the most well-known of serial killers, having committed his crimes almost a century ago, but he did leave "behind a remarkable listing of his crimes and misdeeds" (*Serial Killers . . .*, 1991, p. 85). Born in Minnesota in 1891, Panzram began his life of crime at an early age.

Panzram was born into an impoverished German immigrant household in Minnesota in 1891. "Carl's first years were spent without the attention he desired. In attempts to gain attention, Carl acted out, only to be physically punished and then further ignored" (Singer & Hensley, 2004, p. 467). When only eight years old, Panzram was arrested for disorderly conduct and drunkenness. He was arrested for a number of robberies and sentenced to a juvenile reform school by age 11. At the school, he was sexually and physically abused and, as a form of revenge, he set fire to one of the school buildings. After being released

Previous page: A group loitering and drinking in public. Why do you think individuals or groups might engage in deviant behavior?

from the school, when 14, he "set fire to a warehouse . . . just for fun" (p. 468), and was returned to reform school.

Panzram joined the army at age 16 and received a dishonorable discharge after serving over three years in a military prison. "Before leaving the base, he managed to burn down the military prison workshop" (Singer & Hensley, 2004, p. 468). Following his discharge, Panzram was in and out of prison for a series of burglaries. In his prison terms, Panzram was a difficult inmate, escaping and damaging prison property.

"Before imprisonment, Carl Panzram hated all humanity, but during this period, he turned this hatred toward himself" (Singer & Hensley, 2004, p. 468). Panzram turned to serial killing, traveling the world in search of victims. He later wrote, "In my lifetime I have murdered 21 human beings. I have committed thousands of burglaries, robberies, larcenies, arsons and last but not least I have committed sodomy on more than 1,000 male human beings. For all these things I am not in the least bit sorry . . ." (*Serial Killers . . .*, 1991, p. 85).

After being sentenced to prison for another burglary, Panzram killed a prison staff member, for which he received a death sentence. In 1930, after a lifetime of criminal activity both inside and outside correctional institutions, Panzram was executed (Singer & Hensley, 2004). While an extreme example, Carl Panzram's life and activities beg for explanation. What leads to criminal behavior? Can criminologists provide an answer?

Q Even without further biographical information about Panzram, brainstorm a list of factors—possibly including individual characteristics, social conditions, negative influences, and so on—that *could have* influenced him to commit his deviant acts.

Q Look back at the list you just created. Why would these factors lead an individual down the path of criminal activity?

Q Look back at your list once again. Is there anything that society could do through laws or policies to reduce the harmful impact of these factors?

Conceptualizing Deviance

FOCUSING QUESTION 5.1

What are the characteristics of deviance in society?

There are many activities that are viewed as socially unacceptable, or deviant. These activities range from relatively minor indiscretions (e.g., speaking too loudly in a library) to very serious criminal activities (e.g., murder). **Criminologists** are scholars who study why people commit these types of acts. Criminologists generally seek to answer questions similar to those that you answered following the opening scenario of this chapter. These may be summarized as follows: What causes deviance? Why do these things cause deviance? What steps can we take to reduce deviance?

criminologist
A scholar of criminology, studying crime trends and why persons commit criminal acts.

Unfortunately, there is not a simple answer to these questions. In fact, many criminologists disagree about the causes of deviant behavior and the policy implications that flow from them. The reality is that there are many theories that contain partial answers, but there is no single correct answer that applies in all cases. Therefore, it is important to have a broad understanding of the possible answers, which this chapter will provide (for more thorough evaluations of each theory, excellent sources include Akers & Sellers, 2012, and Shoemaker, 2009). First, however, it is important to review and expand upon the concept of deviance, as introduced in Chapter 4.

As defined in Chapter 4, **deviance** is any departure from behaviors that are typical, acceptable, or expected. Norms and laws, as enforced through the various forms of social control, help identify behaviors labeled as deviant. Therefore, deviance is "any behavior that is likely to be defined as an unacceptable violation of a major social norm

and elicit strong negative reactions by social control agents" (Best & Luckenbill, 1994, pp. 2–3). It is important to have a thorough understanding of deviance before attempting to understand why it occurs. Consider the essentials of the definition just presented.

First, deviance is a behavior. To be deemed a behavior, an *action* must occur, such as when Carl Panzram burned down the reformatory. *Traits,* on the other hand, are not deviant. A trait is a characteristic over which a person has no control. To draw out this distinction, consider hair color as an example. Having naturally blonde (or any other color) hair is a genetically determined trait and, as such, is not deviant. Some people may prefer one hair color to another; this is a personal judgment. But the trait of hair color is not a behavior, and thus, it is not inherently deviant. However, styling hair is an action, and as a result, some hairstyles may be viewed as deviant. For instance, if a person decides to dye his or her hair shamrock green, then this is an action that some—though certainly not all—might label as deviant because it runs counter to social expectations about hairstyling.

The important point here is that to be deviant, a person must do something. This also illustrates that deviance is a social phenomenon rather than one that is defined by physical characteristics. This is what separates the concept of deviance, which is an action in violation of social norms, from personal biases and discriminations that target physical traits over which a person has no control.

Second, deviant behaviors violate social norms, as discussed in Chapter 4. But social norms vary over time and place (see Box 5.1 for an example), as Kai Erikson (2005) described:

> [B]ehavior that is considered unseemly within the context of a single family may be entirely acceptable to the community in general, while behavior that attracts severe censure from members of the community may go altogether unnoticed elsewhere in our culture . . . A man may disinherit his son for conduct that violates old family traditions, a woman may ostracize a neighbor for conduct that violates some local custom, but neither of them are expected to employ those standards when they serve as jurors in a court of law (p. 9).

Therefore, there is no single and universally agreed-upon list of social norms. However, there are some social norms that society feels so strongly about that they are codified into laws. As noted by Erickson, these are the norms—rather than those specific to a family or the traditions of a particular community—that are enforced by judges and juries at criminal trials. For instance, Panzram's actions violated norms of behavior on which there is little disagreement and which have been codified into law. Obviously, arson and murder are viewed as both illegal and unacceptable in most, if not all, circumstances. On the other hand, an unusual hairstyle may be viewed as a deviant violation of norms among some persons but not others, making it a much more situational judgment and not something that is codified into law.

In the study and practice of criminal justice, the focus is primarily on social norms that have been codified in law. However, the explanations of deviance discussed in this chapter apply to any negative deviant behaviors (recall the distinction from positive deviance in Chapter 4), whether they are illegal or simply viewed as distasteful or undesirable. This is important to consider because over time, new laws may be passed that increase the scope of social control by criminalizing behaviors that were once merely viewed as distasteful. As a contemporary example, consider smoking in public places. Once acceptable, the behavior is now often viewed as undesirable and has, in fact, been made criminal in some jurisdictions (see Glantz & Balbach, 2000). To take the issue a step further, as part of the anti-smoking movement in the United States, most correctional agencies have banned smoking in prisons (Kauffman, Ferketich, & Wewers, 2008). In turn, this has generated new concerns about the smuggling of cigarettes into

BOX 5.1

PARADE STRIPPERS

In his article "Parade Strippers: A Note on Being Naked in Public," Craig Forsyth (1992) described the practice of females (and some males) exposing their breasts and other intimate body parts during the New Orleans Mardi Gras celebration (essentially, a street party with parades) in exchange for glass beads and other trinkets thrown by parade float riders and parade observers. This form of public nudity has been compared to nude sunbathing, joining a nudist colony, "streaking," and "mooning."

This is a behavior that is prohibited by criminal law, usually through statutes against indecent exposure. While some arrests are made for indecent exposure (McConnaughey, 2000), "on Mardi Gras day in New Orleans, many things normally forbidden are permitted. People walk around virtually nude [and] women expose themselves . . . Laws that attempt to legislate morality are informally suspended" (Forsyth, 1992, p. 395).

Q Do you consider this form of public nudity to be deviant behavior? If so, explain how it meets the definition of deviance and whether you think it should be classified as crime, sin, and/or poor taste. If not, explain why not.

Q What factors might contribute to making this behavior more acceptable at one place (New Orleans) during one time of year (Mardi Gras) as opposed to others?

Q If you were a police officer in New Orleans, how would you respond to indecent exposure during Mardi Gras? During other times of the year? Is there a difference in your answers? Why or why not?

correctional facilities, whether for smoking or as a form of currency to facilitate exchanges of other items (Lankenau, 2001). As such, conceptions of deviance are truly dynamic, and changes over time can have multiple effects on justice policy and administration.

Third, deviant behaviors elicit negative reactions from social control agents. This may include formal social control (e.g., police officers arresting Panzram for arson) or informal social control (e.g., a parent expressing disapproval of an unusual hairstyle). In fact, these negative reactions complete a feedback loop. When a norm is violated and a punishment or disapproval is given, that serves to further communicate the unacceptability of the behavior (Feinberg, 1965), which in turn reinforces the strength of the norm.

Therefore, defining deviance is sometimes complex, as norms vary and different social control agents treat similar behavior differently. Also, behaviors that were previously considered deviant may be acceptable today, and those that were previously considered acceptable may now be viewed as deviant.

CRIME, SIN, AND TASTE AS FORMS OF DEVIANCE

As noted in the earlier quote from Erikson, not all deviance is criminal. Behaviors that violate a tradition or custom may violate norms and elicit negative reactions but are not necessarily criminal. Smith and Pollack ([1976] 1994) suggest that there are three categories of deviance: crime, sin, and poor taste.

As you learned in Chapter 1, crimes are behaviors that are specifically prohibited by the law. This makes crime a unique form of deviance because it is the only form in which the government (as opposed to other agents of social control) may punish individuals for their deviant behaviors. In addition, crimes are often the most serious of deviant acts, including behaviors such as murder, rape, and robbery.

Sin as a form of deviance stems from behaviors that are religiously prohibited, as described by religious texts, doctrine, or clergy. Sinful behavior may be regulated by clergy (e.g., through expulsion from a religious group) or through informal control exerted by members of religious groups. As you will learn in Chapter 9, in the past, there was little distinction between what was a sin and what was a crime. In fact, religious courts were once the primary legal authorities, and some countries still utilize religious legal systems (e.g., the use of Islamic law in Saudi Arabia; see Bracey, 2006).

Although the United States has a secular (i.e., nonreligious) legal system, there are instances in which religious beliefs have been reflected in the criminal law. For instance, the prohibition of alcohol in the early twentieth century was partially motivated by religious beliefs opposing alcohol (see Okrent, 2010, for an interesting history), and religious beliefs underlay the "blue laws" that once required stores and businesses to remain closed on Sunday.

Poor taste as a form of deviance is regulated by informal social control, which is in turn based on understandings of social norms. In the past, some societies relied on unwritten understandings about what was (and was not) tasteful or acceptable behavior as a basis for law. These were known as traditional legal systems. In the United States, legal codes have always been written, but taste may still influence criminal law. As an example, consider cursing. To some people, foul language is no more than a form of expression. However, to others, foul language is not in good taste, and agents of informal social control may discourage it (through a raised eyebrow from a passerby, a reprimand from a teacher, etc.). In some jurisdictions, this distaste has been formalized by the creation of laws against cursing, as described in Chapter 3.

As part of a school event, high school students in Juneau, Alaska, were permitted to watch the Olympic Torch Relay, which came through town prior to the 2002 Winter Games. One group of students displayed a banner, shown here. One student, who did not take the banner down when told by his principal to do so, was suspended. The principal argued that the banner promoted drug use (*Morse v. Frederick,* 2007). Do you believe this was a deviant behavior? Should the student have been suspended?

Therefore, the various forms of deviance—crime, sin, and taste—overlap to some extent. Smith and Pollack ([1976] 1994) argue that only the most serious deviant acts should be made criminal, and "in regard to those whose conduct really harms no one but themselves, *we should let them alone,* recognizing that to some extent we are all deviants" [emphasis in original] (p. 20).

DEVIANCE IN SOCIETY

What functions does deviance serve in society? Kai Erickson (2005) argued that one function of deviance is to help communities maintain boundaries. Each deviant act is considered along with the norm that was violated; this "sharpens the authority of the violated norm and restates where the boundaries of the group are located" (p. 13). Thus, with each deviant act, the community has an opportunity to reflect on the deviance and decide whether the boundaries of acceptable behavior need to be strengthened, kept the same, or relaxed.

For instance, assume that panhandling (i.e., requesting money from passersby in public places) is viewed as a violation of a community's social norms. With each instance of panhandling, communities may affirm their opposition to it and their resolve to do something about it. As a result, tougher laws against panhandling could be enacted. The community may also refine the norm, such as drawing distinctions that would permit charitable groups to request money in public but prohibit homeless persons from doing so. Furthermore, how the agents of social control respond to panhandling also may change. Whether the police should ask the panhandler to move along, issue a summons, or make an arrest is a tactical decision that reflects community priorities (for additional reading on this example, see Kelling & Coles, 1996). Therefore, the nature of deviance and its evolution directly impact the job of the police officer on the street.

The presence of deviance therefore permits the definition of deviance to evolve, and as it does, persons and communities may revise and redefine their understandings of their norms. Norms and laws are indeed dynamic, continually being revised based on new understandings.

Émile Durkheim ([1938] 1980) had a different perspective on the role of deviance and crime—namely, that crime is a normal and functional part of society. Durkheim first noted that all human societies have crime, even if there are differences in terms of what acts are criminalized. This makes crime a normal, though obviously not desirable, part of society (or what Durkheim called a *social fact*). The only way that any particular crime could be eliminated would be if every single person in society agreed that it was a bad act and that they would never commit it. Durkheim then argued that even if serious crimes were eliminated in this way, people would then turn their attention to criminalizing less serious actions. The process would continue until the law controlled even trivial behavior. For instance, to return to a prior example, if violent crime was eliminated, some might turn their attention to less serious issues, such as criminalizing unusual hairstyles instead of viewing them as a matter of taste.

Durkheim argued that in reality this sort of process would likely not occur because there is a natural diversity of human ideas that makes it impossible for unanimous opinions to develop. This means that there will never be complete agreement on an issue. As long as this is the case, people will continue to disagree (regardless of what the law says) about whether certain behaviors are or are not acceptable, and about what norms should or should not be followed, and crime will therefore continue to exist, as some norms or laws will invariably be broken. This makes crime the normal, but undesirable, feature of society that Durkheim described.

Durkheim also saw crime as necessary to society. His logic was based on the idea that, for society to progress, it needs a diversity of ideas rather than unanimous opinions. However, he believed that it would be impossible to prohibit the diversity of ideas that leads to crime, just described, while permitting the diversity of ideas that leads to

progress. Consider the implications of Durkheim's theory: crimes and other forms of deviance are virtually impossible to eliminate because they are created by natural variations in human thought—ironically, it is variations in human thought that also permit the development of new ideas that allow society to advance.

The arguments set forth by Erickson and Durkheim serve to illustrate that deviance, while appearing to be a simple concept at first glance, is actually a very complex phenomenon. In fact, it relates to a theory of criminology known as **social constructionism** (Lindgren, 2005). This perspective suggests that criminal activity is best understood by studying the processes through which behaviors are defined as deviant or acceptable—which includes the concepts discussed in this, and previous, chapters. The idea underlying this perspective is that we cannot achieve a full understanding of crime unless we review the social forces that influence our definition of it, ranging from the meaning of deviance, to socialization, to ideas about the law, to morality, and more. Social constructionism argues that studying these perspectives will better allow us to analyze not only individual behavior, but also society's response to it. Perhaps most central to social constructionism is that all of these meanings can change as society's preferences and viewpoints change (see generally Edelman, 1988). This is what leads to the name of the theory—the idea is that societies continuously construct and reconstruct their own understandings about deviance and crime through the various processes we have discussed thus far in the text.

social constructionism
In criminological theory, the idea that criminal activity is best understood by studying the processes through which behaviors are defined as deviant or acceptable.

Compare the above description of social constructionism to traditional criminology, which primarily focuses on why individuals engage in behaviors that have already been identified as deviant. Social constructionism helps us understand why behaviors are viewed as deviant or criminal and how those viewpoints change over time; traditional criminology, the subject of the remainder of this chapter, considers why individuals commit those behaviors that are defined as deviant or criminal. Both understandings are important, because taken together, they provide us with a broad view of crime as a social phenomenon. Our discussion will next turn to how traditional criminological perspectives explain why individuals engage in acts of deviance.

Q How should we decide which behaviors to regulate through the criminal law? Do you agree with Smith and Pollack's argument, quoted in this section, about what should be criminalized?

Q Provide examples of various forms of deviance. Are they a crime, sin, or bad taste? How have they been viewed differently over time or between different places? Has social control of the issues (formal or informal) reinforced the strength of the norm being violated?

Q One implication of Durkheim's argument is that as society comes to agreement on the prohibition of serious crimes, attention increasingly turns to the regulation of less serious behaviors. Do you believe this is true? Why or why not?

criminology
The scientific study of crime trends, the nature of crime, and explanations for why persons commit crimes.

classical criminology
A set of explanations for crime based on the concept of free will, or the idea that individuals simply choose whether or not to commit a criminal act.

Some Explanations of Criminal Deviance

FOCUSING QUESTION 5.2

Why do some people engage in criminal deviance?

Think back to the case study at the beginning of the chapter. How did you answer the question about the factors that may have influenced Panzram to commit his criminal acts? In this section, we discuss **criminology**, which is the scientific study of the etiology (i.e., nature and causes) of criminal behavior. Many theories have been developed to explain why people commit crimes. These theories may be divided into two opposing criminological schools of thought: classical criminology and positivism. **Classical criminology**

is based on the concept of free will, viewing the decision to commit crime as a choice freely made by the offender. The **positivist school of criminology** (positivism) is based on the concept of *determinism*, which holds that criminal behaviors are influenced by outside forces. These may include biological, psychological, and sociological factors (Siegel, 2001). Some of the most common theories are summarized in the following sections; see how they compare to your ideas about the causes of Panzram's behavior.

positivist school of criminology
Based on the concept of determinism, this perspective holds that criminal behaviors are influenced by outside forces such as biological, psychological, and sociological factors.

HISTORICAL PERSPECTIVES ON CRIMINOLOGY

Early theories attempted to explain crime based on the supernatural, based on physical characteristics, or by defining crime as an inherited behavior. It is important to note that the theories in this section have been discredited and are presented only to provide historical context.

Demonology. One of the earliest forms of criminological ideas was demonology, which attributed criminal behavior to the influence of evil spirits or demons. Blaming crime on witchcraft is one example. The concept of an evil witch emerged in fourteenth-century Europe. Since that time, witches have been blamed for a variety of social ills. Witchcraft as an explanation for criminal behavior made its way to the New World in the Puritan colony of Massachusetts Bay. Spiritual explanations of crime surfaced when the community believed it had been invaded by a large number of witches (Erikson, 2005). The Salem Witch Trials resulted, including the execution of individuals labeled as witches. Ben-Yehuda (1985) has observed that campaigns against witchcraft served to strengthen the power of the religious authorities who waged them. This is an illustration of the link between sin and crime as conceptualizations of deviance, as well as the connection between informal social control (i.e., religion) and formal social control (i.e., courts of law) in responding to perceptions of deviance.

A number of explanations have been offered to understand the panic over witchcraft in the Massachusetts colony. However, one dominant theme that cannot be overlooked is the role that gender played in the construction of witchcraft. As criminal justice historian Lawrence Friedman (1993) observed, "In some subtle and not so subtle ways, the war against witches was also a war against women" (pp. 46–47). Women who were perceived as violating social norms in a patriarchal (i.e., male-dominated) society have been subjects of persecution not only in the Massachusetts witch trials but also in other witch-hunts worldwide (Levack, 2001).

Phrenology. This was the study of personality traits as revealed by examining bumps and grooves in the skull. This pseudo-science, led by Franz Gall (1758–1828), argued that criminal traits could be determined by the study of the skull's size, weight, shape, and other facial features.

Atavism. Cesare Lombroso (1835–1909), known as the "father of criminology" because he was one of the first to systematically study the causes of crime, believed that criminal behavior was the result of inherited traits. That is, he believed a person could be born as a criminal. Lombroso, a physician with a specialty in psychiatry and legal medicine, "proposed that criminals were biological throwbacks to an earlier evolutionary stage, people more primitive and less highly evolved than their noncriminal counterparts. Lombroso used the term *atavistic* to describe such people" (Vold, Bernard, & Snipes, 1998, p. 32).

Somatotypes. Building on Lombroso's theory, Charles Goring (1870–1919) believed that a person's height and weight were associated with criminal behavior and that offenders tended to be shorter and lighter than nonoffenders. Similarly, William Sheldon claimed that people with different physical builds (what he called different

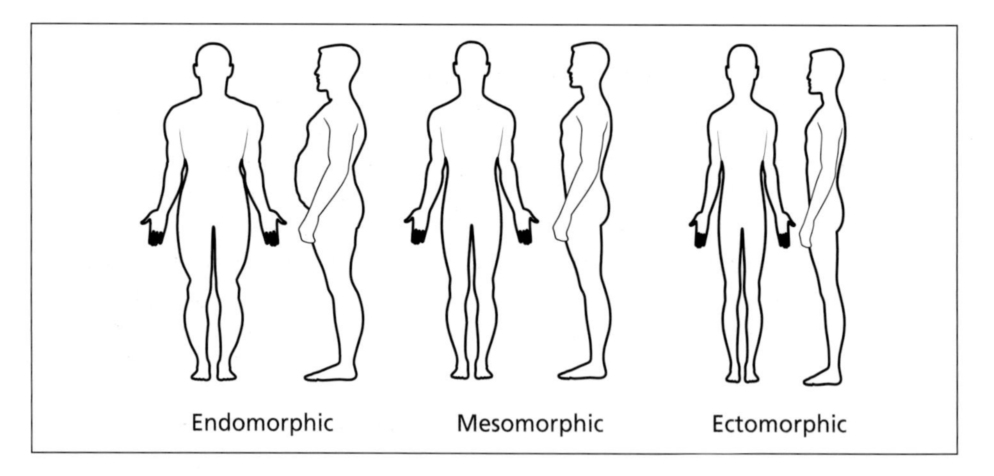

FIGURE 5.1 Sheldon's Somatotypes.

somatotypes) possess different temperaments. He believed that persons who are muscular, active, and aggressive, known as mesomorphs, were more likely to engage in delinquent behavior (see Figure 5.1).

The theories of phrenology, atavism, and somatotypes have two commonalities. First, they all deal with the relationship between physical characteristics and deviance. Second, there is no scientific support for these ideas, and as a result they have generally been discarded by modern criminologists. Research continued along biological lines, as described next.

Family Criminality and Eugenics. Richard Dugdale (1877), while visiting county jails in New York, discovered six incarcerated persons who were blood relatives. He traced their family genetic lines back hundreds of years and reported that the family had a history of criminal activity, including attempted murder, attempted rape, burglary, and theft. Based on his findings, Dugdale concluded that the Jukes (a pseudonym for the family) were a family of degenerates whose environment and heredity led to criminality. This had an impact on thinking about a practice known as eugenics.

Eugenics is the study of genetic factors that may influence future generations. Francis Galton, Charles Darwin's cousin, was considered by most to be the founder of the eugenics philosophy. Galton believed that eugenics was a means to positively influence human evolution by assuring that only the finest reproduced. Galton also argued that persons possessing "bad" genes should be discouraged from reproducing.

Research continued to examine the relationship between crime and genetics. In the twentieth century, psychologist Henry Goddard told a tale of the Kallikak (again, a pseudonym) family. The Kallikaks produced a genetic line of children born outside of marriage, persons deemed sexually immoral by standards of the time (mostly prostitutes), alcoholics, and assorted criminals. "Goddard thought that mental weakness and other undesirable traits were handed down from father and mother to daughter and son" (Friedman, 1993, p. 335).

This led some to advocate sterilization as a means of protecting society from criminals, including even those who had the *potential* for violence and criminality. Eugenics is not limited to sterilization. Other policies derived from eugenics include execution, incarceration for *future* bad acts, and lobotomies for crime prevention (Lanier & Henry, 1998).

Box 5.2 provides additional information about state-mandated sterilization and legal challenges to it. It is important to note that eugenics and notions of biological familial inheritance of criminality have been discredited. These theories were based on overly simplistic notions that bear little resemblance to what modern biological science has learned about the nature of genetic influences on behavior.

BOX 5.2

BUCK V. BELL, 274 U.S. 200 (1927)

In 1924, Virginia adopted a statute authorizing the compulsory sterilization (i.e., a procedure that renders persons unable to have children) of the mentally retarded for the purpose of eugenics. Carrie Buck, an 18 year old, was described by the superintendent of the Virginia State Colony for Epileptics and Feebleminded as "feebleminded" (an archaic term used to label individuals who were mentally retarded or who had certain cognitive impairments) and a genetic threat to society. Carrie was housed at the same institution as her mother, who was also labeled as feebleminded. In addition, Carrie was the mother of a child born outside of marriage who was classified as feebleminded.

The superintendent requested that Carrie be sexually sterilized so she would be unable to have additional children, arguing that it was for the betterment of society. The Supreme Court agreed. In an 8–1 decision, Justice Oliver Wendell Holmes stated:

> It is better for all the world, if instead of waiting to execute degenerate offspring for crime, or to let them starve for their imbecility, society can prevent those who are manifestly unfit from continuing their kind . . . Three generations of imbeciles are enough (274 U.S. 200, p. 208).

Q Do you agree with the Supreme Court ruling? Why or why not?

Q Eugenic sterilization programs were eventually abolished. In fact, in 2002, Virginia Governor Mark Warner formally apologized for Virginia's sterilization program (Virginia governor apologizes, 2002). In 2013, the "Justice for Victims of Sterilization Act" was introduced in the Virginia General Assembly, which would have compensated persons sterilized under Virginia's eugenics program with a one-time $50,000 payment. The bill did not pass. Would you support or oppose this legislation? Why?

Q Today, debate continues about castration (usually through the administration of drugs) of sex offenders. Do some research to find out what arguments have been made for and against this practice. Which side do you think has the better arguments?

XYY Chromosomes. Later research focused more specifically on chromosomal differences and their impact on criminal behavior. Recall from your biology coursework that humans possess 23 pairs of chromosomes. Female chromosome pairs are labeled XX and male chromosome pairs are labeled XY. During the early 1960s, the discovery of an XYY chromosome in some males raised concern about the relationship between the extra Y chromosome and criminality. Some feared that the extra chromosome would lead to aggression and violence. However, subsequent research revealed that there was no relationship between the extra chromosome and criminal violence (Beckwith & King, 1974).

MODERN BIOLOGICAL PERSPECTIVES ON CRIME AND CRIMINALITY

Criminologists have continued to pursue the relationship between biology and crime. After its shaky beginning, the biological perspective on crime and criminality has made a resurgence (see generally Moffitt, Ross, & Raine, 2011). Interestingly, research suggests that one explanation of the witchcraft panic in Salem, referenced above, had a biological component—the effects on the body of intoxication from a poison called ergot that sometimes grows on various grain crops (Caporael, 1976).

Body levels of glucose, a sugar found in the blood, also may be related to criminal behavior. Hypoglycemia, a condition often associated with diabetes, occurs when glucose levels are dangerously low. Individuals in a hypoglycemic state may experience distorted thought patterns or blackouts that can lead to the unintentional commission of deviant or criminal acts; criminal justice professionals must be alert to the symptoms of hypoglycemia, as it is a condition that requires urgent medical treatment (Marks, 2010).

However, modern biological theory goes far beyond conditions such as those described above. Many modern biological theories focus on genetics, in the context of inherited traits that are conducive to crime. The biological perspectives described in this section have been scientifically validated.

Researchers have examined the relationship between crime and heredity by comparing the criminality of identical twins with the criminality of fraternal twins of the same gender. Researcher Karl Christiansen (1977) found that if one identical twin had a criminal conviction, the other twin also had a conviction in 35% of the cases (see also Rowe & Osgood, 1984). More recent twin studies have detected a genetic component for committing acts of intimate partner violence (Hines & Saudino, 2004), adult violent crime (Frisell, Pawitan, Långström, & Lichtenstein, 2012), juvenile aggression (Elev, Lichtenstein, & Moffitt, 2003), and juvenile use of tobacco and illegal drugs (Huizink et al., 2010).

Studies such as these suggest there may be a genetic component to criminal behavior. Unlike prior work, however, the focus is not on specific families passing *crime or criminal behavior* directly to their offspring. Rather, the focus is on identifying particular genes that may influence a variety of behaviors that are associated with a *propensity* to commit crime. "No single gene can deterministically make a person into a criminal. Instead, complex traits are subtly influenced by a great number of genes, the exact number of which is unknown" (Rowe, 2002, p. 100). For instance, genetic differences in the production of neurotransmitters (chemicals in the brain, such as dopamine or serotonin) may produce aggressive or other tendencies in some persons, which if acted upon inappropriately can lead to crime (see Ishikawa & Raine, 2002; Wright, Moore, & Newsome, 2011). Other genes have been associated with a propensity for personality characteristics such as "novelty seeking" (Guo, Roettger, & Cai, 2008, p. 547), which again could lead to criminal activity (committed as a "novelty") if acted upon inappropriately.

Modern biological researchers are also careful to acknowledge that these traits do not cause crime by themselves; rather, the environment in which an individual lives has a significant impact as well (e.g., Guo, Roettger, & Cai, 2008; Beaver, Gibson, DeLisi, Vaughn, & Wright, 2012) through processes described later in this chapter. Also, some persons may channel tendencies toward aggression or novelty seeking through socially acceptable activities, such as sports or skydiving. The social environment can impact how individuals respond to such tendencies. Therefore, the relationship between biology and crime is extraordinarily complex, and new discoveries regularly emerge about the interaction of genes, environment, and human behavior.

THE CLASSICAL SCHOOL OF CRIMINOLOGY

As noted earlier, classical criminology is based on the concept of *free will*, which is the idea that people may choose whether or not to commit a criminal act. This idea has its origins in the eighteenth-century writings of Jeremy Bentham ([1789] 1970). Bentham argued that people are hedonistic, being motivated by the pursuit of pleasure and the avoidance of pain. Therefore, persons who commit criminal acts believe that the potential rewards from their actions will outweigh the potential consequences.

rational choice theory
An explanation for crime suggesting that offenders use a strategic thinking process to evaluate the potential rewards and risks from committing a crime and make their decision accordingly about whether or not to commit the crime.

Rational Choice Theory. A modern version of classical criminology is **rational choice theory**. Using free will as the philosophical base, rational choice theorists believe that

offenders use a strategic thinking process to evaluate rewards and risks. Rational choice theory holds that offenders engage in a rational decision-making process when choosing to commit a criminal act, including a consideration of factors such as the type of offense to be committed to achieve the desired goal, the selection of the victim, the best strategy to utilize in committing the crime, the risk of being caught, the potential sanction (if apprehended), the potential rewards (if successful), and so on. If the benefits outweigh the risks, the offender decides to commit the crime.

Note that the rational choice decision-making process is similar to the process described by Bentham, although rational choice includes consideration of a wider range of variables than pain and pleasure, alone. Rational choice theory also underlies the concept of deterrence, which suggests that crime may be prevented (or deterred) if offenders know they will be caught and swiftly punished for their offenses. Such knowledge could cause a rational offender to decide against committing a crime. Deterrence theory will be more fully discussed in Chapter 10.

Routine Activities Theory. A logical outgrowth of rational choice theory is routine activities theory. Based on research conducted by Lawrence Cohen and Marcus Felson (1979), **routine activities theory** views crime and victimization as a function of individuals' everyday behavior, habits, lifestyles, living conditions, and social interactions. Central to routine activities theory is Cohen and Felson's proposition that crime occurs when three elements converge: a motivated offender, a suitable target, and a lack of capable guardians.

routine activities theory
Views crime and victimization as a function of people's everyday behavior, habits, lifestyle, living conditions, and social interactions. Suggests that crime occurs when three elements converge: a motivated offender, suitable target, and lack of capable guardians.

To be a *motivated offender*, an offender must be willing to commit the offense and be capable of committing it. There are any number of reasons offenders may choose to offend. Although some offenders engage in "deviance as fun" (Riemer, 1981, p. 39) or enjoy the "seductions of crime" (Katz, 1988), motivations often go beyond the statement, "I *want* to commit a crime." Some offenders believe they have nothing to lose or few legitimate alternatives to crime; others have external motivations for committing a crime. For example, if an offender addicted to drugs needs money to buy them, he might decide that robbery is the most effective means to obtain the money.

A *suitable target* can be an object or person. The offender will often select a target that is both vulnerable and that produces the greatest rewards. For example, an armed robber may select a potential robbery victim (or target) based on the time of day, location of the crime, age of the victim, and demeanor of the victim. For instance, when considering the commission of a robbery, an offender may notice two targets: one a physically weak individual openly counting a large amount of money while walking down an empty, unlit alley and the other a bodybuilder on a busy street with no visible sign of valuables. The former would likely be judged the more suitable target. Based on signals of this sort, the potential offender will make the decision of whom, if anyone, to victimize. For property crimes, Clarke and Eck (2003, Section 29) suggest that offenders select targets that are most CRAVED—that is, "Concealable, Removable, Available, Valuable, Enjoyable, and Disposable." These characteristics identify targets that are easy to locate and steal without drawing undue attention. Related to this discussion is a debate around a concept called victim blaming, in which some have argued that victims' behaviors—not just those of the offender—should be considered when attempting to explain crime; see Box 5.3 for discussion of this controversial topic.

Capable guardians are people or objects that may serve as a deterrent to criminal activity. These may include police officers, watchful parents, concerned neighbors, and crime prevention security devices (e.g., alarms, effective lighting, fences), to name a few. When these people or security protections are absent, the likelihood of crime increases. For example, if the potential victim of the robbery in the previous paragraph was walking in a well-lighted area with a group of friends, the potential offender may decide

BOX 5.3

Ethics in Practice

VICTIM BLAMING

As noted in Chapter 1, victimology is the study of why certain people become victims of crime. According to Loseman and Bos (2012), many individuals have a psychological desire to believe that people deserve what they get. This is known as the "just world hypothesis." In other words, it is the idea that good things happen to good people and bad things happen to bad people (of course, different people may define "good" and "bad" differently). When this notion is challenged—that is, when a bad thing has happened to a person who is perceived as good—it can cause psychological discomfort. Sometimes, persons deal with this discomfort by adjusting their thinking to assume that the victim must have deserved the bad act, or brought it on himself or herself. In criminal justice, this can also take the form of victim blaming, in which victims of a crime experience dual victimizations. First, they are victimized by the criminal act itself. Second, they are victimized when society, the media, or the criminal justice system makes assumptions or statements suggesting that they were responsible for their victimization (Karmen, 2012).

Because of the dual victimization that it imposes, victim blaming is controversial. And the matter is complicated by acknowledging that there are various levels of victim involvement in crimes. In some cases, victims do not contribute to their victimization. In other cases, victim facilitation may occur, in which a victim makes it easier for an offender to commit a crime. This is usually an indirect action involving a lack of security precautions. For instance, if a victim leaves a laptop computer unattended in a public place and it is stolen, it would be classified as a victim-facilitated offense. In still other cases, victim precipitation may occur, in which a victim takes steps that more directly lead to a crime, such as by challenging a person to a fight and then becoming the victim of an assault (Karmen, 2012).

Suppose that a 19-year-old college student just left his place of employment and cashed his work check. He headed directly to a house party where he consumed a number of alcoholic beverages. Around 2:00 AM, he left the party and was walking home. He decided to take a shortcut through the alleyway when he was confronted by two armed male subjects who demanded that he empty his pockets. Fearing for his life, he did so and turned the money over to the robbers. The robbers fled the scene.

- Q Did the college student contribute to his own victimization? Why or why not? Could any measures have been taken to prevent this robbery?
- Q Should a victim's actions ever diminish the offender's culpability (i.e., blameworthiness) for an offense? That is, is it ethical for the criminal system to take into account a victim's actions? Explain your answer.
- Q In the 1970s, the modern Victim's Rights Movement began, which promoted rights for victims of crime. The movement developed in response to concerns that offenders' rights were protected while victims received little assistance. Is there an ethical obligation to provide services to victims? If so, to what rights or services do you think victims should be entitled?

that the risks of being identified and apprehended are too great, thereby deterring the robbery due to the guardianship that is present.

- Q What are the strengths and weaknesses of the genetic approach to explaining criminal deviance? How does this relate to the medicalization of deviance, as discussed in the previous chapter?
- Q Do you believe that classical theories explain Carl Panzram's criminal activity? Why or why not?
- Q As a police officer, your sergeant informs you that a number of adult males have been the victim of pickpockets. The crimes are occurring on Main Street during nonbusiness hours. Based on your newly acquired knowledge of the routine activities theory, what steps might you take to resolve the problem?

Psychological Theories of Crime and Criminality

FOCUSING QUESTION 5.3

How can psychological theories explain crime and deviant behavior?

Psychological theories focus on individuals and their thinking processes. With origins in the work of Sigmund Freud, psychological theories have since developed to include a wide range of explanations for deviant behavior.

PSYCHODYNAMIC THEORIES

Developed by Sigmund Freud (1856–1939), **psychodynamic theories** (also known as psychoanalytic theories) propose that human behavior is controlled by a variety of mental processes. Freud believed that the mind could be divided into three levels. The first was the conscious mind, which refers to one's current awareness. The second was the preconscious mind, where many memories are stored. The third was the unconscious mind, which is a warehouse of troublesome memories and feelings that are hidden from immediate awareness. Freud argued that "behaviors could be explained by traumatic experiences in early childhood that left their mark on the individual despite the fact the individual was not consciously aware of those experiences" (Vold et al., 1998, p. 91).

psychodynamic theory
A theory of crime suggesting that human behavior, including crime, is controlled by a variety of mental processes. The theory was developed by Sigmund Freud based on the dynamics of the id, ego, and superego.

To Freud, human behavior was driven by unconscious mental processes involving the id, superego, and ego (Seigel, 2002). The *id* represents the hedonistic side of people, seeking instant gratification and pleasure regardless of the consequences. The id contains urges, impulses, and intense energies (known as the libido, which also includes sexual drives) that may influence criminal activity. The superego represents the extreme opposite of the id. The *superego* is the moral compass of a person, influenced by parental values and societal norms. The ego represents the "umpire" between the id and superego. The *ego* attempts to keep both the id and superego balanced, resulting in appropriate behaviors.

Based on his many years of running an institution for delinquent youth, psychologist August Aichhorn "found that many children in his institution had *underdeveloped* superegos, so that the delinquency and criminality were primarily expressions of an unregulated id. Aichhorn attributed this to the fact that the parents of these children were either absent or unloving, so that the children failed to form the loving attachments necessary for the proper development of their superegos [emphasis in original]" (Vold et al., 1998, pp. 93–94). Aichorn also noted that delinquency could result when a child received "an overabundance of love" (p. 94), thereby spoiling the child by succumbing to the child's every request and demand.

DIFFERENTIAL ASSOCIATION

Edwin Sutherland introduced **differential association theory**, which proposes that criminal behavior is learned from others. Sutherland argued that learning occurs most effectively as a result of face-to-face interactions, usually among intimate social contacts such as family members and close friends. Individuals may learn how to commit crime as well as attitudes that promote criminal behavior (Sutherland, 1947). It is important to note that criminal behavior does not need to be learned solely from other offenders. One can learn criminal behavior from law-abiding people who simply approve of the illegal activity.

differential association theory
Suggests that criminal behavior occurs because offenders learn it from others.

Learning may occur in a number of ways. Social learning theory (also known as observational learning) holds that individuals learn behaviors by watching others. This was illustrated in a classic study by Bandura, Ross, and Ross (1961) in which the

authors determined that children who watched aggressive behavior subsequently behaved aggressively themselves by hitting an inflatable toy. Learning may also occur as a result of reinforcements and punishments in what is known as operant conditioning. According to the theory, behavior can be influenced through four techniques:

- Giving a positive reinforcement (i.e., a desirable reward) after a desired behavior;
- Giving a negative reinforcement (i.e., removing something that a person does not like) after a desired behavior;
- Giving a positive punishment (i.e., administering an unpleasant consequence) after an undesired behavior; or
- Giving a negative punishment (i.e., taking away something that a person likes) after an undesired behavior.

When criminal behaviors are punished or when noncriminal behaviors are reinforced, individuals may learn not to commit crime. However, consider the opposite scenario. When criminal behaviors are reinforced or when noncriminal behaviors are punished, individuals may then learn to commit crime. This often occurs through peer pressure or through association with family, friends, or influential others who engage in or support criminal activity.

neutralization theory
Suggests that crime occurs because offenders justify their criminal behavior through a series of neutralizations or excuses, including denial of responsibility, denial of injury, denial of the victim, condemnation of the condemners, and appeal to higher loyalties.

TECHNIQUES OF NEUTRALIZATION

Gresham Sykes and David Matza (1957) argued that offenders learn to justify their behavior through **neutralization theory**. That is, offenders suppress accepted social values and attitudes and learn to neutralize the negative consequences of their own behavior. Being able to do so allows them to drift into criminal behavior. Sykes and Matza identified five techniques that may neutralize accepted norms; in essence, these are excuses that some offenders may use to justify their criminal behavior. They include: (1) denial of responsibility, (2) denial of injury, (3) denial of the victim, (4) condemnation of the condemners, and (5) appeal to higher loyalties. Table 5.1 describes each in further detail.

TABLE 5.1 Five Techniques of Neutralization

Neutralization Technique	Description	Statement Example
Denial of responsibility	This blames forces beyond the control of the individual. The offender views himself or herself as a victim of circumstance.	"It wasn't my fault."
Denial of injury	The offender does not believe that he or she has caused any great harm to the victim, even if the act did violate the criminal law.	"The store can afford the loss."
Denial of the victim	Even when the offender accepts responsibility, admitting his or her illegal activity, the actions are viewed as rightful retaliation.	"They deserved what they got."
Condemnation of the condemners	Offenders may shift focus from their own actions to judging those who disapprove. They believe that the condemners (i.e., agents of social control) are hypocrites because they also commit similar illegal acts.	"The criminal justice system is corrupt."
Appeal to higher loyalties	The offender is conflicted between violating the law and violating a trust.	"I did it for my best friend."

Source: Sykes & Matza, 1957.

Sykes and Matza also recognized that many offenders do not view themselves as criminals because they only selectively violate the law—disobeying some laws while obeying others. Offenders may drift back and forth between criminality and law-abiding behavior. The neutralization process allows them to do so without having to view themselves as criminals. For instance, an otherwise law-abiding person might shoplift, neutralizing the negative consequences by thinking "no one is really getting hurt" (neutralization 2) and "the store deserved it for leaving merchandise out" (neutralization 3).

PERSONALITY AND CRIME

What role does personality play in criminality? *Personality* refers to an individual's patterns of behavior, mental traits, thoughts, emotions, temperament, and feelings. Personality traits suspected as links to criminal behavior include aggression, hostility, impulsivity, and hyperactivity, to name a few.

Hans Eysenck (1964) proposed that criminals can be distinguished from noncriminals by their lack of conscience and by having other personality traits linked to antisocial behavior (to be discussed momentarily), such as extroversion and neuroticism. *Extreme extroverts* are thrill seekers and impulsive. *Neuroticism* occurs when a person lacks emotional stability and is viewed as irrational, moody, anxious, and tense. Eysenck argued that potential criminals possess both neurotic and extroverted personality traits because they may act in a self-destructive manner without viewing their behavior as harmful or dangerous (Eysenck, 1964).

Michael Gottfredson and Travis Hirschi (1990) have suggested that self-control is a key personality trait that can influence criminality. Specifically, they argue that persons with low self-control are "impulsive, insensitive, physical (as opposed to mental), risk-taking, short-sighted, and nonverbal, and they will tend therefore to engage in criminal and analogous acts" (p. 90). Low self-control is viewed as a stable trait, meaning that it has its origins in childhood and does not change over an individual's lifetime.

Psychoses are also associated with criminal activity. Persons with psychoses lose touch with reality. They may experience delusions (i.e., stable but false beliefs, such as believing that they are a deity or a famous historical figure) and/or hallucinations (e.g., false sensory perceptions, such as hearing voices that are not there in reality). "The psychosis that is most often linked to criminal behavior is schizophrenia, which involves disordered thought patterns characterized by fantasy, delusion, and incoherence . . . Schizophrenia is sometimes associated with acts of violence, including homicide, particularly against people who are thought to be threatening to the schizophrenic" (Conklin, 1998, pp. 175–176).

TABLE 5.2 Diagnostic Criteria for Antisocial Personality Disorder

A pervasive pattern of disregard for and violation of the rights of others, occurring since age 15 years, as indicated by three (or more) of the following:
• Failure to conform to social norms with respect to lawful behaviors, as indicated by repeatedly performing acts that are grounds for arrest. • Deceitfulness, as indicated by repeatedly lying, use of aliases, or conning others for personal profit or pleasure. • Impulsivity or failure to plan ahead. • Irritability and aggressiveness, as indicated by repeated physical fights or assaults. • Reckless disregard for safety of self or others. • Consistent irresponsibility, as indicated by repeated failure to sustain consistent work behavior or honor financial obligations. • Lack of remorse, as indicated by being indifferent to or rationalizing having hurt, mistreated, or stolen from another.

Source: American Psychiatric Association, 2013, p. 659.

antisocial personality
A personality type associated with criminal activity and marked by failure to conform to norms, deceitfulness, impulsivity, aggressiveness, disregard for safety, irresponsibility, and lack of remorse.

Finally, antisocial personality disorder is associated with criminal activity. This does not refer to persons who isolate themselves from others. On the contrary, many **antisocial personality** types, also known as *sociopaths* or *psychopaths,* thrive on personal contact but do so for the purpose of manipulation and deceit. Table 5.2 lists the characteristics of antisocial personalities.

Q What do you see as the strengths and weaknesses of psychodynamic theories of crime?

Q How would the neutralization and personality theories apply to Carl Panzram? Explain your answer.

Q In what ways is crime learned through differential association theory? What prevention programs could be developed that use learning theories to reduce crime?

Sociocultural Theories of Crime and Criminality

FOCUSING QUESTION 5.4

How can sociocultural theories explain crime and deviant behavior?

The psychological theories described in the previous section focus primarily on individual-level explanations for deviant behavior. However, some conditions within society beyond the individual may also influence criminal deviance. Therefore, to more fully understand the causes of deviant behavior, it is important to consider the following sociocultural theories.

SOCIAL DISORGANIZATION THEORY

social disorganization theory
Focuses on the community environmental factors that may lead to crime, including poverty, breakdown of family and social institutions, high turnover of residents, and lack of attachment to the community.

concentric zone theory
Explains criminality in cities by suggesting that multiple zones, diagramed as concentric circles, emerge from the city's center. The theory holds that crime is most likely to occur in the transitional zone, a residential area undergoing change and marked by social disorganization.

The work of sociologists Robert Park, Ernest Burgess, and Roderick McKenzie from the University of Chicago resulted in the development of **social disorganization theory**, which focuses on environmental conditions that lead to crime. Because of its association with the City of Chicago, this is sometimes called the *Chicago School* of criminology. Environmental factors leading to crime may include poverty, the breakdown of families and social institutions, a high turnover of residents (i.e., many persons moving in and then out of the neighborhood), and a lack of bonds to the community. Areas with these characteristics are said to be socially disorganized.

Popularizing social disorganization theory, Clifford Shaw and Henry McKay (1942) developed the **concentric zone theory** to explain criminality in cities. Shaw and McKay divided Chicago into five concentric zones (each two miles wide) to explain social development and crime patterns. Imagine a large circle, beginning at the city's core and spreading outward (illustrated in Figure 5.2). *Zone One* was the downtown, composed primarily of businesses. *Zone Two,* or the "transitional" zone, was formerly a residential community undergoing transition to commercial or industrial uses. *Zone Three* contained the "workingmen's homes," occupied by the working class forced to move from Zone Two as its transition occurred. *Zone Four,* the "residential zone," is where the majority of suburban families resided. *Zone Five,* the "commuter zone," was the most desirable of residential locations, comprising expensive single-family dwellings; residents could drive to the city for work but were far enough away to be distant from the hustle and bustle of city stress (Lanier & Henry, 1998).

Shaw and McKay discovered that Zone Two produced the highest rate of crime and other social problems, including drug abuse, suicide, and mental illness. They theorized that as one resided closer to the business district in an area undergoing transition, there would be minimal community bonding and socialization, a lack of social resources, greater residential transition, and lower levels of security, thereby creating social

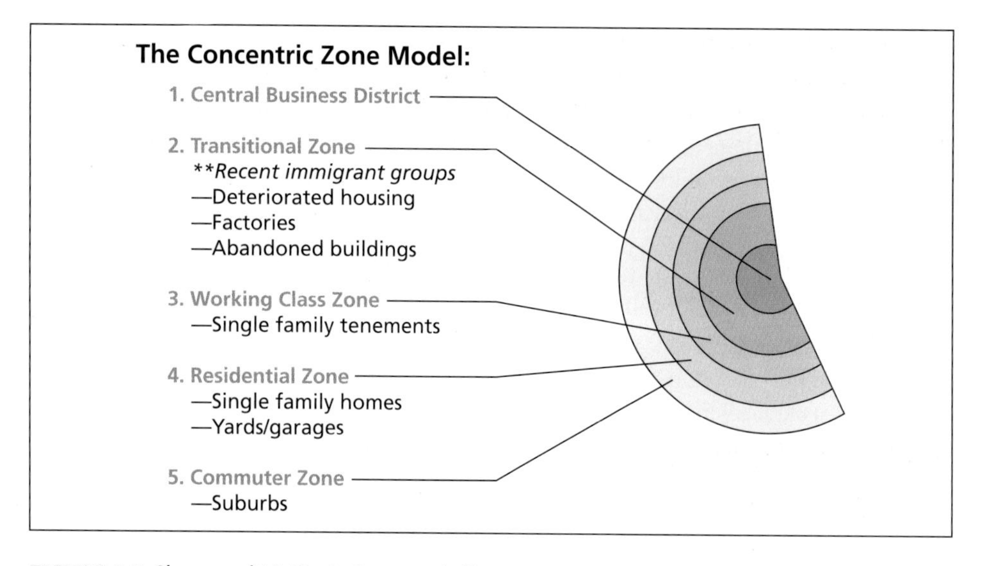

FIGURE 5.2 Shaw and McKay's Concentric Zones.
Source: http://www.csiss.org/classics/uploads/conzone.jpg

disorganization. Today, the concentric zone model has come under some criticism for being too specific to the unique aspects of the time (early twentieth century) and place (Chicago) where it was developed, as other spatial models for understanding urban patterns have since been proposed (e.g., Judd & Simpson, 2011). However, the general concept of social disorganization theory, with its notion that crime varies between neighborhoods because those areas that experience social disorganization also experience more crime, has remained a powerful criminological perspective.

STRAIN THEORY

As defined by Robert Merton (1968), **strain theory** argues that society defines certain goals (principally the accumulation of wealth) as worthy of attainment. Society also identifies the accepted means through which it is expected that the goals will be accomplished (such as having access to education, jobs paying a livable wage with opportunities for advancement, transportation to and from work, and so on). When members of society, predominantly the lower socioeconomic class, fail to achieve socially valued goals because they do not have access to the means of achieving them, frustration (or strain) results. To relieve this frustration, some indigent (i.e., poverty-stricken) persons may seek criminal means—such as stealing, operating an illegal business, and so on—to achieve their goals. Others may reject socially accepted goals in the first place and either seek an escape from society, such as through drug use, or pursue alternate goals of their own choosing, which may include the deliberate pursuit of deviant activities.

strain theory
Suggests that crime occurs when members of society, predominantly the lower socioeconomic class, are unable to achieve goals valued by society (principally, the accumulation of wealth). Failure to achieve goals results in frustration, leading some to turn to criminal activity to achieve goals.

Robert Agnew (1992) expanded the concept of strain theory by suggesting that it could apply to all persons regardless of their socioeconomic status. This was a departure from the preceding theories, which focused primarily on class-based differences. According to Agnew, anyone could experience the kind of strain that results from a failure to achieve a desired goal, the loss of something that a person perceives as bringing value to his or her life, or being faced with unpleasant events or circumstances. The impact of these strains is heightened when "they are (1) greater in magnitude or size, (2) recent, (3) of long duration, and (4) clustered in time" (p. 64). Individuals (again, regardless of income) may address these strains through positive coping strategies or by turning to crime or deviant behaviors. Many factors, including those expressed in other psychological and sociocultural theories, may influence how an individual copes with strain.

DELINQUENT SUBCULTURES

Recall from Chapter 4 the discussion of subcultures, which are groups with norms that differ from those of the broader society. If those norms are deviant and supportive of criminal activity, then members of the subculture may turn to crime. Albert Cohen (1955) argued that juveniles seek to attain status, usually from their peers. Cohen noted that status could be *achieved* (i.e., that which is earned through competition among peers or accomplishments at school) or *ascribed* (that which is acquired through the status already held by family members). According to Cohen, strain occurs when neither ascribed nor achieved status is obtainable, in which case youth reject middle-class values and seek other means of achieving status. To do so, youth may create their own system of values and norms, in turn creating delinquent subcultures, to acquire the status they seek. Cohen argued that this process might lead juveniles to turn to gangs and criminal activity.

Walter Miller (1958) argued that delinquency resulted from efforts to achieve a *different* set of goals from those promoted by social norms—goals that he labeled "lower class culture" (p. 5). Miller highlighted six focal concerns of lower-class culture, including trouble, toughness, smartness, excitement, fate, and autonomy.

Getting into *trouble* or staying out of trouble is a concern in Miller's lower-class culture. While remaining clear of trouble minimizes contact with law enforcement authorities, non-law-abiding behavior may provide status among peers.

Toughness is based on bravery, masculinity, and physical prowess. Miller found that youth raised in single-parent female-headed households may lack positive male role models and, to avoid being called weak or soft, may exaggerate their male bravado.

Smartness is the ability to remain streetwise, including the ability to con others while being careful not to be conned. *Excitement* includes thrills and risks, legal or illegal, to avoid boredom. Excitement may take the form of gambling, drug and alcohol use, joining a gang, or other outlets.

Fate is a function of *external control,* which is a belief that life events are the result of luck and chance rather than hard work and effort. This stems from a belief that individuals possess little control over their lives, accepting the adage "whatever happens, happens." *Autonomy* is the desire to remain independent from authority figures. Authority figures may include parents, police, and teachers.

Criminologists Richard Cloward and Lloyd Ohlin (1960) integrated subcultural deviance and social disorganization theories. Cloward and Ohlin argued that in socially disorganized communities, juveniles may lack adult role models and opportunities for success, whether through legitimate or illegitimate means. They called these juveniles *retreatists,* who resort to drugs, sex, or other activities as a means to escape societal expectations.

SOCIAL CONTROL THEORY

According to criminologist Travis Hirschi (1969), criminal deviance occurs when an individual's bonds to society (i.e., social bonds) are weak or broken. Social bonds are provided by individuals, groups, and organizations that connect a person to the community, including parents, friends, religious groups, clubs, and others. Hirschi identified four components to social bonds: attachment, commitment, involvement, and belief.

Attachment is related to sensitivity. According to Hirschi, if a person is insensitive to the opinions of others and is willing to violate social norms, he or she will feel free to engage in deviant or criminal activity. Conversely, being attached to family, friends, and other social institutions means a person is sensitive to their opinions and therefore less likely to violate norms, in order to avoid negative reactions (this is related to informal social control).

Commitment occurs when a person invests time and energy to meet a personal goal, such as attaining a college degree. Of course, one can be committed to

accomplishing criminal activity as well by focusing attention on deviant behavior. Therefore, persons who are invested in accomplishing *conventional, socially accepted,* goals are less likely to engage in criminal conduct, as they do not want to jeopardize progress toward their goals.

Involvement or participation in conventional activities is a key factor in social control. According to Hirschi, a person engrossed with work, community organizations, and other conventional activities does not have the opportunity to commit deviant acts because he or she is too occupied with other tasks. On the other hand, those with too much idle time are more likely to engage in criminal conduct. In addition, involvement with conventional activities may promote prosocial norms and foster informal social control.

Belief occurs when people share a common set of socially accepted norms, values, and moral principles. Although most persons may understand that deviant acts are wrong, such acts are more likely to occur if the common set of beliefs and values is threatened or absent.

Hirschi's **social bond theory** has been supported by recent research. For example, in a study of adolescent risk-taking, researchers (Vermeersch, T'Sjoen, Kaufman & Van Houtte, 2013) found a strong relationship between a lack of social control and juvenile risk-taking. Furthermore, risk-taking increases when adolescent peers are also risk-takers (see also Boman, Krohn, Gibson, & Stogner, 2012; Intravia, Jones, & Piquero, 2012).

social bond theory
Suggests that crime occurs when an individual's bonds to society are weak or broken. Bonds include attachment to prosocial persons and organizations, commitment to prosocial goals, involvement in prosocial activities, and belief in a common set of prosocial values and morals.

Recall that, with Gottfredson, Hirshi also helped to develop self-control theory, which was classified as a psychological theory of personality in the previous section. Hirschi (2004) now argues that social control and self-control are basically the same. He prefers the use of the term "inhibitors," which he defines as the "factors that one takes into account in deciding whether or not to commit a criminal act" (p. 545). A study of adult offenders drew upon both of Hirschi's perspectives, finding that low levels of social bonding and low self-control were associated with increased likelihood to commit crime (Morris, Gerber, & Menard, 2011). As such, Hirschi's approach has the potential to bridge psychological and sociocultural explanations for crime by drawing on both perspectives.

LABELING THEORY

The idea behind **labeling theory** (which developed from a sociological perspective called *symbolic interaction*) assumes that once society places a label on a person, that individual will self-identify with the label and behave accordingly. In other words, the theory holds that labels serve as self-fulfilling prophecies. For example, if a parent repeatedly tells a child that he is a troublemaker, whether the label is accurate or not, labeling theory would presume that the child would accept and internalize the label and therefore get into trouble.

labeling theory
Assumes that once society places a label on a person, that individual will self-identify with the label and behave accordingly. If a person is labeled as a delinquent, deviant, or criminal, the theory suggests that the person will accept that label and therefore engage in delinquent, deviant, or criminal activity.

Edwin Lemert (1951), a proponent of labeling theory, indicated that the labeling process includes two forms of deviance: primary and secondary. *Primary deviance* is an initial deviant act. Sometimes, committing a deviant act does not negatively stigmatize or label a person. For instance, assume that a student shoplifted merchandise from a store but was never identified or apprehended. Years later, perhaps the student became a prominent business or civic leader. Because the student was never labeled as a thief or criminal, she was able to move past the incident, becoming successful in her profession.

Secondary deviance occurs when an individual commits a deviant or unlawful act—primary deviance—and the incident then comes to the attention of others, including family, friends, or the criminal justice system, any of whom may apply and reinforce a negative label. Unable to remove that negative label, the "deviant" heads in a downward spiral. After accepting and internalizing the label of deviant, the individual starts to act

as though he or she actually is deviant, including the commission of further deviant acts. These subsequent deviant acts, committed as a result of the labeling, are known as the secondary deviance.

conflict criminology
Suggests that crime is a consequence of the oppression of the lower classes by rich and powerful elites.

Marxist criminology
A form of conflict criminology which argues that there is a strong relationship between capitalism, class conflict, and crime. The theory suggests that persons with political power and wealth create laws to suppress the lower class.

For example, assume that the student who shoplifted was apprehended, arrested, taken to jail for booking, taken to court, found guilty, and sentenced to probation. Further assume that the offense became widely known and circulated among the student's friends and family, as well as in the arrest reports posted in the local newspaper. If the student was negatively labeled (e.g., subject to negative remarks labeling her as a criminal, a bad person, or other names), as opposed to being reintegrated into the community (e.g., forgiven, viewed as rehabilitated, offense called a youthful indiscretion), then the process described by labeling theory would begin. The student would consider herself to be a criminal and would find herself treated negatively by others. Internalizing these negative feelings, the student might then turn to additional deviant or criminal activity. The cycle would then repeat itself. This is the essence of labeling theory.

Frank Tannenbaum (1938) described a process he called "the dramatization of the 'evil'" (p. 21), arguing that labeling a child as "evil" plays a vital role in that child's future criminality. The labeled child not only accepts the "tag" but also seeks others who are similarly labeled. Groups of labeled youth may then join together in delinquent subcultures pursuing delinquent enterprises—all as a result of the initial way the child was labeled.

CONFLICT CRIMINOLOGY

The city of Detroit "averages about 14 arsons [deliberately set fires] a day" (Neavling, 2013, para. 11). In recent years, the city's population has declined and the city has had to cut the fire department's budget. Many of the arsons occur in abandoned buildings. How would the various criminological theories presented in this chapter explain arson?

Conflict criminology, also known as *critical criminology, conflict theory, radical criminology*, or *new criminology*, holds that crime is a consequence of the oppression of the lower classes by the rich and powerful elites. In conflict criminology, "[u]nequal distribution of power produces conflict" (Seigel, 2002, p. 174), which becomes the foundation for criminal activity. This theory goes hand in hand with critical theories of law as described in Chapter 3; you may wish to review the two together. There are many varieties of conflict criminology, several of which are profiled here.

Marxist criminology argues that there is a strong relationship between capitalism, class conflict, and crime. The theory argues that individuals with political power and wealth create laws to keep the lower class "in their place." For instance, Marxist theorist Richard Quinney (1970) argued that definitions of crime are created and applied by the powerful elite to shape the enforcement and administration of the criminal law against members of the lower classes.

Feminist criminology (e.g., Jurik, 1999; Wonders, 1999) developed in the late 1960s and gained prominence during the Women's Movement in the early 1970s. Feminist criminologists examine the relationship between gender inequality, male dominance, and the exploitation of women under capitalism. Traditional criminology focuses primarily on male offenders and victims, ignoring gender differences in criminal activity, gender differences in victimization, and inequality in the division of labor (i.e., the exploitation of women in the work force, including salary disparities). Feminist criminologists attempt to address these issues.

Peacemaking criminology is grounded in social justice. "In the peacemaking frame of mind, all imbalances of power *over* . . . others are defined as 'violence' [emphasis in original]" (Pepinsky, 1999b, p. 56). Therefore, traditional forms of punishment, such as incarceration, are

considered counterproductive to justice because they reflect an imbalance of power. Peacemaking criminologists instead argue that the encouragement of communication and relationships can promote justice and heal social wrongs. "Peacemaking is the art and science of weaving and reweaving oneself with others into a social fabric of mutual love, respect, and concern" (Pepinsky, 1999b, p. 59).

feminist criminology
A criminological perspective that examines the relationship between gender inequality, male dominance, and the exploitation of women under capitalism. Feminist criminologists focus on gender differences in crime, female offenders and victims, and gender inequities in the division of labor.

peacemaking criminology
A perspective arguing that the encouragement of communication and relationships can promote justice and heal social wrongs. Views traditional forms of punishment, such as incarceration, as counterproductive because they reflect an imbalance of power.

Q What do you think are the strengths and weaknesses of the sociocultural theories of crime presented in this section? Are there any sociocultural theories that you think are more effective than others in explaining why crime occurs?

Q Do you think any of the sociocultural theories explain Carl Panzram's criminal behavior? If so, explain how.

Q Are there any programs that could be developed to prevent crime by addressing its causes as suggested by the sociocultural theories presented?

The Study of Deviance in Criminal Justice

FOCUSING QUESTION 5.5

Why is the study of deviance important for criminal justice?

This chapter has provided a foundational overview of criminal deviance and theories that explain it. Understanding criminal deviance is essential for the study and practice of criminal justice. In Chapter 3, we argued that it is important for criminal justice students and practitioners to understand the origins of the laws they are studying and enforcing on a daily basis. An understanding of why individuals engage in deviant behavior—and crime, in particular—is equally essential.

If we can understand *why* people commit crimes, we can design policies and programs that will *reduce* crime by addressing its causes. Regrettably, as noted criminal justice scholar Samuel Walker (2006) observed, "most current crime control proposals are nonsense" (p. 11), in part because they "rest on faith rather than facts" (p. 22; see also Lab, 2004). Criminologist James Austin (2003) has gone so far as to label criminology "irrelevant" (p. 557) because it has not received much attention from those responsible for making criminal justice policies. Let this be a challenge to you as a future criminal justice practitioner and scholar: consider how theories of criminal deviance can be applied to prevent crime and then advocate those solutions that have a sound basis and the promise for effectiveness rather than those resting on mere speculation.

A word of caution is in order, though. Understanding the causes of crime is a complex area of study. In fact, there are many theories that were not presented in this chapter, and no single theory of deviance or crime is perfect. Different individuals commit deviant acts for different reasons. Some may be influenced by antisocial personality disorder (a psychological theory), others due to genetic factors (a biological theory), still others due to strain (a sociocultural theory), and many for other reasons altogether (see Box 5.4 for an example of another factor that is associated with crime). Even the same offender may be influenced by different theories at different times. Therefore, it is important to resist the temptation to identify a single "right" theory but rather to consider how each can contribute to our understanding of criminal behavior.

Some criminologists have worked to develop integrated theories, which blend an array of theoretical perspectives to produce a more comprehensive explanation of crime. One type of integrated theory is known as **life course theory**, which explores how involvement in criminal activity changes as offenders grow older and encounter new life circumstances (e.g., marriage, full-time employment, and other major life activities). Life course theories posit that, over the course of a person's life, multiple forces

life course theory
Explores how involvement in criminal activity changes as offenders grow older and encounter new life circumstances.

BOX 5.4

Research in Action

ANIMAL ABUSE AND CRIME

The relationship between animal abuse and crime is well documented. The gradation hypothesis suggests that cruelty to animals at an early age is a cause and step toward subsequent violence directed toward humans (Bierne, 1999). Research has provided support for this hypothesis. Aruke, Levin, Luke, and Ascione (1999) discovered that there is a relationship between animal abuse and a variety of antisocial behaviors, including interpersonal violence, drug offenses, property crimes, and public disorder offenses. Henry (2004) reported that survey respondents who had observed or participated in acts of animal cruelty scored higher on a self-report delinquency scale compared to those who did not. In a study of 180 prison inmates, Overton, Hensley and Tallichet (2012) found that "respondents who had committed recurrent childhood animal cruelty were more likely to have committed recurrent adult violence towards humans" (p. 899), including murder, rape, robbery and battery.

Even witnessing animal abuse can have subsequent negative effects. For instance, research has found that witnessing animal abuse is related to aggression (Felthous, 1979), insensitivity (Ascione, 1993), and even criminal activity (Arluke et al., 1999).

Animal abuse has also been found to be related to crimes of intimate partner violence. For instance, Faver and Strand (2003) report that abusers threaten, hurt, or kill companion animals as a means to control their intimate partners. Ascione et al. (2007) reported that female victims of intimate partner violence residing in shelters were nearly 11 times more likely to report that their partner had hurt or killed pets, compared to women who had not experienced intimate partner violence. They also found that animal abusers used intimidation, threats, and power as a means to control their partners. It is important to note that the relationship between animal abuse and domestic violence is not isolated to heterosexual couples, but may also impact same-sex couples (see Burke & Owen, 2006).

All states have laws against animal abuse, which are supported for two reasons, corresponding to two philosophies of law from Chapter 3. They include viewing animal abuse as a moral wrong, illustrating legal moralism, and recognizing the harmful outcomes that are associated with animal abuse, illustrating legal positivism (Wagner, Owen, & Burke, 2013). The research presented in this box is only a fraction of that which has explored the link between animal abuse and other deviant behaviors, particularly human violence. It does signal that it is an issue worthy of attention from the criminal justice system.

- Q What are the implications of these research findings for criminal justice professionals? Think in terms of the development of law, strategies, and tactics. Explain your answer.
- Q Some jurisdictions have enacted legislation requiring veterinarians to report incidents of animal abuse to law enforcement. What is your opinion of this legislation? What do you think are the advantages and disadvantages?
- Q The PETS Act is a federal law that requires states receiving federal disaster funding to make accommodations for companion animals in the case of evacuations. Should there be a law to require domestic violence shelters to make accommodations for companion animals belonging to victims? Why or why not?

(drawing upon biological, psychological, and sociocultural perspectives) can combine to influence behavior in different ways depending on the stage in life at which a person finds himself or herself (Akers, 2000). Life course theory has been the subject of much study and offers a promising means of integrating a variety of perspectives, including some described in this chapter, to better understand and prevent crime (see Gibson & Krohn, 2013; DeLisi & Beaver, 2011).

Over time, new theories (e.g., integrated theories) emerge to explain crime and deviance as older theories are revisited. As theories change, their implications for criminal justice policy and practice also change.

- Q Having considered the variety of criminological theories presented in this chapter, are there any that strike you as particularly strong explanations of crime? As particularly weak explanations? Why?
- Q Do you think any of the theoretical perspectives presented in this chapter could be integrated to provide a more comprehensive explanation of why crime occurs? If so, how?

Conclusion

Deviant acts are those that violate social norms, including crime. As has been illustrated, there are many possible explanations for deviant behavior. Each explanation is important not only for enhancing our understanding of why crime occurs, but also because each may shape policy recommendations for how to better prevent or respond to crime. Although it is unlikely that we will ever fully understand criminal behavior, and while it is virtually impossible to imagine that a single theory can definitively explain all crimes, it remains important to consider why crime occurs. As new theories continue to emerge, we simultaneously continue the quest of understanding how social control can better address crime. In doing so, however, the values of justice and fairness must be upheld, and it is to these issues that we will turn in Unit III.

Criminal Justice Problem Solving

Youth Gangs

While there is no single definition of a youth gang, they are generally understood as groups with the following characteristics: "The group has three or more members, generally aged 12–24; Members share an identity, typically linked to a name, and often other symbols; Members view themselves as a gang, and they are recognized by others as a gang; The group has some permanence and a degree of organization; The group is involved in an elevated level of criminal activity" (National Gang Center, n.d., para. 2). Regardless of how they have been defined, gangs have a long history in the United States, dating back to the early 1800s (Howell, Egley, Tita, & Griffiths, 2011).

Since that time, gangs have been a topic of conversation for the criminal justice system. Surveys of contemporary law enforcement agencies indicate that gangs are present in urban, suburban, and rural areas, although they are most frequently encountered in large cities. Since 2001, there has been an increase in the percentage of law enforcement agencies indicating that their jurisdiction has a gang problem (Howell, Egley, Tita, & Griffiths, 2011). In 2010, reports from law enforcement agencies suggested that there were approximately 29,400 gangs with approximately 756,000 members in the United States (Egley & Howell, 2012).

Research indicates that joining a gang can produce many negative outcomes. For example, gang members are more likely than non–gang members to become involved in violent criminal activity (Melde, Diem, & Drake, 2012; Melde & Esbensen, 2013). In addition, gang members, when compared to non–gang members, are more focused on social status, are more likely to exhibit anti-authority attitudes, and are more likely to victim-blame (Alleyne & Wood, 2010).

Why do youth join gangs? Decker and Van Winkle (1996) conducted in-depth interviews with 101 active gang members. Each interview took around two hours and addressed a number of issues, one of which was the decision to join a gang. "In declining order of importance, they were: (1) protection, (2) the prompting of friends and/or relatives, (3) the desire to make money through drug sales, and (4) the status associated with being a gang member" (p. 65). Jankowski (1991) conducted research with 37 gangs in a variety of cities. To complete his study, he spent considerable time with each gang, talking to their members and observing and participating in gang activities. This is a form of research known as participant observation. Jankowski found that members joined gangs for the following reasons: the opportunity to make money; as a form of recreation and entertainment; "they see the gang as offering them anonymity" (p. 44); for protection; as a form of rebelling against the expectation that they will be pushed into low-income jobs; and because the gang has a history of being a long-standing part of the community.

Assume that you have been assigned as the supervisor to a gang task force. There have been numerous complaints from concerned community members, teachers, and parents about the increase in gang membership and activity in your city. The police chief has requested that you and your officers take immediate action to rectify the situation. Based on the above material and on your reading of the chapter, address the following questions:

- Q How would theories from this chapter explain the decision to join a gang?
- Q What factors might prevent juveniles from joining gangs? That is, why do some juveniles not join gangs?
- Q Based on your responses to the preceding two questions, and considering the above discussion of why some youths join gangs, what kind of program(s) could reduce the likelihood that juveniles will join gangs?

Perspectives on Justice

Photo Essay: Justice, Privacy, and Enforcement

Unit II showed that both the definitions of deviance and the explanations for it are complex. It is a challenge to understand the sometimes shifting distinctions between those behaviors that are largely viewed as acceptable, those that are viewed as unacceptable but controlled informally, and those that are viewed as unacceptable and regulated through criminal law. For criminal justice professionals, it is the law that guides action. Once a behavior is criminalized, regardless of the reason, the criminal justice system becomes responsible for addressing it, whether through prevention programs targeting the underlying causes of the behavior or through enforcement activities that result in criminal investigations, arrests, prosecutions, and punishments. The goal of the criminal justice system is to seek justice in these activities—a task significant enough that "establish justice" is listed second only to "form a more perfect union" in the goals contained within the preamble of the U.S. Constitution.

But establishing justice is no simple endeavor. It requires considerations about what justice means, how it is to be established, and what limits are imposed on its pursuit. Controversies related to police practices illustrate these dilemmas. What each of the following cases has in common is that the dispute centers on how far the police may go in conducting observations or searches that may have the potential to intrude upon individual privacy. When should law enforcement officers be permitted to conduct searches? Should there be any limits on law enforcement observations of individuals and their behavior? Courts of appeals are generally the arbiters of these questions, as they hear cases about police practices. Each case requires careful consideration of what the pursuit of justice means. In many instances, the issue emerges as a conflict between notions of privacy, on the one hand, and the need for the police to acquire information about criminal cases, on the other.

A phone booth was at the center of one of the most famous cases about search and seizure. In the days before cell phones, phone booths dotted the landscape as sheltered locations from which a person could make a telephone call when away from home or work. In *Katz v. United States,* agents from the Federal Bureau of Investigation (FBI) affixed a device to the exterior of a phone booth, which monitored and recorded what was said inside the booth. This allowed the FBI to obtain evidence that led to Katz's conviction for violation of federal gambling laws, although no warrant had been obtained to permit this electronic surveillance. Was justice upheld in this case? The Supreme Court thought not, expressing concern for Katz's Fourth Amendment rights. Justice Steward wrote for the Court, "the Fourth Amendment protects people, not places. What a person knowingly exposes to the public, even in his own home or office, is not a subject of Fourth Amendment protection. But what he seeks to preserve as private, even in an area accessible to the public, may be constitutionally protected" (*Katz v. United States,* 1967, p. 351). The Court viewed phone booths as areas of privacy, rendering inadmissible the recordings that were made without a warrant. How do you define privacy? Do you think a phone booth meets the definition? What about a pay phone that is not enclosed in a booth?

Are your vehicle's license plates private? Many police agencies now use cameras that have the capability of scanning a vehicle's license plates. The data recorded can be compared to database records to alert police if they encounter a vehicle that is stolen, connected to a crime, or potentially driven by a wanted suspect. Supporters of the program argue that it promotes public safety with little impact on privacy, since license plates are in public view. Opponents of the program argue that the photographic images can intrude upon an individual's privacy and that the scanners can be used to track a vehicle's movements over time (Healey, Toppo, & Meier, 2013). In Virginia, controversy surrounded the decision to use the cameras to record the license plates of all vehicles attending the 2009 presidential inauguration and 2008 campaign rallies for both parties (Bowes, 2013). If you were a judge and a lawsuit was filed challenging the use of license plate scanners (and at least one has been—Rubin & Winton, 2013), how would you rule? What principle(s) would guide your decision?

The Supreme Court case of *Terry v. Ohio* (1968) granted police the authority to conduct a "stop and frisk" of individuals when they had reasonable suspicion that criminal activity might be occurring. The "stop and frisk" allows officers to briefly detain a person and to conduct a pat-down of the outer clothing to check for weapons. In New York City, police implemented an aggressive stop-and-frisk program in 2003. Over the decade that followed, stops increased more than 600%. Yet, only 6% of these stops resulted in an arrest. Moreover, critics charged that the stops were not based on the constitutional standard of reasonable suspicion, but rather were conducted on the basis of racial profiling. Consider that young black men accounted for approximately 25% of all New York City Police Department (NYPD) stops, even though they comprise only about 1.9% of the New York City population. Similarly, young Latino men accounted for 16% of NYPD stops, but comprise only 2.8% of the city's population (see New York Civil Liberties Union, 2012). In 2013, a judge ruled unconstitutional New York City's program on the basis of these racial disparities (*Floyd et al. v. City of New York*, 2013). While some "stop-and-frisks" may continue, there are restrictions, one of which was the judge's order that the NYPD implement a program in which officers wear cameras to record their interactions with the public (Bruinius, 2013). Do you agree with the judge's ruling about the program? Do you think the cameras are a good idea? Why or why not?

Is there a privacy right for bodily fluids? What if they may contain incriminating information? Consider the U.S. Supreme Court case of *Ferguson v. City of Charleston* in which a hospital administered drug tests to pregnant women without their consent. Women who tested positive were subject to arrest. What are the implications of this case for establishing justice? How would you assess the role, needs, and/or rights of the women, the hospital, the police, the fetuses, or the newborns? How would you balance the justice interests of each party? Does the program discriminate against pregnant females, since other persons are not subject to similar testing? The Supreme Court held that the hospital's practice constituted unreasonable search and seizure, stating that "the threat of criminal sanctions to deter pregnant women from using cocaine" was not a sufficient reason to override the requirement of a warrant for this type of testing (*Ferguson v. City of Charleston,* 2001, p. 70). Do you agree or disagree with the decision of the Court?

A more recent controversy has emerged around the issue of body scanners in airports. The scanners are part of preflight screening and "provide a clear image of passengers under their clothes and are meant to find threats that existing metal detectors cannot, like ceramic knives and bomb components" (Wald, 2010, para. 12). How would this correspond with the *Katz* decision? Does it matter whether or not images would be saved or deleted? Does it matter whether the machines have image filters that blur the genital area? Does it matter whether the machine operator sees only the scan image or also the person being scanned? After public protest, the scanners, which some called "virtual strip searches" (Ahlers, 2013, para. 1), were removed from airports and replaced with alternative devices that generate less obtrusive images. What role should public opinion play in criminal justice policy? How should policy makers resolve debates about controversial criminal justice practices?

Justice truly is a balance, and thus the personification of Lady Justice is always shown carrying scales. When law enforcement practices such as those above are challenged, judges review them to determine whether they are acceptable or whether they go too far. If judges decide that they go too far, they may rule them unconstitutional, in which case the evidence collected may be ruled inadmissible in court—even if it is evidence that could prove the guilt of a person accused of a crime. This is called the exclusionary rule, as it requires the exclusion of evidence that is improperly obtained. Do you think that the exclusionary rule is a just practice? This may depend on how you define "justice."

It is important to consider the role of "justice" in "criminal justice." That is the focus of this unit, as we will consider the many ways in which justice may be defined. This may include considerations of whether the right outcomes (however they may be defined) are reached, whether they are conducted in a manner that is fair, and whether they follow the requirements of the Constitution—all of which are illustrated in the above scenarios. As you proceed through the chapters in this unit, you will learn more about the different meanings of justice, how justice policy is made, and how decisions about criminal procedure influence the pursuit of justice in American society.

6

Concepts of Justice

Learning Objectives

(1) Explain the concept of justice. (2) Compare and contrast the various types of justice. (3) Explain distributive justice as it relates to criminal justice issues. (4) Describe how individual and community interests are reflected through distributive justice.

Key Terms

justice
just world
exoneration
procedural justice
social justice
individual justice
vigilante justice
transitional justice
ideology
discourse perspective justice
postmodernism
distributive justice
commutative justice
utilitarian justice
retributive justice
restorative justice
veil of ignorance
mechanical model
authoritarian model
compassionate model
participatory model
justice reinvestment

Key People

Nelson Mandela
Jürgen Habermas
David Schmidtz
Aristotle
Jeremy Bentham
John Rawls
Malcolm Feeley
Bob Altemeyer

Sexting

Case Study

Before reading this case study, take a few moments to reflect on the following question. Make some notes about your answer and be prepared to explain it and share it with your instructor and classmates.

Q What is justice? Think carefully about what justice means to you, how justice can be achieved, and how you might recognize justice.

Assume that a 16-year-old male (Max) and a 16 year-old female (Frieda), both of whom attend the same high school, have been dating for approximately two years. In the past year, the couple has regularly engaged in consensual sexual intercourse. Under the laws of the state in which they reside, it is legal for two 16-year-olds to engage in consensual sexual activity.

Both Max and Frieda have their own cell phones. From time to time, one sends the other a nude photograph accompanied by a sexually explicit text message. The decision to send the photograph and text message is consensual, and both Max and Frieda enjoy receiving and responding to these materials. This practice is known as *sexting,* which may have a variety of legal implications (Joyce, Burke, & Owen, 2009; Walker & Moak, 2010).

Over time, Max and Frieda grow apart, and Frieda decides to end the relationship. This upsets Max, who decides to retaliate. He does so by forwarding to 50 of his friends a nude photograph that Frieda had sent him several months earlier. Frieda soon learns what Max has done, as other students at her school begin to taunt and harass her. As a result, Frieda reports the situation to the school principal, and the school principal notifies the school resource officer (a police officer stationed in the school). At the same time, Frieda's mother hears what has happened and demands justice. Frieda's mother also notifies the news media about the situation, and the local television station runs a news story in which the anchor states, "Sexting is nothing short of an epidemic at this school, and the principal cannot control it." This leads to widespread public outrage.

Facing page: Curtis Sliwa (center) and other members of the Guardian Angels, a volunteer-based crime prevention group. How do you think justice can be achieved?

Q Pause briefly. You are the school resource officer. How do you handle this situation and why? Explain how this corresponds to your definition of justice.

The school resource officer reviews the state's legal code and discovers several provisions that may apply in this case: (1) Section 68a prohibits the production of child pornography, which includes sexually explicit images of persons under 18; (2) Section 68b prohibits transmitting child pornography to others through electronic means; and (3) Section 68c prohibits the possession of child pornography.

The school resource officer interviews Max and Frieda. The officer also obtains a search warrant for Max's cell phone as well as the cell phones of his friends to whom he sent the picture. Frieda voluntarily allows the officer to examine her cell phone. The officer determines that Frieda's cell phone contains 28 sexually explicit images of Max, that Max's cell phone contains 32 sexually explicit images of Frieda, and that Max's friends' cell phones each contain one sexually explicit image of Frieda. The officer then arrests Max, Frieda, and Max's friends on the following charges:

Against . . .	Section and Counts . . .	Rationale . . .
Frieda	Section 68a, 32 counts	For creating 32 sexually explicit images of an underage person (in this case, herself)
	Section 68b, 32 counts	For transmitting each of those images to Max
	Section 68c, 28 counts	For possessing the 28 sexually explicit images sent to her by Max
Max	Section 68a, 28 counts	For creating 28 sexually explicit images of an underage person (in this case, himself)
	Section 68b, 78 counts	For transmitting each of those images to Frieda and for transmitting Frieda's image to his 50 friends
	Section 68c, 32 counts	For possessing the 32 sexually explicit images sent to him by Frieda
Each of Max's 50 friends	Section 68c, 1 count	For possessing the sexually explicit image of Frieda sent by Max

The prosecutor decides to try Max as an adult offender. Max is sentenced to three years of probation and six weekends in jail. He must also permanently register as a sex offender and will be barred from coming within 500 feet of areas where children gather, such as parks and schools (this also means that Max must attend a high school GED program for adults because he is banned from his high school). The prosecutor tries Frieda and Max's friends as juvenile offenders. Each receives one year of juvenile probation, required counseling, and 40 hours of community service; no sex offender registration is required for them.

Q Is the outcome of this case just? Why or why not? How does it correspond to the definition of justice that you provided earlier?

Q Assume that Max was 27 instead of 17. Would this change your answer? Explain.

Q Assume that Frieda was 27 instead of 17. Would this change your answer? Explain.

Q Assume that the parents of Max's friends are angered by the charges. They hold a community protest attended by hundreds of others, demanding that their children not be prosecuted. Should this influence the prosecutor's decision? Explain.

Justice: Fact or Fiction?

FOCUSING QUESTION 6.1

Why does justice matter?

Our ideas about **justice** have been influenced by the culture in which we live and by historical influences too numerous to acknowledge here. Defining justice has been a challenge to philosophers since the days of ancient Greece. The tendencies of idealists and pragmatists and the five concepts of morality (from Chapter 2) have helped shape debates about justice for centuries, as justice has been defined as harmony, as consistent with spirituality, as the quest for truth, and more.

Justice
That which is just. There is no single agreed-upon definition of justice. Rather, conceptions of what does or does not constitute justice have been influenced by culture, history, philosophical perspectives, and more.

However, for many people, justice is like art: they do not know what it is, but they know what they like when they see it. Some people believe that justice is a reality, something that has been achieved through a set of policies and laws. Other people believe that all we can do is aspire toward justice, arguing that perfect justice is illusory and impossible to achieve. Still other people curl their lips mockingly when asked about whether justice exists, believing that there is much *injustice* in the world which may or may not be correctable (for instance, see the discussion of wrongful conviction in Box 6.1). Even so, virtually everyone believes that justice, however it may be defined, is something worth achieving. Ultimately, the criminal justice system is charged with distributing justice throughout society, so it is important for us to give some careful thought to the meanings of justice.

Ideas about justice are also important because they lead to ideas about what is good, or doing the "right thing." If society strives toward justice, then justice becomes a social benchmark. People's actions are weighed against the standards of justice that have been adopted by society. Actions perceived as just are viewed as correct or good, whereas actions perceived as unjust are viewed as incorrect or bad. Ideas about justice are complicated, yet they are not simply theories devoid of meaning. Instead, the quest for justice shapes individuals' lives, and in the case of criminal justice professionals, it shapes their life's work.

The quest for justice may be a natural phenomenon. Evaluating actions against a concept of justice helps fulfill the need to feel certainty about whether something is right or wrong. People strive for feelings of certainty, as doubt causes discomfort (Peirce, 1877). In fact, psychologists have argued that believing in a **just world**, "in which individuals get what they deserve" (Hafer & Bègue, 2005, p. 128), can serve a variety of functions. These include helping to provide order in life, by presuming that justice will provide a guide; maintaining a commitment to long-term goals rather than abandoning them for hedonistic pleasures or in the face of adversity, as the just world specifies that good things will happen to good people; and coping with anger and frustration (for a summary of this line of research, see Hafer & Bègue, 2005).

just world
A world where individuals receive what they deserve. The concept of and belief in a just world has been important in the psychological study of justice.

The quest for justice may also represent the pinnacle of moral reasoning. Recall from Chapter 2 that psychologist Lawrence Kohlberg studied how individuals make decisions about moral dilemmas. One dilemma that Kohlberg (1984) studied posed

BOX 6.1

Ethics in Practice

WRONGFUL CONVICTIONS

The American justice system is structured around the presumption that all accused persons are innocent until proven guilty. Along with this comes the assumption that the criminal justice system is accurate in determining guilt and innocence. But what happens when the system is wrong? An **exoneration** occurs when "a defendant who was convicted of a crime was later relieved of all legal consequences of that conviction through a decision by a prosecutor, a governor or a court, after new evidence of his or her innocence was discovered" (Gross & Shaffer, 2012, p. 7). One report found that almost 2,000 persons were exonerated from 1989 through February 2012.

An in-depth study of 873 of those exonerations found that most of the persons involved had been wrongfully convicted of serious crimes. In fact, 101 had been wrongfully convicted for homicide and sentenced to death; fortunately, they were exonerated before execution. All told, "the defendants had spent more than 10,000 years in prison for crimes for which they should not have been convicted" (Gross & Shaffer, 2012, p. 8), certainly a startling statistic. While it may be a common assumption that DNA evidence is the primary source of exonerations, that is not the case, as DNA was a factor in only 37% of the cases.

Important to recognize is that the report included only those whose wrongful convictions are known, and not those who may still be behind bars but innocent. Groups such as the Innocence Project (n.d.) exist specifically to investigate and work to correct possible wrongful convictions. But why do wrongful convictions occur?

A variety of factors are associated with wrongful convictions. While not an exhaustive list, these include mistaken identification by eyewitnesses, as eyewitness testimony is notoriously unreliable; witnesses who lie, sometimes about who committed a crime and sometimes by making up a crime that did not actually happen; false confessions, which occur more frequently than the public may imagine; the improper use of forensic science, through inappropriate techniques, inaccurate interpretations of results, or lying about results (see Abel, Ellement & Finucane, 2013); poor quality of representation by the defense attorney; investigators focusing their attention on one suspect and ignoring evidence of the suspect's innocence or another person's guilt; or through the use of illegal or unethical practices by persons in the criminal justice system, including prosecutors who do not turn over exculpatory evidence (i.e., that which casts doubt on the defendant's guilt) to the defense, as is required by law (Gross & Shaffer, 2012; Gould, Carrano, Leo, & Young, 2012).

exoneration
Refers to a situation in which a person convicted of a crime is excused from legal consequences after the discovery of evidence of his or her innocence.

the question of whether a man should break into a store to steal a medication that was necessary for his wife's survival but which they could not afford. Kohlberg argued that individuals progress through various stages of moral reasoning during their lifetimes. The lowest stage (Stage 1) is focused on obedience to legal authority out of a fear for punishment, yielding the answer that the man should not steal the drug because he would not want to be punished for doing so. The highest stage (Stage 6), which few persons reach in their lifetimes, is marked by a commitment both to principles of justice and to protesting injustice, even if this requires breaking a law. A person at this stage would most likely indicate that the man should break in and steal the drug because doing so produces a just outcome, valuing the preservation of life over the protection of property. As such, Kohlberg's work suggests that a focus on the principles of justice is the highest point in the development of moral reasoning.

The importance of justice may not be limited to humans, as it may exist in the nonhuman animal kingdom as well. For instance, one study reported that dogs have an innate sense of justice against which they measure actions. When one dog in a pair is rewarded for a task and the other dog is not, the unrewarded dog appears able to identify that he has been treated unfairly (Range, Horn, Viranyi, & Huber, 2009). This could illustrate an irony—that injustice is significant enough to be recognized by a variety of creatures, but justice itself is so complex as to have generated centuries of discussion, only to arrive at tentative (and hotly debated) definitions of what it means.

The opinion of justice officials regarding wrongful conviction appears to be shaped by their occupational roles. The police and prosecutors, who work to apprehend and prosecute offenders, believe that overall error levels are low—understandable, as they do not perceive their work as inaccurate. On the other hand, defense attorneys, who represent those accused of a crime, believe that overall error levels are higher—again understandable, as their job is to question the evidence developed by the police and prosecution. Police, prosecutors, and judges tend not to believe that reforms are necessary in order to reduce wrongful conviction; defense attorneys do (Smith, Zalman, & Kiger, 2011). Contrast this with the finding that the public tends to believe that reforms are necessary in order to protect against wrongful conviction (Zalman, Larson, & Smith, 2012).

Wrongful conviction has an understandably negative impact on the offender who is wrongfully convicted. It also has a negative impact on the families of those wrongfully convicted, and particularly on their children (Jenkins, 2013). Of course, it is also detrimental to the criminal justice system if an innocent person is convicted while the actual guilty party, who may or may not be known, remained free—but how much error is acceptable? A study of criminal justice professionals found that approximately half believed that 0% was the only acceptable rate of wrongful conviction, while slightly more than one-third believed that a wrongful conviction rate up to 1% was acceptable (Ramsey & Frank, 2007).

Q As illustrated above, some believe that it is not acceptable to have wrongful convictions at all, while others believe that a small number of wrongful convictions are tolerable. Review the "Ethics in Practice" box in Chapter 1. The former perspective is a deontological argument and the latter is a utilitarian argument; why? Which do you most agree with?

Q Do you think the government has an ethical obligation to compensate persons who have been wrongfully convicted and then exonerated? If so, how? What theory(ies) of ethics or justice support(s) your answer?

Q Later in the chapter, you will read about the four models of distributive justice (compassionate, participatory, mechanical, authoritarian). Which do you think would be most likely to generate wrongful convictions? Least likely? What reforms would you recommend to avoid wrongful convictions?

From a sociological perspective, the quest for justice has a tremendous impact on society. Because there is no single definition of justice, there are (and always have been and always will be) ongoing debates about what justice is. In the context of these debates, society explores its most controversial issues of public policy. For instance, in debates on abortion, same-sex marriage, the use of the military to intervene in situations overseas, health care reform, and more, each side makes reference to arguments grounded in their concept of justice. As British philosopher John Stuart Mill ([1859] 1981) observed, the ability to engage in informed discussions of these complex issues is necessary for society to make decisions based on the most current ideas and philosophies.

For these reasons, it is important to study theories of justice. An awareness of various justice theories—understanding both those with which you agree and those with which you disagree—enables a full understanding of the multiple sides to a debate, particularly when participants are arguing from different perspectives of justice. This can allow ideas about justice to be reviewed with a full analysis, which in turn results in an improved application and understanding of the law. Criminal justice professionals have the responsibility, and even the obligation, to understand what justice means and how it informs the workings of the criminal justice system, from a police officer's discretion to a judge's sentencing determinations. This chapter will aid you in this understanding.

George Zimmerman's 2013 trial for the murder of Trayvon Martin garnered national attention. Zimmerman, a 28-year-old Hispanic man who was a neighborhood watch patrol coordinator, called 911 to report Martin, a 17-year-old African American high school student, believing him to be suspicious. The two got into an altercation in which Zimmerman fatally shot Martin. Zimmerman asserted self-defense and was acquitted by a jury. Martin was unarmed, carrying only a bag of candy, leading critics to argue that Zimmerman had profiled Martin from the start of the encounter. Here, a demonstrator outside the courtroom displays a sign. What criteria would you use to define a just outcome in this case?

- Q Compare your definition of justice to those of your classmates. How can different definitions lead to differing perceptions of what makes a just world? How can different definitions lead to differing perceptions of what makes a just criminal justice system?
- Q How might differing definitions of justice shape what goals or strategies the criminal justice system, or those employed by it, seek to accomplish?

The Justice in Criminal Justice

FOCUSING QUESTION 6.2

In what ways has justice been defined?

American statesman Daniel Webster once commented, "Justice . . . is the great interest of man on earth. It is a ligament which holds civilized beings and civilized nations together" (1914, p. 533). While a lofty sentiment, the importance of justice and its implications cannot be overstated. Consider American history. According to the Declaration of Independence, the American Revolution (1776–1783) was partially motivated because Great Britain was "deaf to the voice of *justice*" [emphasis added]. The American Civil War (1861–1865) was concerned in large part with the injustice of slavery (see Stampp, 1991). In the late twentieth and early twenty first centuries, substantial debate has emerged about whether American military force should be used to combat injustices (generally contextualized as human rights violations) abroad. Justice, then, is a concept so highly valued that societies are willing to engage in life-and-death struggles about it.

Many of the decisions we make about criminal justice reflect our ideas about justice. Consequently, the type of criminal justice system we prefer is also shaped by our understandings of what justice is (or equally important, what justice is not). Sometimes, we realize that we are uncomfortable with a policy or an action but have difficulty in distinguishing the source of the discomfort. Considering the following perspectives of justice can help us distinguish where discomfort lies or where concerns about justice exist. Can you identify any of the following issues as causing concern in the case about Max and Frieda at the beginning of the chapter?

Procedural justice holds that justice is achieved when the proper procedures are followed. Of course, this begs the question, "What are the proper procedures?" The answer is that the proper procedures are those defined in the Constitution, the Bill of Rights, court decisions, and legal codes. In Chapter 8, you will learn more about the various forms of procedural justice.

procedural justice
Holds that justice is achieved when the proper procedures are followed and addresses the fairness of the procedures used when applying the law. Procedural justice is grounded in the idea that fair procedures are the best guarantees for fair outcomes.

Social justice considers issues of equality and inequality in society. Is there discrimination—in society or in the criminal justice system—based on race, gender, social class, sexual orientation, age, religious belief, disability status, or other factors (see generally Arrigo, 1999b)? To social justice theorists, then, the pursuit of justice is the pursuit of equality. You will learn more about social justice in Chapter 7.

social justice
Considers issues of equality and inequality in society and whether benefits and risks are distributed in a manner that is fair and without discrimination. Argues that the pursuit of justice is the pursuit of equality.

Individual justice is the focus of this chapter. Individual justice primarily focuses on the outcomes that apply to individual persons. The emphasis is less on group equality (as in social justice) or on legal procedures (as in procedural justice) than it is on whether or not the results are correct for the individuals involved (which may mean different things, depending on the theory). For instance, what should be done if a person's home is burglarized? Certainly, we would hope there would not be discrimination based on who the victim or the offender was, which is a matter for social justice. And certainly, we would hope the police and courts would follow the proper procedures in handling the case, which is a matter for procedural justice. But in this chapter, we are most concerned about what happens to the victim and the offender as individuals.

individual justice
Focuses on whether outcomes that apply to individual persons are just.

The remainder of the chapter describes several perspectives through which we can view individual justice. In this section, we will consider five perspectives that have the potential to shape the criminal justice system: vigilante justice, transitional justice, ideological justice, discourse perspective justice, and postmodern justice. Each of these represents its own way for conceptualizing what criminal justice should mean. Afterward, we will move to a discussion of what is arguably the most significant perspective: distributive justice.

VIGILANTE JUSTICE

When people decide to "take the law into their own hands" (Brown, 1969, p. 176), bypassing the criminal justice system (e.g., police, courts, and corrections), **vigilante justice** occurs. Individuals generally engage in vigilante justice (also known as vigilantism) when members of the community agree that it is necessary to do so to protect persons or property. Sometimes, this occurs because there is no established criminal justice system, such as in the early years of the American West. Other times, vigilantism exists alongside an established criminal justice system, perhaps because individuals lack confidence in the system or because they believe they have the right to take steps to protect themselves.

vigilante justice
Occurs when individuals bypass the criminal justice system in resolving a conflict by taking the law into their own hands.

Some forms of vigilante justice operate within the bounds of the law. For instance, the Guardian Angels citizen group was created in 1979 to combat crime in the New York City subway system. Since that time, the group has expanded to other cities and other venues. Members of the Guardian Angels, who are recognized by their distinctive red berets, are citizen volunteers who organize unarmed patrols of public spaces. Research has found that the group has reduced fear of crime, has reduced the frequency of some crimes, and has provided role models for at-risk youth (Pennell, Curtis, Henderson, & Tayman, 1989). The Guardian Angels use legal means to accomplish their goals.

Modern technology has also allowed the development of virtual vigilantism. Solove (2007) notes that "The internet is quickly becoming a powerful norm-enforcement tool. A plethora of websites now serve as forums for people to shame others" (p. 86). Whether with cameras in hand or with the posting of heartfelt comments, the public can readily share its thoughts online. Underlying this is a desire to publicly air grievances and to publicly shame those who are perceived as having done wrong (or perhaps to praise those who are perceived as having done right), and online formats allow it to be conducted in a manner that reaches large audiences. From a historical perspective, it is interesting to note that the criminal justice system long ago moved away from public punishments in the town square; virtual vigilantism has filled the void that was left. However, one concern about virtual vigilantism is that it can sometimes go too far, particularly when a person is wrongly censured or if it leads to permanent labeling, bullying, or further retribution against an individual (Solove, 2007).

Vigilante justice that uses illegal means is more problematic. For instance, if a crime victim chose to exact revenge by assaulting an offender (other than in legally recognized self-defense; see Chapter 9), then that victim could be held accountable through arrest and prosecution. The criminal justice system does not recognize a right to revenge or a right to use illegal means to engage in vigilantism. Rather, all criminal acts are viewed as crimes against the state, which the state then has the sole responsibility for prosecuting and punishing.

TRANSITIONAL JUSTICE

transitional justice
Applies in the unique set of circumstances when a country's government changes and the new government seeks to move away from human rights abuses that occurred under the old government. The transition between governments is marked by a focus on human rights and just outcomes.

As described by Teitel (2002), **transitional justice** applies only in a unique set of circumstances in which (1) a country's government changes and (2) the new government wants to move away from a set of human rights abuses that occurred under the old government. Therefore, as the name suggests, the concern is about ensuring justice during the transition from one governing regime to another, with a concern about human rights at the forefront. Two notable twentieth-century examples illustrate this concept.

A dramatic example was the case of Germany at the end of World War II. One question facing Germany was what the new government should look like after the fall of the Third Reich and the Nazi regime. The Allied nations (United States, France, Soviet Union, and United Kingdom) each occupied a zone of Germany to plan for rebuilding (Paterson, Clifford, & Hagan, 1991). Another question was what should be done to the remaining leaders, including individuals who had planned and implemented the Holocaust. The Allied nations conducted the Nuremberg Trials beginning in 1945, which tried and convicted numerous individuals of war crimes and crimes against humanity (see Marrus, 1997).

The transitional justice experienced by Germany and other post–World War II European countries has had a legacy for modern criminal justice. After the human rights abuses they witnessed during the war, Germany and other European countries moved to abolish the death penalty, labeling it as a human rights violation in its own right. The risk of another Holocaust was too terrifying a prospect to tolerate state-sanctioned penalties of death. Today, to join the European Union, member states must abolish their death penalties (Zimring, 2003). Interestingly, "demonstrations protesting against the United States death penalty have . . . been held in France, Spain, and Norway" (Bohm, 2000, p. 4), in which American capital punishment has been decried as an injustice and a human rights violation. This illustrates how global opinion has changed on this controversial issue, partially as an outgrowth of transitional justice.

This does influence American criminal justice policy. For instance, overseas manufacturers of drugs that have been used in lethal injection executions have taken measures to ensure that they do not sell execution drugs to departments of corrections in the United States (Pilkington, 2013); the European Commission has adopted a similar

rule (Pilkington, 2011). In addition, European countries may not extradite (i.e., return for trial) suspects who have fled from the United States unless assurances are made that the death penalty will not be sought (de Felipe & Martin, 2012).

Another example of transitional justice, also dramatic and one that garnered much attention on the world stage, was the collapse of apartheid in South Africa. Apartheid was state-sanctioned racial segregation in which the all-white government of South Africa repressed the rights, freedoms, and political participation of the majority of the population, who were black. The government's control over the population was sometimes marked by violence aimed at protesters and opponents. Control was also exerted through "the ban, an order from the justice minister" aimed at those who would protest the system, in which they might be prohibited from socializing with others, be given a curfew, be prohibited from working "in a large group (such as in a factory)," and more (Roskin, 2004, p. 510).

Apartheid lasted from the late 1940s to the early 1990s, at which time a new constitution and new government were put into place. Instrumental to the transition was the government's decision to release Nelson Mandela from prison, where he had served 27 years for his role in opposing apartheid in the 1960s. After his release in 1990, Mandela went on to be elected as president of South Africa in 1994. The transition to a new government, and the corresponding move away from the human rights abuses of apartheid, is an example of transitional justice. The transition was not the product of a war; rather, it was motivated by substantial dissent from within and by international politics (Roskin, 2004). As part of the transition, a Truth and Reconciliation Commission (1998) was established. Although the commission found that "the predominant portion of gross violations of human rights was committed by the former state through its security and law-enforcement agencies" (p. 212), the focus was also on the need for "reconciliation" and for "extensive healing and social and physical reconstruction at every level of society" (p. 350).

Transitional justice is rare, as it is limited to circumstances when a government undergoes substantial change. However, as these examples (and others) demonstrate, it is associated with remedying abuses of human rights.

IDEOLOGICAL JUSTICE

To some persons, justice is achieved when their desired ideological system is supported through government policy. An **ideology** is essentially a worldview to which a person subscribes. There are many ideologies with many different belief systems, but what binds them together under this heading is the notion that, to their adherents, society will not be able to achieve justice until its policies reflect those supported by the ideology. Rather than beginning by asking what justice is, or even how it should be accomplished, the analysis begins by asking how can society be more like a preferred ideology, which is presumed to *lead to* justice. That is, the ideology comes first as a collection of beliefs that are assumed to produce justice as a result. The supporters of an ideology may view those who oppose the ideology as standing in the way of justice. Here we will focus on two ideologies near the opposite ends of a spectrum: libertarianism and socialism.

ideology
A worldview to which a person subscribes. Under ideological justice, supporters of an ideology argue that society will not be able to achieve justice until policies are enacted that support their desired ideology.

A libertarian might believe that justice is best accomplished in a society that respects individual rights, particularly the right to own and do as one wishes with property with only the most minimal of government influences (Sargent, 1996). Therefore, any intervention of the law into private property or private rights is viewed as unjust. For instance, libertarians would likely argue that the state should not restrict obscene material, require seat belt usage, criminalize drug possession, or levy more than the most minimal of taxes. Libertarians object to policies that limit what individuals can do with property because they are counter to libertarian ideology and therefore ideologically unjust.

On the other hand, a socialist might believe that justice is best accomplished in a society with a large government that manages public ownership of industries that are viewed as most necessary for a productive society and that provides many services to all members of society. High tax rates are used not only to provide these industries and services but also to control the distribution of wealth. This model of government is known as democratic socialism (Sargent, 1996). Unlike the libertarian, the socialist would argue that an active government is required to promote justice—perhaps arguing that government-funded drug rehabilitation should be made available to any person who desires it, that all educational institutions should be public and well funded, or that economic inequality and social class distinctions should be eliminated.

There are many other ideologies that are beyond the scope of this book (see Sargent, 1996). However, the common theme of ideological justice is that the ideology to which one subscribes defines one's perception of justice.

DISCOURSE PERSPECTIVE JUSTICE

discourse perspective justice
A perspective that emphasizes a public dialog or discourse in which the public then reaches consensus on what is or is not just.

German philosopher Jürgen Habermas (e.g., 1992) developed the concept of **discourse perspective justice**. As the name suggests, the emphasis is on a dialogue—or discourse—about how justice ought to be conceived. Habermas argued that "it is not for the philosopher" (O'Neill, 1997, p. 108) to define justice. This, in and of itself, is a startling proposition because it is in contrast to so many other perspectives, in which philosophers advocating a justice theory specify what they believe justice ought to look like. Rather, Habermas has confidence in the public to engage in conversation about what acceptable norms and principles of justice should be. This does not occur through hypothetical or abstract conversations. In fact, one could argue that we are all surrounded by discourse perspective justice on an almost daily basis, because Habermas envisions discourse occurring "in the context of the real disputes that arise" (O'Neill, 1997, p. 108) in society.

Key to this perspective is that conversations must be conducted logically and ethically in order to best distill the principles that underlie the public's conception of justice. Also key is for the community to reach a consensus on issues of justice, rather than facing a stalemate between opposing sides. Some degree of mutual understanding and compromise therefore become necessary. Again, Habermas clearly values the primacy of community in reaching conclusions about justice. The process of identifying the principles of justice on which the community reaches consensus is accomplished by "the community reasoning aloud through discourse" (Hudson, 2003, p. 155). The minimal requirement for justice, then, focuses on ensuring that processes are in place to allow the discourse, including: "*symmetry* (all are to be given equal rights in discourse) and *reciprocity* (all must pay attention to the views and claims of others) [emphasis in original]" (Hudson, 2003, p. 156). From that necessary starting point, the conversations establishing justice may proceed. Indeed, because they underlie the process that defines justice, these requirements may be considered foundational principles for justice (Hudson, 2003).

At a societal level, discourse perspective justice certainly includes discussion of controversial criminal justice issues, which may occur in a variety of public forums, including but not limited to the mass media (see Barak, 1988). Even on a smaller scale, discourse perspective justice can allow communities, schools, or organizations to engage in conversation about the principles that should be followed to address issues of concern to them. For instance, Pepinsky's (1999b) use of peacemaking criminology to help students resolve an issue related to school cleanliness contained the key elements of discourse perspective justice, as the students met to discuss the principles they thought most fair and just to guide their response. And police-community

collaborations, as can be accomplished through community-oriented policing programs in which the police and public meet to discuss community issues and their potential solutions, can also illustrate discourse perspective principles (for a strong example, see Skogan & Hartnett, 1997). In all cases, the hope is that effective communication will ultimately lead to better justice system outcomes and better treatment of all persons.

POSTMODERN JUSTICE

Recall the discussion of pragmatism in Chapter 2. As you may remember, pragmatists utilize empiricism when structuring their arguments. For a pragmatist to accept something as true or as reality, he or she must observe it or see data about it. That is, for a pragmatist, truth and reality are grounded in measurable observations. This is very similar to the philosophy of modernism, which assumes that there is a *single* reality, and it is a reality based on rational and empirical study. The philosophy of **postmodernism**, on the other hand, holds that there are "many distinct and equally valid realities created by people from many different cultures and subcultures and from many different times and places" (Velasquez, 2002, p. 215). The postmodernist believes that different people create their own narratives (i.e., understandings) of what is real, and furthermore, if they *believe* it is real, then it indeed *becomes* real to them.

postmodernism
A philosophical perspective holding that there are multiple equally valid realities, as individuals create their own narratives and understandings of what is real.

So, what does this mean for justice? One important implication is that, for a postmodernist, there cannot be one single definition of what is just or unjust (and one definition is not necessarily better than another). This is different from idealism because idealists do believe in a particular vision of truth and harmony. It is, however, similar to theories of relativism described in the "Ethics in Practice" box in Chapter 1. As a means for judging whether an action or outcome is just, postmodern justice does not provide much guidance. But perhaps that is its point; as Arrigo (1995) suggests, one goal of postmodern justice is to help understand why different persons and groups have varying definitions of justice, through an exploration of their narratives. In turn, this understanding can possibly help resolve conflicts that emerge based on differing views of justice.

In many ways, postmodern justice reflects the reality of what criminal justice professionals must deal with on a daily basis. While two witnesses to the same criminal event might report seeing very different things, each swears that his or her testimony is "how it really happened." Neither witness is lying. What has happened is that the *actual* reality becomes unimportant; what the witnesses *believe* they saw *becomes* the reality to them. It is the job of the criminal justice professional to figure out how to resolve the accounts in a way that represents the truth in order to pursue justice.

The five perspectives of justice presented thus far have suggested very different views, arguing that justice may be promoted by the public, by historical change, by adherence to an ideology, by open conversation, and by accepting differing perceptions of reality. While each of these perspectives has something to offer to an understanding of justice, they do not provide the primary philosophical foundation of American criminal justice. Rather, the most significant ideas are in the realm of distributive justice, to which the next section turns.

Q How would you assess the strengths and weaknesses of each theory of justice presented in this section? How closely do they correspond (or not correspond) to your definition of justice?

Q How might the theories of justice described in this section influence the resolution of the sexting case described in the chapter's opening?

A Focus on Distributive Justice

FOCUSING QUESTION 6.3

How is distributive justice related to criminal justice?

distributive justice
A perspective on justice that focuses on what individuals are due. As such, distributive justice focuses on the end results of how outcomes are distributed.

It is easy to become overwhelmed when thinking about the multiple ways justice can be defined. The remainder of this chapter focuses on the broad form of justice that is arguably most relevant to the criminal justice system: **distributive justice**. Philosopher of justice David Schmidtz (2006) observed that, at its most basic, "justice concerns what people are due" (p. 7). Think of this as another way of saying that justice is when individuals get what they deserve, a perspective consistent with the "just world hypothesis." While perhaps a simple statement, its implications are substantial. First, we must consider the question of who is due (or deserves) what. From a criminal justice perspective, we start with determining which acts or behaviors should be prohibited under the law. The individuals who commit those acts or behaviors (the "who") are then due something under the law, such as a punishment (the "what"). Second, we must determine what it is, precisely, that the individuals are due. From a criminal justice perspective, this means how to distribute the "results of justice processes—police stops, arrests, verdicts, and sentences—asking whether these results are legitimate" (Castelanno & Gould, 2007, p. 75). In other words, when should an arrest be made versus a warning given? When should an offender be sentenced to prison instead of being placed on probation? Should an offender be required to complete a rehabilitation program? There are many questions of this type that criminal justice professionals address on a daily basis, and the purpose of distributive justice is to ensure that the answers are those that society recognizes as legitimate.

Consider what has happened in distributive justice. The end result of this process is a *distribution* of outcomes (i.e., the stops, arrests, verdicts, and sentences are distributed to those who commit illegal acts). This is why it is known as distributive justice. But how is it to be accomplished? There are a number of ways that we can conceptualize the best approach to giving individuals their due, as described below.

A CLASSIC APPROACH: ARISTOTLE'S COMMUTATIVE JUSTICE

commutative justice
Defines justice as proportionality. Suggests that justice has been met when outcomes are allocated proportionally.

The philosophy of **commutative justice** has its origins in Aristotle's *Nicomachean Ethics* (2000). Under this theory, individuals received their due based on proportionality. Aristotle was concerned about proportionality in exchanges. He wrote, "What is just . . . is what is proportionate. And what is unjust is what violates the proportion" (p. 87). To Aristotle, this applied to voluntary exchanges, such as when a price is established for a good or service (voluntary because individuals can choose whether or not to make the purchase), and to involuntary exchanges, such as when determining the appropriate punishment for an offense (involuntary because the offender may not reject the punishment). Thus, if a good or service has a price that is proportional to its value or if a punishment is in proportion to an offender's crime, then justice has been achieved. The concept of proportionality is explored further in the discussion of punishment in Chapter 10.

AN ECONOMIC APPROACH: BENTHAM'S UTILITARIAN JUSTICE

utilitarian justice
Defines justice as that which provides the greatest good for the greatest number. Also draws upon cost-benefit analysis, comparing the costs and benefits of an action.

In theory, **utilitarian justice** is simple. It has its roots in British philosopher Jeremy Bentham's 1776 work, *A Fragment on Government,* in which Bentham observes, "it is the greatest happiness of the greatest number that is the measure of right and wrong" (para. 2). To determine what is just, then, one must ask the question, *what produces the greatest good for the most people?* A technique called cost–benefit analysis, derived from economics, is often used to arrive at an answer. The first step is to identify the *costs* of an action and then to add up their value. The second step is to identify the *benefits* of an

action and then to add up their value. The final step is to *compare* the value of the costs to the value of the benefits. If the benefits are greater than the costs, then the conclusion is that (to borrow from Bentham) more happiness will be derived than unhappiness, so the action is just.

It is possible to measure utilitarian justice in a purely mathematical fashion. For instance, a study by Cohen (1988) estimated that the average cost of a robbery, in terms of lost money or property as well as the monetary value of a victim's pain and suffering, was $12,594. Cohen then went on to calculate the cost and benefit of extending the length of an average robbery sentence by 10%. He calculated that the benefit, which was the value of the crimes that would be prevented as a result, would be approximately $300 million, whereas the cost of the added prison time would be approximately $336 million. From a utilitarian perspective, this would not be a rational outcome because the increased punishment would produce a loss rather than a benefit. Therefore, the increased prison time would be an unjust outcome on a cost–benefit basis; individuals receive their due only if the benefits outweigh the costs.

It is also possible to conceptualize utilitarian justice as a metaphor instead of adding up actual numbers. Hart and Devlin (from Chapter 3) attempted to examine the costs and benefits of regulating morality, and then each reached his own conclusion about whether it was just to do so. Although not phrased directly in utilitarian terms of costs and benefits, the arguments employed by Hart and Devlin can be interpreted as though they attempted to identify what they believed would produce "the greatest happiness for the greatest number." For Devlin, enforcement of morality produced the greatest happiness by protecting society from immoral activity. For Hart, maximizing freedom produced the greatest happiness by allowing individuals to pursue their preferred (noncriminal) behaviors.

A BELIEF IN PUNISHMENT: RETRIBUTIVE JUSTICE

A commonly accepted notion in society is that if someone commits a crime they deserve to be punished. **Retributive justice**, which we will address in more detail in Chapter 10, holds that individuals are due an unpleasant punishment. "Retributivism is a very straightforward theory of punishment: We are justified in punishing because and only because offenders deserve it" (Moore, 1995, p. 96). This excludes other potential purposes of punishment, such as rehabilitation or using fear of punishment to deter offenders from committing crime.

retributive justice
A perspective of justice which holds that individuals who commit crime are due an unpleasant punishment.

Many people in America believe that the criminal justice system is justified in taking retributive action against criminal behavior, further believing that retribution forms a rationale for law and justice. Indeed, research suggests that the public is most likely to support retribution when people feel a sense of moral outrage, generally against a criminal offense that was deliberately committed. By contrast, for acts that cause harm due to carelessness or an accident, the public is less likely to support retribution (Darley & Pittman, 2003).

Ideas about retribution date back to ancient times, even appearing as a theme in Plato's dialogues. Then, as now, debates occurred as to the worth of retribution as opposed to other approaches, such as restorative justice (Pangle, 2009), a perspective of justice described below.

EVERYONE IS DUE SOMETHING: RESTORATIVE JUSTICE

When a crime occurs, it causes harm to the victim. However, crimes also cause harm to the community and to the offender. For instance, the victim of a robbery has financial losses and the fear of bodily injury (or actual injury). The fabric of the community is harmed because after learning of the robbery, residents might subsequently fear or distrust others, leading to a decline in social interactions. The offender is harmed by

virtue of having stepped outside the accepted bounds of social and legal behavior, which results in an emotional, psychological, or physical (in the case of incarceration) separation from the rest of the community. The goal of **restorative justice** is to take actions to restore the victim, the offender, and society to more desirable conditions that existed before the offense occurred (Hahn, 1998). This expands the scope of distributive justice by arguing that multiple persons and groups are due something in the aftermath of an offense.

restorative justice
Focuses on restoring the victim, offender, and society to the desirable conditions that existed before a criminal offense occurred.

Restorative justice may be understood as an opportunity for the parties to a crime to heal. There are various mechanisms by which this can occur. One is the simple virtue and power of a sincere apology (Lazare, 2004). In some societies, an apology is powerful enough to render further legal action unnecessary (Haley, 1986). Another strategy is the use of mediation in which a mediator (a person with training in conflict management and resolution) confers with the victim and offender to recommend a solution that takes into account the needs or interests of both parties (McGillis, 1998). A more dramatic example is the use of sentencing circles in which multiple parties come together to discuss a criminal incident and negotiate the appropriate solution. For instance, the offender and his or her family, the victim and his or her family, and community members would come together, each sharing his or her perspective. This enables the offender to understand the harms that resulted from the offense and to take accountability for them by accepting a sentence formulated in the group's discussions (Sentencing Circles, n.d.). Restorative justice has proven to be a promising strategy (Latimer, Dowden, & Muise, 2005) though primarily for youthful or minor offenses (Bonta, Jesseman, Rugge, & Cormier, 2006).

Restorative justice can also be understood from a compensatory approach—that is, making efforts to repair the physical or financial damage caused by a crime. In many jurisdictions, there is a crime victims' fund through which the government can provide compensation to victims for their losses. Offenders can be required to pay into the fund, which then helps repair the individuals and the communities that were harmed by their actions. Offenders can also be required to compensate their victims directly, paying for lost items, medical bills, and so on. One judge in Tennessee even made national news for his controversial practice of allowing victims of burglaries to be compensated by taking items from the offender's home (Judge lets victim . . . , 1992).

BUT IS IT FAIR? RAWLS ON JUSTICE

John Rawls was one of the leading contemporary philosophers of justice. Rawls defined "justice as fairness" (Rawls, 2001, p. xvi), so individuals are due that which is identified through a fair process. Of course, this requires us to define fairness, which is perhaps no easier than defining justice. See Box 6.2 to try your hand at defining fairness. Rawls did, however, recommend tools that we can use in an effort to define fairness and thus justice.

Rawls (1999) described a philosophical approach to determining what is fair and just. Specifically, he asks us to use a **"veil of ignorance"** (p. 118) and to make decisions about justice and fairness from an "original position" (p. 15). Let's consider what this means. The veil of ignorance is a technique in which a person must assume that he or she knows nothing whatsoever about his or her background. While under the veil, a person would not know his or her gender, race, age, sexual orientation, socioeconomic background, place of residence, nationality, religion, parentage, job status, education, or any other information. Therefore, a person would not be able to make a self-serving decision at the expense of others. For example, under the veil of ignorance, a wealthy person would not be tempted to

veil of ignorance
A thought experiment used by John Rawls, in which a person is to assume that he or she knows nothing about his or her background. When under the metaphorical veil, individuals are in an original position.

BOX 6.2

JUSTICE AS FAIRNESS

Think about your definition of fairness. What do you think is the fairest way to resolve the following dilemma (adapted from Stone, 2002)?

> Think about the class in which you are using this book. Assume that, one day, your instructor brings to class the most delicious chocolate cake that you can possibly imagine (if you don't care for chocolate cake, then substitute your favorite dessert or food). Of course, everyone in class wants a share. The question is, how should the cake be divided? Why is this the best approach?

Now, compare your answer to that of your classmates. What are the differences? The similarities? Does each answer provide an equally fair outcome? Finally, consider the following concerns (adapted from Stone, 2002). How would you respond to them from the perspective of fairness? It becomes clear that fairness may not be as simple as it appears.

1. Students who missed class complain that they were left out because they would have attended had they known there would be cake. Does it matter why they missed class?
2. Students who did not enroll in the class complain that they were left out because they would have registered for the class had they known there would be cake.
3. Perhaps the cake should be distributed by rank—faculty and teaching assistants with the biggest pieces, seniors with the next largest, juniors with the next largest, and so on. Does rank have its privileges?
4. "A group of men's liberationists stages a protest. Women have always had greater access to chocolate cake, they claim, because girls are taught to bake while boys have to go outdoors and play football" (Stone, 2002, p. 40). The men demand larger shares.
5. Some students have just come from lunch, where they had their own delicious desserts. Students who did not just come from lunch claim that they are more entitled to the cake because they need it more. But the students who had lunch claim they wouldn't have had dessert there had they known about the cake.
6. Students who don't like the cake volunteer to take a smaller share because they wouldn't enjoy it anyway.
7. But what if the students who don't like cake then demand an alternate but equally valuable reward of some sort?
8. Some students claim it would be fairest to put the cake in the middle of the room and just let the chips fall (or the pieces of cake fly) as they may. First come, first served; let the strongest prevail.
9. The cake is so delicious that one piece would hardly be satisfactory. A lottery should be conducted to award the cake as a whole to one lucky person (or large sections, perhaps one-quarter, of the cake to several lucky persons).
10. Some students suggest that a cake supervisor be elected from within the class to manage the distribution of the cake. Candidates for cake supervisor can announce their cake distribution plans, and the class can elect their preferred supervisor. What if the cake supervisor is paid by being given a share of the cake in advance?

create a policy that would deliberately cause harm to others to increase personal wealth. Under the veil, individuals would not know their financial status, and would therefore support policies deemed to be fair to persons of any socioeconomic

background. Likewise, under the veil of ignorance, individuals would not support laws that are discriminatory. Again while under the veil, personal attributes are unknown, so persons would be unlikely to support laws that could be used to discriminate out of fear that such laws might have the potential to be used against them. When this lack of knowledge about personal background is achieved, individuals are said to be in an original position, or a starting point, from which government and policy can then be developed.

Of course, there is no actual cloth that is a real veil of ignorance. Rawls's ideas are simply metaphors about how individuals should approach decisions about justice and fairness. Rawls believed that, in an original position, individuals would agree on principles (recall the discussion of principles, and how they shape rules, from Chapter 2) that are fundamentally fair because they are unable to act in a manner of self-interest that would be fair to some but unfair to others.

Rawls was not writing specifically about criminal justice but about justice in society as a whole. He argued that the veil of ignorance exercise would lead to two principles that should guide society. The first is that all persons should have equal access to the same basic rights, whatever they may be. For instance, to Rawls, an indigent (i.e., poor) defendant should not be denied the right to have an attorney during a trial if that right is available to a wealthy defendant. The U.S. Supreme Court agreed with this principle in *Gideon v. Wainwright* (1963; see Lewis, 1964), holding that indigent defendants in felony cases must be provided with legal representation, even if they cannot afford it. This right was later extended to indigent defendants accused of any crime, felony, or misdemeanor that carried potential jail time (see *Argersinger v. Hamlin,* 1972).

Second, Rawls argued that society must provide equality of opportunity. This means society must not discriminate and all persons should have the same opportunity to succeed. For instance, it is increasingly accepted that a good education is necessary to advance into many leadership positions. Therefore, Rawls's theory would suggest that all persons should have the opportunity to pursue a good education. If an individual is unable to attend a good school for reasons *other than* his or her merit—because, for instance, he or she lives in an area where the schools are dilapidated or because he or she has been discriminated against in an admission decision—then Rawls sees an injustice. Of course, once individuals are given a fair opportunity, their success will vary based on their individual choices, aptitudes, and talents—but the opportunity must be there. In other words, it was equality of opportunity that mattered to Rawls, but this was not a promise that all will be successful in their endeavors. See Box 6.3 for a policy debate on equality of opportunity.

To summarize, Rawls argued that justice is fairness. He then argued that fairness is achieved when society provides the same set of rights and liberties to all persons and when society allows persons an equal opportunity to succeed. If individuals receive their due in accordance with these principles, justice is achieved. Although Rawls's theory has its critics (e.g., Nozick, 1974; Walzer, 1984), it still stands as one of the more important perspectives on contemporary justice.

Q How would any of the models of distributive justice described in this section apply to the resolution of the sexting case at the beginning of the chapter?

Q How would you assess the strengths and weaknesses of each theory of justice presented in this section? How closely do they correspond (or not correspond) to your definition of justice?

Q What features would a just criminal justice system have based on Rawls's principles? Explain.

BOX 6.3

EQUALITY OF OPPORTUNITY

What does equality of opportunity mean? Consider the following actual case.

On March 16, 1996, an individual applying to be a police officer (who will be referred to as the "plaintiff" in the rest of this narrative) completed a written test administered by the Law Enforcement Council of Connecticut, Inc. The Council collated test results and distributed them to 14 Connecticut towns, including New London. The towns used this information when considering candidates for employment in their police agencies.

Among other things, the test measured cognitive abilities. The plaintiff's score on the test was 33. The user's manual for the test suggested two different ranges of scores that it recommended for police patrol officers: 20–28 and 18–30. In either case, the plaintiff's score of 33 exceeded the recommended range.

After taking the test and receiving his score, the plaintiff wanted to apply for an open position with the New London Police. However, the Assistant City Manager informed him that he was not eligible for employment with the town's Police Department, "because he scored too high on the written test . . . New London had decided to consider only applicants who scored between 20 and 27 on the written examination" (*Jordan v. City of New London,* 1999, pp. 2–3).

The plaintiff sued, arguing that his rights of equal opportunity for employment had been violated (see *Jordan v. City of New London,* 1999).

- Q If you were the judge, how you would rule in this case? Why?
- Q The court actually ruled that the city had rational reasons to deny the job to the applicant with the high score, including the argument that overeducated persons would not be satisfied in the job, causing them to leave the position after being hired and trained, and the argument that only considering applicants in a particular range of test scores could help narrow the pool of applicants to a manageable number. How does this compare to your ruling?
- Q Assess the court's ruling using your definition of justice, your definition of fairness, and your definition of equality of opportunity.

Individual and Community Interests in Distributive Justice

FOCUSING QUESTION 6.4

In distributive justice, how can offenders' needs and society's needs be balanced?

You may recall from Chapter 2 that the use of discretion plays a central role in the criminal justice system. For instance, research has found that police officers vary in their ideas about how the law should be enforced (e.g., Muir, 1977), and probation officers vary in their ideas about how probationers should be supervised (e.g., Seiter & West, 2003). These variations can lead two different officers to approach the same situation in very different ways. For instance, one probation officer might see a failed drug test as a reason to revoke probation and send a client back to prison, whereas another probation officer might respond by sending a client to a treatment program. In either case, the probation officer would be using discretion to provide distributive justice—that is, to decide how to provide the client what he or she is due and how to distribute the outcomes of the criminal justice system.

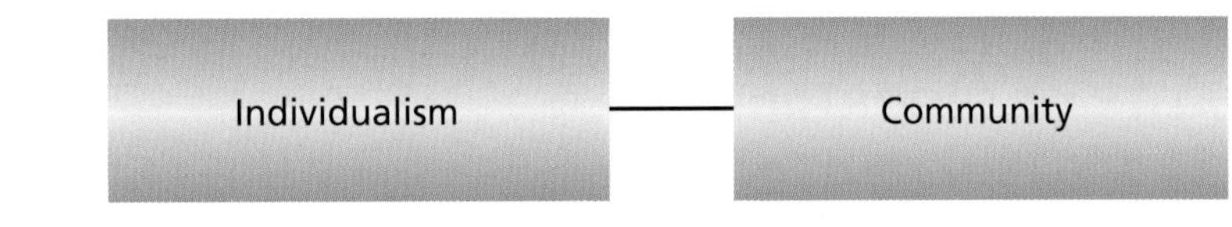

FIGURE 6.1 Balance between Individual and Community.

The application of justice may also differ based on place. The criminal justice system and the ideas about justice that underlie it may vary between states, counties, and towns. You may have heard of places where people believe that the law is applied very strictly, for instance, or of places where the justice system is not so strict. Again, the focus is squarely on distributive justice. Areas with strict enforcement might more freely distribute criminal justice outcomes (e.g., tickets, arrests, lengthy sentences) than areas with lenient enforcement.

In considering these kinds of variations in distributive justice, it is useful to address two questions: What is in the best interest of the individual? And what is in the best interest of the community? For instance, in the case of a noise violation, an individual's interest might be the right to play music at a desired volume, but the community's interest might be for peace and quiet. Of course, these two questions suggest a third: Whose interests should receive the most attention and how should they be balanced?

The difficult task is to select the proper balancing point. It may be tempting to consider the balance on a continuum between two endpoints in which justice emphasizes either the individual or the community. If the balance moves toward the individual, then the needs of the community are sacrificed. If the balance moves toward the community, then the needs of the individual are sacrificed. Figure 6.1 illustrates this model.

However, the model presented in Figure 6.1 is an oversimplification. Instead, it is possible to place a high value on both the individual and on the community at the same time. This leads us to a two-dimensional model, illustrated in Figure 6.2.

The models in Figure 6.2 consider the community, labeled here as "societal needs," and the individual, labeled here as "offender needs" (because it is the offender who generally receives the most attention from the criminal justice system). Four models are illustrated in Figure 6.2 (drawing upon concepts presented in Blake & Mouton, 1964). In parentheses, you will find the focal point of each model. This is the perspective that each model uses to resolve conflicts and to achieve justice. The sections that follow will provide a description of each model and its focal point. As you read, return to Box 6.1 to consider how each model might enable or inhibit wrongful convictions.

MECHANICAL CRIMINAL JUSTICE

mechanical model
A model of justice focusing neither on the needs of society nor on the needs of the offender. The intent of the model is to rigidly and rapidly follow laws and processes without discretion and without consideration of the outcomes they produce.

The **mechanical model** focuses neither on the needs of society nor on the needs of the offender. The intent of the model is to provide social order, and it does so through a focal point of organization. Rather than specifically considering anyone's needs, be they societal or individual, the model holds that society is static and unchanging—almost as though it could be permanently captured in a snapshot. All one needs to maintain order in this unchanging society is an organizational structure that implements the laws and policies that have already been put into place. As long as there is a written code of laws and policies, a police agency that enforces them, a court system that judges them, and a correctional system that punishes violators, the system is assumed to work. There is no need for discretion and little need for judgment beyond what the law says. The dispassionate enforcement of the laws precisely as they are written is the most important element of this model. Its measure of success is whether

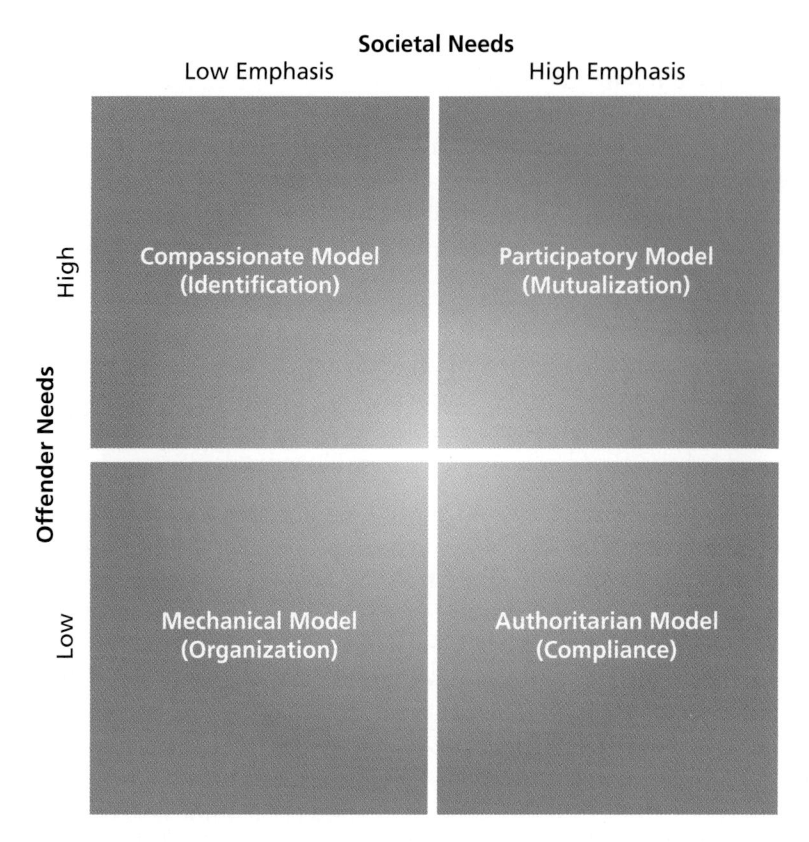

FIGURE 6.2 Distributive Justice Models.

the laws and policies have been followed regardless of what outcomes they may produce or what effects they may have on society or on individuals. Processes matter more than people.

From a distributive justice perspective, criminal justice outcomes are allocated through a very mechanical process without consideration of individual circumstances. Individuals are assumed to have received what they are due if the law has been followed. A decision's impact on the community is also inconsequential, as processes matter more than the actual resolution of a problem. This model is best exemplified in the notion of assembly-line justice, particularly when addressing less serious criminal offenses, which will be discussed further in Chapter 8. Briefly, it is a type of justice in which a busy courtroom works to process as many cases as possible in as short an amount of time as possible, with a greater focus on moving cases along than on trying to identify, or much less address, individual and community needs. As described by Malcolm Feeley (1992),

> In the lower courts trials are rare events, and even protracted plea bargaining is an exception. Jammed every morning with a new mass of arrestees who have been picked up the night before, lower courts rapidly process what the police consider "routine" problems—barroom brawls, neighborhood squabbles, domestic disputes, welfare cheating, shoplifting, drug possession, and prostitution—not "real" crimes. These courts are chaotic and confusing; officials communicate in a verbal shorthand wholly unintelligible to accused and accuser alike, and they seem to make arbitrary decisions, sending one person to jail and freeing the next. (p. 3)

Feeley titled his book about lower courts *The Process Is the Punishment.* In many ways, this is an apt description of mechanical criminal justice.

AUTHORITARIAN CRIMINAL JUSTICE

authoritarian model
A model of justice that focuses on the needs of society but not on the needs of the offender. Under the model, outcomes are highly important but process is not important.

The **authoritarian model** focuses on the needs of society but not on the needs of the offender. Justice is achieved through the focal point of mandating compliance with the laws set forth by the government, which has authority over society. Authoritarianism most specifically refers to a mindset that allows persons to receive direction from someone who desires to provide leadership and authority to them. Altemeyer (1996), the leading expert on authoritarian thought, defines it as a combination of the following:

> Authoritarian submission—a high degree of submission to the authorities who are perceived to be established and legitimate in the society in which one lives; Authoritarian aggression—a general aggressiveness, directed against various persons, that is perceived to be sanctioned by established authorities; [and] Conventionalism—a high degree of adherence to the social conventions that are perceived to be endorsed by society and its established authorities. (p. 6)

Let us consider how this applies to justice. Certain persons or groups in society have authority, which is simply the legal ability to do something. For instance, legislatures have the authority to pass laws, police officers have the authority to arrest persons who break those laws, and courts have the authority to sentence persons found guilty of violating the law. Unlike the mechanical model, outcomes are more important than process. Desired outcomes are those identified by persons or agencies with authority, and the measure of success is whether those outcomes are achieved. If the outcomes are achieved, then justice has been achieved as well. It is important to note that the authoritarian model has little tolerance for disagreement. The law and its enforcement, for instance, are considered absolute. An "us" versus "them" mentality develops in which persons who hold nonconventional values and persons who disagree with desired outcomes are ostracized or labeled as deviant. In addition, the voices of persons and groups without authority often go unheard.

Consider drug enforcement laws as an example. There are laws against certain kinds of drugs, the police enforce those laws, and the courts sentence offenders. So far, this sounds like the mechanical model. However, the authoritarian model does not simply specify that an orderly process should be followed to enforce drug (or any other) laws. The authoritarian model goes a step further, stating that the outcome desired by the law—that is, the elimination of illegal drugs—should be accomplished by any means possible (here we see the focus on the needs of society) whether or not it respects the rights of the offender or other individuals (here we see a lack of focus on the needs of the individual). Rights of procedural justice, such as those discussed in Chapter 8, are viewed negatively, sometimes even as annoyances to be circumvented. Persons who argue against strict enforcement, who are in favor of individual rights, or who advocate for changes in the law (e.g., decriminalizing medical marijuana) are viewed as suspect persons themselves for daring to question the conventional values established by those in authority. Their views are disregarded, and they are labeled as "dangerous" persons who challenge the stability of the system. As you can see, the tone of the authoritarian model is one that tolerates neither dissent nor disobedience.

From a distributive justice perspective, criminal justice outcomes are allocated through loyalty to and compliance with authority. That authority emphasizes that its goals must be accomplished, even if doing so minimizes individual rights and needs. Research has found that some criminal justice professionals demonstrate authoritarian tendencies (see Owen & Wagner, 2008), so an understanding of this model and its implications becomes important.

COMPASSIONATE CRIMINAL JUSTICE

compassionate model
A model of justice that places a higher emphasis on the offender's needs than on society's needs. The model suggests that justice is best achieved by identifying and correcting the needs of the offender that led him or her to commit crime.

The **compassionate model** places a higher emphasis on an offender's needs than on society's needs. However, neither society's needs nor public safety is ignored. The focal point of identification indicates that justice may best be achieved by identifying and correcting the needs of the offender that led him or her to commit crime. In this way,

the compassionate model takes a two-tier approach. First, it emphasizes the importance of preventing crime by anticipating and responding to those needs in advance. For instance, research has identified certain characteristics that increase the risk of a child engaging in delinquent behavior, such as intimate partner violence, negative peer pressure, being "rejected by peers" (Wasserman et al., 2003, p. 7), and more. Programs could then be created to address these issues, leading to reductions in future criminality. Second, the model emphasizes the importance of rehabilitation. Helping offenders to identify their needs and address these concerns in a constructive manner helps to yield justice for the offender and, consequently, for society. This does not render punishment unnecessary but specifies that in the course of punishment, criminal justice professionals should identify and correct the underlying issues that led offenders to commit crime in the first place, thereby lowering the risk for repeat offending. The programs that are instrumental to compassionate justice require partnerships between criminal justice professionals and experts outside the criminal justice system in the fields of psychology, education, social work, and more. For instance, in seeking to prevent juvenile crime, the government might work with child psychologists to develop and staff a program.

If violations of law occur, it communicates that more effort needs to be placed in crime prevention and rehabilitation or that the law itself needs to be modified to reflect changes in societal norms or realities. Violations can also indicate a failure to understand the law and the rationales underlying it, placing the burden on the criminal justice system to educate the public. From a distributive justice perspective, individuals are given their due in an individualized manner after the identification of needs specific to a particular situation and for a particular offender. Justice is only achieved when criminal justice outcomes are distributed in a way that identifies and addresses these needs.

PARTICIPATORY CRIMINAL JUSTICE

The **participatory model** places a high value on both the needs of society and the needs of the offender. To do so, the model uses a focal point of mutualization. This means understanding that meeting one set of needs does not preclude meeting another set of needs. This understanding is based on a commitment to the principles of justice, however they may be defined, and a subsequent commitment to applying those principles in a way that maximizes their value to society and to individuals. The success of the model is measured by the harmony between society and the individuals within it as they work together to promote justice.

participatory model
A model of justice that places a high value on both the needs of society and the needs of the offender. In this model, a variety of participants must work together to create, understand, and apply the law.

An example might prove helpful. Community policing is a popular strategy that we have already briefly mentioned and which you will learn more about in Chapter 11. In short, it involves police officers forming partnerships with the community so they can work together to address issues of crime and disorder. This helps break down barriers that are perceived to exist between the police and the public. As in the compassionate model, the public works with the police to identify and address community needs that lead to an increase in order. However, societal needs are not abandoned, as the police continue their work of patrolling, investigating crime, and so on, but in doing so, the police learn and respond to the community's concerns about which issues should take the highest priority. An effective community policing partnership allows both the public and the police to work together in harmony to achieve justice, focusing both on individual needs and on larger-scale societal concerns.

In this model, all participants in the system must work together to create, understand, and apply the law. In turn, the law must reflect a thorough consideration of perspectives from the public, legislators, criminal justice professionals, and more. The result is a law that truly must be a balance, as diagramed in Figure 6.1, providing rights and freedoms for individuals while also providing sufficient protection for society.

Limited resources and a heavy caseload often lead to busy courtrooms. What style(s) of justice does this illustrate? Should anything be done to reduce the workload of this court?

The participatory model achieves distributive justice through collaboration. Individuals are given their due in a system that allows for public participation in setting priorities and influencing law. As a result, the process that distributes criminal justice outcomes is one for which all members of society have accountability and ownership.

TOWARD JUSTICE

As you can see, justice theory involves many (sometimes conflicting) ideas. If "justice . . . is the great interest of man on earth" as Webster (1914, p. 533) suggests, then it is not an interest on which all persons agree as to its meaning. Different theories of justice can lead to different outcomes in the same case. Yet, it is important to appreciate the variations in justice theory for precisely that reason. The value of justice is powerful enough that "[t]he never ending battle for truth, justice, and the American way" (see Karp, 2009, p. 1) is the call to action for comic book superheroes—and it is also powerful enough to motivate individual actions and societal priorities. Professionals and the public alike must explore the ways justice is defined so we may then understand our own actions and those of others. Doing so can help us look for areas of common agreement, even when disagreements occur about which outcomes are most just.

Of course, this material can only be an introduction to justice theory. As you go through your personal, educational, and professional lives, continue to reflect on what justice means, how it relates to established theories, and how the concept can be refined. Justice is a dynamic concept that makes static definitions difficult. However, continued reflections about justice can advance our understanding of the entire criminal justice enterprise.

All of the forms of justice discussed in this chapter have the potential to shape criminal justice policy. Before moving on, review Box 6.4 and consider how debates about contemporary criminal justice issues are shaped by underlying ideas about the meaning of justice.

BOX 6.4

Research in Action

PURSUING JUSTICE

In 2001, the inaugural issue of the journal *Criminology and Public Policy* was published. The development of the journal was a joint venture between the National Institute of Justice, a research agency within the U.S. Department of Justice, and the American Society of Criminology, an association of academicians and practitioners dedicated to the study of crime and criminal justice. The "journal would have as its mission bridging the gap between policy-relevant research findings and criminal justice policy" (Clear & Frost, 2007). In 2007, the journal published a special issue in which 27 prominent criminologists in a variety of fields pertaining to crime and criminal justice wrote brief essays, each explaining one change they saw as being of central importance to the criminal justice system. While it has been a few years since the issue was published, the topics addressed in the essays remain at the forefront of debates about justice policy.

The recommendations cover a range of issues in the criminal justice system. Some focused on the police, such as recommending efforts to eliminate racial profiling (Alpert, 2007); developing specialized units within police departments to address gang issues, structured around the principles of community-oriented policing (Decker, 2007); developing structures to monitor policing and to investigate allegations of police misconduct, conducted by neutral persons who are not members of the police agency under review (Greene, 2007); requiring police agencies to collect and report data on incidents in which officers use force (Kane, 2007); and requiring police interrogations of suspects to be video recorded (Leo & Richman, 2007).

Others focused on corrections, such as halting the use of the death penalty until the controversies surrounding it can be carefully studied by policy makers and a decision can be made regarding whether to continue its use (Acker, 2007); eliminating mandatory sentences that take away a judge's discretion (Zimring, 2007); promoting further use of restorative justice (Braithwaite, 2007); structuring corrections around the goal of rehabilitation (Cullen, 2007); providing incentives for persons released from prison on parole to participate in rehabilitative programming and to remain crime free (Petersilia, 2007); and for persons on probation, identifying those who are statistically most likely to be homicide victims or offenders and then providing more intensive supervision and services to them (Sherman, 2007).

Closely related to corrections is a focus on offender re-entry, which has as its goal assisting offenders who are released from prison to reduce the likelihood that they will commit subsequent offenses. Possible strategies include re-examining and eliminating some of the prohibitions placed on ex-offenders, such as laws that prohibit them from holding certain jobs, pursuing education, or accessing public assistance programs (Bushway & Sweeten, 2007); in jurisdictions that prohibit felony ex-offenders from voting, changing the laws to allow them to vote (Crutchfield, 2007); unless required due to the nature of the job, prohibiting questions about criminal record in the job application process and deferring background checks until after a job offer has been made, to reduce discrimination against ex-offenders in employment (Henry & Jacobs, 2007); and rather than restricting where convicted sex offenders can live, enforcing restrictions banning high-risk offenders from facilities where children are likely to gather (Walker, 2007).

An additional group of recommendations focused on issues specific to juvenile justice, such as eliminating laws imposing curfews on juveniles, instead seeking other means of addressing juvenile offending (Adams, 2007); ending the use of life sentences for juvenile offenders (Fagan, 2007); identifying and implementing programs designed to address the needs of juveniles at high risk for committing crimes (Jones & Wyant, 2007); reducing reliance on programs such as D.A.R.E. (Drug Abuse Resistance Education), which are not shown to be effective in meeting their goals (Rosenbaum, 2007); and focusing on programs for children that are designed to reduce the likelihood of later offending (Welsh & Farrington, 2007).

Recommendations that do not fall neatly into the above categories include rethinking policies requiring offenders to submit DNA samples to a database (Taylor et al., 2007); emphasizing community-based crime prevention (Acosta & Chavis, 2007); revising sentencing policies, generally, with an emphasis on understanding career criminal offending patterns (Blumstein & Piquero, 2007); improving the efficiency of court processes (Ostrom & Hanson, 2007); designating the Bureau of Justice Statistics to maintain the Uniform Crime Reports, rather than the FBI (Rosenfeld, 2007); focusing increased study on terrorism, its causes, and the most effective responses that balance security with due process (LaFree & Hendrickson, 2007); and finally, and fittingly for the subject of this chapter, ensuring that criminal justice processes are fair (Rottman, 2007).

As you can see, the recommendations cover a variety of areas, many of which have the potential to generate some debate. But how do they correspond to ideas about justice? Consider the questions below.

- Q Review the recommendations and determine which theory or theories of justice (if any) might underlie each. Do you see any trends in terms of what theory or theories of justice are most common in this set of recommendations?
- Q Which of the above recommendations correspond to your definition of justice? Which do not? Why?
- Q Are there any recommendations that you would change or add to the list? If so, explain, and specify what theory of justice underlies your argument.

- Q What are the benefits, disadvantages, and consequences of each model of distributive justice that has been presented?
- Q How would each model of justice discussed in this section apply to the sexting case at the beginning of the chapter?
- Q Should all aspects of the criminal justice system (i.e., police, courts, corrections) subscribe to the same model of justice or to different models? Or does it depend (and if so, on what)? Explain.

Conclusion

What is justice and how do we know when it has been accomplished? This is a question that has vexed humankind for millennia. As illustrated in this chapter, there are many ways to view justice. Certainly, distributive justice is one of the most central to criminal justice practice, with its emphasis on providing individuals what they are due. That is not to discount the other perspectives of justice provided in this chapter, however, as they also can inform the study of criminal justice policy issues. In the next chapter, we will turn to a comparison of different forms of justice (criminal, civil, and social) and also consider how criminal justice policies—strategies that attempt to achieve justice, broadly speaking—are actually made.

Justice Reinvestment

Criminal Justice Problem Solving

justice reinvestment
Programs based on the idea that money spent on incarceration could be better spent on other initiatives to prevent crime.

The premise of **justice reinvestment** is that the money spent on incarceration (sending offenders to prison or jail) could be better spent on other initiatives. Justice reinvestment advocates suggest that "there is no logic to spending a million dollars a year to incarcerate people from one block in Brooklyn—over half for non-violent drug offenses—and return them, on average, in less than three years stigmatized, unskilled, and untrained to the same unchanged block" (Tucker & Cadora, 2003, p. 2).

Instead, justice reinvestment suggests an alternate approach. The general idea is that sentencing laws and strategies should be restructured to send fewer convicted offenders to prison. This will result in decreased spending on prisons. Some of the money that is saved is reinvested into a variety of services and programs that seek to reduce recidivism of released offenders or to prevent crime in general. The remainder of the money that is saved can be used for other purposes, such as funding other state agencies or initiatives and reducing state government expenditures, overall. The concept is an ambitious one, although "many details of justice reinvestment are left up for grabs" (Clear, 2011, p. 587), because there is not one specific way in which it must be accomplished. At least three models have been discussed.

Option #1: Return Funds to Localities to Spend

This option begins by allocating to communities a sum of money in the amount of the projected cost (based on data from prior years) of incarcerating offenders who committed crime in that community. The local jurisdiction is allowed to spend that money as they see fit, so long as the end result is a safer community. If the local courts decide that some high-risk offenders need to be incarcerated, the community pays the state back for doing so. The community is free to use the rest of the money as it wishes, so long as it is invested in community services. In Deschutes County, Oregon, this model was applied to juvenile offenders. The county decided some of the offenders should be incarcerated, and they returned the appropriate amount of money to the state to do so. For other offenders, the county created an intensive public service program in which juveniles "serve[d] their sentences by landscaping local parks, constructing bunk beds for families in need, or partnering with Habitat for Humanity to build homes" (Tucker & Caldora, 2003, p. 6). Surplus funds were spent on "schools, libraries, healthcare, and parks" (Tucker & Caldora, 2003, p. 7). The program did not reduce recidivism, but did produce many community service hours (211 hours per juvenile in the program), creating a positive relationship with the community, and fostering a sense of public service. Victims also reported greater satisfaction with the program than with the typical approach to juvenile crime (see Bradbury, 2002).

Option #2: Develop and Fund Additional Correctional Programming

In this model of justice reinvestment, jurisdictions identify correctional programs and strategies that can be used to reduce recidivism. Funding is provided to these programs and, presuming they are effective, the number of offenders sent to prison decreases, producing cost savings. Many states have adopted this approach; West Virginia is one. West Virginia set a goal of reducing the number of persons who are returned to prison for failing to successfully complete a community sentence (e.g., probation or parole). Based on research identifying substance abuse as a key concern, the state will increase funding for community-based substance abuse treatment in the amount of $5 million per year, among other initiatives. From 2014 through 2018, the state anticipates saving almost $142 million by reducing the prison population. Approximately $25.5 million of those savings will be reinvested into funding the substance abuse treatment and other initiatives, leaving approximately $116.3 million in additional savings for the state (Justice Center, 2013).

Criminal Justice Problem Solving

Justice Reinvestment

continued

Option #3: Pay for Services with Vouchers

Clear (2011) proposed a twofold system. First, offenders in prison could qualify for early release, thereby saving the amount of money that it would have cost to keep them incarcerated for the remainder of their sentence. The money that was saved would be used to provide vouchers to employers willing to hire the offender, important because maintaining employment is a key to successful reentry after release from prison. The vouchers would help the employers pay the ex-offender's wages. Second, offenders who might otherwise be sent to prison could qualify for a community program instead, again saving money. Savings could be used to provide vouchers to community organizations to offset the cost of programs and services offered to help in the supervision or rehabilitation of offenders. As of this writing, this was a conceptual proposal that had not yet been implemented.

What all three options have in common are the following: they are designed to reduce prison populations, which results in cost savings for the government; and some proportion of the cost savings are intended to fund programs that promote community safety by reducing recidivism, preventing crime, or providing supervision and services to offenders. As a concept that is only now being broadly implemented, time will tell if it is able to achieve its noble, but fairly ambitious, goals.

Q What do you think are the advantages and disadvantages of the justice reinvestment program?

Q Which of the three options do you think is most preferable, and why?

Q What philosophy or philosophies of justice do you think the justice reinvestment program illustrates? Explain your answer.

Q How does this program illustrate the relationship between the needs of society and the needs of the offender? Which model(s) of distributive justice (e.g., mechanical, authoritarian, compassionate, participatory) does it illustrate? Explain.

7

Concepts of Justice Policy

Learning Objectives

① Distinguish between criminal justice and civil justice. ② Explain how social justice and political culture influence criminal justice. ③ Explain how criminal justice policy is shaped by government structure. ④ Describe the forces that have shaped the development of criminal justice policy.

Key Terms

victimless crime
parens patriae
statute of limitations
civil justice
tort
preponderance of evidence
social justice
political culture
liberty
equality
public policy
policy window
federalism
National Supremacy Clause
Commerce Clause
agenda setting
problem definition
celebrated case
interest groups
bureaucrats

Key People

Harry Anslinger
David Miller
John Kingdon
Louis Brandeis
Murray Edelman
Samuel Walker
Steven Lab

Case Study

The Quagmire of State Marijuana Policy

The history of American marijuana law has come close to a full circle. Marijuana is derived from cannabis plants. In the nineteenth century, cannabis compounds were sold by pharmacists and traveling salespersons, offering to cure a variety of ailments. At that time, the criminal law did not restrict the use of marijuana (Inciardi, 1992).

By the mid-1930s, most states had passed laws regulating the distribution of marijuana, generally restricting it to those who had a prescription for its medical use (Ferraiolo, 2007). The laws were the product of a public panic about marijuana. The roots of the panic lay in a series of sensationalized and, by most accounts, inaccurate portrayals of marijuana use and its consequences, which appeared in newspapers and magazines. Also, the original *Reefer Madness* film, released in 1936, was specifically designed as an antimarijuana propaganda piece. The public came to fear marijuana and viewed it as a dangerous substance that led to violence and disorder and that was (reflecting the racism prevalent at the time) used by minorities to "have a corrupting influence on white society" (Inciardi, 1992, p. 21).

Enter Harry Anslinger, the director of the Federal Bureau of Narcotics, which was the forerunner of the Drug Enforcement Administration (DEA). In what some have argued was an attempt to gain power for his agency (Inciardi, 1992), Anslinger led the charge against marijuana; in fact, he drafted the antimarijuana law that many states chose to adopt in the 1930s. In 1937, Anslinger was instrumental in the passage of the federal *Marijuana Tax Act*, which essentially outlawed marijuana nationwide by imposing a series of strict restrictions and taxes on its distribution. Subsequent federal laws further controlled and penalized marijuana possession and distribution, and in 1970, it was classified as an illegal Schedule I drug, which defined it as having "no accepted medical use and a high potential for abuse" (Ferraiolo, 2007, p. 158). Since the War on Drugs in the 1980s, federal laws against the possession, sale, and distribution of all illegal drugs, including marijuana, have been strictly enforced as part of "getting tough" on crime and drugs (see Walker, 2006).

Although *federal* law still defines marijuana as an illegal substance, some *states* have taken steps to legally permit marijuana possession and use in certain circumstances.

Previous page: Robbie Callaway, former Chairman of the National Center for Missing and Exploited Children, shows an AMBER Alert kit at a Senate hearing. How do you think criminal justice policy should be made?

CRIMINAL JUSTICE

Criminal justice is, most broadly speaking, the government's response to crime. Characteristics of criminal justice processes will be described and illustrated by Abel and Baker's case.

1. *Criminal justice processes apply only when a crime has been committed.* As described in Chapter 1, crimes are acts or omissions that are specifically listed in a state's criminal code. The criminal code defines the act and indicates whether it is a felony or a misdemeanor. If a person's behavior does not constitute one of the acts or omissions in the criminal code, then no crime has occurred and the criminal justice process is not utilized.

Assume that a statute states: "A person may not intentionally cause or attempt to cause serious physical injury to another," as doing so is the crime of assault in the first degree (Assault . . . , 2011). In the hypothetical example, Baker has intentionally wounded Abel and has done so with the intent of causing injury. Therefore, Baker's conduct meets the criteria for a crime as defined by the quoted criminal code, and the criminal justice processes may be initiated.

On the other hand, if Baker had only said, "Your shirt is ugly and your socks don't match, you contemptible knave," then no crime would likely have occurred, and as a result the criminal justice system would probably not need to be involved in the incident. Next time, Baker will know.

2. *Criminal justice processes are initiated by the state against the accused.* Even though most crimes have victims who experience a direct harm (the exceptions being **victimless crimes**, in which no direct victim is readily identifiable, such as drug use, prostitution, gambling, and others), all crimes are technically considered crimes against the state, or government. If Baker was to be arrested and charged, the case would be *State v. Baker.* The government decides whether charges will be filed and a case will be brought. It is something of a misrepresentation in movies and television programs when a victim says, "I don't want to press charges," because that is not the victim's decision to make; again, it is up to the government. Having said that, it would be difficult for the government to prosecute a case if the victim does not cooperate with the prosecution, so often if a victim does not wish to press charges, the government does not do so.

victimless crime
A category of crime in which no direct victim is readily identifiable. This includes crimes such as drug possession, prostitution, illegal gambling, and others.

The concept of crimes being against the state rather than against individual victims has its roots in the social contract theory described in Chapter 2. Recall that the theory is a metaphor for justice processes in which the state takes responsibility for protecting its citizens. This notion has further roots in English common law, under which the monarch was understood to be the parent and protector of his or her subjects (Custer, 1978), a concept known in Latin as ***parens patriae.*** Casting the state as victim also serves another purpose: it symbolically depersonalizes criminal incidents. It is the state's task, as government, to address and punish crimes. Victims are no longer responsible for producing their own justice. This removes the need for blood feuds in which victims were responsible for enacting their own vigilante justice on an offender. This is of substantial importance because a government's ability to promote justice without having victims turn to vigilantism is associated with the degree of peace in a society (Otterbein & Otterbein, 1965).

parens patriae
A metaphor suggesting that the law (or the government through law) acts as a parent and protector to its subjects. This notion, grounded in the belief that society has a moral obligation to protect its citizens, underlies the theory of legal paternalism.

3. *The agents responsible for initiating the criminal justice process are government employees.* The police investigate crimes and, based on probable cause, arrest persons believed to have committed crimes. The prosecuting attorney files the formal charges and works to resolve criminal cases either through guilty pleas or convictions at trial (the overwhelming majority of cases are resolved through plea bargains and guilty pleas). Both the police and district attorneys are public employees who work for the government.

In the hypothetical tavern situation, assume that someone from the bar calls the police. The police would come and investigate the incident to determine what happened.

In 1975, the Alaska Supreme Court ruled that individuals may possess small amounts of marijuana for personal use, noting "that citizens of the State of Alaska have a basic right to privacy in their homes . . . [which] would encompass the possession and ingestion of substances such as marijuana in a purely personal, non-commercial context in the home" (*Ravin v. State*, 1975, p. 29). In 1996, voters in California approved a measure that legalized medical marijuana (Brown, 2008). As of 2013, more than 69,000 California residents had been issued permission to possess medical marijuana (California Department of Public Health, 2013). In 2008, voters in Massachusetts approved a measure which decriminalized any possession of up to one ounce of marijuana by persons 18 and older, even for recreational purposes. Rather than facing criminal charges, individuals who are caught in possession of an ounce or less will now pay a $100 fine that carries no criminal record and no criminal consequences (*Information for Voters*, 2008). In 2012, voters in Washington and Colorado approved a measure legalizing possession of small amounts (one ounce or less) of marijuana by persons 21 and older, without any penalties (Healy, 2012).

As of this writing, 17 states have decriminalized marijuana to some (even limited) extent, and more than 18 states make some allowance for medical marijuana (Knowles, 2013). Of course, even with these *state* laws, marijuana remains illegal in *federal* law (more on this later).

Q How do you think the law should regulate marijuana? Why? How do debates over the regulation of marijuana correspond to competing philosophies of law?

Q What factors do you think might have influenced the changes in law described above?

Q Assume that a person in Colorado who possesses a small amount of marijuana for personal use is arrested by a federal DEA officer because possession is illegal under federal law (regardless of what Colorado law says). How would you resolve such a case? Why?

Criminal Justice and Civil Justice

FOCUSING QUESTION 7.1

What is the difference between criminal justice and civil justice?

As you learned in Chapter 6, justice is an elusive concept, difficult to define and perhaps equally difficult to fully achieve. In this chapter, we further refine our understanding of justice by exploring three broad venues in which justice can be achieved: criminal, civil, and social. The chapter will then turn to the making of criminal justice policy.

It is important to recognize that, although each accomplishes a different task, criminal, civil, and social justice are not entirely isolated from one another. For instance, the same action can fall under the purview of the criminal justice system and the civil justice system while raising social justice concerns. To help in clarifying the distinctions while highlighting the potential for overlap, this section will track the following hypothetical case.

Hoping for a rousing night "out on the town," Abel stops by his favorite tavern. After ordering and consuming several rounds of shots, Abel notices a female patron at the end of the bar and decides to strike up some conversation. The two hit it off. Their dialogue is interrupted, however, by the arrival of Baker, the patron's jealous ex-boyfriend. Baker takes exception to Abel's conversation (they were only discussing the weather!) and communicates this by breaking several beer bottles over Abel's head. As a result, Abel sustains a concussion (these were heavy beer bottles) as well as a number of cuts that require stitches. Abel's resulting medical bills exceed $10,000, and because Abel is uninsured, he has to pay these bills out of his own pocket.

Upon completing their investigation, they would arrest Baker for his acts against Abel and file an initial charging document. A prosecutor would review the case and the charges against Baker and then would proceed with the case by attempting to secure a guilty plea or a guilty verdict in court.

4. *Because crimes are viewed as acts against society as a whole, there are few time limits placed on when charges may be filed.* For certain legal actions, there is a provision called a **statute of limitations**, which sets time limits on when court processes can be initiated. There is generally no statute of limitations for murder and other very serious crimes. For less serious offenses, there may be statutes of limitations, but generally speaking, the more serious the crime, the longer the time period in which charges can be filed.

statute of limitations
A legal provision that sets time limits on how long after an incident court processes can be initiated.

Assume there is a 15-year statute of limitations for first-degree assault. If Baker had fled the scene after the incident, neither Abel nor the police may have known his identity. If, 10 years later, evidence surfaced (perhaps a long lost video surveillance recording) to indicate that Baker was Abel's assailant, then Baker could be arrested and charged with the crime—even though 10 years had passed.

As a general rule, the more time that elapses between a crime and the filing of charges, the more difficult it is to proceed. Witnesses will grow older and may forget details of the case, evidence may be misplaced or deteriorate, and the police and prosecutors initially involved in the case may have moved on in their careers. However, delayed prosecutions can occur. One such case was dramatized in the film *Ghosts of Mississippi,* which is the story of the trial of Byron De La Beckwith. In 1994, Beckwith was tried and convicted of first-degree murder in the assassination of civil rights leader Medgar Evers—a crime that occurred in 1963. The case was reopened when a prosecutor discovered new evidence in the early 1990s. Upon appeal, the Mississippi Supreme Court upheld the conviction because there was no statute of limitations for murder, which allowed the trial to occur even decades after the offense (*Beckwith v. State of Mississippi,* 1997).

5. *In the criminal justice system, proof of guilt must be beyond a reasonable doubt.* A criminal conviction carries with it many consequences. Depending on the crime and the jurisdiction, they may include, but are not limited to, deprivation of freedom through a prison sentence, inability to hold certain jobs, inability to vote, attaching the label of "convict" or "criminal," and more. Because of these consequences, the state sets a very high bar before it determines guilt. It is difficult to provide a precise definition of "beyond a reasonable doubt." It does not mean absolute certainty beyond any doubt, but at the same time, it does not leave much room for doubt. You will learn more about this concept in Chapter 12.

6. *Upon pleading guilty or being found guilty, a defendant may receive criminal punishment.* Each jurisdiction's legal code defines what that criminal punishment entails. In Baker's case, assume that the punishment specified for assault in the first degree is "imprisonment not exceeding 25 years" (Assault . . . , 2011). The judge could sentence Baker to prison for any amount of time with a maximum of 25 years or suspend part of the prison sentence and require that Baker serve that time on probation (Chapter 13 will explain probation in greater detail). Regardless of Baker's actual sentence, it is a criminal punishment issued by a judge after Baker's conviction.

These characteristics define the criminal justice process. As you can see, it is largely directed by the government and relies on addressing crimes as defined by the legal code.

CIVIL JUSTICE

Civil justice is distinct from criminal justice; it is an entirely different process. However, it is important to recognize that the same incident may be processed through both the criminal justice system and the civil justice system, sometimes with different outcomes. For instance, in 1994, former NFL player, sports commentator, and actor

civil justice
A process, separate from criminal justice, in which private wrongs are addressed through legal action. This generally occurs through the filing of lawsuits by one person, organization, group, etc. against another. A tort is one common type of civil justice action.

O. J. Simpson was criminally charged with the murders of his ex-wife Nicole Brown and her friend Ronald Goldman; in criminal court, he was found not guilty of those charges in 1995 (the case was *People of the State of California v. Simpson*). However, in 1997, Simpson was held accountable in civil court for the death of Goldman and for assault against both Goldman and Brown (in *Goldman v. Simpson* and *Brown v. Simpson,* cases filed by the survivors of the victims) (for further information, see Schuetz & Lilley, 1999). To understand how different outcomes can occur—one in criminal court, one in civil court—based on the same incident, you must understand the differences between criminal justice and civil justice. Consider the following characteristics of civil justice.

1. *Civil justice processes do not require that a crime has been committed.* Under civil justice, individuals may sue when they believe they have been harmed in some way, whether or not the harmful act is codified as a crime. Civil justice covers a wide variety of areas and forms the basis for most study at law schools. To oversimplify, however, one instance in which individuals can pursue civil justice is when they have been physically or emotionally injured as the result of an act. To return to our example, in addition to criminal action, Abel could bring a civil action against Baker, claiming that Baker committed actions that harmed Abel in some way. This type of action is known as a **tort**, or civil wrong. There is no precise statute that lists every specific type of harm that can be addressed in tort law in the way that there are precise statutes that list all types of crimes. Attorneys instead base their arguments, and judges base their decisions, on common law (i.e., established precedents from prior cases), on the particular circumstances of each case, and on how they match broad and general principles that define tort actions.

tort
A harm that is classified as a civil wrong and that forms the basis for action under civil justice processes.

The Abel and Baker case is a situation in which a crime is also a tort. Let's consider a relatively famous case from 1992 in which a tort claim was raised but which was not a criminal act.

> [A woman] sitting in the passenger seat of her grandson's car holding a coffee that she purchased from a drive-through window of a McDonald's . . . opened the lid of her coffee to add cream and sugar, [and] spilled the coffee on herself. The coffee cups were made of Styrofoam and were not particularly sturdy. The sweatpants that [she] was wearing absorbed the coffee and held it next to her skin. A vascular surgeon determined that [she] suffered third degree burns over 6% of her body, including her inner thighs, groin, buttocks, and genital areas. She was hospitalized for eight days, during which time she underwent skin grafting. As a result of the burns and surgery, [she] had permanent scarring on more than 16% of her body. (Ryan, 2003, p. 80)

While an unfortunate occurrence, this was not a criminal event, so it would not be resolved through the criminal justice system. However, as a result of the injury, the victim was able to pursue the case as a tort in civil court.

2. *The civil justice process is initiated by individuals.* In civil justice, acts are not against the state or government; rather, they are against individuals. When one individual tells another person (or a company, or an organization, or whomever) "I'll *SUE* you," they are referring to the initiation of a civil case. Therefore, the civil justice process is only initiated when a person who has been harmed makes the decision to file a lawsuit in a civil court. If Abel were to decide that Baker's criminal punishment was not enough or if Abel wanted to hold Baker further accountable, he could do so by suing him in a civil tort action.

3. *The agents responsible for pursuing civil justice lawsuits are private attorneys.* When an individual has decided to pursue a civil case, he or she generally must hire an attorney to help initiate the proceedings, to conduct necessary inquiries and investigations, and ultimately, to present the case in court (there are some exceptions, such as small

claims court). This attorney is not a government employee but may be in private practice or a member of a law firm. Because attorneys generally charge by the hour or by the case, and cases generally take substantial time to prepare, the civil justice process is more available to those with financial resources than to those without. To pursue a civil case, Abel would have to make an appointment with an attorney to discuss the case. If the attorney agreed to accept the case, he or she would work with Abel to prepare the required documents and to present the case in court.

4. *Civil court places more narrow time limits on bringing a case forward.* There are generally stricter statutes of limitations in civil justice than there are in criminal justice. For instance, for a wrongful injury tort, it is not unusual for there to be a two-year time limit within which civil cases may be filed. If that was the time limit, it would mean that two years and one day after Abel's assault he would no longer be able to bring a civil case against Baker. Again, civil justice refers to private disputes between individuals or organizations, and the courts do not want such issues to linger.

5. *The burden of proof in civil court is by a preponderance of the evidence.* Proof beyond a reasonable doubt is not required. Because individuals will not be deprived of their liberty (by being placed in prison or on probation) and will not lose basic rights (e.g., voting) as a result of losing a civil case, the burden of proof is lower. A **preponderance of evidence** means the judge or jury believes it is "more likely than not" that the defendant injured or harmed the plaintiff, a burden of proof that does not require the same level of certainty as the "beyond a reasonable doubt" threshold for criminal cases. In addition, many of the procedural protections that you will learn about in the next chapter apply only to criminal cases and not civil cases.

6. *Civil justice verdicts do not result in criminal punishment.* If a judge or jury "finds for the plaintiff," it means the person bringing the case wins. However, the defendant

preponderance of evidence
The burden of proof used in deciding cases heard through civil justice processes (it is also used in some criminal justice hearings and in some administrative hearings). It means that the judge or jury believes it is more likely than not that an incident occurred or that one party caused harm to another.

Asset forfeiture is one type of civil court proceeding. In asset forfeiture cases, the government sues to acquire property that was used as an instrumentality of a crime—that is, something that was used to facilitate or commit a criminal offense. Through asset forfeiture, law enforcement agencies have acquired vehicles (as in this picture), computers, money, buildings, and more. The items acquired may be sold, disposed of, or retained for government use. The agency bringing the forfeiture lawsuit bears the burden of demonstrating in civil court that the item was sufficiently connected to the crime. What do you think are the advantages and disadvantages of asset forfeiture? When do you think it should be used?

BOX 7.1

POLICE CIVIL LIABILITY

Qualified immunity is a legal principle specifying that public employees (such as police officers) cannot be sued in civil court unless their conduct is particularly egregious. Qualified immunity does *not* apply, and police officers *can* be sued, if (1) they violate an individual's constitutional rights, such as through an excessive use of force; and (2) in such a case, a reasonable officer would view the use of force as unlawful in the specific circumstance of the case. The Supreme Court has noted in *Graham v. Connor* (1989) that this analysis should be "from the perspective of a reasonable officer on the scene, rather than with the 20/20 vision of hindsight" (p. 396). In addition, *Saucier v. Katz* (2001) specified that qualified immunity is meant "to protect officers from the sometimes 'hazy border between excessive and acceptable force'" (p. 206)

Review the following case in which an officer was sued (using legal language, he was sued by the "respondent" in this case), which ultimately reached the U.S. Supreme Court. The case involved a high speed pursuit and its termination. The pursuit began when an officer "clocked respondent's vehicle traveling at 73 miles per hour on a road with a 55-mile-per-hour speed limit. The deputy activated his blue flashing lights indicating that respondent should pull over. Instead, respondent sped away, initiating a chase down what is in most portions a two-lane road, at speeds exceeding 85 miles per hour . . . In the midst of the chase, respondent pulled into the parking lot of a shopping center and was nearly boxed in by the various police vehicles. Respondent evaded the trap by making a sharp turn, colliding with [a] police car, exiting the parking lot, and speeding off once again down a two-lane highway" (*Scott v. Harris,* 2007, pp. 374–375).

The pursuit was captured on videotape (http://www.supremecourt.gov/media/media.aspx), which the Court described as follows: "we see respondent's vehicle racing down narrow, two-lane roads in the dead of night at speeds that are shockingly fast. We see it swerve around more than a dozen other cars, cross the double-yellow line, and force cars traveling in both directions to their respective shoulders to avoid being hit. We see it run multiple red lights and travel for considerable periods of time in the occasional center left-turn-only lane" (p. 379).

Approximately 10 miles into the pursuit, the officer in the lead requested and received permission to conduct a Precision Intervention Technique (PIT) manuever, which entails using the front quarter of the police vehicle to tap the rear quarter of the vehicle being pursued, causing a spin-out. However, on second thought, the officer decided the vehicles were traveling too fast for a PIT maneuver. Instead, the officer "applied his push bumper to the rear of respondent's vehicle. As a result, respondent lost control of his vehicle, which left the roadway, ran down an embankment, overturned, and crashed. Respondent was badly injured and was rendered a quadriplegic" (p. 375).

The officer was sued in civil court by the driver of the car. The basis of the lawsuit was the driver's claim that the officer used excessive force during the pursuit.

Q How would you rule in the lawsuit? Do you think qualified immunity should apply (in which case the officer could not be sued) or should not apply (in which case a lawsuit against the officer could go forward)? Explain your answer.

Q In recent years, some police agencies have enacted policies limiting when officers are permitted to engage in pursuits (e.g., Lum & Fachner, 2008, pp. 88–90). How would you determine when high speed pursuits are appropriate and when they are not? (You may wish to review research on this topic, including Hill, 2002; Schultz, Hudak, & Alpert, 2009; and Schultz, Hudak, & Alpert, 2010).

Q The Court ruled in favor of the officer, holding that "[t]he car chase that respondent initiated in this case posed a substantial and immediate risk of serious physical injury to others . . . [The officer's] attempt to terminate the chase by forcing respondent off the road was reasonable" (p. 386). Do you agree or disagree with the Court's conclusion? Why?

will not be sentenced to prison or probation or lose any rights. Instead, the defendant will generally be ordered to pay a financial settlement to the plaintiff. This is not a fine paid to the government; rather, it is a sum of money paid directly to the plaintiff. Financial settlements often cover the actual damages incurred in the case for physical injury, and they may also include money to compensate for emotional injury. The settlement can also include punitive damages, which is a sum of money designed to symbolically "punish" the defendant for the damaging acts through a payment to the plaintiff.

Returning to the hot coffee case, a jury found for the plaintiff and also concluded "that McDonald's had engaged in willful, reckless, malicious, or wanton conduct" (Ryan, 2003, p. 82). The jury made the following awards (although the case was appealed and the total amount was later reduced):

> [Punitive damages were] the equivalent of two days of worldwide coffee sales, totaling $2.7 million. With respect to actual damages for medical bills, attorneys' fees, and compensation for loss, [plaintiff] was [also] awarded $200,000. However, the jury determined that [plaintiff] was also at fault in the way she handled the coffee. On this point, the jury determined that [plaintiff] was 20% at fault, which automatically reduced the $200,000 award by 20% to $160,000. (Ryan, 2003, p. 82)

As you can see, civil justice and criminal justice are very different. The primary focus of this text is on criminal justice, but it remains important for you to have a basic understanding of civil justice processes. Not only can the same incident be subject to a civil claim and a criminal case, but criminal justice personnel and agencies can also be sued under civil justice processes by individuals who believe they have been wronged; see Box 7.1 for an example.

Q Assume that a person was arrested for possession of marijuana. How would each of the elements of criminal law apply to the case?

Q One type of civil tort is "wrongful discharge" from a job. Assume that an employee has a physician's prescription for medical marijuana but is fired for violating a company's "zero tolerance" substance abuse policy. If the employee decided to sue the company, how would a wrongful discharge case proceed according to the six elements of civil justice that have been described? If you were the judge, how do you think the case should be resolved?

Q Why do you think we need separate criminal justice and civil justice systems? Would you make any changes to the approach used by either system? Why or why not?

Social Justice and American Values

FOCUSING QUESTION 7.2

How do social justice and political culture influence criminal justice?

Unlike criminal justice and civil justice, **social justice** does not refer to a legal process. Rather, it is an idea or a value to which individuals may subscribe and which, in turn, can shape decisions about civil justice and criminal justice policy issues. Social justice embodies concerns about fairness and equality. Political theorist David Miller (1999) is one of the leading scholars of social justice theory; he states that social justice is

> how the good and bad things in life should be distributed among members of a human society. When, more concretely, we attack some policy or some state of affairs as socially unjust, we are claiming that a person, or more usually a category of persons, enjoys fewer advantages than that person or group of persons ought to enjoy (or bears more of the burdens than they ought to bear), given how other members of the society in question are faring. (p. 1)

social justice
Considers issues of equality and inequality in society and whether benefits and risks are distributed in a manner that is fair and without discrimination. Argues that the pursuit of justice is the pursuit of equality.

Social justice often challenges hegemony, which refers to the influence that is exercised by powerful groups within society. Some debates about social justice stem from fears that those with power use their influence to make decisions that marginalize socially or politically unpopular groups either deliberately or due to a lack of awareness of those groups' needs and concerns. Social justice advocates raise attention to issues in which they observe unjust, unfair, or unequal treatment of persons. As such, social justice overlaps at least partially with critical legal theories (from Chapter 3), critical criminology (from Chapter 5), and the distributive justice concerns with how outcomes are allocated to those to whom they are "due" (from Chapter 6).

There are many issues that can be raised under the umbrella of social justice. One conceptualization is to ask the question, can we have a just society without a particular benefit being available to all members of society? Or are there systematic inequalities or discriminatory behaviors that lead to unequal benefits, which in turn can lead to injustices? Social justice theorists would argue that both criminal and civil justice processes should strive to promote social justice through their decisions and that doing so ought to be a key focus for all legal processes.

In the case of Abel and Baker, one question pertaining to social justice is Abel's lack of health insurance. In the 2010 debates on health care, one pervasive question was precisely about whether it was a social injustice for some persons to be uninsured and to have limited access to health care. This debate emerged as a challenge to the hegemony of the health care system at the time and led to the passage of the Patient Protection and Affordable Care Act, one provision of which was to require that most persons (a small number of exceptions are permitted under the law) acquire a certain level of health insurance coverage. The law, and the issue of health care as a social justice issue in general, continue to be the subject of considerable controversy. While the U.S. Supreme Court upheld the requirement for individuals to have health insurance (*National Federation of Independent Business v. Sebelius,* 2012), vigorous debates have continued on both sides of the issue. But how is social justice specifically related to criminal justice?

Social justice theorists (see Arrigo, 1999a) argue that criminal justice should reflect social justice, linking the two concepts and requiring the criminal justice system to demonstrate fair and equal treatment of all persons under its control, with an emphasis on basic rights. This presumes that we ask questions about what makes a just, fair, and equitable society and then promote a criminal justice system that achieves those goals. Conversely, social justice theorists argue that when an injustice is detected, affirmative steps must be taken to correct the system so it may more effectively promote social justice. Because social philosophies change over time, this can become a continuous process.

As an example, consider health care in prisons. Are inmates entitled to receive health care? And if so, what quality of health care should be provided? This is a social justice question because it considers the distribution of a resource (health care) and whether one group of persons (those in prison) is unfairly denied those resources. For many years, health care in correctional institutions was less than adequate. Consider the following description of one state's correctional health care system through the 1970s (*Ruiz v. Estelle,* 1980):

> Major problems pervade all aspects of the medical care . . . The personnel providing routine medical care are often unqualified; they are also wholly insufficient in numbers and deficiently supervised. The meager medical facilities, inadequately equipped and poorly maintained, do not meet state licensing requirements. Medical procedures are unsound and faulty at all levels of care. Initial processing, sick call methods, and transfer practices are all unnecessarily cumbersome, inefficient, and life-threatening . . . Medical records are so poorly maintained, and the entries

> made therein are so incomplete and inaccurate, as to be either useless or harmful in the day-to-day provision of medical care. (p. 1307)

In 1976, the U.S. Supreme Court ruled "that deliberate indifference to serious medical needs of prisoners" (*Estelle v. Gamble,* 1976, p. 104) is cruel and unusual punishment. One way of understanding this decision is through a social justice lens, with the Supreme Court indicating that provision of health care to inmates is necessary to meet the requirements of fairness and justice. As a result, correctional agencies must create policies that meet this requirement by allowing for proper inmate medical care. Correctional health care continues to be an issue of concern; for a more recent example, see Box 7.2.

As another example, consider a 2010 Arizona state law designed to address illegal immigration, which illustrates the dilemmas that can arise from the perspective of social justice. One of the most controversial provisions of the law is the following:

> For any lawful contact made by a law enforcement official or agency of this state or a county, city, town or other political subdivision of this state where reasonable suspicion exists that the person is an alien who is unlawfully present in the United States, a reasonable attempt shall be made, when practicable, to determine the immigration status of the person. The person's immigration status shall be verified with the Federal Government. (*Senate Bill 1070,* 2010, p. 2)

One fear was that the law would lead to racial profiling by police. Opponents argue that it gives law enforcement too broad of an ability to detain virtually any persons, but in particular persons who appear to be Hispanic, for the purpose of verifying their citizenship. Shortly after the law was passed, President Barack Obama commented that the law could "undermine basic notions of fairness that we cherish as Americans, as well as the trust between police and our communities that is so crucial to keeping us safe" (Archibold, 2010, para. 5). Because of the concerns about discrimination and fairness, this issue invoked concerns pertinent to social justice. It also illustrates conflicts that may occur between criminal justice and social justice.

For instance, some in the criminal justice system might argue that the law was necessary to promote security, order, and enforcement of immigration requirements, with social justice concerns being secondary. At the same time, social justice advocates might argue that the law promotes inequitable outcomes which must be corrected, even if doing so requires changing the law. As is the case with many controversial issues, meaningful dialogue between the two sides could be difficult because each side is arguing from its core values—security on one side and social justice on the other (Sabatier & Jenkins-Smith, 1993). Because beliefs in core values are often strongly held, resolving differences of opinion can take some time, or can require intervention from the courts. The latter was the case for this issue, although different courts reached different decisions. In 2011, the U.S. Court of Appeals upheld a preliminary injunction (i.e., a legal mechanism that temporarily prohibits enforcement of a law) against the section of the law quoted above (*United States v. State of Arizona*). However, in 2012, the U.S. Supreme Court ruled that the provision was permissible (*Arizona v. United States*), particularly if efforts by law enforcement agencies are "reasonable" (as stated in the law) and not excessive or violative of constitutional protections. Still, arguments about the legislation and its social justice impacts continue.

There are many other examples of social justice issues. As a general principle, social justice involves concepts of fairness and equal treatment, particularly when there are concerns about differences between groups. It is also important to note that there are many social justice issues that have not traditionally been the focus of study in criminal justice but which have criminal justice implications nonetheless. Box 7.3 presents one such example pertaining to homelessness.

BOX 7.2

Ethics in Practice

HEALTH CARE AND CALIFORNIA PRISONS

In 2011, the U.S. Supreme Court ruled in the case *Brown v. Plata,* addressing the quality of health care in California state prisons. The case really began many years earlier. In 1990, a lower court found that treatment for serious mental illness in California prisons was inadequate, and in 2001, after a lawsuit was filed, the state itself agreed that medical care was inadequate to meet constitutional requirements. In both of these cases, the state agreed to supervision and oversight as it worked toward correcting the problematic conditions.

The problem for California was a combination of inadequate resources and prison overcrowding. Prisons were filled to nearly double their capacity, leaving too many inmates to be cared for with too few facilities and staff. At the same time, the California state budget was stretched thin, so it was not feasible to build new correctional facilities or to hire additional medical staff and purchase additional medical equipment.

As time went on, those overseeing the situation determined that not enough improvements had been made and the case returned to court. A federal law called the Prison Litigation Reform Act (PRLA) authorizes judges to order states to reduce overcrowding in their facilities, and a three-judge panel in a Federal District Court did exactly that. Specifically, they ordered California to ensure that none of its prisons exceeded 137.5% of their capacity. California prisons exceeded this amount by a total of approximately 46,000 inmates.

There are numerous ways that the state could compy with the order. They could build additional prisons, send inmates to local jails (operated at the county level and generally for short-term confinement of less than a year), or send inmates to facilities in other states that had extra room. Another alternative was to simply release inmates, even if their sentences were not yet completed. Dissatisfied with the District Court's order, California appealed to the U.S. Supreme Court.

The Supreme Court upheld the lower court's order, finding that the state of medical care and mental health care in California's prisons was so inadequate as to violate the Constitutional requirements, and that the order to reduce overcrowding was necessary to ensure that the prisons were able to provide adequate care to those who were incarcerated. The Supreme Court cited a variety of examples of the inadequate medical care brought on by overcrowding:

AMERICAN POLITICAL CULTURE

political culture
The broad set of values that underlie a particular political system. As such, political culture shapes the development of law and policy.

Before concluding a discussion of justice, it is useful to consider values that are held as foundational to American political culture. A **political culture** refers to the broad set of values that underlie a particular political system (see generally Almond & Verba, 1989). In reality, the concept of a political culture is a philosophical oversimplification. There is not one single political culture in most jurisdictions. However, the notion of political culture is important because it is the dominant political culture that tends to shape law and policy.

There is no central repository that officially lists or declares a nation's political culture. Rather, it is derived from the nation's documents (e.g., Constitution, Bill of Rights, Federalist Papers, and Declaration of Independence, among many others) and the nation's social, economic, and political history. Several components of American political culture are briefly surveyed here.

liberty
The freedom and the protection of rights as enumerated in the Constitution and Bill of Rights. Liberty is a fundamental component of American political culture.

Certainly, two of the most preeminent values in American political culture are liberty and equality. **Liberty**, or freedom, is embodied in the first 10 Amendments to the Constitution, the Bill of Rights. From the emphasis on "life, *liberty,* and the pursuit of happiness" [emphasis added] in the Declaration of Independence, liberty has been a key American value. The criminal justice system must balance the need to promote order with a respect for and protection of the many rights and freedoms that are afforded under the Constitution and Bill of Rights both to the innocent and to those accused of crime. You will learn more about these rights in Chapter 8 and Chapter 10.

> Because of a shortage of treatment beds, suicidal inmates may be held for prolonged periods in telephone-booth sized cages without toilets. A psychiatric expert reported observing an inmate who had been held in such a cage for nearly 24 hours, standing in a pool of his own urine, unresponsive and nearly catatonic. Prison officials explained they had 'no place to put him' . . . Wait times for mental health care can range as high as 12 months. In 2006, the suicide rate in California's prisons was nearly 80% higher than the national average . . . Prisoners suffering from physical illness also receive severely deficient care . . . A correctional officer testified that, in one prison, up to 50 sick inmates may be held together in a 12- by 20-foot cage for up to five hours awaiting treatment . . . A prisoner with severe abdominal pain died after a 5-week delay in referral to a specialist; a prisoner with 'constant and extreme' chest pain died after an 8-hour delay in evaluation by a doctor; and a prisoner died of testicular cancer after a 'failure of MDs to work up for cancer in a young man with 17 months of testicular pain.' (pp. 5–7)

Following the Supreme Court's decision, the state of California worked to reduce its inmate population. Many inmates were either moved to local jails or to prisons in other states. Having been given a two-year deadline to do so, when the state reached a point of having only 10,000 inmates beyond the specified limit (Medina, 2013), officials requested permission of the Supreme Court to extend the timeline; the request was refused (*Brown v. Plata,* 2013).

- Q What standard of prison medical care do you think is ethically required?
- Q If you were the Secretary (i.e., Director) of the California Department of Corrections and Rehabilitation, what concerns do you think you would need to balance in determining how to reduce the prison population by 46,000? Which alternative(s) do you think would be most promising? Defend why you believe the alternative(s) are ethically appropriate.
- Q Reducing the prison population by 46,000 inmates is a short-term solution. What do you think should be done in the long term to ensure that this is not a problem in the future?

Equality is also embodied within the Declaration of Independence, which notes that "all men are created *equal*" [emphasis added], and further protected by various constitutional protections and acts of legislation. There has been substantial change and progress over time in ensuring that the political system promotes equality. In the late 1700s, equality was only available to white male property owners who were over the age of 21. Through a series of constitutional amendments and law, equality is now accorded to all persons over 18 regardless of race, gender, or property ownership. In addition, efforts have promoted the expansion of equality to also consider disability status, veteran status, age, sexual orientation, citizenship status, religious affiliation, and more. The criminal justice system must ensure that it functions in a way that does not discriminate or deny rights to certain groups, which is the essence of the concern for social justice described earlier.

Equality
Refers to protections that promote equal rights for all persons without discrimination regardless of characteristics such as race, gender, religion, disability status, veteran status, sexual orientation, income, and more. Equality is a fundamental component of American political culture.

The final value to be discussed is important for the success of any political system. Legitimacy refers to the public's belief in the government's right to govern. That is, it refers to public faith in a particular government or political system. This is essential for criminal justice. If the actors in the criminal justice system—that is, the police, courts, and corrections—are to be effective, they must have the trust of the public. If the public does not place its faith in the criminal justice system, then the social contract is eroded and order may be diminished. Legitimacy may be built by tradition, the creation of policy outcomes that the public views as successful, a common identity shared by the government and the public (e.g., a shared history or a common belief system), and the

BOX 7.3

HOMELESSNESS, SOCIAL JUSTICE, AND CRIMINAL JUSTICE

There are approximately 3.5 million persons in the United States who are homeless—a number that has increased over the past 30 years (National Coalition for the Homeless [NCH], 2009d). Homelessness raises concerns about social justice because it involves a basic human need (i.e., shelter) that is unavailable to a substantial number of people. Homelessness as a social problem is also related to criminal justice. While not an exhaustive list, consider the following links between homelessness and criminal justice.

1. *Domestic violence is a significant cause of homelessness.* Research has found that "a majority of homeless women are victims of domestic violence" and that, of homeless families, "28% . . . were homeless because of domestic violence . . . When a woman decides to leave an abusive relationship, she often has nowhere to go" (National Coalition for the Homeless, 2009a, p. 1). This raises a related concern for social justice and criminal justice in terms of whether female victims of domestic violence, in particular, receive adequate support.
2. *Persons who are homeless are at risk of being victims of crime.* From 1999 through 2008, there were 244 homicides committed against persons who were homeless. The homeless population is also at risk for being targeted as potential victims of antihomeless hate crimes (National Coalition for the Homeless, 2009c). It is the obligation of the criminal justice system to provide protection to persons who are homeless.
3. *Foreclosure is a cause of homelessness and is related to crime.* In the economic downturn of 2008–2009, there was an increase in the number of mortgage foreclosures. Generally, this means that the persons who were living in a foreclosed home had to vacate the property. It is estimated that 21% of persons whose homes were foreclosed spent at least some time living "on the streets" (National Coalition for the Homeless, 2009b, p. 2) and that as many as 10% of homeless persons became homeless because of a mortgage foreclosure. Neighborhoods with higher foreclosure rates experience higher crime rates (Bess, 2008).

Again, homelessness is an issue with implications for social justice and criminal justice. Consider the following policy questions:

Q What can the police do to reduce victimization of the homeless?

Q What policies could be developed to reduce homelessness, especially when it results from a person leaving an abusive home?

Q What services should be provided to assist persons who are homeless?

use of "procedures in which many people have confidence" (Shively, 1999, p. 139). The latter point is particularly important for criminal justice. Indeed, procedural justice, in which criminal justice processes demonstrate fairness and social justice, is one factor that leads citizens to obey the law (Tyler, 2006). Legitimacy, in part through its impact on the effective functioning of the criminal justice system and in part on encouraging citizens to be law abiding, can lead to security in a society.

The values described provide a glimpse into American political culture. Understanding political culture can help place policy debates, including those about criminal justice, in a philosophical context.

- Q Discuss the ways marijuana law could be related to social justice and political culture.
- Q How can criminal justice promote social justice?
- Q How are the values described in the discussion of political culture related to criminal justice, generally? Do you think there are other values that play an important role in American political culture?

The Development of Criminal Justice Policy

FOCUSING QUESTION 7.3

How is criminal justice policy shaped by government structure?

How, then, is justice to be pursued? The criminal justice system is developed and shaped through public policy decisions, as new laws are created and new strategies and tactics are developed. One important observation about criminal justice policy is that effective policy making requires many individuals and organizations to work together in order to establish the laws, procedures, goals, and strategies necessary to produce desired outcomes. Because the criminal justice function comprises many interested persons, agencies, and groups, the more collaboration that occurs, the more likely it is that there will be consistency in policy choices. The sharing of ideas and perspectives may be accomplished through professional organizations (e.g., the International Association of Chiefs of Police for law enforcement; the American Bar Association for the legal community; and the American Correctional Association for corrections), through participation in conferences, through publications, or through interagency partnerships to promote collaborative problem solving. Conversely, if individuals and organizations do not work together, policies are less likely to be consistent and there is greater potential for misunderstanding between persons working in different parts of the system. This reflects the distinction between a system and non-system as described in Chapter 1.

STABILITY AND CHANGE IN PUBLIC POLICY

Political scientist Thomas Dye (1984) defined **public policy** as "whatever governments choose to do or not to do" (p. 2). Criminal justice policy, then, consists of the decisions that governments (whether local, state, or federal) make about what should be done to address crime. It is important to make one initial observation about American public policy, including criminal justice policy. That is, policies tend to be very stable over time. In what Robertson and Judd (1989) call "policy restraint" (p. 1), it is difficult to enact substantial and dramatic change in public policies. In short, the steps that are required to change policy are so difficult and require agreement from so many political actors that change is difficult to accomplish. For instance, laws must generally pass the muster of two legislative bodies, be signed by the chief executive, not be struck down by courts, and be successfully implemented. One positive argument for policy restraint is that it helps promote stability in public policy and therefore stability in the criminal justice process. Stability, in turn, can help build the historical roots that promote legitimacy. If criminal justice policies were to change often, dramatically, and quickly, the public might come to have skepticism in the authority or credibility of the system. At the same time, policy restraint can make it difficult to implement changes that are in fact necessary to improve the criminal justice system.

public policy
The individual and accumulated decisions made by governments (local, state, or federal) about what should be done to address any issue, including crime.

This is not to say that there are never changes in criminal justice policy. However, dramatic change is rare, and once it happens, it tends to become established policy that lasts for a long time (see Baumgartner & Jones, 1993). For dramatic change to occur,

political scientist John Kingdon (1995) argues that three factors must come together at the right time: public perceptions that a problem exists; the availability of a satisfactory solution to solve the problem (often, this solution is prepackaged or advertised by politicians); and a political climate that supports the change. When these factors come together, a **"policy window"** (p. 88) opens and change occurs. The policy window then quickly closes, at which time the policy becomes established and does not dramatically change until the three factors once again converge.

policy window
Based on John Kingdon's theory of public policy, it refers to a time when policy change is most likely to occur for an issue. For a policy window to open for any particular issue, that issue must have been identified as a problem, a solution must be available, and the political climate must support making a change.

Consider the example of marijuana policy. The last major punctuation, or change, in marijuana policy occurred in the 1930s. There was public hysteria, driven by the media, about fear of marijuana, so there were clear public perceptions that a problem existed. The readily available solution, actively promoted by Anslinger, was to criminalize marijuana use. The political climate at the time was receptive to regulation of marijuana. In fact, only one witness (a medical doctor) testified against criminalization at congressional hearings about the law (Ferraiolo, 2007). More recently, in some states, the three criteria have been met and policy windows have opened to allow medical marijuana or limited degrees of decriminalization. However, there is not yet a national consensus in that direction, so there has not been a significant and sustained change in federal marijuana policy.

FEDERALISM

Variation in the law between states is not unusual. Indeed, aside from the most serious of crimes (e.g., murder, rape, robbery) and from rulings of the Supreme Court to which all must adhere (e.g., requiring Miranda warnings prior to custodial interrogation), there are often legal differences between jurisdictions in terms of what is (or is not) criminal, how offenses are defined, how the law is enforced, and so on.

federalism
Having more than one level of government, as in the United States, which has a national government as well as 50 state governments in addition to counties and cities.

This is because of an aspect of government structure called **federalism**, which means that we have two levels of government in the United States: the national (or federal) and the state. These two levels of government are provided for in the U.S. Constitution, each with its own (though sometimes overlapping) powers. There are additional layers of government below the state, including counties, cities or towns, and special districts (which are units that often cross over several local jurisdictions for a single purpose, such as a school district that serves students from several towns). However, the federal and state governments are the most powerful. In fact, a principle known as Dillon's Rule notes that a local government "is a creation of the legislature; it has only the powers which the legislature gives it; and nothing more" (Friedman, 2002, p. 411). This is important because it tells us that the states have very broad powers, but local governments do not. States may delegate to local governments the right, for instance, to have police agencies (as all states do), which may pursue their own strategies and tactics for responding to local crimes. On the other hand, states do not delegate to local governments the right to define criminal laws that would supersede those of the state, although localities do have a very limited ability to define ordinances pertaining to issues such as speed limits, noise violations, and so on.

Consider the implications of federalism. One substantial disadvantage is that it leads to a lack of consistency in terms of the law and its enforcement between different places. For example, Virginia authorizes the death penalty in cases of first-degree murder, but neighboring West Virginia does not. In some counties of Nevada, state-regulated prostitution is legal (see Brents & Hausbeck, 2001); in no other jurisdiction in the United States is this true. Police in some jurisdictions follow an aggressive enforcement approach and arrest all persons found in possession of any marijuana; in other jurisdictions, casual marijuana use, even when criminal, may be ignored (see Johnson, Ream, Dunlap, & Sifaneck, 2008). There is no single pattern to criminal law and justice across the United States. Even in this book, much of what we write is general, and there are differences between jurisdictions too voluminous to list in a single source.

So why have federalism? One benefit of federalism is that it allows jurisdictions, within the bounds of state and federal law, of course, to shape their own responses to their own problems. This is illustrated in Justice Antonin Scalia's opinion in the case of *Harmelin v. Michigan* (1991). The state of Michigan enacted a law requiring a mandatory life sentence for persons in possession of 650 or more grams of cocaine. In upholding the constitutionality of the law after an appeal claiming it to be cruel and unusual, Justice Scalia wrote, "The Members of the Michigan Legislature, and not we, know the situation on the streets of Detroit" (p. 988). Thus, even though the punishment is indeed harsh (a subject for debate in its own right), the Supreme Court acknowledged respect for the judgment of the state of Michigan in determining what its own criminal laws and penalties should be (although state legislators later chose to reduce the penalties).

Federalism also allows that, in the words of Supreme Court Justice Louis Brandeis, "a single courageous state may, if its citizens choose, serve as a laboratory, and try novel social and economic experiments without risk to the rest of the country" (*New State Ice Co. v. Liebmann,* 1932, p. 311). As some states experiment with medical marijuana or decriminalization, other states watch to see how it works. If, after watching, one state or city adopts a policy from another, then policy diffusion has occurred, which is defined as the adoption of the same or similar policy or law by another jurisdiction (see Mooney & Lee, 1999). Some policies diffuse across multiple jurisdictions quickly, particularly when a national-level policy window opens. For instance, Amber Alert, a system providing public notifications and alerts in cases of child abduction, diffused quickly. In 1996, Ambert Alert began as a local initiative in the Dallas–Fort Worth area of Texas; by 2009, Amber Alert had been adopted by every state, as well as Washington, D.C., Puerto Rico, and the U.S. Virgin Islands (Amber Alert, 2010). As an easily implemented and highly visible response to a legitimate area of public concern (see also Makse & Volden, 2011), the policy was a politically popular solution that spread quickly across jurisdictions.

On the other hand, to return to the case study at the beginning of the chapter, changes in marijuana law have occurred more slowly. They raise a variety of complexities, not the least of which is the conflict between state and federal policy; they are less politically popular; and there is not unanimity of public opinion regarding whether laws pertaining to marijuana should or should not be changed. As a result, there has not been the political or popular unanimity or urgency that would result in rapid diffusion of state-level changes in marijuana law.

STATE AND FEDERAL POLICY

Much of the preceding discussion focuses on differences among states. Let's turn our attention to the relationship between federal policy and state policy. Each state has its own complete criminal justice system. Likewise, the federal government has its own complete criminal justice system. Violations of state law are enforced by that state's law enforcement officers, are tried in that state's courts, and are punished by that state's supervised probation or by sentences to that state's prisons. Violations of federal law are enforced by federal law enforcement officers, are tried in federal courts, and are punished by federal-supervised probation or sentences to federal prisons. Therefore, there are really 51 separate criminal justice systems in the United States (and even more if systems of justice in the military, U.S. territories, and Native American tribal governments are included), each with its own processes. How a case is handled depends on whether it is a violation of a state law or a violation of federal law.

One question posed after the marijuana case study at the beginning of the chapter asked you to consider what should happen when a state law conflicts with a federal law—that is, when a state allows some marijuana possession even though it remains illegal under federal law. The **National Supremacy Clause** of the U.S. Constitution

National Supremacy Clause
A clause in the U.S. Constitution that identifies the federal government as the supreme law of the land. This means if there is a conflict between a federal law and a state law, the federal law will take priority.

speaks to this issue: "This Constitution, and the Laws of the United States which shall be made in Pursuance thereof . . . shall be the supreme Law of the Land; and the Judges in every State shall be bound thereby, any Thing in the . . . Laws of any State to the Contrary notwithstanding." Simply stated, federal law trumps state law.

However, the question does become more complex than the clause just cited. Traditionally, the states have had primary authority over criminal law. There were originally very few federal criminal laws, and those that did exist were for instances when a crime was committed against the nation as a whole (i.e., treason), against a federal employee, or on federal property. Otherwise, the federal government stayed out of criminal justice (Miller, 2008). This changed in the twentieth century. Brickey (1996) observed, "In contrast with the 17 crimes that formed the entire body of federal criminal law two centuries ago, there are now more than 3000 federal crimes on the books today" (p. 28). Why the change?

Commerce Clause
A clause in the U.S. Constitution that gives the federal government the power to regulate commerce with other nations and among the states. This clause has allowed the federal government to make and enforce a variety of criminal laws surrounding issues that involve interstate commerce, which may be very broadly defined.

In the twentieth century, the federal government began utilizing the **Commerce Clause** of the U.S. Constitution to define new federal crimes. The clause gives Congress the power "[t]o regulate Commerce with foreign Nations, and among the several States." Here, commerce does not have to mean a business transaction, as we might normally define it. Instead, commerce can be understood more broadly to include any kind of transaction that crosses state lines. Stealing a motor vehicle and crossing state lines was one of the first federal crimes created under the auspices of the Commerce Clause. This law was passed, in part, to make the investigation and prosecution of such crimes more efficient. The federal government could coordinate the investigation and prosecution, which saved states the burden of coordinating investigations, determining which state would prosecute, and so forth. Over time, federal crimes were defined that did not even require the actual criminal event to cross state lines, as long as it affected commerce in some way. For instance, Congress enacted a federal law against carjacking, but the offense itself need not cross state lines. The connection to commerce is that carjacking becomes a federal crime if the car had been, at any time in the past, "transported in interstate commerce," such as when it was delivered from its point of origin to a dealership (Brickey, 1996, p. 30). Through the use of the Commerce Clause, the federal government has greatly expanded its role in criminal justice over the past century.

It is also important to note that, under federalism, the federal government can influence (though not require) states to adopt certain laws and policies through the distribution of federal funding. As one example, the federal government provides money to states for the purpose of highway construction, and "the loss of federal highway construction funds has been a common threat issued by Congress if states do not adopt traffic safety laws . . . [such as a] 21-year old minimum legal drinking age . . . and the 0.08 [blood alcohol content] law [for DUI cases]" (Richardson & Houston, 2009, p. 120). States comply and change their own laws so they can retain federal highway funding. Another example was the adoption of the federal Prison Rape Elimination Act (PREA) in 2003. Sexual assaults violate state law whether they occur inside or outside prison. The PREA did not create a new criminal offense, but rather, made a variety of provisions designed to improve programming, research, and record keeping related to the reduction of sexual assault in correctional institutions. States were provided the opportunity to receive federal monies to assist in achieving these goals. In addition, states would be denied federal funding if they did not meet a series of standards designed to reduce prison sexual assault (for a history of the act, see Schuhmann & Wodahl, 2011).

SEPARATION OF POWERS

Another significant feature of American government is the separation of powers. At the federal and state levels, there are three branches of government: legislative, which makes the laws; judicial, which interprets the laws; and executive, which enforces the

laws. Separating powers into three branches (and at both the state and federal levels) is one feature that makes American government particularly complex, leading to the policy restraint described earlier. This was a deliberate decision by the founders, who were concerned that a single branch of government would gain too much power (see Madison, [1788] 1982). Through a system of checks and balances, each branch of government can counteract the other. (For example, the president can veto a bill from Congress; the courts can rule unconstitutional the acts of other branches; and Congress has authority to deny or confirm appointments of executive officers.) This helps each branch of government safeguard the other, the goal being that only the best policies will ultimately pass muster.

With the exception of the courts, criminal justice agencies typically fall under the executive branch of government. Consider how the legislative and judicial branches may impact policing and correctional agencies. It is the legislature that makes the very laws about what behaviors are or are not criminal. For instance, police officers do not get to make up their own laws but instead must enforce only those that are created by the legislature. The legislature also is responsible for approving the state (or federal) budget. For instance, a prison warden must operate his or her facility without spending more money than was allocated by the state legislature; if the warden believes the funds are insufficient, he or she has little recourse other than to try to persuade the legislature to allocate more money in future years.

The courts hold trials and sentence offenders. A prison warden does not get to pick and choose who is sent to prison, nor does a probation officer get to select which persons will be assigned to his or her caseload. The courts make that decision, and the warden and probation officer must work with the persons who are sent to them regardless of what they may think of the decision. The courts also rule on constitutional and procedural issues, and in doing so, they establish guidelines that police and correctional agencies must follow. If the Supreme Court rules, as it has, that police officers may not use thermal imaging devices (which measure heat) to scan a home (e.g., to detect artificial lights that are used to promote marijuana plant growth) without a warrant, then police officers may not use thermal imaging devices in that way (see *Kyllo v. United States,* 2001).

The point of this discussion is to demonstrate that criminal justice agencies are constrained by the actions of multiple branches of government and must operate within those constraints. It quickly becomes clear that developing criminal justice policy involves not only a consideration of social justice and political culture, but also political structure, as further discussed below.

THEMES IN AMERICAN CRIMINAL JUSTICE POLICY DEVELOPMENT

Even though numerous crimes cross international boundaries (see Box 7.4), criminal justice policies are unique to the countries in which they are made, and there is considerable cross-national variation in terms of how laws are structured and enforced. That being said, there is value in the study of how other countries approach crime and justice, as successes abroad have the potential to suggest approaches that might not otherwise be considered. There have been numerous studies of comparative policing (e.g., Haberfeld & Cerrah, 2008), comparative legal systems (e.g., Jacob, Blankenburg, Kritzer, Provide, & Sanders, 1996), and comparative corrections (e.g., Cavadino & Dignan, 1997), each of which has yielded useful and interesting insights into the phenomena of crime and criminal justice. While some strategies from other countries have successfully been incorporated into American criminal justice practice, such as drawing upon Japanese methods of community policing, there remains a strong caution when trying to borrow ideas from other nations: "it is naïve to try to import institutions that are very much bound to local cultural values, without modifying them to conform to the new context" (Fairchild & Dammer, 2001, pp. 7–8).

BOX 7.4

Research in Action

GLOBAL JUSTICE

While the primary emphasis of this book is on the American criminal justice system, it is important to also spend some time reflecting on global issues of crime and justice. These are matters that cross national boundaries and which have the potential to involve victims or offenders in the United States. Consider the following statistics:

- In 2011, there were 10,283 terrorist attacks worldwide, injuring 25,903 and killing 12,533 (U.S. Department of State, 2012).
- In the United States, "[f]ederally funded human trafficking task forces opened 2,515 suspected incidents of human trafficking for investigation between January 2008 and June 2010" (Banks & Kyckellhahn, 2011, p. 1), most of which were for sex trafficking. The sex trafficking incidents were almost evenly split between child and adult victims.
- From 2006 to 2011, there was an 84% increase in the number of piracy incidents at sea. Piracy appears to be most likely in areas with large coastlines, weak governments, poor economies, and weak military or security forces (Daxecker & Prins, 2013).
- Money laundering occurs when the true source and destination of financial transactions are hidden, making money from illicit enterprises appear to be legally acquired and transferred. Estimates suggest that approximately $2.1 trillion was laundered in 2009 (United Nations Office on Drugs and Crime, 2011a).
- In recent years, countries including the United States have increased efforts to combat media piracy, which is the illegal sharing or sale of copyrighted materials such as movies and music. However, the efforts do not appear to have fully addressed the problem, as illegal media piracy still occurs to the amount of $20 billion in losses per year (Burke, 2010).
- There were "967 seizures of [illegally traded] wildlife and wildlife products between July 1996 and October 2008" (Rosen & Smith, 2010, p. 26). This ranges from ivory trading to furs to live animals to meat. Illegal wildlife trafficking can pose risks to endangered animal populations, health risks to humans, and economic risks to natural resource industries.
- The illegal production and sale of timber amounts to up to $15 billion per year, and due to the scale of timber movement and sales (it is hardly unnoticeable to smuggle stacks of wood or logs), it at times involves corruption of officials to facilitate the trafficking (Graycar & Felson, 2010).
- Illegal international art theft amounts to $6 billion per year (Charney, 2009).

The above is merely a sampling of global crime issues (see also United Nations Office on Drugs and Crime, 2010). The challenge is to determine how to respond.

Q When crime crosses international borders, should countries collaborate in an effort to reduce and prevent criminal activity, to apprehend offenders, and to assist victims? If so, how?

Q What challenges do you think would be involved in international crime control collaborations? Can they be overcome?

Likewise, it is important to study criminal justice policy within the specific context of the country where it is made. In the United States, that includes an understanding of the political culture and attitudes related to morality, law, and justice. It also includes an appreciation for specific criminal justice issues of key interest to the United States, which would certainly include the post–September 11 focus on international terrorism, having a homicide rate that is higher (even with the recent crime drop) than that of most other developd nations (United Nations Office on Drugs and Crime, 2011b), and having the world's highest rate of imprisonment (Walmsley, 2011). And it includes an understanding of the structure of government and politics in the United States, including the stability of public policy, federalism, the relationship between state and federal governments, and the separation of powers.

American criminal justice policy has changed over time (for broad histories, see Walker, 1997; Friedman, 1993), as political culture, relevant issues, and philosophies of governance have changed. Very broadly speaking, the history of American criminal justice policy can be divided into two eras, which were shaped most profoundly by philosophies of governance—and by an attention to alcohol. Through the early twentieth century, criminal justice policy was largely a local and state matter, and one with which the federal government did not, for the most part, become involved. In the late 1800s, states began to explore the prohibition of alcohol. Over time, the movement gained such momentum that the control of alcohol was viewed as a national problem, and from the years of 1920 through 1933, the sale and production of alcohol was banned in the United States in an era known as Prohibition. This was a federal law, as it was in fact established (and later repealed) through an Amendment to the U.S. Constitution, giving it the distinction of being the only criminal law other than treason referenced directly in the document.

The political culture at the time was focused on various social reforms, and alcohol policy became viewed as one of the areas most in need of reform. But it is neither the political culture nor the regulation of alcohol itself that made Prohibition so important to criminal justice history. Rather, it was the impact on the federal government. As Morone (2003) wrote, "Prohibition gave the American government an extraordinary job to do: change the way people lived. What ended up changing most may have been the government itself" (p. 343). The enforcement of Prohibition required the federal government to take a much more active role in criminal justice than it ever had before.

Following Prohibition, the legacy of a strong federal government willing to be involved in issues of criminal justice remained, and as the nation grew and new social issues continued to emerge, the federal government took an increasing role (Robertson, 2012). In the late 1960s, crime became a political issue, as the 1964 presidential election included a discussion of crime control that ultimately led to increased federal attention to criminal justice (Gest, 2001), which has continued to this day. In the late twentieth century, interest groups shaped their advocacy toward the promotion of equality and the protection of rights, in which the federal government played a significant role (Patterson, 2001). In turn, the dual focus—from both federal and state governments—on criminal justice issues is important in helping to maintain public interest in them.

In summary, the federal government's role in criminal justice has expanded dramatically, and we can identify Prohibition as the approximate tipping point between two eras—the first with states having a near-exclusive control over issues of crime and justice, and the second with states and the federal government both heavily involved (sometimes working together and sometimes at odds) in criminal justice. The theme that emerges is that it is important to understand the context in which policy is developed, and in the United States, that means considering the role of state and federal governments. In the next section, we will turn attention to those forces that shape policy making at both levels.

Q What features contribute to restraint in American public policy? What do you think are the advantages and disadvantages of policy restraint? Of federalism?

Q Select a criminal justice policy that interests you. How does it illustrate the features described in this section, including policy windows, federalism, state–federal relations, and separation of powers?

Q Which level of government do you think should have the greatest influence on criminal justice policy—state or federal? Or does it depend on the issue? Explain your answer.

Forces Shaping Criminal Justice Policy

FOCUSING QUESTION 7.4

What forces have a role in shaping the development of criminal justice policy?

Within the political system, there are many forces that come together to shape the development of criminal justice policy. The following discussion highlights several of the most important, beginning with agenda setting and problem definition (see Rochefort & Cobb, 1994).

agenda setting
The process by which an issue is identified as one that needs to be addressed through policy or law. This is often a political process.

Agenda setting refers to the process by which an issue—any issue—is identified as one that needs to be addressed through policy or law. First and foremost, this is a political process. As Murray Edelman (1988) notes, "conditions accepted as inevitable or unproblematic may come to be seen as problems" (p. 12). For instance, the history of marijuana policy illustrates that marijuana, once viewed as unproblematic, was later defined as a very serious problem—based at least in part on a media-driven public panic and on political advocacy, including that by Harry Anslinger. Edelman (1988) also notes that some "damaging conditions may not be defined as political issues at all" (p. 12). For instance, homelessness is a serious problem with numerous implications for the criminal justice system (see Box 7.3), but it has not been at the forefront of public policy debates.

Sharp (1994) suggests that there are three criteria that can identify those issues most likely to be advanced through the agenda setting process. The first is dramatic potential, which refers to the ability to construct an interesting narrative or to identify a high-profile story about the issue. The second is proximity, which refers to the extent to which an issue is seen by the public as something that is personally relevant to them. The third is novelty, which refers to the public's perception that the issue is something new, or a new twist on an existing issue, either of which is necessary to maintain interest. Drug policy provides an example of each. There are numerous high-profile stories, often related to incidents of violence associated with drugs or to celebrity drug use, particularly when they result in death; the public can view drug issues as a threat to health and safety that could consequentially affect them, their families, or friends; and there is constantly a new angle, depending on what type of drug issue is focused upon (Sharp, 1994).

problem definition
Refers to attempts by interested individuals and groups to advocate how a problem ought to be understood. This often occurs after an issue has been placed on the public agenda, as individuals and groups debate the causes of and solutions to the problem in question.

Once an issue is placed on the agenda for discussion, problem definition occurs. **Problem definition** is an attempt by interested individuals and groups to determine "where problems come from and, based on the answer to this question, what kinds of solutions should be attempted" (Rochefort & Cobb, 1994, p. 3). An example will help to illustrate; consider school violence. To determine where problems of school violence come from, fill in the blank: school violence is a __________ problem. Following the 1999 shootings at Columbine High School in Littleton, Colorado, an analysis of newspaper stories found that school violence was identified by the media as a "guns" problem (not enough gun control), as a "pop culture" problem (too much violent media), as a "security" problem (not enough security in schools), and as a "teen life" problem (negative school cultures) (Lawrence & Birkland, 2004, p. 1197). Each of these is a different problem definition for school violence. Individuals and groups have the tendency to select the one definition that they most agree with and to promote it to the exclusion of other possible definitions. This is important because the most politically popular definition drives the types of policies that result. For instance, if "security" is the problem definition most accepted by legislators, then the policies and laws that result will focus primarily on strengthening school security (this indeed was the case; see Lawrence & Birkland, 2004), and less attention will be given to addressing the other aspects of the problem.

Problem definitions can change over time. For instance, media reports defining school shootings as a mental health issue were uncommon after the 1999 Columbine

High School shootings (Lawrence & Birkland, 2004), but were more prevalent following the Sandy Hook Elementary School shootings in Newtown, Connecticut (McLemore & Bissell, 2013). How this will affect policy outcomes remains to be seen.

Research on the death penalty further highlights the power of problem definitions. Over the past 50 years, death penalty problem definitions have changed numerous times, but since the mid-1990s, one of the most frequent has been the concern for executing innocent persons. This has come at the same time that public support for, as well as actual use of, the death penalty has declined. Important to note here is that the problem definition prevalent at the time has an impact on public opinion about the death penalty, and research has found that the prevailing problem definition actually has a greater impact than the murder rate on the number of actual death sentences issued in a year (Baumgartner, De Boef, & Boydstun, 2008).

Clearly, agenda setting and problem definition matter; but where do they come from? Although there are many players in politics and policy making, we will briefly consider four: the media, interest groups, politics and politicians, and bureaucrats.

MASS MEDIA

The media include entertainment programming (movies, television programs, etc.) and news programming (newspapers, television newscasts, news websites, etc.). Both can influence perceptions of crime and criminal justice. Much entertainment programming focuses on crime, as the public seems to enjoy a good detective story. These programs tend to depict work in criminal justice professions as highly exciting, while omitting the routine or mundane parts of the job. The entertainment media also depict much more crime than actually exists; studies have estimated that the homicide rate is 1,000 times higher in fictional television programs than it is in real life. Entertainment programs can influence criminal justice policy by shaping inaccurate perceptions of crime

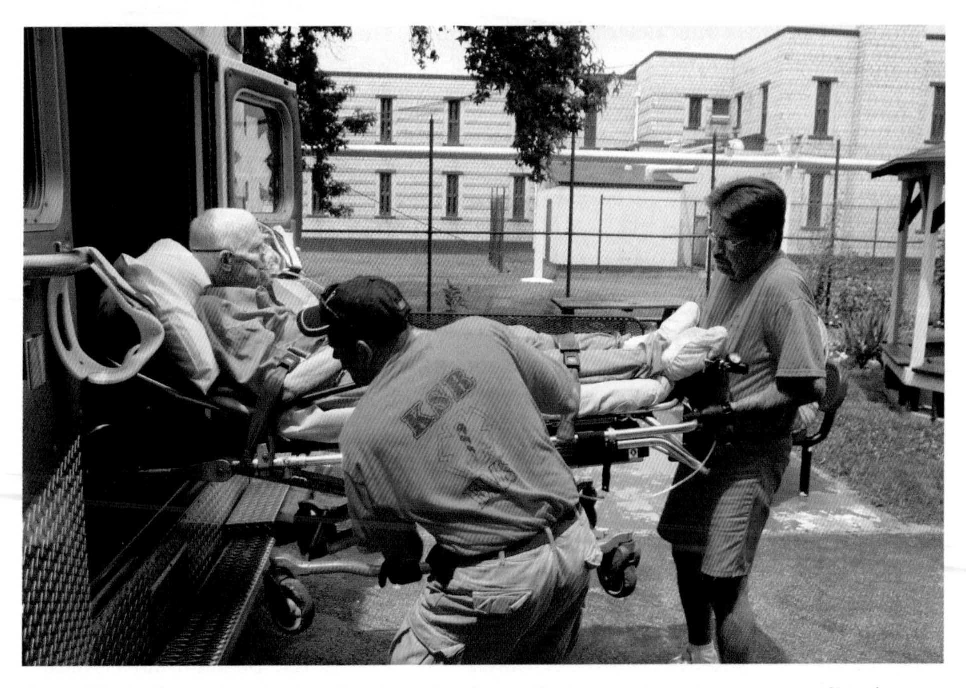

One effect of tougher sentencing laws has been that more inmates are spending longer times in prison. One challenge facing correctional administrators is to determine how to meet the needs of elderly inmates, including health care, appropriate housing units, provision of age-appropriate programming, and more. How could agenda setting and problem definition be applied to this issue? What policy options might be proposed?

and the criminal justice system. In fact, entertainment programs can "generate fear and reinforce popular support for harsher punishment" (Beckett & Sasson, 2004, p. 81).

Similarly, the news media can influence public policy outcomes. Complex news is that which offers "a balanced coverage of diverse viewpoints and ideas toward audiences' understanding of complicated issues" (Sotirovic, 2001, p. 313). When users consume complex news, they are more likely to carefully consider an issue, and this leads to support for criminal justice policies that emphasize efforts to prevent crime rather than only to punish offenders. On the other hand, noncomplex news refers to "the *infotainment* format of various reality-based, pseudo-news, and talk shows [which] emphasizes the drama of events and not their meaning [emphasis in original]" (Sotirovic, 2001, p. 313). When users consume noncomplex news, they are more likely to become fearful of crime, which leads to support for policies that punish offenders but do not prevent crime (Sotirovic, 2001).

In addition to general influences on how the public thinks about crime, the mass media also have the potential to influence the agenda-setting process based on what stories are selected for news coverage. Edelman (1988) notes that supporters and opponents of a variety of issues all vie for media coverage, as it can help bring attention to their causes. Furthermore, the stories that generate attention are those that have the potential for dramatic storytelling, and are often presented in a manner that oversimplifies the true depth or complexity of an issue while emphasizing individuals and personalities rather than broad trends and themes.

Samuel Walker (2006) proposes what he calls the "criminal justice wedding cake" (p. 34) model, observing that criminal cases may be classified into several layers (from largest to smallest, as in a wedding cake). The largest number of cases are fairly routine misdemeanors, generally handled through authoritarian justice processes, and these form the base of the "wedding cake." Moving up to the next layers are various types of felonies, which are more serious but which are not likely to receive a tremendous amount of public attention. The top layer, which is also the smallest layer, is what Walker (2006) labels the **"celebrated cases"** (p. 35). These are the cases or trials which draw substantial amounts of public attention and which are closely followed by the media, both in complex and noncomplex news coverage, demonstrating high levels of drama, oversimplification, and a focus on individuals and personalities. While these are the most atypical cases in the criminal justice system, because of their highly visible media coverage they are also those which most heavily shape public opinion and which raise policy issues considered on the public agenda.

celebrated cases
Cases and trials that draw substantial amounts of public attention and which are closely followed by the media.

For instance, the 1993 abduction and murder of 12-year-old Polly Klass by an offender released from prison on parole became what Walker (2006) would call a "celebrated case" (p. 35), as it received very high levels of media coverage and much public attention. In turn, the public and political dialogue about the case was one factor that led to the adoption of "three strikes" laws in California (requiring lengthy, even life, sentences for repeat offenders), as a response to concern about repeat offending. Advertising media were also instrumental in the adoption of three strikes laws, as numerous commercials were aired both in favor of and in opposition to the three-strikes laws (Page, 2011). You will learn more about three strikes laws, and controversies surrounding them, in Chapter 10.

Through editorial choices, the news media can also shape problem definition. For instance, in a study of gun control policy, Callaghan and Schnell (2001) found that the problem definition most often adopted by the media was that gun control debates reflected concern about a "culture of violence" (p. 193) in the United States. Neither politicians nor interest groups (on either side) identified this as their primary problem definition. The media may have utilized this problem definition because it was the one that generated the greatest audience interest and, in turn, the highest ratings. The media is indeed a powerful force that has the ability to shape discussions and policy making about criminal justice issues.

INTEREST GROUPS

Interest groups are organized groups of individuals who advocate for a particular policy outcome. There are many interest groups pertinent to criminal justice. For example, the National Rifle Association and the Brady Campaign to Prevent Gun Violence are two interest groups on gun issues—the former to advocate for gun ownership rights and the latter to advocate for gun control.

interest groups
Organized groups of individuals who advocate for a particular policy outcome.

One notable example of interest groups is Mothers Against Drunk Driving (MADD). In 1980, MADD was created by Candy Lightner, whose daughter Cari had been killed by an intoxicated driver. The organization was able to raise national attention to the problem of driving under the influence (DUI). By developing and advocating a problem definition that placed the blame on individuals who drove under the influence, MADD's efforts resonated with the emphasis on victim's rights and personal responsibility that were part of the political culture in the 1980s. The alcohol industry also supported MADD, as the problem definition did not place blame for DUI on the alcohol itself but rather on how it was misused by some persons. As a result of MADD's efforts, many new laws and policies have been developed both to prevent and punish DUI (Reinarman, 1988).

Interest groups also include organizations with very broad interests, not focused solely on criminal justice policy concerns. For instance, in 2000, the federal government adopted a law to address the problem of human trafficking, in which individuals are forcibly relocated, often to other countries, for "sex trafficking and subjection to involuntary servitude" (Stolz, 2005, p. 416). Interest groups advocating for the law "included feminist, human rights, democracy-building, services providers (for refugees, prostitutes, and others), and religious organizations" (Stolz, 2005, p. 419), a wide coalition known as an issue network (Smith, 1993). Issue networks often emerge when a variety of groups come together to work to influence policy on an issue, even if they have never worked together before. While not all groups have high levels of resources, and not all groups will agree on all issues, there is a perception that working together is mutually beneficial in terms of the ability to meet at least one mutually agreed-upon policy goal.

Theodore Lowi (1967) attributes significant power to interest groups, suggesting that they are a dominant force in modern politics. Indeed, Lowi envisions the political process as a struggle among competing interest groups, which sometimes eclipse the legislators themselves in terms of the attention they receive and the amount of policymaking power they hold.

The California three strikes law is an example of this. Described in further detail in Chapter 10, the law provides for sentences up to life in prison for a third felony conviction. The California legislature initially rejected three strikes, and it only became law after supporters utilized the initiative process, in which a proposed law is placed on a ballot (a petition with a substantial number of signatures is required to do so) and the voters determine whether or not it should be enacted. California voters were overwhelmingly in favor of three strikes. When three strikes was later challenged for being too tough, an issue network of numerous interest groups representing law enforcement, firefighters, correctional officers, and crime victims came together to defend the law (Page, 2011). It is clear that interest groups have the ability to strongly influence policy development.

POLITICS AND POLITICIANS

It would be difficult to imagine the development of criminal justice policy without considering the role of politics and politicians. Certainly, the media and interest groups influence the political process, but it is ultimately politicians who make most criminal justice policy. Research suggests that politicians, particularly presidents, have the ability to structure agenda setting around their preferred policies and goals. In fact, public opinion about criminal justice issues is more responsive to presidential speeches and

policy statements than it is to actual levels of crime in society (Beckett, 1994; Oliver, 2003). One of the key powers held by politicians is to influence the public opinion and the policy agenda.

Once elevated to the public agenda, some issues are addressed through symbolic, rather than substantive, politics. Most generally, a symbolic solution is one that looks and sounds appealing, thereby conveying the appearance that the issue is being addressed, but which has little actual impact on the issue itself. For instance, the Hate Crime Statistics Act, which required the federal government to maintain data on hate crime victimizations, was viewed as a symbolic means of increasing awareness and demonstrating concern about hate crime (both noble goals) but without taking action to directly address it (Jacobs & Potter, 1998). Likewise, presidential executive orders may be issued to form commissions to study problems and issue proclamations, which again result in increased awareness and concern, but without creating substantive solutions or laws related to criminal justice issues (Oliver, 2001). Symbolic solutions are generally easier to accomplish, politically, than those making more substantive changes to law or policy.

Political decision making is often driven by the Democratic and Republican political parties. There is variation in party beliefs about criminal justice issues between different states and between the national and state-level party organizations (Bridgmon & Bridgmon, 2010). However, perhaps more important is the degree of party competition, which means the likelihood that each party can be successful in the polls (as opposed to knowing that one party is always likely to be the victor, based on local political culture). In states where there is active competition between parties, it is more likely that innovative criminal justice policy initiatives will be proposed, as each party tries to outdo the other by offering what they believe to be the newest and best responses to crime (Williams, 2003).

BUREAUCRATS

bureaucrats
Persons who work within the executive branch of government and agencies that comprise it. They are responsible for implementing policies.

Once policies have been made, they must be implemented, or put into effect. **Bureaucrats**, or persons working within the executive branch of government, have the responsibility for implementing policies. The way bureaucrats implement policy can subsequently shape what a policy actually means. As Michael Lipsky (1980) notes, "bureaucrats make policy in two related respects. They exercise wide discretion in decisions about citizens with whom they interact. Then, when taken in concert, their individual actions add up to agency behavior" (p. 13). As an example, consider police officers enforcing the speed limit. Assume that a stretch of highway has a 55 mile-per-hour (mph) speed limit. Would an officer be legally justified in stopping a motorist who was cruising at 56 mph? Of course. Now assume that officers, as a matter of practice, only stop motorists traveling faster than 60 mph, effectively giving a 5 mph "buffer zone." In practice, this means the *informal* policy is that 60 mph is the "real" speed limit. As citizens learn this (which they will, quickly), motorists will then routinely set their cruise control for 60 mph, confident that they will not be stopped. Consider what has happened here. The law still states that the speed limit is 55 mph. And officers may still stop individuals who travel at 56 mph or faster. However, because of the way the police officers have used their discretion, 60 mph is in perception and in practice functionally the speed limit, and a citizen ticketed for going 56 mph would likely question the legitimacy of the sanction. In this way, the officers have indeed created public policy. This is but one example of what Lipsky (1980) calls "the critical role of street-level bureaucrats" (p. 3) and the important role they play in criminal justice policy.

- How do the media, interest groups, and bureaucracies influence the creation and enforcement of criminal law? Provide examples beyond those described in this section.
- Select a current high-profile criminal justice issue that would illustrate Walker's concept of a "celebrated case." Explain whether it does or does not correspond to the characteristics of criminal justice media coverage described above.
- Try your hand at problem definition. Brainstorm as many responses as you can to this statement: "Marijuana is a _________ issue." Describe what kinds of policies or laws each response would suggest.

Conclusion

Criminal justice and civil justice represent different means by which justice can be achieved, and social justice is an idea emphasizing fair and equitable treatment for all persons. Justice policies are made in an attempt to achieve justice, however it may be defined. There are many influences on justice policy, including political culture and values, government structure, the media, interest groups, bureaucrats—and of course, politics, which underlies them all. These forces come together in shaping the pursuit of justice in the United States. The next chapter explores procedural justice, pertaining to how justice is implemented in practice and the constitutional rights that must be safeguarded in the process.

Criminal Justice Problem Solving

Preschool Crime Prevention

A study by the Washington State Institute for Public Policy (Aos, Miller, & Drake, 2006) found that the implementation of preschool programs for low-income children could reduce crime by approximately 14%. Furthermore, even after paying for the cost of the program, it was estimated to save the state more than $12,000 per child who completed it, through reduced crime and corresponding reductions in criminal justice system expenses. Have you heard of preschool crime prevention programs? If so, that's great. If not, why not? This is a question worth considering.

Steven Lab (2004), former president of the Academy of Criminal Justice Sciences, observed that politicians sometimes abandon programs known to be effective (including preschool) but adopt programs known to be generally ineffective (including Drug Abuse Resistance Education and three strikes laws). Curious as to why, Lab offered four premises as potential explanations.

1. "Politicians look for immediate results that will help them to be reelected" (p. 684).
2. "The emphasis for politicians is on what can be easily counted" (p. 685).
3. "Politicians emphasize those policies and actions that play well in 15-second sound bites" (p. 685).
4. "Political decisions are always focused on the 'issue of the moment'" (p. 685).

Indeed, these four observations would, if accurate, make it difficult for publicly funded preschool programs to gain a foothold. First, the results would not be immediate, as the crime prevention value would not be fully achieved until the preschoolers grew up and lived crime-free lives. Second, because of the time lag, there would not be an easily countable result—at least not for a number of years. Third, it would take more than 15 seconds to fully explain *how* preschool education leads to crime prevention, especially when showing figures to demonstrate that its benefits exceed its costs. Finally, there is not a current public outcry (or "issue of the moment") for which preschool programs are the agreed-upon solution. In addition, there would likely be some philosophical or ideological objections to publicly funded preschool programs.

Lab's implication is that non-experts set the agenda and define the problems and that, for political reasons, it is sometimes difficult to create policies that are based on research and empirical data. However, there is an alternative in evidence-based policy making. In this approach, policy is made "using the highest quality available research evidence on what works best to reduce a specific crime problem and tailoring the intervention to the local context and conditions" (Welsh, 2006, p. 305). This requires careful collaboration between policy makers and experts, including researchers.

Q What do you think could be done to encourage the use of research in policy making?

Q How can political realities, such as those described by Lab, be balanced with evidence, notions of justice, and concern for liberty and equality when making policy? Use preschool programming for crime prevention, or another issue of your choice, as an example.

Q How do you think the factors described in this chapter would affect the development and implementation of preschool programs for crime prevention?

8

Concepts of Criminal Procedure

Learning Objectives

1 Explain the ways that procedural justice can be conceptualized. 2 Compare and contrast Herbert Packer's due process and crime control models. 3 Describe the procedural justice rights contained in the original U.S. Constitution that are relevant to the administration of criminal justice. 4 Discuss the procedural justice rights contained in the Fourth, Fifth, Sixth, and Fourteenth Amendments to the U.S. Constitution and how the exclusionary rule can be used as a remedy for violations of these rights.

Key Terms

substantive due process
procedural justice
crime control model
due process model
habeas corpus
bill of attainder
ex post facto
treason
Bill of Rights
probable cause
reasonable suspicion
exigent circumstances
standing
grand jury
indictment
preliminary hearing
double jeopardy
privilege against self-incrimination
Miranda rights
interrogation
custody
waivers
trial by jury
bench trial
subpoena
Confrontation Clause
Due Process Clause
Equal Protection Clause
exclusionary rule
fruit of the poisonous tree

Key People

John Rawls
John Thibaut
Laurens Walker
Tom Tyler
Herbert Packer

Case Study

When Are Dog Sniffs "Searches"?

In *Florida v. Jardines* (2013), law enforcement officers received an unverified, anonymous tip that Joelis Jardines was growing marijuana in his home. Officers followed up on this tip by conducting warrantless surveillance of Jardines's home. The surveillance included using a dog trained in drug detection to sniff on the front porch of the home. The dog's response suggested the presence of a controlled substance. Based on the dog's positive alert, a judge issued a search warrant allowing police to search inside Jardines's residence. When that search occurred, officers confirmed that the house was being used as a marijuana "grow house" and Jardines was arrested and charged with drug trafficking.

At trial, Jardines attempted to have the evidence against him suppressed. He argued that the use of a drug-detecting dog to sniff the exterior of the house constituted an illegal search because law enforcement officers did not have a warrant to enter onto Jardines's property and use the dog to sniff for evidence of drugs. The U.S. Supreme Court ultimately sided with Jardines because officers physically intruded on Jardines's property, gathering within the "curtilage" of his private residence (the area immediately surrounding the home). Accordingly, the Court ruled that the dog sniff was a substantial government intrusion into the sanctity of Jardines's home and, therefore, constituted a "search" within the meaning of the Fourth Amendment. In holding that this government intrusion went too far, the Court wrote:

> To find a visitor knocking on the door is routine (even if sometimes unwelcome); to spot that same visitor exploring the front path with a metal detector, or marching his bloodhound into the garden before saying hello and asking permission, would inspire most of us to—well, call the police (p. 7)

The Fourth Amendment requires a certain amount of proof, known as "probable cause," before law enforcement officers are permitted to conduct a search. And probable cause cannot be established through information gained in an illegal search. Since the officers

Previous page: An officer and canine searching a school locker area. What principles do you think should guide searches by police officers?

in this case learned what they learned only *after* trespassing onto Jardines's property with the drug-sniffing dog, which the Court ruled unacceptable, it is unlikely that officers would have been able to establish probable cause to obtain a search warrant.

Q Why do you think the framers of the U.S. Constitution required procedural safeguards, such as the existence of probable cause and a judicially issued warrant, as prerequisites for law enforcement officers to enter private property to conduct a search for evidence of a crime?

Q Do you agree with the U.S. Supreme Court's ruling that a dog sniff at the front door of a house where the police suspect drugs are being grown constitutes a search for purposes of the Fourth Amendment and, therefore, should require a warrant supported by probable cause before such a dog sniff can be conducted? Why or why not?

Q Assume that law enforcement officers had never actually physically trespassed onto Jardines' property, but instead used binoculars to look through the home's windows. Do you think the Fourth Amendment should protect the privacy of the home under such circumstances? Explain your reasoning.

Concepts of Procedural Justice

FOCUSING QUESTION 8.1

What does the term "procedural justice" mean?

Due process is the cornerstone of American law. Due process is guaranteed through two clauses in the U.S. Constitution. The clause in the Fifth Amendment restrains the power of the federal government. The clause in the Fourteenth Amendment restrains the power of the state governments. Both due process clauses protect against the arbitrary use of government power in two ways: substantively and procedurally. **Substantive due process** protects against governmental infringement of important rights, like freedom of speech, religion, and the right to privacy (which will be discussed in Chapter 9). **Procedural justice** concerns the fairness of the processes used when applying the law. Procedural justice is grounded in the idea that fair procedures are the best guarantees for fair outcomes. Moreover, if everyone is treated fairly, then it is easier for people to accept outcomes with which they disagree (Deutsch, 2000; Thibaut & Walker, 1975). But how do we know when a procedure is fair?

substantive due process
Protects against governmental infringement of fundamental rights, such as freedom of speech, freedom of religion, and the right to privacy.

procedural justice
Holds that justice is achieved when the proper procedures are followed and addresses the fairness of the procedures used when applying the law. Procedural justice is grounded in the idea that fair procedures are the best guarantees for fair outcomes.

THREE PHILOSOPHICAL MODELS OF PROCEDURAL JUSTICE

In his book *A Theory of Justice* (1971), legal philosopher John Rawls described three models of procedural justice: perfect, imperfect, and pure. A review of these models can help identify the key principles of procedural justice and the differing emphases that may be placed on each of them.

Perfect Procedural Justice: The Accuracy Model. *Perfect procedural justice* exhibits two characteristics. First, there must be some criterion for determining what a fair outcome is. Second, there must be procedures put into place that are designed to facilitate that fair outcome (Rawls, 1971). The first characteristic is supposed to define the "right" or "fair" result. The second sets forth the mechanism to achieve that result. To illustrate this concept, Rawls uses the example of slicing a cake (think back to Box 6.2). He points out that the person slicing the cake normally chooses his or her piece last. As a result, the cake slicer is likely to make all of the pieces the same size because failure to do so could leave him or her with the smallest piece. "'Equal shares for each' is the independent criterion of a fair division; the slicer-picks-last rule is the procedure that reliably produces that outcome" (Solum, 2004, p. 239).

Perfect procedural justice is based on the accuracy model, in which the justice system is structured to produce the "right" result, which generally would be the proper (i.e., accurate) identification and conviction of the guilty party in every case. This somewhat idealistic model strives for accuracy in searching for the truth as the criterion for defining a fair outcome. "Accuracy . . . is provided by elaborate trial procedures, including cross examination, neutral judges and juries, rules of evidence, and representation by counsel" (Solum, 2004, p. 245). Rawls argued that the U.S. system of justice is *not* based on the accuracy model. Instead, Rawls pointed out that legal doctrines often interfere with the accuracy in fact finding required of perfect procedural justice. For instance, the exclusionary rule is a good example. If police violate someone's Fourth Amendment rights by conducting an illegal search and seizure, the evidence seized during the illegal search will likely be inadmissible at trial—even if it is strong evidence of the person's guilt (see *Mapp v. Ohio,* 1961). A higher principle of public policy—namely, protection of constitutional rights—is addressed by this rule. However, it interferes with the overall accuracy of the trial process. Indeed, a guilty person may go free because of the application of the exclusionary rule. (The exclusionary rule is discussed in more detail later in this chapter.)

Imperfect Procedural Justice: The Balancing Model. Imperfect procedural justice occurs when the first characteristic of perfect procedural justice (i.e., the independent criterion for a fair outcome) is present, but the second characteristic—a procedure for guaranteeing the outcome—is missing. Rawls asserts that criminal trials in the United States most closely represent this type of procedural justice. The independent criterion for a fair outcome is present—namely, that someone who is proven to have violated a criminal law should be convicted. Conversely, someone who is not proven to have violated a criminal law should be found not guilty. Yet, the procedures used in criminal courts do not guarantee this outcome. Consider the exclusionary rule again. Its use can sometimes make it difficult to accomplish the first characteristic by interfering with the ability to convict someone who is very likely guilty. But this is because imperfect procedural justice operates within a balancing model.

The balancing model assumes that procedures are designed "to strike a fair balance between the costs and benefits of adjudication" (Solum, 2004, p. 193). This involves a consideration of trade-offs in the judicial process. For example, what is the "cost" of a mistake, such as the wrongful conviction of an innocent person? A series of procedural rights are specified in the U.S. Constitution and the law of evidence to protect against this kind of error. Honoring the constitutional rights of the accused while also attempting to effectively control crime is, in itself, a delicate balance (see Packer, 1968). We will explore the attempt to balance these competing interests later in this chapter.

Pure Procedural Justice: The Participation Model. Finally, pure procedural justice focuses on creating a system with fair procedures that, if followed, are likely though not guaranteed to produce fair outcomes. The process is then more significant than the accuracy of the outcome. Rawls used gambling as an example. Assuming that a number of people place money on a fair bet, whoever winds up with the money is the fair winner. The fact that the winner may have already been a multimillionaire who did not need the money is irrelevant; the fact that one of the people cannot pay the rent as a result of having lost the bet is similarly irrelevant. The actual outcome, therefore, is not what matters in a system of pure procedural justice; rather, what is important is playing by a set of predetermined, mutually agreed-upon, fair rules.

To protect against adjudication procedures based on chance alone (like a coin toss), Rawls states that pure procedural justice must be based on a participation model. The participation model of procedural justice posits "those affected by a decision have the option to participate in the process by which the decision is made" (Solum, 2004,

p. 259). Clearly, parties to a trial are guaranteed a series of rights designed to allow their meaningful participation in the justice process.

However, there are problems with the participation model. First, not all parties can participate equally (see Peterson, Krivo, & Hagan, 2006). For example, those who can afford to hire experienced attorneys and authoritative expert witnesses might have an advantage in court over those who cannot afford to hire such people. Second, racial, ethnic, gender, or sexuality stereotypes and prejudices can affect decisions made by judges and jurors. This, in turn, can give an unfair advantage to some participants while disadvantaging others. Finally, even if it were possible for all participants in the justice system to be on a truly level playing field, the need for accuracy must play a more prominent role than it does in the participation model. That is, participative processes are not enough, by themselves, to ensure justice; rather, there needs to be a "connection between participatory processes and correct outcomes" (Solum, 2004, p. 267). Table 8.1 summarizes Rawls's concepts of procedural justice.

This brief review of theoretical perspectives on procedural justice points to some important principles. First, accuracy matters (drawing upon perfect procedural justice). Second, accuracy is not the only important goal of the system; other principles, such as dignity and respect for people and their rights, must also be taken into account (drawing upon imperfect procedural justice). And third, meaningful participation in processes that adhere to fair rules is also important (drawing upon pure procedural justice). Social psychologists have studied these philosophical principles as they apply to the criminal justice system. Their research teaches us some valuable lessons about what our justice system must do to be perceived as "fair."

SOCIAL PSYCHOLOGICAL FACTORS

In the mid-1970s, John Thibaut and Laurens Walker formed a theory of procedural justice that profoundly influenced research for decades. They argued that the *outcome* of cases (i.e., who "wins" and who "loses") was not as important to the participants' satisfaction as were their perceptions regarding whether the *processes* were fair (e.g., Thibaut & Walker, 1975, 1978). Building on their work, Tom Tyler and his colleagues (2002, 2003) developed a model of three interrelated claims, nicely summarized by O'Hear (2007, pp. 12–13).

> *First,* a person's perception of whether a decision-making process was fair does not depend solely on the outcome, but also on various attributes of the process used to reach the outcome. Those attributes include (1) whether people had an opportunity to state their case ("voice"); (2) whether the authorities were seen as unbiased, honest, and principled ("neutrality"); (3) whether the authorities were seen as benevolent and caring ("trustworthiness"); and (4) whether the people involved were treated with dignity and respect. *Second,* the extent to which decision-making processes are perceived as fair helps shape beliefs regarding the legitimacy of the legal authorities responsible for the decision. And, *third,* the

TABLE 8.1 Summary of Rawls's Three Concepts of Procedural Justice

Criterion	Type of Procedural Justice		
	Perfect	***Imperfect***	***Pure***
Independent criterion for a fair outcome	Yes	Yes	No
Procedure for guaranteeing the outcome	Yes	No	Yes
Model focused upon	Accuracy	Balancing	Participation

> perception that legal authorities have legitimacy enhances the sense that the authorities are entitled to be obeyed. Fair procedures thus promote cooperation with the authorities and compliance with their directives, as well as the development of a more general sense of obligation to obey the law.

Maiese (2004) added an additional criterion requiring that the processes must be transparent. That is, decisions "should be reached through open procedures, without secrecy or deception" (para. 5).

Legitimacy in criminal justice comes only if procedural justice exists and if participants perceive the process as fair. Recall from Chapter 2 that the moral authority of law—the reason people should obey the law—is contingent upon legitimacy (see Raz, 1972). But what does legitimacy mean? Assume, for example, that the criminal justice system operated under the following four conditions that are supported by the research of Tyler and Maiese. First, assume that legal processes were consistently applied. Second, assume that these processes were adjudicated by impartial/neutral people. Third, assume these processes were participatory, meaning that those affected by the decisions have both voice and representation. And fourth, assume that the processes were transparent, meaning that they utilized open procedures without secrecy or deception. Would these criteria create legitimacy in law? Most scholars answer "no." Procedural justice is a necessary component to law's legitimacy, but it is not enough. Laws "must in addition comply with certain values, such as human dignity, liberty, equal concern for all etc., in order to be fully legitimate" (Sadurski, 2006, p. 377). This is why it is important to consider factors such as political culture and social justice, as described in the previous chapter. Furthermore, the *substance* of law must also be fair. In criminal justice, this refers to decisions about which acts should be defined as crimes (drawing upon discussions of legal philosophy from Chapter 3) and what their punishments should be. These concepts are explored in greater detail in Chapters 9 and 10. As you can see, many ideas from the text are interrelated in their shaping of law and criminal justice.

Q Most people would argue that perfect procedural justice is not attainable in criminal trials. What do you think could be done to promote perfect procedural justice? What obstacles might there be to achieving the solutions you propose?

Q What form of procedural justice do you think *Florida v. Jardines* (2013) represents? Explain your answer.

Q Other than those identified by Thibaut, Walker, Tyler, and Maiese, what other values do you think are essential to ensuring that fair procedures are used in the criminal justice system?

Two Models of the Criminal Process

FOCUSING QUESTION 8.2

How does the criminal justice system balance crime control with the rights of the accused?

crime control model
Assembly-line justice with a focus on getting an offender through the criminal justice process as quickly and efficiently as possible. This is one of Herbert Packer's two models of the criminal justice process.

Herbert Packer (1968) described two models of the criminal justice process. The **crime control model** can be viewed as assembly-line justice. Its focus is to move the offender through the criminal justice process as quickly and efficiently as possible. The idea is to arrest, try, convict, and punish offenders with ease and finality. For example, traffic court judges sometimes minimize the time it takes to adjudicate cases. They ask if the defendants would be willing to plead guilty in exchange for a reduced fine, the minimum court costs, and perhaps even the reduction or dismissal of driving points. The people who agree are then pronounced "guilty" and sentenced. The violator benefits because he or she receives a lighter punishment. The judge benefits by having cleared

the courtroom in a timely manner. Thus, the system functions quickly and with efficiency, though not with an attention to individual details.

The crime control model assumes guilt and the need for quick and effective punishment. Under this philosophy, the belief is that if accused persons were not guilty, they would not have been arrested in the first place. Furthermore, in this model the prosecutor, the judge, and often the defense attorney believe the accused is guilty. Proponents of the crime control model recognize the possibility that some of those accused of criminal activity are in fact not guilty. However, punishing a few innocent people is viewed as an acceptable price to pay for controlling crime rapidly and efficiently.

The **due process model**, in contrast, focuses on the rights of the accused. This model assumes that the accused is innocent until proven guilty. If the crime control model is assembly-line justice, the due process model is obstacle-course justice. That is, there are numerous steps that the criminal justice process must go through to assure that only the guilty are punished. If at any point during these many steps there is reasonable doubt that the offender is guilty, then he or she should be removed from the system and set free.

due process model
Focuses on the rights of the accused and advocates formal decision-making procedures, drawing upon the assumption that the accused is innocent until proven guilty. This is one of Herbert Packer's two models of the criminal justice process.

The due process model advocates formal decision-making procedures. Accused persons should have the right to have their day in court. For example, if you wished to contest a traffic ticket in court, you would be able to do so without fear of reprisal. If you were found guilty, the judge should not impose additional fines, court costs, or driving points just because you decided to have your case heard rather than proceeding through the assembly-line process.

The due process model supports the adversarial process, meaning that the prosecution and defense battle it out in a courtroom so that the truth will emerge. This model assumes that a person's freedom is paramount and that there must be conclusive evidence of guilt supported by valid and reliable information before a person can be punished. Furthermore, this evidence is only determined when both sides—the prosecution and defense—have the opportunity to put forward their best cases while contesting the case put forth by the opposing side. The system should be structured carefully to result in the punishment of only those who deserve it.

It should be evident that Packer's two models conflict with each other. Yet, elements from both models work simultaneously throughout the criminal justice process. As described earlier, striking a balance between the two models is one of the reasons John Rawls argues that our criminal justice system is one of imperfect procedural justice.

Q Which do you support more—the due process model or crime control model? Why?

Q Which model is illustrated by the *Florida v. Jardines* case at the beginning of the chapter?

Q How do the due process and crime control models correspond to the three theories of procedural justice described by Rawls? Which model is more consistent with the social psychological research on fairness described earlier? Why?

Procedural Justice in the Original U.S. Constitution

FOCUSING QUESTION 8.3

What procedural criminal justice rights are identified in the text of the original U.S. Constitution?

The U.S. Constitution, consisting of a Preamble and seven Articles, was originally adopted in 1787. It was ratified by the states over the course of the three years that

followed. The Articles of the original Constitution were primarily concerned with the structure and powers of government. However, the text did contain a handful of procedural justice guarantees.

HABEAS CORPUS

Suppose you were imprisoned for a crime you did not commit because, at a state court trial, you were not permitted to cross-examine the prosecution's witnesses against you. Such a trial would violate a number of your constitutional rights. Of course, such errors should not occur. However, if they did, you would have a great argument for the reversal of your conviction on appeal. But what if the appeals process failed to correct this injustice? Article I, Section 9 of the U.S. Constitution guarantees that you could file a petition for a writ of *habeas corpus* in which you ask a federal judge to order your release from state custody. Note that this reflects the concept of federalism discussed in Chapter 7, under which there are both state and federal governments—and under which the federal government has supremacy.

habeas corpus
In a legal context, a writ of *habeas corpus* is a court order directed at someone who has custody of a person ordering the release of that person because his or her incarceration was achieved through unlawful processes.

Literally, *habeas corpus* is Latin for "you have the body." A writ of ***habeas corpus*** is a court order directed at someone who has custody of a person (and, therefore, "has" the person's "body"), ordering the release of that person because his or her incarceration was achieved through unlawful processes. Sometimes referred to as "The Great Writ," *habeas corpus* originated in the courts of England as a means of curbing the authority of the king (Sholar, 2007). Its importance grew over the centuries in England, and by the late 1700s, it was deemed so important that the framers of the U.S. Constitution included it in the first Article. Article I, Section 9, Clause 2 provides that "[t]he Privilege of the Writ of Habeas Corpus shall not be suspended, unless when in Cases of Rebellion or Invasion the public Safety may require it." Since that time, it has been interpreted more broadly than it ever was in England. The Great Writ is considered "the fundamental instrument for safeguarding individual freedom against arbitrary and lawless state action" (*Harris v. Nelson,* 1969, pp. 290–291). The writ of *habeas corpus* is an important form of procedural justice because it provides the mechanism to challenge unlawful incarcerations.

BILLS OF ATTAINDER

Suppose that Congress passes a law declaring one or more persons guilty of a crime and imposing a punishment upon them. For instance, in 1946 a member of Congress "attacked thirty-nine named government employees as 'irresponsible, unrepresentative, crackpot, radical bureaucrats,' and affiliates of 'Communist front organizations'" (*United States v. Lovett,* 1946, pp. 308–309). Congress then conducted an investigation (with few procedural justice protections) of these individuals and ruled that three were "guilty of having engaged in 'subversive activity within the definition adopted by the [Congressional] committee'" (*United States v. Lovett,* 1946, p. 311). The three employees were then removed from their government positions. The U.S. Supreme Court ruled this action unconstitutional, finding that Congress had imposed a punishment (the loss of the opportunity to hold federal employment) upon the individuals after ruling that they were guilty. The process was an unconstitutional bill of attainder because a Congressional action declared a person's guilt and issued a punishment without there having been a trial or judicial process.

bill of attainder
A legislative act that declares someone guilty of a crime and imposes punishment for it in the absence of a trial. The U.S. Constitution prohibits bills of attainder.

A **bill of attainder** is a legislative act declaring someone guilty of a crime and imposing punishment (see Reynolds, 2005) in absence of a trial. Because the determination of guilt is delegated only to the judicial system, and not to the legislature, Article I, Section 9, Clause 3 of the Constitution prohibits Congress from passing bills of attainder. Clause 10 of the same Article and Section similarly prohibits the states from passing bills of attainder. This ensures that all accused persons will have their day in court and that the court will hold all responsibility for determining whether or not persons

are guilty based on evidence introduced at trial. This is important to the concept of procedural justice because it prevents "legislative oppression of those politically opposed to the majority in control" (Pound, [1930] 1998, p. 133). Guilt will only be adduced after a fair judicial process that accounts for relevant evidence.

EX POST FACTO LAWS

Article I, Section 10 of the U.S. Constitution provides: "No State shall . . . pass any . . . *ex post facto* Law." An ***ex post facto*** law is any law that "punishes an act that was not criminal when committed" (West, 2007, p. 243). To return to the case of the fired government bureaucrats, the U.S. Supreme Court suggested that the process had elements of being an *ex post facto* law. The Court observed that Congress "found [the employees] 'guilty' of the crime of engaging in 'subversive activities,' [and] defined that term for the first time," meaning that the rule the employees were accused of violating had been "determined by no previous law" (*United States v. Lovett,* 1946, pp. 316–317). In other words, Congress was not enforcing an existing law but rather had made up a new rule as part of the investigation process. This, in turn, meant that individuals would have had no advance notice of the rule, so they could not have known that they were violating it.

ex post facto
A law punishing an act or behavior that was not criminal when it was committed. *Ex post facto* laws are prohibited under the U.S. Constitution because fairness requires that punishments can only be given when offenders have the opportunity to know that their behavior was criminalized.

Consider a fictional example—suppose that you ate chocolate cake on Monday. Then, on Tuesday, a law went into effect criminalizing the eating of chocolate cake. The *Ex Post Facto* Clause would prohibit your prosecution and/or punishment for having eaten the cake *before* there was a law against doing so. The Supreme Court has also interpreted the *Ex Post Facto* Clause as barring laws that increase the possible punishment an offender may receive for his or her crime *after* the crime was committed or that change the "rules of evidence after the commission of the offense for the purpose of obtaining a conviction" (West, 2007, p. 243). The prohibition of *ex post facto* laws ensures that guilt can be assigned and punishments meted out only when offenders have the opportunity to know that their behavior was criminalized and what the possible consequences are—certainly, a prerequisite for fairness.

TRIAL BY JURY

Article III, Section 2 of the Constitution guarantees that trials for all federal crimes, other than impeachment trials, shall be by jury. The Supreme Court has ruled that this right does not apply to petty crimes, military tribunals, or when the defendant has waived the right to a trial by jury. This right was expanded upon in the Sixth Amendment, discussed later in this chapter in greater detail.

TRIAL FOR TREASON

The only crime defined in the U.S. Constitution is **treason**. The framers were concerned that simply espousing unpopular views in a new democracy might be considered treasonous. Since the First Amendment's protection of free speech was not yet in existence (being adopted after the Constitution), the framers defined the substantive elements of the crime and procedures for proving it to ensure that simple speech could not be interpreted as the crime of treason. Article III, Section 3 states: "Treason against the United States, shall consist only in levying War against them, or in adhering to their Enemies, giving them Aid and Comfort. No Person shall be convicted of Treason unless on the Testimony of two Witnesses to the same overt Act, or on Confession in open Court. . . ."

treason
The only crime defined in the U.S. Constitution, which defines treason as making war against the United States or providing aid and comfort to enemies.

Q Why do you think that the text of the original U.S. Constitution defined only one crime and contained so few procedural justice provisions that are relevant to the criminal process?

Q In response to the terrorist attacks of September 11, 2001, President George W. Bush authorized the indefinite detention of suspected terrorists or enemy combatants at the

U.S. military base in Guantánamo Bay, Cuba. Congress subsequently authorized military commissions to review the cases of these detainees and specifically provided that the decisions of these commissions were not reviewable in U.S. federal courts by means of *habeas corpus*. In *Boumediene v. Bush* (2008), a five-person majority of the justices on the U.S. Supreme Court determined the Congress had unconstitutionally suspended the writ of *habeas corpus* for the Guantánamo detainees. Do you agree that the *habeas corpus* provisions contained in Article I, Section 9, Clause 2 of the U.S. Constitution should apply to the Guantánamo detainees? Explain your reasoning.

Procedural Justice in the Amendments to the U.S. Constitution

FOCUSING QUESTION 8.4

What procedural criminal justice rights are identified in key amendments to the U.S. Constitution?

Bill of Rights
The first 10 amendments to the U.S. Constitution, which identify rights and liberties and restrain the powers of the government through both substantive and procedural due process.

In 1789, Congress adopted 10 constitutional amendments that were ratified by the states within three years. These first 10 Amendments to the Constitution are collectively referred to as the **Bill of Rights**. The Bill of Rights and the Fourteenth Amendment, which was enacted after the U.S. Civil War, expanded on the procedural justice guarantees in the Articles of the original U.S. Constitution with a more comprehensive list of individual rights and liberties that restrain the powers of the government in both substantive and procedural ways.

THE FOURTH AMENDMENT

Article 21 of the Code of Hammurabi (ca. 1750 BCE) stated: "If a man makes a breach into a house, one shall kill him in front of the breach and bury him in it." Some scholars consider this the first statement of law expressing the notion that a "man's home is his castle" (Lasson, 1937). This principle embodies the notion that one's home is sacred and should, therefore, be beyond the reach of unreasonable intrusions—especially from governmental actors, a principle embodied in the Fourth Amendment, which provides:

> The right of the people to be secure in their persons, houses, papers, and effects, against unreasonable searches and seizures, shall not be violated, and no Warrants shall issue, but upon probable cause, supported by Oath or affirmation and particularly describing the place to be searched, and the persons or things to be seized.

A comprehensive review of the Fourth Amendment is beyond the scope of this text. However, in the few pages that follow, we will explore some of the most important principles and cases related to the two clauses of the Fourth Amendment.

Reasonableness. The first clause in the Fourth Amendment is referred to as the Reasonableness Clause. It prohibits unreasonable searches and seizures. "A 'search' occurs when an expectation of privacy that society is prepared to consider 'reasonable' is infringed. A 'seizure' of property occurs when there is some meaningful interference with an individual's possessory interest in that property" (*United States v. Jacobsen,* 1984, p. 113). There is no formula for determining reasonableness; rather, reasonableness is an inherently flexible standard that takes into account all of the circumstances surrounding the actions of law enforcement officials. Generally, though, absent abusive conduct or behavior that "shocks the conscience" (*Rochin v. California,* 1952, p. 172), the reasonableness of search or seizure will turn, in large part, on three factors: (1) whether law enforcement officers trespassed against a defendant's property rights; (2) whether law

enforcement officers violated the defendant's reasonable expectations of privacy; and (3) whether the actions of law enforcement complied with the requirements of the Warrants Clause.

Following English tort law, the U.S. Supreme Court originally adopted a trespass-based approach to the Fourth Amendment by examining whether law enforcement physically intruded into a constitutionally protected area. Thus, in *Olmstead v. United States* (1928), the Court held that wiretapping was not covered by the Fourth Amendment because there had been no physical invasion of the defendant's premises—the wiretap had not been installed on the defendant's property. Similarly, in *Goldman v. United States* (1942), the Court found no search or seizure under the Fourth Amendment when police placed a listening device against a wall in an office that adjoined the defendant's office, again relying on the lack of a physical intrusion.

Until 2012, many legal scholars thought that the trespass-based approach to the Fourth Amendment had been abandoned by the U.S. Supreme Court in *Katz v. United States* (1967). In *Katz,* FBI agents had attached an electronic listening and recording device to the *outside* of a public telephone booth to overhear telephone conversations. They used this device to record the defendant obtaining gambling-related information and placing illegal bets. In a major reversal of its prior precedents (such as *Olmstead* and *Goldman*), the *Katz* Court held that the FBI's actions violated the Fourth Amendment because the use of a recording device violated the defendant's reasonable expectation of privacy in his phone conversations—even though there was no physical intrusion. Since then, the ruling in *Katz* has been understood to govern Fourth Amendment privacy rights. Unreasonable searches under *Katz* focus not on whether or not a trespass occurred, but instead on whether there was a violation of an individual's actual (subjective) expectation of privacy that society is prepared to recognize as objectively reasonable.

For many years, judges and scholars alike interpreted *Katz* as having overruled *Olmstead.* But in *United States v. Jones* (2012), the U.S. Supreme Court clarified that *Katz*'s reasonable expectation of privacy approach supplemented, but did not replace, a trespass-based approach to privacy on one's property. Thus, the current legal interpretation is that the protections of the Fourth Amendment apply whenever there is either a governmental trespass to private property or a governmental invasion of a reasonable expectation of privacy. But, as the discussion in Box 8.1 should make clear, determinations about what constitute reasonable expectations of privacy raise difficult questions on which reasonable people may differ.

Probable Cause and Warrants. The second clause of the Fourth Amendment is called the Warrants Clause. It specifies that warrants must be supported by probable cause, specify where a search is to take place, and describe with particularity who or what is to be seized. **Probable cause** is defined as a "fair probability" based on facts and known circumstances (1) that seizable evidence will be found in a particular location or on a particular person (*Carroll v. United States,* 1925) or (2) that an offense has been or is being committed by the person to be arrested (*Brinegar v. United States,* 1949).

probable cause
A fair probability based on facts and known circumstances. Probable cause is required for an arrest, for the issuance of search and arrest warrants, and for a case to proceed beyond the grand jury and preliminary hearing stages, among other decisions.

Probable cause can be established in a number of ways. Information obtained through a law enforcement officer's own senses—sight, hearing, smell, touch, and taste—often forms the basis of a probable cause determination. But there are numerous methods of establishing probable cause, some of which are presented in Table 8.2. Keep in mind, however, that any single factor may be insufficient to establish probable cause on its own. Rather, probable cause is determined under the *totality of the circumstances* known at the time and must include consideration of whether the information is reasonably trustworthy (*Illinois v. Gates,* 1983).

Exceptions to Probable Cause. Although probable cause is usually necessary to conduct a search, seize evidence, or make an arrest, the Supreme Court has created

BOX 8.1

Ethics in Practice

POLICE SEARCHES THAT INVADE PRIVACY

In *Katz v. United States* (1967), the Supreme Court ruled that the FBI had violated the Fourth Amendment by placing a recording device just outside a public telephone booth. The Court reasoned that the user of the telephone had a subjective expectation of privacy during the call he made from the phone booth. This means that the user subjectively believed that the call would be private. Moreover, the Court found that subjective expectation to be objectively reasonable. This means that the expectation is one that is recognized by and consistent with societal standards.

Katz's formulation of privacy is tied to whether "society" is willing to embrace a subjectively held privacy belief as "reasonable." But when making these determinations, courts rarely, if ever, use public opinion polls or empirical research. Rather, a trial court judge makes his or her best guess and, ultimately, a majority of the Justices on the U.S. Supreme Court settle novel or tough questions. Research, however, suggests the Court's "conclusions about the scope of the Fourth Amendment are often not in tune with commonly held attitudes about police investigative techniques" (Slobogin & Schumacher, 1993, p. 774). In fact, judicial decisions tend to seriously underestimate how citizens view certain police search and seizure tactics as intrusive of privacy.

Fradella, Morrow, Fischer, and Ireland (2011) surveyed people's levels of agreement with key Fourth Amendment precedents. They found significant levels of public agreement with cases in which the courts had protected privacy rights under the Fourth Amendment, but significant levels of public disagreement with cases in which the courts had allowed a range of invasions of privacy over Fourth Amendment challenges. As a result, they concluded that "courts often misjudge what 'society' is prepared to embrace as a reasonable expectation of privacy" (p. 372).

Q Do you agree or disagree with the judicial determinations about whether people have a reasonable expectation of privacy in the circumstances listed below? Why?

Is there a reasonable expectation of privacy . . .

- In garbage placed in sealed plastic bags for collection outside your home? The Supreme Court ruled "no" in *California v. Greenwood* (1988).
- In your bank records? The Supreme Court ruled "no" in *United States v. Miller* (1976).*
- In the numbers dialed from your home telephone? The Supreme Court ruled "no" in *Smith v. Maryland* (1979).
- In your car if the police suspect you have contraband in it? Supreme Court said "no" in *Carroll v. United States* (1925).*

reasonable suspicion
A lower burden of proof than probable cause in which officers can articulate facts and make inferences from them that criminal activity may be afoot. Required for stop and frisks and protective sweeps.

several notable exceptions to this rule. The first important exception is commonly referred to as a stop and frisk. Police are permitted to "stop" suspects based on **reasonable suspicion** of criminal activity—a lower standard of proof than probable cause. Moreover, if they have reasonable suspicion that the suspect may be armed, they may "frisk" the suspect for weapons (*Terry v. Ohio,* 1968). Also, cursory protective sweeps of the passenger compartment of a car may be made if an officer has reasonable suspicion "that the suspect is dangerous and . . . may gain immediate control of weapons" (*Michigan v. Long,* 1983). The same is true for a brief protective sweep of physical premises (*Maryland v. Buie,* 1990).

Exceptions to the Warrant Requirement. The Fourth Amendment does not tell us if warrants are *required* for searches and seizures to be deemed "reasonable" and, therefore, constitutionally valid (see Davies, 1999; Lasson, 1937; Maclin, 1997). While an oversimplification, the courts have responded with a generalized "yes," indicating that warrants are required, but at the same time, courts have created a number of exceptions to the warrant requirement, which are summarized in Table 8.3. For a more detailed examination of a current controversy about cell phone searches, see Box 8.2.

- In your home? The Supreme Court ruled "yes" in *Payton v. New York* (1980), unless some emergency justifies an immediate warrantless entry or unless you grant consent for state actors (i.e., police officers) to enter your home. In *Kyllo v. United States* (2001), the Court said that the privacy expectation in one's home is so special that the Fourth Amendment protects people's homes from being scanned by thermal imaging devices.
- In the open fields around your home if "no trespassing" signs are posted? The Supreme Court ruled "no" in *Oliver v. United States* (1984).*
- In a barn on a landowner's private property that is located many yards away from the main house? The Supreme Court ruled "no" in *United States v. Dunn* (1987).*
- In the contents of your laptop's hard drive when you enter the United States on an international flight or cruise? The Ninth Circuit Court of Appeals said "no" in *United States v. Arnold* (2008).*
- In face-to-face conversations you have with others? The Supreme Court ruled "no" in *United States v. White* (1971), unless the other person is someone with whom you may have a "privileged" (i.e., protected) conversation, such as your attorney, your priest, your psychotherapist, and so forth.
- In high school students *not* being randomly drug tested as a precondition to participating in non-athletic extracurricular activities? The Supreme Court ruled "no," allowing drug testing, in *Board of Education of Indiana School District 92 of Pottawatomie County v. Earls* (2002).*
- In *not* being strip searched after being taken to jail after an arrest for a minor infraction, like a traffic offense or failing to pay a fine? The Supreme Court ruled "no," allowing strip searches, in *Florence v. Board of Chosen Freeholders* (2012).

Q Statistically significant levels of disagreement between the case rulings and the survey of the public reported by Fradella et al. (2011) are marked with an asterisk (*). In light of the fact that "society" appears to reasonably expect privacy in the situations marked by asterisks, do you think the courts have an ethical obligation to overturn their decisions to better protect people's privacy, consistent with public opinion? Even if they are allowed by the courts, do police have an ethical obligation to avoid such invasions of privacy when investigating crimes? Explain your reasoning.

One overarching exception to the Fourth Amendment that should be noted concerns **exigent circumstances**. Exigent circumstances are those "that would cause a reasonable person to believe that entry (or other relevant prompt action) was necessary to prevent physical harm to the officers or other persons, the destruction of relevant evidence, the escape of a suspect, or some other consequence improperly frustrating legitimate law enforcement efforts" (*United States v. McConney,* 1984, p. 1199). This is because the touchstone of the Fourth Amendment is reasonableness, and compliance with the usual requirements of probable cause and a warrant would be *unreasonable* in such emergency, or exigent, situations. For instance, the Supreme Court has allowed warrantless entry based on exigent circumstances such as attempting "to find a suspected felon, armed, within the house into which he had run only minutes before the police arrived" (*Warden v. Hayden,* 1967, p. 299), following a hot pursuit (*United States v. Santana,* 1976), having "an objectively reasonable basis for believing that an occupant is seriously injured or imminently threatened with such injury" (*Brigham City v. Stuart, 2006,* p. 400), and preventing persons inside a residence from destroying evidence (*Kentucky v. King,* 2011).

exigent circumstances
Emergency circumstances when a reasonable person would believe prompt action was necessary to prevent harm, the destruction of evidence, escape, or other such consequences. Exigent circumstances may permit exceptions to Fourth Amendment requirements.

State Action and Standing. It is important to note that the Fourth Amendment generally applies only to conduct by governmental actors (e.g., the police) but not

TABLE 8.2 Methods of Establishing Probable Cause

Methods	How It May Be Used to Establish Probable Cause	
	Information	**Examples**
Collective Police Knowledge	In databases	• Automated Fingerprint Identification System • National DNA Database • National Missing Persons Database • National Unidentified Persons Database
	Shared verbally or in writing	• Citizen complaints • Case files • Broadcasts over police radios • Conversations between investigators
Individual Officer Knowledge	Obtained through senses	• Seeing a crime committed or witnessing possession of real/physical evidence of a crime • Hearing gunfire • Smelling marijuana • Touching an object that reveals its nature as contraband
	Interpreted in light of experience	• Flight by a suspect upon seeing police • Furtive gestures • False, implausible, or evasive answers • Presence at a crime scene or in a high-crime area • Association with other known criminals • Past criminal conduct
Informants	From firsthand accounts	• Eyewitness • Co-conspirators • Eavesdroppers
	From secondhand accounts	• Hearsay information by an informant who obtained information from a credible source who possessed firsthand knowledge of the crime

In 1990, a group of Michigan residents challenged the constitutionality of police setting up sobriety checkpoints to catch drivers operating a motor vehicle while impaired by alcohol or drugs, arguing that the checkpoints violated their Fourth Amendment rights to be free from unreasonable searches and seizures since the stops were not based on any type of individualized suspicion. The U.S. Supreme Court upheld the checkpoints, reasoning that they were effective and necessary to combat drunk driving, while causing only a minimal delay to drivers lawfully operating their vehicles. But dissenting justices found this to be an "insufficient justification" (*Michigan Department of State Police v. Sitz,* 1990, p. 477), arguing that "the net effect of sobriety checkpoints on traffic safety is infinitesimal" (p. 460). How would you rule on this issue?

BOX 8.2

CAN THE POLICE SEARCH CELL PHONES INCIDENT TO AN ARREST?

Should a warrant be required to search an arrested person's cell phone? The U.S. Supreme Court has held that, upon arrest, officers have a broad ability to search a suspect and the area in his or her immediate vicinity (see *Chimel v. California,* 1969). The rationale is that such searches protect officer safety and help to preserve evidence. To conduct a search incident to arrest, officers do not need a warrant or any probable cause beyond that which led to the arrest. But does this extend to the digital information stored within a cell phone that a person is carrying at the time of arrest, such as phone records, text messages, social media posts and chats, photos, videos, and so on? Courts disagree.

The California Supreme Court ruled that cell phones could be searched without a warrant incident to arrest, suggesting that all personal property under the suspect's control at the time of arrest was subject to a search, whether a traditional container in which physical objects could be stored or an electronic container in which digital material was stored (*People v. Diaz,* 2011). The Ohio Supreme Court ruled that cell phones could not be searched incident to arrest, unless it was necessary to protect officer safety or due to an exigent circumstance. The court reasoned that cell phones are different from traditional containers and that individuals have an expectation of privacy in the content of their cell phones, so a warrant should be required before examination (*State v. Smith,* 2009).

Expectations of privacy are often central to the debate about cell phone searches incident to arrest. Consider a case from Virginia in which an individual's cell phone, which he was carrying with him, was seized and inspected after an arrest. The officer inspecting the phone found sexually explicit pictures of the arrestee and his former girlfriend, and then "allegedly alerted several additional Unnamed Officers, deputies, and members of the public 'that the private pictures were available for their viewing and enjoyment'" (*Newhard v. Borders et al.,* 2009, p. 444). Several officers unaffiliated with the case and at least one member of the public were alleged to have viewed the pictures. A federal District Court dismissed the resulting lawsuit against the police department and its officers, holding that qualified immunity applied (see Box 7.1 for further discussion of qualified immunity) and that, while "deplorable, reprehensible, and insensitive," the alleged actions "did not violate any constitutional rights that were 'clearly established' at the time" (p. 450).

In order to balance public safety interests with privacy interests, some courts have taken a more nuanced approach. For instance, a Florida case involved a traffic stop (initially for a speeding violation) in which the officer detected the odor of marijuana from the car, but arrested the driver only for driving on a suspended license. The officer seized the driver's cell phone and, upon inspection, found a photo of marijuana being grown. This photo eventually led to the discovery of marijuana at the driver's residence. A federal District Court ruled:

> Where a defendant is arrested for drug-related activity, police may be justified in searching the contents of a cell phone for evidence related to the crime of arrest, even if the presence of such evidence is improbable. In this case, however, Defendant was arrested for driving with a suspended license. The search of the contents of Defendant's cell phone had nothing to do with officer safety or the preservation of evidence related to the crime of arrest. (*U.S. v. Quintana,* 2008, p. 1300)

The court suppressed evidence from the search, which in turn suppressed the marijuana discovered at the home (under the fruits of the poisonous tree doctrine).

(continued)

BOX 8.2 (continued)

This decision suggested that the acceptability of cell phone searches incident to arrest depends on what the arrest is for, and whether information retained on a cell phone would be relevant to that offense. Of course, it leaves unclear how officers are to make that determination.

As you can see, cell phone searches incident to arrest is an unresolved legal area. Consider the following questions:

- Q Consider the advantages and disadvantages of the approaches developed by the courts in California, Ohio, and Florida. Which do you most agree with, and why?
- Q Do you agree or disagree with the decision in the Virginia case described above? Why?
- Q How does this debate illustrate the conflict between the crime control and due process models? Which forms of procedural justice does each approach illustrate?

conduct by private citizens (*Burdeau v. McDowell,* 1921). However, when private citizens act at the direction of police, they are considered governmental actors for the purposes of the Fourth Amendment (*Coolidge v. New Hampshire,* 1985). Moreover, the terms "governmental actor" or "state actor" are not limited to police or correctional officers. Evidence gathered by governmental inspectors—even teachers in public

TABLE 8.3 Exceptions to the Warrant Requirement

Doctrine	Case(s)	Fourth Amendment Holding
Abandoned Property	*Abel v. Unites States* (1960) *California v. Greenwood* (1988)	The warrantless search and seizure of abandoned items, such as material thrown in the trash, is permissible.
Administrative Searches	*Donovan v. Dewey* (1981) *New York v. Burger* (1981)	Probable cause is not required to conduct administrative inspections for compliance with regulatory schemes such as fire, health, and safety codes (e.g., inspections of jetliners, mining operations, junkyards, pharmacies, gun stores, etc.).
Border Searches	*United States v. Ramsey* (1977) *Illinois v. Andreas* (1983) *United States v. Flores-Montano,* (2004)	Searches conducted at any international border do not require a warrant, probable cause, or even reasonable suspicion. This is based on the "longstanding right of the sovereign to protect itself by stopping and examining persons and property crossing into this country" (*United States v. Ramsey,* p. 616).
Consent Searches	*Schneckloth v. Bustamonte* (1973) *United States v. Matlock* (1974)	Fourth Amendment rights may be voluntarily waived. Thus, if police ask for permission to search without probable cause and/or a warrant and permission is granted voluntarily from someone authorized to give it, any evidence found may be used in a criminal prosecution. The person granting consent need not know that he or she may refuse consent; accordingly, unlike in the *Miranda* setting, police do not have to inform people that a request to conduct a consensual search may be denied (i.e., that people can refuse to give consent).
Inventory Searches	*Colorado v. Bertine* (1987)	After lawfully taking property into custody (such as impounding a car), police may conduct a warrantless search of the property in order to protect the owner's property, to protect police from potential danger, and to guard against claims of theft or loss.

Doctrine	Case(s)	Fourth Amendment Holding
Motor Vehicle Searches	*Carroll v. United States* (1925) *California v. Acevedo* (1991) *Florida v. Jimeno* (1991) *Arizona v. Gant* (2009)	The mobility of motor vehicles justifies warrantless searches of them if there is probable cause to believe that the vehicle contains contraband. This includes any location where the particular contraband might be found, such as the trunk, the glove compartment, luggage, and other containers in the vehicle that could hold the contraband. However, police may not search the passenger compartment of a vehicle incident to a recent occupant's arrest unless it is reasonable to believe that the arrestee might access the vehicle at the time of the search or that the vehicle contains evidence of the offense of arrest (see "searches incident to a lawful arrest," below).
Open Fields Doctrine	*Cady v. Dombrowski* (1973) *Oliver v. United States* (1984) *United States v. Dunn* (1987)	Because one cannot have a reasonable expectation of privacy in open areas, like fields, forests, open water, vacant lots, and the like, police do not have to comply with the Fourth Amendment's mandates of warrants and probable cause to search open areas, even if "no trespassing" signs are posted. Only areas within the "curtilage" of one's home (i.e., the areas immediately adjacent to a home that the owner has taken steps to keep private, like a detached garage, a locked shed or barn, etc.), receive Fourth Amendment protection.
Plain View Doctrine	*Harris v. United States* (1968) *Washington v. Chrisman* (1982)	When a law enforcement officer is legally in a place in which he or she sees contraband or other evidence that provides probable cause to believe criminal activity is afoot, the evidence may be seized without a warrant. The plain view doctrine has been expanded to cover other senses, such as "plain touch" and "plain smell."
Searches Incident to Lawful Arrests	*Chimel v. California* (1969)	Police may search someone who is lawfully arrested "to remove any weapons that the latter might seek to use in order to resist arrest or effect his escape." Police may also search for and seize any evidence on the arrestee's person or in the area within his or her immediate control "in order to prevent its concealment or destruction."
Searches of People under Correctional Supervision	*Hudson v. Palmer* (1984) *Sampson v. California* (2006)	Warrantless and suspicionless searches may be conducted of jail or prison cells as well as of the person of inmates in custody, on probation, or on parole.
Searches of Public Employees and/or Their Work Spaces	*O'Connor v. Ortega* (1987) *National Treasury Employees Union v. Von Raab* (1989) *Skinner v. Railway Labor Executives' Assoc.* (1989)	Neither probable cause nor a warrant is necessary for public employers to conduct searches either for work-related purposes or for investigations of work-related misconduct. This includes noninvasive seizures of bodily fluids to conduct random drug tests on public employees whose job functions make it particularly important for them to be drug-free, such as federal law enforcement agents and railroad conductors.
Special Needs Searches in Public Schools	*New Jersey v. T. L. O.* (1985) *Board of Ed. of Ind. School Dist. 92, Pottawatomie County v. Earls* (2002) *Safford Unified School District v. Redding* (2009)	While the Fourth Amendment applies to searches and seizures conducted by schoolteachers and administrators, neither probable cause nor a warrant is required. There need be only reasonable "grounds for suspecting that the search will turn up evidence that the student has violated or is violating either the law or the rules of the school" (*New Jersey v. T. L. O.*, 1985, p. 342). Moreover, to curb alcohol and drug abuse in schools, random drug testing of students who participate in extracurricular or athletic activities may be conducted without any individualized suspicion or a warrant. Strip searches of students, however, have been held to go too far.

schools—is covered by the Fourth Amendment (*New Jersey v. T.L.O.*, 1985). Thus, it is important for all governmental actors to have a thorough understanding of the Fourth Amendment and of relevant Supreme Court cases to ensure that procedural requirements are met so relevant evidence is not excluded under the exclusionary rule (discussed in detail below)

Finally, for a defendant to challenge a search or seizure on Fourth Amendment grounds, his or her *own* property must have been trespassed by law enforcement, or his or her own reasonable expectation of privacy must have been violated. In other words, a person cannot assert *someone else's* Fourth Amendment rights or raise a challenge on another's behalf. If another person experiences a Fourth Amendment violation, only he or she (or his or her attorney) may challenge it. This is known as the doctrine of **standing**. Standing is a requirement to make a challenge to most alleged violations of constitutional rights, not just Fourth Amendment violations.

standing
A requirement in law that only persons whose direct interests have been involved, or whose rights have been violated, may bring a case or a challenge to evidence in a case. That is, individuals cannot bring a lawsuit or challenge evidence on behalf of someone else.

THE FIFTH AMENDMENT

The Fifth Amendment to the U.S. Constitution provides:

> No person shall be held to answer for a capital, or otherwise infamous crime, unless on a presentment or indictment of a Grand Jury, except in cases arising in the land or naval forces, or in the Militia, when in actual service in time of War or public danger; nor shall any person be subject for the same offense to be twice put in jeopardy of life or limb; nor shall be compelled in any criminal case to be a witness against himself, nor be deprived of life, liberty, or property, without due process of law; nor shall private property be taken for public use, without just compensation.

A number of important procedural justice rights are contained in this Amendment: the right to indictment by a grand jury, the right to be free from double jeopardy, and the privilege against self-incrimination. We will briefly explore each of these concepts.

grand jury
A group of citizens impaneled to hear evidence presented by a prosecuting attorney with the purpose of determining whether sufficient evidence (probable cause) exists to bring to trial a person accused of committing a crime.

Grand Jury. The purpose of a grand jury is to determine whether or not there is sufficient evidence for a person to stand trial for a felony offense. As such, it is a procedural safeguard designed to make sure that persons are not brought to trial unfairly or without probable cause.

A **grand jury** is a group of citizens, often up to 23 people, who review the evidence against a suspect to make sure there is probable cause to believe that the accused has committed a felony. If there is probable cause, then the grand jury returns an **indictment** (sometimes also called a *true bill*). The indictment outlines the facts and circumstances surrounding the crime and the reasons for believing that the accused should stand trial on such charges. If, on the other hand, the grand jury concludes that there is insufficient evidence to make someone stand trial on felony charges, they can refuse to issue an indictment, a process sometimes referred to as issuing a *no bill.* In this case, the process would go no further (unless new evidence was presented), and the accused would not stand trial.

indictment
A written statement issued by a grand jury to indicate that sufficient evidence (probable cause) exists to bring to trial a person accused of a crime.

Because of the Fifth Amendment, all felony cases in the federal system are usually presented to a grand jury. However, the Supreme Court ruled in *Hurtado v. California* (1884) that the right to a grand jury indictment was not so important that it needed to be applied to the states via the Fourteenth Amendment's Due Process Clause. Accordingly, not all states use a grand jury system. Rather, some states have judges make determination of probable cause in open court at a judicial proceeding called a **preliminary hearing**. Similar to a grand jury, if a judge finds probable cause, the case proceeds; if not, the process stops and there is no trial. States that use grand juries often do so because their state constitutions or state laws require it.

preliminary hearing
A hearing held in front of a judge to determine whether or not there is probable cause to believe that a person committed the crime of which he or she stands accused. If probable cause is found, the judge binds over the defendant for trial. If probable cause is not found, the case may be dismissed.

Double Jeopardy. **Double jeopardy** is a complex concept. In its most basic form, double jeopardy bars the same governmental entity from criminally prosecuting and bringing someone to trial twice for the same offense. It also bars "multiple punishments for the same offense" (*Justices of Boston Municipal Court v. Lydon,* 1984, p. 307). However, there are a number of exceptions to these general principles. For example, a second trial for the same offense may occur when the first trial results in a deadlocked or "hung" jury being unable to reach a unanimous verdict (*Blueford v. Arkansas,* 2012). Retrial may also occur when a conviction is reversed on appeal and remanded for a new trial.

Since the concept of double jeopardy only limits successive prosecutions by the *same* governmental sovereign (e.g., the same state), it does not bar a second trial by a different sovereign government, like the federal government or that of another state. For example, assume that someone lies down across the state border between Iowa and Nebraska so that he is simultaneously in both states. If he were shot to death at that moment, both Iowa and Nebraska could place the shooter on trial for murder without violating the Double Jeopardy Clause. Or, if an offender commits a crime that violates both state and federal law, she could be placed on trial in both state and federal court. And finally, keep in mind that the doctrine only applies in criminal, not civil, cases. For instance, someone acquitted of homicide charges in criminal court can still be sued for wrongful death in civil court, which uses a lower burden of proof.

double jeopardy
Bars the same governmental entity from criminally prosecuting someone twice for the same offense or from giving multiple punishments for the same offense. However, there are some exceptions to the general principles of double jeopardy.

Self-Incrimination. The **privilege against self-incrimination** protects a person against being incriminated by his or her own compelled "testimonial communications." A testimonial communication occurs when persons disclose information verbally or in writing. Thus, the privilege against self-incrimination does not prevent the government from forcing someone to appear in a lineup; to give a voice, breath, blood, or handwriting sample; or to be fingerprinted, even if doing so would incriminate him or her. The privilege does, however, allow a person to refuse to testify against him- or herself at a criminal trial. It also allows someone to refuse to answer questions before a trial that might later be used against him or her.

You are probably familiar with the commonly known words of *Miranda v. Arizona* (1966): "You have the right to remain silent. Anything you say can and will be used against you in a court of law. You have the right to have an attorney present during questioning. If you cannot afford an attorney, one will be appointed for you." The Supreme Court ruled in *Miranda* that police had to inform suspects of their ***Miranda* rights** before starting to question someone who is in custody, to ensure that suspects knew of the privilege against self-incrimination. If the police fail to issue such warnings, then the information gained during the interrogation—even a confession—becomes inadmissible under the exclusionary rule. Such statements could not be used unless one of the exceptions listed in Table 8.4 applied.

Contrary to popular belief, *Miranda* rights do not need to be read to someone upon arrest. *Miranda* rights are designed to protect someone in custody from being forced to provide incriminating information about themselves while being interrogated. If there is no interrogation, then *Miranda* does not apply. **Interrogation** includes not only direct questioning but also any statements or actions that are designed to elicit an incriminating response from a suspect (*Rhode Island v. Innis,* 1980). Moreover, for *Miranda* to apply, the interrogation must occur while the suspect is in **custody**. Custody not only includes situations when someone is under formal arrest but also situations that are the "functional equivalent" of arrest. Such situations occur when a reasonable person would no longer feel free "to terminate the interrogation and leave" (*Thompson v. Keohane,* 1995, p. 112).

As a general rule, if a suspect invokes his or her *Miranda* rights during custodial interrogation, then questioning must cease. Since the time *Miranda* was decided, the

privilege against self-incrimination
Specifies that a person may not be compelled to provide testimony against himself or herself.

***Miranda* rights**
Suspects must be advised of the following rights prior to custodial interrogation: You have the right to remain silent. Anything you say can and will be used against you in a court of law. You have the right to have an attorney present during questioning. If you cannot afford an attorney, one will be appointed for you.

interrogation
Questions, statements, or actions that are designed to elicit an incriminating response from a suspect. Miranda warnings must be given prior to custodial interrogation.

custody
Includes situations when someone is under formal arrest and also situations in which a reasonable person would not feel free to end questioning and leave. Miranda warnings must be given prior to custodial interrogation.

BOX 8.3

Research in Action

HOW HAS *MIRANDA V. ARIZONA* AFFECTED POLICE INTERROGATIONS?

In the mid- to late 1990s, Cassell and Hayman (1996) found that in the wake of *Miranda v. Arizona,* confession rates in one jurisdiction decreased by 16% and conviction rates fell 3.8%, leading them to conclude that "*Miranda* may be the single most damaging blow inflicted on the nation's ability to fight crime in the last half century" (p. 1132). In contrast, Stephen Schulhofer (1996) found a 4.1% drop in confession rates and a mere 0.78% decrease in convictions following the inception of *Miranda.* Other researchers concur with Schulhofer, explaining that once officers adjusted to *Miranda* and its limitations, they adapted and began using psychological techniques to exploit *Miranda* to their advantage (Kassin, 2005, 2008; Leo, 1996, 2001b). Indeed, contemporary surveys of law enforcement personnel demonstrate that officers do not consider having to issue *Miranda* warnings to be a hurdle to their investigations (Kassin et al., 2007; Zalman & Smith, 2007). That finding should be unsurprising since more than four out of five suspects choose to waive their *Miranda* rights and talk with police without a lawyer present (Kassin & Norwick, 2004). This high statistic is partly a function of police conduct and partly a function of suspects' mistaken beliefs.

Police employ a variety of strategies to obtain *Miranda* waivers. For example, most interrogators start their attempts to overcome *Miranda* by "strategically establishing rapport with the suspect, offering sympathy and an ally" (Kassin & Norwick, 2004, p. 212). They proceed to deemphasize the importance of *Miranda* warnings as "a mere formality" (p. 212)—an unimportant bureaucratic step that must be followed (Leo, 1996, 2001b). And then they attempt to increase the suspect's perceptions of the benefits of talking with police, relative to its costs, by emphasizing how important it is for the police to learn the suspect's side of the story, often by implying that a brief conversation can clear up the whole matter (Leo, 2001a, 2001b).

On the other side of the interrogation table, a small percentage of suspects simply do not understand their rights and, therefore, waive them without fully comprehending the consequences of that decision (Oberlander & Goldstein, 2001). But even those suspects who understand their rights labor under some mistaken beliefs about the interrogation process. Those who are actually innocent of any wrongdoing, for example, erroneously believe that their innocence will come through during their conversations with police, even when faced with hostile interrogators (Kassin & Norwick, 2004). In other words, people may feel that since they didn't do anything wrong, they not only have nothing to hide, but also have something to gain from talking to police without counsel present, a belief motivated by two naive assumptions: that only criminals need attorneys and that the truth will "come out in the wash" (Kassin, 2008, p. 1312). Yet, trained investigators are not significantly

U.S. Supreme Court has held that mere silence (or "standing mute") is insufficient to invoke the Fifth Amendment privilege against self-incrimination (*Berghuis v. Thompkins,* 2010). Rather, suspects must clearly invoke their *Miranda* rights to receive the protections of the Fifth Amendment (*Salinas v. United States,* 2013).

waiver (of rights)
An instance in which a person knowingly, intelligently, and voluntarily gives up his or her constitutional rights, such as when allowing law enforcement officers to conduct a search or when choosing to answer questions after being advised of Miranda warnings.

Once informed of *Miranda* rights, people are free to waive them. Valid **waivers** of Fifth Amendment rights occur when people voluntarily give up their constitutional rights, such as their right to remain silent. If police used physical force, intimidation, threats, or certain forms of coercion to get suspects to waive their rights, the waiver would be ineffective because it was not voluntary (*Moran v. Burbine,* 1986). The overwhelming majority of the time, however, police abide by the rules designed to protect Fifth Amendment rights and suspects nonetheless waive their *Miranda* rights for the reasons explored in the Box 8.3.

The law of self-incrimination is complicated. There are numerous rules, exceptions to those rules, and exceptions to the exceptions. Our goal here is not to provide you with a detailed understanding of *Miranda* or the privilege against self-incrimination. Rather,

more accurate at detecting truth or deception than untrained laypersons (Vrij, 2008). Moreover, the psychological tactics that most investigators employ, which include trickery and deception, can not only lead an innocent person to unwittingly make incriminating statements, but also can even cause the innocent to falsely confess to things they did not do (Kasssin et al., 2007; Leo, 1996). In fact, laboratory experiments in which researchers created pressured situations induced 18% of suspects in one study to falsely confess something of which they were actually innocent (Russano, Meissner, Narchet, & Kassin, 2005), a number that soared in another study to an astonishing 94% when suspects were confronted with fake evidence of their guilt (Kassin & Kiechel, 2006). Yet, jurors, like most police officers, reject the notion that interrogation tactics elicit false confessions; moreover, they erroneously believe that they can spot a false confession when confronted with one (Blandon-Gitlin, Sperry, & Leo, 2011). It should come as no surprise, then, to learn that false confessions account for roughly 25% of the wrongful convictions overturned by the Innocence Project (2013) using DNA evidence (see also Leo, 2001a).

In contrast, both innocent and guilty suspects alike fear that if they assert their *Miranda* rights, they will be perceived as uncooperative or, even worse, as guilty (Kassin et al., 2007). Yet, the Supreme Court's opinion in the *Miranda* case specifically stated that the Fifth Amendment prohibits the invocation of *Miranda* rights from being interpreted as evidence of guilt at trial. It should be noted, however, that to avail themselves of *Miranda's* protections, suspects must specifically invoke their Fifth Amendment rights, since the Court has determined that the Fifth Amendment does not protect mere silence in the face of an incriminating accusation from being used as circumstantial evidence of guilt (*Salinas v. Texas,* 2013).

In light of how police adapted to *Miranda,* most scholars agree with Schulhofer (1996) that "for all practical purposes, *Miranda's* empirically detectable net damage to law enforcement is zero" (p. 547). On the other hand, *Miranda* helped professionalize police by "eradicating the last vestiges of third-degree [i.e., physical brutality to force confessions] policing interrogation practices" (Leo, 1996, p. 669). Given the move to psychological persuasion over strong-arm tactics, even most law enforcement executives agree that the legacy of *Miranda* has been a positive one for police professionalization (Zalman & Smith, 2007).

Q What can the criminal justice system do to safeguard against false confessions?

Q Some of the psychological strategies used by police to elicit confessions have been controversial. What do you think of these practices? Why do you think they are effective?

Q In 2000, the Supreme Court reaffirmed *Miranda* (*Dickerson v. U.S.*). Do you think that *Miranda* needs to be revised in any way? Why or why not?

you should see that there are a series of procedures in place designed to make sure the criminal justice system treats suspects fairly—the core value of procedural justice.

THE SIXTH AMENDMENT

The Sixth Amendment to the U.S. Constitution states:

> In all criminal prosecutions, the accused shall enjoy the right to a speedy and public trial, by an impartial jury of the State and district wherein the crime shall have been committed, which district shall have been previously ascertained by law, and to be informed of the nature and cause of the accusation; to be confronted with the witnesses against him; to have compulsory process for obtaining witnesses in his favor, and to have the Assistance of Counsel for his defence.

As you see, the text of the Sixth Amendment begins with the phrase "in all criminal prosecutions." That phrase is a bit misleading. It is accurate insofar as the rights in the Amendment are limited to criminal cases and, therefore, do not apply in civil

court, including juvenile delinquency proceedings which are technically civil in nature (*McKeiver v. Pennsylvania,* 1971). However, the word *all* really should read *most,* for reasons that the following sections should make clear.

trial by jury
A trial in which guilt or innocence is determined by a jury of one's peers. The right to a trial by jury exists for felonies and some misdemeanors.

bench trial
A trial in which the judge, rather than the jury, acts as finder of fact (e.g., determining guilt or innocence). Bench trials may occur for some misdemeanors for which trials by jury are not available or when a defendant waives his or her right to a trial by jury.

Jury Trial Rights. Although *all* criminal defendants are entitled to a speedy and public trial (see *Barker v. Wingo,* 1972), the right to have a **trial by jury** depends on the type of case. As a rule, the right to a trial by jury exists only for felonies and for misdemeanors that are not "petty offenses." In *Baldwin v. New York* (1970), the Supreme Court ruled that, for the purpose of the right to trial by jury, a petty offense is any misdemeanor case that carries a potential sentence of less than six months of incarceration. Accordingly, the right to trial by jury only exists when a defendant potentially faces jail time of six months or more. For crimes that carry lower penalties, a **bench trial** will be conducted—a trial in which the judge determines the verdict. A bench trial may also occur in cases when a defendant who is entitled to a trial by jury waives that right with the approval of the court.

Right to Notice of the Charges. Notice of the criminal charges someone is facing is an important right guaranteed by the Sixth Amendment. It provides persons accused of a crime with an opportunity to prepare a defense by knowing precisely which offenses or sections of the criminal code they are charged with violating. Notice is typically provided in two ways. First, written notice is provided in a *charging document.* There are three primary types of charging documents: *indictments* (issued by a grand

Juries are supposed to be from a reasonable cross-section of the community. But that does not necessarily mean that the people summoned for jury duty in any particular case will be "a perfect mirror of the community or accurately [reflect] the proportionate strength of every identifiable group" (*Swain v. Alabama,* 1965, p. 208). For many years potential jurors were summoned to court from voter registration rolls. Today, however, to increase the representativeness of jury pools, people are summoned from telephone lists, motor vehicle or driver's license rolls, and welfare and unemployment lists. How would you determine whether a jury is representative of the community? What could be done to make sure that juries are representative?

jury), *informations* (filed by prosecutors), and *complaints* (signed and sworn by a police officer or victim of a crime). Second, oral notice is given during various pretrial court proceedings, such as the initial appearance and the arraignment. These procedures are discussed in more detail in Chapter 12.

Rights to Call and Confront Witnesses. A defendant has the right to subpoena witnesses to testify on his or her behalf. A **subpoena** is a court order commanding a witness to appear in court at a specific date to provide sworn testimony in a case.

subpoena
A court order commanding a witness to appear in court at a specific date to provide sworn testimony in a case.

To ensure the reliability of evidence, witnesses cannot provide testimony secretly. Rather, they must do so in open court and be subject to cross-examination (*Maryland v. Craig,* 1990). The portion of the Sixth Amendment that guarantees these rights is referred to as the **Confrontation Clause.** "The opportunity for cross-examination . . . is critical for ensuring the integrity of the fact-finding process. Cross-examination is 'the principal means by which the believability of a witness and the truth of his testimony are tested'" (*Kentucky v. Stincer,* 1987, p. 736). The Confrontation Clause significantly limits the use of out-of-court statements by people who are not testifying at trial (see *Crawford v. Washington,* 2004).

Confrontation Clause
The portion of the Sixth Amendment to the U.S. Constitution which guarantees that, in a trial, witnesses must provide their testimony in open court and be subject to cross-examination.

Right to Counsel. Finally, the Sixth Amendment guarantees the right to counsel. Historically, this right meant something very different than it does now. At the time the Sixth Amendment was adopted, the Right to Counsel Clause was included to ensure that people who could afford to hire lawyers were free to do so—a right people still enjoy to this day (Neubauer & Fradella, 2014). But the courts' interpretation of the Sixth Amendment has changed over time. Today, criminal defendants who cannot afford to hire their own attorney must be provided with one free of charge. But, as with other Sixth Amendment guarantees, the right to free counsel does not actually apply in *all* criminal cases; rather, it applies only when a criminal defendant faces potential jail time for either a felony or a misdemeanor offense (*Argersinger v. Hamlin,* 1972; *Gideon v. Wainwright,* 1963).

Of course, the right to counsel does a defendant no good if the attorney does not represent the defendant competently. The Supreme Court has therefore interpreted the Sixth Amendment as guaranteeing the *effective* assistance of counsel (*Strickland v. Washington,* 1984). Accordingly, when a lawyer's performance falls so far below the standard of reasonable competence that the outcome of the case is likely to be unfair or unreliable, the Sixth Amendment provides a remedy for a new trial to occur (*Lockhart v. Fretwell,* 1993).

THE FOURTEENTH AMENDMENT

The Fourteenth Amendment to the U.S. Constitution provides that:

> All persons born or naturalized in the United States, and subject to the jurisdiction thereof, are citizens of the United States and of the State wherein they reside. No State shall make or enforce any law which shall abridge the privileges or immunities of citizens of the United States; nor shall any State deprive any person of life, liberty, or property, without due process of law; nor deny to any person within its jurisdiction the equal protection of the laws. . . .

Arguably, no other provision in the U.S. Constitution is more important to procedural justice than the Fourteenth Amendment in light of its guarantees of due process and equal protection.

Due Process Clause
The provision in the Fourteenth Amendment to the U.S. Constitution that makes nearly all of the criminal procedural rights contained in the Bill of Rights applicable to the states and which serves as an independent source for rights not otherwise listed in the Constitution or Bill of Rights.

Due Process. Recall that most of the provisions that have been discussed originally applied only to the federal government. Although an oversimplification, the **Due Process Clause** of the Fourteenth Amendment was responsible for making nearly all of the

criminal procedural rights guaranteed in the Bill of Rights (and discussed earlier in this chapter) applicable to the states (e.g., *Gitlow v. New York,* 1925). Additionally, the Due Process Clause has been interpreted as providing an independent source for other procedural justice rights that are not specifically enumerated, or listed, in the Constitution or Bill of Rights. For instance, requiring proof beyond a reasonable doubt for criminal convictions (*In re Winship,* 1970) is grounded in the Due Process Clause. Forbidding a state from compelling a criminal defendant to stand trial before a jury while dressed in identifiable prison clothes is another example (*Estelle v. Williams,* 1976).

The Due Process Clause has also been interpreted as the basis for providing substantive rights not explicitly guaranteed in the Constitution. Such substantive rights include the right to privacy (see *Lawrence v. Texas,* 2003), the right of the mentally ill to be free from undue restraints (*Youngberg v. Romeo,* 1982), and the right to refuse medical treatment even if that means a patient will die (*Cruzan v. Director, Missouri Department of Health,* 1990), just to name a few.

Equal Protection Clause
The provision in the Fourteenth Amendment to the U.S. Constitution that serves to guarantee equality, requiring that the law treat similarly situated people in a similar manner without discrimination.

Equal Protection. The **Equal Protection Clause** of the Fourteenth Amendment is a cornerstone of procedural justice. Recall that Tyler's model of procedural justice required that people perceive the justice system as treating people alike, a concern shared by social justice advocates and instrumental to the equality promoted by American political culture. The Equal Protection Clause serves to guarantee equality. Contrary to popular belief, the Equal Protection Clause does not mandate that the law treat everyone the same. Rather, the Clause requires that the law treat *similarly situated people* in a *similar* manner. Thus, the government may not discriminate based on characteristics like race, ethnicity, and religion (see *Brown v. Board of Education,* 1954). If, however, people are not similarly situated, then the law may treat people differently. Consider, for example, that the law may deprive people convicted of certain felony offenses of a variety of rights and privileges that are available to other people who are not similarly situated (those without felony convictions), such as voting rights, the right to lawfully possess a firearm, and the ability to be licensed in certain professions.

THE EXCLUSIONARY RULE

Because the Fourth Amendment originally applied only to the federal government and not to the state and local governments that had primary responsibility for law enforcement, it had little effect for the first 100 years or so of our nation's history. It really was not until the era of Prohibition that federal law enforcement became so active that Fourth Amendment litigation began to become commonplace. In 1914, the Supreme Court had adopted the exclusionary rule in *Weeks v. United States.* The **exclusionary rule** is a remedy for violations of the Fourth Amendment. The rule stipulates that evidence seized by law enforcement officials in violation of a person's constitutional rights cannot be used in criminal trials. The ruling in *Weeks* applied only to federal law enforcement officers and federal trials; as you will see below, it was later extended to also apply to state and local law enforcement and trials. Moreover, if the illegal evidence led law enforcement officers to find additional evidence, then that additional evidence is also inadmissible. This is called the **fruit of the poisonous tree** doctrine. It provides that secondary evidence gathered as a result of some earlier constitutional violation must also be excluded (*Silverthorne Lumber Co. v. United States,* 1920).

exclusionary rule
Stipulates that illegally seized evidence may not be admissible at trial. Established by Supreme Court interpretations of the Fourth Amendment. There are, however, many exceptions to the exclusionary rule.

fruit of the poisonous tree
A doctrine stipulating that further evidence acquired as a result of previously illegally obtained evidence may not be admissible in court.

In *Wolf v. Colorado* (1949), the Supreme Court ruled that the Fourth Amendment's requirements do apply to state and local officials. *Wolf,* however, did not require state courts to apply the exclusionary rule as a remedy for Fourth Amendment violations by state actors. But, the Court did extend the exclusionary rule to the states 11 years later in *Mapp v. Ohio* (1961). Therefore, the exclusionary rule now applies nationally at the federal and state level, and as a result the prosecution may not use illegally obtained evidence in its case-in-chief as substantive evidence of guilt in either federal or state trials.

Although the exclusionary rule was judicially created as a remedy for Fourth Amendment search and seizure violations, the U.S. Supreme Court has extended the reach of the exclusionary rule to other constitutional violations. Thus, the exclusionary rule can be used to suppress incriminating statements, admissions, and even full confessions that were elicited in violation of the Fifth Amendment (*Miranda v. Arizona,* 1966). However, the fruit of the poisonous tree doctrine does not apply to physical evidence derived from statements obtained in violation of *Miranda,* so long as the statements were voluntarily made (*United States v. Pantane,* 2004).

Similarly, the exclusionary rule applies to evidence gained in situations in which the government violates a defendant's Sixth Amendment right to counsel (*Michigan v. Harvey,* 1990). The exclusionary rule has even been extended on due process grounds to suppress the results of unfair pretrial identification procedures, such as lineups that are unnecessarily suggestive (*Manson v. Brathwaite,* 1977). In contrast, the

TABLE 8.4 Exceptions to the Exclusionary Rule

Exception	Key Case(s)	Effect	Example
Independent Source	*Silverthorne Lumber Co. v. United States* (1920) *Segura v. United States* (1984)	Evidence that is tainted by a Fourth Amendment violation is admissible if it is also obtained from an independent source—a source that had nothing to do with the underlying constitutional violation.	In *Segura,* police illegally entered an apartment and remained inside for nearly 19 hours until a search warrant arrived. Even though the entry was illegal, the evidence collected during the search was admissible because the warrant was supported by probable cause established by information independent (that is, separate) from the illegal entry.
Attenuation	*Nardone v. United States* (1939) *Won Sun v. United States* (1963) *United States v. Ceccolini* (1978)	If evidence is obtained in a manner that is so far removed from a constitutional violation that the initial illegality is sufficiently attenuated (meaning weakened), then the evidence is admissible.	In *Ceccolini,* police conducted an illegal search that led them to discover a key witness. That witness was allowed to testify at trial in spite of the illegal entry because the witness's voluntary cooperation with the police sufficiently attenuated the original violation from the testimonial evidence.
Inevitable Discovery	*Murray v. United States* (1988) *State v. Miller* (Supreme Court of Oregon, 1984)	Allows illegally obtained evidence to be admitted if it would have inevitably been discovered by lawful means.	In *Miller,* police violated a defendant's Miranda rights and got him to confess that he had "hurt someone" in his hotel room. During a warrantless search of the room, a dead body was found. The court ruled that the body would have inevitably been discovered by a hotel maid, so evidence from the room (including the body) was admissible in spite of the Miranda violation and the warrantless search of the room.
Good Faith	*United States v. Leon* (1984) *Arizona v. Evans* (1995)	If a police officer acts in good faith reliance on a warrant that he or she reasonably believes to be valid but later is determined to be invalid, the officer's good faith should allow the evidence to be admissible. There is no police misconduct to be deterred when an officer does not know that he or she is doing anything wrong.	In *Evans,* police lawfully stopped a motor vehicle and found that there was an outstanding arrest warrant for the driver. The officer therefore arrested the driver and searched the vehicle, finding marijuana. The warrant, however, had in fact been dismissed, although the officer did not know that. Thus, the initial arrest was invalid. But because the officer acted in good faith reliance on a warrant believed to be valid, the search of the vehicle was upheld.

exclusionary rule does not apply to grand jury proceedings (*United States v. Calandra,* 1974), sentencing hearings (*United States v. Hinson,* 2009), probation or parole revocation proceedings (*Pennsylvania Board of Probation & Parole v. Scott,* 1998), or to any civil cases, including deportation hearings (*INS v. Lopez-Mendoza,* 1984). In addition, the exclusionary rule cannot be used to suppress evidence obtained just because police fail to "knock and announce" their presence when they are supposed to do so before forcibly entering premises to conduct a search authorized by a valid search warrant (*Hudson v. Michigan,* 2006).

Some dislike the exclusionary rule because it sometimes excludes highly relevant evidence from the trial process. So starting in the early 1980s, as support began to shift from the due process model toward the crime control model, the U.S. Supreme Court began to create a series of exceptions to the exclusionary rule that are summarized in Table 8.4.

Q How would you apply the principles of the Fourth Amendment discussed in this section to analyze the *Florida v. Jardines* case, presented at the beginning of the chapter?

Q Do you agree with the Framers of the U.S. Constitution that all of the rights set forth in the Bill of Rights should be afforded to criminal defendants? Which ones, if any, would you eliminate or narrow? Which ones, if any, would you broaden? Explain your reasoning for each change you would make.

Q Are there any rights, beyond those discussed in this chapter, that you think should be provided in criminal proceedings? Explain your answer.

Q The exclusionary rule has been very controversial, leading some to call for abolishing it. What are the arguments for and against the use of the exclusionary rule? Do you think it should continue to be utilized in the criminal justice system? Why or why not? What alternatives might be implemented to insure that police honor citizens' constitutional rights? Explain.

Conclusion

Procedural justice is concerned with the ways laws are enforced. At the heart of this concern is the notion of "fundamental fairness." Philosophy and social psychology can inform us about perceptions of fairness, but the U.S. Constitution is what ultimately sets the minimum requirements for procedural justice. It does so not only by guaranteeing due process and equal protection of the laws but also by guaranteeing a number of specific procedural rights to all who are accused of committing a crime. The criminal justice system attempts to follow its procedures as closely as possible in an ongoing attempt to balance societal needs for crime control with the due process mandates of the Constitution. In Unit IV, we will continue to explore the pursuit of justice through the role of substantive criminal law and punishment.

Surveillance and Technology

Criminal Justice Problem Solving

In 2004, the FBI and members of the Washington, D.C., Metropolitan Police Department came to believe that Antoine Jones, the owner of a nightclub, was trafficking cocaine (*United States v. Jones,* 2012). Without a valid warrant, police subsequently placed a Global Positioning System (GPS) tracking device on his wife's car while it was parked in a public parking lot and then monitored the vehicle's movements for 28 days. At trial, Jones sought to suppress the evidence obtained from the nearly month-long GPS surveillance. The U.S. Supreme Court ultimately sided with Jones, ruling that the government's attachment of the GPS device to the vehicle, and its use of that device to monitor the vehicle's movements, constituted a search under the Fourth Amendment. Therefore, because it was conducted without a warrant, the information obtained was suppressed under the exclusionary rule. Consider the arguments made by several of the Justices on the Court.

Key to Justice Scalia's rationale for a plurality of the Court, in concluding that a search had occurred, was that there had been a physical trespass to Jones's property when the GPS device was attached to the car. Scalia argued that, because there had been an unacceptable trespass, a search had occurred, and it was not necessary to consider whether reasonable expectations of privacy had been violated by the GPS tracking.

Justice Alito wrote a concurring opinion, joined by Justices Ginsburg, Breyer, and Kagan, in which he strongly criticized the majority's resurrection of *Olmstead*'s property-based trespass approach to the Fourth Amendment. Alito argued that *Katz*'s reasonable expectation of privacy framework should have been applied instead. Alito would have upheld the installation and monitoring of the GPS device in the short term. However, he expressed reservations about long-term monitoring, as occurred in the *Jones* case, noting that it would violate expectations of privacy as "the line was surely crossed before the 4-week mark" (Alito concurrence, p. 13). Alito's concurrence freely acknowledges that the availability of technology may reduce expectations of privacy and, therefore, diminish the protections of the Fourth Amendment.

Only Justice Sotomayor's separate concurring opinion embraced the notion that the use of GPS technology to monitor someone's movement would be constitutionally suspect under the Fourth Amendment even in the short term and in the absence of a physical trespass to property. Sotomayor noted that even in the short term, "GPS monitoring generates a precise, comprehensive record of a person's public movements that reflects a wealth of detail about her familial, political, professional, religious, and sexual associations" (Sotomayor concurrence, p. 3). But none of the other members of the Court joined in her decision, leaving us to continue to wonder about the scope of the Fourth Amendment as it applies to tracking technology.

Thus, the Court failed to address a pressing need for law enforcement officers who must continue to wonder whether GPS monitoring *without* a physical trespass (such as when employing real-time, cell phone tracking) is constitutionally permissible, and if so, under what circumstances. Rather, the Court opted for a very narrow decision, which applies only when someone has a property right that is violated by trespass, but lacks a reasonable expectation of privacy (since that issue was not resolved in this case). Such cases will be quite rare. In fact, the case would most likely make a difference in circumstances where trespass impinged upon a property owner's open lands, but the Court seemingly foreclosed even that by writing, "Quite simply, an open field, unlike the curtilage of a home, is not one of those protected areas enumerated in the Fourth Amendment" (p. 10). The Court does not presume a reasonable expectation of privacy in open fields (see *Oliver v. U.S.,* 1984), and stating that open fields are not "enumerated in the Fourth Amendment" suggests that they would not receive Fourth Amendment protection anyway, even if trespass was involved.

Criminal Justice Problem Solving

Surveillance and Technology

continued

But *Jones* left open a particularly challenging question for police and the lower courts alike. Can police monitor suspects' whereabouts by tracking their cell phones? To date, courts are divided. A federal court in Maryland wrote:

> [T]his Court concludes that the Defendants in this case do not have a legitimate expectation of privacy in the historical cell site location records acquired by the government. These records, created by cellular providers in the ordinary course of business, indicate the cellular towers to which a cellular phone connects, and by extension the approximate location of the cellular phone. Put simply, the Fourth Amendment, as currently interpreted, does not contemplate a situation where government surveillance becomes a "search" only after some specified amount of time. (*United States v. Graham,* 2012, pp. 389–390)

Relying on the concurring opinions of Justices Alito and Sotomayor, a court in Massachusetts concluded the opposite, ruling that monitoring cell phone data even at "a single, discrete juncture" violated the defendant's reasonable expectation of privacy since it could reveal personal information about participation in private activities (*Commonwealth v. Pitt,* 2012, p. *8).

Q In the *Jones* case, do you most agree with the perspective offered by Scalia, Alito, or Sotomayor? Or, would you take an entirely different approach to the issue?

Q Do you think police should be able to use cell phone companies' records to triangulate the location of a suspect? Why or why not? Does the length of time of such monitoring matter? How long is too long?

Q Many smartphones are now equipped with GPS. Should police be able to track suspects' movements by monitoring the GPS signals emitted by their phones? Explain your reasoning use the case law summarized in this chapter.

Q What about other forms of technology-based surveillance that can provide law enforcement with long-term, round-the-clock monitoring of suspects, such as video surveillance? How about "smart dust"? These are nanotechnology devices about the size of a cubic millimeter that can track movement, monitor surroundings, take sensor readings, and even broadcast a live video-feed. Might *Katz* (focusing on a reasonable expectation of privacy) and *Jones* (focusing on trespass) be insufficient to protect citizens from high-tech surveillance? How do you think privacy rights should be addressed in the Digital Age?

Penal Social Control

Photo Essay: Bullying

Unit III considered the various ways justice may be constructed: philosophically, politically, and procedurally. Unit IV will explore the two primary means through which justice may be achieved: substantive criminal law and criminal punishment. Substantive criminal law is the listing of acts that have been deemed illegal. This combines the ideas about law and morality from Unit I, the definitions of deviance discussed in Unit II, and the ideals of justice discussed in Unit III, as each shapes the appearance of the laws that the criminal justice system is charged with upholding. Just as there are laws, there are inevitably persons who break them and who are then punished for doing so. There are many debates about what makes a punishment fair, just, and appropriate.

Consider the issue of bullying in schools. Although bullying has occurred for many years, it has only recently come to be viewed as a serious problem that school officials, legislators, and others have worked to address. While states have taken steps to address bullying in their legal codes, the most common response has been to require schools to develop bullying prevention programs and to address bullying in their own discipline codes. However, some have suggested that incidents of bullying should be criminalized and punished under the law. Consider how the law might regulate bullying.

Can bullying be distinguished from assault? For instance, consider this definition of third-degree assault: "A person commits the crime of assault in the third degree if . . . The person purposely places another person in apprehension of immediate physical injury" (Assault in the Third Degree, 2010). Would the scenario pictured meet this definition? Would it be preferable to use third-degree assault charges, or should there be a separate law against bullying? Or should bullying be dealt with through informal social control, bypassing legal regulations entirely? Why?

If bullying were criminalized, the law would have to carefully define it so everyone would know what acts the law prohibited. How would you define bullying? Here is one definition, of a behavior that is prohibited under law in the City of Monona, Wisconsin: "Bullying is a form of harassment and is defined as an intentional course of conduct which is reasonably likely to . . . emotionally abuse, slander, threaten, or intimidate another person and which serves no legitimate purpose"

(An Ordinance Prohibiting Bullying and Harassment, 2013, p. 1). How does this definition match yours? Would you change this definition in any way? In the cartoon, has either character committed an act of bullying? Why?

Bullying can also occur in online forums. Legislators have begun to propose laws to address the problem of cyberbullying. It is important for all laws to be very clear and precise. If laws are not clear, they may be void for vagueness. This means that courts may strike down and render unenforceable laws that are not clear in their description of the prohibited behavior. Consider a cyberbullying law that prohibits communications "about another student . . . which a reasonable person under the circumstances should know would cause the other student to suffer fear of physical harm, intimidation, humiliation, or embarrassment and which serves no purpose of legitimate communication" (Harassing Communications, 2008). Do you believe this law gives adequate notice of what behaviors are prohibited? Why or why not? If not, how could it be improved?

Once a behavior has been defined as a violation of the law or of a rule, a punishment must be associated with it. Enforcement of anti-bullying rules often occurs in school environments. Some schools have identified themselves as bully-free zones, signaling a commitment to reducing bullying behaviors. There are multiple approaches to doing so. What if, under the law, the first incident of bullying resulted in a student's suspension and the second incident resulted in expulsion? This would be known as a zero-tolerance policy, imposing a quick and serious punishment regardless of the circumstances surrounding the incident (see Lyons & Drew, 2006). Do you think this would be a good punishment? Why or why not? What positive or negative effects do you think it might have?

Rather than zero tolerance, another approach is to prevent bullying through the work of school counselors, creating safe and inviting atmospheres within the school as a whole that are intended to prevent bullying from happening in the first place (Stanley, Small, Owen, & Burke, 2012). Which do you think is the better approach: punishing, preventing, or counseling? Why? Ultimately, this is an issue that must be addressed when determining what role punishment ought to play.

What if a jurisdiction determined that parents were responsible for the prevention of bullying? To return to the ordinance from Monona, Wisconsin, cited previously, one provision specifies that parents may be fined if their children (under 18) are cited for bullying twice in a 90-day period. The ordinance specifies that two or more citations in that time suggest that the parent(s) of the child allowed the bullying to occur. And parents are not exempt—the Monona bullying law applies to adults, too, who may be cited for their own bullying behaviors (An Ordinance Prohibiting Bullying and Harassment, 2013). What are the advantages and disadvantages of holding parents accountable for their children's behavior? Do you think this is a good or bad idea? Why do you think the city enacted it?

It quickly becomes clear that the development of criminal law and punishments—even just for a single issue, like bullying—can raise a variety of debates. After an act has been deemed deviant and worthy of formal social control, laws must be carefully crafted and punishments carefully considered. This unit will explore the nature of criminal law and the philosophies of criminal punishment, both of which ultimately shape the work of law enforcement, court, and correctional professionals.

9

Criminal Law

Learning Objectives

1 Describe the evolution of early forms of criminal law to contemporary penal laws in the United States. 2 Explain the primary components of modern criminal law, including *actus reus*, *mens rea*, attendant circumstances, and result. 3 Explain the major classifications of criminal offenses. 4 Differentiate between the major types of criminal defenses. 5 Explain the limits the U.S. Constitution places on the ability to criminalize conduct.

Key Terms

substantive criminal law
restitution
Model Penal Code
actus reus
mens rea
strict liability
attendant circumstances
result
cause-in-fact
proximate cause
crimes against the person
crimes against property
inchoate crimes
defenses
defenses of excuse
defenses of justification
procedural defenses
substantive due process

Case Study

Copyright Infringement

If you have purchased or rented a movie on DVD or Blu-ray, you have probably seen this warning:

> The unauthorized reproduction or distribution of this copyrighted work is illegal. Criminal copyright infringement, including infringement without monetary gain, is investigated by the FBI and is punishable by up to five years in federal prison and a fine of $250,000.

In late May 2008, Barry Gitarts became the first person ever convicted by a federal jury for engaging in criminal copyright infringement involving the illegal online swapping of music. Mr. Gitarts was accused of running a server for an Internet-based piracy group known as the Apocalypse Production Crew (APC). The APC had hundreds of thousands of pirated songs, movies, and games on the server available for illegal downloading. He was sentenced to 18 months in federal prison, two years of supervised release, and a $2,500 fine (U.S. Department of Justice, 2008).

Q Do you agree with the outcome of this case? Why or why not?

Q Should copyright infringement be handled through the criminal justice system or through civil lawsuits for monetary damages? Why?

Q In October 2007, the Recording Industry Association of America won a civil lawsuit for copyright infringement against a Minnesota woman who had illegally shared 24 songs online using a peer-to-peer Internet file-sharing program (Leeds, 2007). The jury imposed $222,000 in damages—$9,250 for each song. Do you agree with the outcome of the case? Explain why or why not. Why do you think this case was handled through the civil justice system and Gitarts's case was criminally prosecuted?

The History of Criminal Law

FOCUSING QUESTION 9.1

How did U.S. criminal law evolve into its present form?

Crime is defined as "an intentional act [or omission] in violation of the criminal law . . . , committed without defense or excuse, and penalized by the state as a felony or misdemeanor" (Tappan, 1947, p. 100). In this chapter, we focus on legal prescriptions and proscriptions—the "rules" of what one must do or must not do, respectively. These

Previous page: Tablet containing the Code of Ur-Nammu, the oldest known legal code. How do you think crimes should be defined under modern criminal law?

rules comprise **substantive criminal law**. The chapter first surveys the history of criminal law with an emphasis on Western society, as that has most directly influenced the American criminal justice system. It will then move to a discussion of criminal offenses, defenses to criminal charges, and constitutionally imposed limits on what behaviors may be made criminal.

substantive criminal law
The area of criminal law that lists and defines specific criminal offenses and the punishments that may be administered to those who commit them.

CRIMINAL LAW IN ANCIENT CIVILIZATIONS

The earliest known written set of laws is the *Code of Ur-Namma* (sometimes called Ur-Nammu) from Sumer around 2100 B.C.E. (Roth, Hoffner, & Michalowski, 1997). This ancient Sumerian code set forth its laws in an "if–then" manner. For example, *if* a man committed the act of kidnapping (the crime), *then* the code specified that he was to be imprisoned and pay a fine in silver (the punishment). This was the pattern in most of the legal codes that followed. In comparison to other ancient legal codes, the punishments in the Code of Ur-Namma were remarkably humane. The code used monetary fines as the predominant form of punishment, even for crimes that inflicted bodily injury. Only crimes viewed as most serious by ancient Sumerian society—murder, robbery, adultery, and rape—were punishable by death (Roth et al., 1997).

The better-known *Code of Hammurabi*, a codification of ancient Babylonian laws, was written approximately 300 years after the Code of Ur-Namma. Like the older Sumerian code, it did not distinguish between civil and criminal law. The Code of Hammurabi was tied to the theology of the time. Hammurabi believed these laws had been given to him by various gods, some of whom had personalities that led them to act arbitrarily. Hammurabi thought having his subjects abide by these divine laws would not only promote justice and fairness in his kingdom but also would keep capricious gods happy (Rosenblatt, 2003). To achieve these goals, the code provided punishments for all types of wrongs. However, unlike the Code of Ur-Namma, the Code of Hammurabi focused much more extensively on retribution, a philosophy of punishment grounded in notions of giving to offenders the type of pain they delivered to their victims (see Chapter 10). In fact, retributive punishment is often interpreted as embodying the principle of *lex talionis*—"an eye for an eye, a tooth for a tooth"—as stated in the code.

The principle of *lex talionis* was continued by the Hebrews in their adaptations of ancient Babylonian law. Indeed, the law of Moses as expressed in Exodus 21:23–25 says: "eye for eye, tooth for tooth, hand for hand, foot for foot, burn for burn, wound for wound, bruise for bruise." However, unlike Babylonian law, compliance with Mosaic Hebrew law was not viewed as having magical powers to control the arbitrary acts of a deity. Rather, Moses saw the law as a moral code dictated by God that represented a contract. Under this covenant, God would not act capriciously but rather would protect His followers as long as they "held up their end of the bargain by adhering to a prescribed ethical tract" (Rosenblatt, 2003, p. 2127). In light of the nature of the covenant, scholars who study biblical law usually do not interpret the expressions of *lex talionis* in Exodus and similar biblical passages as advocating revenge. Instead, the principle represents "a measured and proportionate response to punishable conduct by a member of the community . . . [a] rationality as the defining features of . . . punishment [rather than] the unbridled and unchecked vengeance that had earlier prevailed" (Fish, 2008, p. 61). Indeed, while the death penalty was codified as punishment for numerous offenses, ancient Hebrew law established a variety of procedural obstacles in death penalty cases that rendered actual death sentences highly unlikely outcomes, as the focus of the law was "the sanctity of human life" (Erez, 1981, p. 30).

CRIMINAL LAW IN ANCIENT GREECE AND ROME

Ancient Greek civilization is credited with being both the birthplace of democracy and of Western jurisprudence. The Greeks "invented the revolutionary idea that human

beings are capable of governing themselves through laws of their own making, and seizing control of their destinies" (Rosenblatt, 2003, p. 2129). The Greeks conceptualized law as divinely inspired, but not divinely given. Moreover, the Greeks did not view compliance with the law as being motivated by reverence to their deities. Rather, they saw obedience to the law as part of one's civic duty and, above all, as rational behavior necessary for the orderly control of the universe.

At first, there were few, if any, written laws in ancient Greece. Draco codified the first set of Greek laws in an era when Greece was an oligarchy (ruled by a small, wealthy class). His laws were so oppressive and punitive (indeed, death was the most common penalty) that today we use his name to refer to unduly harsh punishments as "draconian." When Solon became the governor of Athens in roughly 594 B.C.E., Greece was transforming into a more democratic society. Due to Solon's work, the Greeks eventually came to conceptualize crime differently from other ancient civilizations. They began to distinguish between private wrongs, akin to our civil law, and offenses that harmed the community as a whole, akin to our criminal law (Calhoun, 1927). The city-state of Athens led the development of a system of criminal law and procedures. These included the creation of a system to prosecute specific acts before public courts composed of citizens (keep in mind that neither women nor slaves were citizens in Athens). These citizens served in large numbers (often in excess of 500) on juries that decided both guilt and punishment (MacDowell, 1978). However, there was no public prosecutor; proceedings could be initiated by any Athenian citizen. Moreover, many acts that we think of today as crimes, such as homicide and rape, were not viewed as true crimes in ancient Greece (Calhoun, 1927).

restitution
The payment of money to a victim by an offender to compensate the victim for the losses caused by the offender. This concept was present in some ancient Greek legal codes and also is utilized as part of restorative justice models today.

Unlike punishments under other ancient codes, some Greek punishments focused on **restitution**—the payment of money to compensate the victim (like compensatory social control as described in Chapter 4). Still, even after Solon's reforms, punishments for other crimes remained quite harsh, including death, imprisonment, fines, and exile/banishment from the city (a punishment often tantamount to death, as chances for survival were low when completely separated from the community and its resources). In addition, the Greeks used the deprivation of civil rights as a form of punishment, including the loss of the rights to vote, to serve as a juror, to speak in the public forum, or to have a proper burial (see Cohen, 2005).

The distinction, though a blurry one, between civil and criminal law, continued in ancient Rome. The *Lex Duodecim Tabularum*—Law of the Twelve Tables—marginally separated criminal law from other forms of law. However, the punishments for a number of acts that we think of as crimes today were often civil in nature. For example, thefts, assaults, and robberies were treated as civil property violations (see Robinson, 1990). As such, the remedies for these offenses were monetary compensation.

However, by the time of the Emperor Justinian, a clearer division between civil wrongs and true crimes had evolved. Crimes included "treason, adultery, assassination, parricide, kidnapping, and extortion, among others" (Lindgren, 1996, p. 39). Most crimes were punishable by death or by exile enforced by transportation to a far-off land. Other common criminal punishments in ancient Rome included flogging, torture, enslavement, and imprisonment (Lindgren, 1996).

CRIMINAL LAW CHANGES IN EARLY CHRISTENDOM

With the fall of the Roman Empire in the early fifth century, much of western Europe fell under the control of the kings of Germanic tribes from modern-day Scandinavia. Germanic tribal justice blended retributive and restorative justice. Their conceptualization of *lex talionis* was used to support blood feuds—killings to avenge killings. But blood feuds could be avoided through the payment of restitution, even for murder, rape, theft, and assault (Milsom, 1976).

Meanwhile, Christianity grew throughout the first century. This, too, affected criminal law. The ancient Greeks and Romans viewed natural law as a function of the orderly operation of the universe. This belief was premised on the fact that "chaos and unreason cannot explain the order of nature"; therefore, "rules of conduct must rest on certain universal norms that are fixed and permanent in nature" (Rosenblatt, 2003, p. 2130). As Christianity spread through Europe during the Middle Ages, a theological conceptualization of natural law took hold. Largely due to the works of St. Augustine (354–430) and St. Thomas Aquinas (1225–1274), natural law became viewed as the "will of God" (Rosenblatt, 2003, p. 2135). As the power of the Roman Catholic Church grew, interpretations of God's law as expressed in Catholic ecclesiastical (i.e., religious) law, blended with secular (i.e., nonreligious) law such that the distinction between the two became almost impossible to discern. Criminal law trials became searches for the "truth" of God's will in a particular case. Perhaps the best examples of this belief were the notions of trial by combat and trial by ordeal.

Trial by combat appears to have originated in Germanic law (Neilson, [1890] 2009). It was essentially a judicially sanctioned duel in which the parties in a dispute (frequently over land) fought, often until the victor slayed his opponent. After the Norman Conquest of 1066, William the Conqueror introduced the practice in England, where it was sometimes referred to as "wager of battle." The practice eventually dwindled to use in cases affecting royal interests, such as feudal land disputes and the commission of serious crimes. Parliament abolished the practice in the 1810s during the reign of George III (1760–1820).

> In *trial by ordeal,* the accused was made to hold a scalding or burning object and the verdict would depend on the degree of injury—which reflected God's intervention. The judge [often a religious official] would wait for three days to see if the hand had healed, and, if it did, the accused was cleared. In cases where this seventy-two-hour delay seemed too long for the crowd to wait, the trier-of-fact would employ trial by water. This carried immediate results. The accused who floated was guilty. If the accused sank, it was a sign of innocence, even though it might have had other consequences, such as drowning. (Rosenblatt, 2003, pp. 2135–2136)

CRIMINAL LAW IN EARLY ENGLAND

Trial by ordeal was the norm in England at the turn of the second century. But the Norman invasion of England in 1066 marked a major change in the philosophy and administration of law (see Pennington, 1993). William the Conqueror blended Germanic tribal justice with English traditions, many of which had been influenced by Catholic theology and earlier conceptualizations of crime and punishment. By the time Henry II ruled England in the mid- to late twelfth century, English common law began to develop. Under this approach, crimes were no longer private matters but instead were viewed as offenses against the Crown (Rosenblatt, 2003). Because of this shift, the law of the land began to become harmonized into a "common law"—one law that applied consistently throughout the king's lands.

In 1215, King John agreed to the *Magna Carta,* Latin for "great charter." Article 39 of that document provided: "No free man shall be taken, imprisoned, disseised, outlawed, banished, or in any way destroyed . . . except by the lawful judgment of his peers and by the law of the land." The next clause went on to state: "To no one will We sell . . . deny or delay right of justice." Originally, these protections were meant for noblemen, but they quickly grew to apply to all citizens. Once so interpreted, it should be clear that these statements formed the basis of the due process guarantees in the U.S. Constitution (see Chapter 8).

FROM ENGLISH COMMON LAW TO MODERN PENAL LAWS

Tracing the evolution of English common law (see Hale, [1713] 1971) to its maturation in the United States is beyond the scope of this book (see Holmes, [1881] 1991; Langbein, 2003). We note, though, that modern criminal law largely depended on how crimes were defined, and defenses were fashioned in England from the period of Henry II to the time of the American Revolution. Those legal concepts have continued to mature, with modern criminal law being a mixture of the common-law tradition and a series of statutory changes that have been made over the years. The most significant changes to American criminal law occurred from the mid-1960s through the mid-1980s as a result of the American Law Institute (ALI) publishing the ***Model Penal Code*** (MPC) in 1962 and updating it in 1981.

Model Penal Code (MPC)
A set of model criminal laws developed by the American Law Institute in 1962 and updated in 1981, which has formed the basis for revisions to the criminal laws in two-thirds of the American states. By being a model, the code stands as the American Law Institute's conception of what criminal laws ought to look like.

The ALI is a think tank devoted to simplifying and harmonizing the common law across the 50 states to lead to more consistency among states. Comprising judges, lawyers, and scholars from a variety of disciplines, the ALI researches and writes "model" sets of laws governing penal codes, probate codes (the law of wills, trusts, and estates), foreign relations, unfair competition, property, torts, contracts, employment law, and criminal law. Although none of these model sets of laws is the actual law of any particular state, they are highly influential. For example, the MPC has served as the basis for replacing or updating the criminal laws of more than two-thirds of all U.S. states (Robinson, 2008).

Q What do you think of the concept of retributive punishment? Does it achieve justice through revenge, or do you think it is cruel and vengeful? Defend your position.

Q In reviewing the brief history presented in this section, what common themes can you find that are illustrated across the historical legal systems described? Have they influenced the American justice system?

Q Given the significant influence that the MPC has had on statutory criminal law across the United States, why do you think we do not have a single criminal code based on it that applies in all states throughout the country? Should we?

Common Elements of Modern Criminal Law

FOCUSING QUESTION 9.2

Explain the four primary components of modern criminal law.

Under both the common law and the MPC, crimes generally consist of a combination of two or more of four components: *actus reus, mens rea,* attendant circumstances, and a result.

ACTUS REUS

Every crime establishes some act or conduct that is prohibited—the "thing" you are not allowed to do under the criminal law. Such proscribed conduct is called the ***actus reus*** (Latin for the "evil act"). For example, taking the personal property of another (if coupled with the mental state of intent to steal) is the crime of theft. The *actus reus* is the actual taking of the property, as that is the undesired action that is prohibited by law.

actus reus
One component of the legal definition of crime, expressed in a Latin phrase meaning "evil act." The *actus reus* of a crime is the actual act, conduct, or behavior that is prohibited under law.

An *actus reus* must be the result of either a voluntary act or a qualifying omission. A "voluntary act" is a bodily movement performed consciously as a result of effort. For example, punching someone is a voluntary act that would qualify as the *actus reus* for the crime of battery. Similarly, shooting someone is a voluntary act that would qualify as the *actus reus* for a homicide if the victim died. Even speaking certain words can constitute

a voluntary act upon which a criminal prosecution may be based if the words spoken are prohibited. Criminal solicitation (e.g., requesting that someone commit a criminal act) and using fighting words to incite a riot are examples. In contrast, an involuntary act does not qualify as an *actus reus.* Involuntary acts are bodily movements that are not produced by conscious effort, such as reflexes, spasms, or spontaneous convulsions.

An omission—a failure to perform an act of which a person is physically capable—may also qualify as an *actus reus* if the law places an affirmative duty on (i.e., requires) someone to act. Assume that the law tells you that you must do something, but then you fail to do it. Your failure to have done what the law indicated you were supposed to do is an omission that can qualify as an *actus reus.* Examples include failure to yield the right of way and failure to file and pay income taxes. A legal duty to act may also be imposed by relationship. For example, a parent has a legal duty to care for his or her child. A failure to provide for the reasonable health, safety, and welfare of a child is an omission that qualifies as the *actus reus* for the crime of child neglect. A legal duty to act can also be created by contract. Babysitters, lifeguards, and bodyguards agree to act to protect those under their care. If they fail to do so, then such a failure to act could qualify as an *actus reus.*

MENS REA

Most crimes do not impose a criminal sanction for doing an *actus reus* unless it is done with a culpable state of mind, or criminal intent, referred to as the ***mens rea*** (Latin for "evil mind"). *Mens rea* is concerned with the level of intent to commit an *actus reus.* In most cases, if there is no intent to commit the *actus reus,* then there is no crime. Compare two situations. If you were to accidentally and unknowingly pick up a classmate's copy of a textbook while gathering your materials at the end of class and then leave the classroom, you would most likely not have committed a crime. You would have completed the *actus reus* by taking someone else's property, but you would have had no *mens rea,* or intent to do so. If, on the other hand, you saw your classmate's book and purposefully decided to take it because it was in better condition than yours, you would have completed the *actus reus* of taking someone else's property with the *mens rea* of having done so intentionally, therefore committing a crime.

mens rea
One component of the legal definition of crime expressed in the Latin phrase meaning "evil mind." The *mens rea* of a crime is the level of intent the offender had to commit the criminal *actus reus*.

The common-law approach to *mens rea* was quite confusing, using terms like specific intent, general intent, and acting with malice. The *MPC* identified four levels of *mens rea:* purpose, knowledge, recklessness, and negligence (see Table 9.1). The level of *mens rea* often differentiates an accident from a crime, or serious crimes (with a higher level of intent) from petty ones (with a lower level of intent).

A narrow range of crimes are exceptions to the requirement of a union of *actus reus* and *mens rea.* Offenses that are punished *without regard* to the actor's state of mind are referred to as crimes of **strict liability**. A person can be convicted of a strict liability crime for having engaged in the proscribed act (the *actus reus*) even though there was no accompanying criminal intent (*mens rea*). Thus, a person acting without any *mens rea* may nonetheless be convicted of a strict liability crime. Strict liability most frequently attaches to offenses against the public health, safety, and welfare, such as motor vehicle laws and laws regulating the sale of drugs, food, and alcohol. Strict liability has also traditionally been applied to certain morals offenses, such as statutory rape (i.e., sexual intercourse with an underage person) and public intoxication. Assume, for example, that a 22-year-old man has consensual sexual intercourse with a female whom he reasonably believes to be 18, although she is actually 16. Further, assume that the jurisdiction sets the age of consent at 18 years of age. Although she was a willing participant, the man would likely be guilty of the

strict liability
Crimes that do not require criminal intent, or *mens rea*, on the part of the offender. These offenses can therefore be punished without regard to the offender's level of intention (or lack thereof) at the time of the crime.

TABLE 9.1 Levels of *Mens Rea* under the Model Penal Code

Mens Rea	Definition	Example
Purpose	A conscious objective or desire either to engage in prohibited conduct, or to cause a particular illegal result.	Defendant points and shoots a gun at a victim that the shooter intends to kill (without any legally recognized justification or excuse). Victim dies from the gunshot. Defendant acted purposefully (i.e., with specific intent to kill).
Knowledge	*Actual Knowledge:* Subjectively knowing, to a practical certainty, that one is either engaging in prohibited conduct or, alternatively, engaging in conduct that will cause an illegal result. *Constructive Knowledge:* Lacking actual knowledge but remaining willfully blind to circumstances under which a person should have known, to a practical certainty, that one is either engaging in prohibited conduct or, alternatively, engaging in conduct that will cause an illegal result.	Defendant is approached by a stranger who offers $1,000 in cash to drive a locked U-Haul from one city to another. Stranger offers $500 up front, and $500 upon successful delivery of the truck with its contents undisturbed. It turns out that the U-Haul contained marijuana. Defendant was in knowing possession of a controlled substance even though he did not have actual knowledge that the truck contained drugs. He did, however, have constructive knowledge that the U-Haul contained some contraband in light of the circumstances under which the deal was made.
Recklessness	Acting with conscious disregard of a known risk that is both substantial and unjustifiable, resulting in harm.	While drag racing at high speeds on a city street, a driver loses control of the vehicle and causes an accident that kills a bystander. The driver acted recklessly since he knew of, and consciously disregarded, the risk of a serious accident that could be caused by drag racing under such conditions.
Negligence	Unconsciously creating a risk of harm by failing to recognize a substantial and unjustifiable risk that the ordinary, reasonable, prudent person would have recognized.	While hiking, Defendant's girlfriend trips and sprains her ankle. To help her sleep that night, Defendant gives his girlfriend narcotic painkillers and sleeping pills that had been prescribed for him. She dies of an accidental overdose in light of the mixing of these drugs with other medicines she had been taking. Even though Defendant did not think about the possible consequences of giving the drugs to her, he should have been aware of the risk of giving the pills to someone for whom they were not prescribed. Accordingly, Defendant negligently killed his girlfriend.

A police officer working radar. Do you think speeding should be a strict liability offense? Do you think any defenses should apply to excuse speeding?

crime of statutory rape in that jurisdiction because he committed the *actus reus,* and statutory rape has traditionally been punished as a strict liability offense that does not require *mens rea.* Finally, strict liability also may be applied to elements not central to the criminality of an act, such as to attendant circumstances, discussed in the following section.

ATTENDANT CIRCUMSTANCES

The third major component of crime is **attendant circumstances**. These are specific circumstances which must surround the occurrence of an *actus reus* for a crime to have occurred (or for it to be punished in a particular manner). As such, the attendant circumstances vary by offense. For example, the crime of speeding does not take place unless one is traveling on a public roadway. Hence, it is not a crime to race in the Indianapolis 500 because the attendant circumstance of being on a public roadway is not present. Theft is another example. Taking the personal property of another, if coupled with the *mens rea* of specific intent or purpose to steal, constitutes the crime of theft. The *actus reus* is taking property. That taking of property must occur under two attendant circumstances. First, the property must be personal property as opposed to real property like real estate. Second, it must be the property of another person. Thus, if you took property that was actually yours, but you mistakenly believed it to be someone else's, you have not committed the crime of theft because the attendant circumstance of the property belonging to someone else was not met. You may, however, be guilty of attempted theft (more on attempt later).

attendant circumstances
One component of the legal definition of crime, related to specific circumstances which must surround the *actus reus* (criminal act) for a crime to occur or for it to be punished in a particular manner.

As has been stated, strict liability often attaches to attendant circumstances. Assume, for example, that a jurisdiction makes it a felony to "purposefully or knowingly

distribute, sell, or dispense narcotics." Assume that a defendant was arrested and charged with violating this statute when an undercover police officer witnessed the defendant selling cocaine. The *actus reus* of the crime would be the sale or distribution of the cocaine—a controlled and dangerous substance. Such a drug transaction was purposeful, so the *mens rea* of the statute would be satisfied and the defendant could be properly convicted. But assume that the punishment for the offense is higher (e.g., a longer prison term) if the drugs are sold within 1,000 feet of a school. This would make being within 1,000 feet of a school an attendant circumstance for the higher punishment. Even if the defendant did not know there was a school nearby, he or she would nonetheless be properly convicted of distributing drugs within a school zone and could be sentenced to the longer prison term. The fact that the defendant did not know she was selling drugs within a school zone would be irrelevant because the location of the sale is not central to the criminality of the act itself (in this case, selling drugs). The intentional sale of cocaine is what is central to the criminality of the act (i.e., the union of *actus reus* and *mens rea*). The location of the sale is an attendant circumstance to which strict liability may attach.

CAUSATION OF RESULT

The final major component of crime is the **result**—the outcome which actually occurred because of the commission of the *actus reus.* Certain crimes require that a particular result occur. All forms of homicide are an example. One cannot be convicted of any type of homicide unless one's act caused a particular result—namely, the death of another human being.

result
One component of the legal definition of crime related to the requirement that the prosecution must prove that the defendant's behavior (*actus reus*) caused the prohibited result.

When a crime requires a particular result, the prosecution must prove that the defendant's *actus reus,* performed with the requisite *mens rea,* actually *caused* the required result. This process involves the technicalities of the doctrine of causation. Causation in the law requires proof of two distinct types of causation: cause-in-fact and proximate cause. **Cause-in-fact** is what we normally think of as "causing": if a person does some act that directly brings about a particular result, then the person is said to have caused the result. To determine cause-in-fact, ask yourself, "Would the result have occurred *without* the defendant's conduct?" If the answer is "yes," the conduct is not cause-in-fact because the result would have occurred anyway, other than through the defendant's actions. In contrast, if the answer to the question is "no," then conduct is the cause-in-fact of the result because the result would not have occurred had it not been for the defendant's act. The defendant's act is then identified as being responsible for the outcome.

cause-in-fact
One type of causation recognized by the law when linking an *actus reus* with a result. Cause-in-fact has occurred if a person commits an act that directly brings about a particular result and may be determined by asking the question, would the result have occurred without the defendant's conduct? If the answer is "no," cause-in-fact exists.

Consider the drag racing case in the discussion of recklessness in Table 9.1. Assume that, after recklessly disregarding a known risk, the driver of a car in a drag race strikes and injures a pedestrian. Recklessness is the *mens rea,* and striking the pedestrian is the *actus reus.* To determine cause-in-fact, we would ask: Without the defendant's conduct, would the pedestrian have sustained his or her injuries? The answer is most likely "no." The injuries were sustained as a direct result of the collision with the vehicle and otherwise would not have occurred had the race not taken place. Therefore, the defendant's conduct was the cause-in-fact of the victim's injuries.

The law requires more than the direct causation embodied in cause-in-fact to impose criminal liability. The law also requires what is known as proximate cause. **Proximate cause** is concerned with whether there were any other causes (*besides* the defendant's conduct) that *contributed* to the result. If there were no other causes contributing to the result besides the defendant's actions, then proximate cause is established and criminal liability can be imposed. But if there were factors other than the defendant's acts that contributed to the result, a careful proximate cause analysis must be undertaken. When

proximate cause
One type of causation recognized by the law when linking an *actus reus* with a result. Proximate cause asks whether there were any other causes that could lead to the result.

factors other than the defendant's *actus reus* contribute to the result, criminal liability may only be imposed if the result of the *actus reus* was "reasonably foreseeable."

Let's consider an example, again returning to a racing car that strikes a pedestrian. Assume that the pedestrian is seriously injured and taken to the emergency department of a hospital. If, due to a mistake by the treating physician, the pedestrian dies, can homicide charges be filed against the driver of the vehicle? The answer is most likely "yes." At least two factors contributed to the pedestrian's death: first, the individual was struck by a vehicle driven by a person in a reckless manner, and second, the physician erred. Had either of these factors not occurred, the pedestrian would probably still be alive. However, errors in emergency treatment of a crime victim are reasonably foreseeable, and it was the initial collision that led to the need for emergency treatment in the first place. Accordingly, in this example, there is proximate causation, and the driver could be charged with some form of homicide.

On the other hand, assume a different scenario in which the victim sustained only a minor injury. At the hospital, for whatever reason, the physician deliberately mistreated the victim, causing the death. Here, there would not be proximate causation because it would not be reasonable to foresee deliberate malpractice that causes death in the course of treatment for a minor injury. Thus, the perpetrator would likely still face battery charges for causing (even minor) injury but not homicide charges.

Q Presume a statute reads: "A person commits a misdemeanor in the first degree if the person operates or controls a vehicle while under the influence of intoxicating liquor, drugs, or toxic substances if the person is impaired to the slightest degree." Break this crime into its component elements by specifying the *actus reus, mens rea,* result (if any), and attendant circumstances (if any).

Q Recall the FBI warning regarding criminal copyright infringement that we discussed at the start of this chapter. Break this crime into its component elements by specifying the *actus reus, mens rea,* result (if any), and attendant circumstances (if any).

Q What do you think of strict liability? Does imposing criminal liability without any *mens rea* seem fair to you? Why or why not?

Types of Crimes

FOCUSING QUESTION 9.3

What are the major classifications of criminal offenses?

The criminal law divides criminal offenses into four major categories: crimes against the person, crimes against property and habitation, inchoate offenses, and other offenses. We shall explore each of these classifications. Keep in mind that the crimes are presented using very general descriptions; the particulars vary by jurisdiction, as each state and the federal government has its own legal code, with its own provisions. As you review the different types of crime discussed below, consider the scenario presented in Box 9.1.

Crimes in which people are physically victimized are considered the most serious of criminal offenses. Such crimes include homicide, forcible rape, assault, battery, and robbery. These are **crimes against the person**, and their basic elements are summarized in Table 9.2.

crimes against the person
Offenses in which individuals are physically victimized or harmed. These are viewed as the most serious of criminal offenses.

Crimes against property account for the most common types of criminal offenses. Rather than harming people physically, these crimes harm individuals' property, including real estate, goods, and financial resources. This category of crime includes burglary, criminal trespass, arson, fraud, forgery, uttering, receiving stolen property, and a

BOX 9.1

THINKING ABOUT TYPES OF CRIME

Assume the following situation. An offender and two friends meet and decide to steal a valuable painting from a home where the resident is believed to be on vacation. They obtain equipment needed for the break-in and for the movement of the painting. That evening, they succeed in forcing open a window of the home, but are interrupted by the next door neighbor, whom they knock unconscious as they escape. They take the neighbor's wallet and walk to a liquor store. Upon entering the store, one tells the clerk, "Give us what's behind the counter if you know what's good for you," while the other two block the entrance to the store. The clerk hands over money from the cash register. On the way out, the offenders take bottles of their favorite beverages. As they walk down the street, they begin drinking. All are arrested by a police officer after stumbling down the sidewalk, boisterous and inebriated.

- Q Refer to Tables 9.2, 9.3, 9.4, and 9.5. If you were the prosecutor, with what offenses would you charge the individuals in this scenario?
- Q Describe what a prosecutor would need to show to establish the guilt of the defendants (that is, the persons charged with the crime) in this scenario on the charges you identified above (*hint:* consider the four elements of crime—*mens rea*, *actus reus*, attendant circumstances, and causation).

wide variety of theft offenses. These are **crimes against property**, and their basic elements are summarized in Table 9.3.

Crimes that occur as part of the preparation for committing another crime, or in an attempt to commit another crime, are referred to as **inchoate crimes**. This category of crime includes attempt, solicitation, facilitation, aiding and abetting, and conspiracy. These inchoate crimes and their basic elements are summarized in Table 9.4.

There are many other criminal offenses that do not fit neatly into one of the three categories of crime just described. Table 9.5 provides some examples of the ways in which these other offenses are often classified.

- Q Critique the classification of crimes in Tables 9.2 to 9.5. Does it make sense for crimes to be organized in this manner? In what other ways might crimes be categorized?
- Q Why do you think we criminalize attempted or preparatory crimes as inchoate offenses?
- Q Recall the discussion of copyright infringement from the beginning of the chapter. Into what category (crimes against persons, property, etc.) would you classify copyright infringement? Or would you develop a new category for this type of offense? Explain your answer.
- Q As stated earlier, crimes against the person are considered the most serious of crimes and are therefore punished the most severely. But there is a good argument to be made that certain crimes against property, especially major "white-collar offenses" (e.g., corporate negligence, large-scale fraud, etc.) have a much more dramatic effect on society than a single assault or homicide and should be punished as such. Where do you stand on this debate? How should white-collar crimes be classified? Do they fit within existing categories or should they be classified separately?

crimes against property
Offenses that cause harm to an individual's property but do not physically harm the individual.

inchoate crimes
Crimes that occur as part of the preparation for committing another crime or in an attempt to commit another crime, including such acts as attempt, solicitation, facilitation, aiding and abetting, and conspiracy.

TABLE 9.2 Summary of the Elements of the Major Crimes Against the Person

Crime	*Actus Reus*	*Mens Rea*	Result	Attendant Circumstances
Murder	Any act or omission that kills	Purpose or Knowledge (i.e., intent to kill or intent to cause serious bodily harm)	Death of a human being	None
Depraved Heart Murder	Any act or omission that kills	Gross recklessness (i.e., conscious disregard of a known risk of death or serious bodily harm)	Death of a human being	Conduct must manifest an extreme indifference to the value of human life
Voluntary Manslaughter	Any act or omission that kills	Purpose or Knowledge (i.e., intent to kill)	Death of a human being	Killing must have taken place in the heat of passion prompted by legally adequate provocation
Involuntary Manslaughter	Any act or omission that kills	Recklessness or gross negligence (i.e., negligence with a deadly weapon)	Death of a human being	None
Felony Murder	Commission of a qualifying felony that unintentionally kills	Whatever the *mens rea* is for the underlying felony	Death of a human being	(1) Underlying felony must be inherently dangerous; (2) Death must occur during the commission or attempted commission of the felony, or during immediate flight therefrom
Rape	Forcible sexual intercourse	At least recklessness (with regard to whether consent existed)	The penetration, however slight, of a sexual orifice (vagina, anus, mouth)	Without the consent of the victim
Assault and Aggravated Assault	The creation of the immediate apprehension of bodily harm (simple assault) or severe bodily injury (aggravated assault)	Purpose	Victim must have been in apprehension of immediate bodily harm (simple assault) or severe bodily injury (aggravated assault)	Actions must have included more than mere words
Battery and Aggravated Battery	The application of force to the person of another	At least recklessness	Victim must have been touched in an unwanted manner (simply battery), or have been minorly injured (simply battery), or significantly injured (aggravated battery)	None
Robbery	The forcible taking of personal property from a person (or in a person's physical presence)	Purpose (i.e., specific intent to steal)	Property must be taken	(1) Must be personal property; and (2) theft must have been accomplished by force or the threatened use of force

TABLE 9.3 Summary of the Elements of the Major Crimes Against Property

Crime	*Actus Reus*	*Mens Rea*	Result	Attendant Circumstances
Burglary	The unlawful breaking and entering	Purpose (to commit a felony or theft once inside)	Unlawful entry must be into the "structure of another"	"Of another" means the unlawful entry cannot be into one's own premises
Criminal Trespass	Unlawfully entering into or remaining on another's property without the owner's consent	Knowledge (i.e., knowing you have no privilege to enter or remain)	Either the initial entry had to be illegal, or the person must fail to leave when lawfully asked to do so	The entering or remaining on property had to be nonconsensual (i.e., without any legal entitlement to enter or remain on the premises)
Arson	The unlawful burning of a structure	At least recklessness	Structure must be burned, even if just minimally, by fire or explosion damage	The thing burned must be a "structure"
Fraud	Committing any dishonest act (deceit, falsehood, or other fraudulent means) to deprive a victim of his/her property or a lawful right	Purpose (i.e., intentional deception)	The fraud must cause a "deprivation"—some loss, detriment, prejudice, or risk of prejudice to the economic or legal interests of the victim	None
Forgery	Making or altering (by drafting, adding, or deleting) a document	Purpose (i.e., intent to defraud)	None	The document must be a writing with some apparent legal significance (e.g., a check or a contract, not a painting)
Uttering	Offering as genuine any forged document	Purpose (i.e., intent to defraud)	None	The document must be false
Receiving Stolen Property	Receiving possession and control of the stolen personal property of another	Knowledge (i.e., knowing that the property is stolen)	None	The personal property (i.e., not real or intangible property) must have been stolen from a victim by someone other than person receiving the stolen property
Criminal Damage	Damaging or destroying the property of another	At least recklessness	The property must have been damaged by the act of the defendant	The property must have belonged to someone other than the defendant
Theft	The unlawful taking the personal property of another without consent of the rightful owner	Purpose (i.e., intent to steal)	The rightful owner must be deprived of the property	The personal property (i.e., not real or intangible property) must have belonged to someone other than the defendant

TABLE 9.4 Summary of the Elements of the Major Inchoate Crimes

Crime	*Actus Reus*	*Mens Rea*	Result	Attendant Circumstances
Attempt	Attempted to commit a substantive crime	Purpose (i.e., specific intent to commit a substantive criminal offense)	The defendant must have tried but failed to have actually committed the target offense	The attempt must involve the defendant having taken "substantial steps" toward the commission of the crime; mere preparation is insufficient
Solicitation	Inducing or inviting another person to commit a crime	Purpose (i.e., specifically intended that the other person commit the specified crime)	None	None
Facilitation	Providing the means or opportunity for someone else to commit a crime	Knowledge (i.e., knowing that someone intends to commit a crime)	None	None
Aiding and Abetting (Complicity)	Providing aid or encouragement to another person to commit a crime	Purpose (i.e., with the specific intent that the aid or encouragement help or cause the other person to commit a crime)	None	None
Conspiracy	Agreeing to commit a crime or set of crimes with one or more other people	Purpose (i.e., specifically intended that the group commit the specified crime or crimes)	An agreement must be formed	None

TABLE 9.5 A Sample Classification of Other Types of Crimes

Types of Crimes	Examples
Crimes Against Public Administration	Contempt. Perjury. False swearing. Tampering with witnesses or evidence. Obstruction of justice. Bribery. Failure to appear. Tax evasion. Voting fraud.
Crimes Against Public Order	Unlawful assembly. Disturbing the peace. Public drunkenness. Disorderly conduct. Vagrancy. Drug-related offenses. Criminal traffic offenses.
Crimes Against Morality	Adultery. Bigamy. Prostitution. Illegal forms of gambling (i.e., excluding casinos, lotteries, etc.). Obscenity. Statutory rape. Indecent exposure. Public sexual indecency.

Defenses to Crimes

FOCUSING QUESTION 9.4

What are the major types of criminal defenses?

Sometimes, the commission of a crime may be excusable and not require punishment. For example, the intentional killing of a person normally constitutes criminal homicide, but it may be justifiable in war or in self-defense. Similarly, *mens rea* might be formed defectively due to mental illness or mistaken circumstances. The various reasons people should *not* be held criminally responsible for the commission of acts that usually would otherwise constitute crimes are called criminal **defenses**. Defenses to crimes are generally classified in three categories: defenses of excuse, defenses of justification, and procedural defenses. While specifics again may vary by jurisdiction, types of defenses are discussed in further detail, below.

The **defenses of excuse** are those in which a defendant admits to having committed a criminally proscribed *actus reus* but asserts that he or she did so under special circumstances that mitigate or even excuse criminal liability due to a diminished *mens rea*. Thus, excuse defenses are arguments about why an individual person should not be responsible for what might otherwise constitute criminal behavior because of unique *personal* circumstances that serve to diminish *mens rea*. The major defenses of excuse are infancy of age, insanity, mistake, intoxication (both involuntary and voluntary), and duress. A summary of these defenses appears in Table 9.6.

The **defenses of justification** are those in which a defendant admits to having committed a criminally proscribed *actus reus,* and did so with *mens rea,* but asserts that circumstances surrounding the *act* render it justifiable under the law. The major defenses of justification are self-defense, defense of others, defense of property, consent, and execution of public duties. A summary of defenses of justification appears in Table 9.7.

It is important to note the difference between defenses of excuse and defenses of justification. Defenses of excuse suggest that the *person* should be excused for an inability to have a fully formed *mens rea.* Defenses of justification assume that the act was deliberate but argue that it was committed for a reason deemed justifiable under the law.

Procedural defenses are technical defenses created under the law for public policy reasons. Factual guilt, criminal culpability, or situational circumstances are irrelevant to these defenses. Rather, procedural defenses are rooted in concern for due process and other forms of procedural justice, which you learned about in Chapter 8. For instance, procedural defenses might include alleging violations of the right to a speedy trial (and the related defense of the passage of time specified in statutes of limitations), arguing that double jeopardy has occurred, and using the exclusionary rule to prevent illegally obtained evidence from being used to convict someone. Selective prosecution based on race, sex, or a similar characteristic that violates the

defense
Various reasons, recognized under the law, individuals should not be held criminally responsible for the commission of acts that are defined as crimes. If a defendant charged with a crime successfully argues that his or her conduct falls under a recognized defense, then he or she may be found not guilty.

defense of excuse
Defenses in which a defendant admits to having committed an *actus reus* prohibited under the law but asserts that he or she did so under special circumstances that mitigate or excuse criminal liability.

defense of justification
Defenses in which a defendant admits to having committed an *actus reus* prohibited under the law but asserts that circumstances surrounding the act itself render it justifiable.

procedural defense
Technical defenses in which guilt, level of intent, or characteristics of the offense are irrelevant. Procedural defenses include those related to violations of procedural justice rights, immunity, and entrapment.

TABLE 9.6 Defenses of Excuse

Defense	Brief Explanation of the Defense
Infancy of Age	Children under the age of 7 are conclusively presumed to be incapable of forming *mens rea.* Accordingly, they are excused from criminal liability for committing acts that would result in prosecution if they were older. Children between 7 and 14 are similarly presumed to be incapable of forming *mens rea*, but that presumption may be rebutted by relevant evidence to the contrary. If rebutted (i.e., if children between 7 and 14 are shown to be able to form *mens rea*), they usually face delinquency proceedings under the civil jurisdiction of a juvenile court. Children over the age of 14 are rebuttable, presumed to be able to form *mens rea.* Assuming that the capacity to form *mens rea* is not rebutted, children over 14 may be handled in juvenile court or, under certain circumstances, may be transferred to adult court for formal criminal prosecution. Each state has its own provisions for determining when a juvenile may be tried as an adult.
Insanity	In most U.S. jurisdictions, the insanity defense excuses criminal liability if, as a result of a qualifying mental disease or defect, a person lacks the substantial capacity to appreciate the wrongfulness/criminality of his or her actions (see Chapter 4). In a small number of jurisdictions, conduct may also be excused if the person was unable to control his conduct due to a qualifying mental illness, even though the person understood the conduct was wrong (see Chapter 4). Four states have abolished the insanity defense and, as a result, limit the admissibility of evidence regarding mental illnesses to the question of whether the defendant was mentally capable of forming *mens rea*.
Mistake	Factual mistakes that negate *mens rea* may excuse criminal liability if the defendant was actually (subjectively) mistaken and if that mistake was objectively reasonable. Mistakes concerning the meaning or applicability of the law, however, generally do not constitute a criminal defense absent some very rare and highly limited circumstances.
Involuntary Intoxication	Excuses criminal liability if a person lacks the substantial capacity to appreciate the wrongfulness/criminality of his or her actions because the person ingested an intoxicant neither knowing nor having reason to know that he or she was consuming something intoxicating. Alternatively, this defense may also be invoked if someone was forced to take an intoxicating substance under duress.
Voluntary Intoxication	Excuses criminal liability if a person is incapable of forming the requisite *mens rea* of a crime as a result of being significantly intoxicated. Nearly all U.S. jurisdictions limit this defense to mitigate crimes of specific intent (i.e., those requiring purpose or knowledge as the requisite *mens rea*) down to lower levels of criminal liability, to crimes which carry recklessness or negligence as their *mens rea*. Some states, however, do not recognize this defense at all.
Duress	Excuses or mitigates criminal conduct committed out of necessity arising from an emergency situation to avoid serious, imminent bodily harm. The defendant must not have been responsible for having created the emergency giving rise to the necessity to act. The crime committed, however, must have been the lesser of two evils. That is, the harm avoided by committing the crime must be more substantial or more serious than that harm caused by committing the crime. Accordingly, this defense is not available for homicides.

TABLE 9.7 Defenses of Justification

Defense	Brief Explanation of the Defense
Self-Defense	Allows a person who reasonably believes it necessary to use force to defend against an unlawful, imminent attack. The amount of force used must be reasonable. Thus, physical attacks may be repelled by the use of physical force without criminal liability for assault and battery. Similarly, when faced with imminent attack involving deadly force, someone may use deadly force in self-defense without criminal liability for homicide. The use of deadly force, however, is limited in many states by requirements to retreat if the person may do so in safety and/or by requirements to give notice that deadly force will be used in self-defense unless such a warning would be futile.
Defense of Others	People are generally permitted to use force to defend someone else against unlawful, imminent attack to the same extent that the person under attack would have been permitted to use force in self-defense.
Defense of Property	A reasonable amount of non-deadly force may be used to protect one's property. As a general rule (unless a jurisdiction specifically has a law to the contrary), deadly force may not be used to defend property because life is valued more than material possessions.
Consent	A small number of crimes require a lack of consent from the victim as a core element of the offense. Rape, for example, punishes only sexual penetrations that were accomplished without the consent of the victim. Similarly, a theft occurs only if the person whose property was taken did not consent. For such crimes, consent is a defense. Consent may also be a defense to the crime of simple battery. The "victim" of a battery can consent to minor bodily injury as long as that consent was given knowingly, intelligently, and voluntarily. For example, when two boxers enter the ring, they consent to be battered.
Execution of Public Duties	Governmental actors are often permitted to do things that private persons are prohibited from doing under the criminal law. Fire and emergency medical personnel are permitted to violate a number of motor vehicle laws to carry out their official duties. Police officers may use a reasonable amount of force to make a lawful arrest without that force constituting an assault or battery. Police and correctional officers are even permitted to use deadly force under limited circumstances, such as when there is "probable cause to believe that the suspect poses a threat of serious physical harm" (*Tennessee v. Garner,* 1985, p. 11).

An officer attempts to rescue a dog left in a hot car. Concerns about injury or death to dogs left in vehicles prompted California to become the first state to specifically address the issue in its Driver Handbook, which notes that "leaving a dog in a parked car is not only illegal, but carries a penalty of up to $500 in fines and six months in jail if the dog in question is injured or dies as a result" (Barnett, 2010, para. 3). What level of *mens rea* (see Table 9.1) do you think is associated with this offense?

Equal Protection Clause of the Fourteenth Amendment can also be the basis for a procedural defense.

Immunity is another procedural defense that gives a defendant freedom from criminal prosecution due to his or her status as a foreign diplomat or as a cooperating witness for the government in a larger prosecution (e.g., low-level criminals in drug deals or organized crime rings may be offered immunity from prosecution in exchange for their testimony against others).

Finally, procedural defenses also include outrageous governmental conduct, such as entrapment. Entrapment occurs when law enforcement agents induce someone to commit a crime that he or she was not predisposed to commit. For example, assume that an undercover officer solicited a man who has never used a drug before to buy and use drugs. Assume that he initially refused multiple times, but after weeks of applying pressure, he finally was convinced, so he bought and tried the drug. If the undercover officer then arrested him, he would likely assert entrapment as his defense, arguing that the only reason he tried the drug was because of the officer's repeated actions. Outrageous governmental conduct, however, is not limited to entrapment. It can constitute a defense whenever the conduct of law enforcement agents is so outrageous that due process principles would absolutely bar the government from invoking judicial processes to obtain a conviction. For example, the defense was successful in *Metcalf v. Florida* (1994), a case in which police manufactured crack cocaine and then arrested the people who bought the crack from them.

Q Why do you think we have criminal defenses? What would be the consequence of convicting every person who engages in prohibited conduct with the required mental state and then imposing less severe sentences on those who have some justification or excuse for their actions?

Q Do you think it is appropriate to excuse criminal conduct because of youth, mental illness, duress, and the like? Why or why not?

Q Do you think there are any circumstances, other than those listed here, that should serve as a defense to criminal activity?

Constitutional Limitations on Criminalization

FOCUSING QUESTION 9.5

What limits does the U.S. Constitution place on the ability to criminalize conduct?

What conduct should be criminalized? As you should recall from Chapter 4, penal social control is only one way that society can control the behavior of its members. Lawmakers frequently struggle with questions about whether certain conduct should be regulated by the criminal law or by the civil law via compensatory, restorative, or therapeutic social controls. But there is no magic formula to discerning how undesirable behavior should be formally regulated when informal social controls fail.

Many critics argue that lawmakers have created too many crimes, resulting in too much punishment, which, in turn, can produce even greater injustices than the commission of the conduct originally criminalized (e.g., Husak, 2008; Luna, 2005). Consider the fact that it is a federal crime for retailers and distributors of mattresses to remove the tag explaining flammability warnings. Does this really need to be a crime? Might civil fine penalties be sufficient to make sure these mattress tags remain on beds until the consumer decides whether to remove them? The process of creating more and more crimes, especially those that are not traditionally morally blameworthy, is referred to as overcriminalization.

Ideally, common sense, economics, and evidence-based public policies would guide decisions regarding what conduct gets criminalized. But this ideal does not work in reality, largely because of the politics of lawmaking as explained in Chapter 7.

> On occasion, Congress reacts to a crisis . . . in the only way that Congress can act quickly: by passing legislation. There are numerous examples of this phenomenon. The kidnapping of Charles Lindbergh's son led to enactment of the Federal Kidnapping Act, also known as the Lindbergh Law. The murders of Martin Luther King, Jr., and Robert Kennedy by firearms led to the passage of the Gun Control Act of 1968. Just as the murder of Kimber Reynolds and Polly Klaas led to California's "Three Strikes" recidivist law, the rape and murder of Megan Khanka led to the enactment of sex offender registration and notification legislation. Timothy McVeigh's bombing of the Oklahoma City federal building led to enactment of the Antiterrorism and Effective Death Penalty Act. Most of the time, however, legislation steadily drips out of Congress like water falling from a leaky faucet: Congress created more than 450 new crimes from 2000 through 2007, a rate of more than one a week. (Larkin, 2013, p. 725)

Once a criminal law is enacted, it is extraordinarily difficult to get it repealed. Few legislators like to vote to repeal crimes for fear of being accused of being "soft on crime" when they run for reelection (Larkin, 2013). This is especially the case when legislators have adopted laws that are widely perceived as popular because they addressed some "moral panic" created by the intense media attention accompanying the commission of high-profile crimes (Surette, 2011). A *moral panic* describes "a condition, episode, person, or group of persons which emerge to become defined as a threat to societal values and interests" (Cohen, 1972, p. 9). When the media present an issue as a social problem, policy makers often respond with crime control strategies that address the moral panic *surrounding* the issue, rather than creating policies that are based upon empirical data and analysis to address the root causes of the issue itself (Sample & Kadleck, 2008). Griffin

and Miller (2008) describe this process as *crime control theater*—"a public response or set of responses to crime which generate the appearance, but not the fact, of crime control" (p. 160). But it is not just that moral panics contribute to overcriminalization through the process of crime control theater. The real concern is that these laws sometimes undercut the very purposes they are designed to achieve, as illustrated in Box 9.2.

Although media and politics frequently fuel the legislative proclivity to regulate conduct using the criminal law, the U.S. Constitution places certain limits on what behaviors may be criminalized. These limits will be discussed in the following sections.

THE FIRST AMENDMENT

The First Amendment to the U.S. Constitution states: "Congress shall make no law respecting an establishment of religion, or prohibiting the free exercise thereof; or abridging the freedom of speech, or of the press; or the right of the people peaceably to assemble, and to petition the Government for a redress of grievances." This Amendment provides several protections that place limits on the power of government to criminalize speech, religious practices, and the ability to assemble and demonstrate peacefully.

Free Speech and Peaceable Assembly. The free speech protections of the First Amendment generally allow people to speak or write about any topic. People may exercise these liberties alone. Alternatively, people may exercise these rights in small or large groups to share their ideas with others as long as they do so peacefully. For example, a law banning speech critical of governmental policies would be unconstitutional. That would even hold true if people expressed their dissatisfaction with the government by using offensive or profane language (e.g., *Cohen v. California*, 1971). The First Amendment even protects *symbolic speech*—conduct that expresses an idea or opinion, like wearing certain clothes or styling one's hair in a particular unconventional way, accessorizing using buttons or armbands (e.g., *Tinker v. Des Moines*, 1969), or picketing or marching in a parade. Even symbolic hate speech, like burning a cross, may receive some First Amendment protection as symbolic speech depending on the circumstances under which such an act occurs (see *Virginia v. Black*, 2003).

In light of the First Amendment, it is quite rare for a law to ban any type of protected speech or expression. However, criminal statutes may run afoul of the First Amendment by being overbroad. Overbreadth occurs when a law "sweep[s] unnecessarily broadly and thereby invade[s] the area of protected freedoms" (*Zwicker v. Koota,* 1972, p. 250). This typically occurs in cases involving symbolic speech. For example, a law criminalizing flag burning was determined to be unconstitutionally overbroad in *Texas v. Johnson* (1989). The Court held that the law infringed upon people's right to express their dissatisfaction with the government through the symbolic speech embodied in the action of burning the flag.

As with all constitutional rights, there are limits to free speech. Certain categories of speech receive no First Amendment protection. These include defamatory writing and speech (i.e., libel and slander—falsehoods that damage another person's reputation), obscenity, and the use of words "directed to inciting or producing imminent lawless action" (*Brandenburg v. Ohio,* 1969, p. 447). Moreover, the government may limit the time, place, and manner in which the rights to free speech and peaceable assembly are exercised in order to prevent fires, health hazards, obstructions or occupations of public buildings, or traffic problems. For example, no one has the right to "insist upon a street meeting in the middle of Times Square at the rush hour as a form of freedom of speech" (*Cox v. Louisiana,* 1965, p. 554).

Freedom of the Press. The First Amendment generally forbids censorship or other restraints on speech or expression by the media whether in print or in broadcasting (e.g., radio, television, and movies). However, like with free speech, there are limits to this protection. As mentioned earlier, neither defamation nor obscenity receives First

BOX 9.2

Research in Action

ARE LAWS REGULATING SEX OFFENDERS UPON THEIR RELEASE FROM PRISON EFFECTIVE?

Although laws regulating sex offenders after their release from prison date back to 1947, the number and types of such laws have proliferated since the early 1990s. The first major set of such laws required convicted sex offenders to register with their local police department and keep certain information up to date, such as their current addresses, telephone numbers, and employment (Tewksbury & Lees, 2006). Thereafter, some jurisdictions adopted notification laws designed to warn community members when sex offenders lived nearby—an approach that would ultimately be nationally mandated by federal legislation adopted in 2006. Some jurisdictions also adopted one or two other types of laws regulating sex offenders, ranging from requiring sex offenders to wear GPS tracking devices (Levenson & D'Amora, 2007) to placing restrictions on where sex offenders may live, often prohibiting them from residing within so many feet of locations in which children are likely to be found, such as schools and parks (Meloy, Miller, & Curtis, 2008). But are these laws effective at preventing released sex offenders from victimizing more people?

A number of studies have concluded that notification laws are ineffective in reducing sex offense recidivism (Agan, 2011; Prescott & Rockoff, 2011; Veysey & Zgoba 2010). For instance,

> Meloy, Saleh, and Wolff (2007) posited that notification laws are ineffective because sex offender registries are not comprehensive lists of sex offenders, but rather are incomplete due to a number of factors. Specifically, most sex crimes are not reported; plea bargaining allows the offender to negotiate a way out of registering; many mandated offenders do not comply with registration requirements; and most importantly, registration laws often focus on victimizations by strangers—the rarest form of sexual violence. In fact, children are much more likely to be abused by a family member or acquaintance. . . . Consequently, notification laws may provide a false sense of security . . . by misleading people into believing that children are more often victimized by strangers rather than someone they know. . . . In addition, registries contain inaccurate entries due to changes in addresses and data entry mistakes, omissions, and deletions. . . . Finally, it should be noted that notification laws have had some unforeseen consequences. Community notification can cause a decline in home values for households near those of registered sex offenders. . . . They have caused police to incur substantial labor and capital costs to implement community notification programs. . . . Community notification can take a significant toll on an offender's family members economically, socially, psychologically, and even physically. . . . And, finally, notification can cause high rates of socially destabilizing consequences for the offenders themselves, ranging from stress, shame, harassment, job loss, loss of friends, and, in rare cases, even community vigilantism against sex offenders. . . . Notably, all of these consequences

Amendment protection. Similarly, limits on the media's dissemination of information may be permitted if it concerns a matter of national security, such as the location of troops and their combat plans (see, e.g., *New York Times Co. v. United States*, 1971). And as with free speech, the time, place, and manner in which broadcasts are made can be limited. For example, the FCC can bar the broadcast of profane language and sexually explicit material on public airways that may be accessed by children (see *FCC v. Pacifica Foundation*, 1978).

Freedom of Religion. The First Amendment contains two clauses relevant to the freedom of religion. The first is known as the *Establishment Clause*, which the Supreme Court has interpreted as providing a "wall of separation between church and state" (*Everson v. Board of Education*, 1947, p. 16). It prevents local, state, and the federal governments from enacting any law that establishes an official church or from favoring one

can be counterproductive insofar as they can lead to reoffending. (Galeste, Fradella, & Vogel, 2012, p. 7 [internal citations omitted])

Research similarly casts doubt on the effectiveness of GPS monitoring (Turner et al., 2007). For one thing, "GPS only provides notice of offenders who stray from approved locations, but does not prevent deviant activity that occurs within approved geographic locations" (Galeste et al., 2008, p. 7). Additionally, "a significant portion of a probation officer's time, and consequently the jurisdiction's GPS monitoring program staffing resources, are spent responding to alerts produced by the limitations of underdeveloped technology" rather than "responding to violations of criminal behaviors, or precursory behaviors associated with an offending cycle" (Armstrong & Freeman, 2011, p. 180).

Finally, research on residence restrictions suggests that this social control strategy actually *increases* sexual victimization since they "perpetuate the stranger-danger myth that the majority of sex crimes are committed by individuals not known to the victim when research demonstrates otherwise" (Galeste et al., 2012, p. 8; see Meloy, Miller, & Curtis, 2008). Moreover, such restrictions can not only drive offenders to areas where they are less likely to have access to treatment and employment opportunities (Socia, 2011), but also can cause sex offenders to become homeless (California Sex Offender Management Board, 2011). The stressors from both of these factors can actually increase recidivism.

The above research should not suggest that there are no alternatives for managing sex offenders. Treatment programs have been found to reduce recidivism (see MacKenzie, 2006), especially when following the RNR model that is also effective for offender rehabilitation, generally. This model stands for "risk, need, and responsivity," indicating that treatment should focus on "offenders who are likely to reoffend" (those at risk) with strategies focused on "characteristics that are related to reoffending" (addressing need) and "match treatment to the offenders' learning styles and abilities" (responsivity to individual differences) (Hanson, Bourgon, Helmus, & Hodgson, 2009, p. 867).

Q What is your opinion on the various measures described above? Explain your answer.

Q What factors, other than those above, do you think might lead to the ineffectiveness of the various laws regulating sex offenders after release? Do you think the laws could be modified to be more effective?

Q In the U.S. Supreme Court case of *Smith v. Doe,* a convicted sex offender was required to register on Alaska's sex offender registry. Because his offense occurred before the sex offender registry law was passed, he argued that its application to him was an *ex post facto* law. The Court rejected the claim, holding that the registry law was a civil regulation rather than a criminal punishment. Do you agree or disagree with the Court's ruling? Why?

religion over another (or over none at all). For example, laws that criminalized failure to go to weekly religious services or failure to tithe (donate money to a religious organization) would be unconstitutional exercises of the state's police power in light of the protections of the Establishment Clause.

The First Amendment also protects people's rights to act on their beliefs (or to believe nothing at all) in the *Free Exercise Clause.* For instance, the Supreme Court struck down a local ordinance that prohibited the ritual killing of animals (such as "chickens, pigeons, doves, ducks, guinea pigs, goats, sheep, and turtles," some of which are cooked and then consumed after sacrifice) because it infringed upon the religious beliefs of a group that practices animal sacrifice (*Church of Lukumi Babalu Aye v. City of Hialeah,* 1993, p. 525). However, as with other constitutional rights, the freedom to act on religious beliefs is not absolute. With few exceptions, no one may violate otherwise valid laws in the name of freely practicing religion. For instance, laws criminalizing

polygamy are valid even if one's religion condones having multiple spouses (see *Reynolds v. United States,* 1878).

In addition, some governmental restraint on the free exercise of religious beliefs is also permissible in settings where people's rights are already curtailed to some extent, such as in the military or in correctional settings. For instance, the Supreme Court upheld a military regulation prohibiting a service member from wearing his yarmulke, a small cap with religious significance in the Jewish tradition (*Goldman v. Weinberger,* 1986). However, following Congressional action in the wake of the decision, the regulation was subsequently changed to allow some wearing of religious apparel in military settings (Accommodation of Religious Practices, 2009). The Supreme Court has also held that prison inmates may be prohibited from attending religious services, if the prohibition is based on a rule that is necessary to ensure the secure operations of the facility (*O'Lone v. Estate of Shabazz,* 1987). Debates have also occurred in police agencies. In 2012, the Washington, DC, Metropolitan Police Department enacted a policy to allow Sikh (a religion originating in India) officers to wear turbans, beards, and other items (Bahrampour, 2012); however, some other police departments do not, as there is not a consistent policy nationwide.

THE SECOND AMENDMENT

The Second Amendment to the U.S. Constitution states, "A well regulated militia, being necessary to the security of a free state, the right of the people to keep and bear arms, shall not be infringed." In *District of Columbia v. Heller* (2008), the U.S. Supreme Court interpreted the Second Amendment as protecting "an individual right to possess a firearm unconnected with service in a militia, and to use that arm for traditionally lawful purposes, such as self-defense within the home" (p. 577). Two years later, the Court applied the same ruling from the *Heller* case to the states in *McDonald v. City of Chicago* (2010), and invalidated a Chicago ordinance that banned handgun possession by almost all private citizens.

As a result of *Heller* and *McDonald,* it is clear that the Second Amendment places substantive limits on laws regulating firearms. Laws banning the possession of handguns by law-abiding citizens are presumed to be unconstitutional since they interfere with the "the core lawful purpose of self-defense" (*Heller,* 2008, p. 630). On the other hand, like other constitutional rights, the right to bear arms is not unlimited. The Second Amendment does not imply a right to possess weapons suitable for warfare, rather than self-defense, such as bazookas, bombs, grenades, tanks, or biological, chemical, or nuclear weapons. But what of laws directed at other types of guns?

The *Heller* Court specifically endorsed the legality of certain gun control regulations, such as bans on firearm possession by convicted felons and people with serious mental illnesses, bans on carrying firearms "in sensitive places such as schools and government buildings," bans on carrying concealed weapons, and regulations limiting the conditions and qualifications on the commercial sale of firearms (*Heller,* 2008, p. 626). But the constitutionality of a range of other gun-related laws has yet to be decided by the U.S. Supreme Court. Are laws criminalizing the possession of *unregistered* handguns valid? Can firearm registrations be limited to those persons who pass a series of qualifications in the same way that drivers are licensed, such as successful completion of a training course and being photographed? Can firearm registrants be required to be fingerprinted before their licenses are issued? Are laws banning semi-automatic weapons constitutional? How about laws banning possession of firearms with the capacity of shooting more than a certain number of rounds? To date, most lower courts that have considered questions like these have, for the most part, upheld the authority of states and municipalities to regulate firearms in these ways (see Lund, 2012; *Ezell v. City of Chicago,* 2011).

THE FOURTEENTH AMENDMENT: DUE PROCESS AND EQUAL PROTECTION CONCERNS

Due Process Limits on the Reach of Strict Liability. *Mala in se* crimes (Latin for evil "unto itself") are common-law crimes against the person (e.g., murder, rape, aggravated assault) and crimes against property (e.g., theft and arson) that are clearly morally wrong in and of themselves. In contrast, *mala prohibita* offenses are not necessarily inherently bad or evil acts. Rather, *mala prohibita* crimes are those created by statutes or regulations that exist to address public health, safety, and welfare.

As discussed earlier, strict liability imposes criminal penalties for doing a proscribed act without regard to whether there was any corresponding *mens rea.* The U.S. Supreme Court has limited strict liability to crimes that are *mala prohibita;* strict liability may not attach to crimes that are *mala in se* without violating due process (*Morissette v. United States,* 1952). Accordingly, a state could not criminalize a truly accidental killing. However, the criminal law can punish a bartender who serves alcohol to an underage person whom the bartender reasonably believes is over the legal drinking age because the person produced a fake (but realistic) driver's license. Criminalizing such an act without even any negligence may seem harsh, but it is lawful because serving alcohol to a minor is a *malum prohibitum* crime.

Substantive Due Process Limitations on Criminalization. Substantive due process is the notion that certain rights and liberties are so fundamental to the American notion of justice that any governmental infringement upon those rights and liberties should not be tolerated, absent the most serious and compelling reasons. In *Washington v. Glucksberg* (1997), the Supreme Court explained its approach in identifying fundamental rights.

substantive due process
Protects against governmental infringement of fundamental rights, such as freedom of speech, freedom of religion, and the right to privacy.

> First, we have regularly observed that the Due Process Clause specially protects those fundamental rights and liberties which are, objectively, "deeply rooted in this Nation's history and tradition," and "implicit in the concept of ordered liberty," such that "neither liberty nor justice would exist if they were sacrificed." Second, we have required in substantive due process cases a "careful description" of the asserted fundamental liberty interest. (pp. 720–721)

The substantive rights contained in the First Amendment discussed earlier, such as the freedoms of speech, peaceable assembly, and freedom of religion, are all fundamental rights. Other fundamental rights and liberties are not listed in the Constitution but are based on rulings in Supreme Court decisions. The right to privacy is the best example of this. The Supreme Court has interpreted substantive due process to protect a number of privacy rights, ranging from access to contraceptives (e.g., *Griswold v. Connecticut,* 1965) and abortion services (*Roe v. Wade,* 1973) to the right to marry (*Loving v. Virginia,* 1967) and the liberty for adults to engage in certain types of private, consensual sexual conduct (*Lawrence v. Texas,* 2003). The right to privacy as it applies to criminal law is explored in more detail in Box 9.3.

Equal Protection Limitations on Criminalization. Recall from Chapter 8 that the constitutional guarantee of equal protection requires the law to treat similarly situated people in a similar manner. If, however, people are not "similarly situated," then the law may treat different groups of people in disparate ways. Consider the case of *Allam v. State* (1992).

Alaska experimented with legalizing recreational use of small amounts of marijuana in the 1980s. Minors, meaning children age 17 and under, were prohibited from possessing any amount of the drug. Adults 19 years of age or more were permitted to possess less than four ounces of the drug. But the law singled out 18-year-olds for special treatment. Even though Alaskans reach the age of majority at 18 years (and are,

BOX 9.3

Ethics in Practice

WHAT IS THE SCOPE OF THE RIGHT TO PRIVACY?

For most of U.S. history, sodomy was illegal. Sodomy laws criminalized oral and anal sex. These laws were incorporated into U.S. criminal law from English common law. They banned these sex acts between consenting adults—even in private—on the basis of then-prevailing sentiments that such acts were immoral. Sodomy laws applied to those who were married or single, whether heterosexual or homosexual, and to both the active performers and the passive recipients of the acts. The penalties could be quite severe; Georgia classified sodomy as felony punishable by up to 20 years in prison. That law was unsuccessfully challenged in 1986 in *Bowers v. Hardwick* (1986). Over a substantive due process challenge, the Supreme Court rejected the argument that the right to privacy should protect such private, consensual sexual acts. The Court distinguished prior privacy cases like *Griswold v. Connecticut* (1965) and *Roe v. Wade* (1973) by reasoning those cases did not create rights to sexual privacy but rather recognized that the decision to procreate was a private one that ought to lie beyond the reach of the government. In contrast, the Court said, acts of sodomy did not involve procreation. Oral and anal sex, therefore, could be criminalized without violating substantive due process in order to enforce what the Court believed was the widely shared belief in the immorality of these acts.

Seventeen years later, the Supreme Court overruled *Bowers* when it decided *Lawrence v. Texas* (2003). Reversing its earlier premise that criminal law could be used to enforce the moral will of the majority without regard to harm (the classic Hart-Devlin debate as you should recall from Chapter 3), the Court stated that its decision in *Bowers* had failed "to appreciate the extent of the liberty [interest] at stake" (p. 567). The Court reasoned that sodomy laws "have more far reaching consequences, touching upon the most private human conduct, sexual behavior, and in the most private of places, the home," and in doing so, "seek to control a personal relationship that . . . is within the liberty of persons to choose without being punished as criminals" (p. 567). Reasoning that "liberty

therefore, no longer "minors"), they were still prohibited from possessing or using any amount of marijuana. Allam, an 18-year-old who was caught with a small amount of the drug, challenged this law on Equal Protection Clause grounds, arguing that the law unconstitutionally discriminated against 18-year-olds since all other adults in the state were permitted to possess small quantities of the drug. In rejecting his equal protection argument, an appellate court reasoned that the state legislature had a legitimate reason for treating 18-year-olds differently from other adults. Specifically, the court reasoned that 18-year-olds were not similarly situated to other adults because many 18-year-olds are still in high school, where they could easily share the drug with underage minors. Hence, the state legislature had a rational basis for treating one class of adults (those age 18) differently from another class of adults (those 19 and older).

Q Congress passed a law called the Stolen Valor Act, which prohibited individuals from falsely claiming to have received certain military or Congressional honors. The standard penalty was a fine or up to six months in prison, unless an individual falsely claimed to have received the Congressional Medal of Honor, in which case the penalty was a fine or up to a year in prison. The Supreme Court ruled that the law was an unconstitutional infringement upon freedom of speech (*United States v. Alvarez,* 2012). Do you agree or disagree with the Court's ruling? Why?

Q One of the great debates in contemporary society is the degree to which church and state should be separated. In light of the religion clauses in the First Amendment, do you think "faith-based" rehabilitation programs in prisons should be funded by public tax dollars?

Q Critique the decision in *Allam v. State* (1992).

presumes an autonomy of self that includes freedom of thought, belief, expression, and certain intimate conduct" (p. 562), the Court declared all of the remaining sodomy laws in the United States unconstitutional, finding that they violated the substantive due process right to liberty.

Q With which approach to sexual privacy do you agree—the one taken in *Bowers* or the one taken in *Lawrence?* Why?

Q Sodomy laws are an example of societal attempts to enforce public morality through penal social control. Recall from Chapter 3 that H. L. A. Hart and Lord Patrick Devlin engaged in an intellectual debate on whether it was proper to use criminal law in this matter. Do you think it is ethical for those in the majority to enforce their perceptions of morality on others whose moral beliefs differ from theirs? Why or why not?

Q In light of the holding in *Lawrence,* do you think that substantive due process should extend to and invalidate any of the following criminal laws? Explain your reasoning for each, paying particular attention to the moral or ethical arguments in favor of criminalization and opposing criminalization.

- laws criminalizing fornication (i.e., premarital sex) and/or the cohabitation of unmarried persons
- laws criminalizing adultery
- laws criminalizing bestiality (sexual contact with an animal)
- laws criminalizing incest
- laws criminalizing indecent exposure, such as public nudity or public urination
- laws criminalizing public sexual acts

Q Given that the right to privacy is a fundamental right that encompasses "autonomy of self," do you think euthanasia (i.e., assisted suicide) should be legalized on substantive due process grounds? Explain your answer. Include in your response an analysis of the five concepts of morality explored in Chapter 2 and the legal philosophies explored in Chapter 3.

Conclusion

This chapter has traced the evolution of criminal law across several millennia to its current form. It also summarized the major elements common to all types of crime, the classifications of leading crimes and defenses, and the major limitations on criminalization. But the appropriate limits of the criminal law are often subject to deep philosophical differences of opinion. Debates centered on the harm principle, Hart's legal positivism, and Devlin's legal moralism (as described in Chapter 3) continue to this day, as experts and laypersons consider what should (or should not) be criminalized. For example, Luna (2005) compiled a list of dozens of examples of overcriminalization which included arrest and detention for failing to wear a seat belt, jail time for failing to return a library book, and criminal sanctions for frightening pigeons from their nests. Although some of these laws may appear trivial, people punished under them surely do not find them so. It is to the topic of punishment that the next chapter will turn.

Criminal Justice Problem Solving

Zero-Tolerance Policies

Across the United States, more than three-quarters of all school districts have adopted so-called "zero-tolerance" policies that mandate predetermined consequences for violations of certain rules (as one example, recall the discussion on bullying from this unit's photo essay). Some of these policies trigger criminal justice consequences. Consider what happened to Lindsay Brown. In 2001, Lindsay was an 18-year-old high-school senior in Estero, Florida. A few weeks before her graduation, Lindsay, a National Merit Scholar, spent a weekend moving into her own apartment.

> Everything seemed perfect until Monday afternoon when a security officer asked Lindsay to accompany him to the school parking lot. The officer pointed out a kitchen knife lying on the floor of Lindsay's car. She was surprised to see the knife and realized that it must have fallen out of one of her moving boxes. For unknowingly having the kitchen knife in her car, Lindsay was arrested, handcuffed, and hauled off to the Lee County jail. She was suspended from school and banned from graduation events. . . .

Lindsay was charged with felony weapons possession for having a knife on school grounds. After nine-hours in jail—with real criminals—Lindsay's parents bailed her out. A week later, common sense finally interceded when State Attorney Joe D'Alessandro dropped the charge (Heritage Foundation, 2003, paras. 1–2, 4).

Lindsay Brown's case is not unique. A boy scout who brought his pocket knife to school (but never used it as a weapon) was expelled, arrested, and sent to juvenile detention (Heritage Foundation, 2006). A sixth grader who was being taunted and punched by a bully fought back in self-defense. But since he violated his school's zero-tolerance policy concerning violence, he was suspended and criminally charged with "disorderly conduct and fighting in a public place" (Heritage Foundation, 2003, para. 13). A 12-year-old girl was handcuffed, charged as a juvenile, and sentenced to community service for doodling on her desk with an erasable marker (Aull, 2012). Indeed, the growing frequency of student conduct issues making their way into the criminal justice system led criminologist Paul Hirschfield (2008) to write an article provocatively titled, "Preparing for Prison? The Criminalization of School Discipline in the USA."

Research generally fails to support the propositions that zero-tolerance policies reduce school disorder, improve student academic performance, or increase consistency in school discipline (Mendel, 2000; Skiba & Peterson, 1999; Skiba, 2008). In fact, a study conducted by the National Center for Education Statistics (1998) found that schools with no reported crimes were less likely to have zero-tolerance policies than schools that had reported incidents of crime. And, of the schools reporting crimes, within four years of adopting zero-tolerance policies, these schools were less safe than schools without zero-tolerance policies (National Center for Education Statistics, 1998). Additionally, one of the central premises underlying zero-tolerance policies in schools is that the severe, swift, and certain punishments such policies promote are supposed to deter student misconduct. Yet, harsh sanctions such as suspension, expulsion, and arrest are correlated with higher rates of future misbehavior, as well as higher incidence levels of dropping out of school, especially among students of color (Skiba, 2008). Some have referred to this as the "school to prison pipeline," arguing that characteristics of modern education—including zero-tolerance policies—serve to increase the likelihood of future criminality (e.g., Kim, Losen, & Hewitt, 2010). In light of such data, do zero-tolerance policies make zero sense?

Q Explain how the criminal law elements of *actus reus*, *mens rea*, and attendant circumstances would have applied to the charge against Lindsay Brown if her case had been prosecuted. Do you agree with the state attorney's decision to drop the charges?

- Q Do you think zero-tolerance policies against weapons and violence on school grounds are good ideas? Why or why not? What about zero-tolerance policies against drugs? Would your answer change if the drugs at issue were aspirin, Tylenol, or Midol?
- Q Do zero-tolerance policies undermine the concept of *mens rea?* Explain your reasoning.
- Q Do you think that zero-tolerance policies violate students' due process rights? How would you have ruled on such an argument if you had been the judge in any of the students' cases discussed in this section?
- Q Do you think that the sixth grader who fought back against a bully could have successfully argued that the Fourteenth Amendment's Equal Protection Clause should have allowed him to assert self-defense in the same way an adult might have been able to use that defense? Why or why not?

10

Criminal Punishment

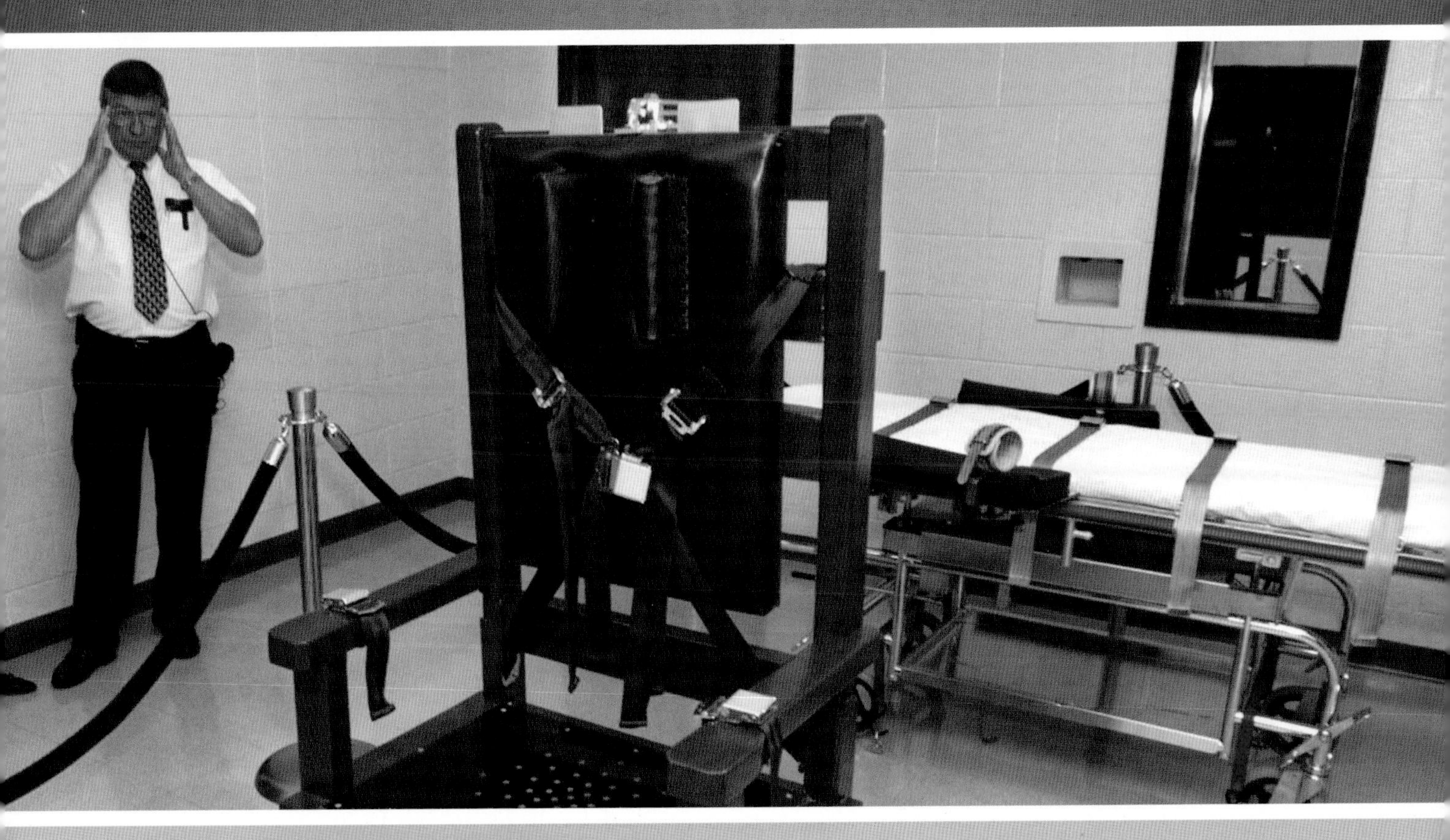

Learning Objectives

1 Explain the concept of punishment. 2 Compare and contrast the five justifications for criminal punishment. 3 Explain how concepts of "dangerous classes" influence punishment decisions. 4 Identify the legal limitations imposed upon criminal punishment. 5 Discuss the future of punishment.

Key Terms

punishment
retribution
just deserts
expiation
general deterrence
specific deterrence
incapacitation
rehabilitation
restitution
restorative justice
dangerous classes
culpability
legality
void for vagueness
bail
fines
cruel and unusual punishment
proportionality
capital punishment

Key People

Gresham Sykes
John Locke
Graeme Newman
Jeremy Bentham
Cesare Beccaria
Sigmund Freud
B. F. Skinner
John B. Watson
Robert Martinson
John Braithwaite
Jerome Skolnick

Three Strikes Laws

Case Study

Leandro Andrade was detained by security personnel at a Kmart store in California for stealing five videotapes valued at $84.70. Two weeks later, Andrade was detained at a different Kmart store after security personnel discovered four videotapes valued at $68.84 in the waistband of his pants. Andrade was arrested and charges were filed against him for petty theft.

Andrade did have a criminal past. In fact, he had been in and out of state and federal prisons for a number of offenses, including misdemeanor theft, residential burglary, transportation of marijuana, and a state parole violation. A heroin addict, Andrade confessed to stealing the videotapes and admitted that he had done so to obtain money to buy the drug.

In cases of petty theft in which the offender has prior convictions, California law allows the offense to count either as a misdemeanor or as a felony (in California, these are known as "wobbler" offenses). It is up to the prosecutor to make that decision. In this case, because Andrade had prior convictions, the prosecutor decided to charge him with a felony. Although the trial judge has the authority to reduce the charge to a misdemeanor, the judge in this case did not do so.

The choice between misdemeanor and felony is important because California has a strict three strikes law. If an offender has two prior convictions for violent or serious felony offenses, then any third felony conviction carries a mandatory prison sentence of 25 years to life. At trial, a jury found Andrade guilty of two counts of petty theft, resulting in a felony conviction. Because Andrade had three prior convictions for first degree burglary of a home, classified under California law as a violent or serious felony, the judge sentenced him to two prison terms of 25 years to life, one for each of the incidents of videotape theft. The sentences were to be served consecutively, meaning that the second prison term begins only after the first term is completed.

Facing page: The electric chair and lethal injection gurney, used to carry out the death penalty. What do you think are the purposes of punishment?

- Q If you were the prosecutor, would you have charged Andrade's thefts as a felony or misdemeanor? Why? Do you think prosecutors should be able to decide whether an act should count as a felony or misdemeanor? Why or why not?
- Q Do you believe that Andrade's punishment was appropriate? Why or why not?
- Q What do you think are the advantages and disadvantages of three strikes laws?
- Q Research has yielded mixed results about three strikes law. Some studies have found that California's law serves to reduce at least some crime (e.g., Helland & Tabarrok, 2007; Chen, 2008), while others have found that it does not, especially when accounting for other factors that can affect crime rates (e.g., Stolzenberg & D'Alessio, 1997; Worrall, 2004). Furthermore, studies on three strikes laws more generally, not limited to California, have found that they may lead to increases in homicide, perhaps because offenders are more likely to kill those who could apprehend or testify against them when facing a third strike (e.g., Marvell & Moody, 2001; Kovandzic, Sloan, & Vieraitis, 2002; Kovandzic, Sloan, & Vieraitis, 2004). How would you weigh these competing research results? To what extent would they shape your opinion about three strikes laws? Why?

Conceptualizing Punishment

FOCUSING QUESTION 10.1

What is punishment?

As described in Chapter 4, social control is a tool used to regulate behavior and, in particular, to ensure that individual behaviors conform to laws and social norms. This chapter explores penal social control, in which the force of law and government-imposed punishments are used to regulate behavior. This chapter's opening case study illustrates the complexities that come with the study of criminal punishment.

punishment
A form of deprivation imposed upon a person as a result of committing a criminal act. Punishments may include, but are not limited to, incarceration (deprivation of freedom), fines (deprivation of money), or physical punishments (deprivation of bodily integrity).

Punishment is most simply defined as a form of deprivation imposed on a person. That is, punishments deprive or take away something that a person desires or values. There are many possible deprivations, including freedom, which is deprived by sending a person to prison; family and friends, contact with whom may be deprived through banishment or social isolation; bodily integrity, which may be deprived through corporal or physical punishments; money, which may be deprived through fines; and life, which may be deprived through the use of the death penalty. In each of these cases, something that a person values is removed as a punishment for wrongdoing.

The concept of deprivations has been important in the study of punishment as a consequence of criminal behavior. In 1958, Gresham Sykes wrote what is considered one of the most important studies of prison life. From his observations of a New Jersey state prison, Sykes reported that prison inmates suffer five deprivations by virtue of being behind bars. These are the deprivation of their liberty, deprivation of goods and services that would be available in the outside world, deprivation of heterosexual relationships, deprivation of individual autonomy or decision making, and deprivation of personal security; each will be discussed in more detail in Chapter 13. For now, it is important to observe that more than 50 years later, Sykes's observations still hold true as accurate descriptors of prison life.

In addition to imposing a deprivation, penal social control must come as a consequence to criminal behavior. That is, criminal punishment may only occur in response to a violation of the criminal law. You may recall legal philosopher H. L. A. Hart from

the discussion of law and morality in Chapter 3. Hart (1968, pp. 4–5) noted that punishment must meet the following five criteria:

1. must involve pain or other consequences normally considered to be unpleasant;
2. must be for an offense against legal rules;
3. must be of an actual or supposed offender for his offense;
4. must be intentionally administered by human beings other than the offender; and
5. must be imposed and administered by an authority constituted by a legal system against which the offense is committed.

Hart's second and fifth criteria differentiate criminal punishment from other sanctions involving similar deprivations. For instance, deprivation of liberty would occur in both of the following situations: a judge imposing a prison term for an offender who committed an armed robbery and a parent placing a child in "time out" for not cleaning his or her room. However, only the former would be considered penal social control, because it is a deprivation in response to a violation of criminal law imposed by a judge within the legal system; the latter falls within the domain of informal social control.

Although this discussion provides a basic definition of punishment, there is wide variation in terms of what specific *types* of punishments are viewed as acceptable. The concept of punishment is socially constructed with variations across time and place. This means that people within a particular society determine which actual punishments will be used and for which criminal offenses. These determinations may be based on factors including political ideology, finances, societal characteristics (i.e., the "mood" of society during that particular point in time), religious beliefs and values, and advances in science (e.g., the latest behavioral modification techniques), to name a few.

For instance, in some countries, legal codes based on religious principles specify that certain offenses should be punished through death by stoning. In the United States, the death penalty is used for a small number of offenses (certain first degree murders that meet criteria designated under the law, as described at the conclusion of this chapter) in some jurisdictions but not others, and in all jurisdictions using the death penalty, lethal injection is the primary form of execution because it is viewed as the most humane method. In other countries, the death penalty has been completely abolished and is viewed as an abuse of a government's power. As another example, consider how a society deals with drug offenders. If a political ideology favors rehabilitating drug offenders, scientific advances must identify sound methods for doing so. Judges could then send drug offenders to treatment centers. However, if citizens were reluctant to pay higher taxes to finance those treatment centers, other alternatives would need to be developed. Therefore, many factors enter into a society's decisions about how to structure criminal punishment, and this results in differences among cities, states, and nations.

Punishments also vary based on factors related to the actual offense, such as its seriousness, the number of victims involved, whether weapons were used, and so on. For instance, consider two hypothetical armed robbers, both of whom entered a bank during business hours, demanded money, and escaped with $12,000. Assume that the first armed robber fired a handgun into the ceiling, causing a customer to faint, and took a teller hostage. Further assume that the second armed robber walked up to the counter, handed the teller a note reading, "I have a gun, give me all the money or I'll use it," and left without further incident. Would the two offenders receive the same punishment? Probably not—the first would likely receive the harsher sentence based on the circumstances of the offense. Therefore, punishment can be individualized to account for the specific actions of an offender.

Q How did Andrade's punishment under California's three strikes law meet the characteristics described in this section?

Q If you were the judge, would you request additional information before announcing a punishment for the hypothetical armed robbers just described? If so, what factors would influence your decision about what punishment to impose?

Justifications for Criminal Punishment

FOCUSING QUESTION 10.2

What are the five justifications for criminal punishment?

When people break the law, it is the government that has the right—some would even say the obligation—to punish them. This gives the government the power to fine, imprison, and in some cases, even kill offenders. Think back to the Hart-Devlin debate in Chapter 3. Even though the two sides disagreed about what constituted a crime, they both agreed that the government should punish crimes, however defined.

Consider the irony of this power. Depriving a person of money, liberty, or life would be viewed as something criminal and immoral if done by an ordinary person. In fact, when done by an ordinary person, deprivation of money is robbery, deprivation of liberty is kidnapping, and deprivation of life is murder. Yet, when done by the government, it would be a fine, imprisonment, and execution, respectively—all within the bounds of the law. So, what gives the government the right to take these actions as a form of criminal punishment when ordinary citizens cannot?

A government "is the only group of people entitled to make decisions that everyone in the state has a duty to accept and obey" (Shively, 1999, p. 134). That is, by its very definition, the government has the unique authority to punish those who do not accept and obey its laws. According to political theorist John Locke, in the absence of government, individuals within the society would have to decide who would be punished and how they would be punished. However, drawing upon the social contract metaphor from Chapter 2, people form an agreement to be governed by a set of rules under the authority of a government. When people make such an agreement, they also delegate the power to punish rule violators to the government (Locke, [1690] 1963). Therefore, the institution of government holds unique powers.

Historically, governments vigorously embraced these powers. In fact, punishments by many early governments were deliberately harsh and were carried out in public view. Offenders were beaten, tortured, and gruesomely executed in deliberate shows of force intended to demonstrate and establish the government's strength and power. Spierenburg (1984) argues that this is a historical pattern, and as governments mature and stabilize, they tend not to make such public displays of force, as citizens become willing to accept the government's authority. At that point, and as the public perceives the government as legitimate, punishments often become more humane.

But perhaps unanswered is the larger question of what the governments, through the criminal justice system, hope to accomplish through the punishment of criminal offenses. In exercising the power to punish, the American criminal justice system relies on five common justifications or goals of punishment. They are retribution, deterrence, incapacitation, rehabilitation, and restitution. The popularity of each justification, like the definition of punishment itself, has varied over time (for an in-depth review of punishment philosophies, see Cullen & Jonson, 2012).

retribution
A justification for punishment grounded in the notion that offenders should be punished because they deserve it. Forms of retribution include revenge, just deserts, and expiation.

RETRIBUTION

Retribution is grounded in the notion that offenders deserve to be punished. There are three competing views of retribution. The first is revenge, which may be conceptualized as "the impulse to get even in the face of injustice" (Barton, 1999, p. xiv). As you learned

in Chapter 9, this view of retribution has its roots in ancient legal codes. For instance, under Hebrew law, principles articulated in Exodus 21:23-25 specify that if there is a serious injury, the remedy is to take "life for life, eye for eye, tooth for tooth, hand for hand, foot for foot, burn for burn, wound for wound, bruise for bruise." This is similar to the Code of Hammurabi (c. 1800 B.C.E.) which stated, among other things, "If a man has destroyed the eye of a free man, his own eye shall be destroyed," and "if he has broken the bone of a free man, his bone shall be broken" (Edwards, 1906, p. 26). Thus, if a victim is wronged, punishment should be designed to get even by imposing the same hardship, with its associated pains, onto the offender.

The second view of retribution is **just deserts**. This, too, is a payback but with less emphasis on individual revenge and one-for-one correspondence between crime and punishment. A person advocating for just deserts would believe that the offender should be punished not only because he or she committed a bad act against an *individual* but also because all criminal acts are viewed as offenses against *society as a whole*. The resulting punishment should be proportional to the crime; that is, the punishment should be equally severe to the offender as the offender's criminal act was to the victim. Therefore, just deserts focuses on the idea that the punishment should fit the crime, imposing a similar pain or hardship on the offender as that which was experienced by the victim, but without resorting to one-on-one revenge (i.e., doing *exactly* the same thing to the offender as the offender did to the victim) or group-based vengeance like blood feuds.

just deserts
A view of retribution focusing on the idea that punishment should be proportional to the crime; that is, punishment should be equally severe to the offender as the offender's criminal act was to the victim.

The third view of retribution is **expiation**, which refers to atonement through suffering. St. Thomas Aquinas, a medieval theologian, was an advocate of this form of punishment. Expiation is based on the idea that crime causes pain to the victim, so the only way for the criminal to repent and learn his or her lesson is through experiencing his or her own pain. Note that expiation introduces an element not found in revenge or just deserts. The pain experienced by the offender should not be imposed solely to get even (be it with an individual or with losses to society) but also to cause the offender to repent and be forgiven. Although expiation is often associated with religious punishment, criminologist Graeme Newman (1983) argued that the American criminal justice system should reserve prisons for offenders who committed the most serious criminal acts (he proposed the use of probation and painful electric shocks as punishments for less serious crimes). In arguing for prisons to be used in this way, Newman writes:

expiation
A view of retribution based on the idea of atonement through suffering. Expiation is based on the idea that crime causes pain to the victim, so the only way for the offender to repent or learn a lesson is through experiencing pain.

> the proper punishment . . . is one that allows for expiation, for a slow learning through a punishment that expresses his crime. It is essential that the basic sin or sins underlying the crime be played out through its opposite so that the individual will learn the evil of his ways. . . . this can only be done through a process of pain and suffering. This is obviously a long and time consuming process, and it is why prison is a most appropriate medium for contrition. (p. 67)

Newman's proposed scheme was not adopted. However, there has been a tension in criminal justice policy debates about the role that retribution, and particularly expiation, should play. As part of sentiments to "get tough" on crime, which emerged during the 1980s, some policy makers and criminal justice agencies chose to pursue what Clear (1994) calls the "penal harm" movement. The movement argues that punishment "is supposed to hurt" and that "harm is justifiable precisely because it is an offender who is suffering" (p. 4). While prisons must abide by the Eighth Amendment's prohibition of cruel and unusual punishment, prison administrators generally have wide latitude to impose a variety of rules, as courts grant deference to their judgments about what is necessary for institutional security. For instance, examples of policies enacted by some facilities under the "penal harm" movement included requiring inmates to wear degrading uniforms, eliminating amenities (whether access to television, certain types of food, pillows, etc.), requiring strict grooming standards, and creating harsh living conditions for inmate populations (see Griffin, 2006).

Arguments in favor of penal harm are generally presented in the context of getting tough on crime, as a punishment for its own sake or in hopes of deterring others (see below). Arguments against it include perceptions that it can erode legitimacy and cause inmates "to respond in a defiant manner" (Griffin, 2006, p. 224), that more effective programming exists (Listwan, Jonson, Cullen, & Latessa, 2008), and that a distinction should be made between proportional penalties and more painful punishments that inflict pain for its own sake, in what Menninger (1968) has called "the crime of punishment" (also the title of his book).

Retribution has long been a part of justice systems. In the United States today, just deserts is the primary form of retribution practiced, although policies such as penal harm also yield some instances of expiation as a punishment philosophy.

DETERRENCE

To *deter* means to discourage someone from doing something. For a punishment to deter, it should have the effect of convincing people not to commit crime. This is usually accomplished through fear of punishment. If a person understands what punishment would likely occur if he or she were caught committing a crime, then that person might choose not to commit the crime. We would then say that person was deterred from committing the crime.

general deterrence
A justification for punishment holding that the imposition of punishment, in general, will prevent (or deter) all persons in the public from committing criminal acts because they will fear being punished if they do so.

There are two types of deterrence: general and specific. **General deterrence** is intended to deter all people from committing crime by making an example out of others who have. The idea is that as members of the public see punishments meted out, they will decide not to commit crime out of a fear of being punished themselves. For instance, general deterrence theory would suggest that every time a person is punished—whether sentenced to prison, jail, probation, or other sanctions—it serves as a reminder to the rest of society that similar crimes will also be punished. Let's consider as an example laws prohibiting text messaging while driving, which most states have enacted (Governors Highway Safety Association, 2013). Under the philosophy of general deterrence, one goal of the law is to cause people not to text while driving out of fear of the punishment they will receive for doing so. Under general deterrence, knowing that another person actually *did* receive a punishment such as a fine for texting while driving—not just that it is *hypothetically* possible to receive one—can also lead others to avoid the behavior, for fear that they too would be caught and punished.

specific deterrence
A justification for punishment that is designed to discourage or prevent individual offenders from committing additional crimes out of fear for being punished again if they do so.

Specific deterrence, sometimes referred to as individual or special deterrence, is not targeted at the general public. Rather, it is designed to discourage or prevent an individual offender from committing any *additional* crimes beyond those for which he or she has already been punished. Specific deterrence would occur if the offender decided that the punishment he or she already experienced was unpleasant and something to avoid in the future. To avoid future punishment, the offender would decide to live a law-abiding lifestyle and would then have been deterred from future criminal activity. For instance, if an individual received a fine for texting while driving, and then decided not to text while driving again in order to avoid the same unpleasant punishment in the future, specific deterrence would have occurred. Note the distinction between general and specific deterrence. General deterrence focuses on the public as a whole, using the threat of punishment to reduce crime. Specific deterrence focuses on an individual offender who has been caught, using the threat of repeated or additional punishment to reduce repeat offending.

The two people who most influenced deterrence theory were Jeremy Bentham ([1789] 1988) and Cesare Beccaria ([1764] 1995). Recall from Chapter 6 that Bentham's theory of justice was based on an analysis of pleasure and pain. This extends to deterrence theory because Bentham believed that offenders, or potential offenders, are rational in thinking through the consequences of their actions. This means that, when deciding on a course of action, people consider the potential for both the pleasure and the pain it

would produce. If the pleasure outweighs the potential pain, Bentham argued that the person will likely engage in the act. This is known as hedonism. If the pain outweighs the pleasure, Bentham argued that the person will be deterred from the action. For instance, in contemplating whether to commit a burglary, an offender might contemplate the value of the goods that could be taken and the happiness those goods would bring, and compare that to the possible punishment that could be given and the pain that punishment would bring. The task for the criminal justice system would be to structure a punishment that was sufficient to outweigh the pleasure of the goods obtained. But this is challenging; how can punishments be structured to maximize deterrent effect?

Beccaria, considered by many to be the founder of the classical school of criminology (see Chapter 5), offered an answer. It is important to understand the context of Beccaria's ideas, which fit into the Enlightenment philosophy of the 1600s and 1700s. In the Enlightenment era, philosophers came to question despotic actions of government—including justice systems viewed as being too draconian—and to advocate for scientific and rational understandings of human behavior and social problems. In this context, Beccaria challenged the criminological notions held by heads of European governments. Instead of utilizing harsh punishments and viewing crime as "the work of the devil" (Vold, Bernard, & Snipes, 1998, p. 16), Becarria suggested that crime could be understood by viewing individuals as rational decision makers, and that punishment could control crime through the principles of deterrence. Beccaria's philosophy actually draws heavily upon the theories of Thomas Hobbes (see Chapter 2), who suggested that one role of government was to "establish laws that administer punishments to deter people from harming one another in their pursuit of their interests" (Cullen and Agnew, 2003, p. 20). Beccaria's work was influential to the leaders of the American Revolution (1775–1783), and that influence continued as the government of the United States was created. Accordingly, deterrence has long been a central philosophy of punishment in the American criminal justice system (Vold, Bernard, & Snipes, 1998).

In order for deterrence to be effective, Beccaria believed that three things are necessary. The first was that the punishment should *swiftly* follow the crime. This is important because the more distance there is between the criminal act and the punishment, the less likely the offender is to associate the punishment with the crime. The second is that the punishment should be *certain.* This means the offender must know that he or she will be punished instead of believing that he or she can get away with the crime. After all, if offenders truly believe that they will get away without being caught, then concerns about potential punishments become moot. The third is that, much like just deserts, the punishment must be *proportional* to the harm caused by the crime. Although Beccaria was an advocate for deterrence, he strongly believed that there are limits to the severity of punishment. Punishments that are too severe can actually be counterproductive to deterrence. For instance, if a punishment is too severe, an offender may perceive the criminal justice system as lacking legitimacy and therefore not feel compelled to abide by its laws; overly harsh punishments can also increase the likelihood that an offender will resort to violence in order to avoid being caught. Beccaria rejected the death penalty and the torture of prisoners, arguing that they could reflect or promote an acceptance of violence by society.

There is great debate over the effectiveness of deterrence (see Nagin, 1998; Apel & Nagin, 2011). To illustrate, assume you are driving your vehicle over the posted speed limit. You glance in your rear-view mirror and notice a police cruiser rapidly approaching your car. Your heart starts to beat rapidly, and you appear to be paying more attention to what is behind you than what is ahead. The police officer activates the vehicle's emergency equipment (lights and siren), and you begin to pull your vehicle over, when the officer passes you and stops the vehicle in front of you. You are relieved. You now make a promise: "I will never speed again." Does the fear of being caught deter you from ever speeding again?

Based on this example, do you believe that deterrence is effective? If not, you are not alone. There are a number of reasons deterrence is often ineffective. First, as suggested earlier, deterrence assumes that people think rationally, but this is not always the case. Mental illness sometimes clouds rational thinking. For instance, a person with schizophrenia suffering from (false) delusions that he is under personal attack may not be deterred from committing harm against another person because he strongly believes that his actions are in self-defense.

It is also important to realize not all decisions are made on a rational basis; in fact, much of human behavior may be motivated by irrational factors. Some psychologists believe this to be the case. For instance, Sigmund Freud believed that human behavior, including criminal behavior, is the product of forces in the unconscious mind. Behaviorists, such as B. F. Skinner and John B. Watson, believed that behavior is produced through a combination of both punishments for negative behavior *and* rewards for good behavior, suggesting that punishment, or the threat of punishment, *by itself* is insufficient to produce change; a system of rewards is also necessary. Neuropsychology is exploring new frontiers in terms of how the biology of the brain may influence behavior. At a more basic level, sometimes individuals just do not think carefully about actions and their consequences. Therefore, it becomes clear that deterrence theory's reliance on rationality as the primary basis for human behavior is likely misplaced.

Second, punishment is usually not swift; it may take years before a criminal case comes to trial, particularly for complicated legal cases, such as those involving murder or other serious crimes. Third, punishment is not certain. There is just no way to predict *if* an offender will be caught and punishment enforced, let alone *how* punishment will be administered. Recall from Chapter 1 that many crimes are not reported to the police, and of those that are reported, most are never cleared or solved. Fourth, punishment is not always proportional. As illustrated earlier, judicial discretion plays a major role in how offenders are sentenced. For similar offenses, one judge may offer probation to the offender, whereas another judge may impose the maximum prison term allowed by law. Fifth, offenders are not always aware of the punishments. You may be thinking that ignorance of the law is no excuse; true enough, but under Bentham's argument, a person must know the potential punishment to enter into the calculus of pleasure versus pain that can lead to deterrence.

INCAPACITATION

incapacitation
A justification for punishment in which punishment is used to remove or reduce the offender's ability to commit criminal activities. The most common form of incapacitation is the use of prison or jail.

Incapacitation is a form of punishment that removes or reduces the offender's ability to commit criminal activities. The most common form of incapacitation is imprisonment. Under this justification of punishment, a person who is confined in prison will be unable to commit crimes against *society*. Notice that the key word here is "society." Crimes can and do occur in a prison setting; for the most part, those crimes are committed by inmates against other inmates or staff members, such as physical assaults, thefts, robberies, and so forth. Even in prison, inmates can be placed into solitary confinement (now known as "administrative segregation"), which is like a jail within the prison. In such a setting, an inmate would be physically separated from other inmates, which would, in turn, render it more difficult for him or her to commit criminal activities in the prison setting. Accordingly, the idea of incapacitation is that removing an offender to prison, or to administrative segregation units within a prison, eliminates or reduces the opportunity for that offender to commit crimes in society—at least for the time that he or she is in prison.

Incapacitation is currently a principal goal of the American criminal justice system. Faith in rehabilitation (discussed below) declined in the 1970s, which provided political momentum for a move toward incapacitation. President Ronald Reagan, elected in 1980, believed that society needed to "get tough" on crime. As a result, the use of prisons as a form of punishment expanded dramatically. This has resulted in what some

criminologists have called "the new penology" (Feeley & Simon, 1992, p. 449), in which prisons are viewed merely as warehouses to hold and incapacitate offenders, keeping them from committing crimes in society until they have to be released back into the community. The notion of prisons as a place for rehabilitation or deterrence is unimportant to the philosophy of incapacitation.

Incapacitation is not limited to confinement in a prison. It can be argued that the death penalty is a form of incapacitation. Execution certainly removes the opportunity for the individual offender to commit another crime. In earlier times, banishment and transportation were popular methods of incapacitation. Banished offenders were expelled from their towns and counties and told never to return, with the threat of execution if they did. Offenders who were "transported" were sent by ship (the means of transportation at the time) to a penal colony. A penal colony is a colonial location or settlement where prisoners were sent to live. In these colonies, offenders raised families and established a society, as it became their new home. Most, if not all, of the penal colonies relied on the prisoners to perform free labor that would benefit the nation's economy. For instance, Great Britain sent offenders to the American colonies and later to Australia to produce goods that were shipped back to Great Britain for sale. Both banishment and transportation assumed that as long as offenders were not in the immediate area, they could do no harm to society.

Incapacitation can also include removing the instrumentalities of the crime—that is, the tools or capabilities that made the crime possible in the first place. For instance, some DUI offenders must forfeit their driver's licenses (and in some cases, their cars), which could render them unable to commit another DUI offense. Likewise, some sex offenders undergo chemical castration, which is meant to reduce or remove their physical ability to commit a sexual offense. While not relying on prison, these examples also may have the effect of incapacitation.

REHABILITATION

Rehabilitation is an attempt to *correct* an offender's behavior to make it conform to the norms of society. To be effective, rehabilitation must be offender specific. Unlike the philosophy of *just deserts*—letting the punishment fit the crime—the viewpoint here is *let the punishment fit, and rehabilitate, the offender*. The focus is on "treating" the offender through therapy, vocational or work-release programs, or educational training, to mention just a few. In theory, if rehabilitation is successful, the violator will return to society "cured" of his or her criminal ways and thereby become a productive member of the community.

rehabilitation
A justification for punishment that views the purpose of punishment as attempting to correct an offender's behavior so it will conform to the law and to social norms. Rehabilitation involves the use of programming (counseling, treatment, education, etc.), rather than fear or pain to correct behavior.

It is interesting to note that the very first prison in the United States, Eastern State Penitentiary, which opened in Philadelphia in 1829, was designed to promote the rehabilitation of offenders. In that prison, offenders were locked in a cell and permitted no human contact for the duration of their sentence. They were provided with a Bible to read, and the idea was that isolated reading and reflection would lead inmates to repent and change their ways.

However, it was not until the mid-twentieth century that rehabilitation gained widespread popularity in the United States. Advocates of rehabilitation strongly believed that treatment of the offender was more humane than other forms of punishment. Furthermore, criminology had advanced to a point where treatment of the offender was believed possible based on theories of what caused, and could therefore prevent, crime. Rehabilitation was also viewed as useful to society by preparing reformed offenders to rejoin society as fully productive members.

In the 1970s, rehabilitation began to lose its popularity. This was in part due to a landmark study by Robert Martinson (1974), which stated, "with few and isolated exceptions, the rehabilitative efforts that have been reported so far have had no appreciable effect on recidivism" (p. 25). That is, the study suggested that rehabilitation

programs were not effective. Summarized as "nothing works," this result was quickly accepted by the public and politicians, and it coincided with the beginning of the get-tough era (discussed above), in which states moved away from rehabilitation and toward incapacitation as a guiding philosophy. This was based in part on political trends, in part on a suspicion of the discretion applied in correctional decisions about the provision and evaluation of inmate rehabilitation, and in part on the interpretation of Martinson's results as suggesting that nothing could ever work (Cullen, 2005).

At the same time, correctional experts began a research program focused on rehabilitation. A follow-up study by Martinson, himself, found that rehabilitation still held promise. Additional evidence mounted to show that rehabilitation could in fact be effective if rehabilitative efforts were properly designed. Keys to successful rehabilitative programming include identifying the behaviors or factors that are most amenable to treatment, designing programs that specifically target those behaviors and patterns, and then determining which programs are most appropriate for which offenders. As a result, experts now know that rehabilitation can be effective (Cullen, 2005).

The new penology of incapacitation continues, but rehabilitation has made a resurgence as well. Interestingly, the public seems to simultaneously support punitive policies and rehabilitation (Cullen, Fisher, & Applegate, 2000). In addition, rehabilitative efforts have been justified as cost-saving correctional alternatives (e.g., Pallone & Hennessy, 2003), as offenders who can be rehabilitated are offenders for whom the state does not have to pay for long-term incarceration. As states experience budget cuts, this seems to have become more important.

restitution
The payment of money to a victim by an offender to compensate the victim for the losses caused by the offender. This concept was present in some ancient Greek legal codes and also is utilized as part of restorative justice models today.

RESTITUTION AND RESTORATION

Restitution is a justification for punishment that requires the offender to pay back the victim—whether an individual, family, or society—for the harm caused by the

Inmates at Cebu Provincial Prison in the Philippines dance to Michael Jackson's song *Thriller*. As part of a program at the prison, inmates audition and spend many hours rehearsing in preparation for dances, many of which have become popular YouTube videos. Introduced as a means of promoting exercise for inmates, the program has promoted teamwork and has been associated with a reduction of violence at the prison (Seno, 2008). What philosophy or philosophies of punishment do you think this illustrates?

offender's criminal behavior. More often than not, restitution involves some type of financial payback. It can also come through community service. Rather than paying the victim back directly with money, community service can symbolically provide restitution by requiring the offender to do something that betters the community harmed by the offense.

Restitution has evolved into a popular strategy called restorative justice. Recall from Chapter 6 that restorative justice goes beyond a mere personal financial settlement; it is a process to restore the health of the community while focusing on the needs of both the victim and the offender. For restorative justice to be effective, the offender must play an active role in the healing process by taking responsibility for his or her actions. By accepting and repaying the harm caused by his or her actions, the offender may be "restored" to society.

restorative justice
Focuses on restoring the victim, offender, and society to the desirable conditions that existed before a criminal offense occurred.

Restorative justice includes a variety of strategies, including the use of mediation or even apologies between victim and offender. For instance, a community dispute resolution center in Durham, North Carolina, provides mediation for low-level criminal complaints, such as "harassment, assault, and related problems among relatives, neighbors, and acquaintances" (McGillis, 1998, p. 3). In cases when both parties agree to participate, the process can provide several advantages over a traditional criminal proceeding. "Mediation provides disputants with the opportunity to communicate face to face, enables disputants to see each other as human beings rather than abstract opponents, and provides opportunities to identify common ground that can lead to the resolution of conflict" (McGillis, 1998, p. 13). This is at the center of what restorative justice encourages—collaborations to address the needs of, and thus heal, those involved in the dispute and the community as a whole. The role that apologies may play in healing has led to increased discussion of their use (see Lazare, 2004), and in fact, apology has played an important form of dispute resolution in some societies, including Japan (Wagatsuma & Rosett, 1986).

One controversial form of restorative justice is shaming. John Braithwaite (1989) argues that there are two forms of shaming. The first and perhaps most effective is reintegrative shaming. This is a strategy whereby the offender is publicly shamed or scolded for his or her actions. The community then forgives the offender and accepts him or her back. The purpose of the shaming is to cause reflection, acknowledgment of wrongdoing, and conformity with social norms, and as such draws heavily upon informal social control. It is reintegrative because the outcome is to allow all parties to heal and for the offender to be accepted upon his or her return as a law-abiding member of society.

Realistically, reintegrative shaming is difficult to implement because members of society rarely forgive and reaccept the offender back into the community. As a result, most modern shaming punishments take the form of disintegrative shaming. Disintegrative shaming labels offenders as deviant, thereby separating them from the community rather than integrating them back into it. For instance, some states use disintegrative shaming as part of their sentences for driving under the influence. Under such a sentence, the offender found guilty of driving under the influence would display a specialized license plate (usually donning a special color). This labels the driver as a violator of the drunken driving statute, shaming that offender. As another example, some judges have required offenders to stand in public places wearing placards that announce their crimes—such as "I am a thief" or "I commit mail fraud." However, in either of these instances, there is no effort to reintegrate the offender through forgiveness and acceptance. Rather, the shaming simply labels the offender and stigmatizes him or her further. As such, disintegrative shaming is not truly a form of restorative justice.

Restitution and restorative justice are utilized to some extent by the American criminal justice system, though perhaps not as heavily as the prior philosophies of punishment. The goals of compensating losses (restitution) and promoting healing (restorative justice) remain to be further studied and debated in terms of their promise as a response to crime.

BOX 10.1

Research in Action

CORPORAL PUNISHMENT

Corporal punishment is defined as "the use of physical force with the intention of causing a child to experience pain, but not injury, for the purpose of correction or control of the child's behavior" (Straus, 2000, p. 1110). While support for corporal punishment in the United States has decreased somewhat over time (Straus & Mathur, 1996), it remains a common practice in the United States and other countries (Straus, 2010).

Corporal punishment is used not only in homes, but in some jurisdictions, in schools, as well. In both cases—homes and schools—corporal punishment is more common in the southern region of the United States (e.g., Owen, 2005; Straus & Stewart, 1999) and is more likely to be supported by conservative Protestants than other religious groups (e.g., Ellison & Sherkat, 1993; Owen & Wagner, 2006). The use of corporal punishment in schools is associated with low levels of social capital, referring in general to the degree to which residents feel connected to their communities and to one another (Owen, 2005; Owen & Wagner, 2006). Research on corporal punishment in the home has found that it is used more frequently by younger parents, lower-income families, African Americans, and mothers (Straus & Stewart, 1999). Even with this variability, though, data are fairly consistent in showing that a majority of children have been spanked at some point in their lives (e.g., Zolotor, Theodore, Runyan, Chang, & Laskey, 2011). There are several policy debates that emerge in discussions of corporal punishment.

First, what is corporal punishment, and at what point does it become abuse? According to Grayson (2006), while corporal punishment is often understood as synonymous with spanking, the methods of corporal punishment may vary widely, including "hitting, slapping, spanking, punching, kicking, choking, electric shock, confinement in small spaces, excessive exercise, and fixed position for long periods of time" (p. 12). Some of the "instruments used to inflict pain upon the child include leather straps, switches, baseball bats, and fists" (Grayson, 2006, p. 12). Laws tend to require the use of corporal punishment to be reasonable, but it is not immediately clear what that means. The vagueness of legal provisions and discretion inherent in their interpretation has led Coleman, Dodge, and Campbell (2010) to argue that "current law fails to give useful guidance to its intended audience" (p. 164).

Second, should corporal punishment be allowed in schools? When permitted, it generally consists of spanking a child with a wooden paddle. At the time of this writing, 19 states allow corporal punishment in their public schools (*Discipline at School,* n.d.), which means that individual school districts in those states can decide whether or not to actually use it. In the landmark case of *Ingraham v. Wright* (1977), the U.S. Supreme Court ruled that spanking a child in school does not constitute

COMPETING PHILOSOPHIES

The five philosophies of punishment discussed above—retribution, deterrence, incapacitation, rehabilitation, and restitution and restorative justice—each convey one possible rationale of punishment. To some extent, all influence the American criminal justice system's approach to punishment. However, many debates have occurred about which philosophy should be the predominant influence on criminal justice policy, and over time, some have become more popular and some less so. The challenge is to determine which best accomplishes the criminal justice system's desired goals and how they should be applied in practice.

It is also important to observe that there are some who believe that current punishment options are inadequate, or even inappropriate, for achieving justice. For instance, Golash (2005) argues that, regardless of the justification for doing so, punishment should be abolished if "it involves depriving people of things to which they have a right (typically, life, liberty, or property)" (p. 2). Similarly, a movement known as penal abolition advocates for abolishing the use of the prison as a punishment alternative

cruel and unusual punishment (under the Eighth Amendment). However, concerns that arise about school corporal punishment include injuries that have resulted from it, the sentiment opposing it in the professional education community, the opposition to it expressed by the public, and the potential for disparities in its use, as it is used disproportionately against male and African American students (see Owen, 2005).

Third, should corporal punishment be allowed in homes? In 31 countries, the majority of which are in Europe, corporal punishment is banned in the home. In the United States in 2007, legislation was proposed in California that would have banned physical discipline of children three and younger as well as the use of belts, paddles, or other implements to spank any child (Vogel, 2007); the law was not passed. Conversely, in 2008, the Indiana Supreme Court upheld the legality of a punishment in which an 11-year-old was struck "five to seven times with either a belt or an extension cord" (*Willis v. State,* 2008, p. 179). Some research studies have distinguished "conditional spanking" from other types, defining it as non-excessive and used only in limited circumstances, "primarily to back-up milder disciplinary tactics (e.g., reasoning or time-out), used for defiance, or used in a controlled manner" (Larzelere & Kuhn, 2005, p. 17). Larzelere and Kuhn (2005) present data to suggest that conditional spanking is an acceptable and effective alternative.

At the same time, other research reaches different conclusions about corporal punishment. For example, in a study of non-abusive corporal punishment by parents, Gershoff (2002) found it to be associated with:

> decreased moral internalization, increased child aggression, increased child delinquent and antisocial behavior, decreased quality of relationship between parent and child, decreased child mental health, increased risk of being a victim of physical abuse, increased adult aggression, increased adult criminal and antisocial behavior, decreased adult mental health, and increased risk of abusing own child or spouse. (p. 544)

Some subsequent research has challenged these negative findings, arguing that they are exaggerated (e.g., Ferguson, 2013); other subsequent research has detected additional negative impacts such as a link between harsh, but non-abusive, corporal punishment in childhood and subsequent diagnosis of mental disorders in adulthood (e.g., Afifi, Mota, Dasiewicz, MacMillan, & Sareen, 2012).

Q What philosophies of punishment underlie the use of corporal punishment?

Q How would you address each of the three policy debates listed above?

Q Based upon these research findings, would you recommend alternatives to corporal punishment? If not, why? If so, what? Do any of the philosophies of punishment influence your answer?

(see Piché & Larsen, 2010). Advocates of punishment reform along these lines often recommend addressing social problems that contribute to crime (e.g., poverty, unemployment), significant expansions of restorative justice concepts (Golash, 2005), and using peacemaking techniques that emphasize empathy for persons rather than obedience to authority (Pepinsky, 1999a). Certainly, debates over punishment philosophy will continue. See Box 10.1 for discussion of a debate related to what does or does not constitute appropriate punishment.

Q What do you think are the advantages and disadvantages of each justification for punishment? Which philosophy of punishment do you think is most promising? Least promising? Explain your answer.

Q Describe how the Andrade case could have been handled under each of the five justifications for punishment. Which do you think is preferable? Why?

Q Do you believe offenders can be rehabilitated? Explain your reasoning.

The Politics of Whom We Punish

FOCUSING QUESTION 10.3

Who is selected for punishment?

dangerous classes
Groups of persons who are targeted for punishment more often than the general population because they are labeled as deviant or dangerous by society. The label may be based on untrue perceptions or discrimination rather than on actual threats.

Now that you understand what punishment is and the justifications for it, the question remains, whom do we punish? You could answer this question by saying that we punish lawbreakers. However, this may be too simplistic a response. There are certain groups of people who are targeted for punishment far more often than the general population. These groups of people are labeled as the **dangerous classes** (see Shelden, 2001). It is important to note that these individuals are not necessarily criminal or inherently bad. They may only be *perceived* as dangerous, generally by persons with social or political power, and then labeled accordingly. This is another example of social construction and labeling within the criminal justice system.

As with the definition of punishment, determining those who are perceived as dangerous classes changes with time, location, circumstances, and so on. Persons placed into the category of "dangerous classes" may be labeled as unworthy of equal treatment, as posing a threat to society, or as otherwise undesirable.

Although the dangerous classes may include persons from selected races, ethnic backgrounds, religious affiliations, sexual orientations, and/or regions, they certainly are not limited to those groups. For instance, police officers often attempt to identify those among the population who fall within the dangerous classes. Some, though not all, police officers are quick to attach a label to law violators. These officers may include in their definition of dangerous classes persons who they believe may cause harm to society or to them personally, such as social deviants, illegal drug users, mentally ill subjects, and juvenile status offenders (i.e., truants, runaways, curfew violators, or others whose offenses are based on their status as juveniles).

According to Jerome Skolnick (1966), police officers develop a perceptual shorthand to assist in the immediate identification of persons believed to pose a personal danger or harm to society. These *symbolic assailants,* as Skolnick called them, are routinely subjected to higher levels of social control than other persons. For example, assume you are a police officer on patrol and you observe two groups loitering on the sidewalk at night. One is a group of religious clergy conversing on a street corner, and the other is a group of teenagers leaning against a building. To which group would you pay more attention? Would you ask either group what their business is or even to move along? Juveniles have traditionally posed problems for the police, and the police have often labeled them as members of the dangerous classes. Note that this is what sometimes leads to profiling. If juveniles are labeled as a dangerous class, then all juveniles may be so labeled, prompting law enforcement suspicion for groups of people regardless of their individual personal attributes.

The point is that some groups are deemed dangerous by those with political, legal, or social power and have accordingly been subject to higher levels of law enforcement. Again, this is based on perceptions, biases, and sometimes discrimination, rather than actual levels of danger.

The importance of understanding the concept of the dangerous classes cannot be overstated. Being labeled as a member of the dangerous class is a means by which society and government identifies, controls, and punishes those targeted individuals and groups. Once tagged a dangerous class, laws may be established to constrain its members. This can result in policies that foster inequality. For instance, when some drug laws were created, certain groups were labeled as dangerous classes and targeted for greater enforcement based on their race. According to Shelden (2001), Hispanics and African Americans were the focus of marijuana drug enforcement during the 1930s; during the 1950s, African Americans were the target of heroin enforcement; and from

the 1980s (and up to the time of this writing), African Americans were the center of attention for the enforcement of crack cocaine. Other racial groups were not so vigorously targeted for drug enforcement, although other racial groups were certainly involved in drug use and drug law violations.

One often cited example was a federal law enacted in 1986 under which "a person convicted of crack cocaine possession received the same mandatory prison term as someone with 100 times the same amount of powder cocaine" (Abrams, 2010, para. 3). This law could have been shaped by the media's portrayal of inaccurate information about crack cocaine (see Hartman & Golub, 1999) or by concerns about violence associated with crack cocaine markets. However, some argued that there was an underlying racial component motivating harsher penalties for crack cocaine, as arrestees were more likely to be African American than arrestees for powder cocaine possession. For instance, in 2009, 79% of persons sentenced under the law for crack cocaine, but only 28% of persons sentenced under the law for power cocaine, were African American, a significant disparity (Kurtzleben, 2010). In wake of the substantial criticism the law generated, it was revised in 2010, bringing the penalties for crack and powder cocaine into closer alignment (Abrams, 2010).

Labeling a group as a dangerous class is not an issue limited to drug laws. It is a human rights issue that results from prejudice and group stereotyping.

Q Can you think of other groups that have been identified as a member of the dangerous classes? If so, which groups? How have those groups experienced higher levels of law enforcement and punishment than others?

Limitations on Criminal Punishment

FOCUSING QUESTION 10.4

Under what circumstances can punishment not be given?

Punishment does not occur without some limits. In fact, there are three philosophical principles that limit punishment under the criminal law: culpability, legality, and proportionality. Punishments may not be given if an individual is not culpable, if criminal laws are not properly constructed, or if the punishment itself violates the Eighth Amendment.

CULPABILITY: A FAIRNESS PRINCIPLE REQUIRING BLAMEWORTHINESS

The criminal law usually requires some level of **culpability**, or blameworthiness, as a prerequisite to criminal punishment. That is, only when individuals are actually guilty of a crime as defined under the law are they subjected to punishment. Recall the discussion of substantive criminal law in Chapter 9. Culpability generally requires both *actus reus*, or a criminal act, and *mens rea*, or criminal intent. The criminal law generally does *not* seek to punish persons who commit acts when they lack free will, such as people who commit acts involuntarily or under duress. The criminal law also generally does not seek to punish persons who lack rationality, such as very young or severely mentally ill offenders. In either case, imposing a punishment would be unjust because the offender would not have had the intent to commit a crime. Recall, however, that there is a class of crimes called strict liability offenses, which punish certain acts even if *mens rea* is lacking. Might these crimes be exceptions to the principle of culpability? Should they be?

culpability
Guilt or responsibility for a criminal offense. Only individuals with culpability may be punished.

One debate surrounding culpability is whether juvenile offenders are equally culpable, and should receive the same kinds of punishments, as adult offenders. Review Box 10.2 for a discussion of how the Supreme Court has addressed this issue.

BOX. 10.2

Ethics in Practice

HOW SHOULD JUVENILES BE PUNISHED?

Should juvenile offenders be treated differently than adults? The Supreme Court has periodically reviewed juvenile court procedures, holding in some cases that the same rules which apply to adults apply to juveniles. These include the right to an attorney, the right to confront their accuser, the right against self-incrimination, the right to be notified of charges (all from *In re Gault,* 1967), and the right to have guilt proven beyond a reasonable doubt (*In re Winship,* 1970). However, juvenile court processes are not required to use a trial by jury (*McKeiver v. Pennsylvania,* 1971), and a federal law specifies that juveniles and adults may not be confined together in correctional settings, such as jails (Juvenile Justice Advisory Council, 1988). Furthermore, juvenile correctional institutions are more closely modeled on principles of rehabilitation, both in their design and in their programming.

The following Supreme Court cases relate specifically to juvenile punishment. All have in common that they raise questions about whether a punishment alternative that would be permissible for an adult offender should be applied to a juvenile offender. Review each case and consider whether you agree or disagree with the outcome.

Roper v. Simmons, 543 U.S. 551 (2005). Seventeen-year-old Christopher Simmons (and two younger friends) broke into Ms. Crook's home, bound her with duct tape and an electrical cord, covered her face and eyes, and then transported her to a state park, where they threw her off a bridge, where she drowned. Even though he was under 18 years of age, he was considered an adult under Missouri law, where the case occurred. Simmons was found guilty and sentenced to death. Justice Kennedy, writing for the majority, noted that juveniles (here meaning persons under the age of 18, regardless of their legal status in a jurisdiction) lack the maturity and understanding of responsibility compared to that which an adult would have. In addition, Justice Kennedy noted that most states already prohibited the death penalty for juvenile offenders. *Outcome:* If an offender was under 18 when a crime was committed, then that offender cannot be sentenced to death for that crime.

Graham v. Florida, 560 U.S. 48 (2010). Terrance Graham, 16 years old, was arrested for attempted robbery and armed burglary resulting in an assault, for which he was tried as an adult. As part of a plea agreement, he was required to spend 12 months in jail followed by a term of probation. Six months after his release from jail, at age 17, Graham was arrested for a home invasion robbery. Because this offense occurred while he was still on probation for the earlier charges, the judge revoked the probation and replaced it with a life sentence for the attempted robbery and armed

NOTICE AND THE PRINCIPLE OF LEGALITY

legality
In punishment theory, legality means that punishment can only be given for crimes as defined by the law and that the punishments given must be within the bounds of the law.

People must be given fair notice of what is expected of them before they can be punished for not having lived up to those expectations. This is the principle of **legality**, which is based on a Latin phrase introduced in Chapter 1: *nullum crimen sine lege, nulla poena sine lege,* meaning there can be no crime without a law that defines it, and there can be no punishment without a law that allows it. This principle is central to notions of fairness and due process, and three implications flow from it.

First, under the principle of legality, no one can be punished for an act that is not expressly labeled as a criminal act by a penal code. Generally speaking, no act can be defined or punished as a crime until a legislature (or the public) votes to include it in their jurisdiction's criminal code. This is important because it ensures advance notice of what is and is not a crime. A police officer cannot make up a law on the spot and arrest a person for it, nor may a court make up a law and then punish a person for it. Laws must be specified before they can be enforced and their violators punished.

burglary. Because Florida, where the crime occurred, had abolished parole, this meant that the sentence was life without parole. Justice Kennedy, writing for the majority, again indicated that juveniles (meaning persons under the age of 18, regardless of their legal status in a jurisdiction) are less culpable than adults due to reduced levels of maturity and understanding of responsibility. In addition, Justice Kennedy found that the severity of a life without parole sentence for a non-homicide offense was not justified by any philosophy of punishment, that it was a sentence rarely given, and that juveniles should be provided some realistic opportunity to become rehabilitated and obtain release. *Outcome:* Offenders who committed a non-homicide offense when under the age of 18 cannot be sentenced to life in prison without the possibility of parole; this means that they must have the *opportunity* to earn release, although release is not guaranteed.

Miller v. Alabama and *Jackson v. Hobbs,* 567 U.S. ___ (2012). These two cases were considered together by the Supreme Court. Evan Miller, 14 years old, was convicted of murder and sentenced to life in prison without parole. Miller, along with a friend, beat Miller's neighbor with a baseball bat and set his trailer on fire. The neighbor died. Kuntrell Jackson, also 14 years old, shot and killed a store clerk during an armed robbery committed with two other juveniles. He was charged with felony murder and aggravated robbery and sentenced to life imprisonment without the possibility of parole. Both offenders were tried as adults and in both cases, the sentence of life without parole was mandatory, meaning that judges were required to impose it and had no discretion to issue a lesser sentence. According to Justice Kagan, who wrote for the majority, juvenile cases (again, juvenile means under the age of 18 regardless of legal status in the jurisdiction) must take into account "the mitigating qualities of youth" (p. 3, slip opinion). *Outcome:* Mandatory sentences of life without parole may not be required when a person under 18 years of age commits a homicide offense; sentencing must "take into account how children are different" (p. 17, slip opinion). Note that this does not prohibit life without parole sentences for homicide offenses committed by juveniles, but specifies such penalties cannot be mandatory.

Q Do you think that there is an ethical requirement to treat juveniles differently from adults when determining what sentences are appropriate as punishments for crime?

Q Do you agree or disagree with the outcomes in the above cases? Why?

Q In each of the above cases, the juvenile offender was tried in adult court. Many states allow this for serious offenses. Is this practice ethical? Why or why not?

Second, criminal laws must be interpreted according to their plain meaning. If the meaning of a criminal law is unclear, most states will interpret it by using common sense and by considering what the lawmakers wanted to accomplish (see *United States v. Brown,* 1948). Some states go a step farther and require their courts to apply only what is precisely stated within a law, bypassing interpretation altogether. This is important because for fair notice to be given, the laws must clearly specify what conduct is being prohibited.

Third, the principle of legality prohibits governments from punishing someone if a criminal law is written too vaguely. If the meaning of a law is too vague, it is deemed **void for vagueness**, and therefore unenforceable. This occurs when a law is written in such a way that persons "of common intelligence must necessarily guess at its meaning and differ as to its application" (Robinson, 2005, p. 356). This is important because it prevents police officers, judges, and citizens from having to guess at the meaning of the law. It also prevents police officers and judges from making up the meaning of law—and from applying made-up meanings unfairly and unequally to groups labeled as the dangerous classes.

void for vagueness
Laws so vague that persons must guess at their meaning, and as a result, such laws are unenforceable. Based on the principle that laws must provide clear descriptions of the conduct that is prohibited.

PROPORTIONALITY AND THE EIGHTH AMENDMENT

The Eighth Amendment of the U.S. Constitution reads: "Excessive bail shall not be required, nor excessive fines imposed, nor cruel and unusual punishment inflicted." This single sentence raises many important issues and debates, some of which are described next.

bail
A financial pledge to ensure that a person accused of a crime will appear in court for trial.

Bail. Bail is not a form of punishment. However, to someone who must post bail, it may feel as though it is a punishment. **Bail** is a financial or property-based pledge to ensure that the accused will appear in court. After being arrested, a person accused of a crime will have a bail hearing before a judge or a magistrate. At that hearing, the judge or magistrate may decide that the accused can be released into the community or on bail. If released on bail, an accused person provides a sum of money or a property title to the court in exchange for being released into the community prior to trial. If the accused person appears in court at the required date and time, the money or property is returned. If the accused fails to appear (FTA) in court, he or she will forfeit the money or property, which will then belong to the court. In addition, an FTA remains on a person's record, and if caught, that person will be compelled to return to court—and almost certainly will not be granted bail again.

Persons who are unable to post their full bail amount may seek the services of bail bond agents. For a fee, usually in the amount of 10% of the bail, the bail bond agent will post the full amount to the court on behalf of the accused. The fee is a cost that is not returned to accused persons, whether or not they appear in court or are found guilty or not guilty, but it does allow them to remain in the community prior to trial. The Supreme Court suggested in 1872 that bail bond agents have wide latitude to pursue those persons who fail to appear in court after securing their services (*Taylor v. Taintor,* 1872), which has given rise to controversies about the authority of bail bounty hunters and has led to laws in some jurisdictions that place limits on their activities.

Note that the Eighth Amendment does *not* require bail to be granted; it simply states that bail shall not be *excessive* if it is granted. In some cases, dangerous persons or those whom the judge believes are likely to flee will not be granted bail at all (see *U.S. v. Salerno,* 1987). The prohibition against excessive bail is designed to protect accused persons from being unnecessarily incarcerated prior to trial when there is not a public safety reason for doing so. When considering the amount of bail and whether or not it is excessive, there are a number of factors that judges may consider.

- *The type of offense committed.* A person who has been arrested for murder may have substantially higher bail, or even be denied bail, than someone arrested for theft. The more serious the crime, the greater potential the accused person will attempt to flee. Therefore, bail is higher for serious offenses.
- *The circumstances surrounding the offense.* Because they are more blameworthy and thus more likely to FTA, higher bail might be set for the "instigators" or initiators of a criminal act.
- *Behavior of the accused.* If the accused resisted arrest or was belligerent to the arresting officer, that can signal a judge that the person might be risky to release, in which case bail may be set at a higher level or denied.
- *The ability of the accused to pay the bail.* Does the accused possess the financial and/or property means to post bail? If so, bail may be set at a level that is affordable to the individual, yet high enough to compel attendance at trial. Some low-risk persons may also be released before trial without having to offer money or property in exchange. This is called release on recognizance (ROR).
- *The accused's chances of not returning for trial.* Bail might be set higher or denied altogether if the accused does not live or work in the area or if the accused does not have immediate family or close friends in the jurisdiction. Individuals without community ties may be more likely to flee.

Excessive Fines. The Eighth Amendment also provides that excessive fines not be imposed. Unlike bail, **fines** are financial penalties that are imposed after the accused has been found guilty of a crime. As such, fines are a form of punishment. The law often provides an upper limit that a fine may not exceed. For instance, a state criminal code might specify that the maximum fine for a low-level misdemeanor is $250 while the maximum fine for a serious felony is up to $100,000. Imposing fines generally depends on judicial discretion, with judges imposing whatever fines—within the legal limit—they believe are appropriate. Fines are usually applied for minor offenses, such as traffic offenses and some misdemeanors, and less frequently applied for more serious felony offenses.

The Eighth Amendment prohibition against excessive fines is difficult to define. This is because it remains unclear as to what "excessive" really means. For an interesting example, consider the use of day fines as described in Box 10.3.

fines
Financial penalties imposed when an offender has been found guilty of a crime.

cruel and unusual punishment
Prohibited under the Eighth Amendment of the U.S. Constitution. However, there are differing legal interpretations as to what constitutes cruel and unusual punishment.

Cruel and Unusual Punishments. The Eighth Amendment to the U.S. Constitution prohibits the imposition of **cruel and unusual punishments**. The Eighth Amendment

BOX 10.3

DAY FINES

Should the American criminal justice system make a greater use of fines? Consider this. In the United States, fines are primarily assigned for traffic offenses and for low-level criminal violations (i.e., misdemeanors). However, in many European countries, fines are utilized much more frequently, even for serious criminal offenses and crimes of violence (i.e., felonies).

One problem with fines is determining the proper amount. Fines that are too high may go unpaid by offenders, and fines that are too low may diminish the seriousness of an offense. One solution, common in European countries but not in the United States, is the use of the day fine. **Day fines** allow judges to assign a fine that is proportional to an offender's daily income. Here's how they work. First, the government assigns a number of fine units based on the severity of each offense. Let's use motor vehicle theft as an example and assume that it is worth 30 fine units. Second, the government determines the value of each fine unit. Let's assume that each fine unit is valued as half of an offender's daily income. Finally, judges do the math. If an offender who makes $80 per day commits motor vehicle theft, that offender's fine would be $1,200 (each fine unit = $40; $40 × 30 fine units = $1,200). If an offender makes $1,000 per day, that offender's fine would be $15,000 (each fine unit = $500; $500 × 30 fine units = $15,000).

Therefore, day fines vary based on an offender's income. In one case, a wealthy driver in Finland who was going 25 miles per hour over the posted speed limit received a $204,000 penalty in a day fine system (Moore, 2007).

- Q Why do you think the United States relies on punishments other than fines for serious criminal offenses?
- Q Is a $204,000 traffic ticket unreasonable in the case described above? Why or why not?
- Q What arguments can you make for and against day fines? What philosophies of punishment do they illustrate?
- Q If day fines were utilized in the United States, do you think they would violate the Eighth Amendment?
- Q Is it possible to develop a "fair" system of fines?

was written to ban inhumane punishment and to ensure fair and equal treatment of offenders. But what is "cruel"? What is "unusual"? As an example, you will probably agree that capital punishment (i.e., the death penalty) for motor vehicle theft is too extreme, but what is it that would make this hypothetical punishment unusual or even cruel?

proportionality
The idea that the punishment should fit the crime. Punishments may be ruled unconstitutional if they are grossly excessive in relation to the crime committed.

One answer is the principle of **proportionality**, which is the idea that the punishment should "fit the crime." Recall that proportionality is important to both just deserts and deterrence as justifications for punishment. It is also important from a legal perspective, as punishments may be unconstitutional when they are grossly excessive in relation to the crime committed. In *Weems v. United States* (1910), the U.S. Supreme Court first signaled that the principle of proportionality was a part of Eighth Amendment jurisprudence.

Of course, this begs the question of how proportionality is determined. Unfortunately, there is no easy answer. Think back to the case study at the beginning of this chapter. Andrade appealed his two 25-years-to-life sentences, and the Supreme Court ultimately ruled that they were not so disproportionate to the crime as to be unconstitutional (*Lockyer v. Andrade,* 2003). Consider the implications of this. For theft of approximately $150 worth of videotapes, Andrade will likely spend the remainder of his life in prison. Of course, Andrade's sentence was based in part on his prior criminal history. However, compare this to a case heard by the Supreme Court 20 years before Andrade's. In *Solem v. Helm* (1983), the defendant had six prior felony convictions, all for nonviolent offenses (burglary, grand larceny, driving while intoxicated, and obtaining money under false pretenses). Upon his seventh felony conviction, which was for check fraud, the defendant was sentenced to life in prison without parole. In that case, however, the Supreme Court ruled that the punishment was cruel and unusual, stating that the defendant "has received the penultimate sentence for relatively minor criminal conduct . . . [and] his sentence is significantly disproportionate to his crime." As you

DUI offenders work on a chain gang. Work includes cleaning up city streets and burying indigent persons (see Ariz. Inmates . . . , 2007). What philosophy or philosophies of punishment does this illustrate? Is it "cruel and unusual punishment" to require inmates to be chained together or to wear the pink shirts?

can see, there is an apparent inconsistency between these two cases. Unfortunately, this has left lawyers, scholars, and justice professionals wondering what disproportionate punishment actually means.

In addition to ensuring that punishments are proportional, the Eighth Amendment was also intended to ban inhumane punishment. This, too, raises a question: what kinds of punishments are inhumane and unacceptable? The first Supreme Court case to explore this issue was *Wilkerson v. Utah* (1878). Here, the Supreme Court upheld executions by firing squad but prohibited burning, disemboweling, and drawing and quartering. In reaching its decision, the Supreme Court wrote, "Difficulty would attend the efforts to define with exactness . . . cruel and unusual punishments; but it is safe to affirm that punishments of torture . . . and all others in the same line of unnecessary cruelty, are forbidden" (pp. 135–136). Thus, even the Supreme Court acknowledged that it is difficult to define cruel and unusual or inhumane punishments beyond banning those of "unnecessary" cruelty.

Box 10.4 provides further background about the Eighth Amendment and cruel and unusual punishment. Try your hand at deciding what is and is not cruel and unusual punishment based on actual court decisions. Some will require you to consider proportionality, and others will require you to consider the humanity or cruelty of the punishment itself.

Q A bartender who serves alcohol to an underage person can be criminally punished for doing so even if the person produced a fake ID. Is that fair? Would the bartender's punishment violate the principle of culpability? Why or why not?

Q The City of Chicago passed an ordinance "which prohibits 'criminal street gang members' from 'loitering' with one another or with other persons in any public place" (eventually overturned by *Chicago v. Morales,* 1999; quotation from pp. 45–46). Do you think this law gives adequate notice of what conduct is prohibited? How would you interpret what this law means? Alternatively, would you rule it void for vagueness? Explain.

Q Do you agree with the decision in *Lockyer v. Andrade?* In *Solem v. Helm?* In *Wilkerson v. Utah?* Explain your answers.

BOX 10.4

WHAT CONSTITUTES CRUEL AND UNUSUAL PUNISHMENT?

In 1789, one reader of the Eighth Amendment observed that "the clause appears to express much humanity, as such, he liked it; but as it appeared to have no meaning, he did not like it" (Veit, Rowling, & Bickford, 1991, p. 180).

It is the Supreme Court that ultimately serves as interpreter of the Eighth Amendment. But has the Court been able to find the meaning of cruel and unusual punishment? You be the judge. In *Ingraham v. Wright* (1977), the Court noted that it "limits the kinds of punishment that can be imposed of those convicted of crimes" (p. 667); in *Solem v. Helm* (1983), the Court indicated that "a criminal sentence must be proportionate to the [offender's] crime" (p. 290); in *Gregg v. Georgia* (1976), the Court specified that "the punishment must not involve the unnecessary and wanton infliction of pain" (p. 173); in *Rhodes v. Chapman* (1981), the Court applied it to "conditions [that] . . . deprive inmates of the minimal civilized measure of life's necessities" (p. 347); and in *Trop v. Dulles* (1958), the Court prohibited punishments that violate "evolving standards of decency that mark the progress of a maturing society" (p.101).

(continued)

BOX 10.4 (continued)

Q How would you define what constitutes cruel and unusual punishment? Do you agree with one or more of the above definitions? Would you develop your own test or set of criteria that would help you identify instances of cruel and unusual punishment? How would you apply your definition to the following issues? Is it cruel and unusual . . .

- to execute homicide offenders who are mentally retarded? The Supreme Court ruled "yes," cruel and unusual, in *Atkins v. Virginia*, 536 U.S. 304 (2002).
- to execute offenders who rape but do not kill an adult? The Supreme Court ruled "yes," cruel and unusual, in *Coker v. Georgia*, 433 U.S. 584 (1977).
- to execute offenders who rape but do not kill children under 12 years of age? The Supreme Court ruled "yes," cruel and unusual, in *Kennedy v. Louisiana*, 128 S. Ct. 2641 (2008).
- to execute an inmate with a three-drug combination, causing unconsciousness, inducing paralysis, and causing cardiac arrest? The Supreme Court ruled "no," not cruel and unusual, in *Baze v. Rees,* 553 U.S. 35 (2008).
- to give a sentence of life without parole for possession of 672 grams of cocaine? The Supreme Court ruled "no," not cruel and unusual, in *Harmelin v. Michigan*, 501 U.S. 957 (1991).
- to punish a person who falsified a document to defraud the government with 15 years of hard labor in chains? The Supreme Court ruled "yes," cruel and unusual, in *Weems v. U.S.*, 217 U.S. 349 (1910).
- to sentence a 17-year-old male who had consensual oral sex with a 15-year-old female to ten years in prison including lifetime registry as a sex offender? The Georgia Supreme Court ruled "yes," cruel and unusual, in *Humphrey v. Wilson*, 282 Ga. 520 (2007).
- to punish a natural-born U.S. citizen by revoking his or her citizenship rights? The Supreme Court ruled "yes," cruel and unusual, in *Trop v. Dulles*, 356 U.S. 86 (1958).
- to allow inmate exposure to high levels of secondhand smoke when prison staff show "deliberate indifference" (p. 30) to its potential medical effects? The Supreme Court ruled "yes" in *Helling v. McKinney,* 509 U.S. 25 (1993).
- as punishment for a prison rule infraction, to punch and kick a handcuffed inmate? The Supreme Court ruled "yes," cruel and unusual, in *Hudson v. McMillian,* 503 U.S. 1 (1992).
- to use physical punishment (i.e., whipping) on prison inmates? The 8th Circuit Court of Appeals ruled "yes," cruel and unusual, in *Jackson v. Bishop*, 404 F.2d 571 (1968).
- to prohibit an offender on probation for nonpayment of child support from having additional children? The Wisconsin Supreme Court ruled "no," not cruel and unusual, in *Wisconsin v. Oakley,* 629 N.W.2d 200 (2001).
- to punish an individual for a medical condition (i.e., addiction to narcotics)? The Supreme Court ruled "yes," cruel and unusual, in *Robinson v. California*, 370 U.S. 660 (1962).

Q How closely did your judgments match those of the courts? Do you see any patterns in what is or is not ruled as "cruel and unusual"?

The Future of Punishment

FOCUSING QUESTION 10.5

How might punishment change in the future?

Although punishment may initially seem to be a simple concept, it involves some fairly sophisticated questions, such as the following:

- What is punishment? How do we define it?
- What do we hope to accomplish through punishment? That is, what is the purpose of punishment?
- Should there be any limits on what kinds of punishments a society can impose? If so, what should those limits be?

After reading this chapter and considering the various issues that have been raised about the philosophy of punishment, how would you answer these questions? Bear in mind that philosophers, legal scholars, and social scientists have struggled with these very questions for centuries and have not been able to distill any absolute answers on which all can agree.

Punishment represents one of the ultimate powers held by the government in any society. Only government has the power to impose criminal punishments, and those punishments can take away rights commonly held by citizens, including the various deprivations noted at the beginning of the chapter. Criminal punishment can go further as well. Even after an offender is released from prison or probation, he or she may be denied the right to vote, to own firearms, to be licensed in certain professions, and even to live in certain areas. In short, the power to punish is precisely that—a far-reaching power of the state that merits close scrutiny.

Punishment is also ever changing. Philosophies about punishment change over time; the United States moved from rehabilitation as a guiding philosophy in the 1960s to incapacitation as a guiding philosophy in the 1980s. Notions of the dangerous classes change over time, given each era's biases and discriminations, but the idea that some groups are under closer surveillance than others has been constant across history. Ideas of the acceptability of certain punishments also change; the death penalty is much less accepted now than it has been previously in American history, but there may be an increased tolerance for lengthy prison sentences even for nonviolent offenders.

Finally, technological advances may change the landscape of punishment in the future. Fabelo (2000) writes of "technocorrections," in which new technologies may enable more sophisticated control of offenders. For instance, global positioning systems (GPS) allow probation officers to track the real-time movement of persons on probation. As tracking systems and computer technologies advance, could the future be a scenario where all known offenders may be tracked in real time on a publicly accessible Internet site? What would be the implications of this in terms of the justifications of punishment, the dangerous classes, and the Eighth Amendment? Ponder this question. Let it serve as an illustration of the importance of reflecting carefully on ideas about punishment.

Q How would you answer the questions posed in this section?

Q One concern about the future of corrections is that the reliance on incapacitation (and the new penology) costs too much money. What alternative punishment strategies could be used to maintain public safety while reducing costs?

Q If you were to design a system of punishment, what would it look like? Which ideas from this chapter would you incorporate? Which would you avoid? Why?

Conclusion

The power to impose punishment is arguably one of the most significant powers held by the state and federal governments. Following conviction for a crime, the government, through the criminal justice system, may compel individuals to surrender their money (through fines), their freedom (through jail and prison), or their lives (through the death penalty). Although punishments may be structured to accomplish a variety of objectives—retribution, deterrence, rehabilitation, incapacitation, or restoration—they must also comply with constitutional provisions primarily grounded in the Eighth Amendment. Like many elements within criminal justice, this illustrates the need for a balance between the achievement of punishment objectives, the protection of society, and the protection of rights. As we move to Unit V, we will turn to an exploration of the agencies within the criminal justice system—the police, courts, and corrections—who must work not only to enforce the law but also to strike the balances required by the Constitution, by notions of justice, and by concepts of law and morality. Their work is indeed challenging but is also necessary for an orderly society.

The Death Penalty

Criminal Justice Problem Solving

capital punishment
The death penalty.

The death penalty (also known as **capital punishment**) is without a doubt the most controversial current issue pertaining to criminal punishment. As society's most severe and final sanction, it merits careful study. The U.S. Supreme Court has acknowledged that "death is a punishment different from all other sanctions" (*Woodson v. North Carolina*, 1976, pp. 303–304), a notion which has led to a series of court cases judging the constitutionality of various aspects of the death penalty. Some cases were presented earlier in Box 10.2. Here we will begin with the two most foundational death penalty cases in modern history, as they have shaped the law by which the death penalty is administered.

In 1972, the Supreme Court temporarily halted executions in the case *Furman v. Georgia*. As a result, offenders who had been sentenced to death had their sentences commuted to prison terms instead. The Court in *Furman* expressed significant concern about how the death penalty was administered in the United States. Justice Stewart captured this sentiment when he wrote, "death sentences are cruel and unusual in the same way that being struck by lightning is cruel and unusual," arguing that they are "so wantonly and freakishly imposed" (pp. 309–310). There was evidence of significant racial discrimination and little consistency in when death sentences were, or were not, handed down.

States attempted to remedy their death penalty laws, and in 1976 the Supreme Court upheld Georgia's death penalty law in *Gregg v. Georgia;* other states using the death penalty followed suit with similar legislation. When charged with a crime that could result in the death penalty, the accused goes through a two-part, or bifurcated, trial. The first part is to determine guilt or innocence, following the standard procedures for criminal trials (as will be described in Chapter 12) with one exception—during jury selection, jurors must indicate if they would be willing to give a death sentence, and if not, they are excluded from the jury (this results in what is called a death-qualified jury). If found guilty, the same jury returns for what is known as the penalty phase, in which they must decide whether to sentence the offender to life in prison or death. In the penalty phase, the prosecution presents evidence of aggravating circumstances for the jury to consider, which are conditions that made the crime particularly heinous. A list of aggravating circumstances is enacted in the state legal code. The defense presents evidence of mitigating circumstances for the jury to also consider, which are factors that may diminish the offender's culpability or alleviate concerns about future dangerousness. If the jury finds beyond a reasonable doubt that one of the specified aggravating circumstances exists, they may issue a death sentence. If they do not, then they may not issue a death sentence.

As of this writing, the death penalty is utilized by 32 states, the federal government, and the U.S. military (Death Penalty Information Center, 2013). But since the Court's decision in *Gregg v. Georgia*, much debate has ensued about the use of capital punishment. In 2000, Illinois Governor George Ryan declared that no more executions would be conducted in his state until a comprehensive study of the death penalty had been completed. A commission studied capital punishment for two years, issuing a comprehensive report to the governor. On the basis of that report, in 2003, Governor Ryan commuted the death sentences (in almost all cases to life without parole) of Illinois inmates on death row due to concerns raised in the report (Turow, 2003). Many other states, and scholars, have engaged in similar studies of capital punishment.

What follows is a listing of some of the most common concerns cited about the death penalty. We provide this not to presuppose that you must oppose the death penalty, but rather because in death penalty debates, these are the issues that emerge from data and discussions. Most research indicates that the death penalty does not deter crime and in some cases may actually increase the homicide rate (e.g., Bailey, 1998); serious errors have been made in two-thirds of all death penalty cases (Gelman, Liebman, West, & Kiss, 2004);

Criminal Justice Problem Solving

continued

significant racial disparities exist in the use of the death penalty (e.g., Williams & Holcomb, 2001); there are concerns about the risk of executing innocent persons (e.g., Turow, 2003); there are concerns about whether persons accused of capital crimes have effective assistance of legal counsel (e.g., Bright, 2010); there are significant geographic disparities, both between states and within states, in terms of the likelihood of whether a death sentence will be sought in a capital murder case (e.g., Ditchfield, 2007); families of homicide victims do not always find closure following an execution (Vollum & Longmire, 2007); implementing the death penalty is very expensive, more so than life imprisonment, because of the legal processes that are involved (e.g., Maryland Commission on Capital Punishment, 2008); public support for the death penalty has declined over time (Gallup, 2013); it is possible that the execution process causes unnecessary pain due to inadequate policies and procedures for administration of lethal injection drugs (Koniaris, Zimmers, Lubarsky, & Sheldon, 2005); there are significant conflicts involving medical ethics regarding the participation of medical personnel in execution processes (Levy, 2005); and European democracies have banned the death penalty as a human rights violation (Zimring, 2003).

As even a brief discussion illustrates, there is quite a bit of debate on death penalty issues. Whether viewed as a means of achieving justice or an injustice, an acceptable penalty or something to be abolished, the issues listed above are those that most frequently surround the issue.

Q Do you think the process approved in *Gregg v. Georgia* remedies the concerns from *Furman v. Georgia*? Would you make any revisions to death sentencing processes?

Q Can the issues of concern pertaining to the death penalty be remedied? If so, how? If not, why not?

Q Arguments for and against the death penalty both invoke the morality of the issue. What moral arguments do you think each side would make?

Q How would you answer what is quickly becoming the most pressing issue facing the criminal justice system: what should be done about the death penalty? Keep it? Reform it? Abolish it?

Overview of Criminal Justice Institutions

Photo Essay: Toward the Future of Criminal Justice

Unit IV addressed the complexities of criminal law and punishment. This unit turns to an examination of the three primary components of the criminal justice system: the police, courts, and corrections. These are the agencies charged with enforcing the criminal law and determining and applying punishments. The work of the actors in the criminal justice process is profoundly shaped by the concepts in each of the previous units. As you read on, consider how issues of morality, deviance, justice, law, and punishment help to shape the role of the police, courts, and corrections.

Each of the chapters that follows provides some historical context for the development of the criminal justice system. Certainly, the criminal justice system is a dynamic entity, which must adapt to changing circumstances and questions about how to best accomplish important goals.

What can be done to increase school safety? Following the tragic 2012 school shooting at Sandy Hook Elementary School in Newtown, Connecticut, many states and localities debated this question. One proposal that received both conservative and liberal support was to place school resource officers (SROs) in more of the nation's schools, including the elementary school level. SROs are police officers who are assigned to work in schools; in addition to law enforcement and crime control functions, they may also assist in developing security measures for the school, work with students in a mentoring capacity, and assist in some classroom instruction on topics of crime and justice. Research on the impact of SROs on crime is mixed, some finding that programs are associated with a reduction in crime and others finding that they are not. There have been successful SRO programs in which the officers have made positive contributions to the school community (James & McCallion, 2013; Raymond, 2010). At the same time, critics argue that having police officers in schools escalates social control, causing "a surge in criminal charges against children for misbehavior that many believe is better handled" (Eckholm, 2013, para. 1) by the teacher, principal, or school authorities, such as "scuffles, truancy, and cursing at teachers" (para. 5). What role do you think SROs should play in schools? Are there any additional steps the police or others can take to address school safety concerns?

Should public areas be monitored by cameras to reduce crime? A simple truism of law enforcement is that it is not possible to place a police officer on every corner. However, technology can be used to supplement police coverage. For instance, London has one of the most noted closed circuit television (CCTV) systems with CCTV covering many city streets. Some of the cameras are equipped with speakers so camera operators may verbally caution potential offenders not to commit deviant acts. Some cameras also utilize facial recognition technology, in which faces recorded on camera are automatically compared to a database of persons wanted for arrest or questioning (see Grinnell & Burke, 2001). The cameras have assisted police in lowering crime rates and reducing fear of crime (Gill & Spriggs, 2005). However, other research has found CCTV to be much more limited in its effectiveness, with the most successful applications found to be in parking areas in the United Kingdom, and when CCTV is paired with other crime prevention measures; some have also argued that the use of CCTV raises privacy concerns (Welsh & Farrington, 2009). There has been debate about whether CCTV systems should be implemented on the streets of American cities. Is CCTV an effective use of police technology? Should it be implemented and, if so, where? If not, why?

How should juvenile offenders be processed under the law? Juveniles (in most jurisdictions, persons under 18) who commit serious offenses may sometimes be tried as adults, in spite of their age; this is known as waiving a juvenile to adult court. But what of juveniles who are not waived to adult court? There is a separate system of juvenile justice which could be (and often is) the subject of its own course. When a juvenile is arrested, the juvenile court has tremendous discretion in terms of how that juvenile is processed. In about half of all cases, juveniles do not go through a formal court process (that is, a proceeding with a judge) but instead either have their charges dismissed or are placed on what is sometimes called informal probation. In informal probation, a juvenile must agree to follow the law and other conditions imposed by a juvenile court officer and if he or she successfully does so, the charge is dismissed (see Sickmund, 2003). Research has found that being processed through the formal juvenile court system has detrimental effects, including an increased likelihood of further offending (Petrosino, Turpin-Petrosino, & Guckenburg, 2010). But that leaves the question—what can be done to address juvenile crime? What alternatives other than formal court processing could be used? In what cases do you think formal processing or waiver to adult court should occur?

How have media portrayals of technology affected courtroom proceedings? In what some have called the "CSI Effect" (Shelton, 2008, p. 2), anecdotal evidence suggests that jurors increasingly want to see the use of scientific evidence in criminal cases. For instance, in one survey, "46 percent [of persons completing the survey] expected to see some kind of scientific evidence in *every* criminal case" (p. 3). Expectations tended to be higher for persons who regularly watched the *CSI* television series. The same study found that persons surveyed would be willing to find a defendant guilty without scientific evidence if there was victim or witness testimony, but not in cases lacking scientific evidence and in which only circumstantial evidence had been presented. These findings led Shelton (2008) to suggest that either prosecutors and defense attorneys should acquire scientific evidence in more cases, or be deliberate in explaining to the jury why scientific evidence was not revelant in the case at hand. Should persons serving on a jury receive training on scientific evidence or other issues prior to hearing a case? In what other ways can the media shape perceptions of the police, courts, or corrections?

How can criminal justice agencies prepare for pandemic flu? Attention to pandemic preparedness increased in the early 2000s. A pandemic, usually occurring with a new strain of flu to which the population does not have immunity, spreads quickly across large areas and places great strain on the health care system, which may not (at least initially) have sufficient resources to quickly address it (About Pandemics, n.d.). Consider the impact of pandemics on probation and parole. It is possible that probation and parole officers could be off work due to illness; preparedness planning "recommends assuming that up to 40% of workers could be absent for as long as two weeks" (Bancroft, 2009, p. 9) in each of multiple waves of illness. In addition, during a pandemic, social distancing is recommended, which refers to avoiding contact with other persons to avoid potential spread of the virus. Yet probation officers must meet with others frequently, both in and outside their offices, as part of their daily work. And officers must be aware that some offenders or their families will become ill, possibly causing them to miss work, miss appointments, or require hospitalization. How would supervision of persons on probation or parole change in a pandemic? What recommendations would you make about how probation and parole officers should approach their work in that circumstance?

Can animal training programs in prison be used to serve the community while also providing benefits to inmate participants? Prisons initially would seem an unlikely place for pets. However, a number of facilities have recognized that Prison Pup Programs can benefit inmates and the community alike (Harkrader, Burke, & Owen, 2004). In the programs, inmates are taught to train service dogs. During training, the dogs spend some time in the prison receiving training and some time with caregivers in the community. After being trained, the dogs enter the community and are paired with persons who benefit from the services they can provide. Research has found that the inmates do benefit from this kind of program, appreciating the ability to help others through their work. In addition, programs can aid in keeping the facility calm and in conveying a greater sense of freedom among inmate participants. Finally, programs are associated with the promotion of "patience . . . parenting skills . . . self esteem . . . [and] social skills" (Turner, 2007, pp. 39–41). If you were a correctional administrator, how would you assess this program? What issues would you have to consider when planning for the implementation of the program?

The work completed by police, court, and correctional personnel forms the backbone of the criminal justice system in the United States. As the examples presented illustrate, the criminal justice system constantly strives to develop new programming alternatives that can help to achieve goals including the maintenance of public safety, the enforcement of the law, and the rehabilitation of offenders. The chapters in Unit V will further explore the origins, development, and current practices of the agencies within the criminal justice system.

11

Core Concepts of U.S. Policing

Learning Objectives

1 Describe the history and philosophies of policing. **2** Explain the culture of policing. **3** Describe the structure of American law enforcement. **4** Identify ethical issues that may arise in policing. **5** Describe how policing strategies have developed over time.

Key Terms

police
political era
professional era
thin blue line
community problem-solving era
watchman style
legalistic style
service style
broken windows policing
working personality
ethics
hot spots policing
community-oriented policing (COP)
problem-oriented policing (POP)
Compstat
focused deterrence

Key People

William Muir
Sir Robert Peel
George Kelling
Mark Moore
James Q. Wilson
Jerome Skolnick
William Westley
Arthur Niederhoffer
Lawrence Sherman
Carl Klockars
Samuel Walker
Herman Goldstein

Policing a Housing Development

Case Study

The New Briarfield Apartments were located in Newport News, Virginia, an East Coast city with 155,000 residents. The apartment complex consisted of 400 one-story wooden units, each containing 4 to 16 apartments arranged in linear groups. Built in the 1940s, the apartments were originally designed and built as temporary housing facilities for workers at a World War II era shipyard. The apartments later served as public housing for low-income families. By the 1980s, the apartments were regarded as one of the worst housing developments in the city.

The apartment residents were primarily low-income African Americans living in female-headed households. Residents lived in fear of crime, sometimes afraid to leave their individual apartments. The apartments had a high crime rate, particularly burglary; for instance, 23% of the occupied units were broken into each year. Twenty percent of the units were vacant, some of which provided hiding places for drug users or dealers. With such a high vacancy rate, it was nearly impossible for the owners of the complex to make a profit; in fact, the owners were facing foreclosure of the property. Over time, the property had physically deteriorated as the temporary structures became run down, conveying the appearance that the facility was not well cared for. Litter, abandoned vehicles, and potholes marked the landscape.

In the 1980s, the city police department had 234 officers and 46 civilian employees. The police tried to respond with traditional strategies—such as patrol, response to calls for service, and occasional efforts by special task forces—but they were proven ineffective (Eck & Spelman, 1987; Wilson & Kelling, 1989). The city purchased the property and demolished the complex in the late 1980's (Davidson, 1989). For a moment, however, assume that this apartment complex still exists. Further assume that you are now the commander of the police district in which the apartments are located, and your chief, the fire chief, and other city agencies are demanding that you "do something" to improve the area and make it safer.

Q What additional information would you want about the New Briarfield Apartment Complex before taking action? Why would this information be useful?

Facing page: Police officer with children in a housing community. What role do you think the police should play in society?

Q What are some potential strategies you could use to reduce crime at the apartment complex? Why do you think these strategies would have the potential to be successful?

Q What other agencies or groups (public or private) could you collaborate with to improve the New Briarfield Apartment Complex? How would working together help improve the situation?

Philosophies of Policing

FOCUSING QUESTION 11.1

How has the police role in society changed over time?

The very mention of the word *police* often evokes a response, sometimes positive, sometimes negative. These responses are often shaped by personal contacts with the police. "In 2008, an estimated 16.9% of U.S. residents age 16 or older had face-to-face contact with police" (Eith & Durose, 2011, p. 1), most for traffic-related issues such as a traffic stop or accident. In most instances, even when treated as a suspect of a crime, persons rated police actions as being respectful and proper to the situation. Perceptions changed notably when police use of force was involved; "most persons who experienced force felt it was excessive" (Eith & Durose, 2011, p. 12). Perceptions of the police are also based on factors other than direct encounters, including stories from friends and relatives, relating their encounters with police officers; media portrayals of police activities, whether through the news or through entertainment programming; and philosophies of moral and ethical behavior and their application to the law enforcement function.

This chapter explores the institution of policing in American society by examining how conceptions of police duties have changed over time, the philosophies of policing that officers bring to the job, the organization of the law enforcement function in the United States, ethical issues faced by police officers, and strategies used by law enforcement agencies to respond to crime and disorder. As you read this chapter, consider how the concepts of law, morality, and justice discussed earlier in the book might also apply to the policing function.

The police role in society is shaped by three key concepts: order maintenance, the right to legitimately use force, and the exercise of discretion. Policing scholar Jerome Skolnick (1966) observed that "the **police** in a democratic society are required to maintain order and to do so under the rule of law" (p. 6). To return to the concept of social control described in Chapter 4, the police are agents of formal social control, ensuring that society's laws are enforced. Functioning under the rule of law also means that the police must follow legally prescribed procedures in enforcing law and order, such as those established in the Bill of Rights, as described in the coverage of procedural justice in Chapter 8.

police
A formal agent of social control and component of the criminal justice system responsible for law enforcement and the maintenance of order.

When enforcing law and maintaining order, the "police are . . . given the right to use coercive force by the state within the state's domestic territory" (Klockars, 1985b, p. 12). This means that a police officer acting within his or her official capacity to maintain order can use whatever force is reasonable and necessary, up to and including deadly force, to protect citizens or officers from imminent harm.

As noted in Chapter 1, the presence of discretion is a fundamental attribute of the criminal justice system. In their daily work, police officers must make many discretionary decisions, and these often relate to distributive justice (as defined in Chapter 6). Discretion is common in policing for a variety of reasons, including the following: limited resources and agency priorities make it impossible to enforce all laws equally all of the time; citizen demands may lead police agencies to focus more extensively on some

laws at the expense of others; and there is sometimes a need for professional judgment made by police officers on a case-by-case basis (consider whether there is ever an "excusable" reason for speeding, for instance). Quite simply, discretion is not unusual; in fact, it is an everyday occurrence in police work (Klockars, 1985b). At the same time, making discretionary decisions is a substantial power held by the police officer on the street which, in part, led William Muir (1977) to describe the police as "streetcorner politicians" (p. 271).

For centuries, the police function has been defined by the duty to enforce law and maintain order with the ability to use force in doing so, all while exercising discretion. However, the application of these principles has changed over time. To better understand the philosophy of policing, we must explore the history of policing.

POLICING IN ENGLAND

We begin our journey in London, England, during the early nineteenth century. London is significant because much of the American criminal justice system was heavily influenced by the English model and because London was the location of the first, modern, organized police department.

In 1829, the first metropolitan police department was formed in England by Sir Robert Peel. Robert Peel was the Home Secretary, responsible for internal security in England, not unlike the U.S. Departments of Justice and of Homeland Security. London was having its share of public disorders, including riots. Peel's goal was to develop a police force that would effectively and efficiently curtail riots, public disorder, and crime. Furthermore, Peel's officers, named Bobbies in a tribute to his first name, were to accomplish these goals without the use of firearms. For personal protection, Bobbies carried only a small truncheon (club) under their coat. To this day, with a few exceptions, British police officers do not carry firearms; furthermore, surveys of British officers find a preference against carrying firearms, even though they can and do face dangerous situations. This is a notable difference from policing in most other countries (Kelly, 2012).

Peel strongly advocated for proactive policing, believing that Bobbies should work to "prevent" crime before it occurs rather than to "react" to crime after it is committed. A positive police–community relationship was also central to Peel's vision, as he argued that the police patrol should provide opportunities for police–public interactions and that the police should act respectfully toward citizens. Finally, Peel believed that officers should be carefully selected and well trained to fulfill their duties (Roberg, Crank, & Kuykendall, 2000).

Peel's law enforcement philosophy proved quite successful in England. Although policing developed around the same time in the United States, it took a very different form. In fact, early policing in the United States was nothing short of chaos, and it took more than 100 years for American policing to aspire to Peel's principles. According to police scholars Kelling and Moore (1988; see also Fogelson, 1977), three historical eras helped shape the role of the police in the United States: the *political era* (1830s to early 1900s), the *professional era* (1930s to 1970s), and the *community problem-solving era* (1970s to present). It was only in the community problem-solving era that American policing began to meet all of Peel's principles. More recent scholars (Oliver, 2006) have suggested that a fourth era of policing—the *homeland security era*—has emerged in the years following the attacks of September 11, 2001.

In reviewing the eras of policing, it is important to see each "metaphorically, providing us with ways to crystallize the complexities of history in simplified terms" (Williams & Murphy, 1990, p. 1). As such, the dates are not firm starting and ending points, and not all police agencies met all characteristics of each era. However, understanding the themes of each era can aid in understanding the historical development of the police in America.

THE POLITICAL ERA (1830s–EARLY 1900s)

political era
The era of American policing from the 1830s to the early 1900s, in which policing was characterized by political undertones and police officers and agencies often fell under the control and influence of local politicians. The era was marked by high levels of corruption.

The **political era** was America's introduction to policing (for a comparison of English and American policing in this time period, see Miller, 1975). As its name implies, early policing in the United States was characterized by political undertones, which bordered on all-out corruption. The police and local politicians frequently had an intimate relationship encouraged by decentralization.

Decentralization means that there is not one central law enforcement agency but rather that each geographic area, whether city, town, or county, has its own police force. This also means that there is not a central philosophy accepted by all law enforcement agencies. Fearful of a strong central government, Americans found local policing more acceptable than having a single national police agency.

Having individual agencies in each jurisdiction allowed for early police forces to be controlled by local politicians, often town council members or the mayor. Rather than serving the public good, the police often engaged in favoritism, sustaining those who supported them. In some departments, officers obtained their jobs by bribing political leaders. For instance, in New York City, promotions once went to the highest bidder: "The going rate in New York was $1,600 for sergeants and $12,000–$15,000 for captains . . . More often the party leaders gave promotions to political favorites" (Fogelson, 1977, p. 29).

Early police officers often lacked professionalism. Reports ranged from regular evasion of duty and drunkenness on the job to "mutual disrespect and brutality . . . between the police and the public" and overlooking criminal activity in exchange for bribes (Walker, 1980, p. 63). Officers were also expected to promote the agenda of the politicians who had appointed them, sometimes even interfering in elections to ensure that the party in power would continue to win at the voting polls.

The police were sometimes used as pawns in larger political disputes as well. In 1853, the New York State legislature became concerned about the amount of power that New York City had accumulated under its mayor at the time, Fernando Wood. In response, the state government established a new New York City police force, under state control (the "Metropolitans"), but did not disband the old police force, which was under city control (the "Municipals"). A riot occurred between the two police forces on the steps of City Hall and "whenever a cop of one force made an arrest, a cop of the other would set the culprit free, and the competing forces routinely raided each other's station houses and freed en masse the prisoners in each other's jails" (Sante, 1991, p. 239).

Some have suggested that the police were able to build community relations during the political era. Police were often selected and assigned to their patrol detail based on their political affiliation, personal contacts, and ethnicity (e.g., Italian officers patrolled the Italian district, Irish officers patrolled the Irish district, etc.). As a result, the police were familiar with their communities and their respective power structures. The police sometimes provided social assistance, such as providing housing and food for the homeless and needy (see Wagner, 2008). However, this was often done for political benefit. If the police helped citizens in the neighborhood, citizens would feel appreciative toward the police, who could then encourage them to support their local politicians at election time. As was typical of the political era, benefits for local politicians were a primary interest (Fogelson, 1977; Kelling & Moore, 1988).

A significant problem that arose during the political era was police discrimination against strangers to the community and members of different ethnic and racial groups. Officers treated these individuals as members of the "dangerous classes," often using brutal force against them. Simply stated, in the political era, it was nearly impossible to maintain a sense of organizational control, leading to police agencies that were ineffective, inefficient, disorganized, and corrupt (Fogelson, 1977; Kelling & Moore, 1988).

Walker (1984) unflatteringly summarized the priorities of police officers in the political era as follows:

> The first was to get and hold the job. The second was to exploit the possibilities for graft [bribery and payoffs] that the job offered. A third was to do as little actual patrol work as possible. A fourth involved surviving on the street, which meant establishing and maintaining authority in the face of hostility and overt challenges to that authority. Finally, officers apparently felt obliged to go through the motions of "real" police work by arresting occasional miscreants. (p. 87)

Clearly, it was time for policing to change.

THE PROFESSIONAL ERA (1930s–1970s)

Political era police agencies were in need of reform, and several factors led to their reform. First, journalists (known as "muckrakers") published articles criticizing the corruption of local governments and called for reform (e.g., Steffens, [1904] 1992). Second, there was an emerging public philosophy promoting good government, which came to be known as the Progressive Movement. Supporters of the movement advocated for civil service (i.e., selection of government employees based on qualifications rather than favoritism), dismantling local political corruption, and encouraging government professionalism. Third, technology led to tactical change. Patrol in automobiles became the central new strategy used by police agencies, made possible in part by radio communication and dispatch. The justification was simple: criminals increasingly had cars, so police should have them as well. The move to motorized patrol replaced the neighborhood-centered policing networks that had been a defining feature of the political era.

The professional era, frequently referred to as the reform era, was led by noted reformers such as former Berkeley, California, police chief August Vollmer, his protégé (and chief of Fullerton, California and Wichita, Kansas, police departments, and later superintending of the Chicago Police Department) Orlando W. Wilson, and Federal Bureau of Investigation Director J. Edgar Hoover. The primary goal of the **professional era** was to remove the political element from policing. This was accomplished in part by organizational changes, such as adopting a military model or rank structure and discipline for police agencies, creating hierarchies that allowed more effective supervision of officers, and developing specialized units (e.g., detective bureaus) to focus on key tasks.

professional era
The era of policing from the 1930s to the 1970s focused on reform, professionalism, and removing political influence from policing.

As the name suggests, during the professional era, police agencies also strived to become more professional. Policing was to be viewed as a profession with training programs, a public service motivation, and an ethical code (similar to doctors, lawyers, teachers, and engineers). Police officers were expected to meet high admission standards, to undergo extensive training, and to be free from corruption.

The professional era's focus was on crime control, crime prevention, and offender apprehension characterized by rapid responses to calls for police service and the use of preventive patrols. It was assumed that the faster the officer responded to a call for service, the greater the chance of apprehending the offender. In addition, police presence was believed to serve as a visual deterrent to potential law violators.

Officers were encouraged to distance themselves from the community in order to minimize the potential for favoritism. This style of policing was often characterized by television's *Dragnet* character Sergeant Friday, who coined the phrase "just the facts, ma'am; just the facts." The role of the police was to respond to a call, learn the facts, respond to them, and leave, without an emphasis on community interaction.

During this time and even to the modern day, policing in the United States has remained decentralized. In the professional era, the Federal Bureau of Investigation and other national law enforcement agencies developed, but the majority of police work was

and continues to be performed at the local level. Yet, even with decentralization, there was a greater emphasis on the consistency of professional practice across agencies. This was accomplished through the efforts of organizations such as the International Association of Chiefs of Police and through the Supreme Court's role in resolving cases about what are and are not proper police practices from a constitutional perspective (many of which focus on the procedural justice concerns described in Chapter 8).

The professional era certainly was an improvement on the corrupt political era, but it was not without its limitations. By creating an impersonal, detached police officer who worked primarily from the confines of a police vehicle, the police and the public were isolated from one another. This created an "us" versus "them" mentality, sometimes known as a **thin blue line** between the police and public. Furthermore, by reducing foot patrol, personal contact between the police and the community was effectively limited to police responses to calls for service. This meant that police–citizen contacts were limited to negative situations in which citizens only saw the police when they were victimized by or accused of committing a crime.

thin blue line
In policing, a division between the police and the public stemming from limited contact between police and public and from an "us" versus "them" mentality sometimes held by police officers. Also associated with the solidarity that emerges among police officers.

According to Kelling and Moore (1988), the professional era was successful during the 1940s and 1950s because social stability prevailed in those decades. However, the 1960s and 1970s were a time of social change, including "the civil rights movement; migration of minorities into cities; the changing age of the population (more youths and teenagers); increases in crime and fear; increased oversight of police actions by courts and the decriminalization and deinstitutionalization movements" (p. 85). As a result of these changes, as well as some instances of police conflict with minority communities, police administrators and scholars began to consider the value of promoting better police–community relations.

THE COMMUNITY PROBLEM-SOLVING ERA (1970s–PRESENT)

The goals of **community problem-solving era** policing are broader than those of the professional era, consisting of crime control, crime prevention, and police–community problem solving, including the use of community-oriented policing (COP) and problem-oriented policing (POP) (discussed later in this chapter). Two government reports in the 1960s emphasized the importance of police–community relations: the *Report by the President's Commission on Law Enforcement and Administration of Justice* (1967) and the *Report of the National Advisory Commission on Civil Disorders* (1968).

community problem-solving era
The era of policing from the 1970s to the present when the goals of the professional era were broadened to include not only crime control but also crime prevention and strengthened police-community relations and collaborations.

It is also worth noting that the values of the community era are politically popular. For instance, in 1994, President Bill Clinton promised in his State of the Union Address to provide funding to communities to put 100,000 new police officers on the street to be deployed in community policing roles (see also Oliver, 2000).

The success of the community problem-solving era of policing is predicated on cooperation and communication between the police and the community. Under this strategy, effective policing cannot be accomplished with detached, impersonal officers; thus, police agencies must adapt their operating philosophies and training programs for community era strategies to be successful.

A community era strategy includes revisiting the days of foot patrol. When foot patrol was the primary means of police patrol, the officer was able to form social bonds within the community. This provided an opportunity for information sharing between the officer and community members. Kelling and Moore (1988) note that in addition to foot patrol, the community era is characterized by

> problem solving, information gathering, victim counseling and services, community organizing and consultation, education, walk-and-ride and knock-on-door programs, as well as regular patrol, specialized patrol, and rapid response to emergency calls for service. Emphasis is placed on information sharing . . . to increase the possibility of crime solution and clearance. (p. 91)

Although the community problem-solving era is a work in progress, it is designed to aid law enforcement, improve the quality of life of its citizenry, and promote citizen satisfaction. While the values of the community problem-solving era still underlie many police activities, Oliver (2006) believes that policing has turned toward a fourth era of policing—the homeland security era.

THE POLICE AND HOMELAND SECURITY: A NEW ERA?

Following the tragic September 11, 2001, terrorist attacks on the World Trade Center buildings in New York City, the Pentagon in Arlington, Virginia, and the downing of the hijacked Flight 93 outside Shanksville, Pennsylvania, attention quickly focused on issues related to homeland security. Less than two weeks after the attacks, President George W. Bush created the White House Office of Homeland Security. By the end of 2002, the U.S. Congress had enacted legislation creating the federal Department of Homeland Security (DHS), which consolidated into one department a variety of agencies with responsibility for homeland security functions (for a historical discussion, see Kettl, 2007). This includes the following law enforcement agencies: U.S. Customs and Border Protection, U.S. Citizenship and Immigration Services, U.S. Immigration and Customs Enforcement, the U.S. Secret Service, the Transportation Security Administration, the U.S. Coast Guard, and the Federal Law Enforcement Training Center (U.S. Department of Homeland Security, 2013).

According to the Department of Homeland Security's official webpage, the DHS mission includes five key areas, which are: "1. Prevent terrorism and enhancing security; 2. Secure and manage our borders; 3. Enforce and administer our immigration laws; 4. Safeguard and secure cyberspace; [and] 5. Ensure resilience to disasters" (U.S. Department of Homeland Security, n.d., para. 7). Note that these mission areas focus on law enforcement functions. As a result, homeland security is an important issue for law enforcement. In addition, these mission areas also go beyond traditional law enforcement, to include domestic and foreign intelligence, information technology, public health, emergency planning, and more. In contributing to homeland security functions, law enforcement agencies inevitably work with professionals in other fields who share a common interest in homeland security.

The significance of homeland security has only grown over time, as many issues have come to be defined as homeland security matters (Kettl, 2007). In addition, the concept of homeland security itself continues to evolve, as new policies and new understandings of preparedness emerge (Caudle, 2012). As noted above, Oliver (2006) has argued that homeland security has become the fourth era of policing. According to Oliver (2006):

> The function of police under Homeland Security is marked by a more focused concentration of its resources into crime control for it is through crime control, enforcement of the criminal law, traffic law, etc., that many potential threats can be exposed and intelligence gathered. In addition, police have begun to take on the role of anti-terrorism by focusing on various passive measures that can reduce the vulnerabilities of their communities to future terrorist attacks. Much of this is being done through local threat assessments, intelligence gathering and intergovernmental information sharing. Another added function of the police is counter terrorism which are those offensive measures taken to respond to terrorist acts through the process of preparedness training, creation of emergency . . . operations centers, large-scale crisis intervention and special reaction team training. Moreover, the collection, processing and analysis of intelligence are also becoming a necessary and crucial function of the police in this current era. (p. 54)

It is important to note that even prior to the events of September 11, 2001, policing was changing. For instance, Kraska and Cubellis (1997) observed that there has

been a "normalization of small-locality police paramilitary units" (p. 607), such as emergency response or SWAT teams, which they call "militarizing Mayberry" (p. 607) (coined after the fictional small town portrayed on television in *The Andy Griffith Show*). This may be attributed to the war on drugs, national police reform efforts, intelligence gathering, and the goal of modernizing criminal justice in general. According to Kraska and Cubellis (1997), an emphasis on paramilitary models of policing has extended beyond large cities and has entered into small-town America, all in the name of security.

According to both Oliver (2006) and Kraska and Cubellis (1997), with greater attention devoted to homeland security and intelligence gathering come potential risks for violations of civil liberties. As a result, the standards for selection, hiring, and training of police officers in this new era of policing may need to be revised and enhanced (Kraska & Cubellis, 1997). Officers must be well-prepared through training and education to strike the appropriate balances between homeland security and civil liberties.

DEVELOPMENTAL THEORIES OF POLICING

As you can see, policing has changed substantially over the past 200 years. Thus far, the discussion has explored *how* policing has changed. A related question is, *why* did we need police in the first place? There is not agreement on the answer to this question. Roberg et al. (2000) provide four theories to explain the development of the police as an institution; scholars disagree about which most accurately explains the emergence of policing. The four theories are disorder theory, crime control theory, urban dispersion theory, and class control theory. The first three theories focus on the role of the police in responding to crime; the fourth focuses on a perspective critical of the historical roots of law enforcement.

Similar to London, many cities in the United States were plagued by riots in the early 1800s. The disorder theory focuses on large-scale disruptive events, suggesting that police agencies were developed to suppress this sort of mob violence. Simply stated, police were needed to curtail large-scale public disorder.

Crime control theory focuses on more "routine," though widespread, forms of disorder. Advocates of the crime control theory believe that as crime increased, social order and systems of informal social control were threatened. This created a public fear of crime, and the police were needed to curb both crime and the fear of crime. This theory supports the notion that as informal social control becomes less effective, formal social control takes over. In this case, as informal social control was perceived to diminish, law enforcement filled the void to provide social order.

The philosophy behind the urban dispersion theory asserted that as cities grew, both predators and potential victims moved to the city, increasing vulnerability to urban crime. Therefore, crime became identified as an urban problem. To combat it, the police were necessary as integral components of urban society to ensure stability (see Monkkonen, 1988).

The class control theory suggests that as urban and industrial growth increased, people from various social and ethnic backgrounds competed for jobs to improve their social status. Similar to conflict theory presented in Chapter 5, class control theory suggested that the modern police were created by the rich and powerful to control the "dangerous classes" and to prevent their upward mobility in society. Policing efforts sometimes targeted the working class. In some cities, the police disrupted strikes, in which workers were advocating for improved working conditions, and aggressively enforced laws regarding issues such as alcohol and gambling in working-class establishments (see Harring, 1983). In a critique of Kelling and Moore's (1988) eras of policing, Williams and Murphy (1990) also noted that there were many discriminatory practices embedded with policing, arguing that only in the community problem-solving era was there the opportunity for correcting past inequalities. For instance, early law

enforcement was called upon to enforce laws pertaining to slavery and then later the Jim Crow laws that allowed racial segregation, which created discord between the police and African American communities. In addition, law enforcement was slow to pursue hiring of minorities and women as fully equal officers, which left departments unrepresentative of the population they were serving.

Q Do you believe that politics still plays a role in policing? If so, how?

Q A key assumption of the professional era is that education benefits police officers. What are the advantages and disadvantages of requiring a college education for police officers?

Q How would you implement community era strategies to address the New Briarfield Apartment situation described at the beginning of the chapter?

Q How would police strategies differ based on each developmental theory noted in this section?

The Culture of Policing

FOCUSING QUESTION 11.2

How does organizational culture influence the police role?

To better appreciate the philosophy of policing, it is important to return to the concept of organizational culture, as described in Chapter 1. As Wilson (1989) observed, "Every organization has a culture, that is, a persistent, patterned way of thinking about the central tasks of and human relationships within an organization. Culture is to an organization what personality is to an individual" (p. 91). Aspects of organizational culture include an agency's norms, values, language, mission, and more. Organizational cultures shape, and are shaped by, the perspectives brought by individuals in the organization, itself. Scholars have studied police organizations and police officer personalities to explore how they influence police practice and behavior.

WILSON'S STYLES OF POLICE BEHAVIOR

In his classic book, *Varieties of Police Behavior*, James Q. Wilson (1974) describes three styles of policing. They are the watchman style, the legalistic style, and the service style. In some cases, an entire department may have one of these styles as its primary focus; in other cases, individual officers within a department may approach their work drawing upon one of these styles.

The central theme of the **watchman style** of policing is keeping the peace and not making waves. Watchman officers are passive and reactive. They will likely ignore many infractions, especially minor ones, and are not concerned about community relations or service calls. The watchman police use whatever discretionary powers are deemed appropriate to maintain order, including the use of informal intervention rather than exercising formal legal authority (e.g., confiscating alcohol from a juvenile rather than charging the juvenile with underage possession). "A watchman-like department is as interested in avoiding trouble as in minding its own business" (Wilson, 1974, pp. 147–148); officers functioning under such a model do not want to draw attention to themselves. Although they certainly will respond to major incidents with their full authority, their overarching goal is to maintain a low profile as long as things in their jurisdiction are doing reasonably well.

At the other extreme of policing is the **legalistic style**. Whether a minor infraction or a major crime, officers strive to enforce the law with the full force of their authority in *every* case. Success is measured by productivity; productivity is measured by statistics. Therefore, the greater the number of arrests and traffic tickets, the more productive the officer and the more successful the agency. Under the legalistic style philosophy,

watchman style
A style of police behavior described by James Q. Wilson in which the purpose of policing is viewed as keeping the peace and not making waves. Officers operating under the watchman style are passive and reactive.

legalistic style
A style of police behavior in which the purpose of policing is to enforce all laws with the full force of police authority in all cases. Officers operating under the legalistic style enforce all laws strictly with little exercise of discretion and measure productivity by statistics, such as number of arrests or tickets.

officers enforce the law because they believe it is the right thing to do—morally, ethically, and legally. Legalistic officers might be heard to say, "We don't make the laws; we simply enforce them." And enforce them they do, with vigor and enthusiasm and with little interest in exercising discretion. Here, "the law is the law," and it must be enforced without consideration of individual circumstances. In this system, the police do not have close interactions with the public. However, they do treat everyone similarly—which usually means vigilantly monitoring for any offenses and giving a ticket or making an arrest for all offenses that are detected.

service style
A style of police behavior in which policing is understood to draw upon the use of discretion to determine the most appropriate response to any given situation. Officers operating under the service style view each situation in its own context and prefer to resolve problems with arrest as a last resort.

The **service style** falls somewhere between the watchman and legalistic styles. Consistent with the values of the community problem-solving era, service style policing is based on the use of discretion to determine the most appropriate response to a situation. Officers are willing to enforce the law aggressively and make arrests when necessary. However, they are also likely to view arrests as a last resort and to prefer seeking alternative solutions to problems. Like the watchman style, officers utilize informal social control to solve problems. Unlike the watchman style, officers are actively engaged with the community, performing routine police work, crime prevention activities, and community service activities, all the while striving to use all of the resources at their disposal to make a community a safe and pleasant place to live without relying on arrests or citations as the only option for doing so.

Therefore, the service style is a proactive approach, seeking to resolve dilemmas and problems before they escalate or to prevent crime in the first place, in both cases exercising discretionary decision making. The legal style, on the other hand, is reactive, responding to offenses with swift and formal enforcement of the laws with little to no discretion. The watchman style is neither reactive nor proactive, instead focused on minimizing police intervention into a situation unless absolutely necessary, and even then at the lowest acceptable level. These styles make for wide variation in how a

Sheriff's deputies respond to a noise complaint at a party attended by 200 persons, mostly teenagers. "Two people were arrested for drinking in public after police said they found large quantities of alcohol at the house and partygoers hiding in bathrooms and closets" (Show, 2012, para. 3). In addition, "parents of minors attending the party were notified by police to come pick up their children" (Show, 2012, para. 9). Which of Wilson's styles of policing does this illustrate, and why? Do you agree or disagree with how the deputies responded to the party?

situation can be handled, depending on the approach taken by different officers or agencies. Box 11.1 discusses broken windows policing. Consider how the three styles just described would apply to the strategy.

BOX 11.1

BROKEN WINDOWS

Is there a relationship between crime and the physical environment? Numerous theories suggest that there is. One of the best known is "broken windows" theory, which was advanced by policing scholars James Q. Wilson and George L. Kelling (1982). The theory suggests that visible signs of disorder can lead to more serious crime. Signs of disorder include physical characteristics of an area, such as broken windows, or actions that occur there, such as loitering. When a neighborhood has signs of disorder, it reflects a lack of caring. This can signal to potential offenders that the neighborhood is ripe for victimization. In addition, if residents perceive their neighborhood as disorderly, they may become fearful and avoid interacting with others outside their homes, resulting in weakened informal social controls. The culmination of these effects is that crime in the area will increase, and the cycle will repeat itself, with the disorder and resulting crime increasing in severity with each repetition.

Broken windows theory does suggest a solution to the foregoing cycle—namely, that if the signs of disorder can be addressed early, then more serious criminal activity can be prevented. **Broken windows policing** is a strategy to reduce disorder in neighborhoods. One form of broken windows policing involves officers "*paying attention* to minor offenses that were essentially ignored in the past" (Sousa & Kelling, 2006, p. 89). This can be done by making arrests, but as described in New York City, "officers . . . were much more likely to informally warn, educate, scold, or verbally reprimand citizens who violated minor offenses . . . officers were mindful of the moral complexities behind their activities" (Sousa & Kelling, 2006, p. 89).

broken windows policing
A strategy to reduce disorder in neighborhoods which focuses police attention on enforcement of minor offenses.

Another form of broken windows policing, much more controversial, is a zero-tolerance approach (see Taylor, 2006) in which *all* perceived disorders are addressed through *formal* police action (arrests or citations). For example, residents may be told to keep their lawns cut or face mandatory fines. Or the police might aggressively enforce laws against all instances of loitering or panhandling (that is, asking passersby for money).

Underlying the above policing strategies is the conceptualization of broken windows theory as a straightforward relationship between disorder and crime, in which the former causes the latter. However, more recent research has suggested that the dynamics are more complex. *Collective efficacy* is a term that refers to "cohesion and mutual trust among neighbors" (Sampson & Raudenbush, 2001, p. 2), which can lead to strong informal social control in a neighborhood. Sampson and Raudenbush (2001) found that collective efficacy was more important than disorder in predicting crime. Areas with high levels of collective efficacy had lower levels of both crime and disorder; in fact, strong collective efficacy was associated with lower levels of crime, even when some disorder was present. This suggests that promoting collective efficacy is a means of reducing both crime and disorder.

- Q What types of disorder do you think might be associated with crime? Why?
- Q What are the advantages and disadvantages of each form of broken windows policing described in this box? Would you utilize this strategy if you were a police chief?In what ways could collective efficacy be developed in a neighborhood? What role could the police play in doing so?
- Q How do you think the watchman, legalistic, and service styles of policing would differ in terms of the responses each would suggest for reducing disorder and increasing collective efficacy?
- Q How could any of the theories described above be applied to the New Briarfield case? Should they be?

POLICE OFFICER PERSONALITIES

Wilson's styles of policing explain three different approaches to police work that can reflect an agency's organizational culture. Other research has explored attributes of officers themselves, which can influence how they approach the job. Several studies are described in this section. Certainly, not all officers demonstrate all attributes described, but taken together, the attributes create what has come to be known as the police officer personality. There is a debate about the source of the police officer personality (see Owen & Wagner, 2008). Some have argued that it is the product of organizational culture, meaning that the working environment of law enforcement produces the attributes described below; others have argued that individuals with these attributes are drawn to policing as a career; and others still suggest that both could have an influence. Regardless, consider how the various attributes of the police officer personality could impact police work.

Jerome Skolnick (1966) noted several qualities of police work that, taken together, make up an officer's "**working personality**" (p. 42). These qualities include:

working personality
Refers to the occupational culture of policing, reflecting elements of police work including danger, authority, social isolation, and solidarity.

- Danger, referring to the risks inherent in police work;
- Authority, reflecting an officer's legal right to make arrests and to use force in appropriate circumstances;
- Social isolation, indicating that police officers often find themselves isolated or removed from other members of the public; and
- Solidarity, in which officers associate primarily with other officers, viewing their colleagues as members of a family bound together by their work.

These values often overlap in police work. For instance, due to the dangerous nature of policing (e.g., confronting armed subjects), police may seek to control situations by creating social distance or separation from the public in order to more dispassionately exert an atmosphere of authority. This can lead officers to become isolated or detached from the public. The resulting social isolation generates police solidarity whereby officers frequently associate with other officers, believing that only fellow officers can truly understand the job and its challenges. This, in turn, can foster an "us" (police) versus "them" (everyone else) mentality.

Skolnick adds that police officers, as a function of their authority, are sometimes responsible for enforcing unpopular laws, laws against relatively minor offenses, and laws against victimless crimes. Sometimes members of the public believe that these represent inappropriate applications of the law (think back to the differing legal philosophies discussed in Chapter 3), in which case they may view the police with distrust. This can lead to perceptions of hypocrisy by the public. "The policeman is apt to cause resentment because of the suspicion that policemen do not themselves strictly conform to the moral norms they are enforcing" (Skolnick, 1966, p. 56). When members of the public believe—whether correctly or incorrectly—that officers sometimes violate the laws they are charged with upholding, it can serve to further isolate the police from the community.

William Westley (1970) concurs with Skolnick, adding that a *code of secrecy* promotes a sense of solidarity among police officers. "Secrecy among the police stands as a shield against the attacks of the outside world . . . Secrecy is loyalty . . . Secrecy is solidarity" (p. 111). That is, there is often an informal code among police officers that "what happens on the streets, remains on the street." The public is viewed as either incapable of understanding or outside the boundaries of trust for sharing such information. This philosophy is reinforced throughout an officer's career, sometimes manifesting itself as a reluctance to report fellow officers who have engaged in wrongdoing, again maintaining the secrecy of what happens on the job. Note that this is different from concerns about confidentiality of protected information (e.g., that which requires

security clearances); the notion of a code of secrecy is much broader, based on the belief that the job should not be discussed with anyone but one's fellow officers. Westley further states that the code of secrecy becomes a part of an officer's morality and therefore a part of the police personality.

The police officer's personality is also shaped by anomie and cynicism (Niederhoffer, 1967). Anomie includes frustration, alienation, despair, and a sense of powerlessness (see Durkheim, 1965). Cynicism is a distrust and pessimistic attitude toward life and career. According to Arthur Niederhoffer, officers begin their career with a sense of commitment and idealism, looking forward to their work as an opportunity to fight crime, vanquish evil, and protect American society. Over time, however, the initial enthusiasm may be diminished by the recognition that not all crime can be prevented or solved, which in turn can lead to disenchantment (recognizing that policing is sometimes less about crime fighting than about public relations), cynicism (coming to dislike the work or to view with pessimism the public, agency administrators, or the department), alienation (social isolation), and finally anomie (feeling a lack of care for work).

Finally, Lefkowitz (1975, 1977) identified a cluster of personality traits centered on authoritarianism (for a comprehensive review, see Owen & Wagner, 2008). This is the notion that the police may come to see themselves as the societal embodiment of the authority of the state (thinking "I am the law"). This can lead to both a rejection of anything different as "abnormal" and a corresponding belief in the need for punishment and discipline for norm breakers, even for those who have not broken a law. This also involves a near-blind acceptance of authority figures, high pressure for conformity (to "fit in"), and a tendency to think rigidly and in oversimplified ways (quickly judging even complex or unclear issues as right or wrong, with no middle ground or room for reflection and analysis). Authoritarianism is a concern because it has been associated with prejudice, a reduced interest in constitutional rights, and a willingness to "accept unfair and illegal abuses of power by government authorities" (Altemeyer, 1996, p. 300).

Many of these values may strike you as negative. However, in a study of the Los Angeles Police Department, Herbert (1997) found that officers' work was guided by a set of six principles, as described here:

> Law, which by legislative fiat defines the permissible parameters of police action; bureaucratic regulations, which seek to determine police procedures more finely through a set of rules that establish a chain of command; adventure/machismo, which constitutes the police as courageous individuals who embrace danger as a test of individual ability; safety, which establishes a set of practices to protect the police from undue harm; competence, which suggests that police should be able to control the public areas for which they are responsible; and morality, which infuses police practice with a sense of right and goodness, in essence because it helps protect society from the "bad guys." (p. 3)

Herbert suggests that an examination of these values can be used as a way to analyze police activities. When all goes well, the six values may act in concert to lead to the appropriate resolution of a situation. When problems arise, it is perhaps because one value becomes too strong and eclipses or dominates the others.

Again, not all of the characteristics apply to all police officers. Over the course of a career, different elements may come and go depending on an officer's assignment, individual attributes, supervisory expectations, and life experiences. As the personality of the officer changes, so may his or her style of patrol. For instance, a police officer with a legalistic approach to policing may soon become disenchanted with the job when suspects are released back into society without serving punishment, thereby

growing very cynical. The officer may decide it's just better to do the bare minimum, maintain order (watchman style), and wait it out until retirement. Conversely, an officer initially operating under the watchman style may later find meaning through interactions with neighborhood residents in community policing activities and become very involved with service style crime prevention. The police personality is dynamic and varies by officer.

For police agencies, administrators, and trainers, the challenge is to determine how to maximize positive aspects of the police personality and minimize the negative aspects. Sometimes this is a matter of degree. For instance, solidarity is useful in that it can build cohesion between officers, leading to effective teamwork. On the other hand, if taken too far, it might be detrimental to community relations. This requires thoughtful reflection which varies based on the environment of each individual police agency. It is to the structure of policing in the United States, with its numerous agencies, to which we now turn.

Q Describe how each of Wilson's styles of policing could be used in the situation at the New Briarfield Apartments. After reviewing your response, which style would you prefer? Why?

Q If you were a police chief, what steps could you take within your agency to promote the positive attributes of the police personality and to help remedy the negative attributes?

Q What similarities and differences do you see among the police personality traits described in this section?

The Structure of American Law Enforcement

FOCUSING QUESTION 11.3

How is law enforcement in the United States organized?

Policing in the United States is fragmented. That is, there are many different police agencies, and historically, there has been little coordination among them, although interagency communications and collaborations have improved over time. For this reason, it is difficult to identify a single police subculture, a single set of policing strategies, or a single definition of the police role; all of these features may vary between agencies. In this section, we examine three levels of law enforcement: local, state, and federal.

In many countries, there is one national police force. This is not the case in the United States (the FBI is one of many federal law enforcement agencies; it is not the national police force). Recall from the discussion of federalism in Chapter 7 that we have multiple levels of government—federal, state and local. Likewise, there are police agencies at the federal, state, and local level. Each level of policing and each agency within those levels differs. For example, two local police departments just miles apart may have separate hiring standards, promotional opportunities, starting salaries, mission statements (that is, the philosophy of law enforcement used to represent community interest), and practices. As a case in point, consider the example of the City and County of St. Louis, Missouri, about which Jones (2000) writes:

> Certainly there is no shortage of police units: the City of St. Louis has its own department . . . , St. Louis County has its own force, and more than sixty of the ninety-plus municipalities [within the County] mount their individual units. Especially in the case of the latter, this allows a variety of policing approaches [by department], ranging from the officer-as-social-worker to the officer-as-code-regulator to the officer-as-crime-fighter." (p. 131)

With over 60 police agencies in the space of a single county, there is tremendous fragmentation in the provision of police services, with agencies drawing upon various policing styles (e.g., Wilson's service style is similar to the officer-as-social-worker and his legalistic style is similar to the officer-as-crime-fighter). However, the various departments do work together, with a Major Case Squad to coordinate investigation of serious crimes that cross jurisdictional boundaries and mutual aid agreements that make provisions for officers from one jurisdiction to assist those in another when there is a need to do so (Jones, 2000).

According to the 2008 Census of State and Local Law Enforcement Agencies (Reaves, 2011), the United States has approximately 765,000 sworn officers (those with the authority to make arrests and use force) in roughly 18,000 public law enforcement agencies. Of those 18,000 agencies, about 12,500 (69%) are local police agencies.

LOCAL POLICE AGENCIES

As just indicated, the vast majority of policing in America is performed by local police agencies. Perhaps surprisingly, most police agencies are not the large city police departments (e.g., New York City with approximately 36,000 sworn officers) such as those featured on television dramas. In fact, about half of all police agencies employ fewer than 10 officers (Reaves, 2011).

Depending on the mission of the local agency, law enforcement goals may differ. However, most local police agencies perform similar duties found in the acronym PEPPAS including: *P*rotecting life and property; *E*nforcing the criminal law; *P*reventing crime; *P*reserving the peace; *A*rresting violators; and *S*erving the community. Most local (city, town, county, etc.) police agencies rely on the military rank structure. For instance, most agencies' hierarchy, from lowest to highest, might look something like this: police officer, sergeant, lieutenant, captain, assistant chief, chief, and perhaps, police commissioner.

Often included under the definition of local law enforcement are sheriffs' departments. In addition to the local law enforcement statistics listed previously, there are 3,063 sheriffs' offices in the United States (Reaves, 2011). Unlike local police chiefs, sheriffs are often elected to their position, and they may or may not have actual law enforcement experience. Sheriffs and their deputies (the law enforcement officers hired by the sheriff) are often responsible for court duties, such as running the local jail, transporting prisoners, serving warrants (and other court documents), and security within the courtroom (serving as a bailiff), and depending on the jurisdiction, may also perform traditional law enforcement duties, including responding to calls for service and conducting investigations.

STATE POLICE AGENCIES

There are 50 state police agencies, also known as the highway patrol in some jurisdictions (Reaves, 2011). The hierarchical rank structure in most state police organizations is similar to the military model noted earlier. In fact, state agencies are often more militaristic in their styles of operations than local agencies, and many state police academies have been compared to military style training.

While their legal mandate focuses on violations of state law, including state highway traffic enforcement and accident investigation, the duties of the state police are similar to local law enforcement, but state police officers have greater jurisdictional freedom; they can investigate criminal activity anywhere within the state.

Sometimes, the overlap of jurisdictions generates conflict between local and state police officers. For example, who has jurisdiction when state police and local police bust a drug ring in the local town? Who receives the recognition for the arrests (which may influence promotion decisions and measures of agency effectiveness)? However,

these conflicts are infrequent, as state and local police generally have a positive working relationship. Furthermore, unless there is a large-scale incident or local agencies need additional resources, state police usually do not become involved in local police operations.

FEDERAL AGENCIES

Of the approximately 120,000 sworn federal law enforcement officers in the United States, most are employed either within the U.S. Department of Homeland Security (approximately 46%) or the U.S. Department of Justice (nearly 33%) (Reaves, 2012). Within each of these federal departments, there are multiple law enforcement agencies. For a listing of the largest federal law enforcement employers, see Table 11.1. Although federal agencies have a hierarchy of command, it differs significantly from local and state police. For instance, the first-level supervisor in a local or state police agency may be a "sergeant," whereas in a federal agency, the supervisor's title may be "agent-in-charge."

The legal mandate of federal officers is the enforcement of federal law, including crimes that cross state boundaries. Federal agents can investigate federal crimes anywhere across the nation, and sometimes abroad, if they affect national security. Unlike state and local police officers, federal agents rarely concern themselves with order

TABLE 11.1 Top Federal Agencies Employing 250 or More Full-Time Officers with Authority to Carry Firearms and Make Arrests, September 2008

Agency	Full-Time Officers
U.S. Customs and Border Protection	36,863
Federal Bureau of Prisons	16,835
Federal Bureau of Investigation	12,760
U.S. Immigration and Customs Enforcement	12,446
U.S. Secret Service	5,213
Drug Enforcement Administration	4,308
Administrative Office of the Courts	4,696
U.S. Marshals Service	3,313
U.S. Postal Inspection Service	2,288
Internal Revenue Service, Criminal Investigation	2,636
Veterans Health Administration	3,128
Bureau of Alcohol, Tobacco, Firearms & Explosives	2,541
U.S. Capitol Police	1,637
National Park Service—Rangers	1,404
Bureau of Diplomatic Security	1,049
U.S. Forest Service	644
U.S. Fish & Wildlife Service	598

Source: Reaves, 2012

maintenance activities. Their duties are much more specific, based on agency, and are usually based on investigations rather than patrol. For instance, the Drug Enforcement Administration (DEA) focuses primarily on drug crimes, the Bureau of Alcohol, Tobacco, and Firearms (BATF) focuses primarily on violations of alcohol, tobacco, and firearm laws, and so on.

The vast majority of collaborative law enforcement efforts prove quite successful, but tensions may still arise. Determining which agencies have authority, and what the roles of those agencies are in a particular operation, can become complicated. For instance, assume that two towns are on either side of a state line and that an incident occurs exactly on the state line. Further assume that it is a motor vehicle accident and, while there are no injuries, a responding officer observes in plain view a stash of illegal drugs and, upon searching the car and its occupants, discovers additional contraband in the form of illegal weapons, counterfeit money, and evidence pertaining to a recent bank robbery. What agencies would have an interest in this scenario? At the very least, the local police from both towns, the state police from both states, the Drug Enforcement Administration, the Bureau of Alcohol, Tobacco, and Firearms, the Secret Service (counterfeiting falls under their jurisdiction), and the Federal Bureau of Investigation (bank robbery falls under their jurisdiction) could be involved. Depending on the circumstances of the case, it is possible that others could become involved, as well.

Q What do you think are the advantages and disadvantages of having multiple local law enforcement agencies rather than a single national agency?

Q Assume that, for a single incident (e.g., that described in the paragraph above), multiple local, state, and federal agencies respond. How should it be determined who is in charge of the response, what role each agency will play, and who will receive credit for the case (for the arrests, for clearing the crime, etc.)?

Q Of the three levels of policing (local, state, and federal), if provided the opportunity, which agency would you prefer to work for? Why?

Ethical Issues in Policing

FOCUSING QUESTION 11.4

What ethical dilemmas may arise in police agencies?

As you recall from Chapter 2, a consideration of morality is essential to the study of criminal justice. Determining what is (or is not) moral is a foundation for professional ethics. In this section, we explore ethical considerations in policing.

Ethics may be viewed as the application of a set of moral thoughts and ideas to determine the right thing to do, often in a professional setting. Although the vast majority of police work is conducted ethically, we will focus on a few police behaviors that violate the ethical standards of law enforcement, many of which fall into the category of police corruption. Police corruption may be defined as an act involving the misuse of authority, often for some personal gain (personal gain may also include a gain for others, such as friends, colleagues or family members). Keep in mind that personal gain does not necessarily mean *financial* rewards, as you will see in a moment.

ethics
The application of morality in a professional setting. Often codified in professional codes of ethics.

LEVELS OF CORRUPTION

Police corruption is not isolated to the street officer. In fact, there have been numerous media accounts of police supervisors, including police chiefs, who have committed unethical and illegal behavior (e.g., a police chief stealing drugs from the property room

to support his addiction). For an example of unethical police activities that received considerable media attention, see Box 11.2.

Although all are unethical, not all instances of corruption are equally severe in terms of how deeply they impact a police organization. In his definitive work on police corruption, Lawrence Sherman (1974) identified four levels of police corruption: (1) rotten apples, (2) rotten pockets, (3) pervasive unorganized corruption, and (4) pervasive organized corruption.

Rotten apples occur when one or more officers independently participate in some form of corrupt activity. For instance, assume a motorist bribes a police officer $20 to avoid a traffic summons. Meanwhile, a fellow officer receives $100 from a local business owner to allow customers to double-park their vehicles, without the fear of a parking citation, in front of her store to improve business sales. Neither officer knows of the other's illegal activity. Corruption would be occurring in this circumstance, but without

BOX 11.2

Ethics in Practice

RAMPART DIVISION

Arguably, one of the most infamous police scandals in the annals of U.S. history occurred during the 1990s within the Los Angeles Police Department's Rampart Division Community Resource Against Street Hoodlums (CRASH) anti-gang unit. The purpose of the CRASH unit was to reduce gang violence, which did decrease after the formation of the unit. However, over time, questions emerged about the unit's practices. According to Weitzer (2002):

> Officers working in Rampart had been accused of framing suspects, falsifying police reports, giving false testimony in court, stealing drugs, and shooting unarmed suspects . . . Seventy officers have been implicated in these crimes, forty have been disciplined for actions in connection with the scandal, and five have been fired. Two hundred lawsuits have been filed against the city by persons who claimed that they were victims of police abuse, and over one hundred tainted criminal convictions have been overturned (Lait & Glover, 2000). Moreover, the Justice Department and the Los Angeles City Council . . . entered into a consent decree to ensure implementation of reforms in the LAPD. (p. 400)

Based on his study of the Rampart scandal, Reese (2005) attributed the problems to a lack of oversight and training. For instance, the CRASH unit was not subjected to traditional oversight:

> Since the data suggested that CRASH was doing an excellent job at reducing crime in the region, a level of trust developed between the members of the CRASH unit and upper management of the LAPD. Because of this trust, certain oversight functions such as audits and control checks were set aside and substituted with good faith. (p. 95)

In turn, the unit was able to operate on its own terms, making discretionary decisions with little regulation. Reese (2005) also observed that discretion is inherent in a police officer's job, and that it would be impossible to provide specific guidance on every type of situation that requires discretionary decision making; however, he suggested that more training is necessary to promote the sound use of discretion. Finally, Reese (2005) argued that the LAPD was insulated from outside scrutiny (such as that provided by a civilian review board), and that internal processes were not sufficient to address problems.

Q Reese (2005) suggests that "many of the Rampart officers believed they were doing the right thing" (p. 96). What factors do you think may have contributed to that feeling?

Q Do you think any reasons other than those listed above may have contributed to the development of the Rampart scandal?

Q What could be done to prevent similar problems in the future?

any coordination between multiple officers; in this circumstance, officers act individually. On the other hand, if the officers had worked as a team and split the total money they received during their patrol shift, they would be known as a rotten pocket, which is a small group of officers working together for unethical purposes.

Often associated with rotten apples and rotten pockets are grasseaters and meateaters (see Knapp Commission, 1972). Grasseaters are officers who accept illegal benefits as a result of some corrupt activity but do so passively. That is, they do not seek out corruption, but may take advantage of it if the opportunity presents itself. Also included in this category are officers who know that corruption is taking place but refuse to report it as part of the *code of secrecy* described earlier. Meateaters are officers who aggressively solicit illegal favors. For instance, if a motorist offered a police officer a $20 bribe to avoid a traffic summons and the officer accepted it, that officer would be considered a grasseater. On the other hand, if upon making the traffic stop the officer told the motorist that he would be willing to accept a bribe or actively demanded a bribe payment, that officer would be considered a meateater.

Sherman (1974) identified two additional levels of police corruption. Pervasive unorganized corruption goes beyond a few grasseaters or rotten apples. This occurs when a large number of officers participate in illegal activity, to the extent that it becomes somewhat characteristic of an agency. For example, in an agency of 100 officers, there may be 10–15 officers accepting illegal favors independently of one another. This conveys the appearance, and perhaps the reality, that corruption is pervasive within the agency. Pervasive organized corruption occurs when meateaters and rotten pockets join forces. This extends corruption and unethical behavior from small groups of officers to well-organized and larger groups of officers, potentially including supervisors and executives. Again, the effect is that corruption becomes pervasive within the agency.

ETHICAL QUESTIONS IN POLICING

Unfortunately, the types of unethical behavior and corrupt activities in policing are almost endless. Some are issues about which there is debate; others are issues in which most view the behavior as unethical. We will discuss several in this section. For each, consider what you would do in the situation—you make the call.

A gratuity is a benefit that a police officer receives simply because he or she is a police officer. This generally takes the form of a police officer being given something, often a financial discount or something tangible, which would not be given to the general public. For instance, assume that a police officer wants to buy a cup of coffee at a convenience store and starts to pay the clerk. The clerk waves the money away and says, "You guys protect the rest of us from crime; your coffee is free." The officer accepts the coffee and leaves. This is an example of a gratuity. Departments differ as to their policies on gratuities—some allowing gratuities under some circumstances and others not—but they have been the subject of frequent ethical debate.

Professional courtesy occurs when a police officer provides a courtesy or special treatment to another law enforcement officer; this sometimes extends to officers' families or other emergency service personnel. For example, assume that an officer, while off duty in his personal vehicle, is stopped for speeding in a neighboring jurisdiction. When the officer from the neighboring jurisdiction approaches the vehicle, the off-duty officer who had been speeding flashes his badge. As a result, the officer who made the traffic stop chooses not to write up a warning or citation. However, had he not been a fellow police officer, a citation would have been given. Of course, this type of situation overlaps with discussions of discretion, generally.

Misuse of authority occurs when a police officer uses his or her position for some sort of personal gain. This is distinguished from passively accepting a gratuity or bribe.

For instance, if while working a traffic detail an officer observed a vehicle driven lawfully by a person he or she finds attractive, and the officer then stopped the vehicle simply to meet the driver and obtain contact information by running the license through Central Records, a misuse of authority would have occurred. This type of action is prohibited by police agencies.

There are numerous other acts that may also represent unethical and corrupt behavior. These include officer theft, breaking and entering, unnecessary use of force, planting evidence, sexual favors (e.g., a citizen offers to perform sexual activity with an officer in exchange for not receiving a citation), kickbacks (e.g., referring an arrestee to a bail bondsman who provides the officer payment for each referral), shakedowns (e.g., meateater demanding money for a monthly payoff from a bar owner to ignore potential violations, such as overcrowding), and racial profiling (enforcing the law against a person or group of people based solely on their race or ethnicity), to name just a few.

THE DIRTY HARRY PROBLEM

As discussed in Chapter 2, moral judgments influence police discretion. Ethics also help to guide officer discretion. But when does a police officer cross the line between good police work and unethical behavior?

Participants in an Occupy Movement protest at the University of California–Davis are pepper-sprayed. In the aftermath of this incident, a task force concluded "that UC Davis police had violated policy and that campus administrators mishandled the November 2011 campus protest" (Ceasar, 2012, para. 11). The students who were pepper-sprayed were compensated in the amount of $30,000 each in a settlement from the university. The officer, who later left the department, received "more than 17,000 angry or threatening emails [and] 10,000 text messages" (Garofoli, 2013, para. 5) and was "awarded more than $38,000 in workers' compensation from the university for suffering he experienced after the incident" (Garafoli, 2013, para. 1). When do you think police use of force is necessary? What are the effects or consequences of police use of force?

In discussing the Dirty Harry problem, Carl Klockars ([1980] 1985a) asks, "when and to what extent does the morally good end warrant or justify an ethically, politically, or legally dangerous means for its achievement?" (p. 50). The Dirty Harry problem takes its name from the 1971 movie starring Clint Eastwood as "Dirty Harry" Callahan, a fictional San Francisco police inspector who will do whatever it takes to apprehend a psychopathic killer who calls himself "Scorpio."

In one scene, Harry tracks Scorpio to an abandoned football stadium. Scorpio is already suffering from a deep knife wound delivered by Harry in an earlier scene. Harry shoots the unarmed Scorpio in the leg with his weapon. With his gun still drawn, Harry approaches Scorpio, who is alive but disabled from the shooting. Harry demands to know the location of a kidnapped girl who Scorpio bragged was buried alive. Without regard to constitutional rights, Harry tortures Scorpio by stomping on Scorpio's open leg wound until he provides the information necessary to locate the girl, who was dead when found. This is an example of illegal means (i.e., unconstitutional interrogation and inappropriate use of force) used for a morally good end (i.e., locating and attempting to rescue a victim).

Situations such as this pose a conundrum, as Klockars ([1980] 1985a) notes: "a police officer, at least in this specific case, cannot be both just and innocent" (p. 58). Obtaining the information could lead to justice, but the officer's actions were clearly illegal; conversely, a police officer acting within the bounds of the law might not be able to extract the confession from Scorpio that would allow the victim to be found, potentially contravening justice. Ultimately, however, police officers are expected to follow the law, consistent with the requirements of constitutional criminal procedure as described in Chapter 8.

CONTROLLING UNETHICAL BEHAVIOR

The vast majority of police officers perform their duties ethically and legally. However, even a few unethical officers or a single high-profile case of police corruption can tarnish the reputation of policing as a whole and lead to a loss of legitimacy for the criminal justice system.

Regardless of the level of policing (local, state, or federal), controlling ethical behavior, misconduct, and corruption is critical for maintaining effective police service. "Exacting ethical standards and a high degree of honesty are perhaps more essential for the police than for any other group in society . . . Nothing undermines public confidence in the police and the process of criminal justice more than the illegal acts of officers" (Task Force Report [1967] 1990, p. 208). So, what can be done to minimize unethical behavior in policing?

First and foremost, police administrators must be willing to recognize and address unethical behavior and corruption. A strategy to address these issues is completing thorough background checks and hiring the proper police candidates, providing effective ethics education and training in the police academy, and continuing to monitor officer behavior throughout their careers. Departments should maintain an effective Internal Affairs Department, or Citizen Review Board, whose responsibility includes investigating police misconduct. Additionally, written policy can specify departmental ethical expectations, and police colleagues can be encouraged to report unethical and illegal police behavior, as it reflects negatively on the entire agency and all its members.

A report by the Community Relations Service (2003) of the U.S. Department of Justice further noted "that good policing must take into consideration two equally important factors: the *values* on which a police department operates, as well as the *practices* it follows [emphasis in original]" (p. v). While focused on the prevention of violence between the police and community, the principles described in the report

similarly serve to promote ethical policing, generally. The values to be emphasized include the following (pp. 4–5):

- The police department must preserve and advance the principles of democracy.
- The police department places its highest value on the preservation of human life.
- The police department believes that the prevention of crime is its number one operational priority.
- The police department will involve the community in the delivery of its services.
- The police department must be accountable to the community it serves.
- The police department is committed to professionalism in all aspects of its operations.
- The police department will maintain the highest standards of integrity.

Attention to ethics in policing has come a long way since the political era. It is important to maintain a focus on ethical issues, to ensure that policing is conducted according to the most professional standards.

Q Earlier, you were asked to consider what you think would be the most appropriate response to the New Briarfield Apartment situation. What ethical problems could potentially emerge during the implementation of your strategy? What could be done to prevent them?

Q Which of the above strategies do you think would be most useful in controlling unethical police activities? Can you think of other strategies to control or monitor unethical or illegal police behavior? Explain.

Q Is it ever appropriate to use unethical (or illegal) police tactics to achieve a desirable outcome? Explain.

Policing Strategies

FOCUSING QUESTION 11.5

How have policing strategies developed over time?

In addition to being ethical, policing strategies should also be effective. For the past half century, scholars have devoted substantial attention to the effectiveness of police operations. Some police strategies appear to be common sense, yet upon closer examination, they have proven to be less effective than previously thought. We will address four of the most classic studies that identified myths of policing. These studies motivated agencies to find creative and more effective methods of policing and helped lead the transition to the community problem-solving era.

MYTHS ABOUT POLICING

Myth 1: The Number of Police Officers Affects Crime. Loftin and McDowall (1982) examined the relationship between reported crime and the number of officers in Detroit during the years 1926 to 1977. Their general conclusion was that the number of officers does not affect crime. That is, increases and decreases in the number of sworn personnel do not, by themselves, lead to an increase or decrease in crime. This suggests that police strategy and tactics are more important than the sheer numbers of officers.

Myth 2: Routine Patrol Deters Crime. For many years, routine preventive patrol was assumed to deter crime. Routine preventive patrol refers to police officers patrolling their assigned beat and watching for signs of trouble or disorder when not responding to calls for service. Patrol has been justified at least in part on the argument that a visible

police presence deters crime. Kelling, Pate, Dieckman, and Brown (1974) examined variations in the level of patrol in 15 Kansas City, Missouri, patrol beats. They randomly assigned the beats to one of three groups: In the group 1 (reactive) beats, officers did not patrol their beats and only entered their assigned areas when dispatched to calls for service; in group 2 (control) beats, officers patrolled their areas normally; and in group 3 (proactive) beats, the level of patrol was doubled or tripled. Results indicated that variations in the level of preventive patrol did not have a significant effect on crime or the fear of crime. The results of this study caused police administrators to rethink the notion that routine preventive patrol can deter crime. As a result, agencies have considered how to more effectively structure police patrols and to deploy officers. One strategy some agencies have turned toward is hot spots policing, described in Box 11.3.

Myth 3: Rapid Response Time Is Essential. Is quicker better? A study of response time in Kansas City, Missouri (Bieck & Kessler, 1977), examined three time intervals. The first was the time between the crime itself and a citizen's call to the police to report it. The second was the time it took for the police to process the call and dispatch a unit to the scene. The third was the time it took for a unit to arrive on the scene after being dispatched. The results found that the latter two time intervals had little impact on solving a crime. The more critical time period was the time between the commission of the crime and reporting it to the police. The average time was 41 minutes—far too long for a rapid response to make much of a difference. Accordingly, unless there is a crime or emergency in progress that is reported immediately, response time is not as significant as it may seem.

Myth 4: The Resourceful Investigator Solves Crimes. Greenwood and Petersilia (1975) examined the investigations of serious crimes reported to the police, including homicide, rape, robbery, aggravated assault, and grand theft (larceny). They discovered that the vast majority of crimes that police investigate were brought to their attention by the public, who also provided officers with suspect identification. That is, the majority of cases were solved with information supplied by the victim to the responding patrol officer rather than requiring in-depth investigations, such as those portrayed on television. In fact, if a suspect is not quickly identified by the victim or other informants, some cases do not even receive further investigation. It is not unusual for cases to be assessed for solvability factors, which are factors that may increase the likelihood of successfully solving the case (e.g., availability of physical evidence, whether the crime is similar to others that have happened in the area, if any suspect description is available, likelihood of recovering stolen property, etc.). Cases with high scores on the solvability factors "are given to the detective division for follow-up investigation; the rest are often closed on the basis of the preliminary investigation and reopened only if additional information is uncovered" (National Institute of Justice, 1994, p. 13).

As you can see, commonly held beliefs about policing may be false. It is important to note, however, that these studies were subject to much scrutiny, review, and challenge; future studies may paint a very different picture. These studies did, however, lead the police administrators to consider new strategies, including team policing, community-oriented policing (COP), and problem-oriented policing (POP)

TEAM POLICING

Team policing served as the forerunner to today's community-oriented policing philosophy. Team policing was developed in Scotland in 1946 but did not become popular in the United States until the early 1970s. The basic concept of team policing is best

BOX 11.3

Research in Action

HOT SPOTS POLICING

Many police agencies across the nation have recognized a need for more effective and efficient crime prevention strategies (see Eck, 2002). As an extension of the community policing and problem-oriented policing movement (see Goldstein, 1990), **hot spots policing** emerged as a new strategy for addressing high-crime places.

As noted in the text, research (Kelling, Pate, Dieckman, & Brown, 1974) indicated that random police patrol was an ineffective crime prevention strategy. This led to the conclusion that what matters most is not how many officers are on patrol, but rather how those officers are most effectively utilized. According to Eck (2005), "a hot spot is an area that has a greater than average number of criminal or disorder events or an area where people have a higher than average risk of victimization" (p. 2). Hot spots can be a single address, a street, or a neighborhood. The concept of hot spots rests on the idea that crime is not evenly distributed; numerous studies have confirmed this, finding that a small number of places tend to generate a large volume of crime (for an overview, see Clarke & Eck, 2007). Research has found that hot spots tend to be stable over time. That is, absent some interruption, high crime areas tend to remain high crime, and low crime areas tend to remain low crime (Weisburd, Bushway, Lum, & Yang, 2004).

Hot spots policing is one potential interruption that may be utilized to reduce crime in hot spot areas. Simply stated, hot spots policing is a crime prevention strategy that involves placing officers where crime is located (see Braga & Weisburd, 2010). This can take the form of significantly higher levels of patrol and police presence or more specific programs implemented in high-crime areas.

Braga, Papachristos, and Hureau (in press) conducted a meta-analysis to explore the effectiveness of hot spots policing. A meta-analysis is a type of study that yields powerful results by using sophisticated statistical techniques to combine the results of numerous—in this case 19—prior studies. Here, the researchers found that "hot spots policing programs generate modest crime control gains" (p. 26) and, furthermore, that they also reduced crime in the areas surrounding the hot spots (this is known as diffusion). In only one study was there a

hot spots policing
A crime prevention strategy that involves placing officers where crime is located. This can take the form of significantly higher levels of patrol and police presence or more specific programs implemented in high-crime areas.

summarized by Smith and Taylor (1985): "Team members are assigned to a specific neighborhood with total responsibility to perform full duties and develop a better relationship with the public. Police–citizen interaction is encouraged. The teams provide 24-hour coverage for that area and officers are assigned on a semi-permanent basis" (p. 40). Thus, each area of the city had its own team to provide all policing services, and the officers on each team worked to build strong relationships with the members of the community. This strategy essentially decentralized policing even further by creating "minidepartments" that served each area of the city.

This sounded great; what could go wrong? According to Samuel Walker (1993), there were a number of problems. First, there was opposition from middle management; with greater responsibility placed on local sergeants and patrol officers, lieutenants and captains resented their loss of authority. Second, some street officers were never informed about the new police strategy and resented those who were selected to participate in it. Third, team policing was designed for decentralization, whereas dispatch technology remained centralized, leading to implementation difficulties. Fourth, the goals of team policing were never made clear: initial planning and implementation were poor. As quickly as team policing arrived, it departed.

community-oriented policing
A policing strategy with the basic philosophy of fostering a positive working relationship between the police and the community.

COMMUNITY-ORIENTED POLICING

Lessons learned from team policing were later incorporated into **community-oriented policing (COP)**, whose basic philosophy is to foster a positive working relationship between the police and the community. While COP strategies may vary depending on agency and community needs, some common themes include: (1) using foot patrol when

significant amount of displacement, which occurs when crime goes down in one area only to increase elsewhere. The hot spots policing programs that were most effective were those that used problem-oriented policing strategies; programs that simply escalated existing policing practices by concentrating them in one location were not as effective.

While hot spots policing has demonstrated effectiveness, there are some concerns worth noting. Namely, in order to be effective, hot spots policing must be based on a careful analysis of the hot spot, finding the best strategy that is applicable for it. Strategies based on zero-tolerance models have the potential to damage police–community relationships and to risk promoting overly aggressive police practices. Rosenbaum (2006) suggests:

> The real question should be, What are the best strategies to combat crime, disorder, and quality of life [offenses] in these hot spots given all that we know about these problems, these locations, and the many resources that can be leveraged (including non-police resources)?" (p. 251)

To assist in researching hot spots and informing the development of appropriate strategies, crime analysis is often used. According to Santos (2013), "crime analysis is the systematic study of crime and disorder as well as other police-related issues—including socio-demographic, spatial, and temporal factors—to assist the police in criminal apprehension, crime and disorder reduction, crime prevention, and evaluation" (p. 2). Many police departments employ crime analysts who work with geographic information systems and statistical analysis to generate data that guides strategy.

Q What benefits do you believe that hot spots policing can provide?

Q What do you think are the advantages and disadvantages of hot spots policing, as a strategy?

Q Assume that your chief asked you to implement a hot spots policing strategy at the New Briarfield apartment complex. What steps would you take in order to do so?

practical to encourage citizens and police to positively interact and communicate; (2) establishing community action groups (e.g., Neighborhood Watch or holding regular community meetings) to allow officers and community members to listen, reflect, and respond to neighborhood issues and concerns; and (3) decentralizing police agencies to allow for easier community accessibility (e.g., by creating police substations). Largely, though, community policing is a *philosophy* that shapes how the police approach their tasks, recognizing members of the community as participants in the law enforcement function.

PROBLEM-ORIENTED POLICING

Developed by Herman Goldstein (1990), **problem-oriented policing (POP)** is a problem-solving strategy designed to involve the police and the community. According to Goldstein, the police need to: (1) become more flexible in problem solving; (2) become more proactive in addressing community problems; (3) maximize the contributions from citizens; (4) empower the patrol officer in the decision-making process; and (5) rethink the organizational structure to become less resistant to change.

problem-oriented policing
A policing strategy designed to help the police identify and respond to the root causes of problems that lead to crime. The emphasis is on making police proactive rather than reactive through use of the SARA model. Also known as POP.

A commonly used problem-solving method is scanning, analysis, response, and assessment (SARA). When used properly, it is a very flexible strategy. It can be used by the patrol officer on the street to address minor problems, and it can be used by police administrators to address citywide problems.

Scanning is examining the environment to identify, confirm, and prioritize problems. Community groups, patrol officers, the news media, or others may bring problems to the attention of the police. Then, police administrators examine the list of problems and determine which need to be addressed first.

Compstat
A policing strategy that integrates computerized crime data and advanced crime mapping to analyze crime patterns, which police supervisors use to develop goals and strategies to reduce crime in their areas.

BOX 11.4

COMPSTAT

Compstat (short for "compare statistics") was developed as part of a problem-oriented policing strategy integrating computerized crime data and advanced crime mapping to analyze crime patterns. It provides police supervisors and police executives with the means to share critical information regarding criminal activity in their jurisdiction through regular meetings at which the data are presented and discussed. Supervisors are expected to develop goals and programs for crime reduction in their areas based on the crime data. As such, they are empowered to engage in problem solving in their jurisdictions and are given the autonomy to develop their own plans for doing so. They are also regularly evaluated on and held accountable for their progress.

Compstat gained popularity after it was implemented in New York City when Police Commissioner William Bratton took office in 1994. Bratton found it disturbing that top police administrators were not fully aware of current crime patterns and statistics. As a result, he held mandatory meetings with jurisdictional police supervisors twice a week requesting (actually, demanding) to know what actions were being taken to reduce crime in their area. They would then have to report on their efforts and results (see Bratton, 1998; Silverman, 1999).

Q What are the advantages and limitations of holding police supervisors accountable through Compstat?

Q Do you think Compstat would be effective in smaller police agencies?

Q Would Compstat have proved useful in the New Briarfield Apartment example?

Analysis refers to understanding the problem and, in particular, the conditions that led to the problem. This makes POP proactive. The police strive to understand why a problem happened, so its underlying causes can be addressed. If the underlying causes are not addressed, the problem will continue. The analysis stage generally requires careful research and analysis of data. See Box 11.4 for discussion of Compstat, a program aimed at the analysis of crime trends.

Response is the development and implementation of solutions to the problem based on attacking its causes. One key element of problem-oriented policing is to promote partnerships between the police and other organizations. As a result, the police seek the assistance of other private or public agencies who can contribute to a solution. This is important because it acknowledges that crime prevention involves many facets of society beyond law enforcement.

Assessment refers to the evaluation of the strategy. Was the problem solved? If so, there was success. If not, the police may go back to the analysis stage once again and work on a new response to the problem.

AN EXAMPLE OF PROBLEM-ORIENTED POLICING: RICHMOND'S SECTOR 213

The response by Richmond, Virginia, to crime in one area of the city (Sector 213) illustrates the problem-oriented policing process, and also community policing strategies for responding to crime. The first step, *scanning*, occurred as data indicated that crime in the area had increased, coupled with a high level of citizen complaints and police officer observations that the area had long experienced crime and disorder. On

the basis of this information, the area was identified as one in need of attention. The second step, *analysis,* revealed some potential causes of the crime problems. Some properties in the area were run-down and not maintained, leaving hiding places for drugs, guns, and prostitution. Some landlords were not local and did not regularly check their properties. Community members were fearful and, as a result, believed there was little they could do (Richmond Police Department, 2007).

The *response* drew upon a variety of interventions, coordinated by one officer on special assignment to the area. Consistent with principles of community-oriented policing, the officer walked foot patrols and talked to residents. "People in the area saw him on a daily basis, walking the streets, the alleys. They grew to know and trust him. He would throw a football with the kids. Before long the community was feeding him information, which he acted on" (Richmond Police Department, 2007, pp. 8–9). Consistent with principles of problem-oriented response, the officer collaborated with the city's Department of Public Works, Department of Public Utilities, Animal Control, Public Library, local health care providers, and more, all collaborating to clean up the area, enforce code violations, assist local residents, and maintain a safe community. The *assessment* found that crime decreased significantly after the response, including a 47% reduction in violent crime (Richmond Police Department, 2007).

With a focus on community policing and problem solving, today's police leaders better understand the importance of police–community cooperation. Creative police strategies have been developed, incorporated, and debated to meet community needs and demands. Increased attention has been devoted to the examination of the police subculture and its effect on police and community values. This allows police agencies to best serve citizens in their communities.

Q Do you think there is a way to address the four myths identified to enhance the effectiveness of police practice?

Q How could the various strategies described in this section be applied in the New Briarfield Apartments?

Conclusion

An exploration of police history reveals that the police role in society has changed over time. Policing strategies have also changed over time, particularly in light of research about what does (or does not) work in police practice. As the front-line enforcers of the law, the police are often a person's first point of contact with the criminal justice system, whether that person is a victim or an offender. No doubt policing will continue to change in the future as new priorities and technologies emerge. Regardless of the focus or the technologies, police agencies and police professionals must maintain their commitment to providing ethical and effective public service. The next chapter turns to the courts, which are responsible for hearing criminal cases, many of which are referred to them through the work of the police.

Criminal Justice Problem Solving

Focused Deterrence

Consider the following scenario as described by the police department in High Point, North Carolina (Fealy, 2006):

> High Point is a city of approximately 95,000 in central North Carolina (it adjoins the much larger city of Greensboro) with a furniture-industry industrial base. The city is 60% white and 30% African-American; some 13% of the population and 10% of families live below the poverty line. High Point started experiencing serious drug activity and gun violence in the mid 1990s, when its homicide rate climbed higher than Greensboro and nearby Winston-Salem . . .
>
> [The newly appointed police chief's] first tour of the city was enough to show chronic street-corner dealing, crack houses, prostitution, and drive-through drug buyers. These markets were exclusively in poor minority neighborhoods, though drug and sex buyers often came from outside. The markets drove a wide range of crime; community complaints were chronic. [The High Point Police Department] and its partners did a great deal of street drug enforcement, warrant service, and investigation of mid-level dealers, but to no effect; some of High Point's open-air markets dated back 40 years to the first heroin epidemic. (pp. 2–3)

The criminal behaviors in this description—drug sales and prostitution—are fairly common problems in many communities. In High Point, church leaders and other community members became frustrated. In fact, members of some congregations were unable to enter their respective parking lots on Sunday mornings because the cars of patrons waiting for prostitutes blocked the entrance. Appalled by the traffic congestion and the reason for the congestion, the pastors of the churches and their congregations sought assistance from the police and also committed to help the police.

focused deterrence
A policing strategy in which offenders are told how their actions have caused harms to the community; are offered resources to help them stop offending; and are told that if they do not stop offending, an aggressive enforcement campaign will be launched against them by the police.

To address the situation, the police department used a strategy called **focused deterrence**, which has several characteristics (see Kennedy, 2011). It begins with a meeting between the police and concerned members of the community, in which each engages in an honest dialogue with the other. This includes understanding the perspectives of the other, and a dual commitment from both to work together to address the crime problems the community is most concerned about. In High Point, the meeting revealed, and helped to heal, long-standing misunderstandings between the police and community.

The police then identify a group of offenders that they wish to target. In High Point, the primary concern was with open-air drug sales (that is, those conducted on public streets, often in plain view of others) and the violence that accompanies them. Through much research, the police identified 16 active open-air drug dealers, a much smaller number than they had anticipated. Once the 16 were identified, the police worked to make cases against them, through investigations and undercover work. Four offenders who were found to be involved in gun crimes or violence were arrested; the remaining 12 offenders were not, although the evidence against them for other offenses was kept on file.

The 12 offenders were then invited to attend a meeting at which they received several messages. First, community leaders, clergy, and family members explained to offenders how their actions had caused them, and the community as a whole, harm and pain. Second, offenders were offered resources to help them stop offending, such as treatment or employment programs. Third, offenders were told that evidence had already been gathered against them and that the drug dealing in the area was to stop. If it did not, they were told, an aggressive enforcement campaign would be launched against them, including the use of "any and all legal tools (or levers) to sanction" them (Kennedy, 2006, pp. 156–157). This included evidence that had already been gathered, which would be sufficient to immediately arrest many of them, as well as any new evidence that could be discovered.

Evidence suggests the intervention was effective. Kennedy (2011) wrote, "There hasn't been a homicide, a shooting, or a reported rape in the West End since May, 2004. It's been six and a half years, as I write this. The community has its streets back. People started going outside, using the parks, fixing up their houses . . . The overt [drug] market is *gone* [emphasis in original]" (p. 183). Evidence also suggests that many of the former drug dealers responded to the strategy and sought and received employment (Fealy, 2006). Corsaro, Hunt, Hipple, and McGarrell (2012) have called for additional research on this type of strategy, but suggest that this is a strategy that holds promise for violence reduction.

The program's goal is to deter offending, but it is specifically focused on a small number of offenders—hence the name of this strategy, focused deterrence. Consider the following questions about the focused deterrence model.

Q Why do you think this program was successful?

Q What are the advantages and disadvantages of focused deterrence as a policing strategy? Would there be any challenges in implementing it?

Q What is your opinion of focused deterrence as a policing strategy? Explain your answer.

Q Do you think focused deterrence would work for other types of crime? If not, why? If so, what offenses?

12

Core Concepts of U.S. Court Systems

Learning Objectives

1 Describe the organizational structure and jurisdiction of the criminal court system in the United States. 2 Discuss the primary roles of each member of the courtroom workgroup. 3 Explain each of the major pretrial judicial processes in the sequence in which they usually occur in felony cases. 4 Describe what occurs during each major step of the criminal trial process. 5 Analyze the process of judicial review and its potential impact on public policy. 6 Compare and contrast the process and philosophies of legal reasoning.

Key Terms

adjudication
jurisdiction
hierarchical jurisdiction
subject matter jurisdiction
geographic jurisdiction
courtroom workgroup
felony
misdemeanor
initial appearance
grand jury
preliminary hearing
arraignment
discovery
exculpatory evidence
plea bargaining
motion
summons
voir dire
peremptory challenges
petit jury
presumption of innocence
evidence
beyond a reasonable doubt
indeterminate sentencing
determinate sentencing
appeal
certiorari
habeas corpus
judicial review
legal reasoning
drug court

Shipwreck

Case Study

In 1884, a small yacht set sail from England to Australia carrying four crewmen—three grown men and a boy. A storm capsized the yacht, causing it to sink. The crew escaped on a small lifeboat. At first, they survived on rainwater, some turnips they had brought with them, and a turtle they captured at sea. But by the 18th day, they had gone without food for a full week and were hundreds of miles from land. The captain suggested to one of his crewmen that they draw lots so that one of them could be killed and the others could survive by eating the sacrificed member of the crew. Although the idea was initially rejected, two men eventually agreed to kill the boy in the hopes of fostering their own survival. They selected the boy because he was, in their opinion, the closest to death from starvation. They also took into account that the grown men had families, whereas the boy had not yet married or fathered children. The captain stabbed the boy in the neck, and for the next four days, the three men survived by eating the boy's body and drinking his blood. The three men were then rescued by a passing ship.

The three men were charged with and convicted of murder because they premeditatedly killed the boy when he was not threatening any danger to them. The court rejected the notion that people should be able to kill others out of necessity, outside of self-defense. Not only did the judges find no precedent to support a necessity defense for murder, but they also refused to create such a defense. While the judges were sympathetic to the men's plight, they were concerned with recognizing a defense in which individuals could choose who lived and who died because someone perceived it necessary to kill. The judges also pointed out that the defendants "might possibly have been picked up the next day by a passing ship, or they might possibly not have been picked up at all; in either case it is obvious that the killing of the boy would have been an unnecessary and profitless act" (*Regina v. Dudley & Stephens*, 1884, Opinion of Coleridge, C. J., para. 2).

Q If you had been the prosecutor in the case, would you have charged the defendants with murder or some less serious crime? Explain your reasoning.

Q Do you agree with the decision of the court to convict the defendants of murder? Do you find the reasons offered by the judges in support of their decision to convict the defendants (and reject the defense of necessity) persuasive? Why or why not?

Q The defendants were originally sentenced to death on the murder charge. The queen later commuted their sentences to six months in prison. Which sentence do you prefer? Or would you issue a different sentence entirely? Why? How is "justice" achieved under any of the sentences?

Facing page: A trial in progress. How do you think courtroom decisions should be made?

The Structure of the U.S. Court System

FOCUSING QUESTION 12.1

How are U.S. courts organized?

adjudication
The formal process for resolving legal disputes in courts of law.

jurisdiction
The authority given to a court to hear and adjudicate a particular dispute. There are multiple forms of jurisdiction, including hierarchical, subject matter, and geographic.

hierarchical jurisdiction
The organization of state and federal court systems in which a case begins in a court of original jurisdiction where factual determinations are made.

Adjudication is the formal process for resolving legal disputes in courts of law. The court system in the United States is fragmented. The federal government has its own court system, and each of the 50 states also has its own court system. **Jurisdiction** refers to the authority given to a court to hear and adjudicate (that is, make a ruling about) a particular dispute. There are multiple forms of jurisdiction, including hierarchical, subject matter, and geographic. It is important to understand the different types of jurisdiction because they determine which court (among the many that exist) will ultimately be responsible for issuing a verdict or making a ruling in a particular case.

HIERARCHICAL JURISDICTION

State and federal courts are organized in a hierarchy, as illustrated by Figure 12.1. **Hierarchical jurisdiction** refers to the organization of a court system which distinguishes between courts of original jurisdiction and appellate courts, each with its own responsibilities, as described below. Assume that a defendant is arrested for assault. We will follow his case through the hierarchical jurisdiction of the courts.

A court with *original jurisdiction* is where a case begins. Courts with original jurisdiction consider evidence and make both factual and legal determinations in a case. That is, these courts decide what happened and how the law should apply to the situation. These are also known as *trial courts,* in which a single judge presides over the proceedings. The primary function of trial courts is to resolve factual disputes. Thus, at hearings and trials, trial courts usually hear testimony from witnesses, examine physical and scientific evidence, make judgment about the credibility of the witnesses and other

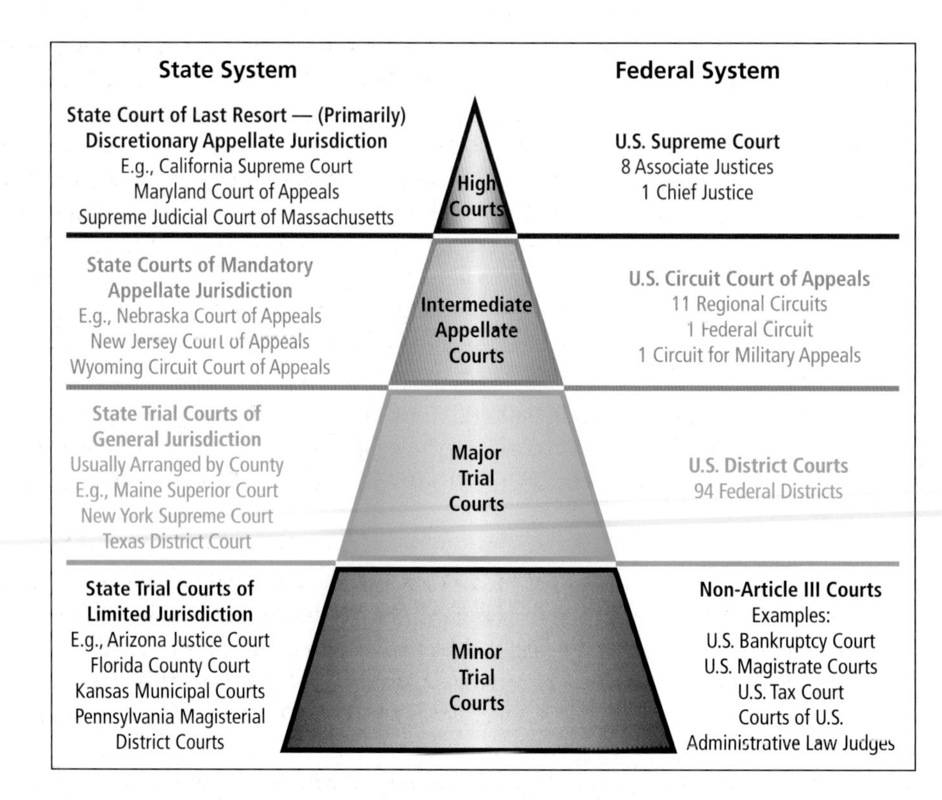

FIGURE 12.1 Overview of the Structure of the Dual Court System in the United States.

evidence, and then reach a decision that resolves the facts that are in dispute. In the case of the assault, the prosecutor would present evidence arguing that the defendant committed the assault, such as testimony from witnesses at the scene, images recorded by video cameras at the scene, testimony from medical professionals about the nature of the victim's injuries, and more. The defense attorney would challenge the evidence introduced by the prosecutor and perhaps call other witnesses testifying that the defendant was not even in town on the night of the incident. The judge would ensure that the trial proceeded fairly and according to legal rules, and a jury would determine whether or not the evidence was sufficient to convict the defendant. If the defendant were found guilty, the judge would issue a sentence as punishment for the offense (e.g., fines, probation, jail, prison).

The trial courts of original jurisdiction in the federal system are called Federal District Courts. As of the writing of this book, there are 94 federal districts—one or more per state and in various territories such as the District of Columbia, Puerto Rico, Guam, and the Virgin Islands (see Figure 12.2). The trial courts of original jurisdiction in the various state court systems go by many different names, as illustrated by Figure 12.1.

In contrast, courts with *appellate jurisdiction* review the proceedings of a lower court of original jurisdiction. Unlike trial courts, appellate courts do not conduct trials and rarely make factual determinations about the events surrounding an alleged criminal offense. Rather, a panel of judges reviews the transcripts from a trial court of original jurisdiction and the legal arguments offered by each party (the prosecution and the defense) to rule on whether the decision is in accordance with applicable law. That is, the work of appellate courts concerns questions about the interpretation or application of laws, not questions of fact. If the defendant charged with assault was found guilty, he might choose to appeal, and the appellate court would review issues such as whether he had a fair trial, whether the evidence was obtained legally, and whether the law had been applied correctly—all matters of interpretation and application of the law. The appellate court would not attempt to determine whether the defendant had actually been in the fight.

In the federal system and in approximately 40 U.S. states, there are enough appeals that the appellate courts are divided into two layers. The losing party in a court of original jurisdiction has the right to appeal the case to the intermediate court of appeals. In the federal system, this court is called the U.S. Circuit Court of Appeals. There are 14 federal judicial circuits: eleven are based on geographic divisions across the United States (see Figure 12.2), one is in the District of Columbia to hear appeals related to the many federal agencies located there, one handles patent and customs claims (the U.S. Circuit Court of Appeals for the Federal Circuit), and one hears appeals from military courts (the U.S. Court of Appeals for the Armed Forces). Most states also call their intermediate appellate court some variation on the term *court of appeals*.

All states have a court of last resort—the highest court in the state, which serves as the final decision maker on all appeals concerning matters of state law. The federal system also has a high court of last resort, the U.S. Supreme Court, which is the final arbitrator of all cases concerning questions of federal law and constitutional interpretation.

There are some rare exceptions to the hierarchies just described. For example, U.S. district courts (ordinarily courts of original jurisdiction) have appellate jurisdiction over federal courts that were not established under Article III of the U.S. Constitution, such as bankruptcy courts, magistrate courts, and the courts of various administrative federal agencies. Similarly, the U.S. Supreme Court (ordinarily an appellate court of last resort) serves as a court of original jurisdiction in a small number of cases, such as those involving foreign ambassadors and cases in which one U.S. state sues another. In these cases, the Supreme Court does make factual determinations in the case rather than functioning strictly as an appellate court.

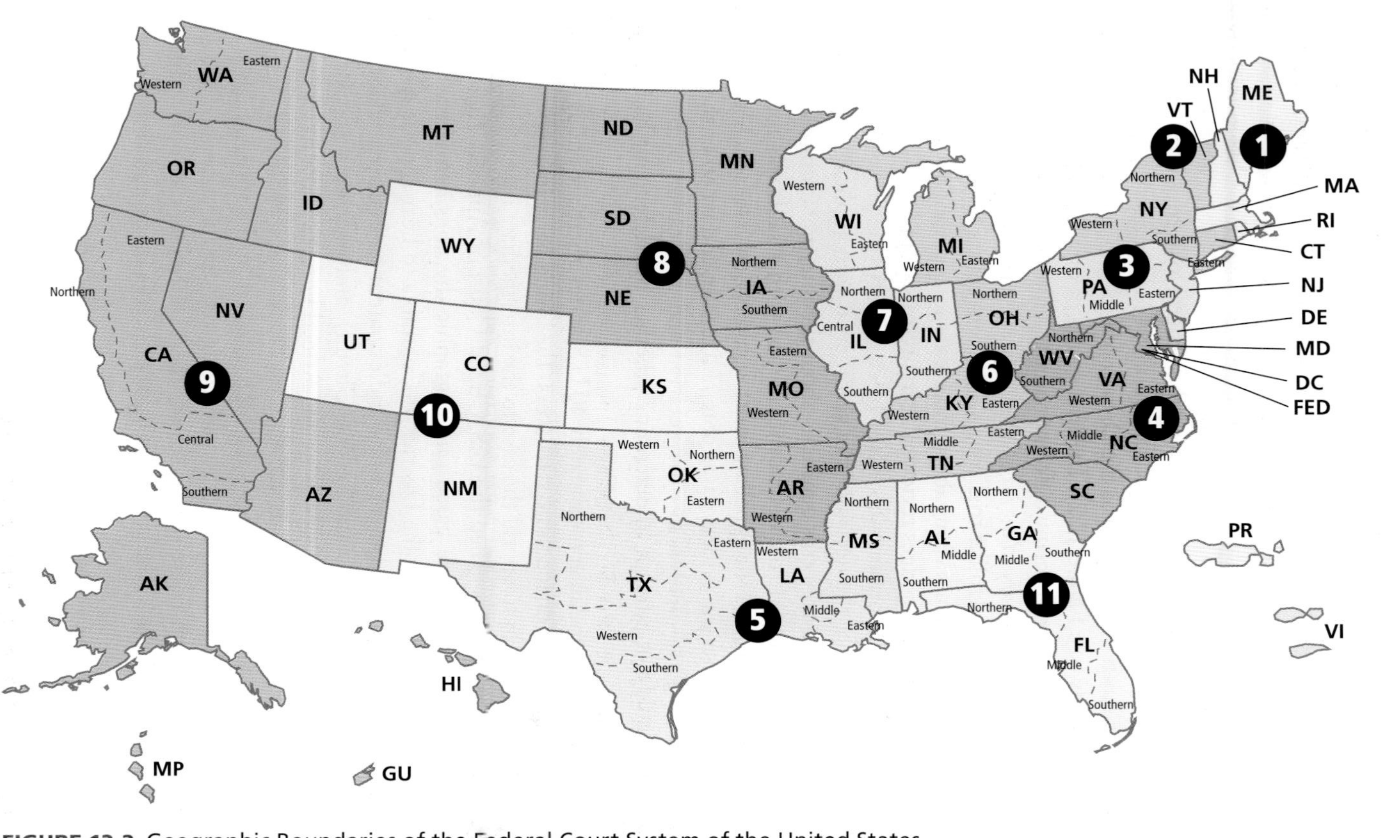

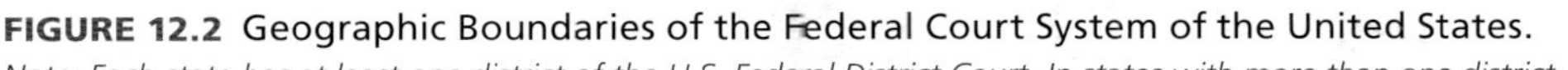
FIGURE 12.2 Geographic Boundaries of the Federal Court System of the United States.
Note: Each state has at least one district of the U.S. Federal District Court. In states with more than one district, the dashed line indicates the boundary between districts. The color-coded and numbered areas are the circuits of the U.S. Circuit Court of Appeals.

OTHER FORMS OF JURISDICTION

The type of case that may be adjudicated by a court of original jurisdiction is called **subject matter jurisdiction**. Courts of *limited subject matter jurisdiction* are specialized, hearing cases only on certain topics. Courts of *general subject matter jurisdiction* hear all other types of cases.

subject matter jurisdiction
A form of jurisdiction based on the subject matter of a case. Courts of limited subject matter jurisdiction hear cases only on certain topics; courts of general subject matter jurisdiction hear all other types of cases.

All federal courts are courts of limited subject matter jurisdiction, meaning that they can adjudicate only certain types of disputes. Federal courts have the subject matter jurisdiction to hear cases presenting *federal questions*. These include violations or interpretations of federal laws or regulations, such as federal crimes, social security, taxes, broadcasting, international trade, and bankruptcy. Federal courts may also adjudicate certain state law claims when *diversity of citizenship* exists (i.e., the parties to a lawsuit are all from different states and the dispute involves at least a certain amount of money). Federal appellate courts may also hear cases requesting the appellate review of state court decisions, policies, or laws (often to determine whether or not they are constitutional).

Cases that do not fall within the subject matter jurisdiction of the federal courts are adjudicated in state courts. But even within a state court system, the trial courts of original jurisdiction are usually split between two layers: minor trial courts and major trial courts. Minor trial courts typically have limited subject matter jurisdiction over traffic cases, civil cases involving "small claims" (relatively small amounts of money), municipal ordinance violations, juvenile offenses, probate matters (the administration of the estates of people who have died), and family law (e.g., divorce, adoption, child custody). In contrast, major trial courts have general subject matter jurisdiction over all remaining cases that are not specifically assigned to a court of limited subject matter jurisdiction. This includes major criminal offenses, personal injury or contract lawsuits for larger sums of money than the small claims limit, real estate disputes, workers' compensation claims, and most issues involving the internal governance of business entities such as trusts, partnerships, and corporations.

Geographic jurisdiction refers to the geographic area where a court is located and over which it is empowered to adjudicate cases. In most state systems, those geographic areas tend to run along the county line boundaries. In the federal system, the geographic jurisdiction of federal courts is set by district (see Figure 12.2).

geographic jurisdiction
A type of jurisdiction based on location, in which a court is empowered to hear cases that originated within the geographic area (whether county, district, or other geographic unit) over which that court has authority.

The three types of jurisdiction—hierarchical, subject matter, and geographic—are considered together when determining where a case should be heard. That is, when charging a suspect with a crime, when making an appeal, or when preparing a civil case, the court to hear the case must be at the appropriate place in the hierarchy of court structure, authorized to hear the subject matter of the issue at hand, and in the correct geographical area.

Q Do you think the U.S. court systems are well organized? Explain.

Q If the shipwreck case had occurred in the United States, what courts do you think might have been involved? Why?

Q Research the court structure in your state. What are the courts of original jurisdiction? What are the appellate courts? What courts have special subject matter jurisdiction? How is geographic jurisdiction assigned?

The Courtroom Workgroup

FOCUSING QUESTION 12.2

Who are the members of the courtroom workgroup and what do they do?

courtroom workgroup
The working relationship that develops among court employees, including judges, prosecutors, defense attorneys, and others.

The **courtroom workgroup** refers to the working relationship among court employees (Eisenstein & Jacob, 1977). Rather than having an adversarial relationship, as often

portrayed in novels and television, attorneys and judges in criminal courts frequently know one another from repeat encounters in professional and social circles. Through their interactions, attorneys and judges develop informal norms that help guide the processing of cases. Although each person is dedicated to his or her role—the prosecutor representing the state, the defense representing the accused, and the judge serving as legal referee of the proceedings—over time, each comes to know the style of the other to the point where all can anticipate how a case will be processed. This helps the courtroom function smoothly and leads to an efficient system of handling cases. Police officers also may become part of the courtroom workgroup because they regularly testify in court, often in similar cases before the same judges and attorneys.

JUDGES

Judges preside over state and federal courts. Their primary role is to serve as a referee, enforcing the rules of procedure and evidence. Sometimes, however, judges are faced with tough decisions about what the law means. This is especially true for appellate judges whose decisions often set public policy. Although judges are supposed to be completely impartial, there is no doubt that their particular judicial philosophies affect their decision making (see Carter & Burke, 2010).

In the federal system, all judges—including those who serve on the U.S. Supreme Court—are nominated by the president and must be confirmed by a majority vote of the U.S. Senate. If confirmed, the judges enjoy life tenure, meaning that they remain federal judges until they die or retire, unless they do something so unethical that they are impeached from office by the Senate (which is very rare). As you might imagine, given the process of becoming a federal judge, nominees tend to have highly accomplished legal careers even before they are nominated (Goldman, 1999).

Five states grant the power to appoint judges to the governor or the legislature. Sixteen states use a merit selection process for selecting judges. That means a nonpartisan nominating committee screens applicants for judgeships and then makes recommendations (depending on the state) to the state bar association, the justices of the state high court, the members of the state legislature, or the governor, who then fills judicial vacancies based on the recommendations of the committee. In the remaining states, judges are elected either in partisan (affiliated with a political party) or nonpartisan elections. Once on the bench, rather than enjoying life tenure as their federal counterparts do, most state judges are subject to formal reelection or voter recall through retention elections (in which voters indicate whether a current judge should or should not remain in office, rather than voting to select a judge from among multiple candidates on a ballot).

Given that methods of selecting judges vary so dramatically, researchers have attempted to determine if one method is superior to another in terms of placing high-quality judges on the bench. Box 12.1 examines what research has found about judicial selection.

PROSECUTORS

Crimes are considered offenses against the state. Governmental officials called *prosecutors* are responsible for prosecuting violations of criminal law. Prosecutors go by many names in different states, including district attorneys, commonwealth's attorneys, state's attorneys, and county attorneys. In the overwhelming majority of states, prosecutors' offices are arranged by county, with each county having a lead prosecutor who is elected to local office. The lead prosecutor employs a staff of lawyers who litigate cases in court.

In the federal system, each federal district has a chief prosecutor called the U.S. Attorney. These positions are political appointments to four-year terms made by the president of the United States and confirmed by the Senate. Therefore, U.S. attorneys

may change when a new administration is elected to office. Each U.S. Attorney's office employs a cadre of lawyers called *Assistant U.S. Attorneys*, who hold their positions regardless of the political party in power at the time; they assist the U.S. Attorney in preparing cases and presenting them in court.

Although prosecutors report to the attorney general of their state (and U.S. Attorneys report to the U.S. Attorney General), most prosecutors' offices enjoy a great deal of autonomy. Prosecutors may exercise a great deal of discretion when making decisions like whom to charge with which crimes and whether to agree to a plea bargain or take a case to trial. Prosecutors are sometimes called the "gatekeepers" of the criminal justice system because of their power to determine who will appear in court and on what charges. Because of this discretionary ability, prosecutors are the most powerful of the primary court actors. The overwhelming majority of prosecutors exercise this power with the dignity and integrity their offices demand. Unfortunately, however, as explored in Box 12.2, instances of prosecutorial misconduct can significantly undermine the cause of justice that prosecutors are supposed to uphold.

DEFENSE ATTORNEYS

Recall from Chapter 8 that the Sixth Amendment to the U.S. Constitution provides that "[i]n all criminal prosecutions, the accused shall enjoy the right . . . to have the Assistance of Counsel for his defence." The interpretation of that language, however, has changed over time. The right to have a *defense attorney* (also known as defense counsel) was not recognized under English common law or in colonial America (Finnegan, 2009). The Sixth Amendment was originally intended to protect wealthy people from being told that they could not hire lawyers to represent them. It was not until well into the twentieth century that the U.S. Supreme Court began to interpret the Sixth Amendment in the way that we understand it today. In fact, it was not until *Gideon v. Wainwright* (1963) that the Court declared that criminal defendants facing felony charges in state courts had the right to the assistance of an attorney even if they could not afford to hire one for themselves. In *Argersinger v. Hamlin* (1972), the Court extended the right to counsel to defendants in misdemeanor cases who were facing a potential sentence of incarceration in jail.

A defendant who can afford to do so may hire his or her own private attorney. This occurs in roughly 20% of all criminal cases (Neubauer & Fradella, 2014). In the remaining criminal cases, defendants cannot afford to hire defense counsel; accordingly, the government provides a lawyer at no expense to the defendant. Unlike people who hire their own lawyers, indigent defendants (i.e., those who cannot afford their own representation) typically have little or no say in who represents them. Rather, a lawyer is appointed by the state in one of three ways in order to represent an indigent defendant. In jurisdictions that have busy enough criminal court systems to make it economically feasible to run a public defender's office, the state employs a group of criminal defense attorneys whose full-time job is to represent indigent defendants. In other jurisdictions, the state hires private attorneys on a case-by-case basis to represent criminal defendants. And in sparsely populated areas, the state may even take bids from attorneys in private practice who are willing to represent criminal defendants.

Whether defense counsel is privately retained or appointed, Walsh and Hemmens (2008) explain that defense attorneys have five primary roles.

> (1) to ensure that the defendants' rights are not violated (intentionally or in error); (2) to make sure the defendants know all of their options before they make a decision; (3) to provide the defendants with the best possible defense, without violating ethical and legal obligations; (4) to investigate and prepare the defense; and (5) to argue for lowest possible sentence or best possible plea bargain. (p. 103)

BOX 12.1

Research in Action

JUDICIAL SELECTION METHODS

As previously explained, there are four primary methods used to select judges in the United States: (1) direct election of judges by citizens in partisan elections (in which judicial candidates run as members of a political party; (2) direct election of judges by citizens in nonpartisan elections (in which judicial candidates run for office without any formal political party affiliation; (3) appointment of judges by elected officials (the U.S. president, the governor, a state legislature); and (4) the *Missouri Plan.* The Missouri Plan is a type of "merit selection" in which a nominating body (usually involving a state bar association which, in turn, utilizes lawyers, judges, and laypersons) screens people interested in judicial office. The nominating body then forwards to the governor a list of persons it has deemed suitable for appointment, from which the governor chooses whom to select as a new judge. After a designated period of service, the judge must stand for retention election, in which the public votes on whether or not the judge should keep his or her position (this gives citizens the opportunity to remove judges after a period of time if they have not performed well on the bench).

Those who favor judicial elections argue that judges, like other public officials, should be accountable to the people (Bogard, 2003; Bonneau & Gann-Hall, 2009). After all, having to stand for reelection builds in "a structural incentive to avoid unpopular rulings" (Pozen, 2008, p. 276). And being accountable to the electorate is more likely to cause judges to be pragmatic, rather than to adhere to a particular judicial philosophy (Sunstein, 2007).

Others counter that elections place a higher value on accountability to the public over independence in judicial decision making (American Bar Association [ABA], 2003; Geyh, 2003). They argue that judges are not like governmental officials in the executive and legislative branches. Rather, judges are supposed to be above politics, serving the cause of justice as independent, impartial arbiters (Moyer, 2005). Indeed, making tough decisions that may not be popular with the general public is part and parcel of being a good judge (ABA, 2003; Croley, 1995). Additionally, those who oppose judicial elections assert that appointing judges is not only more likely to promote diversity on the bench—a proposition for which the empirical evidence is mixed (see Reddick, Nelson, & Caufield, 2010)—but also results in higher quality judges as a function of selectees being screened for appointment to the bench (Behrens & Silverman, 2002; Sobel & Hall, 2007).

At one time, judicial elections were "sleepy, low-key affairs," largely as a function of "[c]odes of conduct [which] prevented candidates from announcing their views on controversial topics, criticizing other candidates, or directly soliciting campaign contributions" (Pozen, 2008, pp. 266–267). But times have changed, especially as a result of the U.S. Supreme Court's decision in *Republican Party of Minnesota v. White* (2002), which ruled that the First Amendment to the U.S. Constitution's guarantee of free speech mandates that candidates for judicial office be permitted to announce their views on controversial political and legal topics. Since then, "[p]ublic trust and the appearance of impartiality have likewise suffered" (Pozen, 2008, p. 304; see also ABA, 2003; Cann & Yates, 2008). Indeed, more than 70% of Americans "believe that campaign contributions

The Sixth Amendment right to counsel only applies when triggered by the occurrence of a critical stage of a criminal prosecution, such as postindictment lineups, arraignments, preliminary hearings, trials, and sentencing hearings (Marcus, 2009). The right does *not* apply in civil cases, including *habeas corpus* or immigration proceedings; individuals who can afford to do so may hire an attorney in civil cases, but indigent persons are not provided with an attorney by the state.

OTHER COURTROOM WORKGROUP MEMBERS

Although judges, prosecutors, and defense attorneys are the primary actors in criminal cases, courthouses employ a wide range of professionals who keep the courthouse running. Court security staff help ensure that the courthouse and the people in it are kept safe. Court clerks file cases, manage case dockets, and attend to financial and human

have at least some influence on judges' decisions in the courtroom, versus only five percent who believe that campaign contributions have no influence" (Pozen, 2008, p. 304). Messy political elections, especially those involving negative campaign advertisements, combined with unlimited campaign contributions that are permissible in the wake of *Citizens United v. Federal Election Commission* (2010), have only served to erode further the public's confidence in an independent, impartial, and fair-minded judiciary (Carrington, 2011).

Some research suggests that the various selection methods do not produce significant differences in levels of judicial integrity as measured by judicial misconduct. Goldschmidt, Olson, and Ekman (2009) concluded that although there were "statistically significant differences across the methods of judicial selection and a majority of the categories of judicial misconduct, none of these differences could be considered substantively strong or overwhelming" (p. 477). But the American Judicature Society (Reddick, 2010) concluded that merit selection systems "produce fewer unfit judges than judicial elections" (p. 7).

On the whole, although merit selection tends to place candidates on the bench who hold undergraduate and law degrees from more prestigious schools than other selection methods do (Glick & Emmert, 1987), most research concludes that the method of selection does not affect the overall quality of judges in terms of characteristics like intelligence, temperament, legal ability and experience, and fair-mindedness (Choi, Gulati, & Posner, 2010; Flango & Ducat, 1979). There is also some support for the proposition that the varying methods of selection do not significantly affect the quality of the decisions judges reach (Gann-Hall, 1992). But these propositions are disputed. Some empirical studies support the notion that appointed judges are the most independent and, therefore, are less likely to engage in strategic decision making in certain types of cases (Epstein, Knight, & Shvetsova, 2002; Pinello, 1995). And research conducted after *Republican Party of Minnesota v. White* (2002) suggests that "judicial quality is low in states that utilize elections to select their judges" (Sobel & Hall, 2007, p. 79). Another recent study conducted in the wake of the *Citizens United* decision that drew on four years of data from all 50 U.S. states found that "elected judges are more likely to decide in favor of business interests as the amount of campaign contributions received from those interests increases. In other words, every dollar of direct contributions from business groups is associated with an increase in the probability that the judge in question will vote for business litigants" (Kang & Shepherd, 2011, p. 69). In light of the concerns about judicial elections, might merit selection be the best way to place judges on the bench? Or should philosophical concerns about the importance of an accountable, democratically elected judiciary trump the concerns raised by recent research?

- Q Which method of judicial selection does your state use?
- Q What do you think are the advantages and disadvantages of each method of selecting judges?
- Q Which method of judicial selection do you most prefer? Why? Or would you recommend modifications to, or a method different from, those described above?

resource administration. Law clerks help judges conduct research and write opinions. Court reporters transcribe court proceedings so that a written record is maintained in the event of an appeal. Translators make sure that language barriers do not prevent people from understanding the courtroom proceedings. Bailiffs help maintain order in courtrooms. Secretaries schedule hearings and trials and coordinate the calendars of judges and attorneys.

Numerous correctional professionals work in most courthouses. Probation officers, for example, conduct investigations into defendants' backgrounds and report their findings to help judges fashion appropriate sentences. Pretrial services representatives oversee the administration of bail and make arrangements to release qualified pretrial detainees from custody. And representatives from a range of pretrial diversion programs evaluate defendants and make recommendations (generally for low-risk or

BOX 12.2

Ethics in Practice

PROSECUTORIAL MISCONDUCT

The very first standard listed in the National District Attorneys Association's (2009) National Prosecution Standards states:

> 1–1.1: The prosecutor is an independent administrator of justice. The primary responsibility of a prosecutor is to seek justice, which can only be achieved by the representation and presentation of the truth. This responsibility includes, but is not limited to, ensuring that the guilty are held accountable, that the innocent are protected from unwarranted harm, and that the rights of all participants, particularly victims of crime, are respected. (p. 2)

Yet, stories of prosecutorial misconduct fill the news and scholarly journals. One of the more sensational prosecutorial misconduct cases occurred in 2006 when assistant prosecutor Mike Nifong violated a number of ethical rules in the wake of a stripper having accused members of the Duke University lacrosse team of sexually assaulting her during a party (see Mosteller, 2007). Nifong made false and inflammatory statements to the media that could have interfered with the defendants' Sixth Amendment rights to a fair trial had the charges not ultimately been dropped. He also improperly commented on the defendants' invocation of their right to remain silent. And, perhaps most egregiously, he allowed the charges to pend against the defendants for months while concealing DNA evidence that showed the defendants were innocent.

Nifong's actions appear to have been motivated by a desire to be elected as the next district attorney of Durham County, North Carolina. The case presented him with an opportunity to run as a crusader for racial justice since the alleged victim was black and the men she accused were white students attending an expensive and prestigious private university. Nifong won the election with strong support from the African American community in the county. But Nifong was ultimately disbarred (meaning he was stripped of his license to practice law) for his unethical behavior (Mosteller, 2007).

The Duke University lacrosse case is unusual, but not unique. Rubin (2011), for example, documented a series of egregious cases in New York City in which prosecutorial misconduct of constitutional dimension—the withholding or concealing of *exculpatory evidence* (evidence that tends to cast doubt on a defendant's guilt)—sent innocent people to prison for crimes they did not commit. Other more common forms of prosecutorial misconduct include making improper statements (i.e., those not permitted under the rules of evidence and procedure), suborning perjury (knowingly presenting false testimony), making material misstatements of law or fact to a judge or jury, and prosecuting a case for vindictive reasons. Perhaps surprisingly to the layperson, however, prosecutors who engage in unethical behavior rarely face any serious sanctions. In fact, a number of reasons work in combination with each other to insulate prosecutors from the consequences of most unethical behavior (Gershman, 1986). Arguably, though, the most important of these reasons might be two U.S. Supreme Court rulings.

In *Imbler v. Pachtman* (1976), the Court held that, unlike police and correctional actors who can be sued for their unethical actions, prosecutors are protected from all civil liability connected with their litigation of criminal cases. This immunity even extends to actions performed in bad faith, such as intentionally withholding exculpatory evidence or knowingly using fabricated evidence. The Court reasoned that it is "better to leave unredressed

first-time offenders) concerning their placement into drug and alcohol treatment, anger management classes, and a range of other programs premised on the therapeutic and conciliatory styles of social control (see Chapter 4) which, if successfully completed, might allow a defendant to avoid formal adjudication, including the attendant penal social controls and the criminal record that comes with it.

Finally, there are even members of the public who come to court with sufficient frequency that they might become members of the courtroom workgroup. Bail agents post bail bond to secure the release of the defendants who hire them. Some newspapers

the wrongs done by dishonest officers than to subject those who try to do their duty to the constant dread of retaliation" (*Imbler v. Pachtman,* 1976, p. 428). The Court assumed that disciplinary proceedings at work and before the bar would be a sufficient deterrent to most prosecutorial misconduct. But that assumption has turned out to be incorrect. Studies repeatedly demonstrate not only that prosecutorial misconduct frequently contributes to wrongful convictions (Joy, 2006), but also that prosecutors "are rarely held accountable in disciplinary proceedings for their misconduct" (McDonald-Henning, 2012–2013, pp. 221–222; Rubin, 2011).

Twenty-five years later, the U.S. Supreme Court decided *Connick v. Thompson* (2011), a civil case in which Thompson had sued the Orleans Parish District Attorney's Office for its failure to properly train and supervise its prosecutors. That office had prosecuted Thompson for attempted robbery. During his trial, prosecutors failed to turn over a lab report that, if Thompson's attorney had known about it, could have been used to show that blood on the victim's pants from the robber was Type B, different from Thompson's Type O blood type. Without that exculpatory evidence, Thompson was wrongfully convicted. He was subsequently charged with murder, in a case unrelated to the attempted robbery. Thompson did not take the stand in his own defense during the murder trial because of his prior conviction for attempted robbery, which could have been used against him had he testified. He was convicted and sentenced to death. A month before his scheduled execution 14 years later, Thompson's private investigator discovered the lab report. Both his attempted robbery and murder convictions were vacated. After the state retried Thompson on the murder charge and a jury acquitted him, Thompson sued the district attorney's office, arguing that the office had been deliberately indifferent to an obvious need to train prosecutors to avoid constitutional violations, such as failing to turn over exculpatory evidence like the lab report. The jury awarded Thompson $14 million ($1 million for each year he spent on death row). The U.S. Supreme Court ultimately reversed this award, holding that a prosecutor's office cannot be held civilly liable for failure to train its prosecutors based on a single instance of constitutional violations by prosecutors or even a handful of dissimilar cases in which prosecutors fail to turn over exculpatory evidence. Rather, a pattern of similar abuses must be shown before civil liability can attach for a municipality's failure to train its employees.

- **Q** What do you think of the outcome in the Duke Lacrosse case? Was justice served? Explain your reasoning.
- **Q** What factors do you think might lead some prosecutors to misbehave? Why do you think they are so infrequently disciplined for such misbehavior? (For an excellent and easy-to-understand explanation of the various answers to both of these questions see Gershman, 1986).
- **Q** Review the holding in *Imbler v. Pachtman.* Should absolute immunity from civil suits be provided when prosecutors unintentionally commit unethical acts—in other words, when those acts are a result of negligence? Do you think this is fair? Is it good public policy? Do you feel differently concerning unethical acts that are intentionally committed in bad faith? Why or why not?
- **Q** Do you agree with the outcome in *Connick v. Thompson?* Why or why not?
- **Q** What do you think could be done to help reduce prosecutorial misconduct and the number of wrongful convictions to which such misconduct contributes?

and television stations assign reporters to cover courthouse events. Psychologists, social workers, and other counselors provide support services for victims of certain crimes. Some courthouses use specially trained child advocates to assist child witnesses and victims navigate judicial processes. And some witnesses—such as certain police officers, investigators, and expert witnesses—appear in court with such regularity that they, too, become members of the courtroom workgroup.

It takes the coordinated efforts of all of these members of the courtroom workgroup to make the criminal justice system function properly.

Q What role would each member of the courtroom workgroup have in the case presented at the beginning of this chapter?

Q What do you think are the advantages and disadvantages of selecting local prosecuting attorneys through elections? Do you think prosecutors should be selected through election or by other means? Why?

Q What do you think are the advantages and disadvantages of having a state-funded public defender's office? Of contracting with private attorneys? Which method do you think is preferable for appointing an attorney for an indigent defendant? Why?

Criminal Pretrial Processes

FOCUSING QUESTION 12.3

What judicial processes occur before a criminal trial?

felony
The most serious crimes, which are generally punished by a sentence of a year or more in prison and/or a substantial fine.

misdemeanor
Less serious offenses that are generally punished by a sentence of less than a year in jail and/or a small to moderate fine.

Criminal offenses are broadly classified into two categories: felonies and misdemeanors. The distinction between the categories is based on the seriousness of the crime and the maximum possible punishment that can be given for it (see Table 12.1 for an example from one state; but note that each state, and the federal government, varies in terms of how they classify crimes and punishments). **Felonies** are the most serious crimes, and they usually can be punished by a sentence of a year or more in prison and/or a substantial fine. **Misdemeanors** are less serious offenses, and they are usually punished by a sentence of less than a year in jail and/or a small to moderate fine. For instance, robbery is generally a felony, whereas disorderly conduct is generally a misdemeanor. Lawmakers, when writing legal codes, specify whether acts are classified as felonies or misdemeanors.

The following discussion outlines steps in processing a *felony* case. Misdemeanor cases are often handled less formally through assembly-line processes as described in

TABLE 12.1 Punishments for Felonies and Misdemeanors in Virginia (from Most Serious Offenses to Least Serious Offenses)

Offense Category	Authorized Punishments
Class 1 Felony	Death or life in prison and a fine up to $100,000
Class 2 Felony	20 years to life in prison and a fine up to $100,000
Class 3 Felony	5 to 20 years in prison and a fine up to $100,000
Class 4 Felony	2 to 10 years in prison and a fine up to $100,000
Class 5 Felony	1 to 10 years in prison *or* up to 12 months in jail and a fine up to $2,500
Class 6 Felony	1 to 5 years in prison *or* up to 12 months in jail and a fine up to $2,500
Class 1 Misdemeanor	Up to 12 months in jail and a fine up to $2,500
Class 2 Misdemeanor	Up to 6 months in jail and a fine up to $1,000
Class 3 Misdemeanor	A fine up to $500
Class 4 Misdemeanor	A fine up to $250

See Punishment for Conviction of a Felony (2008) and Punishment for Conviction of a Misdemeanor (2000).

Chapters 6 (discussion of mechanical model) and 8 (discussion of the crime control model). However, trials can—and do—occur in misdemeanor cases. When a misdemeanor is processed, though, grand juries are not used, and there is not always a right to a trial by jury, as you will learn later (you may also wish to refer to Figure 1.5 in Chapter 1).

INITIAL APPEARANCE

When someone is arrested, the law requires that the person be taken before a neutral judicial officer for an **initial appearance**. The initial appearance is also known as a *Gerstein* hearing after the U.S. Supreme Court case that mandated it, *Gerstein v. Pugh* (1975). The initial appearance protects the rights of an arrested person by reviewing the law enforcement officer's decision that there was probable cause for an arrest, which is required by the Fourth Amendment. The initial appearance is supposed to occur within 48 hours of a person's arrest. Delays beyond 48 hours require the government to prove "extraordinary circumstances" for the longer delay (*County of Riverside v. McLaughlin*, 1991).

Initial appearance
When a judge or magistrate informs an accused person of the charges against him or her, the possible penalties, and the right to retain counsel or have an attorney appointed if indigent.

Several other things typically occur at an initial appearance, although technicalities differ by jurisdiction. The defendant is always informed of charges and possible penalties. The defendant is usually provided with a copy of any charging documents and informed of the right to retain counsel or, if indigent, to have an attorney appointed. In addition, bail may be preliminarily granted or denied; a full bail hearing usually occurs later as a separate proceeding. And in more than 75% of all *misdemeanor* cases, a defendant pleads guilty to the offense charged at the initial appearance (Neubauer & Fradella, 2014).

CHARGING

Criminal defendants may be formally charged with committing a crime in three primary ways: by a *complaint* filled out by a police officer or private citizen accusing a person of committing a crime; by an *indictment* returned by a grand jury; or by an *information*, which is a document presented by a prosecutor to a judge at a preliminary hearing. Regardless of which method is used, a charging document must include the crime being charged; the person being charged; when and where the alleged acts occurred; the possible penalties; and most important, a written statement of the facts of the offense. A complaint is commonly used for *misdemeanor* charges. Indictments and informations are used primarily for *felony* charges.

Before standing trial on felony charges, an accused has the right to have the evidence against him or her reviewed to make sure there is sufficient evidence to warrant moving forward with a trial. There are two distinct judicial processes used to achieve this goal: grand jury proceedings and preliminary hearings. Defendants are entitled to have one or the other but not both.

Recall from Chapter 8 that the Fifth Amendment to the U.S. Constitution guarantees the right to a grand jury indictment in all federal felony prosecutions. About half of the states also provide this right. A **grand jury** is a group of citizens that typically ranges in size from 16 to 23 people (although a handful of states use grand juries as small as 3 to 5 people). Its purpose is to serve as a check on prosecutorial power by listening to evidence of criminal wrongdoing presented by a prosecutor and to determine whether that evidence is sufficient to make someone stand trial. If the grand jury finds, by a simple majority vote, that there is probable cause to believe a person has committed the offense, it issues an indictment (also known as a *true bill*), and the case moves forward. If, on the other hand, the grand jury finds insufficient evidence to issue an indictment, it issues a *no bill*, the case does not move forward, and the accused person does not have to stand trial for the alleged offense.

grand jury
A group of citizens impaneled to hear evidence presented by a prosecuting attorney with the purpose of determining whether sufficient evidence (probable cause) exists to bring to trial a person accused of committing a crime.

Grand juries usually sit for a fixed period ranging from 1 to 18 months. In spite of their purpose of restraining unbridled prosecutorial authority, grand juries rarely return

a no bill. Instead, they tend to rubber-stamp the requests of prosecutors (see Washburn, 2008), meaning that virtually all cases brought to a grand jury result in an indictment that sends the case forward. This is largely because grand jury proceedings are held in secret (not in open court) and only the prosecutor presents evidence; neither the defendant nor his or her counsel is usually present. In fact, a defendant may not even know that a grand jury is investigating his or her alleged involvement in a crime.

preliminary hearing A hearing held in front of a judge to determine whether or not there is probable cause to believe that a person committed the crime of which he or she stands accused. If probable cause is found, the judge binds over the defendant for trial. If probable cause is not found, the case may be dismissed.

A **preliminary hearing** is another proceeding designed to determine if a defendant must stand trial on felony charges. Preliminary hearings are used as checks on prosecutorial authority in jurisdictions that do not use grand juries. They are also used in grand jury jurisdictions when a defendant waives the right to a grand jury indictment. Unlike grand jury proceedings, preliminary hearings are held in open court before a judge. Both the prosecution and the defense may present evidence and arguments. A judge then determines if there is probable cause. If the judge finds there is probable cause to believe the defendant committed the felony or felonies charged, then the judge *binds over* the defendant for trial. If, however, the judge determines that probable cause is lacking, the judge may reduce felony charges to misdemeanor charges or may dismiss the charges completely, depending on what the evidence warrants.

ARRAIGNMENT

arraignment A judicial proceeding at which a person accused of a crime is formally advised of the charges by the reading of the charging document in open court, advised of his or her rights, and asked to enter a plea (e.g., guilty, not guilty, *nolo contendere*) to the charges.

After a defendant is indicted by a grand jury or bound over for trial by a judge at a preliminary hearing, the next step is to hold an arraignment. An **arraignment** is a formal proceeding in which the charging document is read to the defendant in open court, and the defendant is asked to enter a formal plea on each charge. Defendants generally have two options: guilty or not guilty. If the defendant pleads not guilty, the case is scheduled for trial. If the defendant pleads guilty—something that usually only occurs if the prosecution and defense have agreed to a plea bargain (discussed later)—then the case is scheduled for sentencing. In some jurisdictions, a defendant may be permitted to plead *nolo contendere* (no contest), which allows a defendant to admit that there is sufficient evidence such that a conviction at trial is highly likely. However, unlike with a guilty plea, with a *nolo contendere* plea the defendant is not required to actually admit guilt. In some jurisdictions, this means that a *nolo contendere* plea cannot be used against a person in a civil (noncriminal) court trial pertaining to the same set of facts (recall from Chapter 7 that a single incident may result in both criminal and civil actions). Finally, in most U.S. jurisdictions, a mentally ill defendant may enter a plea of not guilty by reason of insanity (see Chapter 4). Contrary to popular belief, such pleas occur in less than 1% of all felony cases. Moreover, when insanity pleas are entered, they are unsuccessful approximately 75% of the time (Perlin, 1997).

DISCOVERY

discovery The process by which the parties (defense and prosecution) to a criminal case exchange relevant information about that case. The purpose of discovery is to prevent unfair surprises at trial.

exculpatory evidence Any evidence that may be favorable to the defendant in a criminal trial, either by casting doubt on the defendant's guilt or mitigating the defendant's culpability. The prosecution must disclose all exculpatory evidence to the defense as part of the discovery process.

Discovery is the process by which the parties exchange relevant information about a case. Although there is no constitutional right to discovery in criminal cases, a series of statutes, judicial decisions, and court rules have established obligations to disclose certain information as part of a defendant's due process rights to a fair trial. For example, both sides must disclose a list of witnesses who may be called at trial. Similarly, the parties must disclose relevant evidence, including results or reports of physical examinations, scientific tests, or experiments on evidence. Additionally, the prosecution must disclose all **exculpatory evidence** to the defense (*Brady v. Maryland,* 1963). Exculpatory evidence is any evidence that may be favorable to the defendant at trial either by tending to cast doubt on the defendant's guilt or by tending to mitigate the defendant's culpability. The prosecution must also disclose any prior inconsistent statements of prosecutorial witnesses so that the defense may conduct meaningful cross-examinations of the prosecution's witnesses (see Demands for Production of Statements and Reports of Witnesses, 1970, also known as the Jencks Act). Collectively, all of the information disclosed is supposed to prevent unfair surprises at trial.

PLEA BARGAINING

Contrary to the jury trials favored in television and film portrayals, the vast majority of criminal cases never go to trial. Rather, they are resolved by a plea bargain. **Plea bargaining** is the process by which a defendant agrees to plead guilty in exchange for some consideration from the government. "Plea bargaining dominates the modern American criminal process. Upwards of 95% of all state and federal felony convictions are obtained by guilty plea" (Covey, 2008, p. 1238).

plea bargaining
The process by which a defendant agrees to plead guilty in exchange for some consideration from the government, such as a lower charge, fewer counts, or a reduced sentence. Approximately 95% of felony cases are resolved by plea bargaining.

Plea bargaining usually takes one of three forms. In *charge bargaining*, the defendant pleads guilty to a less serious charge than the one in the charging document. For example, someone charged with the felony of aggravated assault may plead guilty to a misdemeanor assault charge to avoid not only the felony conviction but also the increased prison time that would come with the more serious charge. In *count bargaining*, someone charged with multiple offenses pleads guilty to only some of the charges in exchange for the others being dropped. This, in turn, reduces the overall sentence the defendant will receive. For example, someone charged with eight counts of bank robbery may plead to one or two counts and face punishment just for those counts rather than for all of the robberies. Finally, *sentence bargaining* occurs when a defendant pleads guilty to the crime originally charged but does so in exchange for a lesser sentence than would likely have been imposed if the defendant had been convicted at trial. For example, someone facing the death penalty for a homicide might plead guilty to murder if a sentence of life is recommended as part of a plea bargain.

Whatever form of plea bargaining is used, the plea agreement in any case must be agreed upon by the prosecutor, defense counsel, and the defendant. Once a plea agreement is negotiated, it is ultimately up to a judge to accept the plea and enter judgment in accordance with the agreement. If the judge refuses to accept the terms of a plea bargain, the defendant may withdraw from the plea agreement and seek a trial.

PRETRIAL MOTIONS

A **motion** is a formal request asking a court to make a specific ruling. Motions may be made orally or in writing and may concern any number of substantive or procedural issues. In criminal justice, however, the most important motion that can be made before a trial is the *motion to suppress*. In such a motion, a defendant charged with a crime asks a judge to suppress (or prohibit) certain evidence from being considered at trial because it was gathered in violation of the defendant's constitutional rights. Recall from Chapter 8, for example, that searches for and seizures of evidence must comply with the requirements of the Fourth Amendment. Similarly, custodial interrogations that lead a suspect to make incriminating statements (sometimes even full confessions) must have been obtained in accordance with the rights in the Fifth and Sixth Amendments to the U.S. Constitution. If evidence was obtained in violation of any of these constitutional rights, then a defendant may file a motion to suppress the evidence. If granted by a judge, the suppressed evidence is excluded and may not be used to establish the defendant's guilt at trial. Thus, granting a motion to suppress may seriously affect the outcome of a criminal case. However, such motions are relatively rare. They are filed in less than 8% of all criminal cases (Nardulli, 1983). Moreover, such motions are granted in less than 2% of the cases in which they are filed (Uchida & Bynum 1991).

motion
A formal request asking the court to make a specific ruling on an issue or question. Motions may address any number of substantive or procedural issues, but the most significant is a motion to suppress evidence that was gathered in violation of a defendant's constitutional rights.

Q Why do you think initial appearances must be held within 48 hours, barring exceptional circumstances?

Q If you were a criminal defendant facing felony charges, which process would you prefer to protect your rights—the grand jury process or a preliminary hearing? Why?

Q Do you think "surprises" should be allowed at criminal trials? Explain.

Q What are the advantages and disadvantages of plea bargaining?

Criminal Trial Processes

FOCUSING QUESTION 12.4

What happens during and after a criminal trial?

The Sixth Amendment to the U.S. Constitution guarantees the right to a speedy, public, and impartial trial by jury for defendants who stand accused of crimes. The Supreme Court, however, has carved out two significant exceptions to this rule. First, because juvenile cases are civil actions as opposed to being truly criminal in nature, juveniles in most states do not have a right to a trial by jury (see *McKeiver v. Pennsylvania,* 1971). Second, the right to a jury trial does not apply to petty charges, defined by the Supreme Court as any case in which the punishment is a fine, community service, the loss of a privilege such as one's driver's license, or incarceration for fewer than six months (*Baldwin v. New York,* 1970; *Blanton v. City of North Las Vegas,* 1989).

When the right to trial by jury does not exist or when a defendant elects to waive his or her right to a trial by jury (as they often do in cases when they believe a jury would be biased against them for some reason), a judge assumes the role of the jury as the trier of fact. Such proceedings are called *bench trials* because the case is tried by the judge, who sits on "the bench."

summons
A court order that directs a recipient to appear in court at a specific time on a specific date. Among other uses, the summons is the mechanism by which potential jurors are compelled to appear in court to participate in the jury selection process.

voir dire
A term for the process in which the venire of potential jurors is sworn to tell the truth and then questioned to screen out persons who may not be able to make a fair and impartial decision in the case (this is known as being stricken for cause). Potential jurors can also be excused with peremptory challenges.

peremptory challenge
Allows the prosecution or defense to excuse a potential juror during the *voir dire* process without specifying a cause. Each side is typically permitted only a limited number of peremptory challenges, and they may not be used to exclude jurors on the basis of race or gender.

petit jury
The group of jurors empaneled to hear a particular criminal case, at the conclusion of which they render a verdict. In most states, petit juries in criminal trials are composed of 12 jurors.

JURY SELECTION

In jury trials, the jury must be selected before a trial can begin. Jury selection is a complicated process that varies significantly not only from state to state, but even from courtroom to courtroom within the same courthouse. However, there are several steps that commonly occur almost everywhere. First, court personnel need to assemble a group of potential jurors. This task is usually executed by a jury administrator or clerk of the court who issues summonses to potential jurors. A **summons** is a court order that directs a recipient to appear in court at a specific time on a specific date. The group of people who respond to the summons by coming to court to participate in the jury selection process are called the *venire.*

Next, the venire is questioned in court in a process known as ***voir dire***, a Latin term meaning "to speak the truth." During *voir dire,* the venire is sworn to tell the truth and is then asked a variety of questions designed to screen out people who cannot make a fair and impartial decision in the case. Some judges allow the lawyers in the case to ask the questions; other judges prefer to ask the questions themselves. Either way, the questions are supposed to help the court determine who should be excused from serving on the jury because they are partial to one side of the case or because they are biased about the nature of the case. These parties are excused from jury service for cause (also known as being stricken for cause). For example, people who were the victims of significant thefts may not be able to be fair and impartial jurors in a burglary case. In some jurisdictions, each side may also be permitted to excuse a few potential jurors without cause. These are called **peremptory challenges**. Peremptory challenges may be used for nearly any reason, ranging from the prosecution or defense not liking the way someone looked at them to thinking that the potential juror may not believe the arguments they plan to make during trial. Peremptory challenges may not, however, be used in a discriminatory manner. It violates the constitutional guarantee of equal protection of the law for lawyers to use their peremptory strikes to exclude potential jurors on the basis of race or gender (*Batson v. Kentucky,* 1986; *J. E. B. v. Alabama ex rel. T. B.,* 1994).

Once the *voir dire* process is completed, the judge will impanel and swear the **petit jury**—the people who will listen to the evidence over the course of the trial and then render a verdict. In most states, criminal juries are comprised of 12 petit jurors. However, some states use juries composed of fewer than 12 jurors. The U.S. Supreme Court approved of juries as small as 6 persons in *Williams v. Florida* (1970). As indicated in Table 12.2, the size of a jury affects whether or not verdicts that are not unanimous may be permitted under the law.

PRESUMPTIONS AND EVIDENCE

At the start of a criminal trial, the jury is guided by two presumptions, which are conclusions that the jury is *required* to make in the absence of sufficient evidence being introduced at trial to overcome or *rebut* the presumption. The *presumption of sanity* applies in all criminal trials. All defendants are presumed to be sane—legally responsible for their actions—unless they are proven insane at trial. Because sanity is an issue in only a miniscule number of criminal cases, the presumption of sanity is rarely even mentioned. The second is the **presumption of innocence**. All criminal defendants are presumed innocent until proven guilty beyond a reasonable doubt. This means the defendant does not have to prove his or her innocence. Rather, the prosecutor bears the burden of proof to overcome or rebut the presumption of innocence by introducing sufficient evidence to prove the defendant guilty beyond a reasonable doubt. If the prosecutor does not or cannot introduce such evidence or if the defense attorney is able to introduce reasonable doubt, then the defendant is acquitted (found "not guilty").

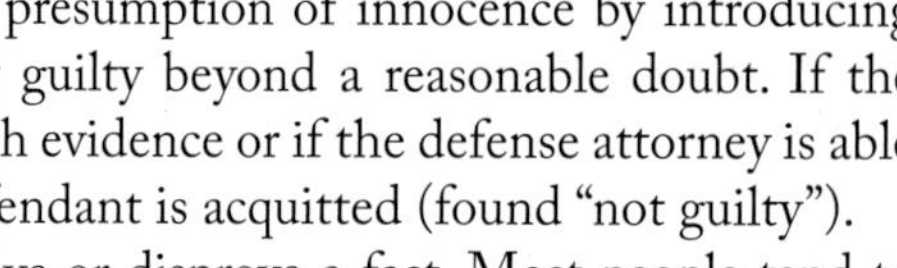

presumption of innocence
Presumes that all criminal defendants are innocent until their guilt has been proven beyond a reasonable doubt. This is a presumption that the jury (or judge in a bench trial) is required to make at a criminal trial.

Evidence is anything that helps to prove or disprove a fact. Most people tend to think of evidence as *real* or *physical evidence*—tangible objects like clothes, weapons, drugs, documents, and so forth, but there are three other types of evidence that are commonly used in criminal trials. Evidence also includes *testimony,* or the responses of sworn witnesses to the questions posed to them by attorneys or the judge, and *scientific evidence,* or the results of scientific or forensic testing on real or physical evidence. *Demonstrative evidence* includes maps, photos, diagrams, computer simulations, and other aids designed for use at trial to help demonstrate some fact to the judge or jury.

evidence
Anything that helps prove or disprove a fact. May include physical evidence, sworn testimony, scientific evidence, or demonstrative evidence.

Expert witness testifies for the defense in the trial of Dr. Conrad Murray, convicted of involuntary manslaughter in the death of music star Michael Jackson. As the title suggests, expert witnesses must qualify as experts on the subject matter about which they testify. They can be questioned in court not only about their areas of expertise, but also about facts such as their educational background, number of times they have previously served as an expert witness, and amount of compensation they receive for testifying. What factors would you consider when determining whether a witness was an expert on a topic? Which would be most important?

TABLE 12.2 Order of Presentation at Trial

Procedure	What Happens
Opening Statements	The parties present an overview of their case. This normally includes their "theory" of the case and an outline or road map of the evidence they plan to present over the course of trial. The prosecution usually goes first because it bears the burden of persuasion.
Prosecution's Case-in-Chief	The prosecution calls witnesses and presents other evidence in an attempt to prove the defendant's guilt. When a prosecutor calls a witness, a *direct examination* is conducted. Direct examinations are comprised of a series of open-ended questions (e.g., who, what, when, where, how, why). When the prosecutor finishes the direct examination of any witness, the defendant is guaranteed the right to conduct a *cross-examination*. Questions on cross-examination tend to be closed ended in that they typically ask for a "yes" or "no" answer. Cross-examination questions usually focus on undermining the credibility of the witness by exploring inconsistencies, inaccuracies, biases, or inadequacies of observation.
Motion for Judgment of Acquittal	While not required, the defense may move for a *judgment of acquittal* at the end of the prosecution's case-in-chief. This motion asks the judge to dismiss the case because no reasonable jury could find the defendant guilty in light of the evidence presented by the prosecution. These motions are rarely granted.
Defense's Case-in-Chief	The defense conducts direct examination of its witnesses and presents other evidence in an attempt to create reasonable doubt about the defendant's guilt. The prosecution can then cross-examine witnesses called by the defense.
Renewed Motion for Judgment of Acquittal	The defense may (but is not required to) renew its motion for acquittal after presenting its case-in-chief. Again, these motions are rarely granted.
Rebuttal Case by Prosecution	While not routine, the prosecution may be permitted to introduce additional evidence after the defense has closed its case-in-chief. Such evidence is usually limited to rebutting evidence presented by the defense.
Closing Arguments	Both the prosecution and the defense are permitted to summarize their respective cases to the jury and present arguments why the verdict should be in their favor. Usually, the prosecution makes its closing argument first, then the defense makes it closing argument, and finally, the prosecution gets the "last word" during rebuttal.
Jury Instructions	The judge instructs the jury as to the applicable law that is relevant in the case. The timing of jury instructions varies and may be at the start of the trial, before closing arguments, or after the closing arguments have been made.
Jury Deliberations	The jury leaves the courtroom to conduct their deliberations in private.
Verdict	In most criminal trials, the jury deliberates until all members of the jury vote to either convict or acquit the defendant. A handful of states allow 12-person verdicts that are not unanimous. If a 6-person jury is used, the verdict must be unanimous. If the jury cannot reach consensus to agree on a verdict, a judge may declare a *hung jury*, which results in the jury being discharged and the case being retried or dismissed.
Postverdict Motions	The parties may (but are not required to) introduce various motions. For example, if the defendant is convicted, defense counsel might move to allow the defendant to remain free on bail pending sentencing. Alternatively, the defense may move for a new trial or for a judgment of acquittal.
Sentencing	The imposition of sentence upon a convicted defendant normally takes place at a sentencing hearing a number of weeks after the verdict. The court must impose a sentence that is authorized under the governing criminal statutes.
Judgment	The case formally ends when the clerk of the court enters a final judgment in the case. In a criminal case, the judgment reveals whether the defendant was acquitted or convicted on each count charged and, if convicted, what sentence was imposed.

Prosecutors try to build a case by using all of the types of evidence they have to rebut the presumption of innocence. Their goal is to prove all elements of a crime **beyond a reasonable doubt**. This term is difficult to define. It cannot be quantified; rather, it is an inherently qualitative concept. The Federal Judicial Center offered the following definition of reasonable doubt—one that U.S. Supreme Court Justice Ruth Bader Ginsburg thought was clear enough to understand that she cited it favorably in *Victor v. Nebraska* (1994, p. 27):

beyond a reasonable doubt
The burden of proof necessary to find a defendant guilty of a crime, whether in a trial by jury or a bench trial.

> Proof beyond a reasonable doubt is proof that leaves you firmly convinced of the defendant's guilt. There are very few things in this world that we know with absolute certainty, and in criminal cases the law does not require proof that overcomes every possible doubt. If, based on your consideration of the evidence, you are firmly convinced that the defendant is guilty of the crime charged, you must find him guilty. If on the other hand, you think there is a real possibility that he is not guilty, you must give him the benefit of the doubt and find him not guilty.

TRIAL

Although the order in which a criminal trial unfolds varies somewhat from state to state, most trials proceed in the order presented in Table 12.2. The ultimate goal of a criminal trial is to reach a verdict. In criminal cases, the two possible outcomes are either "guilty" or "not guilty." In insanity defense cases (which, recall, are very rare), there is also the possibility of a verdict such as "not guilty by reason of insanity" or "guilty except insane" (see Fradella, 2007).

SENTENCING

If a defendant is convicted, the trial court judge must sentence the defendant to some sort of criminal punishment (see Chapters 10 and 13). Although sentencing is technically a part of the judicial process, it is important to note that all three branches of government play a role in the process. In the penal code of a given jurisdiction, the legislature sets the permissible range of punishments that a judge may impose

Members of the media record proceedings in a courtroom. Some jurisdictions allow cameras to film or photograph trials in progress; others do not. What do you think are the advantages and disadvantages of allowing cameras in the courtroom? Do you think they should be permitted?

(as illustrated in Table 12.1). When a jurisdiction uses an **indeterminate sentencing** scheme, the statute sets a range of permissible sentences for a given offense (usually a minimum and a maximum) and leaves it to the sentencing judge to impose whatever sentence he or she feels is fair under the particular facts of a case. Because this can lead to great disparities in sentences, some jurisdictions have adopted **determinate sentencing** schemes. In their strictest form, determinate sentencing schemes may require a judge to impose a particular sentence for a given crime; such sentences are called *mandatory sentences.* In their more common form, however, determinate sentencing schemes use *sentencing guidelines* (see Chapter 3) that specify a minimum, maximum, and presumptive term for each crime. The sentencing judge is supposed to impose the presumptive term in the case, adding to it only if there are aggravating circumstances (e.g., factors which render the circumstances surrounding an offense or the harms it causes worse than a typical offense of that type) and subtracting from it only if there are mitigating circumstances (e.g., factors which render the circumstances surrounding an offense or the harms it causes less severe than a typical offense of that type).

indeterminate sentencing
A method of sentencing in which a statute sets a broad range of permissible sentences for an offense (usually a minimum and a maximum) and leaves it to the sentencing judge to impose whatever sentence he or she feels is fair, given the particular facts of a case.

determinate sentencing
A method of sentencing that limits judges' discretion by requiring specific sentences for a particular crime (as in a mandatory sentence) or by providing sentencing guidelines that use numerical scales and tables to arrive at the recommended sentence for a particular case.

The executive branch exercises a significant role in the sentencing process through the recommendations of the prosecutor. The executive branch can also control sentences by pardoning offenders or commuting their sentences through the actions of a governor, the president, or through agencies like a clemency board or a parole board.

Probation officers also play an important role in sentencing. In some states, probation officers are employees in the executive branch of government, usually in the state's Department of Corrections. In other states and the federal government, probation officers are employees of the judicial system. In either case, probation officers have an influence over criminal sentencing through the recommendations they make. In the federal courts and in most states, after a defendant is convicted, a sentencing hearing is scheduled, perhaps four to six weeks after the trial. In the meantime, probation officers prepare a *presentence investigation report* (PSI). This report summarizes the circumstances leading up to the commission of the offense; the defendant's social, educational, family, and financial background; the existence of any mitigating factors, such as drug or alcohol dependence; and the defendant's criminal history. The report may also contain the probation officer's perceptions of the defendant's level of remorse, the officer's professional judgment about the defendant's risk of reoffending, and the officer's recommendation for sentencing the offender. This report gives the sentencing judge a great deal of information that the judge can then use when deciding how to impose a just sentence within the applicable type of sentencing scheme. These reports are very influential, as judges often agree to impose sentences in accordance with the sentencing recommendations made by probation officers in the PSI (Spohn, 2008).

POSTCONVICTION REVIEW

After a sentence has been imposed and a final judgment has been entered in a case, a convicted defendant has the right to file an **appeal**. Recall that appellate courts rarely focus on issues of guilt or innocence but most often consider whether the law was properly applied, whether the pretrial and trial processes were fair, and so on. Unlike at trial, no evidence is presented during an appeal. Rather, appeals are decided by panels of judges who review the case record (i.e., the transcripts of trial testimony, the documents received into evidence at trial, and the rulings of the trial court judge) as well as the arguments that lawyers make. These legal arguments are usually made in written form in a document called a *brief.* Sometimes, appeals courts will also hear *oral arguments* from the lawyers in the case. The judges on an appellate court review all of these materials to make sure that the criminally accused received a fair trial and a legal

appeal
In criminal cases, the defendant has the right to file an appeal requesting that an appellate court review the decision made by a lower court.

sentence. Thus, the primary purpose of initial appeals from trial court judgments is the correction of errors.

If minor legal errors were made during a trial that were unlikely to have affected the overall outcome of the case, appeals courts call such mistakes *harmless error.* Such errors do not result in the reversal of a conviction on appeal. If, however, significant mistakes were made at trial that likely contributed to an unfair verdict, then the court will rule these mistakes to constitute *prejudicial or reversible error* and overturn the conviction on that basis. Such an outcome is rare. In fact, criminal convictions are reversed on appeal in less than 8% of cases (Neubauer & Fradella, 2014). The overwhelming majority of cases end after the first appeal is resolved because every defendant is entitled to one appeal as a matter of right. After an initial appeal is decided, subsequent appeals to even higher levels of appellate courts are not guaranteed as a matter of right. Instead, subsequent appeals proceed at the discretion of their higher court. In other words, the high courts of most states are able to pick and choose which cases they want to hear; the same is true in the federal system with the U.S. Supreme Court. Moreover, error correction is rarely the primary purpose of such discretionary appeals; rather, high courts primarily exercise their discretion to hear appeals for purposes of policy formation.

People seeking appellate review of their case *after* their initial appeal may ask a higher court to hear their case by filing a petition for a writ of certiorari. Such a writ is an order from a higher appellate court to a lower appellate court to send the record of the case to the higher court for review. ***Certiorari*** is rarely granted. Unlike intermediate appellate courts whose primary function is error correction, discretionary appeals at high courts are usually selected for public policy reasons or to resolve disagreements in how lower courts have ruled on constitutional questions. In fact, the U.S. Supreme Court typically hears only 80 to 90 cases each year, rejecting between 7,000 and 15,000 other petitions for *certiorari* that the Court receives each year. This small caseload is primarily a function of the fact that the U.S. Supreme Court tends to accept only cases in which uniform policy pronouncements are needed in order to settle matters of significant national importance. "Stated another way, [the] error correction [function of initial appeals] is concerned primarily with the effect of the judicial process on individual litigants, whereas policy formulation [function of discretionary appeals] involves the impact of the appellate court decision on other cases" (Neubauer & Fradella, 2014, p. 437). The U.S. Supreme Court's role in policy formulation is explored further later in this chapter.

certiorari
Persons seeking appellate review of their case after their initial appeal may ask a higher court to hear their case by filing a petition for a writ of *certiorari. Certiorari* is rarely granted.

When all appeals are exhausted, a criminal defendant might still be able to turn to the civil justice system to seek relief through applications for a writ of ***habeas corpus*** (see Chapter 8). A person in custody may seek a writ arguing that one or more errors of constitutional dimension (i.e., not merely procedural mistakes) occurred at trial that subsequent appeals failed to correct. As you might imagine, courts grant such postconviction relief rather infrequently.

habeas corpus
In a legal context, a writ of *habeas corpus* is a court order directed at someone who has custody of a person ordering the release of that person because his or her incarceration was achieved through unlawful processes.

Q If you had been one of the defendants in the shipwreck case, would you have preferred a jury trial or a bench trial? Why?

Q What type of person would you have wanted on the jury if you had been the prosecutor in the shipwreck case? What if you were the defense attorney? Explain your reasoning.

Q If you were a judge, which type of sentencing scheme would you prefer? Why?

Q If you were imposing sentence on the defendants in the shipwreck case, which facts of the case, if any, would you consider to be aggravating factors that would cause you to impose a harsher sentence? What mitigating factors would cause you to impose a more lenient sentence?

Judicial Review

FOCUSING QUESTION 12.5

How can judicial review impact public policy?

High courts often hear cases that involve the use of judicial review, which can profoundly affect justice policy. Recall from Chapter 7 that Article VI of the U.S. Constitution contains the *National Supremacy Clause,* which declares that the Constitution is the "Supreme Law of the Land." What happens if Congress or a state legislature were to enact a law that conflicts with a provision of the Constitution? In the 1803 landmark case of *Marbury v. Madison,* the U.S. Supreme Court declared that it is the role of the courts to resolve such conflicts. Courts exercise the power of **judicial review** when they invalidate laws enacted by a legislature or rules made by an executive agency because the laws or rules violate or conflict with the Constitution.

judicial review
The power of the courts to invalidate laws enacted by a legislature or rules made by an executive agency if they violate or conflict with the U.S. Constitution. In criminal justice, judicial review is often focused on issues of substantive due process or procedural justice.

Even before *Marbury v. Madison,* the authors of the Federalist Papers (including Alexander Hamilton, the first Secretary of the Treasury; John Jay, the first Chief Justice of the Supreme Court; and James Madison, the fourth President of the United States) argued that the Constitution's protections "of particular rights or privileges would amount to nothing" without judicial review because there would be no means for enforcing them (Hamilton, Madison, & Jay, [1788] 2003, p. 379). Advocates of judicial review also assert that it makes "[t]he United States . . . a more just society" than it would have been if constitutional rights had been left to more political government institutions (Dworkin, 1986, p. 356). Critics counter that judicial review amounts to judges substituting their own judgments for those of elected officials and for the will of the public. Disagreements about which "rights" ought to exist in a just society, as illustrated by ongoing debates regarding abortion, same-sex marriage, euthanasia, and other controversial issues, have led some modern commentators to reject judicial review on the grounds that such disputes should be resolved through the legislative process and based on the public's preferences.

But what happens when the will of the majority perpetuates an injustice? For example, when the United States was founded, slavery was legally acceptable. Even when slavery was abolished after the Civil War, the law still allowed discrimination against African Americans. Had the U.S. Supreme Court not invalidated the concept of "separate, but equal" in *Brown v. Board of Education* (1954), segregation would have remained legal until legislators corrected this injustice. Because courts are in a unique position to address inequality in society, defenders of judicial review argue that it is fundamental to the functioning of a just democracy. In fact, the courts have frequently been the branch of government to which minority groups have turned, often successfully, in their struggles for equality (Frymer, 2003).

Clearly, the power of judicial review affects public policy. When the Supreme Court ruled that the death penalty may not be given to persons who were under 18 at the time of their offense (*Roper v. Simmons,* 2005), it was a policy decision that impacted state sentencing laws. When the Supreme Court ruled that the Second Amendment right to "keep and bear arms" applied to the states (*McDonald v. City of Chicago,* 2010), state and local governments had to revisit their laws about firearms. In short, courts—especially the U.S. Supreme Court—make policy through the power of judicial review. Whether addressing injustices or inequalities or issuing constitutional rulings, the decisions of the Supreme Court have the potential to shape federal, state, and local laws, criminal justice agency practices, justice system policies, and more.

Q Should courts have the ability to invalidate a law enacted by a legislative body because the judges believe that the law violates someone's rights? Explain your answer.

Q Do you think judicial review is fundamental to democracy or inconsistent with it? Explain your position.

Legal Reasoning

FOCUSING QUESTION 12.6

How do judges decide cases?

Judges interpret and apply the law, whether a trial court judge ruling on the admissibility of a piece of evidence or a Supreme Court justice ruling on the constitutionality of a police practice. However, it is misleading to speak of "the law" as a simple set of rules whose meaning is clearly understood; "law is a language, not simply a collection of rules" (Carter & Burke, 2010, p. 5). When grappling with the language of the law, judges must engage in careful decision making to ensure that the law is properly understood and applied. Doing so is central to the legitimacy of the courts in a democracy. At its most basic level, **legal reasoning** concerns the processes by which judges "justify how and why they use their power" when interpreting and applying the law (Carter & Burke, 2010, p. 8). We expect such decisions to be coherent, logical, and well reasoned. But judicial philosophies clearly play a role in the adjudication process.

legal reasoning
The processes by which judges make decisions about how to interpret and apply the law.

PHILOSOPHIES OF LEGAL REASONING

The traditional view of legal reasoning is called *legal formalism.* It states that "judges apply the relevant law to the relevant facts and arrive at a decision" (Friedrichs, 2006, p. 53), such that: law + facts = decision. Logic lies at the heart of this theory of legal reasoning. In fact, legal formalism rejects the notion that ethical, political, philosophical, or policy considerations should play any role in judicial decision making, even if applying the law precisely as it is written may result in an outcome judges think undesirable. This assumes that there is little role for discretion in the law; whatever the law says is what should happen. Legal formalism has been criticized as too mechanical, especially because the facts of a case are often in dispute and the law is sometimes unclear or imprecise. Moreover, legal formalism assumes that there is a single "correct" answer when, in fact, there may be no such thing.

Legal realism suggests that legal reasoning is an act of interpretation involving the evaluation of arguments made by opposing parties. This analysis may require judges to consider factors *beyond* the law to resolve uncertainties in cases. This does not mean that judges simply guess or that they select an answer that suits their personal values. Instead, legal realism suggests that judges should be guided by certain basic principles, such as fairness, when deciding how the law should be applied in a case. Some legal realists go further. Those who advocate *legal instrumentalism* think that judges should make decisions that promote "good" or "desirable" outcomes. With this approach, judges craft decisions to achieve justice, serve broad social interests, and foster good public policy.

Legal realism remained the dominant school of legal reasoning from the turn of the twentieth century to the late 1940s. By the 1950s, other schools of thought began to emerge. *Legal process theories* tried to harmonize legal formalism and legal realism by offering "neutral principles" that judges could use to resolve unclear cases. Some legal process theorists believe that judges should try to understand the *original intent* of a constitution or statute (Fallon, 1994; Young, 2005). Others argue that judges should consider "general ethical principles and widely shared social goals" (Hart & Sacks, 1958, pp. 158–159). Still others maintain that judges should consider government structure, such as the separation of powers and federalism, and how that would affect decisions (Wechsler, 1954). Many of the legal process approaches still have influence today, although they have been critiqued for allowing judges to draw upon their own ideologies (Wells, 1991). Determining which neutral principles to use, and then how to use them, is in part a value decision leading to inconsistencies between judges.

The *law and economics* movement emerged in the 1970s, primarily from classic utilitarian assumptions that people are rational decision makers who will maximize

their own best interest. This approach advocates that the law should be interpreted (and cases should be decided) in a way that distributes economic costs and benefits to promote economic efficiency and maximize wealth (Friedman, 2000; Polinsky, 2003; Posner, 1993). Although this approach was popular through the 1980s, it has been criticized for its focus on economic interests over noneconomic interests, most notably social justice (Edelman, 2004; Friedrichs, 2006). It still remains, however, a leading conservative theory of legal reasoning.

The leading liberal theory is called the *jurisprudence of rights,* a modern extension of legal realism. Those who subscribe to the jurisprudence of rights, most notably Ronald Dworkin (1978, 1986), argue that the primary extralegal consideration that should guide judges is an ethics of "rights." This school of thought advocates going beyond the text of constitutions or statutes to examine the moral implications of the adjudication *process.* Moreover, the moral questions are examined from a perspective that promotes equality—both of opportunity and of outcome. That is, fairness for all, especially for those least able to protect their own rights and interests, is the guiding principle judges use when deciding cases under this approach.

Based on neo-Marxist notions of power, *critical legal studies* (CLS) began in the late 1970s and has gained influence since then. It argues that law *is* politics. As such, law is "hegemonic"—designed to maintain the status quo in society, meaning that it perpetuates the privileges and disadvantages that come with people's standing in the social hierarchy. Critical legal studies critiques legal reasoning that serves the interests of the wealthy and powerful at the expense of the poor and less powerful (see Kelman, 1987; Kennedy, 1997). The CLS movement produced several offshoots that focus on ways the legal system has systematically oppressed particular groups in society. *Critical race theory* focuses on the experiences of racial and ethnic minorities with the legal system (see Crenshaw, Gotanda, Peller, & Thomas, 1995; Delgado & Stefancic, 2001; Lawrence & Matsuda, 1997). The school of *feminist jurisprudence* focuses on gender inequality in society as a function of law (see Baer, 1999; MacKinnon, 2007; West, 1988). And *postmodern jurisprudence* borrows from all of these critical schools to focus on the intersection of race, gender, gender identity, religion, social class, sexual orientation, and the like to study structural inequalities in law and society, often by using literary theory to deconstruct the meaning of words in legislation and judicial decisions (Douzinas, Warrington, & McVeigh, 1993; Minda, 1996).

Critical and postmodern theories remain controversial and out of the mainstream for two reasons. First, they reject the notion of any objective truth or reality and the empirical methods of science and social science. Rather, they use the methods of literature, such as discourse analysis, narrative, storytelling, and rhetoric. Second, they focus on criticism at the expense of offering ideas for workable reform (Farber & Sherry, 1997). Yet critical and postmodern legal theories have undoubtedly exposed some of the shortcomings of more traditional approaches to legal decision making. This, in turn, has helped to sensitize legal actors (especially through changes in legal education) to social justice concerns about racism, sexism, homophobia, and other issues.

THE PROCESS OF LEGAL REASONING

Regardless of their philosophy of adjudication, philosophy of law, or philosophy of justice, we expect that all judges will explain *how* they arrived at their ultimate decision in a case. Carter and Burke (2010) constructed a model that explains the four primary criteria that judges may consider. Their model is presented in Figure 12.3. As you see, the facts of a case and the applicable law are only two of the factors; social background facts and value judgments also play a role.

The degree to which any of these factors might influence a judge's decision varies from case to case and also varies based on the judge's legal philosophy. For an example of legal reasoning, see Box 12.3.

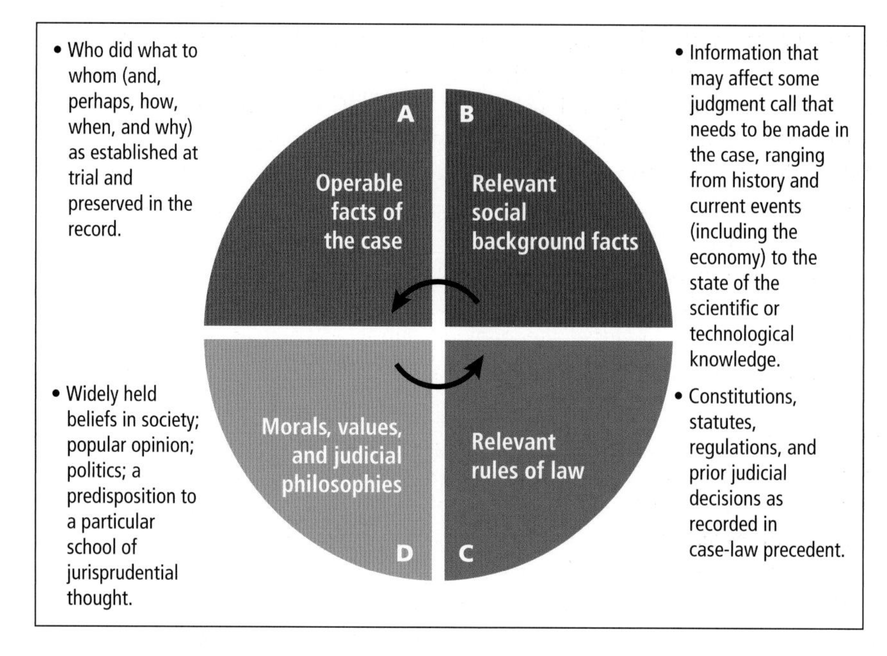

FIGURE 12.3 The Four Primary Components of Legal Reasoning.
Adapted from: Carter & Burke, 2010

Q How would each legal philosophy described address the shipwreck case study from the beginning of the chapter? Be sure to include analyses of the charge, the conviction, the original sentence, and the actual punishment.

Q Which philosophy (or philosophies) of legal reasoning do you most agree with? Why?

BOX 12.3

AN EXERCISE IN LEGAL REASONING

Consider the following hypothetical scenario, variations of which have been debated by legal scholars and students for years (see Hart, 1958; Schlag, 1999):

> Assume that a law prohibits bringing a vehicle into a city's park. Individuals who break the law must pay a fine not to exceed $1,000. The law was passed out of concern for the well-being of the park. You are a judge, and you are well aware of this law. You now have to rule on the following incidents:

1. A townsperson driving through town decides to take a shortcut through the park.
2. An ambulance driver takes his ambulance into the park to rescue a sick park visitor.
3. A local veterans' group donates a jeep as part of a war memorial in the park.
4. A child brings a motorized remote-control car into the park.

Q How should "vehicle" be defined?

Q What does it mean to "bring a vehicle" into the park?

Q Compare and contrast how each of these cases would be resolved by a legal formalist, a legal realist, and a legal process theorist who subscribes to the notion of original intent.

(*continued*)

BOX 12.3 (continued)

Q How would you resolve each of these cases? In each, which elements from Figure 12.1 would be most important in your decision? Why?

Legal reasoning is related to perceptions of law and justice. Review material from previous chapters, as necessary, to answer these questions:

Q What was your preferred theory of law from Chapter 3? How would it apply to the four incidents listed above?

Q What was your preferred theory of justice from Chapter 7? How would it apply to the four incidents listed above?

Consider the consistencies between your preferred resolution to the preceding cases, your preferred philosophy of law, and your preferred philosophy of justice. Compare your results to those of your classmates. Your conversations should help illustrate how and why different jurists may approach the same case in different ways.

Conclusion

The courts are often one of the first institutions that individuals think of when they hear "criminal justice" because of the role the courts play in adjudicating criminal cases. Although trials are rare, with plea bargains far more common, the courtroom workgroup plays an essential role in the resolution of criminal cases. Prosecuting attorneys, defense attorneys, judges, and other members of the courtroom workgroup labor to see cases through the pretrial and, if necessary, the trial processes described in this chapter, all the while maintaining an emphasis on justice. Appellate courts also have a significant impact on criminal justice, particularly through the power of judicial review and constitutional interpretation, which results in decisions that can shape criminal justice policies and practices nationwide. The topic of the next chapter is the correctional system in the United States, which (not surprisingly) the courts directly affect. Judges determine how offenders are sentenced to the various correctional alternatives, and the power of judicial review establishes the limits of punishments that correctional agencies may impose.

Problem-Solving Courts

Criminal Justice Problem Solving

Recall from the Research in Action Box (Box 4.3) in Chapter 4 that many U.S. jurisdictions have developed specialized mental health courts to apply formal social control to mentally ill offenders using a combination of the therapeutic and penal styles of social control. Mental health courts are just one example of *problem-solving courts*—specialized courts designed to address the underlying problems of the defendants who appear in them, rather than just to punish the commission of crimes.

According to the U.S. Bureau of Justice Assistance ([BJA], n.d., para. 1–9), a division of the U.S. Department of Justice,

> Problem-solving courts began in the 1990s to accommodate offenders with specific needs and problems that were not or could not be adequately addressed in traditional courts. Problem-solving courts seek to promote outcomes that will benefit not only the offender, but the victim and society as well. Thus problem-solving courts were developed as an innovative response to deal with offenders' problems, including drug abuse, mental illness, and domestic violence. Although most problem-solving court models are relatively new, early results from studies show that these types of courts are having a positive impact on the lives of offenders and victims and in some instances are saving jail and prison costs.
>
> In general, problem-solving courts share some common elements:
>
> - Focus on outcomes. Problem-solving courts are designed to provide positive case outcomes for victims, society and the offender (e.g., reducing recidivism or creating safer communities).
> - System change. Problem-solving courts promote reform in how the government responds to problems such as drug addiction and mental illness.
> - Judicial involvement. Judges take a more hands-on approach to addressing problems and changing behaviors of defendants.
> - Collaboration. Problem-solving courts work with external parties to achieve certain goals (e.g., developing partnerships with mental health providers).
> - Non-traditional roles. These courts and their personnel take on roles or processes not common in traditional courts. For example, some problem-solving courts are less adversarial than traditional criminal justice processing.
> - Screening and assessment. Use of screening and assessment tools to identify appropriate individuals for the court is common.
> - Early identification of potential candidates. Use of screening and assessment tools to determine a defendant's eligibility for the problem-solving court usually occurs early in a defendant's involvement with criminal justice processing.

Today, there are many types of problem-solving courts in operation in the United States, including domestic violence courts, DUI courts, elder courts, veterans' courts, and prisoner reentry-courts. But the oldest and most widely adopted types of specialized courts are drug courts.

drug court
A collaborative, team-based program designed to help drug offenders in which the prosecuting attorney, defense attorney, probation officer, substance abuse treatment counselor, and judge meet regularly to review and reward (or punish) each offender's progress (or lack thereof).

A **drug court** program is a collaborative, team-based effort that includes a drug offender and the prosecuting attorney, defense attorney, probation officer, substance abuse treatment counselor, and judge. Rather than simply sentencing an offender and moving on, the court meets regularly and offenders report often on their progress, one key component of which is drug testing and substance abuse treatment. At each progress report, the judge may offer rewards to offenders who have shown progress and may issue sanctions to offenders who have not. The concept is unique in that it creates a courtroom partnership centered on providing rehabilitation that is individualized to meet each

Criminal Justice Problem Solving

Problem-Solving Courts

continued

offender's needs. Offenders who successfully complete the program may have their charges dropped or may receive lesser charges or penalties than offenders who do not go through the program (see MacKenzie, 2006).

The first drug court was created in Dade County, Florida, in 1989. Since then, drug courts have grown in importance (Belenko, 2001). Almost 2,800 drug courts were in operation by 2013 with even more being planned (Bureau of Justice Assistance, 2013). Studies concluded that overall treatment retention in drug courts "is substantially better than in other community-based treatment programs for offenders" (p. 25; see also Belenko, DeMatteo, & Patapis, 2007; Goldkamp, White, & Robinson, 2001; Government Accountability Office [GAO], 1997, 2005). Most studies have also reported lower recidivism rates for drug court participants than for comparison groups (Belenko, 2001; Belenko et al., 2007; Gottfredson, Najaka, & Kearley, 2003; GAO, 2005), even over periods as long as 10 years (Finigan, Carey, & Cox, 2007; Mackin et al., 2009). And cost analyses of drug courts have found a net cost savings to the criminal justice system, largely as a function of crime reduction (Belenko, 2007; Hoyt, McCollister, French, Leukefeld, & Minton, 2004; Huddleston, Marlowe, & Casebolt, 2008; Mackin et al., 2009; Marlowe, 2010).

In spite of the research supporting the efficacy of drug courts, they are not without their critics. For example, the Drug Policy Alliance (2011) and the Justice Policy Institute (2011) both oppose drug courts because these courts seek to control drug addiction through the criminal justice system, rather than purely through therapeutic interventions by health professionals. Thus, if people try, but fail, to overcome their drug problems through drug court participation, they face incarceration. Both of these organizations also point out that the money used to fund drug courts could be spent on addiction treatment services that could reach far many more people in need than those who are selected for drug court participation. Finally, the National Association of Criminal Defense Lawyers (2009) criticizes drug courts because they typically require defendants to give up their Sixth Amendment trial rights and plead guilty as a prerequisite to participating in the drug court programs.

- Q Critique the concept of problem-solving courts.
- Q Do you support the expansion of drug courts? Why or why not?
- Q Do you think the model of problem-solving courts, of which drug courts are one example, should be extended to other types of issues or offenses? If so, what types of issues, and why? If not, why not?
- Q How might problem-solving courts evolve to address some of the shortcomings their critics raise?

13

Core Concepts of U.S. Correctional Theory and Practice

Learning Objectives

1 Describe the goals of the American correctional system. 2 Explain how essential tensions explain conflicts concerning correctional policy. 3 Explain how correctional instituions have developed over time. 4 Explain how community corrections have developed over time.

Key Terms

corrections
incarceration
recidivism
essential tension
conflict theory
prison-industrial complex
correctional boot camps
correctional institution
jail
prison
solitary system
congregate system
reformatory system
farm system
security level
classification
total institution
mortification
pains of imprisonment
contraband
prisonization
importation hypothesis
deprivation hypothesis
panacea phenomenon
transportation
mark system
parole
probation
suspended sentence
split sentence
truth in sentencing
intermediate sanctions
halfway house
day reporting center
electronic monitoring
house arrest
intensive supervision probation (ISP)

Key People

Jonas Hanway
John Howard
Hans Toch
David Garland
Michel Foucault
Jonathan Simon
Thomas Kuhn
Erving Goffman
Gresham Sykes
Donald Clemmer
Alexander Maconochie
Walter Crofton
John Augustus

Case Study

Weightlifting in Prison

Should inmates in correctional institutions be permitted to participate in weightlifting as a form of recreation? Consider the following information.

Research suggests that the public does not strongly support weightlifting in prison (see Applegate, 2001). Reasons for objecting vary. Some believe it makes prisons too pleasant and less of a deterrent to crime; others believe "weight lifting simply permits inmates to become more physically dangerous" (Lenz, 2002, p. 517). Still others are concerned about the cost of weightlifting equipment, although Lenz (2002) found that the public is more likely to support weightlifting when it is paid for by the inmates instead of by tax dollars.

Partly in response to these concerns, Congress passed a bill including the Zimmer Amendment (named for its sponsor, Republican Congressman Dick Zimmer from New Jersey) in 1996. "Provisions of this 'no-frills' bill directly affect prison recreation activities by prohibiting the purchase and replacement of weightlifting equipment and musical instruments and the showing of R-rated movies" (Kahler, 2008, p. 92). As a federal law, the Zimmer Amendment only applies to federal prisons and not those operated by state or local governments. However, other states have pursued similar legislation (Lenz, 2002).

The views of correctional administrators, however, differ from those of the public and of politicians. In fact, two-thirds (66.7%) of correctional administrators in one study supported maintaining prison weightlifting activities (Tewksbury & Mustaine, 2005). The American Correctional Association also supports prison weightlifting (Kahler, 2008). Like

Previous page: The "Roundhouse" at Stateville Correctional Center in Illinois. What purposes do you think prisons serve in American society?

other recreational activities, weightlifting keeps inmates busy, which is important for the orderly operation of a prison. In addition, weightlifting can be used as a reward or incentive for good inmate behavior (Lenz, 2002).

Furthermore, weightlifting "reduces tension, builds self-esteem, and teaches the necessity of cooperation [e.g., through inmates 'spotting' for each other]" (Kahler, 2008, p. 92). Research has found that weightlifting in prison can reduce inmates' levels of aggression and anger (Wagner, McBride, & Crouse, 1999) and is also associated with lower levels of depression and stress among inmates (Bukaloo, Krug, & Nelson, 2009). As a result, it is possible that weightlifting could be beneficial not only for institutional management but also for rehabilitating offenders.

Q Should prison inmates be permitted to lift weights? Why or why not? How would you respond to the arguments raised by the opposing side?

Q How is your answer shaped by your opinions of what purposes correctional institutions ought to accomplish?

Q Recall from Chapter 2 the discussion of idealism and pragmatism. Compare and contrast how an idealist and a pragmatist would address the issue of prison weightlifting.

The Scope and Purpose of American Corrections

FOCUSING QUESTION 13.1

How large is the American correctional system, and what goals should it accomplish?

In the American criminal justice system, correctional agencies are responsible for carrying out sentences imposed by the criminal courts. Sentences may range from probation to prison to execution, depending on the crime and jurisdiction. The federal government maintains its own correctional agencies (e.g., the Federal Bureau of Prisons and U.S. Probation and Pretrial Services), as do each of the 50 states (generally through a state Department of Corrections). Individuals sentenced in federal court are under the jurisdiction of federal agencies, and those sentenced in a state court are under the jurisdiction of that state's correctional agency or agencies. Local jurisdictions (cities and counties) may also operate correctional systems, primarily for misdemeanor offenders from their local areas.

Corrections is a huge industry in the United States. In 2010 alone (the most recent data available at the time of this writing), total spending on corrections in the United States totaled more than $80 billion (Kyckelhahn & Martin, 2013). This annual expenditure funded the supervision of more than 4.8 million probationers and parolees, approximately 1.5 million inmates in state and federal prisons, and more than 748,000 inmates in local jails. In 2010, this amounted to 1 out of every 33 persons in the United States being under some form of correctional supervision (Glaze & Parks, 2012). The distinctions between probation, parole, jails, and prisons will be clarified later in the chapter. For now, one key point is that the correctional component of the criminal justice system entails significant expenditures and directly affects many people.

corrections
The component of the criminal justice system responsible for carrying out sentences imposed by the criminal courts. May include prisons, jails, probation, parole, and other alternatives.

There is another key point to draw from this discussion. The United States makes extensive use of **incarceration** (prison and jail sentences) as a form of punishment. In fact, the United States has the world's highest incarceration rate, with 743 residents per 100,000 confined in prison or jail. Even the next highest countries, Rwanda and Russia, are substantially lower, at 595 and 568 per 100,000, respectively. For a point of comparison, the incarceration rate in England and Wales is 153 per 100,000 (Walmsley,

incarceration
The use of sentences to correctional institutions (prisons and jails) as a form of punishment.

2011). If incarceration rates remain approximately the same as they were in the first decade of the twenty-first century, it is estimated that one person out of fifteen (or 6.6% of the population) will spend some time in a state or federal prison, and that does not even include those who will spend time in local jails (Bonczar, 2003).

It is important to dispel the popular notion that the United States is the world's leader in incarceration because crime is so prevalent. Gottschalk (2006) observed, "the fact is that mass imprisonment [in the United States] is only weakly related to the underlying crime rates" (p. 26). As described in Chapter 1, overall crime rates in the United States are not dramatically higher than those in other industrial democracies. Although lethal violence is more common in the United States, this by itself does not account for the degree to which U.S. incarceration rates eclipse those of other nations. The incarceration rate was 138 persons per 100,000 in 1980, after which it increased dramatically to 743, as noted above. Some factors contributing to the increase included fear of crime, political campaigns and legislation focused on "getting tough" on crime, and the use of imprisonment as a strategy in the War on Drugs (Austin & Irwin, 2001; Pratt, 2009).

With corrections accounting for such a large share of the government's budget and affecting so many people, what should it seek to accomplish? The very name—corrections—suggests a degree of optimism, with a hope that offenders could be rehabilitated or corrected so that they would no longer engage in illegal activity. Indeed, in the eighteenth century, correctional reformers such as Jonas Hanway and John Howard advocated for the development and use of prisons instead of the death penalty and other physical punishments common at the time. Their rationale was that the prison was an instrument of rehabilitation and a place where inmates would reflect on their deeds and "discover the right principles to guide [their] life" (McGowen, 1995, p. 86), based in part on religious introspection.

Two millennia earlier, Plato made a similar argument. While imprisonment was not a common punishment at all in ancient society, in Book 10 of the *Laws,* Plato recommended that certain offenders should be imprisoned for a sentence of five years or more but with a goal of rehabilitation. During their time in prison, inmates would "have no intercourse with the other citizens, except with members of the nocturnal council [a moral authority], and with them let them converse with a view to the improvement of their soul's health" ([360 B.C.E.] 1892, p. 286). Ideally, reform would occur as a result.

recidivism
A measure of how often former offenders commit new crimes.

Unfortunately, the contemporary correctional system does not fully meet the goal of offender reformation. The **recidivism** rate is a measure of how often former offenders commit new crimes. A nationwide study of inmates released from prison in 2004 found that recidivism rates were fairly high. Within three years of release, 43.4% of released inmates were sent back to prison. Approximately half (22.3%) returned to prison for having committed a new crime, and approximately half (21%) returned for having violated a condition, or special rule, of their release (Pew Center, 2011). The latter are referred to as *technical violations,* which include such things as failing a drug test, failing to report for a meeting with a parole officer, leaving the jurisdiction without permission, not abiding by a curfew or residence restrictions, if imposed, and so on. Probation fared better, as only 16% of persons on probation in 2011 were returned to prison or jail either for committing a new crime or for committing a technical violation by violating the rules of probation supervision (Maruschak & Parks, 2012). Still, these data suggest that the correctional ideal is not easily achieved.

There are five frequently acknowledged philosophies of punishment. One is rehabilitation, which is the most closely linked to the concept of correction. As described in Chapter 10, support for rehabilitation has declined over time, as "getting tough" on crime has been the more popular approach. The other philosophies are retribution, or the idea that offenders deserve unpleasant punishment; deterrence, or the idea that the

threat of punishment should discourage the public from committing crimes and that punishment should discourage offenders from repeating criminal acts; incapacitation, or removing an offender's ability to commit crimes against society, generally by confining the offender in prison; and restitution, or compensating a victim or society for losses caused by crime. The challenge for correctional agencies is to determine which of these philosophies (or other ideas) should underlie correctional practice and how much to emphasize each.

A mission statement is one way correctional agencies articulate the philosophies and goals to which they subscribe. This can help us make sense out of competing philosophical perspectives. Consider the following mission statements:

Nevada Department of Corrections (2010): "Protect the public by confining convicted felons according to the law, while keeping staff and inmates safe" (para. 1).

Illinois Department of Corrections (2002): "Protect the public from criminal offenders through a system of incarceration and supervision which securely segregates offenders from society, assures offenders of constitutional rights and maintains programs to enhance the success of offenders' reentry into society" (para. 1).

Arkansas Department of Correction (n.d.): "Provide public safety by carrying out the mandates of the courts; provide a safe, humane environment for staff and inmates; provide programs to strengthen the work ethic; provide opportunities for spiritual, mental, and physical growth" (para. 2).

Note that there are similarities and differences among the mission statements. This is exactly the point of the discussion. It is difficult to identify a single or uniform philosophy that expresses the precise nature or purpose of corrections across all agencies and jurisdictions.

This leaves the dilemma as expressed by correctional luminary Hans Toch (1997): "Those who look for philosophical consistency in prison policies are apt not to find it" (p. 4). Likewise, David Garland (2001) sees little philosophical consistency in contemporary corrections, arguing that "we lack any . . . agreement, any settled culture, or any clear sense of the big picture" (p. 4). Garland also argues that a new vision for corrections has emerged based on the "culture of control."

The culture of control is marked by a "desire for security, orderliness, and control, for the management of risk and the taming of chance" (Garland, 2001, p. 194). Garland argues that this idea currently dominates the thinking of the public, politicians, and some correctional personnel. As a result, the agents of formal social control (i.e., the criminal justice system) take on more and more authority to use rules, technology, and surveillance to control deviant behaviors of any sort—and the severity of punishments for deviant behavior escalates during the process.

This is similar to an argument advanced by French philosopher Michel Foucault (1977). Foucault viewed the development of the prison as motivated by a desire to limit government power by limiting its ability to issue arbitrary and excessive punishments. As prisons became popular (in place of other, more brutal, punishments), they came to be used as tools of discipline, creating "docile bodies" (p. 135) through a system of surveillance and control. For instance, constant surveillance ultimately led to total control over persons. As Foucault noted (drawing upon an idea posed earlier by Jeremy Bentham), if individuals knew that at any moment they could (unknowingly) be under the observation of an authority figure with the power to punish them for wrongdoing, then they would always act as though they were under observation—and this would mean acting in a positive or law-abiding manner to avoid being detected or punished for violating a rule.

Once such a system of control was established, Foucault argued, the temptation would exist to extend it even beyond punishment for crime, but also to other areas of society. Instead of being restricted to corrections, the culture of control could lead

toward "an indefinite discipline" (p. 227), in which individuals' compliance could be measured for social norms that by their very nature were fully unattainable. For instance, could "disciplinary methods and examination procedures" (p. 227) be used to measure compliance with norms such as truthfulness, etiquette, work ethic, timeliness, and courtesy? The result would be a constant surveillance and emphasis on control of behavior. In turn, Foucault asked, "Is it surpising that prisons resemble factories, schools, barracks, hospitals, which all resemble prisons" (p. 228)?

This notion is echoed by Jonathan Simon's (2007) description of "governing through crime" (p. 5). Simon argues that efforts for control and surveillance have extended beyond the criminal justice system to also impact families, schools, and workplaces, where individuals are subjected to an increased amount of monitoring, regulation, rigid rules, and zero-tolerance policies. As such, the notion of a culture of control may be felt in other areas of society besides corrections or criminal justice. Interestingly, studies of online communities with "perfect surveillance" (Wang, Haines, & Tucker, 2011), as exact keystrokes and transactions can be recorded and analyzed, have also suggested that, while there is an increasing presumption that control and surveillance are essential to security, informal social controls and collective efficacy must still play a central role in the regulation of human behavior. Accordingly, the balance of correctional philosophies is multifaceted.

As control and surveillance increase, so does the potential for conflict with constitutional rights. The Constitution is a benchmark for what is or is not legally permissible within corrections, as policies are judged against its provisions about rights and liberties. A careful balance must then be struck between formal social control and individual freedoms, a role that generally falls to the courts. In fact, lawsuits alleging constitutional violations have historically been a significant force for reform in the correctional system and have helped to define acceptable correctional philosophies and to discard unacceptable practices (see Feeley & Rubin, 1998).

Q If you were the leader of a correctional agency, what philosophy or mission of corrections would you emphasize? Why? How would your answer influence weightlifting in prisons?

Q Do you think the lack of consistency in current correctional practice is a problem? Why or why not?

Q Can you identify any examples of a culture of control or of governing through crime? What philosophies of justice (from Chapter 6) do you think these concepts represent?

Four Essential Tensions Underlying Correctional Philosophy and Policy

FOCUSING QUESTION 13.2

How do essential tensions explain conflicts about correctional policy?

essential tension
A concept described by Thomas Kuhn that reflects a conflict between ideals of what should be and the observable world as it actually is.

If correctional policy is not based on one single philosophy, how does it develop? The concept of an **essential tension**, developed by philosopher of science Thomas Kuhn (1977), refers to a conflict between ideals of *what should be* and the observable world *as it actually is.* A consideration of essential tensions provides a framework that can help us understand forces that shape the development of correctional policy.

THE ESSENTIAL TENSION OF FINANCE

Money and budgets are the most profound of the essential tensions. Correctional agencies are funded by tax dollars allocated by legislatures. A correctional agency may have impressive goals or ideas for innovative programs, but without money to fund them,

those goals or programs will go unrealized. For instance, changing economic conditions have had a dramatic effect on correctional policy:

> financial crisis, complicated by the rise in correctional expenses and in their relative share of the budget, has yielded a new set of correctional discourses and practices, fueled by a language of scarcity. Under this framework, perceptions are changed, and policies are created, with short-term savings in mind . . . correctional techniques are chosen and discussed mainly through their impact on taxpayers' wallets. (Aviram, 2010, pp. 2–3)

Budgetary concerns can become a de facto guiding philosophy by allowing the budget to be the primary driver of correctional policy. In response to budget reductions, states have closed prisons, shifted priorities (e.g., reducing treatment programs, even those required by law), and changed laws so that fewer persons are sentenced to prison (Gramlich, 2010). In fact, for the first time since 1972, state prison populations decreased slightly (by 0.3%) in 2009. Budgetary concerns were one contributor to the decrease, as "states began to realize they could effectively reduce their prison populations, and save public funds, without sacrificing public safety" (*Prison Count 2010,* 2010, p. 3; see also Brown, 2012). Additional reductions in state-level incarceration have continued, declining 2.3% between 2008 and 2012 (Carson & Golinelli, 2013); whether these declines will continue, and how they may impact state budgets, remains to be seen.

Of course, it is logical that finances are important. But viewed as an essential tension, it is the pragmatic reality of finance—rather than idealistic goals or values—that can sometimes drive correctional practice. This reflects the simple truism that correctional agencies can only do that which they can afford to do. Reflecting the economic concept of opportunity cost, in which the expenditure of money for one item precludes its use to purchase another, agencies must choose how to allocate scarce funds. This sometimes leads to a disconnect in which correctional agencies are criticized for not doing more, whether to provide a secure environment, to rehabilitate, or to promote other goals, yet the reason is that they do not have funds to do so.

There is also a **conflict theory** perspective of finance as a driver of correctional policy. Conflict theorists argue that decisions are made to benefit (financially or otherwise) those who hold power in society (see generally Siegel, 2001). The conflict perspective is perhaps best exemplified by the notion of a **prison-industrial complex**, meaning "a set of bureaucratic, political, and economic interests that encourage increased spending on imprisonment, regardless of the actual need" (Schlosser, 1998, p. 54). This concept is sometimes levied as a criticism against prison privatization (that is, the operation of correctional facilities by private companies, as described in Chapter 2) or to suggest that providers of prison equipment and services, sold to correctional agencies, have an interest in sustaining high levels of imprisonment (Gottschalk, 2006).

conflict theory
Argues that decisions are made to benefit (financially or otherwise) those who hold power in society.

prison-industrial complex
A conflict theory perspective of corrections, suggesting that increased spending on incarceration is not driven by need but rather by political and economic interests.

Notions of a prison-industrial complex are also proferred as an explanation for new prison construction. From 1960 to 1995, the American prison population increased dramatically, and 829 new prisons were constructed. Supporters of new prison construction argue that it brings economic benefits, jobs, and growth to the communities where the prisons are built (Hooks, Mosher, Rotolo, & Lobao, 2004). Critics of new prison growth argue that "the use of prisons as money-makers for struggling rural communities has become a major force driving criminal justice policy . . . regardless of [other] policy rationales" (Huling, 2002, p. 213). However, research has found that new prisons do not tend to produce economic benefits for the communities in which they are built (Hooks, Mosher, Genter, Rotolo, & Lobao, 2010; Hooks et al., 2004).

Whether attributed to opportunity cost or a prison-industrial complex, financial concerns can and do drive correctional policy decision making. This creates the essential tension between what corrections ought to do (based on goals and philosophies) and what corrections actually does (driven by finances).

THE ESSENTIAL TENSION OF RESEARCH

Regardless of the funding available, pragmatic thinkers would hope that correctional policy is justified based on solid research about strategies and tactics that work versus those that do not. Even in times of fiscal stress, agencies can maximize effectiveness by conducting research to inform their decisions.

Sadly, this is not always the case. Steven Lab (2004), former president of the Academy of Criminal Justice Sciences, argues that criminal justice research is, at best, not actively sought and, at worst, totally ignored when criminal justice policy is made. Lab places part of the blame on scholars themselves for not disseminating research results more broadly and more clearly and for not making the effort "to step forward when bad decisions are being made [to] discourage the adoption of ill-conceived policies" (p. 692). However, even when research is presented, it does not always influence policy.

Indeed, correctional policy is sometimes based on inaccurate perceptions grounded in "common sense" rather than on empirical evidence (Cullen, Blevins, Trager, & Gendreau, 2005, p. 53). However, common sense is not always correct. **Correctional boot camps** provide an example. The idea of a boot camp is that offenders who are at moderate risk for committing additional crimes should be placed in a program lasting several months. In the program, offenders would live in a military-style environment, subject to drills with confrontational strategies and physical labor designed to build discipline (e.g., a "drill sergeant" correctional officer yelling at an inmate and then requiring him to do 50 pushups). Justifications for boot camps were largely grounded on the common-sense belief that such a program *ought* to work.

correctional boot camps
A punishment alternative in which offenders live in a military-style environment, subject to drills with confrontational strategies and physical labor designed to build discipline.

The problem was that the program did *not* often work. In fact, prior research (largely ignored in the development of correctional boot camps) had found that military service, in general, was not an effective tool for rehabilitating offenders. Research on the correctional boot camps themselves similarly found that they were not effective in reducing recidivism (MacKenzie, 2006). When research on the ineffectiveness of boot camps in Georgia was released, a spokesperson for the governor stated, "we don't care what the study thinks," and a correctional administrator stated "that academics were too quick to ignore the experiential knowledge of people 'working in the system' and rely on research findings" (Vaughn, 1994, in Cullen et al., 2005, p. 60). Yet, it is the systematic collection and analysis of empirical data—that is, research—which leads to conclusions about what is or is not effective. Such evidence was lacking for boot camps, as one report stated: "research on adult boot camps in Georgia and Illinois found no difference in recidivism [between boot camp participants and a comparison group]. An evaluation of Washington's Work Ethic Camp (WEC) actually found higher rates of recidivism, from high rates of revoked parole" (Parent, 2003, p. 7). It is also interesting to note, however, that the same report found that boot camps may be more effective *if* they "offered more intensive treatment and postrelease supervision" (p. 9). But the treatment and supervision were key, rather than the military model of the camps, which was *not* shown to be effective.

Could a process that more deliberately included the input of researchers have resulted in a better correctional alternative than boot camps? This question illustrates the essential tension that emerges when there is research pertaining to a policy decision, but that research is disregarded in the policy-making process. In such cases, idealistic notions or popular ideas may instead justify correctional policy, which in some cases can lead to adopting or maintaining policies that are not effective in meeting their goals.

THE ESSENTIAL TENSION OF DISCRETION

Recall from Chapter 1 the discussion of criminal justice both as bureaucracy and profession. These concepts form the basis for the third essential tension: discretion. Bureaucracies are driven by rules and procedures that all personnel are expected to

follow carefully and deliberately. On the other hand, a profession comprises individuals who are expected to exercise their own judgment when determining how to resolve a situation.

There are pros and cons to either approach. A reliance on *rules and procedures* helps to ensure fairness and consistency while grounding decisions in agreed-upon principles that may not be overruled by an individual employee. A reliance on *professional judgment* allows for the unique circumstances of each individual case to be considered while allowing the professional to draw upon past experience and expertise in solving a problem (Schneider, Ervin, & Snyder-Joy, 1996). Many agencies have developed quantitative (numbers-based) scales in order to guide decisions and limit discretion. Scales usually pose a series of questions, with answers scored on a point system. Deviations from the recommended outcomes must usually be justified in writing. Examples pertinent to corrections include:

- *Probation Supervision.* Some offenders, rather than being sent to prison, serve their time on probation. While on probation, they may live and work in the community, but they also must follow some special rules and report regularly to a probation officer. When determining how much supervision a person on probation needs from a probation officer, many agencies use a numerical scale to determine what level of risk an individual offender poses (e.g., see Domurad, 1999).
- *Classification.* When an offender is sentenced to prison, the Department of Corrections must decide which prison is most appropriate for him or her (e.g., minimum, medium, or maximum security). Numerical scales are often used to guide this decision (e.g., see Federal Bureau of Prisons, 2006). See Box 13.1 for an example.
- *Parole Release.* In some states, prison inmates may be released on parole before the end of their sentence. To receive parole, inmates must be approved by a parole board, which determines if the inmate has been rehabilitated. Some parole boards use numerical scales to help them make parole release decisions (e.g., see Keilin, 2001).
- *Revocation.* If a person on probation violates a law or a rule of probation (e.g., leaving the state without permission of the probation officer), then the probation may be revoked and the person sent back to prison. Some states use numerical scales to determine whether or not a violation is serious enough to send the person to prison (e.g., see Virginia Criminal Sentencing Commission, n.d.).

Research has found that probation officers do not perceive numerical scales to be particularly effective, and that they would prefer more discretion rather than being constrained by the results of a scale (Schneider et al., 1996). Herein lies the essential tension. Some may feel that the most appropriate decision making occurs when well-trained professionals are able to provide individualized attention to the specifics of each case, justified by the recognition that no two cases or offenders are identical. On the other hand, correctional case processing often relies on a bureaucratic approach that minimizes discretion, justified out of a concern for consistency or fairness. This may lead to philosophical differences and disagreements about policy between those who approach corrections work from a bureaucratic model and those who view it as a profession.

THE ESSENTIAL TENSION OF INVISIBILITY

Right now, how much specific information do you know about the workings of prison and probation? For most people, the answer is "not much." Of the three primary areas of criminal justice—the police, courts, and corrections—correctional agencies are most hidden from public view. Through the study of civics and American government in high school, people generally have an idea about what the courts do. People generally

BOX 13.1

OFFENDER CLASSIFICATION SCALE

As noted in the text, after a judge sentences an offender to prison, the Department of Corrections (if a state prison) or Federal Bureau of Prisons (if a federal prison) must decide the prison and security level to which the offender will be assigned. This is a process known as classification. Below is an example of a quantitative scale used in classification decisions (based on Instructions for Initial . . . , 2008). You may wish to look ahead to Table 13.1 for a definition of maximum, medium, and minimum security prisons.

Total points in the following categories to determine the appropriate security level.

Crime Category	*A [most serious] = 0* *B = 5* *C = 10* *D [least serious] = 20*	
History of Violence	*In prior incarceration*	*Any (from list) within past seven years = 0* *None = 10*
	Other	*Prior violent felony conviction = 0* *None = 5*
Detainers	*Wanted for other felony charge or warrant = 0* *Wanted by immigration and customs enforcement = 8* *None = 10*	
Escape History	*Any within last ten years = 0* *None = 6*	
Age	*Under 29 = 0* *29 or older = 6*	
Presumptive Security Level:	*0–37 Points: Maximum* *38–47 Points: Medium* *48 or More Points: Minimum*	

Q Why do you think each of the factors was selected for inclusion in the table? Are there any you would change? Are there any you would add?

Q Under some circumstances, inmates can receive an "override," which would allow them to be sent to a security level different from the one indicated by points alone. What factors do you think should be considered in allowing "overrides"?

Q Quantitative scales, such as the one above, are "objective" classification systems. Another approach is to use "subjective" classification, in which "decisions were made based on intuition and experience" (Carlson, 2008, p. 73). What do you think are the advantages and disadvantages of each? Which do you prefer? Why?

have an idea about the nature and purpose of police work through officers' work in the community. Of course, the ideas about the courts and policing may not be fully developed or entirely accurate, but they are often better than the public understanding of corrections. As Farrington (1992) observed, "We 'put our criminals behind bars.' We 'send them down the river.'... All of these phrases are suggestive of a general out-of-sight, out-of-mind mentality regarding our nation's penal institutions and those who inhabit them" (p. 18).

The information the public holds about corrections usually comes from the media. Although some excellent documentaries exist about correctional institutions (prisons and jails), the news media rarely explore the range of issues facing correctional agencies (see Welch, Weber, & Edwards, 2000). Correctional alternatives besides prison are infrequently covered in the news, public affairs documentaries, or popular entertainment.

With the billions of dollars spent annually on corrections, it is ironic that correctional agencies are so far removed from public awareness. This leads to the essential tension at stake here. With corrections being an invisible and unknown entity to most persons, meaningful conversations about correctional policy become both challenging and uncommon. This compounds the difficulty of attempting to seek policies that articulate a guiding philosophy for correctional practice.

SUMMARY OF THE CONCEPT OF ESSENTIAL TENSIONS

Much correctional policy is shaped by the four essential tensions that have been discussed. Each involves a give and take, as people with differing opinions advocate to have their preferred policies adopted. These essential tensions also shape other areas of criminal justice, such as policing and the courts. However, they are particularly important for corrections because of the general lack of correctional theory. Were there a sound, constitutionally valid, well-established, and empirically verified uniform philosophy guiding contemporary correctional practice, the four essential tensions would be less important because that philosophy could then guide key correctional decisions. Until agreement on such a philosophy emerges, however, debates will likely continue to be shaped by factors reflected in the essential tensions.

Q How would each essential tension influence policy about weightlifting in prison?

Q Are there remedies to the conflicts posed by the essential tensions? Why or why not?

History and Practice of Institutional Corrections

FOCUSING QUESTION 13.3

How have correctional institutions changed over time?

The study and practice of corrections is typically subdivided into two areas . The first is institutional corrections , which includes issues related to prisons and jails, as discussed in this section. The second is community corrections, which includes correctional alternatives that take place outside prisons and jails, as discussed later in the chapter.

Correctional institutions are secure facilities designed to house persons accused or convicted of a crime. There are two types of correctional institutions. A **jail** is a short-term facility usually operated by a county sheriff. Jails hold persons accused (but not convicted) of crimes who are awaiting trial, including persons who were denied bail or pre-trial release. In addition, jails also hold convicted offenders who have short sentences, usually of less than one year. A **prison** is a long-term facility operated by the state or federal government. Prisons hold convicted offenders who have been sentenced to longer terms, usually of a year or more.

A HISTORICAL SURVEY OF CORRECTIONAL INSTITUTIONS

In the colonial era and the early years of the American republic, correctional institutions were not widely used for punishment. In fact, there were no prisons to speak of, and jails were used for one of two purposes: to hold persons awaiting trial or punishment (but not as punishment itself) or to hold persons who could not pay their debts (a debtor's prison).

correctional institution
A secure facility designed to house persons accused or convicted of a crime. Jails and prisons are the two primary types of correctional institutions.

jail
A correctional institution holding persons accused of a crime who are awaiting trial and offenders who are sentenced to less than one year. Jails are short-term facilities usually operated by a county sheriff.

prison
A correctional institution holding persons who are sentenced to more than a year. Prisons are long-term facilities operated by the state or federal government.

Typical punishments included the death penalty, physical beatings, banning offenders from an area (banishment), fines, or public shaming (discussed in Chapter 10). In shaming, offenders were placed in the town square and restrained by an apparatus such as the stocks, which secured the person's feet, or the pillory, which secured the person's hands or head, so he or she could not move or leave (Rothman, 1995).

It was against this backdrop that correctional institutions developed. In 1776, the Walnut Street Jail opened in Philadelphia. The operations of this jail were influenced by reforms introduced in England and also by Quaker philosophies (popular in Pennsylvania at the time) that decried the death penalty and instead sought rehabilitation of inmates. As a result, the jail was no longer viewed as a place to wait for punishment; it became a place to send offenders for the specific purposes of punishment and reform. At the same time, the establishment of early correctional institutions also helped to increase the power of the state government. The Walnut Street Jail was ultimately transformed into a Pennsylvania state prison in 1794, clearly establishing the state as having primary responsibility for offenders who committed serious crimes (i.e., felonies). This demonstrated that state authority for social control exceeded that of local governments (Takagi, 1975).

Three models of correctional institutions developed in nineteenth-century America: the solitary system, based on Eastern State Penitentiary in Pennsylvania; the congregate system, based on Auburn State Prison in New York; and prison farms, common in the southern United States. Each is described in the following paragraphs (see Box 13.2 for a discussion of a fourth system that enjoyed limited popularity).

solitary system
An early method of incarceration in which inmates remained in individual cells with little to no human contact for the duration of their sentence. The goal was to promote offender rehabilitation through self-introspection.

The **solitary system** (also known as the Pennsylania system) was modeled on practices at the Walnut Street Jail. The goal of the solitary system was to promote offender rehabilitation through self-introspection. The institution most closely associated with the solitary system was Eastern State Penitentiary, which opened in Philadelphia, Pennsylvania, in 1829. Eastern State Penitentiary was designed to completely isolate the offender. The utter silence of the institution was remarkable. Inmates were to have no human contact from the time they were admitted to the time they were released. They wore hoods when taken to their cells, so they could not interact with staff or with any inmates who happened to be out of their cells. Inmates were to stay in their individual cells without leaving for the duration of their sentences. Each cell had a heavy wooden door so the inmate was isolated from the corridor along which his or her cell was located. So inmates could periodically see the outdoors, each cell did have its own small private exercise yard, separated from others by high walls (Friedman, 1993). Inmates could read the Bible and reflect on their past deeds, working toward rehabilitation. They also could engage in some work projects that could be completed without leaving the cell (Rothman, 1995). The idea was that complete separation from other human beings would cause inmates to become penitent (hence the name "penitentiary"), recognizing and repenting for their criminal acts and turning away from future criminal activity.

congregate system
An early method of incarceration in which inmates lived in individual cells during the night but worked in factories and had meals in dining halls during the day. Absolute silence was required of inmates, even when outside their cells.

The **congregate system** (also known as the Auburn system) was based on Auburn State Prison, opened in 1816 in Auburn, New York. Auburn was promoted as a less expensive alternative to the solitary system and one that could generate revenue for the state through inmates' work in prison factories (Rothman, 1995). Like the solitary system, absolute silence was expected in congregate prisons. However, the inmates were not completely isolated from one another. At night, inmates lived in solitary cells. However, during the day, they moved from their cells to a dining hall for meals and then to work in factories (Friedman, 1993). Inmates who broke the rule of silence received harsh physical punishments. The development of the congregate system was prompted by a desire for prisons to rehabilitate, in addition to punish. The strict discipline was intended to lead to reformation of the inmate, but with a prison less costly than one designed on the solitary model (Rothman, 1995).

BOX 13.2

THE REFORMATORY SYSTEM

The **reformatory system** provided an alternative to the harsh environments of many nineteenth-century prisons. Elmira Reformatory, one of the most recognized, opened in New York in 1876. Its founder, Zebulon Brockway, envisioned it as a more effective alternative to other prisons, particularly for young adult offenders. Inmates who were successful in the institution's programs could earn early release, and inmates progressed through grades toward this goal. Designed as a rehabilitative institution (Rotman, 1995), the elements of Elmira Reformatory included the following (excerpts quoted from Brockway, 1910, pp. 99–101):

1. "[The structure] should be salubriously situated and, preferably, in a suburban locality . . . The whole should be supplied with suitable modern sanitary appliances and with an abundance of natural and artificial light."
2. "Clothing for the prisoners, not degradingly distinctive but uniform, yet fitly representing the respective grades or standing of the prisoners . . . For the sake of health, self-respect, and the cultural influence of the general appearance, scrupulous cleanliness should be maintained and the prisoners kept appropriately groomed."
3. "A liberal prison dietary designed to promote vigor . . . Deprivation of food, by a general regulation, for a penal purpose, is deprecated . . . More variety, better quality and service of foods for the higher grades of prisoners is serviceably allowed . . ."
4. "A gymnasium completely equipped with baths and apparatus; and facilities for field athletics."
5. "Facilities for special manual training sufficient for about one-third of the resident population . . . [including] mechanical and freehand drawing; sloyd in wood and metals; cardboard constructive form work; clay modeling; cabinet making; chipping and filing; and iron molding."
6. "Trades instruction . . . conducted to a standard of perfect work and speed performance that insures the usual wage value to their services."
7. "A regimental military organization of the prisoners with a band of music, swords for officers, and dummy guns for the rank and file of prisoners . . . The regular army tactics, drill, and daily dress parade should be observed."
8. "School of letters with a curriculum that reaches from an adaptation of the kindergarten . . . through various school grades up to the usual high-school course."
9. "A well-selected library for circulation, consultation, and under proper supervision, for occasional semi-social use."
10. "The weekly institutional newspaper, in lieu of all outside newspapers, edited and printed by the prisoners under due censorship."
11. "Recreating and diverting entertainments . . . provided in the great auditorium; not any vaudeville nor minstrel shows, but entertainments of such a class as the middle cultured people of a community would enjoy."
12. "Religious opportunities, optional."
13. "Definitely planned, carefully directed, emotional occasions . . . for a kind of irrigation [utilizing] music, pictures, and the drama."

Q What elements of the reformatory system do you think are useful? What elements do you dislike? Explain your answer in the context of what you believe are the goals of corrections.

reformatory system
An early method of incarceration designed for young offenders, with an emphasis on education, vocational instruction, and rehabilitation.

farm system
A historical method of incarceration used primarily in the American South in which inmates lived and worked on large prison farms. The prison farms were operated primarily by the inmates themselves, some of whom served as guards over the other inmates. Severe physical punishment was common at the prison farms.

A very different system emerged in some southern states, which developed **farm systems**. It is important to note that some prisons today have farms that are operated by inmates, but the concept of a farm *system* is very different from any current practice. In a farm system, inmates lived together in large bunkhouses similar to barracks. Farms were largely operated by the inmates themselves. There were few civilian employees, so certain inmates were selected to guard others and were even armed to do so. Very little money was invested in the prison farms, but they were expected to generate revenue for the state by selling produce. Very few services were provided for inmates, and some had to sell their blood to earn money for items such as clothing, health care, and other essentials. Inmates who violated the few rules that existed were punished (often by other inmates) by whippings, electric shock, or by other physical means. The farm system was marked by high levels of violence and questionable security (see Feeley & Rubin, 1998; *Holt v. Sarver,* 1970).

Over time, each of these three systems was abandoned. The prison farm system was ruled unconstitutional and replaced with more traditional correctional institutions (e.g., *Holt v. Sarver,* 1970). The solitary system was criticized because complete isolation could cause mental distress and because separate cells and yards for each individual inmate were expensive. The congregate system was the one most adopted by other states, but the system of strict silence and the practice of housing only one inmate per cell were abandoned due to overcrowding (Rothman, 1995). As discussed in Chapter 10, a shift occurred over time with less emphasis placed on the prison serving as a rehabilitative force and more emphasis on incapacitation, modeled after the "get tough on crime" philosophy.

CURRENT PRACTICE IN CORRECTIONAL INSTITUTIONS

In a contemporary prison, inmates typically live with a cellmate, have opportunities for work or programming during the day (including recreation, religious services, counseling, education or vocational training, and more), and interact regularly with other inmates and correctional staff. There is, however, substantial variation in prisons in terms of their design, programs offered, and security level.

You may visualize a prison as containing cell blocks arranged in long rows with cells on one or both sides of a long corridor. Some prisons, particularly older institutions, are designed this way. However, many newer prisons utilize a pod-style design in which cells surround a central day room, as illustrated in Figure 13.1 (each grouping of cells and day room is known as a "pod"). Inmates may gather for recreation,

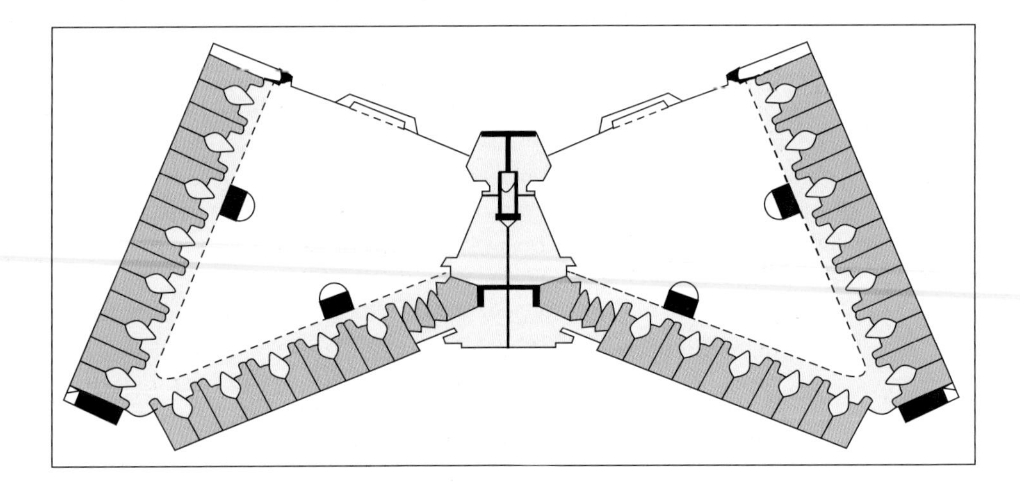

FIGURE 13.1 Pod-Style Design.
Source: Goldman, 2003

programming, or other prosocial activities in the large open day room. In addition, inmates and correctional staff may interact there. These characteristics facilitate a strategy known as unit management, in which multiple activities are contained within the pod; staff within the pod (e.g., correctional officers and correctional counselors) can then work more closely with inmates to promote meaningful counseling. The unit management philosophy is associated with reductions in inmate violence and other rule violations (Bayens, Williams, & Smykla, 1997).

It is also important to note that there are different types of prison facilities. Perhaps the most familiar distinction is that based on **security level**. Within each state and the federal government, there are low (minimum), medium, and high (maximum) security prisons. Differences between security levels center on issues such as how much freedom inmates have within the institution, what types of programming opportunities are available to inmates, and how much security is incorporated into the facility (fences, towers, number of correctional officers, etc.). Table 13.1 provides additional information about security levels. Note that the largest number of inmates are in medium security; by comparing the percentage of insitutions to the percentage of offenders, also note that minimum security facilities are generally smaller than medium or maximum security facilities.

security level
In corrections, the differences between minimum, medium, and maximum-security prisons centering on issues such as how much freedom inmates have within the institution, what types of programming are available, and how many security features are incorporated into the facility.

As discussed previously, offenders who are sentenced to prison go through an initial **classification** process in which correctional officials determine their security level and assign them to a prison. It is common for offenders to be reclassified multiple times during their sentences based on their adjustment and their behavioral record. For instance, inmates who began in maximum security can be moved to medium security if their record has been positive. Inmates can also be moved to higher security levels, if necessary. See Box 13.3 for a discussion of controversies surrounding "supermax" prisons.

classification
The process by which correctional officials determine the prison and security level to which an inmate should be assigned.

THEORETICAL PERSPECTIVES ON PRISON LIFE

Regardless of the type of institution, there are two theoretical perspectives that provide a context for understanding correctional institutions and life within them. They are the work of Erving Goffman (1961) on "total institutions" (p. 4) and the work of Gresham Sykes (1958) on the "pains of imprisonment" (p. 63).

TABLE 13.1 State and Federal Institutional Security Levels[a]

Level	Definition[b]	Percentage of Institutions[c]	Percentage of Inmates[c]
Minimum	"These facilities often have a greatly reduced level of staff supervision and generally have no perimeter security such as a fence. These institutions are utilized to house offenders with no history of violence or sex offenses, and those confined in this type of facility generally are serving short sentences."	53.2%	21.7%
Medium	"Facilities in this category have secure perimeters (generally double fences with armed vehicles that patrol the outside of the fence line) and more security personnel. Inmates serving various sentences may be housed at this level."	26.4%	42.4%
Maximum	"These penitentiaries are for offenders with histories of violence and for those who represent a threat to others . . . Inmate housing is typically in cells, and perimeter security is significant (walls or double fences, often with armed towers)."	20.4%	35.9%

[a] Data include prisons and community-based residential facilities
[b] From Cooksey, 2008, pp. 61–62
[c] Calculated from Stephan, 2008.

BOX 13.3

Research in Action

SUPERMAX PRISONS

Most states and the federal government have at least one supermax prison, which is a level above traditional maximum security, operated as follows:

> inmates are confined in their cells for 22 to 23 hours a day (Fellner & Mariner, 1997; NIC, 1997; Riveland, 1999). These institutions limit human contact to instances when medical staff members, clergy members, or counselors stop in front of inmates' cells during routine rounds. Physical contact is limited to being touched through security doors by correctional officers while being put in restraints or having restraints removed. Most verbal communication occurs through intercom systems (Riveland, 1999). (Pizarro & Stenius, 2004, p. 251)

Inmates are assigned to supermax prisons by correctional staff based on their behaviors in other prisons. It is not the severity of an inmate's crime, but rather the nature of an inmate's behavior in prison, that is considered in supermax assignments (Pizarro & Stenius, 2004). In a study of one state's supermax facility, Mears and Bales (2010) found that there was wide variability in supermax confinement, with some inmates spending relatively short times and others spending the majority of their sentence in supermax. The majority of supermax inmates had multiple stays there. Similarly, Pizarro and Stenius (2004) had observed that some jurisdictions lacked specific criteria guiding decisions about how long inmates should be detained in supermax before being moved to other facilities.

Pizarro, Stenius, and Pratt (2006) identified a number of influences leading to the popularity of supermax prisons, including the reduced emphasis on rehabilitation and increased focus on using prisons to separate offenders from society—going one step further with supermaxes and separating inmates identified as disruptive from other inmates. This also fits within the get-tough-on-crime movement and the notion that newly constructed supermax prisons could drive local economies. Research has also found a majority of the public to be supportive of supermax prisons (Mears, Mancini, Beaver, & Gertz, 2013).

Safety is one primary goal of supermax facilities, whether by reducing violence, preventing escape, improving inmate behavior, minimizing gang activity, lowering recidivism, and providing a means to punish disruptive inmates (Mears & Watson, 2006). While wardens tend to be supportive of supermax facilities, one study found that many also believed supermax prisons can produce negative effects (Mears & Castro, 2006).

total institution
A concept described by Erving Goffman in which an institution controls all aspects of a person's life. Correctional institutions are one example of a total institution, as the institution controls all aspects of an inmate's life.

The concept of a **total institution** is a powerful descriptor of the prison (Goffman also suggests that nursing homes, mental hospitals, boarding schools, the military, monasteries, and other social organizations meet the criteria of total institutions). To understand Goffman's (1961) concept of a total institution, first consider life *outside* a total institution as he describes it: "A basic social arrangement in modern society is that the individual tends to sleep, play [i.e., engage in recreational activities], and work in different places, with different co-participants, under different authorities, and without an over-all rational plan" (pp. 5–6). For instance, an individual might sleep at home and work in an office. While at home, she might interact with family members and while at work she might interact with office colleagues. At home, the family unit develops a system for making decisions and resolving conflicts, while at work a boss takes on these tasks. In other words, there is separatation between different areas of one's life.

A total institution is the exact inverse. The inmate in a prison sleeps, engages in recreation, and works in the same place—the prison. The inmate does these activities with the same co-participants (all other inmates) while under the supervision and direction of the same authorities (correctional officers supervise the inmate's cell, the recreational areas, and the work areas). The institutional experience as a whole is

Research tends to verify that there are concerns about supermax prisons. In theory, the use of supermax prisons should reduce violence in other prisons, as disruptive inmates are relocated to the supermax facility. But, research has not found them to have an impact on the level of violence between inmates, and has found mixed results on violence against staff—some jurisdictions seeing a decrease, others an increase, and others no impact (Briggs, Sundt, & Castellano, 2003; Sundt, Castellano, & Briggs, 2008). Inmate accounts suggest that supermax, "instead of isolating the most negative elements . . . has elevated their status and extended their reach into the minds and hearts of more prisoners" (Hartman, 2008, p. 172) and that "conditions are designed to test their control, to 'create stress' and 'make us antisocial' in a purposeful effort to produce negative effects" (Rhodes, 2004, p. 54). Research also suggests that supermax does not reduce recidivism—compared to similar inmates who were *not* held in supermax, those who were have been found to have higher violent recidivism rates (Mears & Bales, 2009) and higher overall recidivism rates, if in supermax facilities at the time of their release (Lovell, Johnson, & Cain, 2007).

One of the most notable concerns about supermax confinement is its impact on mental health. One study found that almost half of inmates in supermax had a serious mental illness, brain damage, psychiatric symptoms, or evidence of self-harm (Lovell, 2008). This has led some (e.g., Hafemeister & George, 2012) to criticize holding the mentally ill in supermax as cruel and unusual punishment. Other scholars have argued that supermax confinement, itself, causes psychological harm (Haney, 2003), leading some health professionals to call for its discontinuation (Shalev, 2011; Metzner & Fellner, 2010). A study of one state's efforts to reduce its supermax population, including removal from supermax of inmates with serious mental illness, found that the changes were associated with a decrease in violence and a decrease in the use of force against inmates (Kuppers et al., 2009).

Supermax prisons remain controversial. Consider these questions:

- Q Do supermax prisons illustrate any of the essential tensions of corrections?
- Q Some support the continuation of supermax prisons, others a reduction in their use, and others still a complete discontinuation of their use. Which would you prefer? Why?
- Q Can supermax confinement be modified to avoid the negative outcomes described above, but to maintain the focus on safety as a goal?

designed to accomplish some goals (although as noted earlier, there is not easy agreement in American corrections as to what those goals are).

The scope of control in a total institution includes aspects of life that would not be regulated on the outside, such as acceptable hairstyles, what food can be consumed, and what materials may be read. Also unlike life outside a total institution, inmate misconduct in one area of life—for instance, work in a prison factory—can result in negative consequences in another area of life—such as revoked recreational privileges or even changing the inmate's living quarters to a higher security prison. Thus, the control over the inmate is total in a total institution.

Inmates entering a total institution undergo what Goffman (1961) refers to as **mortification**, which essentially means a loss of personal identity. The name is replaced with an identification number, institutional clothing replaces individual attire, personal property that reflects one's interests is limited, institutional rules diminish individualism and unique identity, and in a prison, others at the institution—staff and inmate alike—quickly become aware of the inmate's most personal information, as documented in official records (the contents of which quickly spread through the institutional grapevine).

mortification
The loss of personal identity that comes with admission to a total institution, such as a prison or jail.

pains of imprisonment
As described by Gresham Sykes, five deprivations, or things that are withheld from inmates: liberty, goods and services, heterosexual relationships, autonomy, and security. Taken together, these deprivations partially define the prison experience.

contraband
Any item that prison or jail inmates are not permitted to possess.

It is within this setting that inmates experience the **pains of imprisonment** as described by Sykes (1958), based on his study of a New Jersey prison. The pains of imprisonment take the form of five things (tangible and intangible) that are withheld from inmates during the time of their incarceration. These include:

- *Deprivation of Liberty.* Most obviously, the inmate is not at liberty in society due to being incarcerated in a prison. Contacts with the outside world are also limited, as mail is inspected, telephone calls are monitored, visits are subject to numerous regulations, and the Internet is not available.
- *Deprivation of Goods and Services.* Sykes suggests that, in a culture that values possessions as signs of affluence and status, "material possessions are so large a part of the individual's conception of himself that to be stripped of them is to be attacked at the deepest layers of personality" (p. 69). Prison rules specify items that inmates may not possess. Any item that inmates are not permitted to possess is called **contraband**, which includes items that are illegal for anyone (e.g., illegal drugs), items that are prohibited only to inmates (e.g., R-rated movies are prohibited under the Zimmer Amendment), and items that inmates may have only in limited quantities (e.g., if an inmate has 11 books but the rules only allow him to have 10, then the 11th book is contraband).
- *Deprivation of Heterosexual Relationships.* Prisons are usually segregated by gender. Sykes suggests that this results in the inmate being "figuratively castrated by his involuntary celibacy" (p. 70). However, sexual activity does occur in

California correctional officer examines cell phones confiscated from inmates in prison. Cell phones are considered contraband when possessed by inmates, and prison administrators and officers have worked to develop strategies to detect and confiscate them (Burke & Owen, 2010). What deprivations of prison do you think this illustrates? Why do you think prison staff are concerned about inmates having cell phones? What strategies could be developed to prevent cell phone smuggling, possession, and use in prison?

(Boyer, Clark, Kett, Salisbury, Sitkoff, & Woloch, 1993). At that time, rehabilitation was still a favored approach to handling offenders and crime was viewed as one of many social problems that could be solved with the right programs.

CURRENT PRACTICE IN COMMUNITY CORRECTIONS

All states currently utilize probation, and it is in fact the most common criminal sentence (see Glaze & Bonczar, 2009). However, parole is less common than it once was. In the 1990s, many states adopted **truth in sentencing**, which stipulates that offenders sentenced to prison must serve a certain portion of their time—usually 85% (see Rosich & Kane, 2005)—with no release (on parole or otherwise) prior to that time. This conflicts with parole's presumption that offenders may be sufficiently rehabilitated to earn release much earlier in their sentences. As a result, some states have abolished parole, and many inmates now serve close to their full sentence regardless of participation in programs or rehabilitative efforts. This represents the panacea phenomenon, as parole and early release (once viewed as a solution) came to be viewed as problematic, resulting in truth in sentencing being imposed as a new solution. Ironically, truth in sentencing has now come to be viewed as problematic due to the essential tension of finance (e.g., Scott-Hayward, 2009)—inmates staying in prison for longer periods of time, with early release unavailable, results in higher correctional costs. In addition, some research has also found that rule violations increase when truth in sentencing is implemented and parole is abolished, as early release is not available as an incentive to promote good behavior (Memory, Guo, Parker, & Sutton, 1999).

In addition to probation and parole, many other correctional alternatives have been developed since the 1960s. Because these alternatives fall on a continuum between probation at one end and prison at the other, they are known as **intermediate sanctions**. Boot camp, discussed earlier in this chapter, is an intermediate sanction. Various community-based facilities, similar in premise to Crofton's open prison, also exist. For instance, offenders may live at a **halfway house**, a residential facility that provides various educational and counseling programs in a setting that is more homelike and has greater freedoms than a prison or jail. Research on halfway houses is mixed, some finding that they reduce recidivism and some finding that they do not (La Vigne, 2010). Or, offenders may be required to attend a **day reporting center**, which is similar to a halfway house in the programs that are offered, but inmates are only required to check in daily rather than live there. Some research has found day reporting centers to be effective at reducing recidivism (e.g., Champion, Harvey, & Schanz, 2011), while other research has not (e.g., Boyle, Ragusa-Salerno, Lanterman, & Marcus, 2013). Part of the variation in results could be due to the wide variation in types of programs that are offered at the facility, as halfway houses and day reporting centers can vary widely in the types of services they provide.

An intermediate sanction that has increased in popularity is **electronic monitoring**. Offenders sentenced to this program must wear a device, usually in an ankle bracelet, which monitors their location. This may be used for offenders who are given curfews, for offenders who are prohibited from being in certain locations (e.g., sex offenders may not be allowed on school grounds), or for offenders who are under **house arrest** (meaning they may not leave their homes). Again, studies have been mixed, some finding electronic monitoring to be effective in preventing subsequent offending (e.g., Bulman, 2010) and others not (e.g., MacKenzie, 2006). It is possible that the variation in results could be due to differences in how programs are implemented and monitored, the quality of the technology used, and the population of offenders assigned to electronic monitoring (e.g., offenses committed, prior record, and so on).

Many probation offices utilize an intermediate sanction that is designed for offenders who are high risk or who have not been successful on regular probation.

truth in sentencing
Stipulates that offenders sentenced to prison must serve a certain portion of their time, usually 85%, and no early release (on parole or otherwise) may occur prior to that time. The federal government and many states have adopted truth in sentencing.

intermediate sanctions
A range of correctional alternatives that lie on a continuum between probation and prison.

halfway house
A type of correctional facility that provides educational and counseling programs in a homelike setting and offers offenders greater freedoms than a prison or jail. Halfway houses are an intermediate sanction.

day reporting center
A facility offering programs for offenders, but rather than living at the facility, offenders are only required to check in daily. Day reporting centers are an intermediate sanction.

electronic monitoring
A program in which offenders must wear a device, usually in an ankle bracelet, that monitors their location. Often used in combination with house arrest. Electronic monitoring is an intermediate sanction.

house arrest
An intermediate sanction in which offenders may live at home but are not permitted to leave their home. Electronic monitoring is generally used to enforce house arrest.

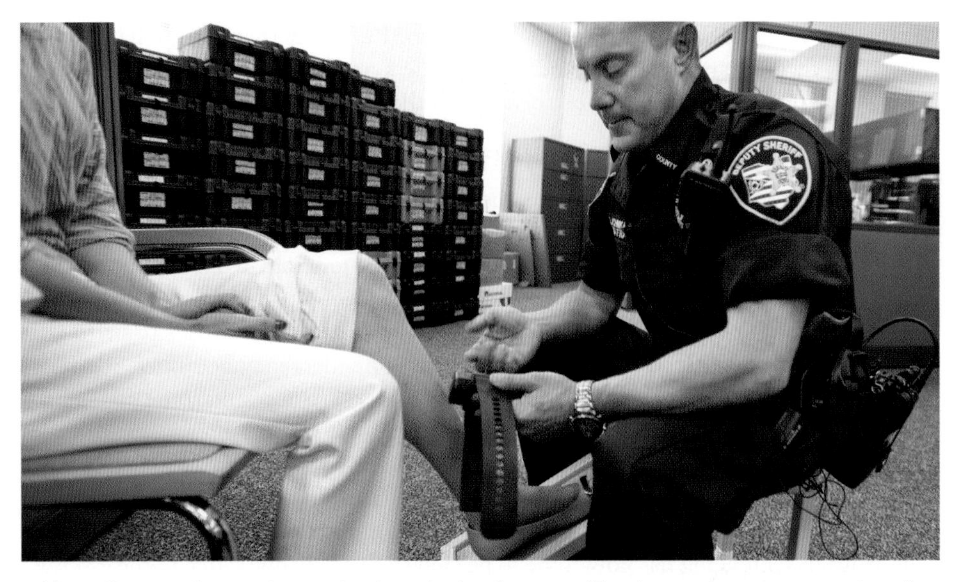

Officer fits an electronic monitoring device for an offender on house arrest. In what circumstances do you think electronic monitoring is an appropriate sentence? What do you think are the advantages and disadvantages?

intensive supervision probation
A highly structured form of probation designed for high-risk offenders or offenders who have not been successful on regular probation. Also known as ISP, it requires more frequent meetings and closer supervision than traditional probation.

Known as **intensive supervision probation (ISP),** it is a much more structured form of probation. Traditional probation requires only weekly or monthly meetings between the offender and probation officer, but ISP requires more regular meetings, several times per week, with much closer monitoring of the offender's activities. Although regular probation officers may supervise up to 100 (or more) offenders at one time, ISP officers are responsible for much fewer—around 25 or 30—again enhancing surveillance. Some research has found that ISP does not reduce recidivism; in fact, some data suggest that offenders on ISP are found to violate probation rules more often, possibly because the enhanced surveillance increases the likelihood of being caught (e.g., MacKenzie, 2006).

As has been the case for other intermediate sanctions, however, the research is mixed, with some findings indicating that ISP can reduce recidivism without increasing the likelihood that offenders are returned to prison for probation rule violations, particularly if the case loads are kept low (i.e., no more than 30 probationers supervised by one officer; see Jalbert, Rhodes, Flygare, & Kane, 2010). The latter point is particularly important, as there is sometimes a tendency for caseloads to increase as officers feel pressured to take on "just one more case," often due to the essential tension of finance and a lack of sufficient resources to maintain ideal workloads. Once again, it is important to consider possible explanations for the mixed findings. One study (Lowenkamp, Flores, Holsinger, Makarios, & Latessa, 2010) found that ISP programs focused on principles of effective treatment (e.g., a rehabilitation model) were more effective than those focused primarily on supervision and control—illustrating that consideration of the punishment philosophy can have a practical impact on program effectiveness.

The above discussion illustrates that correctional agencies have sought a variety of intermediate sanctions to provide a range of options between probation and prison. Studies of program effectiveness have been mixed, but one general principle of effective programming is to ensure that offenders are placed in the programs best suited for them, individually, based on a consideration of their level of risk and needs (see generally Cullen, 2005). Box 13.5 provides additional examples of community-based corrections by exploring one state's menu of options.

BOX 13.5

THE RANGE OF COMMUNITY SANCTIONS

The Ohio Office of Criminal Justice Services (2005) developed a guide to the range of community-based sanctions available in the state. In considering a wide range of sentencing possibilities, the Office noted: "Using a mix of prevention, intervention, education, treatment, and traditional incarceration, community corrections works to prevent, treat, and rehabilitate criminals in addition to handing down punishment for a crime" (p. 1). Some of the community sanctions include:

Financial Sanctions

- *Fines,* or payment of an amount of money as punishment for an offense
- *Fees,* in which the offender pays back the state for costs associated with handling the case
- *Super Fines,* of up to one million dollars for certain types of offenses specified under law, including aggravated felonies or crimes where "there are three or more victims, [or] the offender has previous convictions with the current offense [involving] three victims" (p. 7)
- *Restitution,* or money paid to the state that is then distributed to victims as compensation for their losses

Non-Residential Sanctions

- *Pretrial Diversion,* in which an offender's completion of an assigned program will result in charges being dismissed
- *Probation,* as discussed in the text
- *Day Reporting,* as discussed in the text
- *House Arrest,* requiring offenders to remain in their homes
- *Electronic Monitoring,* as discussed in the text
- *Community Service,* in which "an offender works for a public or non-profit agency without pay" (p. 19)
- *Drug Treatment,* emcompassing a range of programs that offenders may be required to attend
- *Drug Testing,* to ensure that offenders are not using illegal drugs
- *Intensive Supervision Probation,* as discussed in the text
- *Monitored Time,* in which low-risk offenders are "subject to no conditions other than leading a law-abiding life" (p. 23)
- *Curfew,* in which offenders must be home at certain times
- *Counseling, Employment, Education, or Training,* including a wide range of programs offenders can be required to attend on these issues
- *Victim-Offender Mediation,* allowing victims and offenders to meet to allow restitution and healing
- *License Violation Report,* for persons whose "occupations require a license to practice" (p. 27), in which the license-granting agency is notified of the person's conviction
- *Domestic Violence Counseling Program,* which may be required in some domestic violence cases

Residential Sanctions

- *Community-Based Correctional Facilities,* in which offenders may spend up to six months while participating in a variety of counseling, educational, employment, training, substance abuse, and other programming
- *Work Release,* allowing offenders in jails or other residential facilities to continue going to work each day, returning to the jail or facility for the remainder of the day

(continued)

BOX 13.5 (continued)

- *Halfway Houses,* as discussed in the text
- *Transitional Control,* in which prison inmates with 180 days or less remaining to serve are placed in residential facilities and required to wear an electronic monitoring device
- *Alternative Residential Facilities,* or other licensed facilities in which offenders may reside to receive services or programming, "such as a non-secure substance abuse facility, [or] a mental health residential facility" (p. 46)

Based on your review of these alternatives, consider the following questions:

Q Are there any alternatives listed above that you like more or less than others? Why? Do you have any ideas for alternatives that should be added to the list?

Q How would you determine which programs would be appropriate for which offenders?

Q Are there any types of cases in which you think the above programs should be used? Are there any in which you think they should not be used?

American corrections has come a long way from the time of confining offenders in stocks in the public square. Shaped by competing philosophies and the essential tensions described earlier, correctional policy continually strives to discover the next panacea for responding to crime. However, crime control requires more than the panacea phenomenon. As Dean-Myrda and Cullen (1998) noted, a rational, thoughtful, and informed approach to correctional policy is necessary. Such an approach would seek to retain and improve upon the positive aspect of programs, rather than rejecting those that are not perfect: "In the end, we should contemplate the wisdom of entering a post-panacea period in which simple solutions are forfeited in the pursuit of meaningful, if incremental, progress in an arena—crime control—that has been stubbornly resistant to the quick fix" (p. 15).

Q What do you think are the advantages and disadvantages of community corrections?

Q What factors do you think are necessary in order for probation, parole, and intermediate sanctions to be effective? How do you think intermediate sanctions should be changed, if at all, to promote their effectiveness at reducing recidivism?

Q Can you identify examples of the panacea phenomenon? Is Dean-Myrda and Cullen's recommendation possible? What would be necessary to make it so?

Conclusion

As we close this text, we hope that you have found the study of criminal justice to be a dynamic and interesting pursuit. In Chapter 1, we defined criminal justice as society's response to crime. A simple and broad definition, it perhaps obscured the true complexity of a field to which you have now given considerable thought. As you move forward, we hope you are a more sophisticated observer of criminal justice than before you began reading this text. We leave you with a challenge—one that all students, scholars, and practitioners of criminal justice should consider: what will be your contribution to the field of criminal justice? Striving for justice is an ancient pursuit and one in which the criminal justice system is but a single component, but it is through careful thought and reflection that the system ultimately advances. The future is yours.

Voting Rights

Criminal Justice Problem Solving

According to The Sentencing Project (2013), roughly 5.85 million U.S. citizens are unable to vote in elections due to voting disenfranchisement laws that are applied in most states to persons under correctional supervision. Consider the following:

- 48 states and the District of Columbia prohibit inmates from voting while incarcerated for a felony offense.
- Only two states—Maine and Vermont—permit persons in prison to vote.
- 35 states prohibit persons on parole from voting and 31 of these states exclude persons on probation as well.
- Four states deny the right to vote to all persons with felony convictions, even after they have completed their sentences. Seven others disenfranchise certain categories of ex-offenders and/or permit application for restoration of rights for specified offenses after a waiting period . . .
- Each state has developed its own process of restoring voting rights to ex-offenders but most of these restoration processes are so cumbersome that few ex-offenders are able to take advantage of them. (p. 1)

Disenfranchisement laws have ancient Greco-Roman roots; they were used throughout Europe and incorporated in the laws of U.S. colonies (Varnum, 2008). But "over time, these laws became both more common and more severe" (p. 116). Indeed, when African American men were granted the right to vote after the Civil War, "many Southern states tailored their criminal disenfranchisement laws, along with other voting qualifications, to increase the effect of these laws on black citizens" (Shapiro, 1993, p. 540). Today, nearly 7.7% of African American adults in the United States are barred from voting due to criminal convictions, which is more than three times the national average of 2.5%. The figure is as high as 20% of all African-American adults in some states, including Florida, Kentucky, and Virginia (Sentencing Project, 2013). The United States is the only democracy in the world where some states disenfranchise convicted felons for the rest of their lives, even after they have fully served their sentences.

In *Richardson v. Ramirez* (1974), the U.S. Supreme Court upheld California's felony disenfranchisement law, rejecting the argument that the laws violated the Equal Protection Clause of the Fourteenth Amendment to the U.S. Constitution. Eleven years later, though, the Court revisited the matter in *Hunter v. Underwood* (1985). In that case, two men had been convicted of passing bad checks—a misdemeanor under state law. Yet, they were denied the right to vote under a provision of the Alabama State Constitution that disenfranchised those convicted of "any crime . . . involving moral turpitude" (p. 223). In that case, the Court found that the law had been intentionally designed to disenfranchise African Americans. Accordingly, the Court declared the law unconstitutional as a violation of the Equal Protection Clause of the Fourteenth Amendment. However, other voter disenfranchisement laws remain intact, as listed above.

Q Why do you think states have chosen to enact voting disenfranchisement laws? Do you agree or disagree with these laws? Why?

Q What philosophy of punishment (refer to Chapter 10) do you think underlies voter disenfranchisement laws?

Q Many scholars and commentators have called for either the repeal of voting disenfranchisement laws or their invalidation by the courts. Do you think the federal constitutional guarantee of the "equal protection of the laws" serves as a legitimate basis for invalidating the nation's felony disenfranchisement laws? Why or why not?

REFERENCES

Abel, D., Ellement, J. R., & Finucane, M. (2013). Annie Dookhan, alleged rogue state chemist, may have affected 40,323 people's cases, review finds. *Boston.com.* Available: http://www.boston.com/metrodesk/2013/08/20/annie-dookhan-alleged-rogue-state-chemist-may-have-affected-more-than-people-cases-review-finds/asc530gqHcQFEik4MLRpgI/story.html

Abercrombie, N., Hill, S., & Turner, B. S. (2006). *Dictionary of sociology* (5th ed.). New York: Penguin Books.

About pandemics. (n.d.). *Flu.gov.* Available: http://www.flu.gov/pandemic/about/index.html

Abrams, J. (2010, July 29). Congress passes bill to reduce disparity in crack, powder cocaine sentencing. *Washington Post.* Available: http://www.washingtonpost.com/wp-dyn/content/article/2010/07/28/AR2010072802969.html

Accommodation of Religious Practices within the Military Setting, Department of Defense Instruction Number 1300.17 (2009, February 10).

Acker, J. R. (2007). Impose an immediate moratorium on executions. *Criminology and Public Policy, 6,* 641–650.

Acosta, J., & Chavis, D. (2007). Build the capacity of communities to address crime. *Criminology and Public Policy, 6,* 651–662.

Adams, K. (2007). Abolish juvenile curfews. *Criminology and Public Policy, 6,* 663–670.

Adler, M. (1947). The doctrine of natural law in philosophy. *University of Notre Dame Natural Law Institute Proceedings, 1,* 65–84.

Afifi, T. O., Mota, N. P., Dasiewicz, P., MacMillan, H. L., Sareen, J. (2012). Physical punishment and mental disorders: Results from a nationally representative US sample. *Pediatrics, 130,* 1–9.

AFL-CIO. (2013). Sexual orientation. Retrieved from http://www.aflcio.org/Issues/Civil-and-Workplace-Rights/Your-Rights-at-Work/Sexual-Orientation

Agan, A. Y. (2011). Sex offender registries: Fear without function? *Journal of Law and Economics, 54*(1), 207–239.

Agnew, R. (1992). Foundations for a general strain theory of crime and delinquency. *Criminology, 30,* 47–87.

Ahlers, M. M. (2013, May 30). TSA removes body scanners criticized as too revealing. *CNN.* Available: http://www.cnn.com/2013/05/29/travel/tsa-backscatter

Akers, R. L. (2000). *Criminological theories: Introduction, evaluation, and application* (3rd ed.). Los Angeles: Roxbury.

Akers, R. L., & Jensen, G. F. (2007). *Social learning theory and the explanation of crime: Advances in criminological theory series* (new ed.). Edison, N.J.: Transaction Publishers.

Akers, R. L., & Sellers, C. S. (2012). *Criminological theories: Introduction, evaluation, and application* (6th ed.). New York: Oxford University Press.

Allam v. State, 830 P.2d 435 (Alaska App. 1992).

Alleyne, E., & Wood, J. (2010). Gang involvement: Psychological and behavioral characteristics of gang members, peripheral youth, and non-gang youth. *Aggressive Behavior, 36,* 423–436.

Almond, G. A., & Verba, S. (1989). *The civic culture: Political attitudes and democracy in five nations.* Newbury Park, Calif.: Sage Publications.

Alpert, G. P. (2007). Eliminate race as the only reason for police-citizen encounters. *Criminology and Public Policy, 6,* 671–678.

Altemeyer, B. (1996). *The authoritarian specter.* Cambridge, Mass.: Harvard University Press.

Amber Alert. (2010, January). *Amber Alert timeline.* Available: http://www.ojp.usdoj.gov/newsroom/pdfs/amberchronology.pdf

American Bar Association (2003). *Justice in jeopardy: Report of the commission on the 21st century judiciary.* Chicago: Author.

American Law Institute. (1981). *Model penal code.* Washington, D.C.: American Law Institute. (Original work published 1962)

American Psychiatric Association. (2013). *Diagnostic and statistical manual of mental disorders* (5th ed., DSM-5). Arlington, VA: American Psychiatric Publishing.

Amethyst Initiative. (n.d.). Available: http://www.theamethystinitiative.org/

An Ordinance Prohibiting Bullying and Harassment, City of Monona Ordinance No. 5–13–645 (2013).

Anderson, E. A. (2005). *Out of the closet and into the courts: Legal opportunity, structure, and gay rights litigation.* Ann Arbor: University of Michigan Press.

Anti-Defamation League. (2012). *Anti-Defamation League state hate crime statutory provisions.* Available: http://www.adl.org/assets/pdf/combating-hate/ADL-hate-crime-state-laws-clickable-chart.pdf

Aos, S., Miller, M., & Drake, E. (2006). *Evidence-based public policy options to reduce future prison construction, criminal justice costs, and crime rates.* Olympia: Washington State Institute for

Public Policy. Available: http://www.wsipp.wa.gov/rptfiles/06-10-1201.pdf

Apel, R., & Nagin, D. S. (2011). General deterrence: A review of recent evidence. In J. Q. Wilson & J. Petersilia (Eds.), *Crime and public policy* (pp. 411–436). New York: Oxford University Press.

Applegate, B. K. (2001). Penal austerity: Perceived utility, desert, and public attitudes toward prison amenities. *American Journal of Criminal Justice, 25,* 253–268.

Applegate, B. K., Cullen, F. T., Link, B. G., Richards, P. J., & Lanza-Kadue, L. (1996). Determinates of public punitiveness toward drunk driving: A factorial survey approach. *Justice Quarterly, 13*(1), 57–79.

Archibold, R. C. (2010, April 23). Arizona enacts stringent law on immigration. *New York Times.* Available: http://www.nytimes.com/2010/04/24/us/politics/24immig.html?scp=1&sq=arizona%20enacts%20stringent%201aw%200n%20immigration&st=cse

Argersinger v. Hamlin, 407 U.S. 25 (1972).

Aristotle. (2000). *Nicomachean ethics* (R. Crisp, Trans.). New York: Cambridge University Press.

Ariz. inmates convicted of DUI wear pink. (2007, December 12). *USA Today.* Available: http://usatoday30.usatoday.com/news/nation/2007-12-12-dui-chain-gang_N.htm

Arizona v. United States, 567 U.S. __ (2012).

Arkansas Department of Correction. (n.d.). *Goals.* Available: http://www.adc.arkansas.gov/goals_objectives.html

Arluke, A., Levin, J., Luke, C., & Ascione, F. (1999). The relationship of animal abuse to violence and other forms of antisocial behavior. *Journal of Interpersonal Violence, 14,* 963–975.

Armstrong, G. S., & Freeman, B. C. (2011). Examining GPS monitoring alerts triggered by sex offenders: The divergence of legislative goals and practical application in community corrections. *Journal of Criminal Justice, 39*(2), 175–182.

Arrest for Violation of Order–Penalties–Good Faith Immunity for Law Enforcement Officials, Missouri Revised Statutes, § 455.085 (2010).

Arrigo, B. A. (1999a). In search of social justice: Toward an integrative and critical (criminological) theory. In B. A. Arrigo (Ed.), *Social justice, criminal justice: The maturation of critical theory in law, crime, and deviance* (pp. 253–272). Belmont, Calif.: West/Wadsworth.

Arrigo, B. A. (Ed.). (1999b). *Social justice, criminal justice: The maturation of critical theory in law, crime, and deviance.* Belmont, Calif.: West/Wadsworth.

Arrigo, B. (1995). The peripheral core of law and criminology: On postmodern social theory and conceptual integration. *Justice Quarterly, 12,* 447–472.

Ascione, F. (1993). Children who are cruel to animals: A review of research and implications for developmental psychology. *Anthrozoos, 6,* 226–247.

Ascione, F., Weber, C., Thompson, T., Heath, J., & Maruyama, M. (April, 2007). Battered pets and domestic violence: Animal abuse reported by women experiencing intimate violence and by non-abused women. *Violence against Women, 13,* 354–373.

Assault in the First Degree, Maryland Criminal Law Code, § 3-202 (2011).

Assault in the Third Degree, Missouri Revised Statutes, § 565.070 (2010).

Associated Press. (2006, March 25). Bear wrestler insists critics are off-base. *USA Today.* Available: http://www.usatoday.com/news/nation/2006-03-25-bearwrestling_x.htm

Associated Press. (2002, July 10). *ACLU fights Pennsylvania police on profanity arrests.* Available: http://www.firstamendmentcenter.com/news.aspx?id=3680

Atkins v. Virginia, 536 U.S. 304 (2002).

Atwater v. City of Lago Vista, 532 U.S. 318 (2001).

Aull, E. H. (2012). Zero tolerance, frivolous juvenile court referrals, and the school-to-prison pipeline. *Ohio State Journal on Dispute Resolution, 27*(1), 179–206.

Austin, J. (2003). Why criminology is irrelevant. *Criminology and Public Policy, 2,* 557–564.

Austin, J., & Irwin, J. (2001). *It's about time: America's imprisonment binge* (3rd ed.). Belmont, Calif: Wadsworth.

Aviram, H. (2010). Humonetarianism: The new correctional discourse of scarcity. *Hastings Race and Poverty Law Journal, 7,* 1–52.

Axelrod, R. (1984). *The evolution of cooperation.* New York: Basic Books.

Baer, J. A. (1999). *Our lives before the law: Constructing a feminist jurisprudence.* Princeton, N.J.: Princeton University Press.

Bahrampour, T. (2012, May 16). D.C. police to allow Sikh officers to wear beards, religious items on job. *Washington Post.* Available: http://articles.washingtonpost.com/2012-05-16/local/35455142_1_sikh-officers-sikh-american-legal-defense-punjab

Bailey, W. C. (1998). Deterrence, brutalization, and the death penalty: Another examination of Oklahoma's return to capital punishment. *Criminology, 36,* 711–733.

Baker-Brown, I. (1866). On the curability of certain forms of insanity, epilepsy, catalepsy, and hysteria in females. London: Robert Hardwicke.

Baldwin v. New York, 399 U.S. 66 (1970).

Bancroft, P. (2009). *Pandemic influenza preparedness and response planning: Guidelines for community corrections.* Lexington, KY: American Probation and Parole Association. Available: https://www.ncjrs.gov/pdffiles1/Archive/228287NCJRS.pdf

Bandura, A., Ross, D., & Ross, S. A. (1961). Transmission of aggression through imitation of aggressive models. *Journal of Abnormal and Social Psychology, 63,* 575–582.

Banks, D., & Kyckellhahn, T. (2011, April). *Characteristics of suspected human trafficking incidents, 2008–2010.* Washington, D.C.: U.S. Department of Justice. Available: http://www.bjs.gov/content/pub/pdf/cshti0810.pdf

Barak, G. (1988). Newsmaking criminology: Reflections on the media, intellectuals, and crime. *Justice Quarterly, 5,* 565–587.

Barker v. Wingo, 407 U.S. 514 (1972).

Barnett, L. (2010, August 25). Text warning drivers about the dangers of leaving dogs in hot cars to be added to California's

driver's manual. *Los Angeles Times.* Available: http://latimesblogs.latimes.com/unleashed/2010/08/text-warning-drivers-about-the-dangers-of-leaving-dogs-in-hot-cars-to-be-added-to-california-drivers.html

Barton, C. K. B. (1999). *Getting even: Revenge as a form of justice.* Chicago: Open Court.

Batson v. Kentucky, 476 U.S. 79 (1986).

Baumgartner, F. R., De Boef, S. L., & Boydstun, A. E. (2008). *The decline of the death penalty and the discovery of innocence.* New York: Cambridge University Press.

Baumgartner, F. R., & Jones, B. D. (1993). *Agendas and instability in American politics.* Chicago: University of Chicago Press.

Bayens, G. J., Williams, J. J., & Smykla, J. O. (1997, September). Jail type and inmate behavior: A longitudinal analysis. *Federal Probation, 61*(3), 54–62.

Baze v. Rees, 553 U.S. 35 (2008).

Bear Wrestling, Revised Missouri Statutes, § 578.176 (2010).

Beaver, K. M., Gibson, C. L., DeLisi, M., Vaughn, M. G., & Wright, J. P. (2012). The interaction between neighborhood disadvantage and genetic factors in the prediction of antisocial outcomes. *Youth Violence and Juvenile Justice, 10,* 25–40.

Beccaria, C. (1995). On crimes and punishments. In R. Bellamy (Ed.), R. Davies & V. Cox (Trans.), *On crimes and punishments, and other writings* (pp. 1–114). New York: Cambridge University Press. (Original work published 1764)

Beck, A. J., Berzofsky, M., Caspar, R., & Krebs, C. (2013). *Sexual victimization in prisons and jails reported by inmates, 2011–2012.* Washington, DC: Bureau of Justice Statistics. Available: http://www.bjs.gov/content/pub/pdf/svpjri1112.pdf

Beck, A. J., Harrison, P. M., Berzofsky, M., Caspar, R., & Krebs, C. (2010). *Sexual victimization in prisons and jails reported by inmates, 2008–2009.* Washington, D.C.: U.S. Department of Justice. Available: http://bjs.ojp.usdoj.gov/content/pub/pdf/svpjri0809.pdf

Beckett, K. (1994). Setting the public agenda: "Street crime" and drug use in American politics. *Social Problems, 41,* 425–447.

Beckett, K., & Sasson, T. (2004). *The politics of injustice: Crime and punishment in America* (2nd ed.). Thousand Oaks, Calif.: Sage Publications.

Beckett, K., & Sasson, T. (2000). *The politics of injustice: Crime and punishment in America.* Thousand Oaks, Calif.: Pine Forge Press.

Beckwith v. State of Mississippi, 707 S0.2d 547 (Supreme Court of Mississippi, 1997).

Beckwith, J., & King, J. (1974). XYY syndrome—A dangerous myth. *New Scientist, 64,* 474–476.

Behavioral Analysis Unit, National Center for the Analysis of Violent Crime. (2008). Serial murder: Multi-disciplinary perspectives for investigators. Washington, D.C.: Federal Bureau of Investigation. Available: http://www.fbi.gov/stats-services/publications/serial-murder/serial-murder-july-2008-pdf

Behrens, M. A., & Silverman, C. (2002). The case for adopting appointive judicial selection systems for state court judges, *Cornell Journal of Law & Public Policy, 11,* 273–314.

Belenko, S. (2001). Research on drug courts: A critical review: 2001 update. New York: The National Center on Addiction and Substance Abuse at Columbia University. Retrieved from http://www.drugpolicy.org/

Belenko, S., DeMatteo, D., & Patapis, N. (2007). In D. W. Springer & A. R. Roberts (Eds.), *Handbook of forensic mental health with victims and offenders: Assessment, treatment, and research* (pp. 385–423). New York: Springer Publishing Company.

Ben-Yehuda, N. (1985). *Deviance and moral boundaries.* Chicago: University of Chicago Press.

Bentham, J. (1988). *The principles of morals and legislation.* Amherst, N.Y.: Prometheus Books. (Original work published 1789)

Bentham, J. (1970). *An introduction to the principles of morals and legislation* (J. H. Burns & H. L. A. Hart, Eds.). London: Athlone Press. (Original work published 1789)

Bentham, J. (1776). *A fragment on government.* Available: http://www.efm.bris.ac.uk/het/bentham/government.htm

Berghuis v. Thompkins, 560 U. S. 370 (2010).

Bess, M. (2008, October). Assessing the impact of home foreclosures in Charlotte neighborhoods. *Geography and Public Safety, 1*(3), 2–5. Available: http://www.cops.usdoj.gov/files/RIC/Publications/GPS-V011_iss3.pdf

Best, J. (1999). *Random violence: How we talk about new crimes and new victims.* Berkeley: University of California Press.

Best, J. (1990). *Threatened children: Rhetoric and concern about child-victims.* Chicago: University of Chicago Press.

Best, J., & Luckenbill, D. F. (1994). *Organizing deviance* (2nd ed.). Upper Saddle River, N.J.: Prentice Hall.

Bieber v. People, 856 P.2d 811 (Colo. 1993), cert. denied, 510 U.S. 1054 (1994).

Bieck, W., & Kessler, D. A. (1977). *Response time analysis.* Kansas City, Mo.: Kansas City Board of Police Commissioners.

Black, D. (1998). *The social structure of right and wrong* (Rev. ed.). New York: Academic Press.

Black, D. (1989). *Sociological justice.* New York: Oxford University Press.

Black, D. (1984). *Toward a general theory of social control* (Vol. 1). Orlando, Fla.: Academic Press.

Black, D. (1976). *The behavior of law.* New York: Academic Press.

Blake, R., & Mouton, J. (1964). *The managerial grid: The key to leadership excellence.* Houston, Tex.: Gulf.

Blakely v. Washington, 542 U.S. 296 (2004).

Blandon-Gitlin, I., Sperry, K., & Leo, R. A. (2011). Jurors believe interrogation tactics are not likely to elicit false confessions: Will expert witness testimony inform them otherwise? *Psychology, Crime & Law, 17*(3), 239–260.

Blanton v. City of North Las Vegas, 489 U.S. 538 (1989).

Blonder, I. (2010). Public interests and private passions: A peculiar case of police whistleblowing. *Criminal Justice Ethics, 29,* 258–277.

Blueford v. Arkansas, 132 S. Ct. 2044 (2012).

Blumstein, A., & Piquero, A. R. (2007). Restore rationality to sentencing policy. *Criminology and Public Policy, 6,* 679–688.

Blumstein, A., & Wallman, J. (Eds.). (2000). *The crime drop in America.* New York: Cambridge University Press.

Board of Education of Indiana School District 92 of Pottawatomie County. v. Earls, 536 U.S. 822 (2002).

Bogard, D. (2003). *Republican Party of Minnesota v. White:* The lifting of judicial speech restraint. *University of Arkansas at Little Rock Law Review, 26,* 1–18.

Bohm, R. M. (2000, November–December). The future of capital punishment in the United States. *ACJS Today,* pp. 1, 4–6.

Boman, J., Krohn, M., Gibson, C., & Stogner, J. (November, 2012). Investigating friendship quality: An exploration of self-control and social control theories' friendship hypotheses. *Journal of Youth & Adolescence, 41,* 1626–1540.

Bonczar, T. P. (2003, August). Prevalence of imprisonment in the U.S. population, 1974–2001. *Bureau of Justice Statistics Special Report.* Available: http://bjs.ojp.usdoj.gov/content/pub/pdf/piusp01.pdf

Bonneau, C. W., & Gann-Hall, M. (2009). *In defense of judicial elections.* New York: Routledge.

Bonta, J., Jesseman, R., Rugge, T., & Cormier, R. (2006). Restorative justice and recidivism: Promises made, promises kept? In D. Sullivan & L. Tifft (Eds)., *Handbook of restorative justice: A global perspective* (pp. 108–120). New York: Routledge.

Boumediene v. Bush, Nos. 06–1195 & 06–1196 (June 12, 2008).

Bowers v. Hardwick, 478 U.S. 186 (1986).

Bowes, M. (2013, August 18). Police recorded license plates at Obama inauguration. *Richmond Times-Dispatch.* Available: http://www.timesdispatch.com/news/local/crime/state-police-recorded-license-plates-at-obama-inauguration/article_32678a59-f9e1–5e46–8336- d5f4ba076cb7.html

Boyer, P. S., Clark, C. E., Kent, J. F., Salisbury, N., Sitkoff, H., & Woloch, N. (1993). *The enduring vision: A history of the American people* (2nd ed.). Lexington, Mass.: D. C. Heath.

Boyle, D. J., Ragusa-Salerna, L. M., Lanterman, J. L., & Marcus, A. F. (2013). An evaluation of day reporting centers for parolees: Outcomes of a randomized trial. *Criminology and Public Policy, 12,* 119–143.

Bracey, D. H. (2006). *Exploring law and culture.* Long Grove, Ill.: Waveland Press.

Bradbury, B. (2002, June 28). Deschutes County delinquent youth demonstration project (Report No. 2002–29). Salem: Oregon Secretary of State. Available: www.sos.state.or.us/audits/ pages/state_audits/full/2002/2002–29. pdf

Brady v. Maryland, 373 U.S. 83 (1963).

Braga, A., Papachristos, A., & Hureau, D. (in press). The effects of hot spots policing on crime: An updated systematic review and meta-analysis. *Justice Quarterly.*

Braga, A., & Weisburd, D. (2010). *Policing problem places: Crime hot spots and effective prevention.* New York: Oxford University Press.

Braithwaite, J. (2007). Encourage restorative justice. *Criminology and Public Policy, 6,* 689–696.

Braithwaite, J. (1989). *Crime, shame and reintegration.* New York: Cambridge University Press.

Brandenburg v. Ohio, 395 U.S. 444 (1969).

Branti v. Finkel, 445 U.S. 507 (1980).

Bratton, W. (1998). *Turnaround: How America's top cop reversed the crime epidemic.* New York: Random House.

Brents, B. G., & Hausbeck, K. (2001). State-sanctioned sex: Negotiating formal and informal regulatory practices in Nevada brothels. *Sociological Perspectives, 44,* 307–332.

Brickey, K. F. (1996). The Commerce Clause and federalized crime: A tale of two thieves. *Annals of the American Academy of Political and Social Science, 543,* 27–38.

Bridgmon, S. L., & Bridgmon, P. B. (2010). Ideality and party responsibility within the law and justice policy domain. *Criminal Justice Policy Review, 21,* 223–238.

Briggs, C. S., Sundt, J. L., & Castellano, T. C. (2003). The effect of supermaximum security prisons on aggregate levels of institutional violence. *Criminology, 41,* 1341–1376.

Brigham City v. Stuart, 547 U.S. 398 (2006).

Bright, S. B. (2010). The right to counsel in death penalty and other criminal cases: Neglect of the most fundamental right and what we should do about it. *Journal of Law in Society, 11,* 1–30.

Brinegar v. United States, 338 U.S. 106 (1949).

Brockway, Z. R. (1910). The American reformatory prison system. In C. R. Henderson (Ed.), *Correction and prevention: Vol. I. Prison reform* (pp. 88–107). New York: Russell Sage Foundation.

Brown v. Board of Education, 347 U.S. 483 (1954).

Brown v. Plata, 570 U.S. ___ (2013).

Brown v. Plata, 563 U.S. ___ (2011).

Brown, E. G. (2008, August). *Guidelines for the security and non-diversion of marijuana grown for medical use.* Sacramento: California Department of Justice. Available: http://www.ag.ca.gov/cms_attachments/press/pdfs/n1601_medicalmarijuanaguidelines.pdf

Brown, E. K. (2012). Foreclosing on incarceration? State correctional policy enactments and the great recession. *Criminal Justice Policy Review, 24,* 317–337.

Brown, J. S. (1952). A comparative study of deviations from sexual mores. *American Sociological Review, 17,* 135–146.

Brown, R. M. (1969). The American vigilante tradition. In H. D. Graham & T. R. Gurr (Eds.), *Violence in America: Historical and comparative perspectives* (pp. 144–218). New York: Signet Books.

Bruinius, H. (2013, August 14). Body cams for N.Y.C. police as a check on "stop and frisk": a good idea? *Christian Science Monitor.* Available: http://www.csmonitor.com/ USA/Justice/2013/0814/Body-cams-for-N.Y.C.-police-as-a-check-on-stop-and-frisk-a-good-idea

Buck v. Bell, 274 U.S. 200 (1927).

Buckaloo, B. J., Krug, K. S., & Nelson, K. B. (2009). Exercise and the low-security inmate: Changes in depression, stress, and anxiety. *Prison Journal, 89,* 328–343.

Bulman, P. (2010, December). Electronic monitoring reduces recidivism. *Corrections Today,* pp. 72–73.

Burdeau v. McDowell, 256 U.S. 465 (1921).

Bureau of Justice Assistance. (2013). *Drug courts.* Washington, D.C.: U.S. Department of Justice, Office of Justice Programs. Retrieved from https://ncjrs.gov/pdffiles1/nij/238527.pdf

Bureau of Justice Assistance. (2007). *Building an offender reentry program: A guide for law enforcement.* Available: https://www.bja.gov/publications/reentry_le.pdf

Bureau of Justice Assistance. (n.d.). What are problem-solving courts? Available: https://www.bja.gov/evaluation/ program-adjudication/problem-solving-courts.htm

Bureau of Justice Statistics. (2013). *Justice expenditure and employment extracts, 2010—preliminary.* Available: http://www.bjs.gov/index.cfm?ty=pbdetail&iid=4679

Bureau of Justice Statistics. (2010). *The justice system.* Available: http://bjs.ojp.usdoj.gov/content/justsys.cfm

Bureau of Justice Statistics. (1992). *Survey of inmates of local jails. Special report: Drunk driving.* Washington, D.C.: U.S. Government Printing Office.

Burger v. State, 163 S.E.2d 333 (Ga. App. 1968).

Burke, L. (2010). International media pirates: Are they making the entertainment industry walk the plank? *Business, Entrepreneurship, and the Law, 4,* 67–91.

Burke, L. O., & Vivian, J. E. (2001). The effect of college programming on recidivism rates at the Hampden County House of Correction: A 5-year study. *Journal of Correctional Education, 52,* 160–162

Burke, T. (2001, May). The passive alcohol sensor. *Law and Order, 49*(5), 53–55.

Burke, T. W., & Owen, S. (2010, July). Cell phones as prison contraband. *FBI Law Enforcement Bulletin*, pp. 10–15.

Burke, T. & Owen, S. (2006, January/February). Same-sex domestic violence: Is anyone listening? *The Gay & Lesbian Review, 13,* 6–7.

Bush, G. W. (2004, January 20). Address before a Joint Session of the Congress on the State of the Union. Available: http://www.presidency.ucsb.edu/ws/index.php?pid=29646

Bushway, S. D., & Sweeten, G. (2007). Abolish lifetime bans for ex-felons. *Criminology and Public Policy, 6,* 697–706.

Buzawa, E. S., & Buzawa, C. G. (2003). *Domestic violence: The criminal justice response* (3rd ed.). Thousand Oaks, Calif.: Sage Publications.

Calhoun, G. M. (1927). *The growth of criminal law in ancient Greece.* Berkeley: University of California Press.

California Department of Public Health. (2013, August 8). *Medical Marijuana Program (MMP) facts and figures.* Available: http://www.cdph.ca.gov/programs/MMP/Documents/MMP%20Fact%20and%20Figures.pdf

California Sex Offender Management Board. (2011). *Homelessness among California's registered sex offenders: An update.* Sacramento, Calif.: Author. Retrieved from http://www.casomb.org/docs/Residence_Paper_Final.pdf

California v. Greenwood, 486 U.S. 35 (1988).

Callaghan, K., & Schnell, F. (2001). Assessing the democratic debate: How the news media frame elite policy discourse. *Political Communication, 18,* 183–212.

Callahan, L. A., Steadman, H. J., McGreevy, M. A., & Robbins, P. C. (1991). The volume and characteristics of insanity defense pleas: An eight-state study. *Bulletin of the American Academy of Psychiatry and Law, 19*(4), 331–338.

Campbell, D. L., Dodge, K. A., & Campbell, S. K. (2010). Where and how to draw the line between reasonable corporal punishment and abuse. *Law and Contemporary Problems, 73,* 107–165.

Cann, D. M., & Yates, J. L. (2008). Homegrown institutional legitimacy: Assessing citizens' diffuse support for their state courts. *American Politics Research,* 36, 297–329.

Cantor, D., & Lynch, J. P. (2000). Self-report surveys as measures of crime and criminal victimization. In D. Duffee (Ed.), *Criminal justice 2000: Vol. 4. Measurement and analysis of crime and justice* (pp. 85–138). Washington, D.C.: U.S. Department of Justice. Available: http://www.ncjrs.gov/criminal_justice2000/v014_2000.html

Caporael, L. R. (1976). Ergotism: The Satan loosed in Salem? *Science, 192*(4234), 21–26.

Carlson, P. M. (2008). Inmate classification. In P. M. Carlson & J. S. Garrett (Eds.), *Prison and jail administration: Practice and theory* (2nd ed., pp. 71–81). Sudbury, Mass.: Jones and Bartlett Publishers.

Carlson, P. M., & Garrett, J. S. (2008). *Prison and jail administration: Practice and theory* (2nd ed.). Boston: Jones and Bartlett.

Carrington, P. D. (2011). Public funding of judicial campaigns: The North Carolina experience and the activism of the Supreme Court. *North Carolina Law Review, 89,* 1965–2010.

Carroll v. United States, 267 U.S. 132 (1925).

Carroll-Ferrary, N. L. (2006/2007). Incarcerated men and women, the Equal Protection Clause, and the requirement of "similarly situated." *New York Law School Law Review, 51,* 595–617.

Carson, E. A., & Golinelli, D. (2013, July). *Prisoners in 2012—advance counts.* Washington, DC: Bureau of Justice Statistics. Available: http://www.bjs.gov/content/pub/pdf/p12ac.pdf

Carson, E. A., & Sabol, W. J. (2012, December). *Prisoners in 2011.* Bureau of Justice Statistics. Available: http://www.bjs.gov/content/pub/pdf/p11.pdf

Carter, L. H., & Burke, T. F. (2010). *Reason in law* (8th ed.). Upper Saddle River, N.J.: Pearson/Longman.

Cassell, P. G., & Hayman, B. S. (1996). Police interrogation in the 1990s: An empirical study of the effects of *Miranda. UCLA Law Review, 43,* 839–931.

Castellano, T. C., & Gould, J. B. (2007). Neglect of justice in criminal justice theory: Causes, consequences, and alternatives. In D. E. Duffee & E. R. Maguire (Eds.), *Criminal justice theory: Explaining the nature and behavior of criminal justice* (pp. 71–92). New York: Routledge.

Catalano, S. (2012, November). *Intimate partner violence, 1993–2010.* Available: http://www.bjs.gov/content/pub/pdf/ipv9310.pdf

Caudle, S. L. (2012). Homeland security: The advancing national strategic position. In D. G. Kamien (Ed.), *The McGraw-Hill homeland security handbook: Strategic guidance for a coordinated approach to effective security and emergency management* (2nd ed., pp. 71–98). New York: McGraw-Hill.

Cavadino, M., & Dignan, J. (1997). *Penal systems: A comparative approach.* Thousand Oaks, Calif.: Sage Publications.

Ceasar, S. (2012, September 26). UC to pay nearly $1 million in UC Davis pepper-spray settlement. *Los Angeles Times.* Available: http://latimesblogs.latimes.com/lanow/2012/09/uc-davis-pepper-spray.html

Champion, D. R., Harvey, P. J., & Schanz, Y. Y. (2011). Day reporting center and recidivism: Comparing offender groups in a western Pennsylvania county study. *Journal of Offender Rehabilitation, 50,* 433–446.

Charney, N. (2009). Art crime in context. In N. Charney (Ed.), *Art and crime: Exploring the dark side of the art world* (pp. xvii–xxv). Santa Barbara, Calif.: Praeger.

Chen, E. Y. (2008). Impacts of "three strikes and you're out" on crime trends in California and throughout the United States. *Journal of Contemporary Criminal Justice, 24,* 345–370.

Chicago v. Morales, 527 U.S. 41 (1999).

Chimel v. California, 395 U.S. 752 (1969).

Choi, S. J., Gulati, G. M., & Posner, E. A. (2010). Professionals or politicians: The uncertain empirical case for an elected rather than appointed judiciary. *Journal of Law, Economics, and Organization, 26,* 290–336.

Christiansen, K. (1977). A preliminary study of criminality among twins. In S. Mednick & K. Christiansen (Eds.), *Biosocial bases of criminal behavior* (pp. 89–108). New York: Gardner.

Christie, N. (2004). *A suitable amount of crime.* New York: Routledge.

Christy, A., Poythress, N. G., Boothroyd, R. A., Petrila, J., & Mehra, S. (2005). Evaluating the efficiency and community safety goals of the Broward County mental health court. *Behavioral Sciences and the Law, 22,* 227–243.

Church of Lukumi Babalu Aye v. City of Hialeah, 508 U.S. 520 (1993).

Citizens United v. Federal Election Commission, 558 U.S. 310 (2010).

City of Indianapolis v. Edmond, 531 U.S. 32 (2000).

Clark v. Arizona, 548 U.S. 735 (2006).

Clarke, R. V., & Eck, J. E. (2007). *Understanding risky facilities.* Problem-Oriented Guides for Police, Problem-Solving Tools Series (No. 6). Washington, DC: U.S. Department of Justice. Available: http://www.popcenter.org/tools/pdfs/risky_facilities.pdf

Clarke, R., & Eck, J. (2003). *Become a problem-solving crime analyst in 55 small steps.* London: Jill Dando Institute of Crime Science

Clear, T. R. (2011). A private-sector, incentives-based model for justice reinvestment. *Criminology and Public Policy, 10,* 585–608.

Clear, T. R. (1994). *Harm in American penology: Offenders, victims, and their communities.* Albany: State University of New York Press.

Clear, T. R., Cole, G. F., & Reisig, M. D. (2009). *American corrections* (8th ed.). Belmont, Calif.: Thomson Higher Education.

Clear, T. R., & Frost, N. A. (2007). Informing public policy. *Criminology and Public Policy, 6,* 633–640.

Clear, T. R., Harris, P. M., & Baird, S. C. (1992). Probationer violations and officer response. *Journal of Criminal Justice, 20,* 1–12.

Clemmer, D. (1940). *The prison community.* New York: Holt, Rinehart and Winston.

Cloward, R. A., & Ohlin, L. E. (1960). *Delinquency and opportunity: A theory of delinquent gangs.* New York: Free Press.

Cochran, J. K., & Bromley, M. L. (2003) The myth (?) of the police sub-culture. *Policing: An International Journal of Police Strategies and Management, 26*(1), 88–117.

Cohen v. California, 403 U.S. 15 (1971).

Cohen, A. (1955). *Delinquent boys: The culture of the gang.* New York: Free Press.

Cohen, D. (2005). Crime, punishment, and the rule of law in classical Athens. In M. Gagarin & D. Cohen (Eds.), *The Cambridge companion to ancient Greek law* (pp. 211–235). Cambridge, UK: Cambridge University Press.

Cohen, D. (1996). Law, social policy, and violence: The impact of regional cultures. *Journal of Personality and Social Psychology, 70,* 961–978.

Cohen, L., & Felson, M. (1979). Social change and crime rate trends: A routine activities approach. *American Sociological Review, 44,* 588–608.

Cohen, M. A. (1988). Pain, suffering, and jury awards: A study of the cost of crime to victims. *Law and Society Review, 22,* 537–555.

Cohen, S. (1972). *Folk devils and moral panics: The creation of the mods and rockers* (2nd ed.). New York: St. Martin's Press.

Cohn, A. W. (1974, June). Training in the criminal justice nonsystem. *Federal Probation,* pp. 32–37.

Cohn, E. G., Rotton, J., Peterson, A. G., & Tarr, D. B. (2004). Temperature, city size, and the southern subculture of violence: Support for social escape/avoidance (SEA) theory. *Journal of Applied Social Psychology, 34,* 1652–1674.

Coker v. Georgia, 433 U.S. 584 (1977).

Colorado v. Bertine, 479 U.S. 367 (1987).

Commonwealth v. Pitt, 2012 WL 927095 (Mass. Super. Ct. 2012).

Commonwealth v. Tate, 893 S.W.2d 368 (Ky. 1995).

Community Relations Service. (2003). *Principles of good policing: Avoiding violence between police and citizens.* Washington, DC: U.S. Department of Justice. Available: http://www.justice.gov/archive/crs/pubs/principlesofgoodpolicingfina1092003.pdf

Conklin, J. E. (2003). *Why crime rates fell.* Boston: Allyn & Bacon.

Conklin, J. E. (1998). *Criminology* (6th ed.). Boston: Allyn & Bacon.

Conrad, P., & Schneider, J. W. (1992). *Deviance and medicalization: From badness to sickness* (2nd ed.). Philadelphia: Temple University Press.

Conrad, P., & Schneider, J. W. (1980). *Deviance and medicalization: From badness to sickness.* St. Louis: C. V. Mosby.

Cooksey, M. B. (2008). Custody and security. In P. M. Carlson & J. S. Garrett (Eds.), *Prison and jail administration: Practice and Theory* (2nd ed., pp. 61–69). Sudbury, Mass.: Jones and Bartlett Publishers.

Coolidge v. New Hampshire, 403 U.S. 443 (1985).

Corsaro, N., Hunt, E. D., Hipple, H. K., & McGarrell, E. F. (2012). The impact of drug market pulling levers policing on neighborhood violence: An evaluation of the High Point drug market intervention. *Criminology and Public Policy, 11,* 167–199.

Cosden, M., Ellens, J., Schnell, J., & Yamini-Diouf, Y. (2005). Efficacy of a mental health treatment court with assertive community treatment. *Behavioral Sciences and the Law, 23,* 199–214.

Cosgrove, L., & Krimsky, S. (2012). A comparison of DSM-IV and DSM-5 panel members' financial associations with industry: A pernicious problem persists. *PLoS Medicine, 9*(3), 1–4.

Council of State Governments. (2013). Mental health. Retrieved from http://csgjusticecenter.org/mental-health/

County of Riverside v. McLaughlin, 500 U.S. 44 (1991).

Covey, R. D. (2008). Fixed justice: Reforming plea bargaining with plea-based ceilings. *Tulane Law Review, 82,* 1237–1290.

Cox v. Louisiana, 379 U.S. 536 (1965).

Crawford v. Washington, 541 U.S. 36 (2004).

Crenshaw, K., Gotanda, N., Peller, G., & Thomas, K. (Eds.). (1995). *Critical race theory: The key writings that formed the movement.* New York: New Press.

Croley, S. P. (1995). The majoritarian difficulty: Elective judiciaries and the rule of law. *University of Chicago Law Review, 62,* 689–790.

Crutchfield, R. D. (2007). Abandon felon disenfranchisement policies. *Criminology and Public Policy, 6,* 707–715.

Cruzan v. Director, Missouri Department of Health, 497 U.S. 261 (1990).

Cullen, F. T. (2007). Make rehabilitation corrections' guiding paradigm. *Criminology and Public Policy, 6,* 717–727.

Cullen, F. T. (2005). The twelve people who saved rehabilitation: How the science of criminology made a difference. *Criminology, 43,* 1–42.

Cullen, F. T., & Agnew, R. (2003). *Criminological theory: Past to present,—Essential readings* (2nd ed.). Los Angeles: Roxbury.

Cullen, F. T., Blevins, K. R., Trager, J. S., & Gendreau, P. (2005). The rise and fall of boot camps: A case study in common-sense corrections. *Journal of Offender Rehabilitation, 40,* 53–70.

Cullen, F. T., Fisher, B. S., & Applegate, B. K. (2000). Public opinion about punishment and corrections. *Crime and Justice, 27,* 1–79.

Cullen, F. T., & Gilbert, K. E. (1982). *Reaffirming rehabilitation.* Cincinnati, Oh.: Anderson.

Cullen, F. T., & Jonson, C. L. (2012). *Correctional theory: Context and consequences.* Thousand Oaks, Calif.: Sage Publications.

Cunningham, W. C., Strauchs, J. J., & Van Meter, C. W. (1990). *The Hallcrest Report II: Private security trends 1970–2000.* Stoneham, Mass.: Butterworth-Heinemann.

Curra, J. O. (1999). *The relativity of deviance.* Thousand Oaks, Calif.: Sage Publications.

Custer, L. B. (1978). The origins of the doctrine of *parens patriae. Emory Law Journal, 27,* 195–208.

Daneker, M. D. (1993). Moral reasoning and the quest for legitimacy. *American University Law Review, 43,* 49–84.

Darley, J. M., & Pittman, T. S. (2003). The psychology of compensatory and retributive justice. *Personality and Social Psychology Review, 7,* 324–336.

Davidson, H. (1996). No consequences: Re-examining parental responsibility laws. *Stanford Law and Policy Review, 7,* 23–30.

Davidson, M. (1989 April 19). Housing authority proposes using grant for New Briarfield. *Daily Press.* http://articles.dailypress.com/1989-04-19/news/8904190176_1_housing-authority-subsidized-housing-elder-grant-program

Davies, T. Y. (1999). Recovering the original Fourth Amendment. *Michigan Law Review, 98,* 547–750.

Dawson, M. (2006). Intimacy and violence: Exploring the role of victim–defendant relationship in criminal law. *Journal of Criminal Law and Criminology, 96,* 1417–1449.

Daxecker, U., & Prins, B. (2013). Insurgents of the sea: Institutional and economic opportunities for maritime piracy. *Journal of Conflict Resolution, 57,* 940–965.

de Beaumont, G., & de Tocqueville, A. (1964). *On the penitentiary system in the United States and its application in France* (F. Lieber, Trans.). Carbondale: Southern Illinois University Press. (Original work published 1833)

de Felipe, M. B., & Martin, A. N. (2012). Post 9/11 trends in international judicial cooperation: Human rights as a constraint on extradition in death penalty cases. *Journal of International Criminal Justice, 10,* 581–604.

Dean-Myrda, M. C., & Cullen, F. T. (1998). The panacea pendulum: An account of community as a response to crime. In J. Petersilia (Ed.), *Community corrections: Probation, parole, and intermediate sanctions* (pp. 3–18). New York: Oxford University Press.

Death Penalty Information Center. (2011). *Facts about the death penalty.* Available: http://www.deathpenaltyinfo.org/documents/FactSheet.pdf

Death Penalty Information Center. (2013). *States with and without the death penalty.* Available: http://www.deathpenaltyinfo.org/states-and-without-death-penalty

Decker, S. H. (2007). Expand the use of police gang units. *Criminology and Public Policy, 6,* 729–734.

Decker, S. H., & Van Winkle, B. (1996). *Life in the gang: Family, friends, and violence.* New York: Cambridge University Press.

Deflem, M. (2006). *Sociological theory and criminological research: Sociology of crime, law, and deviance* (Vol. 7). San Diego, Calif.: Elsevier/JAI Press.

Deitrick, S., Beauregard, R. A., & Kerchis, C. Z. (1999). Riverboat gambling, tourism, and economic development. In D. R. Judd & S. S. Fainstein (Eds.), *The tourist city* (pp. 233–244). New Haven, Conn.: Yale University Press.

Delaware v. Prouse, 440 U.S. 648 (1979).

Delgado, R., & Stefancic, J. (2001). *Critical race theory: An introduction.* New York: New York University Press.

DeLisi, M., & Beaver, K. (2011). *Criminological theory: A life-course approach.* Sudbury, Mass.: Jones and Bartlett Publishers

Demands for Production of Statements and Reports of Witnesses, 18 U.S.C. § 3500 (1970).

Dennis, J. P. (2012). Gay content in newspaper comics. *The Journal of American Culture, 35*(4), 304–314.

Dershowitz, A. M. (1994). *The abuse excuse and other cop-outs, sob stories, and evasions of responsibility.* Boston: Little, Brown.

Deutsch, M. (2000). Justice and conflict. In M. Deutsch & P. T. Coleman (Eds.), *The handbook of conflict resolution: Theory and practice* (pp. 41–64). San Francisco: Jossey-Bass.

Devlin, P. (1977). Morals and the criminal law. In K. Kipnis (Ed.), *Philosophical issues in law* (pp. 54–65). Englewood Cliffs, N.J.: Prentice Hall. (Original work published 1965)

Dickerson v. United States, 530 U.S. 428 (2000).

Dirks-Linhorst, P. A., & Linhorst, D. M. (2012). Recidivism outcomes for suburban mental health court defendants. *American Journal of Criminal Justice, 37,* 76–91.

Discipline at School. (n.d.). The Center for Effective Discipline. Available: http://www.stophitting.com/index.php?page=states banning.

District of Columbia v. Heller, 554 U.S. 570 (2008).

Ditchfield, A. (2007). Challenging the intrastate disparities in the application of capital punishment statutes. *Georgetown Law Review, 95,* 801–830.

Dixon, J. (2008). Mandatory domestic violence arrest and prosecution policies: Recidivism and social governance. *Criminology and Public Policy, 7,* 663–670.

Doe v. City of Trenton, 143 N.J. Super. 128 (Superior Court of New Jersey, Appellate Division, 1976).

Domurad, F. (1999). So you want to develop your own risk assessment instrument. *Topics in Community Corrections,* pp. 11–16. Available: http://nicic.gov/pubs/1999/period160.pdf

Douzinas, C., Warrington, R., & McVeigh, S. (1993). *Postmodern jurisprudence: The law of text in the texts of law.* New York: Routledge.

Drug Policy Alliance. (2001). *Drug courts are not the answer: Toward a health-centered approach to drug use.* New York: Author.

Dryburgh, M. M. (2009). Personal and policy implications of whistle-blowing: The case of Corcoran State Prison. *Public Integrity, 11,* 155–170.

Dugdale, R. (1877). *The Jukes: A study in crime, pauperism, and heredity.* New York: Putnam.

Durham v. United States, 214 F.2d 862 (D. C. Cir. 1954).

Durkheim, É. (1980). The rules of sociological method. In S. H. Traub & C. B. Little (Eds.), *Theories of deviance* (pp. 3–21). Itasca, Ill.: F. E. Peacock Publishers. (Original work published 1938)

Durkheim, É. (1965). *The division of labor in society.* Glencoe, Ill.: Free Press.

Durkheim, É. (1938). Rules for distinguishing between the normal and the pathological. In É. Durkheim, *Rules of the sociological method* (pp. 64–75). New York: Free Press.

Duwe, G., & Clark, V. (2013). The effects of private prison confinement on offender recidivism: Evidence from Minnesota. *Criminal Justice Review, 38,* 375–394.

Dworkin, R. (2000). *Must our judges be philosophers? Can they be philosophers?* Presentation for the New York Council for the Humanities Scholar of the Year Lecture.

Dworkin, R. (1986). *Law's empire.* Cambridge, Mass.: Harvard University Press.

Dworkin, R. (1978). *Taking rights seriously.* Cambridge, Mass.: Harvard University Press.

Dworkin, R. (1966). Lord Devlin and the enforcement of morals. *Yale Law Journal, 75,* 986–1005.

Dye, T. (1984). *Understanding public policy.* Englewood Cliffs, N.J.: Prentice Hall.

Eaton, D. K., Kann, L., Kinchen, S., Shanklin, S., Flint, K. H., Hawkins, J., Harris, W. A., Lowry, R., McManus, T., Chyen, D., Whittle, L., Lim, C., & Wechsler, H. (2012, June 8). Youth Risk Behavior Surveillance—United States, 2011. *Morbidity and Mortality Weekly Report, Surveillance Summaries, 61*(4), 1–162. Available: http://www.cdc.gov/mmwr/pdf/ss/ss6104.pdf

Eck, J. E. (2005). Crime hot spots: What they are, why we have them, and how to map them. In *Mapping crime: Understanding hot spots* (pp. 1–14). Washington, DC: U.S. Department of Justice. Available: https://www.ncjrs.gov/pdffiles1/nij/209393.pdf

Eck, J. (2002). Preventing crime at places. In L. Sherman, D. Farrington, B. Welsh, & D. L. MacKenzie (Eds.), *Evidence-based crime prevention* (pp. 241–294). New York: Routledge.

Eck, J., & Maguire, E. (2000). Have changes in policing reduced violent crime? An assessment of the evidence. In A. Blumstein & J. Wallman (Eds.), *The Crime drop in America* (pp. 207–265). New York: Cambridge University Press.

Eck, J. E., & Spelman, W. (1987). *Problem-solving: Problem-oriented policing in Newport News.* Washington, D.C.: U.S. Department of Justice.

Eckholm, E. (2013, April 12). With police in schools, more children in court. *New York Times.* Available: http://www.nytimes.com/2013/04/12/education/with-police-in-schools-more-children-in-court.html?pagewanted=all&_r=0

Edelman, L. B. (2004). Rivers of law and contested terrain: A law and society approach to economic rationality. *Law and Society Review, 38,* 181–97.

Edelman, M. (1988). *Constructing the political spectacle.* Chicago: University of Chicago Press.

Edwards, C. (1906). *The oldest laws in the world.* London: Watts.

Egan, K. (2007). Morality-based legislation is alive and well: Why the law permits consent to body modification but not sadomasochistic sex. *Albany Law Review, 70,* 1615–1642.

Egley, A., & Howell, J. C. (2012, April). *Highlights of the 2010 National Youth Gang Survey.* Juvenile Justice Fact Sheet. Available: http://www.ojjdp.gov/pubs/237542.pdf

Ego-depletion and self-affirmation as underlying aspects of blaming of innocent victims. *Social Justice Research, 25,* 1–13.

Eisenstein, J., & Jacob, H. (1977). *Felony justice: An organizational analysis of criminal courts.* Boston: Little, Brown.

Eith, C., & Durose, M. R. (2011, October). *Contacts between police and the public, 2008.* Bureau of Justice Statistics Special Report (No. NCJ 234599). Available: http://www.bjs.gov/content/pub/pdf/cpp08.pdf

Eitzen, D. S., & Baca-Zinn, M. (Eds.). (1998). *In conflict & order: Understanding society* (8th ed.). Upper Saddle River, N.J.: Pearson/Allyn & Bacon.

Elder, R. W., Shults, R. A., Sleet, D. A., Nichols, J. L., & Thompson, R. (2002). Effectiveness of sobriety checkpoints for reducing alcohol-involved crashes. *Traffic Injury Prevention, 3,* 266–274.

Elev, T. C., Lichtenstein, P., & Moffitt, T. E. (2003). A longitudinal behavioral genetic analysis of the etiology of aggressive and nonaggressive antisocial behavior. *Development and Psychopathology, 15,* 383–402.

Elkins, B. E. (1994). Idaho's repeal of the insanity defense: What are we trying to prove? *Idaho Law Review, 31,* 151–171.

Ellison, C. G., & Sherkat, D. E. (1993). Conservative Protestantism and support for corporal punishment. *American Sociological Review, 58,* 131–144.

Elrod v. Burns, 427 U.S. 347 (1976).

Epstein, L., Knight, J., & Shvetsova, O. (2002). Selecting selection systems. In S. B. Burbank & B. Friedman (Eds.) *Independence at the crossroads: An interdisciplinary approach.* (pp. 191–227). Thousand Oaks, Calif.: Sage Publications.

Erez, E. (1981). Thou shalt not execute: Hebrew law perspective on capital punishment. *Criminology, 19,* 25–43.

Erikson, K. T. (2005). *Wayward Puritans: A study in the sociology of deviance.* Boston: Allyn & Bacon. (Original work published 1966)

Erke, A., Goldenbeld, C., & Vaa, T. (2009). The effects of drink-driving checkpoints on crashes: A meta-analysis. *Accident Analysis and Prevention, 41,* 914–923.

Estelle v. Gamble, 429 U.S. 97 (1976).

Estelle v. Williams, 425 U.S. 401 (1976).

Everson v. Board of Education, 330 U.S. 1 (1947).

Eysenck, H. J. (1964). *Crime and personality.* Boston: Houghton Mifflin.

Ezell v. City of Chicago, 651 F.3d 684 (7th Cir. 2011).

Fabelo, T. (2000, May). "Technocorrections": The promises, the uncertain threats. *Sentencing and Corrections: Issues for the 21st Century* (No. 5). Washington, D.C.: National Institute of Justice.

Fagan, J. (2007). End natural life sentences for juveniles. *Criminology and Public Policy, 6,* 735–746.

Fagan, K. (2013, August 2). Gun-death drop sparks debate on where credit lies. *San Francisco Chronicle.* Available: http://www.sfgate.com/crime/article/Gun-death-drop-sparks-debate-on-where-credit-lies-4704627.php

Fairchild, E., & Dammer, H. R. (2001). *Comparative criminal justice systems* (2nd ed.). Belmont, Calif.: Wadsworth.

Fallon, R. H., Jr. (1994). Reflections on the Hard and Wechsler paradigm. *Vanderbilt Law Review, 47,* 943–987.

Farber, D. A., & Sherry, S. (1997). *Beyond all reason: The radical assault on truth in American law.* New York: Oxford University Press.

Farrell, G., Tilley, N., Tseloni, A., & Mailley, J. (2010). Explaining and sustaining the crime drop: Clarifying the role of opportunity-related theories. *Crime Prevention and Community Safety, 12,* 24–41.

Farrington, K. (1992). The modern prison as total institution? Public perception versus objective reality. *Crime and Delinquency, 38,* 6–26.

Faver, C. & Strand, E. (2003). Domestic violence and animal cruelty: Untangling the web of abuse. *Journal of Social Work Education, 18,* 237–253.

FCC v. Pacifica Foundation, 438 U.S. 726 (1978).

Fealy, J. (2006). *Eliminating overt drug markets in High Point, North Carolina (application for the 2006 Herman Goldstein Award).* Available: http://www.popcenter.org/library/awards/goldstein/2006/06–20(F).pdf

Federal Bureau of Investigation. (2013). *Hate crime statistics 2012: Incidents and offenses.* Available: http://www.fbi.gov/about-us/cjis/ucr/hate-crime/2012/topic-pages/incidents-and-offenses/incidentsandoffenses_final

Federal Bureau of Investigation. (2012a). *Crime in the United States 2011: Clearances.* Available: http://www.fbi.gov/about-us/cjis/ucr/crime-in-the-u.s/2011/crime-in-the-u.s.-2011/clearances

Federal Bureau of Investigation. (2012b). *Crime in the United States: Property crime.* Available: http://www.fbi.gov/about-us/cjis/ucr/crime-in-the-u.s/2011/crime-in-the-u.s.-2011/property-crime/property-crime

Federal Bureau of Investigation. (2012c). *Crime in the United States 2011: Region.* Available: http://www.fbi.gov/about-us/cjis/ucr/crime-in-the-u.s/2011/crime-in-the-u.s.-2011/offenses-known-to-law-enforcement/standard-links/region

Federal Bureau of Investigation. (2012d). *Crime in the United States 2011: Violent crime.* Available: http://www.fbi.gov/about-us/cjis/ucr/crime-in-the-u.s/2011/crime-in-the-u.s.-2011/violent-crime/violent-crime

Federal Bureau of Investigation. (2012e). *Hate crime statistics 2011: Methodology.* Available: http://www.fbi.gov/about-us/cjis/ucr/hate-crime/2011/resources/methodology

Federal Bureau of Investigation. (2011). *Crime in the United States, 2011: Expanded homicide data table 14.* Available: http://www.fbi.gov/about-us/cjis/ucr/crime-in-the-u.s/2011/crime-in-the-u.s.-2011/tables/expanded-homicide-data-table-14

Federal Bureau of Investigation. (2004). Uniform Crime Reporting handbook. Available: http://www.fbi.gov/about-us/cjis/ucr/additional-ucr-publications/ucr_handbook.pdf

Federal Bureau of Investigation. (n.d.). *UCR data online.* Available: http://www.ucrdatatool.gov/index.cfm

Federal Bureau of Prisons. (2006, September 12). *Inmate security designation and custody classification* (Policy P5100.08). Washington, D.C.: Federal Bureau of Prisons. Available: http://www.bop.gov/policy/progstat/5100_008.pdf

Feeley, M. M. (1992). *The process is the punishment: Handling cases in a lower criminal court.* New York: Russell Sage Foundation.

Feeley, M. M., & Rubin, E. L. (1998). *Judicial policy making and the modern state: How the courts reformed America's prisons.* New York: Cambridge University Press.

Feeley, M. M., & Simon, J. (1992). The new penology: Notes on the emerging strategy of corrections and its implications. *Criminology, 30,* 449–474.

Feinberg, J. (1971). Legal paternalism. *Canadian Journal of Philosophy, 1,* 105–124.

Feinberg, J. (1965). The expressive function of punishment. *Monist, 49*(3), 397–423

Fellner, J., & Mariner, J. (1997). *Cold storage: Super-maximum security confinement in Indiana.* New York: Human Rights Watch.

Felson, M. (2002). *Crime and everyday life* (3rd ed.). Thousand Oaks, Calif.: Sage Publications.

Felthous, A. (1979). Childhood antecedents of aggressive behavior in male psychiatric patients. *Bulletin of the American Academy of Psychiatry and Law, 8,* 104–110.

Ferguson v. City of Charleston, 532 U.S. 67 (2001).

Ferguson, C. J. (2013). Spanking, corporal punishment and negative long-term outcomes: A meta-analytic review of longitudinal studies. *Clinical Psychology Review, 33,* 196–208.

Ferraiolo, K. (2007). From killer weed to popular medicine: The evolution of American drug control policy, 1937–2000. *Journal of Policy History, 19,* 147–179.

Finckenauer, J. O., & Gavin, P. W. (1999). *Scared straight: The panacea phenomenon revisited.* Prospect Heights, Ill.: Waveland Press.

Finigan, M. W., Carey, S. M., & Cox, A. (2007). *Impact of a mature drug court over 10 years of operation: Recidivism and costs (Final report).* Portland, Ore.: NPC Research.

Finnegan, S. (2009). Pro se criminal trials and the merging of inquisitorial and adversarial systems of justice. *Catholic University Law Review, 58,* 445–499.

Fish, M. J. (2008). An eye for an eye: Proportionality as a moral principle of punishment. *Oxford Journal of Legal Studies, 28,* 57–71.

Flango, V., & Ducat, C. (1979). What difference does method of judicial selection make? *Justice System Journal, 5,* 25–43.

Florida v. Jardines, 133 S. Ct. 1409 (2013).

Floyd et al. v. City of New York, 08 Civ. 1034 (SAS) (U.S. District Court, Southern District of New York, 2013).

Fogelson, R. M. (1977). *Big-city police.* Cambridge, Mass.: Harvard University Press.

Forsyth, C. J. (1992, October–December). Parade strippers: A note on being naked in public. *Deviant Behavior, 13,* 391–403.

Foucault, M. (1977). *Discipline and punish: The birth of the prison* (A. Sheridan, Trans.). New York: Vintage Books.

Fox, J. A. (2000). Demographics and U.S. homicide. In A. Blumstein & J. Wallman (Eds.), *The Crime Drop in America* (pp. 288–317). New York: Cambridge University Press.

Fradella, H. F. (2013). Guns, mental illness, and public policy. Unpublished manuscript.

Fradella, H. F. (2007). *Mental illness and criminal defenses of excuse in contemporary American law.* Bethesda, Md.: Academica Press.

Fradella, H. F. (2007). From insanity to beyond diminished capacity: Mental illness and criminal excuse in the post-*Clark* era. *University of Florida Journal of Law and Public Policy, 18,* 7–92.

Fradella, H. F. (2003). Faith, delusions, and death: A case study of the death of a psychotic inmate as a call for reform. *Journal of Contemporary Criminal Justice, 19,* 98–113.

Fradella, H. F. (2000). Minimum mandatory sentences: Arizona's ineffective tool for the social control of DUI. *Criminal Justice Policy Review, 11,* 113–135.

Fradella, H. F., Morrow, W. J., Fischer, R. G., & Ireland, C. E. (2011). Quantifying *Katz:* Empirically measuring reasonable expectations of privacy in the Fourth Amendment context. *American Journal of Criminal Law, 38*(3), 289–373.

Frances, Allen J. (2012, Dec. 2). DSM-5 is guide, not bible—Ignore its ten worst changes: APA approval of DSM-5 is a sad day for psychiatry. *Psychology Today.* Retrieved May 31, 2013 from http://www.psychologytoday.com/blog/dsm5-in-distress/201212/dsm-5-is-guide-not-bible-ignore-its-ten-worst-changes

Friedman, D. D. (2000). *Law's order: What economics has to do with law and why it matters.* Princeton, N.J.: Princeton University Press.

Friedman, L. M. (2002). *American law in the twentieth century.* New Haven, Conn.: Yale University Press.

Friedman, L. M. (1993). *Crime and punishment in American history.* New York: Basic Books.

Friedrichs, D. O. (2006). *Law in our lives: An introduction* (2nd ed.). Los Angeles: Roxbury.

Frisell, T., Pawitan, Y., Långström, N., & Lichtenstein, P. (2012). Heritability, assortative mating and genetic differences in violent crime: Results from a total population sample using twin, adoption, and sibling models. *Behavior Genetics, 42,* 3–18

Frymer, P. (2003). Acting when elected officials won't: Federal courts and civil rights enforcement in U.S. labor unions, 1935–1985. *American Political Science Review, 97,* 483–499.

Fukunaga, K. K., Paswark, R. A., Hawkins, M., & Gudeman, H. (1981). Insanity plea: Interexaminer agreement and concordance of psychiatric opinion and court verdict. *Law and Human Behavior, 5*(4), 325–328.

Furman v. Georgia, 408 U.S. 238 (1972).

Gabor, T. (1994). *Everybody does it! Crime by the public.* Toronto: University of Toronto Press.

Galeste, M. A., Fradella, H. F., & Vogel, B. L. (2012). Sex offender myths in print media: Separating fact from fiction in U.S. newspapers. *Western Criminology Review, 13*(2), 4–24.

Gallup. (2013, January 9). U.S. *Death penalty support stable at 63%.* Available: http://www.gallup.com/poll/159770/death-penalty-support-stable.aspx

Gallup. (2013, June 12). *Americans disapprove of government surveillance programs.* Available: http://www.gallup.com/poll/163043/americans-disapprove-government-surveillance-programs.aspx

Gallup. (2012). *Honesty/ethics in professions.* Available: http://www.gallup.com/poll/1654/honesty-ethics-professions.aspx#1

Gallup. (n.d.). *Civil liberties.* Available: http://www.gallup.com/poll/5263/Civil-Liberties.aspx

Gann-Hall, M. (1992). Electoral politics and strategic voting in state supreme courts. *Journal of Politics, 54,* 427–446.

Garcetti v. Ceballos, 547 U.S. 410 (2006).

Garland, D. (2001). *The culture of control: Crime and social order in contemporary society.* Chicago: University of Chicago Press.

Garofoli, J. (2013, October 23). UC Davis pepper-spray officer awarded $38,000. *San Francisco Chronicle.* Available: http://www.sfgate.com/politics/joegarofoli/article/UC-Davis-pepper-spray-officer-awarded-38-000-4920773.php

Geller, W. A., & Morris, N. (1992). Relations between federal and local police. *Crime and Justice, 15,* 231–348.

Gelman, A., Liebman, J. S., West, V., & Kiss, A. (2004). A broken system: The persistent patterns of reversals of death sentences in the United States. *Journal of Empirical Legal Studies, 1,* 209–261.

Gershman, B. L. (1986). Why prosecutors misbehave. *Criminal Law Bulletin, 22*(2), 131–143.

Gershoff, E. (2002). Corporal punishment by parents and associated child behaviors and experiences: A meta-analytic and theoretical review. *Psychological Bulletin, 128,* 539–579.

Gerstein v. Pugh, 420 U.S. 103 (1975).

Gerstenfeld, P. B. (2004). *Hate crimes: Causes, controls, and controversies.* Thousand Oaks, Calif.: Sage Publications.

Gest, T. (2001). *Crime and politics: Big government's erratic campaign for law and order.* New York: Oxford University Press.

Geyh, C. G. (2003). Why judicial elections stink. *Ohio State Law Journal, 64,* 43–79.

Gibbs, J. C. (2014). *Moral development and reality: Beyond the theories of Kohlberg, Hoffman, and Haidt* (3rd ed.). New York: Oxford University Press.

Gibson, C. L., & Krohn, M. D. (Eds.). (2013). *Handbook of life-course criminology: Emerging trends and directions for future research.* New York: Springer.

Gideon v. Wainwright, 372 U.S. 335 (1963).

Gill, M., & Spriggs, A. (2005, February). *Assessing the impact of CCTV.* Home Office Research Study 292. London: Home Office.

Gingerich v. Commonwealth, 382 S.W.3d 835 (Supreme Court of Kentucky, 2012).

Gitlow v. New York, 268 U.S. 652 (1925).

Glantz, S. A., & Balbach, E. D. (2000). *Tobacco war: Inside the California battles.* Berkeley: University of California Press.

Glaze, L. E., & Parks, E. (2012, November). *Correctional populations in the United States, 2011.* Washington, D.C.: Bureau of Justice Statistics. Available: http://www.bjs.gov/content/pub/pdf/cpus11.pdf

Glick, H. R., & Emmert, C. (1987). Selection systems and judicial characteristics: The recruitment of state supreme court judges. *Judicature, 70,* 228–235.

Goffman, E. (1961). *Asylums: Essays on the social situation of mental patients and other inmates.* New York: Anchor Books.

Golash, D. (2005). *The case against punishment: Retribution, crime prevention, and the law.* New York: New York University Press.

Goldkamp, J. S., White, M. D., & Robinson, J. B. (2001). Do drug courts work? Getting inside the drug court black box. *Journal of Drug Issues, 31*(1), 27–72.

Goldman v. Weinberger, 475 U.S. 503 (1986).

Goldman, M. (2003, July). *Jail design review handbook.* Washington, D.C.: U.S. Department of Justice. Available: http://nicic.gov/pubs/2003/018443.pdf

Goldman, S. (1999). *Picking federal judges: Lower court selection from Roosevelt through Reagan.* New Haven, Conn.: Yale University Press.

Goldschmidt, J., Olson, D., & Ekman, M. (2009). The relationship between method of judicial selection and judicial misconduct. *Widener Law Journal, 18,* 455–481.

Goldstein, H. (1990). *Problem-oriented policing.* New York: McGraw-Hill.

Goodnow, F. J. (1997). Politics and administration. In J. M. Shafritz & A. C. Hyde (Eds.), *Classics of public administration* (4th ed., pp. 27–29). Fort Worth, Tex.: Harcourt Brace College Publishers. (Original work published 1900)

Gostin, L. O. (2006, April 26). Physician-assisted suicide: A legitimate medical practice? *Journal of the American Medical Association, 295*(16), 1–3.

Gottfredson, D. C., Najaka, S. S., & Kearley, B. (2003). Effectiveness of drug treatment courts: Evidence from a randomized trial. *Criminology and Public Policy, 2*(2), 171–196.

Gottfredson, M. R., & Hirschi, T. (1990). *A general theory of crime.* Stanford, Calif.: Stanford University Press.

Gottschalk, M. (2006). *The prison and the gallows: The politics of mass incarceration in America.* New York: Cambridge University Press.

Gould, J. B., Carrano, J., Leo, R., & Young, J. (2012). *Predicting erroneous convictions: A social science approach to miscarriages of justice.* Available: https://ncjrs.gov/pdffiles1/nij/grants/241389.pdf

Gove, S. K., & Nowlan, J. D. (1996). *Illinois politics and government: The expanding metropolitan frontier.* Lincoln: University of Nebraska Press.

Government Accountability Office. (2005). *Adult drug courts: Evidence indicates recidivism reductions and mixed results for other outcomes.* Washington, D.C.: Author.

Government Accountability Office. (1997). *Drug courts: Overview of growth, characteristics, and results.* Washington, D.C.: Author.

Governors Highway Safety Association. (2013, August). *Distracted driving laws.* Available: http://www.ghsa.org/html/stateinfo/laws/cellphone_laws.html

Graham v. Connor, 490 U.S. 386 (1989).

Graham v. Florida, 560 U.S. 48 (2010).

Gramlich, J. (2010, May 19). For state prisons, cuts present new problems. *Stateline.* Available: http://www.stateline.org/live/printable/story?contentID=485663

Graycar, A., & Felson, M. (2010). Situational prevention of organised timber theft and related corruption. In K. Bullock, R. V. Clarke, & N. Tilley (Eds.), *Situational prevention of organised crimes* (pp. 81–92). Portland, Ore.: Willan Publishing.

Grayson, J. (2006). Corporal punishment in schools. *Virginia Child Protection Newsletter, 76,* 12–14, 16.

Greene, J. R. (2007). Make police oversight independent and transparent. *Criminology and Public Policy, 6,* 747–754

Greenwood, P. W., & Petersilia, J. (1975). *The Criminal investigation process: Vol. 1. Summary and policy recommendations* (R-1776). Santa Monica, Calif.: Rand.

Greer, K. R. (2000). The changing nature of interpersonal relationships in a women's prison. *Prison Journal, 80,* 442–468.

Gregg v. Georgia, 428 U.S. 153 (1976).

Gregorian, D., Gearty, R., Molloy, J., & Miller, F. (2013, March 12). 'Cannibal cop' Gilberto Valle faces life in prison after jury finds him guilty of conspiracy to kidnap and illegal use of federal databases. *New York Daily News.* Retrieved from http://www.nydailynews.com/new-york/cannibal-faces-life-guilty-conspiracy-kidnap-illegal-databases-article-1.1286075

Griffin, M. L. (2006). Penal harm and unusual conditions of confinement: Inmate perceptions of "hard time" in jail. *American Journal of Criminal Justice, 30,* 209–226.

Grinnell, M. S., & Burke, T. W. (2005, December). An examination of national and international DNA databases (Part 1). *Campbell Law Observer, 26*(10), 3–4.

Grinnell, M., & Burke, T. (2001, November). Face recoginition technology. *Law and Order,* pp. 36–40.

Griswold v. Connecticut, 381 U.S. 153 (1965).

Grogger, J. (2000). An economic model of recent trends in violence. In A. Blumstein & J. Wallman (Eds.), *The crime drop in America* (pp. 266–287). New York: Cambridge University Press.

Gross, S. R., & Shaffer, M. (2012). *Exonerations in the United States, 1989–2012: Report by the National Registry of Exonerations.* Available: http://www.law.umich.edu/special/exoneration/Documents/exonerations_us_1989_2012_full_report.pdf

Grube, G. M. A. (Trans.). (1992). *Plato's Republic.* Indianapolis, Ind.: Hackett.

Guo, G., Roettger, M. E., & Cai, T. (2008). The integration of genetic propensities into social-control models of delinquency and violence among male youths. *American Sociological Review, 73,* 543–568.

Haberfeld, M. R., & Cerrah, I. (Eds.). (2008). *Comparative policing: The struggle for democratization.* Los Angeles, Calif.: Sage Publications.

Habermas, J. (1992). *Moral consciousness and communicative action* (C. Lenhardt & S. W. Nicholsen, Trans.). Cambridge, Mass.: MIT Press.

Hafemeister, T. L., & George, J. (2012). The ninth circle of hell: An Eighth Amendment analysis of imposing prolonged supermax solitary confinement on inmates with a mental illness. *Denver University Law Review, 90,* 1–54.

Hafer, C. L., & Bègue, L. (2005). Research on just-world theory: Problems, developments, and future challenges. *Psychological Bulletin, 131,* 128–167.

Haggin, P. (2012). Obama signs federal ban on "bath salt" drugs. *Time.* Available: http://newsfeed.time.com/2012/07/10/obama-signs-federal-ban-on-bath-salt-drugs/

Hahn, P. H. (1998). *Emerging criminal justice: Three pillars for a proactive justice system.* Thousand Oaks, Calif.: Sage Publications.

Hale, M. (1971). *The history of the common law of England,* (C. M. Gray, Ed.). Chicago: University of Chicago Press. (Original work published 1713)

Haley, J. O. (1986). Comment: The implications of apology. *Law and Society Review, 20,* 499–507.

Hamdan v. Rumsfeld, 548 U.S. 507 (2006).

Hamdi v. Rumsfeld, 542 U.S. 507 (2004).

Hamilton, A., Madison, J., & Jay, J. (2003). *The federalist (with letters of Brutus),* (T. Ball, Ed.). Cambridge, UK: Cambridge University Press. (Original work published 1788)

Haney, C. (2003). Mental health issues in long-term solitary and "supermax" confinement. *Crime and Delinquency, 49,* 124–156.

Hanson, R. K., Bourgon, G., Helmus, L., & Hodgson, S. (2009). The principles of effective correctional treatment also apply to sexual offenders: A meta-analysis. *Criminal Justice and Behavior, 36,* 865–891.

Harassing Communications, Kentucky Revised Statutes, § 525.080 (2008).

Harkrader, T., Burke, T. W., & Owen, S. S. (2004, April). Pound puppies: The rehabilitative uses of dogs in correctional facilities. *Corrections Today,* pp. 74–79.

Harlow, C. W. (1999). *Prior abuse reported by inmates and probationers.* Washington, D.C.: Office of Justice Programs. Available: http://www.bjs.gov/content/pub/pdf/parip.pdf

Harmelin v. Michigan, 501 U.S. 957 (1991).

Harring, S. L. (1983). *Policing a class society: The experience of American cities, 1865–1915.* New Brunswick, N.J.: Rutgers University Press.

Harris v. Nelson, 394 U.S. 286 (1969).

Hart, H. L. A. (1994). *The concept of law.* New York: Oxford University Press. (Original work published 1961)

Hart, H. L. A. (1971). Immorality and treason. In R. A. Wasserstrom (Ed.), *Morality and the law* (pp. 49–54). Belmont, Calif.: Wadsworth. (Original work published 1959)

Hart, H. L. A. (1968). *Punishment and responsibility: Essays in the philosophy of law.* New York: Oxford University Press.

Hart, H. L. A. (1958). Positivism and the separation of law and morals. *Harvard Law Review, 71,* 593–629.

Hart, H. M., & Sacks, A.M. (1958). *The legal process: Basic problems in the making and application of law.* Cambridge, Mass.: Tentative edition, mimeographed copy.

Hartman, D. M., & Golub, A. (1999). The social construction of the crack epidemic in the print media. *Journal of Psychoactive Drugs, 31,* 423–433.

Hartman, K. E. (2008). Supermax prisons in the consciousness of prisoners. *Prison Journal, 88,* 169–176.

Healey, J. R., Toppo, G., & Meier, F. (2013, July 18). You can't hide from cops with license plate scanners. *USA Today.* Available: http://www.usatoday.com/story/money/cars/2013/07/17/license-plate-scanners-aclu-privacy/2524939/

Healy, J. (2012, November 7). Voters ease marijuana laws in 2 states, but legal questions remain. *New York Times.* Available: http://www.nytimes.com/2012/11/08/us/politics/marijuana-laws-eased-in-colorado-and-washington.html?_r=0

Heitzeg, N. A. (1996). *Deviance: Rulemakers and rulebreakers.* Belmont, Calif.: Wadsworth.

Helland, E., & Tabarrok, A. (2007). Does three strikes deter? A nonparametric estimation. *Journal of Human Resources, XLII,* 309–330.

Helling v. McKinney, 509 U.S. 25 (1993).

Henry, B. (October, 2004). The relationship between animal cruelty, delinquency, and attitudes toward the treatment of animals. *Society and Animals, 12,* 185–207.

Henry, J. S., & Jacobs, J. B. (2007). Ban the box to promote ex-offender employment. *Criminology and Public Policy, 6,* 755–762.

Henry, N. (1995). *Public administration and public affairs* (6th ed.). Englewood Cliffs, N.J.: Prentice Hall.

Herbert, S. (1997). *Policing space: Territoriality and the Los Angeles Police Department.* Minneapolis: University of Minnesota Press.

Herinckx, H. A., Swart, S. C., Ama, S. M., Dolezal, C. D., & King, S. (2005). Rearrest and linkage to mental health services among defendants of the Clark County mental health court program. *Psychiatric Services, 56*(7): 853–857.

Heritage Foundation, The. (2006). Case studies: The end of the pocket knife. Retrieved from http://www.overcriminalized.com/CaseStudy/Rankin-End-of-Pocket-Knife.aspx

Heritage Foundation, The. (2003). Case studies: Criminalizing kids I: True tales of zero tolerance overcriminalization. Retrieved from http://www.overcriminalized.com/CaseStudy/Tales-of-Zero-Tolerance-One.aspx

Hess, K. M., & Wrobleski, H. M. (2003). *Police operations: Theory and practice* (3rd ed.). Belmont, Calif.: Wadsworth.

Hickey, E. W. (2010). *Serial murderers and their victims* (5th ed.). Belmont, Calif.: Wadsworth/Cengage Learning.

Hill, J. (2002, July). High-speed police pursuits: Dangers, dynamics, and risk reduction. *FBI Law Enforcement Bulletin,* pp. 14–18. Available: http://www.fbi.gov/stats-services/publications/law-enforcement-bulletin/2002-pdfs/july021eb.pdf

Hines, D. A., & Saudino, K. J. (2004). Genetic and environmental influences on intimate partner aggression: A preliminary study. *Violence and Victims, 19,* 701–718.

Hirschfield, P. J. (2008). Preparing for prison? The criminalization of school discipline in the USA. *Theoretical Criminology, 12*(1), 79–101.

Hirschi, T. (2004). Self-control and crime. In R. F. Baumeister & K. D. Vohs (Eds.), *Handbook of self-regulation: Research, theory, and applications* (pp. 537–552). New York: Guilford Press.

Hirschi, T. (1969). *Causes of delinquency.* Berkeley: University of California Press.

Hobbes, T. (1963). Leviathan or the matter, form, and power of a commonwealth ecclesiastical and civil. In J. Somerville & R. E. Santoni (Eds.), *Social and political philosophy* (pp. 139–168). New York: Anchor Books. (Original work published 1651)

Hoffmann, D. E., & Weber, E. (2010, April 22). Medical marijuana and the law. *New England Journal of Medicine, 362,* 1453–1457.

Holmes, O. W. (1991). *The common law.* Mineola, N.Y.: Dover. (Original work published 1881)

Holt v. Sarver, 309 F.Supp. 362 (U.S. District Court for the Eastern District of Arkansas, 1970).

Hooks, G., Mosher, C., Genter, S., Rotolo, T., & Lobao, L. (2010). Revisiting the impact of prison building on job growth: Education, incarceration, and county-level employment, 1976–2004. *Social Science Quarterly, 91,* 228–244.

Hooks, G., Mosher, C., Rotolo, T., & Lobao, L. (2004). The prison industry: Carceral expansion and employment in U.S. counties, 1969–1994. *Social Science Quarterly, 85,* 37–57.

Hoover, N. C., & Pollard, N. J. (2000). *Initiation rites in American high schools: A national survey.* Available: http://www.alfred.edu/hs_hazing/

Hough, R. M., & Tatum, K. M. (2012). An examination of Florida policies on force continuums. *Policing: An International Journal of Police Strategies and Management, 35,* 39–54.

Howell, J. C., Egley, A., Tita, G. E., & Griffiths, E. (2011, May). *U.S. gang problem trends and seriousness, 1996–2009.* National Gang Center Bulletin, No. 6. Available: http://www.nationalgangcenter.gov/Content/Documents/Bulletin-6.pdf

Hoyt, W. H., McCollister, K. E., French, M. T., Leukefeld C., & Minton, L. (2004). Economic evaluation of drug court: Methodology, results, and policy implications. *Evaluation and Program Planning, 27*(4), 381–396.

Huddleston, C. W., Marlowe, D.B., & Casebolt, R. (2008). *Painting the current picture: A national report card on drug courts and other problem solving court programs in the United States* (Vol. 2, No. 1). Alexandria, Va.: National Drug Court Institute.

Hudson v. McMillian, 503 U.S. 1 (1992)

Hudson v. Michigan, 547 U.S. 586 (2006).

Hudson, B. (2003). *Justice in the risk society.* Thousand Oaks, Calif.: Sage Publications.

Huff-Corzine, L., Corzine, J., & Moore, D. C. (1986). Southern exposure: Deciphering the South's influence on homicide rates. *Social Forces, 65,* 904–924.

Huizink, A. C., Levälahti, E., Korhonen, T., Dick, D. M., Pulkkinen, L., Rose, R. J., & Kaprio, J. (2010). Tobacco, cannabis, and other illicit drug use among Finnish adolescent twins: Causal relationship or correlated liabilities? *Journal of Studies on Alcohol and Drugs, 71,* 5–14.

Huling, T. (2002). Building a prison economy in rural America. In M. Mauer & M. Chesney-Lind (Eds.), *Invisible punishment: The collateral consequences of mass imprisonment* (pp. 197–213). New York: New Press.

Human Rights Campaign. (2013). *LGBT equality at the Fortune 500.* Available: http://www.hrc.org/resources/entry/lgbt-equality-at-the-fortune-500

Humphrey v. Wilson, 282 Ga. 520 (2007).

Hunter v. Underwood, 471 U.S. 222 (1985).

Hurtado v. California, 110 U.S. 516 (1884).

Husak, D. (2008). *Overcriminalization: The limits of the criminal law.* New York: Oxford University Press.

Illinois Department of Corrections. (2002). *Illinois Department of Corrections Mission Statement.* Available: http://www.idoc.state.il.us/mission_statement.shtml

Illinois v. Gates, 462 U.S. 213 (1983).

Imbler v. Pachtman, 424 U.S. 409 (1976).

In re Gault, 387 U.S. 1 (1967)

In re Winship, 397 U.S. 358 (1970)

Inciardi, J. A. (1992). *The war on drugs II: The continuing epic of heroin, cocaine, crack, crime, AIDS, and public policy.* Mountain View, Calif.: Mayfield.

Information for Voters: The 2008 ballot questions. (2008). Boston: Mass. Secretary of the Commonwealth. Available: http://www.sec.state.ma.us/ele/elepdf/IFV_2008.pdf

Ingraham v. Wright, 430 U.S. 651 (1977).

Innocence Project. (2013). *DNA exonerations nationwide.* Retrieved from http://www.innocenceproject.org/Content/DNA_Exonerations_Nationwide.php

Innocence Project. (n.d.). Available: http://www.innocenceproject.org/

Instructions for initial custody designation. (2008). Washington State Department of Corrections Policy (No. DOC 310.150 Attachment 1). Available: http://www.doc.wa.gov/policies/default.aspx?show=300

International Association of Chiefs of Police. (n.d.). *Model policy on standards of conduct.* Available: http://www.theiacp.org/PoliceServices/ProfessionalAssistance/Ethics/ModelPolicyonStandardsofConduct/tabid/196/Default.aspx#ConceptsIssues

Intravia, J., Jones, S., & Piquero, A. (2012). The roles of social bonds, personality, and perceived costs: An empirical investigation into Hirschi's "New" Control Theory. *International Journal of Offender Therapy & Comparative Criminology, 56,* 1182–1200.

Irwin, J. (1998). The jail [excerpt]. In T. J. Flanagan, J. W. Marquart, & K. G. Adams (Eds.), *Incarcerating Criminals: Prisons and Jails in Social and Organizational Context* (pp. 227–236). New York: Oxford University Press. (Original work published in 1985)

Isaacson, W. (2003). *Benjamin Franklin: An American life.* New York: Simon & Schuster.

Ishikawa, S. S., & Raine, A. (2002). Behavioral genetics in crime. In J. Glicksohn (Ed.), *The neurobiology of criminal behavior* (pp. 81–110). Norwell, Mass.: Kluwer Academic Publishers.

J. E. B. v. Alabama ex rel. T. B., 511 U.S. 127 (1994).

Jackson v. Bishop, 404 F.2d 571 (1968).

Jacob, H., Blankenburg, E., Kritzer, H. M., Provine, D. M., & Sanders, J. (1996). *Courts, law and politics in comparative perspective.* New Haven, Conn.: Yale University Press.

Jacobs, J. B., & Potter, K. (1998). *Hate crimes: Criminal law and identity politics.* New York: Oxford University Press.

Jacobs, J. B., & Potter, K. A. (1997). Hate crimes: A critical perspective. *Crime and Justice, 22,* 1–50.

Jalbert, S. K., Rhodes, W., Flygare, C., & Kane, M. (2010). Testing probation outcomes in an evidence-based practice setting: Reduced caseload size and intensive supervision effectiveness. *Journal of Offender Rehabilitation, 49,* 233–253.

James, N., & McCallion, G. (2013). *School resource officers: Law enforcement officers in schools.* Congressional Research Service report (No. R43126). Available: http://www.fas.org/sgp/crs/misc/R43126.pdf

Jankowski, M. S. (1991). *Islands in the street: Gangs and American urban society.* Berkeley: University of California Press.

Janofsky, J. S., Vandewalle, M. B., & Rappeport, J. R. (1989). Defendants pleading insanity: An analysis of outcome. *Bulletin of the American Academy of Psychiatry and Law, 17,* 203–211.

Jay, T. (1992). *Cursing in America: A psycholinguistic study of dirty language in the courts, in the movies, in the schoolyards and on the streets.* Philadelphia: John Benjamins.

Jenkins, S. (2013). Secondary victims and the trauma of wrongful conviction: Families and children's perspectives on imprisonment, release, and adjustment. *Australian and New Zealand Journal of Criminology, 46,* 119–137.

Jiang, S., & Fisher-Giorlando, M. (2002). Inmate misconduct: A test of the deprivation, importation, and situational models. *Prison Journal, 82,* 335–358.

Johnson, B., Golub, A., & Dunlap, E. (2000). The rise and decline of hard drugs, drug markets, and violence in inner-city New York. In A. Blumstein & J. Wallman (Eds.), *The crime drop in America* (pp. 164–206). New York: Cambridge University Press.

Johnson, B. D., Ream, G. L., Dunlap, E., & Sifaneck, S. J. (2008). Civic norms and etiquettes regarding marijuana use in public settings in New York City. *Substance Use and Misuse, 43,* 895–918.

Johnson, L. M. (2008). A place for art in prison: Art as a tool for rehabilitation and management. *Southwest Journal of Criminal Justice, 5,* 100–120.

Jolley, J. (2008, April 3). 21's a bust? Seven states debate lowering drinking age. *ABC News.* Available: http://abcnews.go.com

Jones, E. T. (2000). *Fragmented by design: Why St. Louis has so many governments.* St. Louis, Mo.: Palmerston and Reed Publishing.

Jones, P. R., & Wyant, B. R. (2007). Target juvenile needs to reduce delinquency. *Criminology and Public Policy, 6,* 763–771.

Jordan v. City of New London, 1999 U.S. Dist. LEXIS 14289 (U.S. District Court for the District of Connecticut, 1999).

Joy, P. A. (2006). The relationship between prosecutorial misconduct and wrongful convictions: Shaping remedies for a broken system. *Wisconsin Law Review, 2006,* 399–429.

Joyce, J., Burke, T. W., & Owen, S. S. (2009, September). Can you see me now? The legal implications of "sexting." *Campbell Law Observer, 30,* 1, 4–6.

Judd, D. R., & Simpson, D. (Eds.). (2011). *The city revisited: Urban theory from Chicago, Los Angeles, and New York.* Minneapolis: University of Minnesota Press.

Judge lets victim take from thief. (1992, April 10). *Wilmington Morning Star,* p. 3B.

Jurik, N. C. (1999). Socialist feminism, criminology, and social justice. In B. A. Arrigo (Ed.), *Social justice, criminal justice: The maturation of critical theory in law, crime, and deviance* (pp. 31–50). Belmont, Calif.: West/Wadsworth.

Justice Center of the Council of State Governments. (2013). *Justice reinvestment in West Virginia.* Available: http://csgjusticecenter.org/wp-content/uploads/2013/06/BJA.JR-West-Virginia_v5.pdf

Justice for Victims of Sterilization Act of 2013, House Bill No. 1529 (2013).

Justice Policy Institute. (2011). *Addicted to courts: How a growing dependence on drug courts impacts people and communities.* Washington, D.C.: Author.

Justices of Boston Municipal Court v. Lydon, 466 U.S. 294 (1984).

Juvenile Justice Advisory Council. (1988). Juveniles and jail removal: Kids in jail . . . what the new law means. Washington, D.C.: U.S. Department of Justice. Available: https://www.ncjrs.gov/pdffiles1/Digitization/113176NCJRS.pdf

Kade, W. J. (2000). Death with dignity: A case study. *Annals of Internal Medicine, 132,* 504–506.

Kahler, H. L. (2008). Recreation. In P. M. Carlson & J. S. Garrett (Eds.), *Prison and jail administration: Practice and theory* (2nd ed., pp. 91–98). Sudbury, Mass.: Jones and Bartlett Publishers.

Kane, R. J. (2007). Collect and release data on coercive police actions. *Criminology and Public Policy, 6,* 773–780.

Kang, M. S., & Shepherd, J. M. (2011). The partisan price of justice: An empirical analysis of campaign contributions and judicial decisions. *New York University Law Review, 86,* 69–130.

Kant, I. (2004). The moral law. In L. J. Pojman (Ed.), *The moral life: An introductory reader in ethics and literature* (2nd ed., pp. 316). New York: Oxford University Press.

Kant, I. (2002). *Groundwork for the metaphysics of morals* (A. W. Wood, Trans.). New York: Vail-Ballou Press. (Original work published 1785)

Kappeler, V. E., & Potter, G. W. (2005). *The mythology of crime and criminal justice* (4th ed.). Long Grove, Ill.: Waveland Press.

Karmen, A. (2012). *Crime victims: An introduction to victimology* (8th ed.). Belmont, Calif.: Wadsworth.

Karp, L. N. (2009). *Truth, justice, and the American way: What Superman teaches us about the American dream and changing values within the United States.* (Thesis submitted to Oregon State University). Available: http://ir.library.oregonstate.edu/jspui/bitstream/1957/11926/1/Thesis_LKarp.pdf

Kassin, S. M. (2008). Confession evidence: Commonsense myths and misconceptions. *Criminal Justice and Behavior, 35*(10), 1309–1322.

Kassin, S. M. (2005). On the psychology of confessions: Does innocence put innocents at risk? *American Psychologist, 60*(3), 215–228.

Kassin, S. M., & Kiechel, K. L. (1996). The social psychology of false confessions: Compliance, internalization, and confabulation. *Psychological Science, 7,* 125–128.

Kassin, S. M., Leo, R. A., Meissner, C. A., Richman, K. D., Colwell, L. H., Leach, A. M., & La Fon, D. (2007). Police interviewing and interrogation: A self-report survey of police practices and beliefs. *Law and Human Behavior, 31*(4), 381–400.

Kassin, S. M., & Norwick, R. K. (2004). Why people waive their Miranda rights: The power of innocence. *Law and Human Behavior, 28*(2), 211–221.

Katz v. United States, 389 U.S. 347 (1967).

Katz, J. (1988). *Seductions of crime.* New York: Basic Books.

Kauffman, R. M., Ferketich, A. K., & Wewers, M. E. (2008). Tobacco policy in American prisons, 2007. *Tobacco Control, 17,* 357–360.

Keilin, S. (2001, December). *An overview of Texas parole guidelines.* Austin, Tex.: Criminal Justice Policy Council. Available: http://www.bop.gov/policy/progstat/5100_008.pdf

Kelling, G. L., & Coles, C. M. (1996). *Fixing broken windows: Restoring order and reducing crime in our communities.* New York: Free Press.

Kelling, G. L., & Moore, M. H. (1988). The evolving strategy of policing. In S. G. Brandl & D. E. Barlow (Eds.), *Classics in policing* (pp. 71–95). Cincinnati, Oh.: Anderson.

Kelling, G. L., Pate, T., Dieckman, D., & Brown, C. E. (1974). *The Kansas City preventive patrol experiment: A summary report.* Washington, D.C.: Police Foundation.

Kelly, J. (2012, September 19). Why British police don't have guns. *BBC News Magazine.* Available: http://www.bbc.co.uk/news/magazine-19641398

Kelman, M. (1987). *A guide to critical legal studies.* Cambridge, Mass.: Harvard University Press.

Kennedy v. Louisiana, 128 S. Ct. 2641 (2008).

Kennedy, D. M. (2011). *Don't shoot: One man, a street fellowship, and the end of violence in inner-city America.* New York: Bloomsbury.

Kennedy, D. M. (2006). Old wine in new bottles: Policing and the lessons of pulling levers. In D. Weisburd & A. A. Braga (Eds.), *Police innovation: Contrasting perspectives* (pp. 155–170). New York: Cambridge University Press.

Kennedy, D. (1997). *A critique of adjudication [fin de siècle].* Cambridge, Mass.: Harvard University Press.

Kentucky v. King, 563 U.S. ___ (2011).

Kentucky v. Stincer, 482 U.S. 730 (1987).

Kettl, D. F. (2007). *System under stress: Homeland security and American politics* (2nd ed.). Washington, D.C.: C.Q. Press.

Kim, C. Y., Losen, D. J., & Hewitt, D. T. (2010). *The school-to-prison pipeline: Structuring legal reform.* New York: New York University Press.

King, J. (2003). *Hate crime: The story of a dragging in Jasper, Texas.* New York: Pantheon Books.

Kingdon, J. W. (1995). *Agendas, alternatives, and public policies* (2nd ed.). New York: HarperCollins.

Kirp, D. L., & Bayer, R. (1999). The politics of needle exchange. In E. B. Sharp (Ed.), *Culture wars and local politics* (pp. 178–192). Lawrence: University Press of Kansas.

Kirschner, S. M., & Galperin, G. J. (2001). Psychiatric defenses in New York County: Pleas and results. *The Journal of the American Academy of Psychiatry and the Law, 29*(2), 194–201.

Klinger, D. A., & Brunson, R. K. (2009). Police officers' perceptual distortions during lethal force situations: Informing the reasonableness standard. *Criminology and Public Policy, 8,* 117–140.

Klinger v. Department of Corrections, 31 F.3d 727 (U.S. Court of Appeals for the Eighth Circuit, 1994).

Klockars, C. B. (1985a). The Dirty Harry problem. In F. A. Elliston & M. Feldberg (Eds.), *Moral issues in police work* (pp. 55–71). Lanham, Md.: Rowman & Littlefield. (Original work published 1980)

Klockars, C. B. (1985b). *The idea of police.* Beverly Hills, Calif.: Sage Publications.

Knapp Commission report on police corruption. (1972). New York: Braziller.

Knowles, D. (2013, June 6). Vermont becomes 17th state to decriminalize marijuana, making possession of less than an ounce of pot punishable by fine. *New York Daily News.* Available:http://www.nydailynews.com/news/national/vermont-decriminalizes-possession-small-amounts-pot-article-1.1365354

Kohlberg, L. (1984). *Essays on moral development: Vol. 2. The psychology of moral development.* San Francisco: Harper & Row.

Kohlberg, L., & Hersh, R. H. (1977). Moral development: A review of the theory. *Theory into Practice, 16,* 53–59.

Koniaris, L. G., Zimmers, T. A., Lubarsky, D. A., & Sheldon, J. P. (2005). Inadequate anesthesia in lethal injection for execution. *The Lancet, 365,* 1412–1414.

Koo, J., Rosentraub, M. S., & Horn, A. (2007). Rolling the dice? Casinos, tax revenues, and the social costs of gaming. *Journal of Urban Affairs, 29,* 367–381.

Koppel, N. (2007, August 30). Are your jeans sagging? Go directly to jail. *New York Times.* Available: http://www.nytimes.com/2007/08/30/fashion/30baggy.html

Kovandzic, T. V., Sloan, J. J., & Vieraitis, L. M. (2004). "Striking out" as crime reduction policy: The impact of "three strikes" laws on crime rates in U.S. cities. *Justice Quarterly, 21,* 207–239.

Kovandzic, T. V., Sloan, J. V., & Vieraitis, L. M. (2002). Unintended consequences of politically popular sentencing policy: The homicide promoting effects of "three strikes" in U.S. cities (1980–1999). *Criminology and Public Policy, 1,* 399–424.

Kraska, P., & Cubellis, L. (December, 1997). Militarizing Mayberry and beyond: Making sense of American paramilitary policing. *Justice Quarterly, 14,* 607–629.

Kuhn, T. (1977). *The essential tension: Selected studies in scientific tradition and change.* Chicago: University of Chicago Press.

Kuppers, T. A., Dronet, T., Winter, M., Austin, J., Kelly, L., Cartier, W., Morris, T. J., Hanlon, S. F., Sparkman, E. L., Kumar, P., Vincent, L. C., Norris, J., Nagel, K., & McBride, J. (2009). Beyond supermax administrative segregation: Mississippi's experience rethinking prison classification and creating alternative mental health programs. *Criminal Justice and Behavior, 36,* 1037–1050.

Kurtzleben, D. (2010, August 3). Data show racial disparity in crack sentencing. *U.S. News and World Report.* Available: http://www.usnews.com/news/articles/2010/08/03/data-show-racial-disparity-in-crack-sentencing

Kyckelhahn, T., & Martin, T. (2013, July 1). *Justice expenditure and employment extracts, 2010—preliminary.* Washington, D.C.: Bureau of Justice Statistics. Available: http://www.bjs.gov/index.cfm?ty=pbdetail&iid=4679

Kyllo v. United States, 533 U.S. 27 (2001).

La Vigne, N. G. (2010, February 3). Statement at a Hearing to the House of Representatives Oversight and Government Reform Subcommittee on Federal Workforce, Postal Service, and the District of Columbia. Available from the Urban Institute: http://www.urban.org/UploadedPDF/901322_lavigne_testimony_halfwayhome.pdf

Lab, S. P. (2004). Crime prevention, politics, and the art of going nowhere fast. *Justice Quarterly, 21,* 681–692.

Laband, D. N., & Heinbuch, D. H. (1987). *Blue laws: The history, economics, and politics of Sunday-closing laws.* Lexington, Mass.: D. C. Heath.

LaFree, G., & Hendrickson, J. (2007). Build a criminal justice policy for terrorism. *Criminology and Public Policy, 6,* 781–790.

Lait, S., & Glover, S. (December 29, 2000). Rampart scandal expected to take a continuing toll. *Los Angeles Times.* Available: http://articles.latimes.com/2000/dec/29/local/me-5954

Lamb, H. R., & Bachrach, L. L. (2001). Some perspectives on deinstitutionalization. *Psychiatric Services, 52,* 1039–1045.

Langan, P. A., & Levin, D. J. (2002). *Recidivism of prisoners released in 1994.* Washington, D.C.: U.S. Department of Justice. Available: http://www.ojp.usdoj.gov/bjs/pub/pdf/rpr94.pdf

Langbein, J. H. (2003). *The origins of adversary criminal trial.* New York: Oxford University Press.

Langton, L., & Planty, M. (2011). *Hate crime, 2003–2009.* Washington, D.C.: U.S. Department of Justice. Retrieved from http://www.bjs.gov/content/pub/pdf/hc0309.pdf

Lanier, M. M., & Henry, S. (1998). *Essential criminology.* Boulder, Colo.: Westview Press.

Lankenau, S. E. (2001). Smoke 'em if you got 'em: Cigarette black markets in U.S. prisons and jails. *Prison Journal, 81,* 142–161.

Larkin, P. J. (2013). Public choice theory and overcriminalization. *Harvard Journal of Law & Public Policy, 36,* 715–793.

Larzelere, R. E., & Kuhn, B. R. (2005). Comparative child outcomes of physical punishment and disciplinary tactics: A meta-analysis. *Clinical Child and Family Psychology Review, 8,* 1–37.

Lasson, N. B. (1937). *The history and development of the Fourth Amendment to the United States Constitution.* Baltimore: Johns Hopkins University Press.

Latimer, J., Dowden, C., & Muise, D. (2005). The effectiveness of restorative justice practices: A meta-analysis. *Prison Journal, 85,* 127–144.

Lattimore, P. K., Steffey, D. M., & Visher, C. A. (2010). Prisoner reentry in the first decade of the twenty-first century. *Victims and Offenders, 5,* 253–267.

Lawrence v. Texas, 539 U.S. 558 (2003).

Lawrence, C. R., III, & Matsuda, M. J. (1997). *We won't go back: Making the case for affirmative action.* Wilmington, Mass.: Houghton Mifflin.

Lawrence, R. G., & Birkland, T. A. (2004). Guns, Hollywood, and school safety: Defining the school-shooting problem across public arenas. *Social Science Quarterly, 85,* 1193–1207.

Lazare, A. (2004). *On apology.* New York: Oxford University Press.

Lee, H., & Vaughn, M. S. (2010). Organizational factors that contribute to police deadly force liability. *Journal of Criminal Justice, 38,* 193–206.

Leeds, J. (2007, October 7). Labels win suit against song sharer. *New York Times,* p. C1.

Lefkowitz, J. (1977). Industrial-organizational psychology and the police. *American Psychologist, 5,* 346–364.

Lefkowitz, J. (1975). Psychological attributes of policemen: A review of research and opinion. *Journal of Social Issues, 31,* 3–26.

Lemert, E. (1951). *Social pathology: A systematic approach to the theory of sociopathic behavior.* New York: McGraw-Hill.

Lenz, N. (2002). "Luxuries" in prison: The relationship between amenity funding and public support. *Crime and Delinquency, 48,* 499–525.

Leo, R. A. (2001a). False confessions: Causes, consequences, and solutions. In S. D. Westervelt & J. A. Humphrey (Eds.) *Wrongly convicted: Perspectives on failed justice* (pp. 36–54). Newark, N.J.: Rutgers University Press.

Leo, R. A. (2001b). Questioning the relevance of *Miranda* in the twenty-first century. *Michigan Law Review, 99,* 1000–1029.

Leo, R. A. (1996). The impact of *Miranda* revisited. *Journal of Criminal Law and Criminology, 86,* 621–692.

Leo, R. A., & Richman, K. D. (2007). Mandate the electronic recording of police interrogations. *Criminology and Public Policy, 6,* 791–798.

Lerch, C., Burke, T., & Owen, S. (2008, September/October). Familial DNA: It's all in the family. *Police and Security News,* pp. 56–60.

Levack, B. P. (Ed.). (2001). *Gender and witchcraft.* New York: Routledge.

Levenson, J. S., & D'Amora, D. A. (2007). Social policies designed to prevent sexual violence. The emperor's new clothes? *Criminal Justice Policy Review, 18,* 168–199.

Levy, C. J. (2005). Conflict of duty: Capital punishment regulations and AMA medical ethics. *Journal of Legal Medicine, 26,* 261–274.

Lewis, A. (1964). *Gideon's trumpet.* New York: Vintage Books.

Lewis, P. G., Provine, D. M., Varsanyi, M. W., & Decker, S. H. (2013). Why do (some) city police departments enforce federal immigration law? Political, demographic, and organizational influences on local choices. *Journal of Public Administration Research and Theory, 23,* 1-25.

Lindgren, J. (1996). Why the ancients may not have needed a system of criminal law. *Boston University Law Review, 76,* 29–57.

Lindgren, S. (2005). Social constructionism and criminology: Traditions, problems and possibilities. *Journal of Scandinavian Studies in Criminology and Crime Prevention, 6,* 4–22.

Lipsky, M. (1980). *Street-level bureaucracy: Dilemmas of the individual in public services.* New York: Russell Sage Foundation.

Listwan, S. J., Jonson, C. L., Cullen, F. T., & Latessa, E. J. (2008). Cracks in the penal harm movement: Evidence from the field. *Criminology and Public Policy, 7,* 423–465

Locke, J. (1963). An essay concerning the true original extent and end of civil government. In J. Somerville & R. E. Santoni (Eds.), *Social and political philosophy* (pp. 169–204). New York: Anchor Books. (Original work published 1689)

Lockhart v. Fretwell, 506 U.S. 364 (1993).

Lockyer v. Andrade, 538 U.S. 63 (2003).

Loffreda, B. (2001). *Losing Matt Shepard.* New York: Columbia University Press.

Loftin, C., & McDowall, D. (1982, June). The police, crime & economic theory: An assessment. *American Sociological Review, 47,* 393–401.

Loseman, A., & Bos, K. (March, 2012). A self-regulation hypothesis of coping with an unjust world: Ego-depletion and self-affirmation as underlying aspects of blaming of innocent victims. *Social Justice Research, 25,* 1–13.

Lovell, D. (2008). Patterns of disturbed behavior in a supermax population. *Criminal Justice and Behavior, 35,* 985–1004.

Lovell, D., Johnson, L. C., & Cain, K. C. (2007). Recidivism of supermax prisoners in Washington state. *Crime and Delinquency, 53,* 633–656.

Loving v. Virginia, 388 U.S. 1 (1967).

Lowenkamp, C. T., Flores, A. W., Holsinger, A. M., Makarios, M. D., & Latessa, E. J. (2010). Intensive supervision programs: Does program philosophy and the princples of effective intervention matter? *Journal of Criminal Justice, 38,* 368–375.

Lowi, T. (1967). The public philosophy: Interest-group liberalism. *American Political Science Review, 61,* 5–24.

Lucas, P. (2009, July 27). Businesses using music to deter crime and loitering. *Seattle Times.* Available: http://seattletimes.nwsource.com/html/entertainment/2009543344_music27m.html

Lum, C., & Fachner, G. (2008). *Police pursuits in an age of innovation and reform: The IACP police pursuit database.* Alexandria, Va.: International Association of Chiefs of Police. Available: http://www.theiacp.org/LinkClick.aspx?fileticket =IlJDjYrusBc%3D&tabid=392

Luna, E. (2005). Overcriminalization: The politics of crime. *American University Law Review, 54,* 703–746.

Lund, N. (2012). Second Amendment standards of review in a *Heller* world. *Fordham Urban Law Journal, 39,* 1617–1636.

Lundahl, B. W., Kunz, C., Brownell, C., Harris, N., & Van Vleet, R. (2009). Prison privatization: A meta-analysis of cost and quality of confinement indicators. *Research on Social Work Practice, 19,* 383–394.

Lynch, J. P., & Addington, L. A. (2007). *Understanding crime statistics: Revisiting the divergence of the NCVS and the UCR.* New York: Cambridge University Press.

Lyons, W., & Drew, J. (2006). *Punishing schools: Fear and citizenship in American public education.* Ann Arbor: University of Michigan Press.

MacCoun, R. J., & Reuter, P. (2001). *Drug war heresies: Learning from other vices, times, and places.* New York: Cambridge University Press.

MacDowell, D.M. (1978). *The law in classical Athens.* Ithaca, N.Y.: Cornell University Press.

MacKenzie, D. L. (2006). *What works in corrections: Reducing the criminal activities of offenders and delinquents.* New York: Cambridge University Press.

Mackin, J. R., Lucas, L. M., Lambarth, C. H., Waller, M. S., Weller, J. M., Aborn, J. A., Linhares, R., Allen, T. L., Carey, S. M., & Finigan, M. W. (2009). *Baltimore City district court adult drug treatment court 10-year outcome and cost evaluation.* Portland, Ore.: NPC Research: Portland.

MacKinnon, C. A. (2007). *Women's lives, men's laws.* Cambridge, Mass.: Belknap/Harvard University Press.

Maclin, T. (1997). The complexity of the Fourth Amendment: A historical review. *Boston University Law Review, 77,* 925–974.

Madison, J. (1982). The Federalist No. 51. In G. Wills (Ed.), *The Federalist Papers by Alexander Hamilton, James Madison, and John Jay* (pp. 261–265). New York: Bantam Books. (Original work published 1788)

Maiese, M. (2004). Procedural justice. In G. Burgess & H. Burgess (Eds.), *Beyond intractability.* Boulder: Conflict Research Consortium, University of Colorado. Available: http://www .beyondintractability.org/essay/procedural_justice/

Makse, T., & Volden, C. (2011). The role of policy attributes in the diffusion of innovations. *The Journal of Politics, 73,* 108–124.

Mann, J. (2011). Delivering justice to the mentally ill: Characteristics of mental health courts. *Southwest Journal of Criminal Justice, 8*(1), 44–58.

Manson v. Brathwaite, 432 U.S. 98 (1977).

Mapp v. Ohio, 367 U.S. 643 (1961).

Marbury v. Madison, U.S. (1 Cranch) 137 (1803).

Marcus, P. (2009). Why the United States Supreme Court got some (but not a lot) of the Sixth Amendment right to counsel analysis right. *St. Thomas Law Review, 21,* 142–189.

Markkula Center for Applied Ethics. (2009). *A framework for thinking ethically.* Available: http://www.scu.edu/ethics/ practicing/decision/framework.html

Marks, V. (2010). Forensic aspects of hypoglycemia. *Diabetic Hypoglycemia, 2*(3), 3–8.

Marlowe, D.B . (2010). *The facts on adult drug courts.* Washington, D.C.: National Association of Drug Court Professionals.

Marrus, M. R. (1997). *The Nuremberg War Crimes Trial, 1945–1946: A documentary history.* New York: Bedford/St. Martin's.

Martinson, R. (1974, Spring). What works? Questions and answers about prison reform. *Public Interest, 35,* 22–54.

Maruschak, L. M., & Parks, E. (2012). *Probation and parole in the United States, 2011.* Washington, D.C.: Bureau of Justice Statistics. Available: http://www.bjs.gov/content/pub/pdf/ ppus11.pdf

Marvel, T. B., & Moody, C. E. (2001). The lethal effects of three-strikes laws. *Journal of Legal Studies, 30,* 89–106.

Maryland Commission on Capital Punishment. (2008). *Final report to the General Assembly.* Available: http://www.goccp .maryland.gov/capital-punishment/documents/death-penalty-commission-final-report.pdf

Maryland v. Buie, 494 U.S. 325 (1990).

Maryland v. Craig, 497 U.S. 836 (1990).

Maryland v. King, 569 U.S. ___ (2013).

Mazerolle, L., & Ransley, J. (2006). The case for third-party policing. In D. Weisburd & A. A. Braga (Eds.), *Police innovation: Contrasting perspectives* (pp. 191–206). New York: Cambridge University Press.

McCaghy, C. H., Capron, T. A., Jamieson, J. D., & Harley Carey, S. H. (2007). *Deviant behavior: Crime, conflict, and interest groups* (8th ed.). Upper Saddle River, N.J.: Pearson/ Allyn & Bacon.

McCleary, R., Nienstedt, B. C., & Erven, J. M. (1982). Uniform Crime Reports as organizational outcomes: Three time series experiments. *Social Problems, 29,* 361–372.

McCollough, T. E. (1991). *The moral imagination and public life: Raising the ethical question.* Chatham, N.J.: Chatham House Publishers.

McConnaughey, J. (2000, February 28). Police warn on Mardi Gras flashing, bead tossing. *The Pittsburgh Post-Gazette,* p. A6.

McCreary, J. R. (2013). "Mentally defective" language in the Gun Control Act. *Connecticut Law* Review, *45,* 813–864.

McDevitt, J., Levin, J., & Bennett, S. (2002). Hate crime offenders: An expanded typology. *Journal of Social Issues, 58,* 303–317.

McDonald v. City of Chicago, 561 U.S. ___ (2010).

McDonald-Henning, K. (2012–2013). The failed legacy of absolute immunity under *Imbler*: Providing a compromise approach to claims of prosecutorial misconduct. *Gonzaga Law Review, 48,* 219–278.

McGillis, D. (1998, September). *National Institute of Justice Program Focus: Resolving community conflict: The dispute settlement center of Durham, North Carolina.* Washington, D.C.: U.S.

Department of Justice. Available: http://www.ncjrs.org/pdffiles/172203.pdf

McGowen, R. (1995). The well-ordered prison: England, 1780–1865. In N. Morris & D. J. Rothman (Eds.), *The Oxford history of the prison: The practice of punishment in Western society* (pp. 78–109). New York: Oxford University Press.

McKeiver v. Pennsylvania, 403 U.S. 528 (1971).

McLemore, D. M., & Bissell, K. L. (2013). *"Evil visited this community today": News media framing of the Sandy Hook school shootings.* Paper presented at the Association for Education in Journalism and Mass Communication (Washington, D.C.).

McLure, J. (2013, May 20). Vermont passes law allowing doctor-assisted suicide. *NBC News Health.* Available: http://www.nbcnews.com/health/vermont-passes-law-allowing-doctor-assisted-suicide-6C10003656

McNeil, D. E., & Binder, R. L. (2007). Effectiveness of a mental health court in reducing criminal recidivism and violence. *American Journal of Psychiatry, 164,* 1395–1403.

Mears, D. P., & Bales, W. D. (2010). Supermax housing: Placement, duration, and time to reentry. *Journal of Criminal Justice, 38,* 545–554.

Mears, D. P., & Bales, W. D. (2009). Supermax incarceration and redivisism. *Criminology, 47,* 1131–1166.

Mears, D. P., & Castro, J. L. (2006). Wardens' views on the wisdom of supermax prisons. *Crime and Delinquency, 52,* 398–431.

Mears, D. P., Cochran, J. C., Siennick, S. E., & Bales, W. D. (2012). Parole visitation and recidivism. *Justice Quarterly, 29,* 888–918.

Mears, D. P., Mancini, C., Beaver, K. M., & Gertz, M. (2013). Housing for the "worst of the worst" inmates: Public support for supermax prisons. *Crime and Delinquency, 59,* 587–615.

Mears, D. P., & Watson, J. (2006). Towards a fair and balanced assessment of supermax prisons. *Justice Quarterly, 23,* 232–270.

Medina, J. (2013, January 21). California sheds prisoners but grapples with courts. *New York Times.* Available: http://www.nytimes.com/2013/01/22/us/22prisons.html?pagewanted=1

Melde, C., Diem, C., Drake, G. (2012). Identifying correlates of stable gang membership. *Journal of Contemporary Criminal Justice, 28,* 482–498.

Melde, C., & Esbensen, F. (2013). Gangs and violence: Disentangling the impact of gang membership on the level and nature of offending. *Journal of Quantitative Criminology,* 29, 143–166.

Meloy, M. L., Miller, S. L., & Curtis, K. M. (2008). Making sense out of nonsense: The deconstruction of state-level sex offender residence restrictions. *American Journal of Criminal Justice, 33*(2), 209–222.

Memory, J. M., Guo, G., Parker, K., & Sutton, T. (1999). Comparing disciplinary infraction rates of North Carolina Fair Sentencing and Structured Sentencing inmates: A natural experiment. *Prison Journal, 79,* 45–71.

Mendel, R. A. (2005). *Less hype, more help: Reducing juvenile crime, what works—and what doesn't.* Washington, DC: American Youth Policy Forum. Retrieved from www.aypf.org/publications/mendel/MendelRep.pdf

Mendelsohn, B. (1963) The origin of victimology. *Excerpta Criminologica, 3,* 239–256.

Menninger, K. (1968). *The crime of punishment.* New York: The Viking Press.

Merton, R. K. (1968). *Social theory and social structure.* New York: Free Press.

Metcalf v. Florida, 635 So. 2d 11 (Fla. 1994).

Metzner, J. L., & Fellner, J. (2010). Solitary confinement and mental illness in U.S. prisons: A challenge for medical ethics. *Journal of the American Academy of Psychiatry and the Law, 38,* 104–108.

Michigan Department of State Police v. Sitz, 496 U.S. 444 (1990).

Michigan v. Boomer, 250 Mich. App. 534 (Court of Appeals of Michigan, 2002).

Michigan v. Harvey, 494 U.S. 344 (1990).

Michigan v. Long, 463 U.S. 1032 (1983).

Mielke, H. W., & Zahran, S. (2012). The urban rise and fall of air lead (Pb) and the latent surge and retreat of societal violence. *Environment International, 43,* 48–55.

Mill, J. S. (1981). On liberty. In M. Curtis (Ed.), *The great political theories* (Vol. 2, pp. 190–204). New York: Avon Books. (Original work published 1859)

Miller v. Alabama and *Jackson v. Hobbs,* 567 U.S. ___ (2012).

Miller, D. (1999). *Principles of social justice.* Cambridge, Mass.: Harvard University Press.

Miller, L. L. (2008). *The perils of federalism: Race, poverty, and the politics of crime control.* New York: Oxford University Press.

Miller, R. D. (1997). The continuum of coercion: Constitutional and clinical considerations in the treatment of mentally disordered persons. *Denver University Law Review, 74,* 1169–1214.

Miller, W. B. (1958). Lower class culture as a generating milieu of gang delinquency. *Journal of Social Issues, 14,* 5–19.

Miller, W. R. (1975, Winter). Police authority in London and New York (1830–1870). *Journal of Social History,* pp. 81–101.

Milsom, S. F. C. (1976). *The legal framework of English feudalism.* Cambridge, UK: Cambridge University Press.

Minda, G. (1996). *Postmodern legal movements: Law and jurisprudence at century's end.* New York: New York University Press.

Miranda v. Arizona, 384 U.S. 436 (1966).

Mishra, S., & Lalumière, M. (2009). Is the crime drop of the 1990s in Canada and the USA associated with a general decline in risky and health-related behavior? *Social Science and Medicine, 68,* 39–48.

Missouri Department of Corrections. (2013, July). *Rules and regulations governing the conditions of probation, parole, and conditional release.* Jefferson City: Missouri Department of Corrections.

Moffitt, T. E., Ross, S., & Raine, A. (2011). Crime and biology. In J. Q. Wilson & J. Petersilia (Eds.), *Crime and public policy* (pp. 53–87). New York: Oxford University Press.

Mohr, L. B. (1996). *The causes of human behavior: Implications for theory and method in the social sciences.* Ann Arbor: University of Michigan Press.

Monkkonen, E. H. (1988). *America becomes urban: The development of U.S. cities and towns 1790–1980.* Berkeley: University of California Press.

Mooney, C. Z., & Lee, M. (1999). The temporal diffusion of morality policy: The case of death penalty legislation in the American states. *Policy Studies Journal, 27,* 766–780.

Moore, L. (2007, March 18). Sticking it to the scofflaw. *U.S. News & World Report, 142,* 47.

Moore, M. E., & Hiday, V. A. (2006). Mental health court outcomes: A comparison of re-arrest and re-arrest severity between mental health court and treatment court participants. *Law and Human Behavior, 30,* 659–674.

Moore, M. S. (1995). The moral worth of retribution. In J. G. Murphy (Ed.), *Punishment and Rehabilitation* (3rd ed., pp. 94–130). Belmont, Calif.: Wadsworth Publishing.

Moran v. Burbine, 475 U.S. 412 (1986).

Morgan, B., Morgan, F., Foster, V., & Kolbert, J. (2000). Promoting the moral and conceptual development of law enforcement trainees: A deliberate psychological educational approach. *Journal of Moral Education, 29,* 203–218.

Morgan, G. (1986). *Images of organization.* Newbury Park, Calif.: Sage Publications.

Morissette v. United States, 342 U.S. 246 (1952).

Morn, F. (1995). *Academic politics and the history of criminal justice education.* Westport, Conn.: Greenwood Press.

Morone, J. A. (2003). *Hellfire nation: The politics of sin in American history.* New Haven, Conn.: Yale University Press.

Morris, R. G., Gerber, J., & Menard, S. (2011). Social bonds, self-control, and adult criminality: A nationally representative assessment of Hirschi's revised self-control theory. *Criminal Justice and Behavior, 38,* 584–599.

Morrison, G. B., & Garner, T. K. (2011). Latitude in deadly force training: Progress or problem? *Police Practice and Research, 12,* 341–361.

Morse v. Frederick, 441 U.S. 393 (2007).

Moses, M. C. (1995). *Keeping incarcerated mothers and their daughters together: Girl Scouts Beyond Bars.* Washington, D.C.: National Institute of Justice. Available: https://www.ncjrs.gov/pdffiles/girlsct.pdf

Mosteller, R. P. (2007). The Duke lacrosse case, innocence, and false identifications: A fundamental failure to "do justice." *Fordham Law Review, 76,* 1337–1412.

Moyer, T. J. (2005). Commission on the 21st century judiciary. *Akron Law Review, 38,* 555–565.

Muir, W. K. (1977). *Police: Streetcorner politicians.* Chicago: University of Chicago Press.

Murray, J. (2005). Policing terrorism: A threat to community policing or just a shift in priorities? *Police Practice and Research, 6,* 347–361.

Musgrave, C. T., & Stephenson, B. W. (1983). Moral development of individuals selecting careers in law enforcement: Implications for selection and training. *Journal of Police Science and Administration, 11,* 358–362.

Nagin, D. S. (1998). Criminal deterrence research at the outset of the twenty-first century. In M. Tonry (Ed.), *Crime and justice: A review of research* (Vol. 23, pp. 1–42). Chicago: University of Chicago Press.

Narain, J. (2008, April 18). Sorry, wrong house: Drug squad's sledgehammer raid nets a dinner lady drinking tea. *Daily Mail.* Available: http://www.dailymail.co.uk/news/article-560279/Sorry-wrong-house-Drug-squads-sledgehammer-raid-nets-dinner-lady-drinking-tea.html

Nardulli, P. F. (1983). The societal cost of the exclusionary rule: An empirical assessment. *American Bar Foundation Research Journal, 8*(3), 585–609.

National Association of Criminal Defense Lawyers. (2009). *America's problem-solving courts: The criminal costs of treatment and the case for reform.* Washington, D.C.: Author.

National Center for Education Statistics. (1998, March). *Violence and discipline problems in U.S. public schools: 1996–97.* Washington, D.C.: Office of Educational Research and Improvement, U.S. Department of Education.

National Coalition of Anti-Violence Programs. (2012). *2011 report on lesbian, gay, bisexual, transgender, queer, and HIV-affected hate violence.* New York: Author. Retrieved from: http://www.avp.org/storage/documents/Reports/2012_NCAVP_2011_HV_Report.pdf

National Coalition for the Homeless. (2009a). *Domestic violence and homelessness.* Available: http://www.nationalhomeless.org/factsheets/domestic.pdf

National Coalition for the Homeless. (2009b). *Foreclosure to homelessness: The forgotten victims of the subprime crisis.* Available: http://www.nationalhomeless.org/factsheets/foreclosure.pdf

National Coalition for the Homeless. (2009c). *Hate crimes and violence against people experiencing homelessness.* Available: http://www.nationalhomeless.org/factsheets/Hatecrimes.pdf

National Coalition for the Homeless. (2009d). *How many people experience homelessness?* Available: http://www.nationalhomeless.org/factsheets/How_Many.pdf

National Conference of State Legislatures. (2013, November 21). *Defining marriage: State defense of marriage laws and same-sex marriage.* Available: http://www.ncsl.org/research/human-services/same-sex-marriage-overview.aspx

National Conference of State Legislatures. (2010, November). *State whistleblower laws.* Available: http://www.ncsl.org/issues-research/labor/state-whistleblower-laws.aspx

National Conference of State Legislatures. (2008). *States with littering penalties.* Available: http://www.ncsl.org/issues-research/env-res/states-with-littering-penalties.aspx

National District Attorneys Association. (2009). *National prosecution standards* (3rd ed.). Alexandria, Va.: Author.

National Federation of Independent Business v. Sebelius, 567 U.S. ___ (2012).

National Gang Center. (n.d.). *Frequently asked questions about gangs.* Available: http://www.nationalgangcenter.gov/About/FAQ#q1

National Institute of Corrections. (1997). *Supermax housing: A survey of current practices, special issues in corrections.* Longmont, Colo.: National Institute of Corrections Information Center.

National Institute of Justice. (1994). *25 years of criminal justice research.* Washington, D.C.: U.S. Department of Justice. Available: https://www.ncjrs.gov/pdffiles1/nij/151287.pdf

Neavling, S. (2013, July 13). Detroit arson a persistent problem as city services decline. *Huffpost Detroit*. Available: http://www.huffingtonpost.com/2013/07/15/detroit-arson_n_3591149.html

Neilson, G. (2009). *Trial by combat*. Clark, N.J.: The Lawbook Exchange. (Original work published 1890)

Neubauer, D. W., & Fradella, H. F. (2014). *America's courts and the criminal justice system* (11th ed.). Belmont, Calif.: Wadsworth/Cengage.

Nevada Department of Corrections. (2010). *State of Nevada Department of Corrections*. Available: http://www.doc.nv.gov

New Jersey v. T. L. O., 469 U.S. 325 (1985).

New State Ice Co. v. Liebmann [Brandeis dissent], 285 U.S. 262 (1932).

New York Civil Liberties Union. (2012, May 9). Stop-and-Frisk 2011. Available: http://www.nyclu.org/files/publications/NYCLU_2011_Stop-and-Frisk_Report.pdf

New York Times Co. v. United States, 403 U.S. 713 (1971).

Newhard v. Borders et al., 649 F.Supp. 2d 440 (U.S. District Court for the Western District of Virginia, 2009).

Newman, D. W. (2003). September 11: A societal reaction perspective. *Crime, Law and Social Change, 39*, 219–231.

Newman, G. (1983). *Just and painful: A case for the corporal punishment of criminals*. New York: Macmillan.

Niederhoffer, A. (1967). *Behind the shield: The police in urban society*. New York: Anchor Books.

Nozick, R. (1974). *Anarchy, state, and utopia*. Malden, Mass.: Blackwell.

O'Hear, M. M. (2007). Plea bargaining and procedural justice (Marquette Law School Legal Studies Paper No. 07-02). Retrieved from http://ssrn.com/abstract=982220

O'Lone v. Estate of Shabazz, 482 U.S. 342 (1987).

O'Neill, S. (1997). *Impartiality in context: Grounding justice in a pluralist world*. Albany: State University of New York Press.

O'Reilly, K. B. (2010, January 18). Physician-assisted suicide legal in Montana, court rules. *American Medical News*. Available: http://www.amednews.com/article/20100118/profession/301189939/6/

Oberlander, L. B., & Goldstein, N. E. (2001). A review and update on the practice of evaluating Miranda comprehension. *Behavioral Sciences and the Law, 19*(4), 453–471.

Office of Criminal Justice Services. (2005). *Justice alternatives: Ohio statutory community sanctions for adult and juvenile offenders*. Columbus, Ohio: Office of Criminal Justice Services. Available: http://www.publicsafety.ohio.gov/links/ocjs_CorrectionsBB.pdf

Okrent, D. (2010). *Last call: The rise and fall of prohibition*. New York: Scribner.

Oliver v. U.S., 466 U.S. 170 (1984).

Oliver, W. M. (2006). The fourth era of policing: Homeland security. *International Review of Law, Computers and Technology, 20*, 49–62

Oliver, W. M. (2003). *The law and order presidency*. Upper Saddle River, N.J.: Prentice Hall.

Oliver, W. M. (2001). Executive orders: Symbolic politics, criminal justice policy, and the American presidency. *American Journal of Criminal Justice, 26, 1–21.*

Oliver, W. M. (2000). The third generation of community policing: Moving through innovation, diffusion, and institutionalization. *Police Quarterly, 3*, 367–388.

Ostrom, B. J., & Hanson, R. A. (2007). Implement and use court performance measures. *Criminology and Public Policy, 6*, 799–806.

Otterbein, K. F., & Otterbein, C. S. (1965). An eye for an eye, a tooth for a tooth: A cross-cultural study of feuding. *American Anthropologist, 67*, 1470–1482.

Overton, J., Hensley, C., & Tallichet, S. (March, 2012). Examining the relationship between childhood animal cruelty motives and recurrent adult violent crimes toward humans. *Journal of Interpersonal Violence*, 27, 599–915.

Owen, S. (2005). The relationship between social capital and corporal punishment in schools: A theoretical inquiry. *Youth and Society, 37*, 85–112.

Owen, S. S., Burke, T. W., & Vichesky, D. (2008). Hazing in student organizations: Prevalence, attitudes, and solutions. *Oracle: The Research Journal of the Association of Fraternity Advisors, 3*, 40–58. Available: http://www.afa1976.0rg/Portals/0/documents/Oracle/Oracle_v013_iss1%200wen.pdf

Owen, S., & Burke, T. (2003, February). The Court of Appeals made the correct decision. *Campbell Law Observer*, pp. 3, 16.

Owen, S. S., Fradella, H. F., Burke, T. W., & Joplin, J. (2006). Conceptualizing justice: Revising the introductory criminal justice course. *Journal of Criminal Justice Education, 17*, 3–22.

Owen, S. S., & Wagner, K. (2008). The specter of authoritarianism among criminal justice majors. *Journal of Criminal Justice Education, 19*, 30–53.

Owen, S. & Wagner K. (2006). Explaining school corporal punishment: Evangelical Protestantism and social capital in a path model. *Social Justice Research, 19*, 471–499.

Packer, H. L. (1968). *The limits of the criminal sanction*. Palo Alto, Calif.: Stanford University Press.

Page, J. (2011). *The toughest beat: Politics, punishment, and the prison officers union in California*. New York: Oxford University Press.

Pallone, N. J., & Hennessy, J. J. (2003). To punish or to treat: Substance abuse within the context of oscillating attitudes toward correctional rehabilitation. *Journal of Offender Rehabilitation, 37*, 1–25.

Pangle, L. S. (2009). Moral and criminal responsibility in Plato's *Laws*. *American Political Science Review, 103*, 456–473.

Parent, D. G. (2003). *Correctional boot camps: Lessons from a decade of research*. Washington, D.C.: U.S. Department of Justice. Available: http://www.ncjrs.gov/pdffiles1/nij/197018.pdf

Parkes, H. B. (1932). Morals and law enforcement in colonial New England. *New England Quarterly, 5*, 431–452.

Parsons, T. (1951). *The social system* (new ed.). New York: Free Press.

Paterline, B. A., & Petersen, D. M. (1999). Structural and social psychological determinants of prisonization. *Journal of Criminal Justice, 27*, 427–441.

Paterson, T. G., Clifford, J. G., & Hagan, K. J. (1991). *American foreign policy: A history since 1990* (3rd ed., Rev.). Lexington, Mass.: D. C. Heath.

Patterson, J. T. (2001). The rise of rights and rights consciousness in American politics, 1930s-1970s. In B. E. Shafer & A. J. Badger (Eds.), *Contesting democracy: Substance and structure in American political history, 1775–2000* (pp. 201–223). Lawrence: University Press of Kansas.

Payton v. New York, 445 U.S. 573 (1980).

Peirce, C. S. (1877, November). The fixation of belief. *Popular Science Monthly, 12,* 1–15. Available: http://www.peirce.org/writings/p107.html

Peltz, J. (2010, April 1). "Stop the Sag" billboards battle low-slung pants. *NBCNews.com.* Available: http://www.msnbc.msn.com/id/36132246/ns/us_news-life/

Pennell, S., Curtis, C., Henderson, J., & Tayman, J. (1989). Guardian Angels: A unique approach to crime prevention. *Crime and Delinquency, 35,* 378–400.

Pennington, K. (1993). *The prince and the law, 1200–1600: Sovereignty and rights in the Western legal tradition.* Berkeley: University of California Press.

Pennsylvania Board of Probation & Parole v. Scott, 524 U.S. 357 (1998).

People v. Diaz, 51 Cal. 4th 84 (Supreme Court of California, 2011).

Pepinsky, H. (1999a). Empathy works, obedience doesn't. *Criminal Justice Policy Review, 9,* 141–167.

Pepinsky, H. (1999b). Peacemaking primer. In B. A. Arrigo (Ed.), *Social justice, criminal justice: The maturation of critical theory in law, crime, and deviance* (pp. 51–70). Belmont, Calif.: Wadsworth.

Perlin, M. L. (1997). The borderline which separated you from me: The insanity defense, the authoritarian spirit, the fear of faking, and the culture of punishment. *Iowa Law Review, 82,* 1375–1426.

Perrone, D., & Pratt, T. C. (2003). Comparing the quality of confinement and cost-effectiveness of public versus private prisons: What we know, why we do not know more, and where to go from here. *Prison Journal, 83,* 301–322.

Petersilia, J. (2007). Employ behavioral contracting for "earned discharge" parole. *Criminology and Public Policy, 6,* 807–814.

Peterson, R., Krivo, L., & Hagan, J. (2006). *The many colors of crime: Inequalities of race, ethnicity, and crime in America.* New York: New York University Press.

Petrosino, A., Turpin-Petrosino, C., & Guckenburg, S. (2010). Formal system processing of juveniles: Effects on delinquency. *Campbell Systematic Reviews, 2010*(1). Available: http://www.campbellcollaboration.org/lib/project/81/

Pew Center on the States. (2011). *State of recidivism: The revolving door of America's prisons.* Available: http://www.pewtrusts.org/uploadedFiles/wwwpewtrustsorg/Reports/sentencing_and_corrections/State_Recidivism_Revolving_Door_America_Prisons%20.pdf

Piché, J., & Larsen, M. (2010). The moving targets of penal abolitionism: ICOPA, past, present and future. *Contemporary Justice Review, 13,* 391–410.

Pierce, P. A., & Miller, D. E. (2004). *Gambling politics: State government and the business of betting.* Boulder, Colo.: Lynne Rienner Publishers.

Pilkington, E. (2013, May 15). British drug company acts to stop its products being used in US executions. *The Guardian.* Available: http://www.theguardian.com/world/2013/may/15/death-penalty-drugs-us-uk

Pilkington, E. (2011, December 20). Europe moves to block trade in medical drugs used in US executions. *The Guardian.* Available: http://www.theguardian.com/world/2011/dec/20/death-penalty-drugs-european-commission

Pinello, D. R. (1995). *The impact of judicial-selection method on state-supreme-court policy: innovation, reaction, and atrophy.* Westport, Conn.: Greenwood Press.

Pizarro, J. M., Stenius, V. M. K., & Pratt, T. C. (2006). Supermax prisons: Myths, realities, and the politics of punishment in American society. *Criminal Justice Policy Review, 17,* 6–21.

Pizarro, J., & Stenius, V. M. K. (2004). Supermax prisons: Their rise, current practices, and effect on inmates. *Prison Journal, 84,* 248–264.

Plato. (1892). *Laws.* In B. Jowett (Trans.), *The Dialogues of Plato* (Vol. 5, pp. 1–361). London: Oxford University Press. (Original work published 360 B.C.E.)

Polinsky, A.M. (2003). *An introduction to law and economics.* Chicago: Aspen Publishers.

Posner, R. A. (2003). *Law, pragmatism, and democracy.* Cambridge, Mass.: Harvard University Press.

Posner, R. A. (1993). *The problems of jurisprudence.* Cambridge, Mass.: Harvard University Press.

Pound, R. (1998). *Criminal justice in America.* New Brunswick, N.J.: Transaction Publishers. (Original work published 1930)

Pozen, D. E. (2008). The irony of judicial elections. *Columbia Law Review, 108,* 265–330.

Pratt, T. C. (2009). *Addicted to incarceration: Corrections policy and the politics of misinformation in the United States.* Los Angeles: Sage.

Pratt, T. C., Gaffney, M. J., Lovrich, N. P., & Johnson, C. L. (2006). This isn't CSI: Estimating the national backlog of forensic DNA cases and the barriers associated with case processing. *Criminal Justice Policy Review, 17,* 32–47.

Prescott, J. J., & Rockoff, J. E. (2011). Do sex offender registration and notification laws affect criminal behavior? *Journal of Law and Economics, 54*(1), 161–206.

President's Commission on Law Enforcement and the Administration of Justice. (1967). *The challenge of crime in a free society.* Washington, D.C.: U.S. Government Printing Office.

Prison count 2010: State population declines for the first time in 38 years. (2010, April). Pew Center on the States. Available: http://www.pewcenteronthestates.org/uploadedFiles/Prison_Count_2010.pdf?n=880

Punishment for Conviction of a Felony, Code of Virginia § 18.2–10 (2008).

Punishment for Conviction of a Misdemeanor, Code of Virginia § 18.2–11 (2000).

Quinney, R. (1970). *The social reality of crime.* Boston: Little, Brown.

Rachels, J., & Rachels, S. (2010). *The elements of moral philosophy* (6th ed.). New York: McGraw-Hill.

Raes, K. (2001). Legal moralism or paternalism? Tolerance or indifference? Egalitarian justice and the ethics of equal concern. In P. Alldridge & C. H. Brants (Eds.), *Personal autonomy, the private sphere and the criminal law: A comparative study* (pp. 25–47). Portland, Ore.: Hart.

Rafter, N. (2010). Silence and memory in criminology: The American Society of Criminology 2009 Sutherland address. *Criminology, 48,* 339–355.

Ramsey, R. J., & Frank, J. (2007). Wrongful conviction: Perceptions of criminal justice professionals regarding the frequency of wrongful conviction and the extent of system errors. *Crime and Delinquency, 53,* 436–470.

Rand, M. R., & Rennison, C. M. (2002). True crime stories: Accounting for differences in our national crime indicators. *Chance, 15*(1), 47–51.

Range, F., Horn, L., Viranyi, Z., & Huber, L. (2009). The absence of reward induces inequity aversion in dogs. *Proceedings of the National Academy of Sciences, 106,* 340–345.

Rasul v. Bush, 542 U.S. 466 (2004).

Ravin v. State, 537 P.2d 494 (Supreme Court of Alaska, 1975).

Rawls, J. (2001). *Justice as fairness: A restatement.* Cambridge, Mass.: Harvard University Press.

Rawls, J. (1999). *A theory of justice* (Rev. ed.). Cambridge, Mass.: Harvard University Press.

Rawls, J. (1971). *A theory of justice.* Cambridge, Mass.: Belknap/Harvard University Press.

Raymond, B. (2010). *Assigning police officers to schools.* U.S. Department of Justice, Office of Community Oriented Policing Services, Problem-Oriented Guides for Police Response Series (No. 10). Available: http://www.popcenter.org/Responses/pdfs/school_police.pdf

Raz, J. (1972). Legal principles and the limits of law. *Yale Law Journal, 81*(5), 823–854.

Reaves, B. A. (2012, June). *Federal law enforcement officers, 2008* Washington, D.C.: Bureau of Justice Statistics.

Reaves, B. A. (2011, July). *Census of state and local law enforcement agencies, 2008.* Washington, D.C.: Bureau of Justice Statistics.

Reddick, M. (2010). *Judging the quality of judicial selection methods: Merit selection, elections, and judicial discipline.* Chicago: American Judicature Society. Retrieved from http://www.judicialselection.us/uploads/documents/Judging_the_Quality_of_Judicial_Sel_8EF0DC3806ED8.pdf

Reddick, M., Nelson, M. J., & Caufield, R. P. (2010). *Examining diversity on state courts: How does the judicial selection environment advance—and inhibit—judicial diversity?* Chicago, ILL: American Judicature Society. Retrieved from http://www.judicialselection.com/uploads/documents/Examining_Diversity_on_State_Courts_2CA4D9DF458DD.pdf

Redlich, A. D., Hoover, S., Summers, A., & Steadman, H. J. (2010). Enrollment in mental health courts: Voluntariness, knowingness, and adjudicative competence. *Law and Human Behavior, 34,* 91–104.

Reese, R. (2005). *Leadership in the LAPD: Walking the tightrope.* Durham, N.C.: Carolina Academic Press.

Regina v. Dudley & Stephens, 4 QB D 273 (High Court of Justice, 1884).

Reiman, J. (2001). *The rich get richer and the poor get prison: Ideology, class, and criminal justice* (6th ed.). Boston: Allyn & Bacon.

Reinarman, C. (1988). The social construction of an alcohol problem: The case of Mothers Against Drunk Drivers and social control in the 1980s. *Theory and Society, 17,* 91–120.

Report by the President's Commission on Law Enforcement and Administration of Justice. (1967). Washington, D.C.: U.S. Government Printing Office.

Report of the National Advisory Commission on Civil Disorders. (1968). New York: Bantam Books.

Republican Party of Minnesota v. White, 536 U.S. 765 (2002).

Rest, J. R., & Navárez, D. (Eds.). (1994). *Moral development in the professions: Psychology and applied ethics.* Hillsdale, N.J.: Lawrence Erlbaum Associates

Reynolds v. United States, 98 U.S. 145 (1878).

Reynolds, J. (2005). The rule of law and the origins of the bill of attainder clause. *St. Thomas Law Review, 18,* 177–205.

Rhode Island v. Innis, 446 U.S. 291 (1980).

Rhodes v. Chapman, 452 U.S. 337 (1981).

Rhodes, L. A. (2004). *Total confinement: Madness and reason in the maximum security prison.* Berkeley: University of California Press.

Richardson v. Ramirez, 418 U.S. 24 (1974).

Richardson, L. E., & Houston, D. J. (2009). Federalism and safety on America's highways. *Publius: The Journal of Federalism, 39,* 117–137.

Richmond Police Department. (2007). *Sector 213: From blight to bliss.* Application for the 2007 Herman Goldstein Award for Excellence in Problem-Oriented Policing. Available: http://www.popcenter.org/library/awards/goldstein/2007/07–38.pdf

Riemer, J. W. (1981). Deviance as fun. *Adolescence, 16,* 39–43.

Riveland, C. (1999). *Supermax prisons: Overview and general considerations.* Washington, D.C.: U.S. Department of Justice, National Institute of Corrections.

Roberg, R., Crank, J., & Kuykendall, J. (2000). *Police and society* (2nd ed.). Los Angeles: Roxbury.

Robertson, D. B. (2012). *Federalism and the making of America.* New York: Routledge.

Robertson, D. B., & Judd, D. R. (1989). *The development of American public policy: The structure of policy restraint.* Glenview, Ill.: Scott, Foresman.

Robey v. State, 456 A.2d 953 (Md. App. 1983)

Robinson v. California, 370 U.S. 660 (1962).

Robinson, P. H. (2013). Natural law and lawlessness: Modern lessons from pirates, lepers, Eskimos, and survivors. *University of Illinois Law Review, 2013,* 433–506.

Robinson, P. H. (2008). *Criminal law: Cases and controversies* (2nd ed.). New York: Aspen.

Robinson, P. H. (2005). Fair notice and fair adjudication: Two kinds of legality. *University of Pennsylvania Law Review, 154,* 335–398.

Robinson, O. F. (1990). *Criminal law of ancient Rome.* Baltimore: Johns Hopkins University Press.

Rochefort, D. A., & Cobb, R. W. (1994). Problem definition: An emerging perspective. In D. A. Rochefort & R. W. Cobb, *The politics of problem definition: Shaping the policy agenda* (pp. 1–31). Lawrence: University Press of Kansas.

Rochin v. California, 342 U.S. 165 (1952).

Roe v. Wade, 410 U.S. 113 (1973).

Rogers, J. L., Bloom, J. D., & Manson, S. M. (1984). Insanity defenses: Contested or conceded? *American Journal of Psychiatry, 141*(7), 885–888.

Room, R., Turner, N. E., & Ialomiteanu, A. (1999). Community effects of the opening of the Niagara casino. *Addiction, 94,* 1449–1466.

Roper v. Simmons, 543 U.S. 551 (2005).

Rosen, G. E., & Smith, K. F. (2010). Summarizing the evidence on the international trade in illegal wildlife. *EcoHealth, 7,* 24–32.

Rosen, M. (1999). Insanity denied: Abolition of the insanity defense in Kansas. *Kansas Journal of Law & Public Policy, 8,* 253–262.

Rosenbaum, D. P. (2007). Just say no to D.A.R.E. *Criminology and Public Policy, 6,* 815–824.

Rosenbaum, D. P. (2006). The limits of hot spots policing. In D. Weisburd & A. A. Braga (Eds.), *Police Innovation: Contrasting Perspectives* (pp. 245–263). New York: Cambridge University Press.

Rosenberg, R. S. (2013, Apr. 12). Abnormal is the new normal: Why will half of the U.S. population have a diagnosable mental disorder? *Slate.* Retrieved from http://www.slate.com/articles/health_and_science/medical_examiner/2013/04/diagnostic_and_statistical_manual_fifth_edition_why_will_half_the_u_s_population.html

Rosenblatt, A. M. (2003). The law's evolution: Long night's journey into day. *Cardozo Law Review, 24,* 2119–2147.

Rosenfeld, R. (2007). Transfer the Uniform Crime Reporting program from the FBI to the Bureau of Justice Statistics. *Criminology and Public Policy, 6,* 825–834.

Rosenfeld, R. (2000). Patterns in adult homicide: 1980–1995. In A. Blumstein & J. Wallman (Eds.), *The crime drop in America* (pp. 130–163). New York: Cambridge University Press.

Rosenfeld, R., Messner, S. F., & Baumer, E. P. (2001). Social capital and homicide. *Social Forces, 80,* 283–309.

Rosich, K. J., & Kane, K. M. (2005, July). Truth in sentencing and state sentencing practices. *NIJ Journal, 252,* 18–21.

Roskin, M. G. (2004). *Countries and concepts: Politics, geography, culture* (8th ed.). Upper Saddle River, N.J.: Pearson/Prentice Hall.

Ross, E. A. (1901). *Social control: A survey of the foundations of order.* New York: Macmillan.

Ross, H. L., McCleary R., LaFree, G. (1990). Can the threat of jail deter drunk drivers? The Arizona case. *Journal of Criminal Law and Criminology, 81,* 156–170.

Roth, M. T., Hoffner, H. A., & Michalowski, P. (1997). *Law collections from Mesopotamia and Asia Minor* (2nd ed.). Atlanta: Scholars Press.

Rothman, D. J. (1995). Perfecting the prison: United States, 1789–1865. In N. Morris & D. J. Rothman (Eds.), *The Oxford history of the prison: The practice of punishment in Western society* (pp. 110–129). New York: Oxford University Press.

Rotman, E. (1995). The failure of reform: United States, 1865–1965. In N. Morris & D. J. Rothman (Eds.), *The Oxford history of the prison: The practice of punishment in Western society* (pp. 168–197). New York: Oxford University Press.

Rottman, D. B. (2007). Adhere to procedural fairness in the justice system. *Criminology and Public Policy, 6,* 835–842.

Rousseau, J. J. (1963). The social contract. In J. Somerville & R. E. Santoni (Eds.), *Social and political philosophy* (pp. 205–238). New York: Anchor Books. (Original work published 1762)

Rowe, D. C. (2002). *Biology and crime.* Los Angeles: Roxbury.

Rowe, D., & Osgood, D. W. (1984). Heredity and sociological theories of delinquency: Reconsideration. *American Sociological Review, 49,* 526–540.

Rubin, J. B. (2011). The Supreme Court assumes errant prosecutors will be disciplined by their offices or the bar: Three case studies that prove that assumption wrong. *Fordham Law Review, 80,* 537–572.

Rubin, J., & Winton, R. (2013, May 6). Privacy groups file lawsuit over license plate scanners. *Los Angeles Times.* Available: http://articles.latimes.com/2013/may/06/local/la-me-ln-license-plate-lawsuit-20130506

Ruiz v. Estelle, 503 F.Supp. 1265 (U.S. District Court for the Southern District of Texas, 1980).

Russano, M. B., Meissner, C. A., Narchet, F. M., & Kassin, S. M. (2005). Investigating true and false confessions within a novel experimental paradigm. *Psychological Science, 16,* 481–486.

Rutan v. Republican Party of Illinois, 497 U.S. 62 (1990).

Ryan, P. S. (2003). Revisiting the United States application of punitive damages: Separating myth from reality. *ILSA Journal of International and Comparative Law, 10,* 69–93.

Saad, L. (2011, July 11). *Americans express mixed confidence in criminal justice system.* Available: http://www.gallup.com/poll/148433/americans-express-mixed-confidence-criminal-justice-system.aspx

Sabatier, P. A., & Jenkins-Smith, H. C. (1993). *Policy change and learning: An advocacy coalition approach.* Boulder, Colo.: Westview Press.

Sachdev, P. S. (2013). Is DSM-5 defensible? *Australian and New Zealand Journal of Psychiatry, 47*(1), 10–11.

Sadler, M. S., Correll, J., Park, B., & Judd, C. M. (2012). The world is not black and white: Racial bias in the decision to shoot in a multiethnic context. *Social Issues, 68,* 286–313.

Sadurski, W. (2006). Law's legitimacy and "democracy-plus." *Oxford Journal of Legal Studies,* 26, 377–409.

Salinas v. United States, No. 12–246 (Jun. 17, 2013).

Sample, L. L., & Kadleck, C. (2008). Sex offender laws: Legislators' accounts of the need for policy. *Criminal Justice Policy Review, 19*(1), 40–62.

Sampson, R. J., & Raudenbush, S. W. (2001, February). *Disorder in urban neighborhoods: Does it lead to crime?* National Institute of Justice Research in Brief. Available: https://www.ncjrs.gov/pdffiles1/nij/186049.pdf

Sante, L. (1991). *Low life: Lures and snares of old New York.* New York: Vintage Books.

Santos, R. (2013). *Crime analysis with crime mapping.* Los Angeles, CA: Sage.

Saracho, O. N., & Spodek, B. (2007). *Contemporary perspectives on socialization and social development in early childhood education.* Charlotte, N.C.: Information Age.

Sargent, L. T. (1996). *Contemporary political ideologies: A comparative analysis* (10th ed.). New York: Harcourt Brace College Publishers.

Saucier v. Katz, 533 U.S. 194 (2001).

Schlag, P. (1999). No vehicles in the park. *Seattle University Law Review, 23,* 381–389.

Schlosser, E. (1998, December). The prison-industrial complex. *Atlantic Monthly,* pp. 51–77.

Schmidt, M. F. H., & Sommerville, J. A. (2011). Fairness expectations and altruistic sharing in 15-month-old human infants. *PLoS One, 6,* e23223.

Schmidtz, D. (2006). *Elements of justice.* New York: Cambridge University Press.

Schneider, A. L., Ervin, L., & Snyder-Joy, Z. (1996). Further exploration of the flight from discretion: The role of risk/need instruments in probation supervision decisions. *Journal of Criminal Justice, 24,* 109–121.

Schouten, R. & Silver, J. (2012). Almost a psychopath: The insanity defense. *Psychology Today.* Retrieved from http://www.psychologytoday.com/blog/almost-psychopath/201208/the-insanity-defense

Schretlen, D., & Arkowitz, H. (1990). A psychological test battery to detect prison inmates who fake insanity or mental retardation. *Behavioral Sciences and the Law, 8*(1), 75–84.

Schuetz, J., & Lilley, L. S. (1999). *The O. J. Simpson trials: Rhetoric, media, and the law.* Carbondale: Southern Illinois University Press.

Schug, R. A., & Fradella, H. F. (2014). *Mental illness and crime.* Thousand Oaks, Calif.: Sage.

Schuhmann, R. A., & Wodahl, E. J. (2011). Prison reform through federal legislative intervention: The case of the Prison Rape Elimination Act. *Criminal Justice Policy Review, 22,* 111–128.

Schulhofer, S. J. (1996). *Miranda*'s practical effect: Substantial benefits and vanishingly small social costs. *Northwestern University Law Review, 90,* 500–563.

Schultz, D. P., Hudak, E., & Alpert, G. P. (2010, March). Evidence-based decisions on police pursuits: The officer's perspective. *FBI Law Enforcement Bulletin,* pp. 1–7. Available: http://www.fbi.gov/stats-services/publications/law-enforcement-bulletin/2010-pdfs/march101eb

Schultz, D. P., Hudak, E., & Alpert, G. P. (2009, April). Emergency driving and pursuits: The officer's perspective. *FBI Law Enforcement Bulletin,* pp. 1–7. Available: http://leb.fbi.gov/2009-pdfs/leb-april-2009

Scott v. Harris, 550 U.S. 372 (2007).

Scott-Hayward, C. S. (2009, July). *The fiscal crisis in corrections: Rethinking policies and practices.* New York: Vera Institute of Justice. Available: http://www.vera.org/files/The-fiscal-crisis-in-corrections_July-2009.pdf

Segal, J. A., & Spaeth, H. J. (1993). *The Supreme Court and the attitudinal model.* New York: Cambridge University Press.

Seigel, L. (2002). *Criminology: The core.* Belmont, Calif.: Wadsworth.

Seiter, R. P., & West, A. D. (2003). Supervision styles in probation and parole: An analysis of activities. *Journal of Offender Rehabilitation, 38,* 57–75.

Senate Bill 1070 [Senate Engrossed], Arizona State Senate (2010). Available: http://www.azleg.gov/legtext/491eg/2r/bills/sb1070s.pdf

Seno, A. A. (2008, January 15). Dance is part of rehabilitation at Philippine prison. *New York Times.* Available: http://www.nytimes.com/2008/01/15/world/asia/15iht-inmates.1.9223130.html?pagewanted=all

Sentencing circles. (n.d.). Available: http://www.nij.gov/topics/courts/restorative-justice/promising-practices/sentencing-circles.htm

Sentencing Project. (2013, June). *Felony disenfranchisement laws in the United States.* Available: http://sentencingproject.org/doc/publications/fd_bs_fdlawsinus_Jun2013.pdf

Serial killers and murderers. (1991). Lincolnwood, Ill.: Publications International.

Shalev, S. (2011). Solitary confinement and supermax prisons: A human rights and ethical analysis. *Journal of Forensic Psychology Practice, 11,* 151–183.

Shapiro, A. L. (1993). Challenging criminal disenfranchisement under the Voting Rights Act: A new strategy. *Yale Law Journal, 103,* 537–566.

Sharkey, J. (1999, December 19). Mental illness: Defining the line between behavior that's vexing and certifiable. *New York Times.* Available: http://query.nytimes.com/gst/fullpage.html?res=9400E1D81330F93AA25751C1A96F958260

Sharp, E. B. (2005). *Morality politics in American cities.* Lawrence: University Press of Kansas.

Sharp, E. B. (1994). Paradoxes of national antidrug policymaking. In D. A. Rochefort & R. W. Cobb (Eds.). *The politics of problem definition: Shaping the policy agenda* (pp. 98–116). Lawrence: University Press of Kansas.

Shaw, C. R., & McKay, H. D. (1942). *Juvenile delinquency in urban areas.* Chicago: University of Chicago Press.

Shelden, R. G. (2001). *Controlling the dangerous classes: A critical introduction to the history of criminal justice.* Boston: Allyn & Bacon.

Shelton, D. E. (2008, March). The "CSI effect": Does it really exist? *NIJ Journal, 259,* 1–6.

Sherman, L. W. (2007). Use probation to prevent murder. *Criminology and Public Policy, 6,* 843–850.

Sherman, L. W. (1974). Toward a sociological theory of police corruption. In L. Sherman (Ed.), *Police corruption: A sociological perspective* (pp. 1–39). New York: Anchor Books.

Sherman, L. W., & Berk, R. A. (1984). The specific deterrent effects of arrest for domestic assault. *American Sociological Review, 49,* 261–272.

Sherman, L. W., Gottfredson, D. C., MacKenzie, D. L., Eck, J., Reuter, P., & Bushway, S. D. (1998, July). Preventing crime: What works, what doesn't, what's promising. *National Institute of Justice Research in Focus.* Available: http://www.ncjrs.gov/pdffiles/171676.pdf

Shively, W. P. (1999). *Power and choice: An introduction to political science* (6th ed.). New York: McGraw-Hill.

Shoemaker, D. J. (2009). *Theories of delinquency: An examination of explanations of delinquent behavior* (6th ed.). New York: Oxford University Press.

Sholar, J. A. (2007). *Habeas corpus* and the war on terror. *Duquesne Law Review, 45,* 661–700.

Show, C. (2012, June 17). The moment police broke up raucous graduation party of 200 teenagers...thrown by boy whose parents were out of town. *Daily Mail.* Available: http://www.dailymail.co.uk/news/article-2160863/Police-break-California-drinking-house-party-thrown-18-year-old-boy-200-teenagers-showed-up.html

Sickmund, M. (2003, June). *Juveniles in court.* Juvenile Offenders and Victims National Report Series Bulletin. Available: https://www.ncjrs.gov/html/ojjdp/195420/contents.html

Siegel, L. J. (2001). *Criminology: Theories, patterns, and typologies* (7th ed.). Belmont, Calif.: Wadsworth.

Silver, E., Cirincione, C., & Steadman, H. J. (1994). Demythologizing inaccurate perceptions of the insanity defense. *Law and Human Behavior, 18,* 63–70.

Silverman, E. B. (1999). *NYPD battles crime: Innovative strategies in policing.* Boston, Mass.: Northeastern University Press.

Silverthorne Lumber Co. v. United States, 251 U.S. 385 (1920).

Simon, J. (2007). *Governing through crime: How the war on crime transformed American democracy and created a culture of fear.* New York: Oxford University Press.

Sims, D. (2008, September 8). USDA pins Sam Mazzola's bear-wrestling act. *The Plain Dealer.* Available: http://blog.cleveland.com/metro/2008/09/usda_pins_sam_mazzolas_bearwre.html

Singer, S. D., & Hensley, C. (2004). Applying social learning theory to childhood and adolescent firesetting: Can it lead to serial murder? *International Journal of Offender Therapy and Comparative Criminology, 48,* 461–476.

Sinha, D. (1996). Culture as the target and culture as the source: A review of cross-cultural psychology in Asia. *Psychology and Developing Societies, 8*(1), 83–105.

Skiba, R. (2008). Are zero tolerance policies effective in the schools? *American Psychologist, 63*(9), 852–862.

Skiba, R., & Peterson, R. (1999). The dark side of zero tolerance: Can punishment lead to safe schools? *Phi Delta Kappan, 80*(5), 372–376, 381–382.

Skogan, W. G., & Hartnett, S. M. (1997). *Community policing, Chicago style.* New York: Oxford University Press.

Skolnick, J. (1966). *Justice without trial: Law enforcement in democratic society.* New York: John Wiley.

Slow-moving vehicle emblem or reflective tape required, Kentucky Revised Statutes, §189.820 (2012).

Smith v. Doe, 538 U.S. 84 (2003).

Smith v. Maryland, 442 U.S. 735 (1979).

Smith, A. B., & Pollack, H. (1994). Deviance as crime, sin, and poor taste. In P. A. Adler & P. Adler (Eds.), *Constructions of deviance: Social power, context, & interaction* (pp. 11–25). Belmont, Calif.: Wadsworth. (Original work published 1976)

Smith, B., Zalman, M., & Kiger, A. (2011). How justice officials view wrongful convictions. *Crime and Delinquency, 57,* 663–685.

Smith, M. J. (1993). *Pressure, power, and policy: State autonomy and policy networks in Britain and the United States.* Pittsburgh: University of Pittsburgh Press.

Smith, R., & Taylor, R. (1985, December). A return to neighborhood policing: The Tampa, Florida experience. *Police Chief,* pp. 39–44.

Sobel, R. S., & Hall, J. C. (2007). The effect of judicial selection processes on judicial quality: The role of partisan politics. *CATO Journal, 27*(1), 69–82.

Socia, K. M. (2011). The policy implications of residence restrictions on sex offender housing in upstate NY. *Criminology and Public Policy, 10*(2), 351–389.

Solem v. Helm, 463 U.S. 277 (1983).

Solove, D. J. (2007). *The future of reputation: Gossip, rumor, and privacy on the internet.* New Haven, Conn.: Yale University Press.

Solum, L. B. (2004). Procedural justice. *Southern California Law Review, 78,* 181–321.

Sotirovic, M. (2001). Affective and cognitive processes as mediators of media influences on crime policy preferences. *Mass Communication and Society, 4,* 311–329.

Sousa, W. H., & Kelling, G. L. (2006). Of "broken windows," criminology, and criminal justice. In D. Weisburd & A. A. Braga (Eds.), *Police innovation: Contrasting perspectives* (pp. 77–97). New York: Cambridge University Press.

Southern Poverty Law Center. (2010). The math: Anti-LGBT hate violence. Montgomery, AL: Author. Retrieved from http://www.splcenter.org/the-anti-gay-lobby-the-family-research-council-the-american-family-association-the-demonization-of—3#.Ua6HV_Pn90k

Spelman, W. (2000). The limited importance of prison expansion. In A. Blumstein & J. Wallman (Eds.), *The crime drop in America* (pp. 97–129). New York: Cambridge University Press.

Spierenburg, P. C. (1984). *The spectacle of suffering.* New York: Cambridge University Press.

Spohn, C. (2009). *How do judges decide?: The search for fairness and justice in punishment.* Thousand Oaks, Calif.: Sage Publications.

Spohn, C. C. (2008). *How do judges decide? The search for fairness and justice in punishment* (2nd ed.). Thousand Oaks, Calif.: Sage Publications.

Sport England. (2002). *Positive futures: A review of impact and good practice, summary report.* London: Sport England. Available: www.sportengland.org

Spreitzer, G. M., & Sonenshein, S. (2004). Toward the construct definition of positive deviance. *American Behavioral Scientist, 47,* 828–847.

Stampp, K. M. (1991). *The causes of the Civil War* (Rev. ed.). New York: Simon & Schuster.

Stanley, P. H., Small, R., Owen, S. S., & Burke, T. W. (2012). Humanistic perspectives on addressing school violence. In M. B. Scholl, A. S. McGowan, & J. T. Hansen (Eds.), *Humanistic perspectives on contemporary counseling issues* (pp. 167–189). New York: Routledge.

State v. Crenshaw, 659 P.2d 488 (Wash. 1983).

State v. Grimsley, 444 N.E.2d 1071 (Ohio App. 1982).

State v. Smith, 124 Ohio St.3d (Supreme Court of Ohio, 2009).

Steffens, L. (1992). *The shame of cities.* New York: Hill and Wang. (Original work published 1904)

Steinbrook, R. (2008). Physician-assisted death from Oregon to Washington State. *New England Journal of Medicine, 359,* 2513–2515.

Stephan, J. J. (2008). *Census of state and federal correctional facilities, 2005.* Washington, D.C.: Bureau of Justice Statistics. Available: http://www.bjs.gov/content/pub/pdf/csfcf05.pdf

Stimson, G., Grant, M., Choquet, M., & Garrison, P. (2007). *Drinking in context: Patterns, interventions, and partnerships.* New York: Routledge.

Stolz, B. (2005). Educating policymakers and setting the criminal justice policymaking agenda: Interest groups and the "Victims of Trafficking and Violence Act of 2000." *Criminal Justice, 5,* 407–430.

Stolzenberg, L., & D'Alessio, S. J. (1997). "Three strikes and you're out": The impact of California's new mandatory sentencing law on serious crime rates. *Crime and Delinquency, 43,* 457–469.

Stone, D. (2012). *Policy paradox: The art of political decision making* (3rd ed.). New York: W. W. Norton and Company.

Stone, D. (2002). *Policy paradox: The art of political decision making* (Rev. ed.). New York: W. W. Norton.

Stone, T. H. (1997). Therapeutic implications of incarceration for persons with severe mental disorders: Searching for rational health policy. *American Journal of Criminal Law, 24,* 283–358.

StopHazing.org. (n.d.). *State anti-hazing laws.* Available: http://www.stophazing.org/laws.html

Stowell, J. I., Messner, S. F., McGeever, K. F., & Raffalovich, L. E. (2009). Immigration and the recent violent crime drop in the United States: A pooled, cross-sectional time-series analysis of metropolitan areas. *Criminology, 47,* 889–928.

Straus, M. A. (2010). Prevalence, societal causes, and trends in corporal punishment by parents in world perspective. *Law and Contemporary Problems, 73,* 1–30.

Straus, M. (2000). Corporal punishment and primary prevention of physical abuse. *Child Abuse and Neglect, 24,* 1109–1114.

Straus, M. A., & Mathur, A. K. (1996). Social change and the trends in approval of corporal punishment by parents from 1968 to 1994. In D. Frehsee, W. Horn, & K. D. Bussmann (Eds.), *Family violence against children: A challenge for society* (pp. 91–105). New York: Walter de Gruyter.

Straus, M. & Stewart, J. (1999). Corporal punishment by American parents: National data on prevalence, chronicity, severity, and duration, in relation to child and family characteristics. *Clinical Child and Family Psychology Review, 2,* 55–70.

Strickland v. Washington, 466 U.S. 668 (1984).

Sundt, J. L., Castellano, T. C., & Briggs, C. S. (2008). The sociopolitical context of prison violence and its control: A case study of supermax and its effect in Illinois. *Prison Journal, 88,* 94–122.

Sunstein, C. R. (2007). If people would be outraged by their rulings, should judges care? *Stanford Law Review, 60,* 155–212.

Surette, R. (2011). *The media, crime, and criminal justice: Images and realities* (4th ed.). Belmont, Calif.: Wadsworth/Cengage.

Survey methodology for Criminal Victimization in the United States. (n.d.). Available: http://www.bjs.gov/content/pub/pdf/ncvs_methodology.pdf

Sutherland, E. H. (1947). *Principles of criminology.* New York: Harper & Row.

Swain v. Alabama, 380 U.S. 202 (1965).

Swedberg, R. (2004). *The Max Weber dictionary: Key words and central concepts.* Stanford, Calif.: Stanford University Press.

Sykes, G. M. (1958). *The society of captives: A study of a maximum security prison.* Princeton, N.J.: Princeton University Press.

Sykes, G. M., & Matza, D. (1957, December). Techniques of neutralization: A theory of delinquency. *American Sociological Review, 22,* 664–670.

Takagi, P. (1975, December). The Walnut Street Jail: A penal reform to centralize the powers of the state. *Federal Probation, 39,* 18–26.

Talbott, J. A. (2004). Deinstitutionalization: Avoiding the disasters of the past. *Psychiatric Services, 55,* 1112–1115. (Original work published 1979)

Tamanaha, B. (2004) *On the rule of law.* New York: Cambridge University Press.

Tannenbaum, F. (1938). *Crime and the community.* New York: Ginn.

Tappan, P. W. (1947). Who is the criminal? *American Sociological Review, 12*(1), 96–102.

Task Force Report. (1990). Salem, N.H.: Ayer. (Original work published 1967)

Taylor v. Taintor, 83 U.S. 366 (1872).

Taylor, P. (2005). Biocentric egalitarianism. In L. P. Pojman (Ed.), *Environmental ethics: Readings in theory and application* (4th ed., pp. 117–131). Belmont, Calif.: Wadsworth/Thomson Learning. (Original work published1981)

Taylor, R. B. (2006). Incivilities reduction policing, zero tolerance, and the retreat from coproduction: Weak foundations and strong pressures. In D. Weisburd & A. A. Braga (Eds.), *Police innovation: Contrasting perspectives* (pp. 98–114). New York: Cambridge University Press.

Taylor, R. B., Goldkamp, J. S., Weiland, D., Breen, C., Garcia, R. M., Presley, L. A., & Wyant, B. R. (2007). Revise policies mandating offender DNA collection. *Criminology and Public Policy, 6,* 851–862.

Teitel, R. G. (2002). *Transitional justice.* New York: Oxford University Press.

Tennessee v. Garner, 471 U.S. 1 (1985).

Terry v. Ohio, 392 U.S. 1 (1968).

Tewksbury, R., & Lees, M. (2006). Perceptions of sex offender registration: Collateral consequences and community experiences. *Sociological Spectrum, 26,* 309–334.

Tewksbury, R., & Mustaine, E. E. (2005). Insiders' views of prison amenities: Beliefs and perceptions of correctional staff members. *Criminal Justice Review, 30,* 174–188.

Texas v. Johnson, 491 U.S. 397 (1989).

Thibaut, J., & Walker, L. (1975). *Procedural justice: A psychological analysis.* Hillsdale, N.J.: Erlbaum.

Thompson v. Keohane, 516 U.S. 99 (1995).

Thornberry, T. P., & Krohn, M. D. (2000). The self-report method for measuring delinquency and crime. In D. Duffee (Ed.), *Criminal justice 2000: Vol. 4. Measurement and analysis of crime and justice* (pp. 33–83). Washington, D.C.: U.S. Department of Justice. Available: http://www.ncjrs.gov/criminal_justice2000/vol_4/04b.pdf

Thurman v. City of Torrington, 595 F.Supp. 1521 (U.S. District Court for the District of Connecticut, 1984).

Tinker v. Des Moines Independent Community School District, 393 U.S. 503 (1969).

Toch, H. (1997). *Corrections: A humanistic approach.* Monsey, N.Y.: Criminal Justice Press.

Trop v. Dulles, 356 U.S. 86 (1958).

Trupin, E., & Richards, H. (2003). Seattle's mental health courts: Early indicators of effectiveness. *International Journal of Law and Psychiatry, 26*(1), 33–53.

Truth and Reconciliation Commission of South Africa. (1998). *TRC final report* (Vol. 5). Available: http://www.justice.gov.za/trc/report/finalreport/Volume%205.pdf

Tucker, S. B., & Cadora, E. (2003, November). Justice reinvestment. *Ideas for an Open Society, 3*(3), 1–8. Available: http://www.soros.org/resources/articles_publications/publications/ideas_20040106/ideas_reinvestment.pdf

Tunnell, K. D. (2008). Illegal dumping: Large and small scale littering in rural Kentucky. *Southern Rural Sociology, 23*(2), 29–42

Turner, S., Jannetta, J., Hess, J., Myers, R., Shah, R., Werth, R., & Whitby, A. (2007). *Implementation and early outcomes for the San Diego High Risk Sex Offender (HRSO) GPS pilot program.* Irvine: University of California, Irvine, Center for Evidence-Based Corrections. Retrieved from http://ucicorrections.seweb.uci.edu/files/2013/06/HRSO_GPS_Pilot_Program.pdf

Turner, W. G. (2007, June). The experiences of offenders in a prison canine program. *Federal Probation, 27*(1), 38–43.

Turow, S. (2003). *Ultimate punishment: A lawyer's reflections on dealing with the death penalty.* New York: Picador.

Tyler, T. R. (2006). *Why people obey the law.* Princeton, N.J.: Princeton University Press.

Tyler, T. R., & Huo, Y. J. (2003). Procedural justice, legitimacy, and the effective rule of law, *Crime and Justice, 30,* 283–357.

Tyler, T. R., & Huo, Y. J. (2002). *Trust in the law: Encouraging public cooperation with the police and courts.* New York: Russell Sage Foundation.

U.S. Department of Homeland Security. (2013, April 10). Available: http://www.dhs.gov/xlibrary/assets/dhs-orgchart.pdf

U.S. Department of Homeland Security. (n.d.). *Our mission.* Available: http://www.dhs.gov/our-mission

U.S. Department of Justice. (2010). *Criminal victimization in the United States, 2008 statistical tables.* Available: http://www.bjs.gov/content/pub/pdf/cvus08.pdf

U.S. Department of Justice. (2008, September 19). *Member of music piracy group sentenced to 18 months in prison* (U.S. Department of Justice press release). Available: http://washingtondc.fbi.gov/dojpressrel/pressrel08/wf091908b.htm

U.S. Department of Justice. (2004). *The nation's two crime measures.* Available: http://www.bjs.gov/content/pub/pdf/ntcm.pdf

U.S. Department of State. (2012, July 31). *National Counterterrorism Center: Annex of statistical information.* Available: http://www.state.gov/j/ct/rls/crt/2011/195555.htm.

Uchida, C. D., & Bynum, T. S. (1991). Search warrants, motions to suppress and lost cases: The effects of the exclusionary rule in seven jurisdictions. *Journal of Criminal Law and Criminology, 84*(4), 1034–1066.

United Nations Office on Drugs and Crime. (2011a, October). *Estimating illicit financial flows resulting from drug trafficking and other transnational organized crime.* Vienna, Austria: United Nations Office on Drugs and Crime. Available: http://www.unodc.org/documents/data-and-analysis/Studies/Illicit_financial_flows_2011_web.pdf

United Nations Office on Drugs and Crime. (2011b). *2011 global study on homicide: Trends, contexts, data.* Vienna, Austria: United Nations Office on Drugs and Crime. Available: http://www.unodc.org/documents/data-and-analysis/statistics/Homicide/Globa_study_on_homicide_2011_web.pdf

United Nations Office on Drugs and Crime. (2010). *The globalization of crime: A transnational organized crime threat assessment.* Vienna, Austria: United Nations Office on Drugs and Crime. Available: http://www.unodc.org/documents/data-and-analysis/tocta/TOCTA_Report_2010_low_res.pdf

United States v. Alvarez, 567 U.S. ___ (2012).

United States v. Arnold, 523 F.3d 941 (9th Cir. 2008).

United States v. Booker, 543 U.S. 220 (2005).

United States v. Brown, 333 U.S. 18 (1948).

United States v. Calandra, 414 U.S. 338 (1974).

United States v. Dunn, 480 U.S. 294 (1987).

United States v. Flores-Montano, 541 U.S. 149 (2004).

United States v. Graham, 846 F. Supp. 2d 384 (D. Md. 2012).

United States v. Hinson, 585 F.3d 1328 (10th Cir. 2009).

United States v. Jacobsen, 466 U.S. 109 (1984).

United States v. Jones, 565 U.S. ___ (2012).

United States v. Kyllo, 533 U.S. 27 (2001).

United States v. Lovett, 328 U.S. 303 (1946).

United States v. Matlock, 415 U.S. 164 (1974).

United States v. McConney, 728 F.2d 1195, 1199 (9th Circuit), *cert. denied,* 469 U.S. 824 (1984).

United States v. Martinez-Fuerte, 428 U.S. 543 (1976).

United States v. Miller, 425 U.S. 435 (1976).

United States v. Pantane, 542 U.S. 630 (2004).

United States v. Quintana, 594 F. Supp. 2d 1290 (U.S. District Court for the Middle District of Florida, 2008).

United States v. Salerno, 481 U.S. 739 (1987).

United States v. Santana, 427 U.S. 38 (1976).

United States v. State of Arizona, No. 10–16645 (U.S. Circuit Court of Appeals for the Ninth Circuit, 2011).

United States v. White, 401 U.S. 745 (1971).

United States v. Windsor, 570 U.S. ___ (2013).

van der Does, L., Newman, S., & Dawson, A. (2004). *High-quality pre-kindergarten: The key to crime prevention and school success in Tennessee.* Washington, D.C.: Fight Crime: Invest in Kids. Available: http://www.fightcrime.org/sites/default/files/reports/TNprek.pdf

Van Maanen, J. (1974). Working the street: A developmental view of police behavior. In H. Jacob (Ed.), *The potential for reform of criminal justice* (pp. 83–129). Beverly Hills, Calif.: Sage Publications.

Van Voorhis, P., & Presser, L. (2001). *Classification of women offenders: A national assessment of current practices.* Washington, D.C.: National Institute of Corrections. Available: http://static.nicic.gov/Library/017082.pdf

Van Vugt, E., Gibbs, J., Jan Stams, G., Bijleveld, C., Hendriks, J., & van der Laan, P. (2011). Moral development and recidivism: A meta-analysis. *International Journal of Offender Therapy and Comparative Criminology, 55,* 1234–1250.

Varnum, T. G. (2008). Let's not jump to conclusions: Approaching felon disenfranchisement challenges under the Voting Rights Act. *Michigan Journal of Race and Law, 14,* 109–142.

Vars, F. E., & Young, A. A. (2013). Do the mentally ill have a right to bear arms? *Wake Forest Law Review, 48,* 1–24.

Vaughn, M. (1994, Fall). Boot camps. *The Grapevine, 2,* 2.

Veit, H. E., Rowling, K. R., & Bickford, C. B. (Eds.). (1991). *Creating the Bill of Rights: The documentary record from the First Federal Congress.* Baltimore: Johns Hopkins University Press.

Velasquez, M. (2002). *Philosophy: A text with readings* (8th ed.). Stamford, Conn.: Wadsworth.

Vermeersch, H., T'Sjoen, G., Kaufman, J., & Van Houtte. (2013). Social science theories on adolescent risk-taking: The relevance of behavioral inhibition and activation. *Youth & Society, 45,* 27–53.

Veysey, B. M., & Zgoba, K. M. (2010). Sex offenses and offenders reconsidered: An investigation of characteristics and correlates over time. *Criminal Justice and Behavior, 37,* 583–595.

Victor v. Nebraska, 511 U.S. 1 (1994).

Virginia Criminal Sentencing Commission. (n.d.). *Sentence revocation report.* Richmond: Virginia Criminal Sentencing Commission. Available: http://www.vcsc.state.va.us/worksheets_2007/SSR_booklet2007.pdf

Virginia governor apologizes for eugenics law. (2002, May 2). *USA Today.* Available: http://usatoday30.usatoday.com/news/nation/2002/05/02/virginia-eugenics.htm

Virginia v. Black, 538 U.S. 343 (2003).

Virkkunen, M. (1987). Metabolic dysfunctions among habitually violent offenders: Reactive hypoglycemia and cholesterol levels. In S. A. Mednick, T. E. Moffitt, & S. A. Stack (Eds.), *The causes of crime: New biological approaches* (pp. 292–311). New York: Cambridge University Press.

Vogel, N. (2007, February 23). Spanking ban plan revisited. *Los Angeles Times.* Available: http://articles.latimes.com/2007/feb/23/local/me-spank23

Vold, G. B., Bernard, T. J., & Snipes, J. B. (1998). *Theoretical criminology* (4th ed.). New York: Oxford University Press.

Vollum, S., & Longmire, D. R. (2007). Covictims of capital murder: Statements of victims' family members and friends made at the time of execution. *Violence and Victims, 22,* 601–619.

Vrij, A. (2008). *Detecting lies and deceit: Pitfalls and opportunities.* Chichester, UK: Wiley.

Wagatsuma, H., & Rosett, A. (1986). The implications of apology: Law and culture in Japan and the United States. *Law and Society Review, 20,* 461–498.

Wagner, A. (2008). *Good order and safety: A history of the St. Louis Metropolitan Police Department, 1861–1906.* St. Louis: Missouri History Museum.

Wagner, K., Owen, S., & Burke, T. (2013). What makes a crime? The perceived harmfulness, wrongfulness, and seriousness of offenses against nonhuman animals. Manuscript submitted for publication.

Wagner, M., McBride, R. E., & Crouse, S. F. (1999). The effects of weight-training exercise on aggression variables in adult male inmates. *Prison Journal, 79,* 72–89.

Wald, M. L. (2010, January 12). Mixed signals on airport scanners. *New York Times.* Available: http://www.nytimes.com/2010/01/13/us/13scanners.html

Walker, J. T. (2007). Eliminate residency restrictions for sex offenders. *Criminology and Public Policy, 6,* 863–870.

Walker, J. T., & Moak, S. (2010, February). Child's play or child pornography: The need for better laws regarding sexting. *ACJS Today, 35,* 1, 3–9.

Walker, S. (2006). *Sense and non-sense about crime and drugs: A policy guide* (6th ed.). Belmont, Calif.: Wadsworth.

Walker, S. (1997). *Popular justice: A history of American criminal justice.* New York: Oxford University Press.

Walker, S. (1993). Does anyone remember team policing? Lessons of the team policing experience for community policing. *American Journal of Police, 12*(1), 33–56.

Walker, S. (1984). "Broken windows" and fractured history: The use and misuse of history in recent police patrol analysis. *Justice Quarterly, 1,* 75–90.

Walker, S. (1980). *Popular justice: A history of American criminal justice.* New York: Oxford University Press.

Walmsley, R. (2011). *World prison population list* (9th ed.). London: International Centre for Prison Studies. Available: http://www.idcr.org.uk/wp-content/uploads/2010/09/WPPL-9-22.pdf

Walsh, A., & Hemmens, C. (2008). *Law, justice, and society: A sociolegal introduction.* New York: Oxford University Press.

Walshok, M. L. (1971). The emergence of middle-class deviant subcultures: The case of swingers. *Social Problems, 18*(4), 488–495.

Walzer, M. (1984). *Spheres of justice: A defense of pluralism and equality.* New York: Basic Books.

Wang, V., Haines, K., & Tucker, J. V. (2011). Deviance and control in communities with perfect surveillance—the case of Second Life. *Surveillance and Society, 9,* 31–46.

Warden v. Hayden, 387 U.S. 294 (1967).

Washburn, K. K. (2008). Restoring the grand jury. *Fordham Law Review, 76,* 2333–2388.

Washington v. Glucksberg, 521 U.S. 702 (1997).

Wasserman, G. A., Keenan, K., Tremblay, R. E., Coie, J. D., Herrenkohl, T. I., Loeber, R., & Petechuk, D. (2003). *Risk and protective factors of child delinquency* (Child Delinquency Bulletin Series). Available: http://www.ncjrs.gov/pdffiles1/ojjdp/193409.pdf

Weber, M. (1997). Bureaucracy. In J. M. Shafritz & A. C. Hyde (Eds.), *Classics of public administration* (4th ed., pp. 37–43). Fort Worth, Tex.: Harcourt Brace College Publishers. (Original work published 1946)

Webster, D. (1914). *The great speeches and orations of Daniel Webster.* Boston: Little, Brown.

Wechsler, H. (1954). The political safeguards of federalism: The role of the states in the composition and selection of the national government. *Columbia Law Review, 54,* 543–560.

Weeks v. United States, 232 U.S. 383 (1914).

Weems v. United States, 217 U.S. 349 (1910).

Weisburd, D., Bushway, S., Lum, C., & Yang, S. (2004). Trajectories of crime at places: A longitudinal study of street segments in the city of Seattle. *Criminology, 42,* 283–322.

Weiser, B. (2013a, March 12). "Ugly thoughts" defense fails as officer is convicted in cannibal plot. *New York Times.* Retrieved from http://www.nytimes.com/2013/03/13/nyregion/gilberto-valle-is-found-guilty-in-cannibal-case.html?pagewanted=all&_r=0

Weiser, B. (2013b, March 12). Psychiatrist to testify on deviance of officer. *New York Times.* Retrieved from http://www.nytimes.com/2013/01/08/nyregion/psychiatrist-to-testify-about-deviance-at-officers-trial.html

Weitzer, R. (2002). Incidents of police misconduct and public opinion. *Journal of Criminal Justice, 30,* 397–408.

Welch, M., Weber, L., & Edwards, W. (2000). "All the news that's fit to print": A content analysis of the correctional debate in the *New York Times. Prison Journal, 80,* 245–264.

Wellman, C. (2006, Spring). A defense of stiffer penalties for crimes. *Hypatia, 21*(2), 62–80.

Wells, M. (1991). Behind the parity debate: The decline of the legal process tradition in the law of federal courts. *Boston University Law Review, 71,* 609–644.

Welsh, B. C. (2006). Evidence-based policing for crime prevention. In D. Weisburd & A. A. Braga (Eds.), *Police innovation: Contrasting perspectives* (pp. 305–321). New York: Cambridge University Press.

Welsh, B. C., & Farrington, D. P. (2011). Evidence-based crime policy. In M. Tonry (Ed.), *The Oxford handbook of crime and criminal justice* (pp. 60–92). New York: Oxford University Press.

Welsh, B. C., & Farrington, D. P. (2009). Public area CCTV and crime prevention: An updated systematic review and meta-analysis. *Justice Quarterly, 26,* 716–745.

Welsh, B. C., & Farrington, D. P. (2008). Effects of improved street lighting on crime. *Campbell Systematic Reviews, 13.* Available: www.campbellcollaboration.org/lib/download/223/

Welsh, B. C., & Farrington, D. P. (2007). Save children from a life of crime. *Criminology and Public Policy, 6,* 871–880.

West, A. (2007). The Georgia legislature strikes with a vengeance! Sex offender residency restrictions and the deterioration of the *ex post facto* clause. *Catholic University Law Review, 57,* 239–268.

West, R. (1988). Jurisprudence and gender. *University of Chicago Law Review, 55,* 1–72.

Westley, W. A. (1970). *Violence & the police: A sociological study of law, custom, and morality.* Cambridge, Mass.: MIT Press.

White Tail Park v. Stroube, 413 F.3d 451 (2005).

White, M. D., & Klinger, D. (2012). Contagious fire? An empirical assessment of the problem of multi-shooter, multi-shot deadly force incidents in police work. *Crime and Delinquency, 58,* 196–211.

Widom, C. S., & Maxfield, M. G. (2001, February). *An update on the "cycle of violence"* [National Institute of Justice Research in Brief]. Available: http://www.ncjrs.gov/pdffiles1/nij/184894.pdf

Wilkerson v. Utah, 99 U.S. 130 (1878).

Williams v. Florida, 399 U.S. 78 (1970).

Williams, H., & Murphy, P. V. (1990, January). The evolving strategy of police: A minority view. *Perspectives on Policing,* No. 13. Available: https://www.ncjrs.gov/pdffiles1/nij/121019.pdf

Williams, J. (2003). Criminal justice policy innovation in the states. *Criminal Justice Policy Review, 14,* 401–422.

Williams, M. R., & Holcomb, J. E. (2001). Racial disparity and death sentences in Ohio. *Journal of Criminal Justice, 29,* 207–218.

Willis v. State, 888 N.E.2d 177 (Supreme Court of Indiana, 2008).

Wilson, J. Q. (1989). *Bureaucracy: What government agencies do and why they do it.* New York: Basic Books.

Wilson, J. Q. (1974). *Varieties of police behavior.* New York: Atheneum Publishers.

Wilson, J. Q., & Kelling, G. L. (1989, February). Making neighborhoods safe. *Atlantic Monthly,* pp. 46–52.

Wilson, J. Q., & Kelling, G. L. (1982, March). Broken windows: The police and neighborhood safety. *Atlantic Monthly, 211,* 29–38.

Wilson, W. (1997). The study of administration. In J. M. Shafritz & A. C. Hyde (Eds.), *Classics of public administration* (4th ed., pp. 14–26). Fort Worth, Tex.: Harcourt Brace College Publishers. (Original work published 1887)

Wintemute, G. (2000). Guns and gun violence. In A. Blumstein & J. Wallman (Eds.), *The crime drop in America* (pp. 45–96). New York: Cambridge University Press.

Wisconsin v. Oakley, 629 N.W.2d 200 (Supreme Court of Wisconsin, 2001).

Wolf v. Colorado, 338 U.S. 25 (1949).

Wolfe, N. T. (1981). Mala in se: A disappearing doctrine? *Criminology, 19,* 131–143.

Wolfenden Report: Report of the Committee of Homosexual Offenses and Prostitution. (1963). New York: Stein and Day.

Wonders, N. A. (1999). Postmodern feminist criminology and social justice. In B. A. Arrigo (Ed.), *Social justice, criminal justice: The maturation of critical theory in law, crime, and deviance* (pp. 111–128). Belmont, Calif.: West/Wadsworth.

Woodson v. North Carolina, 428 U.S. 280 (1976).

Worrall, J. L. (2004). The effect of three-strikes legislation on serious crime in California. *Journal of Criminal Justice, 32,* 283–296.

Wright, J. P., Moore, K., & Newsome, J. (2011). Molecular genetics and crime. In K. M. Beaver & A. Walsh (Eds.), *The Ashgate Research Companion to biosocial theories of crime* (pp. 93–114). Burlington, Vt.: Ashgate Publishing.

Wright, K. N. (1981). The desirability of goal conflict within the criminal justice system. *Journal of Criminal Justice, 9,* 209–218.

Yates, J., & Gillespie, W. (2002). The problem of sports violence and the criminal prosecution solution. *Cornell Journal of Law and Public Policy, 12,* 145–168.

Young, E. A. (2005). Institutional settlement in a globalizing judicial system. *Duke Law Journal, 54,* 1143–1261.

Youngberg v. Romeo, 457 U.S. 307 (1982).

Zalman, M., Larson, M. J., & Smith, B. (2012). Citizens' attitudes toward wrongful convictions. *Criminal Justice Review, 37,* 51–69.

Zalman, M., & Smith, B. W. (2007). The attitudes of police executives toward *Miranda* and interrogation policies. *Journal of Criminal Law and Criminology, 97,* 873–940.

Zender, L. (1995). Wayward sisters: The prison for women. In N. Morris & D. J. Rothman (Eds.), *The Oxford history of the prison: The practice of punishment in Western society* (pp. 328–361). New York: Oxford University Press.

Zimring, F. E. (2007). Protect individual punishment decisions from mandatory penalties. *Criminology and Public Policy, 6,* 881–886.

Zimring, F. E. (2003). *The contradictions of American capital punishment.* New York: Oxford University Press.

Zimring, F. E., & Hawkins, G. (1997). *Crime is not the problem: Lethal violence in America.* New York: Oxford University Press.

Zolotor, A. J., Theodore, A. D., Runyan, D. K., Chang, J. J., & Laskey, A. L. (2011). Corporal punishment and physical abuse: Population-based trends for three-to-11-year-old children in the United States. *Child Abuse Review, 20,* 57–66.

Zwicker v. Koota, 389 U.S. 241 (1972).

GLOSSARY

A posteriori. Reasoning that is based on empiricism, grounded in observations, data, and experiences. Most associated with pragmatism. (Chapter 2)

A priori. Reasoning that occurs without empiricism and which may stem from sources including tenacity, authority, or common-sense arguments offered without evidence. Most associated with idealism. (Chapter 2)

Actus reus. One component of the legal definition of crime, expressed in a Latin phrase meaning "evil act." The *actus reus* of a crime is the actual act, conduct, or behavior that is prohibited under law. (Chapter 9)

Adjudication. The formal process for resolving legal disputes in courts of law. (Chapter 12)

Agenda setting. The process by which an issue is identified as one that needs to be addressed through policy or law. This is often a political process. (Chapter 7)

Agents of direct social control. Those who attempt to punish or neutralize organizations and individuals who deviate from society's norms. Such agents include social welfare agencies, science and medicine, and government. Compare to **agents of ideological social control**. (Chapter 4)

Agents of ideological social control. Those who attempt to shape the consciousness of people in society by influencing ideas, attitudes, morals, and values. Such agents include the family, educational institutions, religion, organized sports, the media, and the government and help to maintain the status quo by persuading citizens to willingly comply with laws. Compare to **agents of direct social control**. (Chapter 4)

Aggravating circumstances. In capital cases, where a death sentence may be given, these are conditions specified in law that make a crime particulalry heinous. In the second phase of a bifurcated trial, jurors must find beyond a reasonable doubt that one or more aggravating circumstances were present in order to give a death sentence. In other cases, factors which render the circumstances surrounding an offense or the harms it causes worse than a typical offense of that type; may be considered in the application of sentencing guidelines. *See also* **mitigating circumstances, bifurcated trial**, **sentencing guidelines**. (Chapter 10; Chapter 12)

Antisocial personality. A personality type associated with criminal activity and marked by failure to conform to norms, deceitfulness, impulsivity, aggressiveness, disregard for safety, irresponsibility, and lack of remorse. Also known as *psychopath* or *sociopath.* (Chapter 5)

Apartheid. A former policy in South Africa, abolished in the 1990s, of state-sanctioned racial segregation in which the all-white government repressed the rights, freedoms, and political participation of the majority of the population, who were black. (Chapter 6)

Appeal. In criminal cases, the defendant has the right to file an appeal requesting that an appellate court review the decision made by a lower court. Appeals may be filed after a sentence has been imposed and final judgment entered in a case and primarily focus on substantive due process and procedural justice rather than on factual issues of guilt or innocence. (Chapter 12)

Appellate jurisdiction. A court that reviews the proceedings of a lower court of original jurisdiction. *See also* **appeal**. (Chapter 12)

Application of law. One of the six concepts of law, addressing whether the law is applied uniformly by all or in a manner that leaves room for interpretation. *See also* **six concepts of law**. (Chapter 3)

Arraignment. A judicial proceeding at which a person accused of a crime is formally advised of the charges by the reading of the charging document in open court, advised of his or her rights, and asked to enter a plea (e.g., guilty, not guilty, *nolo contendere*) to the charges. (Chapters 1, 12)

Atavism. A historical theory of criminology holding that persons were born criminals as the result of inherited traits. This theory has been discredited by modern criminologists. (Chapter 5)

Atavistic. Under the theory of **atavism**, the term referred to persons who were born criminals. (Chapter 5)

Attendant circumstances. One component of the legal definition of crime, related to specific circumstances which must surround the *actus reus* (criminal act) for a crime to occur or for it to be punished in a particular manner. (Chapter 9)

Attitudinal model. A model of judicial decision making which suggests that courts decide cases based on the judges' attitudes and values. (Chapter 3)

Authoritarian model. A model of justice that focuses on the needs of society but not on the needs of the offender. Under the model, outcomes are highly important but process is not important. Compare to **compassionate model**, **mechanical model**, and **participatory model**. (Chapter 6)

Bail. A financial pledge to ensure that a person accused of a crime will appear in court for trial. The accused person posts a sum of money (or a property title) to the court in exchange for being released prior to trial; if the accused appears for trial, the money or property title is returned. Bail bond agents may post the bail for an accused person in exchange for a fee that is not returned. (Chapter 10)

Banishment. A type of punishment in which offenders were banned from, and prohibited from returning to, an area. (Chapters 9, 13)

Bench trial. A trial in which the judge, rather than the jury, acts as finder of fact (e.g., determining guilt or innocence). Bench trials may occur for some misdemeanors for which trials by jury are not available or when a defendant waives his or her right to a trial by jury. Compare to **trial by jury**. (Chapters 1, 8, 12)

Beyond a reasonable doubt. The burden of proof necessary to find a defendant guilty of a crime, whether in a trial by jury or a bench trial. Although a higher standard than probable cause but a lower standard than absolute certainty, there is no precise way to quantify how much proof it takes to reach the standard of beyond a reasonable doubt. (Chapter 12)

Bifurcated trial. The two-part trial used in capital cases, where the death penalty is a possible sentence. The first part of the trial is to determine guilt or innocence and the second part is to determine whether to sentence the offender to life in prison or to death. (Chapter 10)

Bill of attainder. A legislative act that declares someone guilty of a crime and imposes punishment for it in the absence of a trial. The U.S. Constitution prohibits bills of attainder. (Chapter 8)

Bill of Rights. The first 10 amendments to the U.S. Constitution, which identify rights and liberties and restrain the powers of the government through both substantive and procedural due process. (Chapter 8)

Binds over. Refers to when a judge in a preliminary hearing finds that there is probable cause to believe a defendant committed a felony and accordingly holds that the defendant must stand trial. *See also* **preliminary hearing**. (Chapter 12)

Blue laws. Laws that required businesses to be closed, and prohibited other activities, on Sundays. Over time, most of these laws have been repealed. (Chapter 1)

Bobbies. The name given to police officers in England in the 1800s; named for Sir Robert Peel, who created the first metropolitan police department in 1829. (Chapter 11)

Brief. A written document that is used to make legal arguments in the appeals process. *See also* **appeal**. (Chapter 12)

Broken windows policing. A strategy to reduce disorder in neighborhoods which focuses police attention on enforcement of minor offenses. (Chapter 11)

Bureaucratic agency. An organization that is governed by rules and procedures, is organized in a hierarchy with clear lines of supervision, requires substantial amounts of paperwork, and requires training of employees. Criminal justice agencies are bureaucratic agencies. (Chapter 1)

Bureaucrats. Persons who work within the executive branch of government and agencies that comprise it. They are responsible for implementing policies. (Chapter 7)

Capital punishment. The death penalty. (Chapter 10)

Cause-in-fact. One type of causation recognized by the law when linking an *actus reus* with a result. Cause in fact has occurred if a person commits an act that directly brings about a particular result and may be determined by asking the question, would the result have occurred without the defendant's conduct? If the answer is "no," cause-in-fact exists. Compare to **proximate cause**. (Chapter 9)

Celebrated cases. Cases and trials that draw substantial amounts of public attention and which are closely followed by the media. *See also* **criminal justice wedding cake model**. (Chapter 7)

Certiorari. Persons seeking appellate review of their case after their initial appeal may ask a higher court to hear their case by filing a petition for a writ of *certiorari*. *Certiorari* is rarely granted. (Chapter 12)

Charge bargaining. A form of plea bargaining in which the defendant pleads guilty to a less serious charge than the one in the charging document. *See also* **plea bargaining**. Compare to **count bargaining** and **sentence bargaining**. (Chapter 12)

Civil justice. A process, separate from criminal justice, in which private wrongs are addressed through legal action. This generally occurs through the filing of lawsuits by one person, organization, group, etc., against another. A tort is one common type of civil justice action. (Chapter 7)

Class control theory. A developmental theory of American policing suggesting that the police were created by the rich and powerful to control and prevent the upward mobility of those (often members of the working class) perceived as dangerous classes. *See also* **dangerous classes**. (Chapter 11)

Classical criminology. A set of explanations for crime based on the concept of free will, or the idea that individuals simply choose whether or not to commit a criminal act. (Chapter 5)

Classification. The process by which correctional officials determine the prison and security level to which an inmate should be assigned. (Chapter 13)

Clearance rate. A statistic indicating the percentage of cases that are solved, or cleared, usually through the arrest of a suspect. (Chapter 1)

Code of ethics. A statement that guides employees about moral questions and ethical expectations specific to a particular workplace or working environment. Professions have codes of ethics that can guide professionals in discretionary decision making. (Chapter 1)

Code of Hammurabi. A well-known codification of ancient Babylonian laws from around 1800 B.C.E. The code focused heavily on retribution and the principle of *lex talionis*. (Chapter 9)

Code of Ur-Namma. The earliest known set of written laws, from Sumer around 2100 B.C.E. The code used monetary fines as the predominant form of punishment. (Chapter 9)

Collective efficacy. Cohesion and mutual trust among neighbors, which can lead to strong informal social control in a neighborhood. Synonym for **social capital**. (Chapter 11)

Collective judgment. The consensus that members of a society would reach about which behaviors are morally acceptable and which behaviors are morally unacceptable. This was instrumental to Patrick Devlin's theory of legal moralism. (Chapter 3)

Commerce Clause. A clause in the U.S. Constitution that gives the federal government the power to regulate commerce with other nations and among the states. This clause has allowed the federal government to make and enforce a variety of criminal laws surrounding issues that involve interstate commerce, which may be very broadly defined. (Chapter 7)

Community problem-solving era. The era of policing from the 1970s to the present when the goals of the professional era were broadened to include not only crime control but also crime prevention and strengthened police–community relations and collaborations. Compare to **homeland security era**, **political era**, and **professional era**. (Chapter 11)

Community-oriented policing. A policing strategy with the basic philosophy of fostering a positive working relationship between the police and the community. Also known as COP, there are many approaches to community-oriented policing, and it is currently popular in the United States. (Chapter 11)

Commutative justice. Defines justice as proportionality. Suggests that justice has been met when outcomes are allocated proportionally. (Chapter 6)

Compassionate model. A model of justice that places a higher emphasis on the offender's needs than on society's needs. The model suggests that justice is best achieved by identifying and correcting the needs of the offender that led him or her to commit crime. Compare to **authoritarian model**, **mechanical model**, and **participatory model**. (Chapter 6)

Compensatory social control. Focuses on providing restitution to the victim of a harmful act. This is typically accomplished through the civil justice system. Compare to **conciliatory social control**, **penal social control**, and **therapeutic social control**. (Chapter 4)

Complaint. A document completed by a police officer or private citizen accusing a person of committing a crime. (Chapter 12)

Compstat. A policing strategy that integrates computerized crime data and advanced crime mapping to analyze crime patterns, which police supervisors use to develop goals and strategies to reduce crime in their areas. (Chapter 11)

Concentric zone theory. Explains criminality in cities by suggesting that multiple zones, diagramed as concentric circles, emerge from the city's center. The theory holds that crime is most likely to occur in the transitional zone, which is described as a residential community undergoing transition to commercial or industrial uses and marked by social disorganization. (Chapter 5)

Conciliatory social control. Attempts to create and preserve social harmony via dispute resolution. This is accomplished through practices such as mediation. Compare to **compensatory social control**, **penal social control**, and **therapeutic social control**. (Chapter 4)

Conflict criminology. Suggests that crime is a consequence of the oppression of the lower classes by rich and powerful elites. (Chapter 5)

Conflict theory. Argues that decisions are made to benefit (financially or otherwise) those who hold power in society. (Chapter 13)

Confrontation Clause. The portion of the Sixth Amendment to the U.S. Constitution which guarantees that, in a trial, witnesses must provide their testimony in open court and be subject to cross-examination. (Chapter 8)

Congregate system. An early method of incarceration in which inmates lived in individual cells during the night but worked in factories and had meals in dining halls during the day. Absolute silence was required of inmates, even when outside their cells. (Chapter 13)

Contraband. Any item that prison or jail inmates are not permitted to possess. (Chapter 13)

Corporal punishment. The use of physical force with the intention of causing a child to experience pain, but not injury, for the purpose of correction or control of the child's behavior. (Chapter 10)

Correctional boot camps. A punishment alternative in which offenders live in a military-style environment, subject to drills with confrontational strategies and physical labor designed to build discipline. (Chapter 13)

Correctional institution. A secure facility designed to house persons accused or convicted of a crime. Jails and prisons are the two primary types of correctional institutions. *See also* **jail** and **prison**. (Chapter 13)

Corrections. The component of the criminal justice system responsible for carrying out sentences imposed by the criminal courts. May include prisons, jails, probation, parole, and other alternatives. (Chapter 13)

Corruption. Occurs when professional ethics are disregarded or when professionals engage in illegal activities. (Chapter 11)

Count bargaining. A form of plea bargaining in which a defendant charged with multiple offenses pleads guilty to only some of the charges in exchange for the others being dropped. *See also* **plea bargaining**. Compare to **charge bargaining** and **sentence bargaining**. (Chapter 12)

Courtroom workgroup. The working relationship that develops among court employees, including judges, prosecutors, defense attorneys, and others. (Chapter 12)

Craft. A career field in which entry into and training for the occupation are accomplished through an apprenticeship model, with current practitioners mentoring others into the field. Some have debated whether criminal justice is a profession or a craft. (Chapter 1)

Crime. Any behavior that the government chooses to regulate by passing a law prohibiting it (punishing those who engage in the behavior, called a *crime of commission*) or by passing a law requiring it (punishing those who do not do so, called a *crime of omission*). A more formal definition of crime is an intentional act or omission in violation of the criminal law, committed without defense or justification, and penalized by the government as a felony or misdemeanor. (Chapters 1, 9)

Crime control model. Assembly-line justice with a focus on getting an offender through the criminal justice process as quickly and efficiently as possible. This is one of Herbert Packer's two models of the criminal justice process. Compare to **due process model**. (Chapter 8)

Crime control theory. A developmental theory of American policing suggesting that police agencies were created to address an increase in crime and disorder as informal systems of social control were perceived to become less effective. (Chapter 11)

Crimes against property. Offenses that cause harm to an individual's property but do not physically harm the individual. (Chapter 9)

Crimes against the person. Offenses in which individuals are physically victimized or harmed. These are viewed as the most serious of criminal offenses. (Chapter 9)

Criminal justice. The study of society's response to crime, including crime prevention and the work of the criminal justice system. (Chapter 1)

Criminal justice system. The collection of criminal justice agencies (e.g., police, courts, corrections) and how they are structured to work together in processing criminal cases. (Chapter 1)

Criminal justice wedding cake model. An approach to classifying criminal cases into routine misdemeanors, serious felonies, and celebrated cases. *See also* **celebrated cases**. (Chapter 7)

Criminologist. A scholar of criminology, studying crime trends and why persons commit criminal acts. (Chapter 5)

Criminology. The scientific study of crime trends, the nature of crime, and explanations for why persons commit crimes. (Chapters 1, 5)

Critical legal studies. A theory of legal reasoning which emerged in the 1970s and argues that law is politics and designed to maintain the status quo in society. Critical race theory, feminist jurisprudence, and postmodern jurisprudence are variations of critical legal studies. (Chapter 12)

Critical race theory. A perspective of legal reasoning drawing upon critical legal studies and focusing on the experience of racial and ethnic minorities with the legal system. (Chapter 12)

Critical theories of law. A legal philosophy holding that the law was created and is used by powerful individuals to help them remain in power. (Chapter 3)

Cruel and unusual punishment. Prohibited under the Eighth Amendment of the U.S. Constitution. However, there are differing legal interpretations as to what constitutes cruel and unusual punishment. (Chapter 10)

Culpability. Guilt or responsibility for a criminal offense. Only individuals with culpability may be punished. (Chapter 10)

Culture of control. The idea described by David Garland suggesting that American correctional systems, and the criminal justice system in general, are marked by a desire for security, order, control, and risk management, with an increased use of rules, technology, and surveillance to control deviant behaviors. (Chapter 13)

Custody. Includes situations when someone is under formal arrest and also situations in which a reasonable person would not feel free to end questioning and leave. *Miranda* warnings must be given prior to custodial interrogation. *See also* **interrogation**. (Chapter 8)

Dangerous classes. Groups of persons who are targeted for punishment more often than the general population because they are labeled as deviant or dangerous by society. The label may be based on untrue perceptions or discrimination rather than on actual threats. (Chapter 10)

Dark figure of crime. Refers to the amount of crime that is not reported to the police or other authorities. An example is the gap between the official Uniform Crime Report crime rates and those suggested by the National Crime Victimization Survey. (Chapter 1)

Data. Careful and systematic observations that are analyzed to draw a conclusion about a research question. Examples of data include statistics, interviews, survey responses, and more. (Chapter 2)

Day fines. A type of fine that is scaled according to an offender's income rather than being the same for all persons who commit an offense. (Chapter 10)

Day reporting center. A facility offering programs for offenders, but rather than living at the facility, offenders are only required to check in daily. Day reporting centers are an intermediate sanction. (Chapter 13)

Death-qualified jury. A jury selected to hear a capital case, where the death penalty is a possible sentence. A death-qualified jury is composed of persons who, during the jury selection process, indicate that they would be willing to impose the death penalty. (Chapter 10)

Debtor's prison. A type of facility (no longer in current use) used in the colonial era to hold persons who could not pay their debts. (Chapter 13)

Decarceration. A movement in the 1960s and 1970s emphasizing a reduced use of jails and prisons, instead focusing on community-based, sometimes therapeutic, forms of social control. (Chapter 4)

Decentralization. The lack of a single centralized national police force; instead, each geographic area, such as a state, city, town, or county, has its own police force. Related to federalism, this reflects the structure of American policing. (Chapter 11)

Defense. Various reasons, recognized under the law, individuals should not be held criminally responsible for the commission of acts that are defined as crimes. If a defendant charged with a crime successfully argues that his or her conduct falls under a recognized defense, then he or she may be found not guilty. *See also* **defense of excuse**, **defense of justification**, and **procedural defense**. (Chapter 9)

Defense attorneys. Lawyers who represent persons accused of a crime. Defense attorneys may be private attorneys hired by accused persons who can afford to do so, private attorneys appointed by the court to represent indigent persons, or state employees whose full-time job is to represent indigent persons. (Chapter 12)

Defense of excuse. Defenses in which a defendant admits to having committed an *actus reus* prohibited under the law but asserts that he or she did so under special circumstances that mitigate or excuse criminal liability. These defenses center on suggesting that the defendant was unable

to have a fully formed *mens rea*. Defenses of excuse include infancy of age, insanity, mistake, intoxication, and duress. (Chapter 9)

Defense of justification. Defenses in which a defendant admits to having committed an *actus reus* prohibited under the law but asserts that circumstances surrounding the act itself render it justifiable. These defenses assume that an act was deliberate, with *mens rea,* but argue that the reasons for the act were justifiable under the law. Defenses of justification include self-defense, defense of others, defense of property, consent, and execution of public duties. (Chapter 9)

Deinstitutionalization. A movement in the 1960s and 1970s in which persons were released from mental hospitals in favor of community-based, often therapeutic, social control. (Chapter 4)

Deity. What one believes about the nature of a supreme being. (Chapter 2)

Delinquent subcultures. A criminological theory suggesting that some youth create their own system of values and norms, or their own subculture, to acquire the status they seek. In doing so, members of the subculture may turn to crime. (Chapter 5)

Democratic socialism. A model of government in which a democracy seeks to use taxes and regulation to achieve goals of a **socialist** ideology. (Chapter 6)

Demonology. A historical perspective on criminology that attributes criminal behavior to the influence of evil spirits or demons. This theory has been rejected by modern criminologists. (Chapter 5)

Demonstrative evidence. A form of evidence that includes items such as maps, photos, diagrams, computer simulations, and other aids designed for use at trial to help demonstrate some fact to the judge or jury. *See also* **evidence**. Compare to **physical evidence**, **scientific evidence**, and **testimony**. (Chapter 12)

Deprivation hypothesis. An explanation for prisonization suggesting that the nature of the prison environment and its deprivations shape inmate behavior. Compare to **importation hypothesis**. (Chapter 13)

Determinate sentencing. A method of sentencing that limits judges' discretion by requiring specific sentences for a particular crime (as in a mandatory sentence) or by providing sentencing guidelines that use numerical scales and tables to arrive at the recommended sentence for a particular case. Compare to **indeterminate sentencing**. (Chapter 12)

Deviance. Behaviors that violate society's expectations, beliefs, standards, or values. As such, deviance refers to any departure from behaviors that are typical, acceptable, or accepted. Therefore, deviant behaviors violate social norms and often generate negative reactions from the agents of social control. Crime is one form of deviance. (Chapters 1, 4, 5)

Differential association theory. Suggests that criminal behavior occurs because offenders learn it from others. (Chapter 5)

Diffusion. Occurs when a crime prevention program reduces crime in the area where it is implemented and in the surrounding areas, as well. Opposite of **displacement**. (Chapter 11)

Dillon's Rule. The principle that local governments are creations of the legislature, meaning that local governments only have as much power as state governments decide they should have. This means that local governments are not as important as the state and federal governments under American federalism. (Chapter 7)

Dirty Harry problem. A dilemma faced by law enforcement officers when considering whether it is ever acceptable to use an ethically inappropriate method to achieve a morally good result. The Dirty Harry problem is the subject of many discussions about police ethics and procedural justice. (Chapter 11)

Discourse perspective justice. A perspective that emphasizes a public dialogue or discourse in which the public reaches consensus on what is or is not just. (Chapter 6)

Discovery. The process by which the parties (defense and prosecution) to a criminal case exchange relevant information about that case. The purpose of discovery is to prevent unfair surprises at trial. (Chapter 12)

Discretion. A criminal justice professional's ability to use professional judgment rather than being constrained by rigid rules when making decisions about how to handle a case. Discretion is common throughout the criminal justice system. (Chapter 1)

Discretion in law. One of the six concepts of law, which considers whether discretion should or should not be encouraged in the enforcement of the law. *See also* **six concepts of law**. (Chapter 3)

Disintegrative shaming. A form of shaming that, as a result of public shaming or scolding, labels offenders as deviant, thereby separating them from the community rather

than reintegrating them into it. Compare to **reintegrative shaming**. (Chapter 10)

Disorder theory. A developmental theory of American policing that suggested large-scale disruptive events and the need to suppress mob violence led to the development of police agencies. (Chapter 11)

Displacement. Occurs when crime goes down in an area where a crime prevention program is implemented, but increases in other locations. Opposite of **diffusion**. (Chapter 11)

Dissenting opinion. An opinion in a Supreme Court (or other appellate court) case written by justices who disagree with the majority opinion. Although a dissenting opinion does not become law, it does serve as a statement of a justice's beliefs. (Chapter 3)

Distributive justice. A perspective on justice that focuses on what individuals are due. As such, distributive justice focuses on the end results of how outcomes are distributed. (Chapter 6)

Diversity of citizenship. Occurs when parties to a lawsuit are all from different states. When this occurs in disputes involving a certain amount of money, federal courts may adjudicate state law claims. (Chapter 12)

DNA database. Files maintained by state and federal governments that archive DNA (deoxyribonucleic acid) samples from known offenders. When DNA is retrieved in an unsolved case, it can be compared to the samples in the database to see if there is a match. (Chapter 1)

Double jeopardy. Bars the same governmental entity from criminally prosecuting someone twice for the same offense or from giving multiple punishments for the same offense. However, there are some exceptions to the general principles of double jeopardy. (Chapter 8)

Drug court. A collaborative, team-based program designed to help drug offenders in which the prosecuting attorney, defense attorney, probation officer, substance abuse treatment counselor, and judge meet regularly to review and reward (or punish) each offender's progress (or lack thereof). (Chapter 12)

Due Process Clause. The provision in the Fourteenth Amendment to the U.S. Constitution that makes nearly all of the criminal procedural rights contained in the Bill of Rights applicable to the states. Also serves as an independent source for other procedural justice rights or substantive due process rights not otherwise listed in the Constitution or Bill of Rights. (Chapter 8)

Due process model. Focuses on the rights of the accused and advocates formal decision-making procedures, drawing upon the assumption that the accused is innocent until proven guilty. This is one of Herbert Packer's two models of the criminal justice process. Compare to **crime control model**. (Chapter 8)

Effective assistance of counsel. Guaranteed by the Sixth Amendment to the U.S. Constitution. If a lawyer's performance falls so far below the standard of reasonable competence that the outcome of the case is likely to be unfair or unreliable, then a defendant has been denied effective assistance of counsel and a new trial may occur. (Chapter 8)

Electronic monitoring. A program in which offenders must wear a device, usually in an ankle bracelet, that monitors their location. Often used in combination with house arrest. Electronic monitoring is an intermediate sanction. *See also* **house arrest**. (Chapter 13)

Emergency management. The study of preparation for, response to, and recovery from disaster or crisis situations. (Chapter 1)

Empiricism. The notion that the answers to questions should be grounded in the collection and analysis of data. This approach guides scholars in criminal justice and other fields. (Chapter 2)

Entrapment. A procedural defense that occurs when law enforcement agents induce someone to commit a crime that he or she was not predisposed to commit. (Chapter 9)

Equal protection. In legal terms, treating persons consistent with the concept of equality. (Chapter 8)

Equal Protection Clause. The provision in the Fourteenth Amendment to the U.S. Constitution that serves to guarantee equality, requiring that the law treat similarly situated people in a similar manner without discrimination. (Chapter 8)

Equality. Refers to protections that promote equal rights for all persons without discrimination regardless of characteristics such as race, gender, religion, disability status, veteran status, sexual orientation, income, and more. Equality is a fundamental component of American political culture. (Chapter 7)

Essential tension. A concept described by Thomas Kuhn that reflects a conflict between ideals of what should be and the observable world as it actually is. (Chapter 13)

Establishment Clause. One of two clauses in the First Amendment to the U.S. Constitution relevant to

religious freedom. The Establishment Clause prohibits laws that establish an official state religion or that favor one religion over another. Compare to **Free Exercise Clause**. (Chapter 9)

Ethics. The application of morality in a professional setting. Often codified in professional codes of ethics. (Chapter 11)

Eugenics. The study of genetic factors that may influence future generations. Was also a term used to refer to programs, since discredited, that used medical interventions to sterilize persons who were labeled as having bad genes. (Chapter 5)

Evidence. Anything that helps prove or disprove a fact. May include physical evidence, sworn testimony, scientific evidence, or demonstrative evidence. (Chapter 12)

Ex post facto. A law punishing an act or behavior that was not criminal when it was committed. *Ex post facto* laws are prohibited under the U.S. Constitution because fairness requires that punishments can only be given when offenders have the opportunity to know that their behavior was criminalized. (Chapter 8)

Exclusionary rule. Stipulates that illegally seized evidence may not be admissible at trial. Established by Supreme Court interpretations of the Fourth Amendment. There are, however, many exceptions to the exclusionary rule. (Chapter 8)

Exculpatory evidence. Any evidence that may be favorable to the defendant in a criminal trial, either by casting doubt on the defendant's guilt or mitigating the defendant's culpability. The prosecution must disclose all exculpatory evidence to the defense as part of the discovery process. (Chapter 12)

Exigent circumstances. Emergency circumstances when a reasonable person would believe prompt action was necessary to prevent harm, the destruction of evidence, escape, or other such consequences. Exigent circumstances may permit exceptions to Fourth Amendment requirements. (Chapter 8)

Exoneration. Refers to a situation in which a person convicted of a crime is excused from legal consequences after the discovery of evidence of his or her innocence. (Chapter 6)

Expiation. A view of retribution based on the idea of atonement through suffering. Expiation is based on the idea that crime causes pain to the victim, so the only way for the offender to repent or learn a lesson is through experiencing pain. (Chapter 10)

External/relational social control. A type of informal social control that depends on a person's interactions with others, in which positive or negative reactions from others lead individuals to conform to social norms. Compare to **internal or self-control**. (Chapter 4)

Farm system. A historical method of incarceration used primarily in the American South in which inmates lived and worked on large prison farms. The prison farms were operated primarily by the inmates themselves, some of whom served as guards over the other inmates. Severe physical punishment was common at the prison farms. (Chapter 13)

Federalism. Having more than one level of government, as in the United States, which has a national government as well as 50 state governments in addition to counties and cities. (Chapter 7)

Felony. The most serious crimes, which are generally punished by a sentence to a year or more in prison and/or a substantial fine. Compare to **misdemeanors** and **infractions**. (Chapter 12)

Feminist criminology. A criminological perspective that examines the relationship between gender inequality, male dominance, and the exploitation of women under capitalism. Feminist criminologists focus on gender differences in crime, female offenders and victims, and gender inequities in the division of labor. (Chapter 5)

Feminist jurisprudence. A perspective of legal reasoning drawing upon critical legal studies and focusing on gender inequality in society as a function of law. (Chapter 12)

Fines. Financial penalties imposed when an offender has been found guilty of a crime. (Chapter 10)

Focal point of law. One of the six concepts of law, focused on how the success of the law is judged. Success of the law may be based on its outcomes or on its processes. *See also* **six concepts of law**. (Chapter 3)

Focused deterrence. A policing strategy with a three-step process. First, groups of offenders are told by family and community leaders how their actions have caused harms to the community. Second, offenders are offered resources to help them stop offending. Third, offenders are told that if they do not stop offending, an aggressive enforcement campaign will be launched against them by the police. (Chapter 11)

Folkways. Norms that are less formal and that tend not to be based on moral foundations. Compare to **mores**. (Chapter 4)

Forensic science. The application of scientific principles to cases progressing through the legal system, generally to aid in investigations and to prepare evidence for trials. (Chapter 1)

Formal social control. Mechanisms exercised by the government to control human behavior and to cause persons to conform to norms and obey laws. Criminal justice and criminal law are the most important tools of formal social control. Compare to **informal social control**. (Chapter 4)

Formation of law. One of the six concepts of law, considering how the law is created; the formation of law may be rational or irrational. *See also* **six concepts of law**. (Chapter 3)

Foundation of law. One of the six concepts of law, addressing the ideas or notions on which the law is based. Foundations of law may include public morality or private morality. *See also* **six concepts of law**. (Chapter 3)

Free Exercise Clause. One of two clauses in the First Amendment to the U.S. Constitution relevant to religious freedom. The Free Exercise Clause protects individuals' rights to act upon or practice their religious beliefs. Compare to **Establishment Clause**. (Chapter 9)

Fruit of the poisonous tree. A doctrine stipulating that further evidence acquired as a result of previously illegally obtained evidence may not be admissible in court. (Chapter 8)

General deterrence. A justification for punishment holding that the imposition of punishment, in general, will prevent (or deter) all persons in the public from committing criminal acts because they will fear being punished if they do so. Compare to **specific deterrence**. (Chapter 10)

General subject matter jurisdiction. A court that hears cases on a variety of topics. Courts of general subject matter jurisdiction hear those cases that are not heard in courts of limited subject matter jurisdiction. Compare to **limited subject matter jurisdiction**. (Chapter 12)

Geographic jurisdiction. A type of jurisdiction based on location, in which a court is empowered to hear cases that originated within the geographic area (whether county, district, or other geographic unit) over which that court has authority. (Chapter 12)

Governing through crime. An idea described by Jonathan Simon suggesting that efforts for control and surveillance once reserved to the criminal justice system have extended to families, schools, and workplaces, where individuals are subject to an increased amount of monitoring, regulation, and zero-tolerance policies. (Chapter 13)

Grand jury. A group of citizens impaneled to hear evidence presented by a prosecuting attorney with the purpose of determining whether sufficient evidence (probable cause) exists to bring to trial a person accused of committing a crime. If such evidence is found, the grand jury issues an indictment. Failure to find such evidence results in dismissal of a case. *See also* **indictment**. (Chapters 1, 8, 12)

Grasseaters. Police officers who accept illegal benefits as a result of corrupt activity but who do so passively rather than actively seeking opportunities for unethical conduct. Compare to **meateaters**. (Chapter 11)

Gratuity. A situation in which a police officer is given a benefit (e.g., a discount or something for free) that is not available to other members of the general public. Gratuities are a subject of debate in discussions of police ethics. (Chapter 11)

Great Society. A collection of social programs promoted by President Johnson aimed at eradicating a variety of social problems, including poverty, inadequate health care, racial injustice, pollution, and more. (Chapter 13)

Guardian Angels. A citizen group created in 1979 to combat crime in the New York City subway system. Since that time, the group has expanded to other cities and other venues. (Chapter 6)

Habeas corpus. In a legal context, a writ of *habeas corpus* is a court order directed at someone who has custody of a person ordering the release of that person because his or her incarceration was achieved through unlawful processes. This provides the mechanism by which unlawful incarcerations may be challenged. (Chapters 8, 12)

Halfway house. A type of correctional facility that provides educational and counseling programs in a homelike setting and offers offenders greater freedoms than a prison or jail. Halfway houses are an intermediate sanction. (Chapter 13)

Harm principle. The idea advanced by John Stuart Mill that a society (through the law) should only concern itself with actions that pose a direct harm to others. (Chapter 3)

Harmless error. Minor legal errors that were unlikely to have affected the overall outcome of a case. If appealed, harmless errors do not result in the reversal of a conviction. Compare to **prejudicial/reversible error**. (Chapter 12)

Harmony. The idea that when things are in their proper order, it represents beauty. (Chapter 2)

Hart-Devlin debate. An intellectual exchange between British legal philosophers H. L. A. Hart and Patrick Devlin focused on the role of morality in the law. *See also* **legal moralism** and **legal positivism**. (Chapter 3)

Hate Crime Statistics Act. A law requiring the federal government to maintain data on hate crime victimizations. (Chapter 7)

Hedonism. The idea that individuals will commit an act if the potential pleasure outweighs the potential pain but will not commit an act if the potential pain outweighs the potential pleasure to be gained. This was instrumental to Jeremy Bentham's theories and to the ideas of general and specific deterrence. (Chapter 10)

Hegemony. The influence that is exercised by powerful groups in society. (Chapter 7)

Heuristic. A tool, usually a philosophical idea or perspective, used to reduce decision-making complexity by providing guidance in answering questions. (Chapter 3).

Hierarchical jurisdiction. The organization of state and federal court systems in which a case begins in a court of original jurisdiction where factual determinations are made. These decisions may be appealed to a court of appellate jurisdiction, which reviews the proceedings of the court of original jurisdiction to ensure that laws and procedures were properly applied. (Chapter 12)

Homeland security. The identification of and response to threats to national security, with a particular emphasis on terrorism. (Chapter 1)

Homeland security era. An era of policing that focuses on crime control to expose threats and gather intelligence, and also on tasks related to the prevention of terrorist attacks. Compare to **community problem-solving era**, **political era**, and **professional era**. (Chapter 11)

Hot spots. An area that has a greater than average number of criminal or disorder events or an area where people have a higher than average risk of victimization; hot spots can be a single address, a street, or a neighborhood. (Chapter 11)

Hot spots policing. A crime prevention strategy that involves placing officers where crime is located. This can take the form of significantly higher levels of patrol and police presence or more specific programs implemented in high-crime areas. (Chapter 11)

House arrest. An intermediate sanction in which offenders may live at home but are not permitted to leave their home. Electronic monitoring is generally used to enforce house arrest. *See also* **electronic monitoring**. (Chapter 13)

Idealist. An advocate of the philosophical perspective of idealism, which evaluates actions and decisions based on how well they meet broad goals or theoretical ideas. Compare to **pragmatist**. (Chapter 2)

Idealistic theories of law. Theories of law grounded in the idealistic perspective. The theories include legal naturalism, rights and interpretive jurisprudence, critical theories of law, and legal paternalism. Common ideas underlying idealistic theories include a strong connection between law and morality and the use of law to draw upon history and tradition in pursuit of ultimate truths. (Chapter 3)

Ideology. A worldview to which a person subscribes. Under ideological justice, supporters of an ideology argue that society will not be able to achieve justice until policies are enacted that support their desired ideology. (Chapter 6)

Immunity. A procedural defense that gives the defendant freedom from criminal prosecution due to his or her status as a foreign diplomat or as a cooperating witness for the government in a larger prosecution. (Chapter 9)

Imperfect procedural justice. A model of procedural justice described by John Rawls in which a criterion is identified for determining what a fair outcome is, but procedures do not guarantee that the fair outcome will be accomplished. Imperfect procedural justice balances sometimes competing interests, such as due process and crime control. Compare to **perfect procedural justice** and **pure procedural justice**. (Chapter 8)

Importation hypothesis. An explanation for prisonization suggesting that inmates bring their attitudes and life experiences from the outside into prison, and these shape their behavior in the prison environment. Compare to **deprivation hypothesis**. (Chapter 13)

Incapacitation. A justification for punishment in which punishment is used to remove or reduce the offender's ability to commit criminal activities. The most common form of incapacitation is the use of prison or jail, with the idea that removing the offender from society will reduce the offender's ability to commit crime. (Chapter 10)

Incarceration. The use of sentences to correctional institutions (prisons and jails) as a form of punishment. *See also* **correctional institution**. (Chapter 13)

Inchoate crimes. Crimes that occur as part of the preparation for committing another crime or in an attempt to commit another crime, including such acts as attempt,

solicitation, facilitation, aiding and abetting, and conspiracy. (Chapter 9)

Indeterminate sentencing. A method of sentencing in which a statute sets a broad range of permissible sentences for an offense (usually a minimum and a maximum) and leaves it to the sentencing judge to impose whatever sentence he or she feels is fair, given the particular facts of a case. Compare to **determinate sentencing**. (Chapter 12)

Indictment. A written statement issued by a grand jury to indicate that sufficient evidence (probable cause) exists to bring to trial a person accused of a crime. Also known as a true bill, the indictment indicates the specific offense with which the accused is charged, including a description of the facts and circumstances surrounding the crime that led the grand jury to find probable cause. (Chapters 1, 8, 12)

Indigent. In criminal justice, refers to defendants who are unable to afford legal representation. (Chapter 6)

Individual justice. Focuses on whether outcomes that apply to individual persons are just. (Chapter 6)

Informal social control. Tools used to control behavior in everyday social life, including social control exercised by peers, communities, families, and groups. This forms the basis of the socialization process. Compare to **formal social control**. (Chapter 4)

Information. A formal, written document accusing a person of a crime. The document is prepared by the prosecuting attorney and submitted to a judge for his or her consideration at a preliminary hearing. (Chapters 1, 12)

Infraction. Low-level offenses that are violations of laws or ordinances but are not classified as either felonies or misdemeanors. Many traffic violations are infractions. Compare to **felony** and **misdemeanor**. (Chapter 1)

Inhibitors. In self-control and social control theories, the factors that a person takes into account in deciding whether or not to commit a crime. (Chapter 5)

Initial appearance. When a judge or magistrate informs an accused person of the charges against him or her, the possible penalties, and the right to retain counsel or have an attorney appointed if indigent. A decision may also be made about whether to grant bail. The initial appearance is to occur within 48 hours of a person's arrest. (Chapters 1, 12)

Initiative/referendum elections. Elections in which the public, as a whole, votes directly on whether or not certain laws should be passed. (Chapter 3)

Insanity. A legal defense that refers to the defendant's state of mind at the time a criminal offense is committed. Definitions of insanity vary by jurisdiction. (Chapter 4)

Intensive supervision probation. A highly structured form of probation designed for high-risk offenders or offenders who have not been successful on regular probation. Also known as ISP, it requires more frequent meetings and closer supervision than traditional probation. (Chapter 13)

Interest groups. Organized groups of individuals who advocate for a particular policy outcome. (Chapter 7)

Intermediate sanctions. A range of correctional alternatives that lie on a continuum between probation and prison. (Chapter 13)

Internal or self-control. A type of informal social control related to conscience in which an individual internalizes norms and acts according to them. Compare to **external or relational social control**. (Chapter 4)

Interrogation. Questions, statements, or actions that are designed to elicit an incriminating response from a suspect. *Miranda* warnings must be given prior to custodial interrogation. *See also* **custody**. (Chapter 8)

Issue network. A coalition of interest groups that work together to shape policy on an issue of common interest. (Chapter 7)

Jail. A correctional institution holding persons accused of a crime who are awaiting trial and offenders who are sentenced to less than one year. Jails are short-term facilities usually operated by a county sheriff. (Chapter 13)

Judges. Those who preside over state and federal courts. The primary role of the judge is to enforce the rules of criminal procedure and criminal evidence. (Chapter 12)

Judicial review. The power of the courts to invalidate laws enacted by a legislature or rules made by an executive agency if they violate or conflict with the U.S. Constitution. In criminal justice, judicial review is often focused on issues of **substantive due process** or **procedural justice**. (Chapter 12)

Jurisdiction. The authority given to a court to hear and adjudicate a particular dispute. There are multiple forms of jurisdiction, including hierarchical, subject matter, and geographic. (Chapter 12)

Jurisprudence. The academic and philosophical study of law. (Chapter 3)

Jurisprudence of rights. A modern extension of legal realism which argues that the primary consideration, other than the law, that should guide judges is an ethics of rights, in which fairness is the guiding principle to be used when deciding cases. (Chapter 12)

Just deserts. A view of retribution focusing on the idea that punishment should be proportional to the crime; that is, punishment should be equally severe to the offender as the offender's criminal act was to the victim. (Chapter 10)

Just world. A world where individuals receive what they deserve. The concept of and belief in a just world has been important in the psychological study of justice. (Chapter 6)

Justice. That which is just. There is no single agreed-upon definition of justice. Rather, conceptions of what does or does not constitute justice have been influenced by culture, history, philosophical perspectives, and more. (Chapter 6)

Justice reinvestment. Programs based on the idea that money spent on incarceration could be better spent on other initiatives to prevent crime. (Chapter 6)

Labeling theory. Assumes that once society places a label on a person, that individual will self-identify with the label and behave accordingly. If a person is labeled as a delinquent, deviant, or criminal, the theory suggests that the person will accept that label and therefore engage in delinquent, deviant, or criminal activity. (Chapter 5)

Law and economics. A movement emerging in the 1970s advocating that the law should be interpreted (and cases decided) in a way that distributes economic costs and benefits in a manner that promotes economic efficiency and maximizes wealth. (Chapter 12)

Law and legal studies. The study of legal issues in law school or prelaw programs of which criminal law is one component. Also included are civil law, constitutional law, jurisprudence, legal research, philosophy of law, and more. (Chapter 1)

Law Enforcement Assistance Administration. An agency created by Congress to distribute funds to improve criminal justice administration and practice. Known as LEAA, the agency was created in 1968 and abolished in 1982; the Office of Justice Programs has continued some of LEAA's functions. (Chapter 1)

Law Enforcement Education Program. A program created by the Law Enforcement Assistance Administration to fund college-level criminal justice education. Known as LEEP, the program was restructured in 1979 and discontinued soon thereafter. (Chapter 1)

Legal formalism. The traditional view of legal reasoning holding that judges apply law to the facts of the case to arrive at logical decisions separate from any ethical, political, philosophical, or policy considerations. (Chapter 12)

Legal instrumentalism. Philosophy of legal reasoning holding that judges should make decisions that promote good or desirable outcomes. Judges operating under this approach make decisions to achieve justice, serve broad social interests, and foster good public policy. (Chapter 12)

Legal moralism. The idea that popular notions of morality should influence decisions about what behaviors the law ought to regulate. This was the perspective held by Patrick Devlin in the Hart-Devlin debate. (Chapter 3)

Legal naturalism. A legal theory espousing a belief in the concept of natural law. *See also* **natural law**. (Chapter 3)

Legal paternalism. A legal theory holding that the government creates and enforces law to protect individuals from engaging in risky behaviors or making decisions that might harm them. (Chapter 3)

Legal positivism. A philosophy that views the law solely as a human creation rather than as an attempt to discover, confirm, or enforce higher moral standards. This was the perspective held by H. L. A. Hart in the Hart-Devlin debate. (Chapter 3)

Legal pragmatism. A legal theory arguing that the law should be based on empirical evidence rather than on grand concepts such as morality. (Chapter 3)

Legal process theories. An approach to legal reasoning that attempts to harmonize legal formalism and legal realism by offering neutral principles that judges could use to resolve unclear cases. However, determining which neutral principles to use and how to use them is a value decision which can lead to inconsistencies between judges. (Chapter 12)

Legal realism. A legal theory with a primary focus on the decision-making processes of the courts. The theory holds that the courts create law through their accumulated decisions, meaning that the law becomes whatever the courts say it is. Legal realism suggests that legal reasoning is an act of interpretation, requiring judges to consider factors beyond the law to resolve uncertainties in cases. In this approach, judges craft decisions to achieve justice, serve broad social interests, and foster good public policy. (Chapters 3, 12)

Legal reasoning. The processes by which judges make decisions about how to interpret and apply the law. (Chapter 12)

Legalistic style. A style of police behavior described by James Q. Wilson in which the purpose of policing is to

enforce all laws with the full force of police authority in all cases. Officers operating under the legalistic style enforce all laws strictly with little exercise of discretion and measure productivity by statistics, such as number of arrests or tickets. Compare to **service style** and **watchman style**. (Chapter 11)

Legality. In punishment theory, legality means that punishment can only be given for crimes as defined by the law and that the punishments given must be within the bounds of the law. (Chapter 10)

Legitimacy. Exists when citizens accept that their government has the right to govern them. Governments without legitimacy may face protest, disobedience, or revolution. (Chapter 2)

Lex talionis. The retributive principle of punishment illustrated by the phrase "an eye for an eye, a tooth for a tooth . . ." This was the idea that offenders should have the same harm applied to them as they applied to their victims. (Chapter 9)

Libertarian. An ideological perspective holding that society should respect individual rights with only minimal government influence, particularly the right to own and do as one wishes with property. (Chapter 6)

Liberty. The freedom and the protection of rights as enumerated in the Constitution and Bill of Rights. Liberty is a fundamental component of American political culture. (Chapter 7)

Life course theory. Explores how involvement in criminal activity changes as offenders grow older and encounter new life circumstances. (Chapter 5)

Limited subject matter jurisdiction. A specialized subject matter jurisdiction. Courts of limited subject matter jurisdiction only hear cases on certain topics. Compare to **general subject matter jurisdiction**. (Chapter 12)

Magna Carta. A document signed by King John in England in 1215. The document established basic rights of procedural justice for citizens accused of a crime and was one source for the types of due process protections granted under the U.S. Constitution and Bill of Rights. *Magna Carta* is Latin for "great charter." (Chapter 9)

Majority opinion. The opinion in a Supreme Court (or other appellate court) case providing the Court's ruling, which becomes the law of the land. Compare to **dissenting opinion**. (Chapter 3)

Mala in se. A Latin phrase for criminalized acts that are universally (or nearly universally) viewed as being inherently evil or bad, such as murder or rape. Compare to ***mala prohibita***. (Chapter 1)

Mala prohibita. A Latin phrase for criminalized acts that have been made illegal not because they are viewed as being inherently wrong but because a legislature or government has chosen to criminalize them nonetheless. Compare to ***mala in se***. (Chapter 1)

Mandatory sentence. A sentencing structure in which a law passed by a legislature requires a judge to impose a particular sentence for a crime. (Chapter 12)

Marijuana Tax Act. A federal law passed in 1937 that had the effect of outlawing marijuana nationwide by imposing a series of strict restrictions and taxes on its distribution. (Chapter 7)

Mark system. Used by Alexander Maconochie at the Norfolk Island prison colony; inmates accumulated marks or points for positive behaviors and, upon collecting a sufficient number of marks, could receive special privileges and eventual release. (Chapter 13)

Marxist criminology. A form of conflict criminology which argues that there is a strong relationship between capitalism, class conflict, and crime. The theory suggests that persons with political power and wealth create laws to suppress the lower class. (Chapter 5)

Meateaters. Police officers who actively solicit corrupt or unethical activities. Compare to **grasseaters**. (Chapter 11)

Mechanical model. A model of justice focusing neither on the needs of society nor on the needs of the offender. The intent of the model is to rigidly and rapidly follow laws and processes without discretion and without consideration of the outcomes they produce. Compare to **authoritarian model**, **compassionate model**, and **participatory model**. (Chapter 6)

Media piracy. The illegal sharing or sale of copyrighted materials such as movies and music. (Chapter 7)

Medical model of deviance. A way of explaining deviance that underlies therapeutic social control. Under the model, deviance is defined objectively as a disease, and treatment of the disease is sought in accordance with the therapeutic style of social control. (Chapter 4)

Medicalization of deviance. Defining a deviant behavior as an illness or a symptom of an illness and then providing medical intervention to treat the illness. Incorporates elements of the medical model of deviance and therapeutic formal social control. (Chapter 4)

Mens rea. One component of the legal definition of crime expressed in the Latin phrase meaning "evil mind." The *mens rea* of a crime is the level of intent the offender had to

commit the criminal *actus reus*. Levels of intent include committing a crime with purpose, knowledge, recklessness, or negligence. (Chapter 9)

Mental health courts. A specialized type of problem-solving court for offenders with mental illnesses. Mental health courts focus on therapeutic social control. (Chapter 4)

Mesomorphs. Under the criminological theory of somatotypes, persons who are muscular, active, and aggressive and therefore viewed as more likely to engage in delinquent behavior. This theory has been discredited by modern criminologists. (Chapter 5)

***Miranda* rights.** In 1966, the Supreme Court ruled in the case *Miranda v. Arizona* that suspects must be advised of the following rights prior to custodial interrogation: You have the right to remain silent. Anything you say can and will be used against you in a court of law. You have the right to have an attorney present during questioning. If you cannot afford an attorney, one will be appointed for you. *See also* **custody** and **interrogation**. (Chapter 8)

Misdemeanor. Less serious offenses that are generally punished by a sentence of less than a year in jail and/or a small to moderate fine. Compare to **felony** and **infraction**. (Chapter 12)

Mission statement. A written statement of the philosophies that guide an agency or organization. (Chapter 13)

Missouri Plan. A method of judicial selection in which a nominating body screens persons interested in judicial office and recommends names to the governor; from that list, the governor chooses who will be appointed as a judge; and after appointment, the judge will stand for a retention election in which voters determine whether or not the judge should continue to serve. (Chapter 12)

Misuse of authority. Occurs when a police officer uses his or her position for some sort of personal gain. Generally viewed as a violation of police ethics. (Chapter 11)

Mitigating circumstances. In capital cases, where a death sentence may be given, these are factors that may diminish the offender's culpability or alleviate concerns about future dangerousness. The defense presents evidence of mitigating circumstances in the second stage of the bifurcated trial. In other cases, factors which render the circumstances surrounding an offence or the harms it causes less severe than a typical offense of that type; may be considered in the application of sentencing guidelines. *See also* **aggravating circumstances; bifurcated trial; sentencing guidelines**. (Chapter 10; Chapter 12)

***Model Penal Code* (MPC).** A set of model criminal laws developed by the American Law Institute in 1962 and updated in 1981, which has formed the basis for revisions to the criminal laws in two-thirds of the American states. By being a model, the code stands as the American Law Institute's conception of what criminal laws ought to look like. (Chapter 9)

Money laundering. Occurs when the true source and destination of financial transactions are hidden, making money from illicit enterprises appear to be legally acquired and transferred. (Chapter 7)

Morality. Judgments about what behaviors or actions societies or individuals view as right or wrong, good or bad. Morality may also be viewed as an ongoing process in which society or individuals continually reflect on norms, values, and standards when determining the best solution to a dilemma. (Chapters 1, 2)

Mores. Norms that are formally expressed and that tend to have moral underpinnings. Compare to **folkways**. (Chapter 4)

Mortification. The loss of personal identity that comes with admission to a total institution, such as a prison or jail. (Chapter 13)

Motion. A formal request asking the court to make a specific ruling on an issue or question. Motions may address any number of substantive or procedural issues, but the most significant is a motion to suppress evidence that was gathered in violation of a defendant's constitutional rights. *See also* **motion to suppress**. (Chapter 12)

Motion to suppress. A motion in which a defendant charged with a crime asks a judge to suppress, or prohibit, certain evidence from being considered at trial because it was gathered in violation of the defendant's constitutional rights. *See also* **motion**. (Chapter 12)

National Crime Victimization Survey. A survey conducted by the Bureau of Justice Statistics to determine how many persons have been the victims of criminal acts. Also known as the NCVS, this is an example of a victimization survey. (Chapter 1)

National Incident-Based Reporting System. Crime data collected by the Federal Bureau of Investigation with more detailed information than available in the Uniform Crime Reports. Also known as NIBRS, the data are often used by researchers to analyze crime patterns. (Chapter 1)

National Supremacy Clause. A clause in the U.S. Constitution that identifies the federal government as the

supreme law of the land. This means if there is a conflict between a federal law and a state law, the federal law will take priority. (Chapters 7, 12)

Natural law. A belief that there are universally accepted principles of human behavior meant to apply to all persons in all places and that law should discover, reflect, and enforce these principles. (Chapter 3)

Neutralization theory. Suggests that crime occurs because offenders justify their criminal behavior through a series of neutralizations or excuses, including denial of responsibility, denial of injury, denial of the victim, condemnation of the condemners, and appeal to higher loyalties. (Chapter 5)

No bill. Issued when a grand jury finds insufficient evidence to issue an indictment. *See also* **grand jury** and **indictment**. (Chapter 12)

Nolo contendere. A Latin term for a plea in which a person accused of a crime does not challenge the charges and accepts a penalty but without admitting guilt for the offense. (Chapter 12)

Nonsystem. An idea expressing lack of coordination between criminal justice system agencies. This may be due to fragmentation between agencies, the prevalence of discretion, and lack of agreement on criminal justice goals and philosophies. (Chapter 1)

Nulla poena sine lege. A Latin phrase meaning that no punishment can be given by a court unless there is a law that authorizes it. (Chapter 1)

Nullum crimen sine lege. A Latin phrase meaning that no behavior can be considered a crime unless there is a law enacted that prohibits it. (Chapter 1)

Oral argument. Arguments made by parties to a case before judges in an appellate court. *See also* **appeal**. (Chapter 12)

Original jurisdiction. Court where a case begins, which considers evidence and makes both factual and legal determinations in the case. (Chapter 12)

Original position. A state achieved under the veil of ignorance in which one has a lack of knowledge about his or her personal background. John Rawls argues that this is the starting point from which government and policy should be developed, as it minimizes a focus on self-interest. *See also* **veil of ignorance**. (Chapter 6)

Overbreadth. Occurs when a law intrudes upon constitutionally protected freedoms, in which case the law may be ruled invalid, unconstitutional, and unenforceable. (Chapter 9)

Pains of imprisonment. As described by Gresham Sykes, five deprivations, or things that are withheld from inmates: liberty, goods and services, heterosexual relationships, autonomy, and security. Taken together, these deprivations partially define the prison experience. (Chapter 13)

Panacea phenomenon. A cycle described by Finckenauer and Gavin in which a new criminal justice intervention is proposed but with unrealistic expectations; the intervention is implemented but does not meet the unrealistic goals set for it; frustration builds and the program is labeled a failure; and policy makers develop a new intervention, at which point the cycle repeats itself. (Chapter 13)

Paradigm. Philosophical tendencies or worldviews held by individuals that they use to help them make decisions. (Chapter 2)

Parens patriae. A metaphor suggesting that the law (or the government through law) acts as a parent and protector to its subjects. This notion, grounded in the belief that society has a moral obligation to protect its citizens, underlies the theory of legal paternalism. (Chapters 3, 7)

Parole. A process allowing the early release of an offender after serving part of his or her sentence. Release may be granted by a parole board if the inmate has demonstrated that he or she is rehabilitated and poses a low risk to society. (Chapter 1)

Participatory model. A model of justice that places a high value on both the needs of society and the needs of the offender. In this model, a variety of participants must work together to create, understand, and apply the law. Compare to **authoritarian model**, **compassionate model**, and **mechanical model**. (Chapter 6)

Peacemaking criminology. A perspective arguing that the encouragement of communication and relationships can promote justice and heal social wrongs. Views traditional forms of punishment, such as incarceration, as counterproductive because they reflect an imbalance of power. (Chapter 5)

Penal abolition. A movement advocating for abolishing the use of prisons as a punishment alternative. (Chapter 10)

Penal harm movement. Refers to a set of policies enacted beginning in the 1980s to "get tough" on crime by enacting retributive rules and unpleasant conditions in prisons. (Chapter 10)

Penal social control. Views the violator of a social norm that has been codified into criminal law as an offender who is deserving of official condemnation and punishment.

This is accomplished through the criminal justice system. Compare to **compensatory social control**, **conciliatory social control**, and **therapeutic social control**. (Chapter 4)

Perceptual shorthand. A concept described by Jerome Skolnick, in which police officers use labels and perceptions to make rapid judgments about which persons are believed to pose a personal danger or harm to society. Persons so identified are known as symbolic assailants and may routinely be subjected to higher levels of social control than other persons, whether or not an actual threat exists. (Chapter 10)

Peremptory challenge. Allows the prosecution or defense to excuse a potential juror during the *voir dire* process without specifying a cause. Each side is typically permitted only a limited number of peremptory challenges, and they may not be used to exclude jurors on the basis of race or gender. (Chapter 12)

Perfect procedural justice. A model of procedural justice described by John Rawls in which a criterion is identified for determining what a fair outcome is, and then procedures are put into place to achieve that fair outcome. Perfect procedural justice strives for accuracy when searching for the truth. Compare to **imperfect procedural justice** and **pure procedural justice**. (Chapter 8)

Pervasive organized corruption. A level of police corruption identified by Lawrence Sherman describing agencies where corruption and unethical behavior are well organized and involve many officers, potentially including supervisors. (Chapter 11)

Pervasive unorganized corruption. A level of police corruption identified by Lawrence Sherman where a large number of rotten apples in an agency participate in illegal activity. *See also* **rotten apples**. (Chapter 11)

Petit jury. The group of jurors empaneled to hear a particular criminal case, at the conclusion of which they render a verdict. In most states, petit juries in criminal trials are composed of 12 jurors. (Chapter 12)

Phrenology. A historical theory in criminology that was the study of personality traits as revealed by an examination of the bumps and grooves in the skull. This theory has been discredited by modern criminologists. (Chapter 5)

Physical evidence. Tangible objects that are used as evidence in a criminal trial; also known as real evidence. *See also* **evidence**. Compare to **testimony**, **scientific evidence**, and **demonstrative evidence**. (Chapter 12)

Pillory. An apparatus located in a public area for the purpose of shaming offenders. The device restrained offenders by securing their head and hands so they could not move or leave, thereby placing the offender on public display. Compare to **stocks**. (Chapter 13)

Plea bargaining. The process by which a defendant agrees to plead guilty in exchange for some consideration from the government, such as a lower charge, fewer counts, or a reduced sentence. Approximately 95% of felony cases are resolved by plea bargaining. *See also* **charge bargaining**, **count bargaining**, and **sentence bargaining**. (Chapter 12)

Pod-style design. A modern style of prison design in which cells surround a central day room where inmates may gather for recreation, programming, or other prosocial activities. Each grouping of cells and day room is known as a pod. (Chapter 13)

Police. A formal agent of social control and component of the criminal justice system responsible for law enforcement and the maintenance of order. (Chapter 11)

Policy diffusion. Occurs when a policy or law created in one jurisdiction is adopted by other jurisdictions. (Chapter 7)

Policy window. Based on John Kingdon's theory of public policy, it refers to a time when policy change is most likely to occur for an issue. For a policy window to open for any particular issue, that issue must have been identified as a problem, a solution must be available, and the political climate must support making a change. (Chapter 7)

Political culture. The broad set of values that underlie a particular political system. As such, political culture shapes the development of law and policy. *See also* **liberty**, **equality**, and **legitimacy**. (Chapter 7)

Political era. The era of American policing from the 1830s to the early 1900s, in which policing was characterized by political undertones and police officers and agencies often fell under the control and influence of local politicians. The era was marked by high levels of corruption. Compare to **community problem-solving era**, **homeland security era**, and **professional era**. (Chapter 11)

Positivist school of criminology. Based on the concept of determinism, this perspective holds that criminal behaviors are influenced by outside forces such as biological, psychological, and sociological factors. (Chapter 5)

Postmodern jurisprudence. A perspective of legal reasoning drawing upon critical legal studies and focusing on the intersection of race, gender, gender identity, religion, social class, sexual orientation, and other perspectives to study inequalities in law and society, often using literary theory to interpret legislation and judicial decisions. (Chapter 12)

Postmodernism. A philosophical perspective holding that there are multiple equally valid realities, as individuals create their own narratives and understandings of what is real. Postmodern perspectives on justice recognize these differences and have as a goal helping to understand why different persons and groups have differing conceptions of what is just. (Chapter 6)

Pragmatist. An advocate of the philosophical perspective of pragmatism, in which actions and decisions are evaluated based on empiricism and the analysis of data. Compare to **idealist**. (Chapter 2)

Prejudicial/reversible error. Significant mistakes made in a criminal trial that are likely to contribute to an unfair verdict. These errors may result in overturning a conviction. Compare to **harmless error**. (Chapter 12)

Preliminary hearing. A hearing held in front of a judge to determine whether or not there is probable cause to believe that a person committed the crime of which he or she stands accused. If probable cause is found, the judge binds over the defendant for trial. If probable cause is not found, the case may be dismissed. *See also* **information**. (Chapters 1, 8, 12)

Preponderance of evidence. The burden of proof used in deciding cases heard through civil justice processes (it is also used in some criminal justice hearings and in some administrative hearings). It means that the judge or jury believes it is more likely than not that an incident occurred or that one party caused harm to another. (Chapter 7)

Prescriptive norms. Norms that specify what individuals should or are encouraged to do. Compare to **proscriptive norms**. (Chapter 4)

Presentence investigation report. A report prepared by probation officers containing information about the offender and the nature of the offense. Commonly known as PSI, its purpose is to aid a judge in determining the sentence for a case. (Chapter 12)

Presumption of innocence. Presumes that all criminal defendants are innocent until their guilt has been proven beyond a reasonable doubt. This is a presumption that the jury (or judge in a bench trial) is required to make at a criminal trial. (Chapter 12)

Presumption of sanity. Presumes that defendants are sane (i.e., legally responsible for their actions), unless they are proven insane at trial (through successful use of the insanity defense). This is a presumption the jury (or judge in a bench trial) is required to make at a criminal trial. *See also* **insanity.** (Chapter 12)

Pretrial release. A decision to allow a person to remain free rather than held in jail prior to a trial in criminal court. (Chapter 1)

Principles. Expressions about broad ideas about how the world (or some part of it) ought to work. Principles often form the basis for the creation of rules. *See also* **rules**. (Chapter 3)

Prison. A correctional institution holding persons who are sentenced to more than a year. Prisons are long-term facilities operated by the state or federal government. (Chapters 1, 13)

Prison-industrial complex. A conflict theory perspective of corrections, suggesting that increased spending on incarceration is not driven by need but rather by political and economic interests. (Chapter 13)

Prison Rape Elimination Act (PREA). A federal law designed to improve programming, research, and record keeping related to the reduction of sexual assault in correctional institutions. (Chapter 7)

Prisonization. An inmate's acceptance of the unique culture of the prison environment, including (but not limited to) its norms, jargon, lifestyle, and conditions. Prisonization has been explained by the **importation hypothesis** and the **deprivation hypothesis**. (Chapter 13)

Privilege against self-incrimination. Specifies that a person may not be compelled to provide testimony against himself or herself. The *Miranda* warnings are given prior to custodial interrogation to ensure that suspects are aware of the privilege against self-incrimination. *See also* ***Miranda* rights**. (Chapter 8)

Probable cause. A fair probability based on facts and known circumstances. Probable cause is required for an arrest, for the issuance of search and arrest warrants, and for a case to proceed beyond the grand jury and preliminary hearing stages, among other decisions. Compare to **reasonable suspicion**. (Chapter 8)

Probation. A punishment given by a judge that allows the offender to remain in the community instead of being sent to jail or prison. Often part of a **suspended sentence**. (Chapter 13)

Problem definition. Refers to attempts by interested individuals and groups to advocate how a problem ought to be understood. This often occurs after an issue has been placed on the public agenda (through agenda setting), as individuals and groups debate the causes of and solutions to the problem in question. (Chapter 7)

Problem-oriented policing. A policing strategy designed to help the police identify and respond to the root causes of problems that lead to crime. The emphasis is on making police proactive rather than reactive through use of the SARA model. Also known as POP, it is currently a popular strategy in the United States. See also **scanning, analysis, response, and assessment**. (Chapter 11)

Problem-solving courts. Specialized courts designed to address the underlying problems of the defendants who appear in them, rather than just to punish the commission of crimes. (Chapter 12)

Procedural defense. Technical defenses in which guilt, level of intent, or characteristics of the offense are irrelevant. Procedural defenses include those related to violations of procedural justice rights, immunity, and entrapment. *See also* **immunity** and **entrapment**. (Chapter 9)

Procedural justice. Holds that justice is achieved when the proper procedures are followed and addresses the fairness of the procedures used when applying the law. Procedural justice is grounded in the idea that fair procedures are the best guarantees for fair outcomes. (Chapters 6, 8)

Profession. A career field that meets criteria including a common educational background, adoption of an ethical code, performing specialized tasks, having mechanisms for quality control, prestige as a member of the profession, and lifetime membership in the profession. Some have debated whether criminal justice is a profession or a craft. *See also* **craft** (Chapter 1)

Professional courtesy. Occurs when a police officer provides a courtesy or special treatment to another law enforcement officer (e.g., not giving an officer a ticket if he is stopped for speeding). Professional courtesy is a subject of debate in discussions of police ethics. (Chapter 11)

Professional era. The era of policing from the 1930s to the 1970s focused on reform, professionalism, and removing political influence from policing. Compare to **community problem-solving era, homeland security era**, and **political era**. (Chapter 11)

Prohibition. The time in American history from 1920 to 1933 when alcohol use was banned by the Eighteenth Amendment to the U.S. Constitution. Prohibition was repealed by the Twenty-first Amendment to the U.S. Constitution. (Chapter 1, 7)

Proportionality. The idea that the punishment should fit the crime. Punishments may be ruled unconstitutional if they are grossly excessive in relation to the crime committed. (Chapter 10)

Proscriptive norms. Norms that specify what individuals should not or are encouraged not to do. Compare to **prescriptive norms**. (Chapter 4)

Prosecutors. Government officials who are responsible for prosecuting (charging and bringing to trial) violations of criminal law. Prosecutors are sometimes called the "gatekeepers" of the criminal justice system because of their power to determine who will appear in court and on what charges. (Chapter 12)

Protective sweep. A brief examination of an area conducted for officer safety purposes. Reasonable suspicion that a suspect is dangerous and may have access to weapons must exist to conduct a protective sweep. *See also* **reasonable suspicion**. (Chapter 8)

Proximate cause. One type of causation recognized by the law when linking an *actus reus* with a result. Proximate cause asks whether there were any other causes that could lead to the result. If not, the defendant may be criminally liable for the result; if so, the defendant may be liable only if a reasonable person would have foreseen that the defendant's specific *actus reus* would lead to the result. Compare to **cause-in-fact**. (Chapter 9)

Psychodynamic theory. A theory of crime suggesting that human behavior, including crime, is controlled by a variety of mental processes. The theory was developed by Sigmund Freud based on the dynamics of the id, ego, and superego. (Chapter 5)

Public policy. The individual and accumulated decisions made by governments (local, state, or federal) about what should be done to address any issue, including crime. (Chapter 7)

Punishment. A form of deprivation imposed upon a person as a result of committing a criminal act. Punishments may include, but are not limited to, incarceration (deprivation of freedom), fines (deprivation of money), or physical punishments (deprivation of bodily integrity). (Chapter 10)

Pure procedural justice. A model of procedural justice described by John Rawls that focuses on creating a system with fair procedures that, if followed, are likely but not guaranteed to produce fair outcomes. Pure procedural justice is based on a participation model in which persons affected by a decision have the opportunity to participate in the process (e.g., a trial) by which that decision is made. Compare to **imperfect procedural justice** and **perfect procedural justice**. (Chapter 8)

Putative backlash. May occur after a formerly deviant behavior has been vindicated. Occurs when the behavior is

either recriminalized or redefined as deviant. *See also* **vindication**. (Chapter 4)

Qualified immunity. A legal principle specifying that public employees cannot be sued in civil court unless their conduct is particularly egregious. (Chapter 7)

Quantitative scales. Numerical scales. In criminal justice settings, the results of quantitative scales are used to guide decisions and thereby limit discretion. (Chapter 13)

Rate. A standardized measure that allows comparison of data between areas with different populations. Often used when reporting crime data, crime rates are calculated by dividing the number of offenses by the population of an area and then multiplying by 100,000. The resulting number indicates how many offenses occur per 100,000 persons in a particular location. (Chapter 1)

Rational choice theory. An explanation for crime suggesting that offenders use a strategic thinking process to evaluate the potential rewards and risks from committing a crime and make their decision accordingly about whether or not to commit the crime. (Chapter 5)

Rationale for law. One of the six concepts of law, related to the purpose law serves in society; answers may include the enforcement of morality or the protection of individual rights. *See also* **six concepts of law**. (Chapter 3)

Reasonable expectation of privacy. Refers to an expectation of privacy that society views as a reasonable one. Significant because the protections of the Fourth Amendment apply when there is governmental intrusion upon a reasonable expectation of privacy. (Chapter 8)

Reasonable suspicion. A lower burden of proof than probable cause in which officers can articulate facts and make inferences from them that criminal activity may be afoot. Required for stop and frisks and protective sweeps. Compare to **probable cause**. (Chapter 8)

Recidivism. A measure of how often former offenders commit new crimes. (Chapter 13)

Reformatory system. An early method of incarceration designed for young offenders, with an emphasis on education, vocational instruction, and rehabilitation. (Chapter 13)

Rehabilitation. A justification for punishment that views the purpose of punishment as attempting to correct an offender's behavior so it will conform to the law and to social norms. Rehabilitation involves the use of programming (counseling, treatment, education, etc.), rather than fear or pain to correct behavior. (Chapter 10)

Reintegrative shaming. A form of shaming in which the offender, after being publicly shamed or scolded, is forgiven and accepted back into the community. Compare to **disintegrative shaming**. (Chapter 10)

Restitution. The payment of money to a victim by an offender to compensate the victim for the losses caused by the offender. This concept was present in some ancient Greek legal codes and also is utilized as part of restorative justice models today. (Chapter 9)

Restorative justice. Focuses on restoring the victim, offender, and society to the desirable conditions that existed before a criminal offense occurred. (Chapter 6)

Result. One component of the legal definition of crime related to the requirement that the prosecution must prove that the defendant's behavior (*actus reus*) caused the prohibited result. **Cause-in-fact** and **proximate cause** are two types of causation that can be used to link an *actus reus* with a result. (Chapter 9)

Retribution. A justification for punishment grounded in the notion that offenders should be punished because they deserve it. Forms of retribution include revenge, **just deserts**, and **expiation**. (Chapter 10)

Retributive justice. A perspective of justice which holds that individuals who commit crime are due an unpleasant punishment. (Chapter 6)

Revocation. Occurs when a person on probation or parole commits a new crime or violates the rules of probation or parole and is removed from probation or parole and sent to prison as a result. (Chapter 13)

Rotten apples. A level of police corruption identified by Lawrence Sherman in which one or more officers independently participate in some form of corrupt activity. (Chapter 11)

Rotten pocket. A level of police corruption identified by Lawrence Sherman in which a group of officers work together for corrupt or unethical purposes. (Chapter 11)

Routine activities theory. Views crime and victimization as a function of people's everyday behavior, habits, lifestyle, living conditions, and social interactions. Suggests that crime occurs when three elements converge: a motivated offender, suitable target, and lack of capable guardians. (Chapter 5)

Rule. An externally imposed guideline that shapes behavior in some way. Rules are generally based on, and derived from, broader principles. *See also* **principles**. (Chapter 3)

Scanning, analysis, response, and assessment. The four steps used in problem-oriented policing. Commonly referred to as SARA. (Chapter 11)

Scientific evidence. A form of evidence that includes the results of scientific or forensic testing on real or physical evidence. *See also* **evidence**. Compare to **physical evidence**, **testimony**, and **demonstrative evidence**. (Chapter 12)

Search. Occurs when an expectation of privacy that society is prepared to consider reasonable is infringed by a governmental actor. (Chapter 8)

Search incident to arrest. A search of a suspect and the area in his or her immediate control after an arrest, conducted for the purpose of protecting officer safety and preventing the destruction of an evidence. No warrant or probable cause is required beyond that which led to the arrest. (Chapter 8)

Security administration. The identification and management of risk in public, commercial, or residential settings. This provides the basis for the private security industry. (Chapter 1)

Security level. In corrections, the differences between prisons centering on issues such as how much freedom inmates have within the institution, what types of programming are available, and how many security features are incorporated into the facility. Typical security levels include minimum, medium, and maximum. (Chapter 13)

Seizure. Occurs when there is some meaningful interference with an individual's possessory interest in property by a governmental actor. (Chapter 8)

Self. A philosophical concept that represents how one views humanity. (Chapter 2)

Self-report study. One way of measuring the amount of crime in society by administering surveys that ask persons to report whether or not they have committed certain criminal acts. (Chapter 1)

Sentence bargaining. A form of plea bargaining in which a defendant pleads guilty to the crime originally charged but does so in exchange for a lesser sentence than would likely have been imposed if the defendant had been convicted at trial. *See also* **plea bargaining**. Compare to **count bargaining** and **charge bargaining**. (Chapter 12)

Sentencing guidelines. A system of sentencing designed to reduce discretion and promote consistency in sentencing. In this approach, judges use specified formulas, generally based on an offender's prior record and seriousness of the crime committed, to determine sentences. (Chapter 3; Chapter 12)

Serial murderer. Offenders who have killed two or more victims over time. (Chapter 5)

Service style. A style of police behavior described by James Q. Wilson in which policing is understood to draw upon the use of discretion to determine the most appropriate response to any given situation. Officers operating under the service style view each situation in its own context and prefer to resolve problems with arrest as a last resort. Compare to **legalistic style** and **watchman style**. (Chapter 11)

Six concepts of law. A framework for understanding the role of law in society by considering the foundation, rationale, formation, application, focal point, and use of discretion in law. (Chapter 3)

Social bond theory. Suggests that crime occurs when an individual's bonds to society are weak or broken. Bonds include attachment to prosocial persons and organizations, commitment to prosocial goals, involvement in prosocial activities, and belief in a common set of prosocial values and morals. (Chapter 5)

Social capital. Patterns of social relationships among people. Areas with high social capital have strong social relationships among community members. Synonym for **collective efficacy**. (Chapter 1)

Social constructionism. In criminological theory, the idea that criminal activity is best understood by studying the processes through which behaviors are defined as deviant or acceptable. (Chapter 5)

Social contract theory. A philosophical explanation for the origins of government, in which individuals willingly give up complete freedom to do as they please in exchange for a more secure society governed by laws enforced by a government. (Chapter 2)

Social control. The processes by which society controls individual and group behaviors. The term is now often used to refer to the ways deviant behaviors are controlled, both informally and formally. (Chapter 4)

Social disorganization theory. Focuses on the community environmental factors that may lead to crime, including poverty, breakdown of family and social institutions, high turnover of residents, and lack of attachment to the community. (Chapter 5)

Social justice. Considers issues of equality and inequality in society and whether benefits and risks are distributed in

a manner that is fair and without discrimination. Argues that the pursuit of justice is the pursuit of equality. (Chapter 6, 7)

Social norms. Societal judgments about what individuals should or should not do. Norms are based on widely shared values about what are good or bad, correct or incorrect, behaviors. (Chapter 4)

Socialist. An ideological perspective favoring a society with a large government structure that manages public ownership of industries viewed as most necessary for a productive society and that provides many public services to all members of society. (Chapter 6)

Socialization. The process by which individuals learn a society's or culture's norms and also learn to conform to them. (Chapter 4)

Socially constructed. The idea that societies and individuals construct their own understandings about what certain ideas mean. This helps to explain why different societies or different localities define crimes in different ways, as each may have its own understanding of what crime means. (Chapter 1)

Solitary system. An early method of incarceration in which inmates remained in individual cells with little to no human contact for the duration of their sentence. The goal was to promote offender rehabilitation through self-introspection. (Chapter 13)

Solvability factors. Factors that may increase the likelihood of successfully solving a case, such as the availability of physical evidence, whether the crime is similar to others that have happened in the area, if any suspect description is available, likelihood of recovering stolen property, etc. (Chapter 11)

Somatotypes. A historical theory of criminology suggesting that a person's height and weight were associated with criminal behavior and that individuals with different physical builds, or somatotypes, possess different temperaments. This theory has been discredited by modern criminologists. *See also* **mesomorphs.** (Chapter 5)

Specific deterrence. A justification for punishment that is designed to discourage or prevent individual offenders from committing additional crimes out of fear of being punished again if they do so. Compare to **general deterrence**. (Chapter 10)

Split sentence. A sentence in which offenders first spend some time in jail (or prison) after which they are released to serve a probation sentence in the community. (Chapter 13)

Standing. A requirement in law that only persons whose direct interests have been involved, or whose rights have been violated, may bring a case or a challenge to evidence in a case. That is, individuals cannot bring a lawsuit or challenge evidence on behalf of someone else. (Chapter 8)

State of nature. A philosophical idea describing an environment in which there is little order because there is no justice system or government. (Chapter 2)

Statute of limitations. A legal provision that sets time limits on how long after an incident court processes can be initiated. (Chapter 7)

Stocks. An apparatus located in a public area for the purpose of shaming offenders. The device restrained offenders by securing their feet so they could not move or leave, thereby placing the offender on public display. Compare to **pillory**. (Chapter 13)

Stop and frisk. Briefly detaining a person and performing a limited pat-down of the outer clothing when there is reasonable suspicion of criminal activity. (Chapter 8)

Strain theory. Suggests that crime occurs when members of society, predominantly the lower socioeconomic class, are unable to achieve goals valued by society (principally, the accumulation of wealth). Failure to achieve goals results in frustration, leading some to turn to criminal activity to achieve goals. (Chapter 5)

Strategy. The broad approach that an agency or organization uses to address a problem or issue. A strategy is a broad plan that is put into effect through the use of various specific tactics. Compare to **tactics**. (Chapter 2)

Stratification. Differences between members of a society that occur when persons and groups are divided in a hierarchical manner. This results in levels of inequality from which persons at the top of the hierarchy benefit, whereas those at the bottom suffer. (Chapter 4)

Strict liability. Crimes that do not require criminal intent, or *mens rea,* on the part of the offender. These offenses can therefore be punished without regard to the offender's level of intention (or lack thereof) at the time of the crime. (Chapter 9)

Subculture. A group that shares a set of norms that are different from those of the larger society. (Chapter 4)

Subject matter jurisdiction. A form of jurisdiction based on the subject matter of a case. Courts of limited subject matter jurisdiction hear cases only on certain topics; courts of general subject matter jurisdiction hear all other types of

cases. *See also* **general subject matter jurisdiction** and **limited subject matter jurisdiction**. (Chapter 12)

Subpoena. A court order commanding a witness to appear in court at a specific date to provide sworn testimony in a case. (Chapter 8)

Substantive criminal law. The area of criminal law that lists and defines specific criminal offenses and the punishments that may be administered to those who commit them. (Chapter 9)

Substantive due process. Protects against governmental infringement of fundamental rights, such as freedom of speech, freedom of religion, and the right to privacy. The rights protected under substantive due process include those specified in the Constitution and Bill of Rights as well as those held through the Due Process Clause. (Chapters 8, 9)

Summons. A court order that directs a recipient to appear in court at a specific time on a specific date. Among other uses, the summons is the mechanism by which potential jurors are compelled to appear in court to participate in the jury selection process. (Chapter 12)

Supermax prison. A high-security prison operating at a level above traditional maximum security, in which inmates spend the majority of the day in their cells and have limited human contact; inmates are assigned to supermax prisons based on their behaviors in other prisons. (Chapter 13)

Suspended sentence. A type of sentence in which a judge gives an offender a prison sentence but sets the prison sentence aside to allow the offender to serve his or her time on probation instead. If the offender violates the terms of probation or commits a new crime, the judge may revoke the probation and require the offender to serve the original prison sentence. *See also* **probation**. (Chapter 13)

Sworn employee. Employees of criminal justice agencies who are authorized to enforce criminal law, such as having the authority to arrest and detain persons suspected of criminal activity. (Chapter 1)

Symbolic speech. Conduct that expresses an idea or opinion. Although not verbal or written speech, symbolic speech receives First Amendment protection. (Chapter 9)

Tactics. Specific actions that are taken to implement the broad idea outlined in a strategy. Compare to **strategy**. (Chapter 2)

Team policing. A policing strategy developed in Scotland in 1946 in which a team of police officers was assigned to a specific neighborhood with the responsibility for performing all police services for that neighborhood. The strategy proposed decentralizing policing by creating numerous mini-departments within a city. The strategy was attempted but never became popular in the United States. (Chapter 11)

Technical violation. Occurs when a person violates the rules of probation or parole; this can be the basis for removal from probation or parole, resulting in the offender being sent to prison. (Chapter 13)

Teleology. A philosophical concept suggesting that a vast and purposeful universe with an underlying order creates meaning. (Chapter 2)

Testimony. A form of evidence comprised of the responses of sworn witnesses to the questions posed to them by attorneys or the judge. *See also* **evidence**. Compare to **physical evidence**, **scientific evidence**, and **demonstrative evidence**. (Chapter 12)

Therapeutic social control. Views the deviant person as someone who needs help to become nondeviant or "normal." This is often accomplished through science and medicine. Compare to **compensatory social control**, **conciliatory social control**, and **penal social control**. (Chapter 4)

Thin blue line. In policing, a division between the police and the public stemming from limited contact between police and public and from an "us" versus "them" mentality sometimes held by police officers. Also associated with the solidarity that emerges among police officers. (Chapter 11)

Tort. A harm that is classified as a civil wrong and that forms the basis for action under civil justice processes. (Chapter 7)

Total institution. A concept described by Erving Goffman in which an institution controls all aspects of a person's life. Correctional institutions are one example of a total institution, as the institution controls all aspects of an inmate's life. (Chapter 13)

Transitional justice. Applies in the unique set of circumstances when a country's government changes and the new government seeks to move away from human rights abuses that occurred under the old government. The transition between governments is marked by a focus on human rights and just outcomes. (Chapter 6)

Transportation. A practice used through the 1800s in England in which offenders were sent to live in overseas colonies and prohibited from returning to England. (Chapter 13)

Treason. The only crime defined in the U.S. Constitution, which defines treason as making war against the United States or providing aid and comfort to enemies. (Chapter 8)

Trial by jury. A trial in which guilt or innocence is determined by a jury of one's peers. The right to a trial by jury exists for felonies and some misdemeanors. Compare to **bench trial**. (Chapter 8)

Trial by ordeal. A type of criminal trial once used in which offenders had to perform physical feats or tests, the results of which were used to determine guilt or innocence. (Chapter 9)

Trial court. A court in which a single judge presides over the proceedings; the primary function of trial courts is to resolve factual disputes. (Chapter 12)

True bill. When a grand jury issues an indictment, it is also known as a true bill. *See also* **grand jury** and **indictment**. (Chapter 12)

Truth in sentencing. Stipulates that offenders sentenced to prison must serve a certain portion of their time, usually 85%, and no early release (on parole or otherwise) may occur prior to that time. The federal government and many states have adopted truth in sentencing. (Chapter 13)

Typical crime. A crime in which one individual or group victimizes another individual or group, usually through direct physical harm or property loss. Also known as *street crime,* this stands in contrast to white-collar crimes committed in the arena of finance or by corporations. (Chapter 1)

Ultimate truth. A belief held by idealists that there are certain absolute notions or ideas (i.e., truths) that guide or should guide human action. (Chapter 2)

Uniform Crime Report. An annual report of the number of crimes reported to the police, prepared by the Federal Bureau of Investigation. Also known as the UCR, this stands as the official source of crime data in the United States. (Chapter 1)

Unit management. A modern strategy of correctional management implemented in prisons with pod-style design. Under unit management, multiple activities are conducted within the pod, and staff can work more closely with inmates, promoting meaningful counseling and reducing inmate violence and rule violations. *See also* **pod-style design**. (Chapter 13)

Urban dispersion theory. A developmental theory of American policing suggesting that the growth of cities led crime to be identified as an urban problem and that the police were necessary to ensure the stability of urban society. (Chapter 11)

Utilitarian justice. Defines justice as that which provides the greatest good for the greatest number. Also draws upon cost–benefit analysis, comparing the costs and benefits of an action. (Chapter 6)

Veil of ignorance. A thought experiment used by John Rawls, in which a person is to assume that he or she knows nothing about his or her background. When under the metaphorical veil, individuals are in an original position. *See also* **original position**. (Chapter 6)

Venire. The group of persons who are summoned to court as potential jurors and who then participate in the ***voir dire*** process for jury selection. (Chapter 12)

Victimless crime. A category of crime in which no direct victim is readily identifiable. This includes crimes such as drug possession, prostitution, illegal gambling, and others. (Chapter 7)

Victim blaming. When society, the media, or the criminal justice system make assumptions or statements suggesting that victims were in some way responsible for their own victimization. (Chapter 5)

Victimology. The study of why persons or entities (e.g., businesses, organizations) become victims of crime. (Chapter 1)

Vigilante justice. Occurs when individuals bypass the criminal justice system in resolving a conflict by taking the law into their own hands. (Chapter 6)

Vindication. Occurs when a behavior once viewed as deviant is no longer viewed as deviant. (Chapter 4)

Void for vagueness. Laws so vague that persons must guess at their meaning, and as a result, such laws are unenforceable. Laws may be struck down under judicial review if they are void for vagueness. Based on the principle that laws must provide clear descriptions of the conduct that is prohibited. (Chapter 10)

Voir dire. A Latin term for the process in which the venire of potential jurors is sworn to tell the truth and then questioned to screen out persons who may not be able to make a fair and impartial decision in the case (this is known as being stricken for cause). Potential jurors can also be excused with **peremptory challenges**. (Chapter 12)

Voting disenfranchisement laws. Laws that prohibit persons convicted of a felony from voting. States differ in the

type and extent of disenfranchisement laws they have, if any. (Chapter 12)

Waiver (of rights). An instance in which a person knowingly, intelligently, and voluntarily gives up his or her constitutional rights, such as when allowing law enforcement officers to conduct a search or when choosing to answer questions after being advised of *Miranda* warnings. (Chapter 8)

Watchman style. A style of police behavior described by James Q. Wilson in which the purpose of policing is viewed as keeping the peace and not making waves. Officers operating under the watchman style are passive and reactive. Compare to **legalistic style** and **service style**. (Chapter 11)

Wolfenden Report. A report issued by a British government commission in 1963 regarding the legal status of homosexuality and prostitution. The report formed the basis for the Hart-Devlin debate. (Chapter 3)

Working personality. Refers to the occupational culture of policing, reflecting elements of police work including danger, authority, social isolation, and solidarity. (Chapter 11)

Youth Risk Behavior Study. A survey of high school students administered regularly by the Centers for Disease Control to measure the frequency of high-risk behaviors. (Chapter 1)

INDEX

Page numbers in italic indicate figures or tables, bold indicates photographs.

D

Q

R

S

T

U

V

W

X

Y

Z

PHOTO CREDITS

Page 1: AP Photo/Roswell Daily Record, Mark Wilson; **2:** (top) AL.com/Landov, (bottom left) ©iStockPhoto.com/asiseeit, (bottom right) ©iStockPhoto.com/imageegami; **3:** (top) Shutterstock, (bottom) Karsten Moran; **4:** (left) Chicago History Museum, (right) AP Photo; **14:** NGT/National Geographic Creative; **26:** Anne Cusack/Los Angeles Times/March 18, 2010; **32–33:** Bureau of Justice Statistics, 2010; **38:** Getty Images/William Henry Pyne; **39:** (top) AP Photo/North Wind Archives, (bottom) Eastern State Penitentiary Historic Site; **40:** (top) AP Photo/Mark Lennihan, (middle) Getty Images/Thinkstock, (bottom) Getty Images/Brendan Smialowski; **42:** AP Photo/Richard Sheinwald; **47:** Cavendish Press; **62:** AP Photo/Eau Claire Leader-Telegram, Chuck Rupnow; **67:** Chris James; **81:** AP Photo/Charles Krupa; **92:** AP Photo; **96:** AP Photo/Jamie-Andrea Yanak; **97:** (top) Getty Images/NBC Universal, (bottom) Getty Images/Joel Auerbach/Stringer; **98:** (top left) Tattoo by Kevin Stiles. Bristol, Connecticut, USA, (top right) Sarah Elaine Schenkelberg, (bottom left) AP Photo/Robert Mecea; **99:** iStockPhoto; **109:** AP Photo/Dan Cepeda, Star-Tribune; **110:** AP Photo/Denver Post, RJ Sangosti; **123:** Golden Pixels/Super Stock; **128:** Zuma Press/Clay Good; **144:** AP Photo; **150:** Getty Images/Bryan Mullenix; **151:** (top) AP Photos/Star Tribune, Jim Gehrz, (bottom) AP Photo/Seth Wenig; **152:** (top) Cultura Limited/SuperStock, (bottom) Getty Images/Scott Olson/Staff; **153:** Shutterstock; **154:** Getty Images/New York Daily News/Contributor; **160:** AP Photo/Alex Menendez; **176:** AL.com/Landov; **181:** AP Photo/Dennis Cook; **187:** Brazos County Sherriff Department; **203:** Ackerman + Gruber; **209:** Getty Images/Shelly Katz; **222:** AP Photo/Norman Shapiro **230:** iStockPhoto/dcdebs; **238:** public domain; **239:** (top) CALVIN AND HOBBES ©1995 Watterson. Dist. by UNIVERSAL UCLICK. Reprinted with permission. All rights reserved, (middle) Shutterstock, (bottom) Getty Images/plherrera; **240:** (top) Houston Community Newspapers, (bottom) iStockPhoto; **241:** The Schøyen Collection, MS 2064; **249:** AJC; **259:** Irfan Khan/Los Angeles Times; **270:** AP Photo/Mark Humphrey; **280:** AP Photo; **290:** AP Photo/Matt York; **298:** (top) AP Photo; **299:** (top) AP Photo, (bottom) ©iStockPhoto/Windzepher; **300:** (top) AP Barksdale Air Force Base, (bottom) Shutterstuck/dragon_fang; **301:** AP Photo/Patrick Semansky; **302:** Getty Images/Steve Liss; **312:** San Diego County Sherriff's Department; **322:** AP Photo/The Enterprise, Wayne Tilcock; **332:** Naples Daily News; **349:** AP Photo/Paul Buck; **351:** Beaumont Enterprise/Dave Ryan; **357:** Adapted from Carter, L.H., & Burke, T.F. (2007). *Reason in Law* (7th ed.). New York: Pearson Longman; **361:** David Leventi/www.davidleventi.com; **374:** Goldman, 2003; **378:** AP Photo/Rich Pedroncelli; **384:** AP Photo/The Cincinnati Enquirer, Carrie Cochran.